Developmental Physical Education for All Children

4TH EDITION

David L. Gallahue, EdD
Indiana University

Frances Cleland Donnelly, PED
West Chester University

HUMAN KINETICS

Library of Congress Cataloging-in-Publication Data

Gallahue, David L.
    Developmental physical education for all children / David L. Gallahue,
Frances Cleland Donnelly.--4th ed.
        p. cm.
Rev. ed. of: Developmental physical education for today's children. 3rd
ed. c1996.
Includes bibliographical references and index.
    ISBN 0-7360-3388-2 (Hard Cover)
    1. Physical education for children. 2. Movement education. 3. Motor
learning. 4. Physical education for children--Study and teaching. I.
Donnelly, Frances Cleland, 1951- II. Gallahue, David L. Developmental
physical education for today's children. III. Title.
    GV443 .G232 2003
    372.86--dc21
                            2002010770

ISBN: 0-7360-3388-2

This book is a revised edition of *Developmental Physical Education for Today's Children (3rd ed.),* published in 1996 by Brown & Benchmark.

The Web addresses cited in this text were current as of August 2002, unless otherwise noted.

Acquisitions Editor: Scott Wikgren; **Developmental Editor:** Joanna Hatzopoulos Portman; **Assistant Editor:** Derek Campbell; **Copyeditor:** Joyce Sexton; **Proofreader:** Erin Cler; **Indexer:** Marie Rizzo; **Permission Manager:** Dalene Reeder; **Graphic Designer:** Robert Reuther; **Graphic Artist:** Denise Lowry; **Photo Manager:** Leslie A. Woodrum, **Cover Designer:** Keith Blomberg; **Photographer (cover):** Leslie A. Woodrum; **Photographer (interior):** Leslie A. Woodrum, except where noted; **Art Manager:** Kelly Hendren; **Illustrators:** Denise Lowry and Roberto Sabas

Printed in China   10   9   8   7   6   5   4   3   2   1

Human Kinetics
Web site: www.HumanKinetics.com

United States: Human Kinetics, P.O. Box 5076, Champaign, IL 61825-5076
800-747-4457
e-mail: humank@hkusa.com

Canada: Human Kinetics, 475 Devonshire Road Unit 100, Windsor, ON N8Y 2L5
800-465-7301 (in Canada only)
e-mail: orders@hkcanada.com

Europe: Human Kinetics, 107 Bradford Road, Stanningley, Leeds
LS28 6AT, United Kingdom
+44 (0) 113 255 5665
e-mail: hk@hkeurope.com

Australia: Human Kinetics, 57A Price Avenue, Lower Mitcham, South Australia 5062
08 8277 1555
e-mail: liahka@senet.com.au

New Zealand: Human Kinetics, P.O. Box 105-231, Auckland Central
09-523-3462
e-mail: hkp@ihug.co.nz

As always, *to the sunshine of my life:* Ellie, David Lee, Jennifer, and Dan

David Gallahue

To my friends and colleagues who *inspire* me, and to my family who have always offered *unconditional love and support:* Mom, Dad, Libby, Vic, Zach, Ryan, and Jim

Fran Cleland Donnelly

Contents in Brief

PART III THE DEVELOPMENTAL PROGRAM 331

PART IV THE SKILL THEMES 415

PART V   THE CONTENT AREAS   565

PART VI   THE PROGRAM STRANDS   639

Contents

CHAPTER 26   **672**
Developing the Feeling Child

Preface

Developmental Physical Education for All Children, 4th Edition is written for students in physical education, early childhood education, and elementary education. It is especially designed for those taking a first course in children's physical education and physical activity, although it is also used for more advanced courses because of its comprehensive and in-depth coverage of important topics.

The most distinguishing feature of this text is that it is written from a developmental perspective. Children are, therefore, viewed first and foremost from where they *are* in terms of their motor, cognitive, and affective development (e.g., individual appropriateness) rather than where they *should* be (age-group appropriateness). To that end, the physical activity orientation to children's physical education and the movement education perspective are merged and cooperatively applied. Our knowledge of children's motor development, movement skill learning, and physical activity and fitness enhancement serves as the conceptual framework for the developmental approach advocated here.

This edition of *Developmental Physical Education for All Children* has been completely updated and extensively revised. The book maintains its integrity as being much more than a "cookbook" or text void of a consistent philosophical approach. A number of learning aids help readers focus on essential concepts and practical pointers. The developmental approach advocated here attempts to apply our knowledge of children's growth and motor development in a comprehensive manner that recognizes the essential concept of the individuality of the learner in terms of his of her motor, cognitive, and affective development.

Each chapter opens with a **key concept** and **chapter objectives**. These represent the essential points to be covered in the chapter and are intended to focus the reader on the critically important information that follows. Each chapter closes with a list of **excellent readings** that have been selected because of their overall quality, relevance to the topic being discussed, and general reader accessibility. **Web resources** are included in each chapter where appropriate. These resources have been selected because of the accuracy, relevancy, and in-depth coverage of topics.

Within each chapter there are several helpful learning aids. **Teaching Tips** provide the reader with a quick and easy reference tool for making practical application to the information being discussed. **Concept** boxes in the margins distill the discussion into its essential concepts. **Reality Checks** provide real-life vignettes illustrating how information being discussed may be put to practical use. Take time to reflect on the Real-World Situations prior to answering the Critical Questions. Finally, important terms are indicated in boldface and repeated under the heading **Terms to Remember** at the end of each chapter. These are intended to serve as a self-check of important word meanings. A brief **summary** concludes each chapter. Its intent is to condense the information contained in the just completed chapter and to provide a list of up-to-date **Excellent Readings** on the topic.

Developmental Physical Education for All Children is organized so that teachers can easily use the text in its entirety in a single course or divide the chapters for use in two separate courses. Parts I, II, and III ("The Learner," "The Teacher," "The Developmental Program") focus on essential background information for successful teaching. These first 17 chapters can be effectively incorporated into a full semester methods course. Parts IV, V, and VI ("The Skill Themes," "The Content Areas," "The Program Strands"), the last nine chapters, can easily be used in a course focusing on developmental movement experiences for preschool and elementary school children.

Part I, "The Learner," focuses on the child from a developmental perspective. Chapter 1, "An Overview of Developmental Physical Education," is critically important to making maximum use of the rest of the text. The aims and goals of children's physical education are discussed, followed by a thorough definition of *developmental* physical education. Next, the motor, cognitive, and affective components of developmental physical education are briefly introduced, as are the movement skill theme and program strand approach to teaching children's physical education. Chapter 2, "Childhood Growth and Motor Development," introduces important factors that affect children's growth patterns and motor development. In addition, this chapter outlines motor, cognitive, and affective characteristics during the periods of early and later childhood in an attempt to help the reader form a generalized, age-appropriate view of the normally developing child. Chapters 3 and 4, "Movement Skill Acquisition" and "Physical Activity and Fitness Enhancement," focus on these two topics as the unique and primary outcomes of the developmental physical education program. Chapter 3 contains the categories of movement, phases and stages of motor development, and levels of learning a new movement skill. Chapter 4 discusses the components of physical fitness, principles of fitness development, and the weaving of physical activity into children's lifestyle. Chapters 5 and 6, "Cognitive Learning" and "Affective Growth," deal with important additional outcomes of quality physical education. Chapter 5 focuses on the cognitive concept and perceptual-motor outcomes of children's physical education. Self-concept development, positive socialization, and character education are included in Chapter 6. Chapter 7, "Children With Disabilities," concludes part I. This chapter focuses on the physical activity needs of children with disabilities and describes for teachers categories of limiting con-

ditions that affect these children. A wealth of Teaching Tips can be found in this chapter that will be of particular help to the novice teacher.

Part II, "The Teacher," contains six chapters that provide the reader with a realistic view of both the art and the science of teaching. Chapters 8 and 9, "Effective Teaching" and "Facilitating Learning," are essential to understanding the role of the teacher. Chapter 8 discusses the teacher's responsibilities, stages in becoming an effective teacher, characteristics of effective teachers, and both verbal and nonverbal communication techniques. Chapter 9 takes a close look at positive discipline and classroom management and offers a variety of practical suggestions intended to help lead children to improved self-control. Chapter 10, "Teaching Styles," is a critical element of this text. This chapter discusses important factors to consider when utilizing a particular teaching style. No amount of reading, however, will show students how to use the spectrum of teaching styles effectively. It is therefore critically important to follow up this chapter by having students observe master teachers at work and, most important, to experience a variety of actual teaching situations. Chapter 11, "Planning for Success," takes an in-depth look at skill themes and lesson planning. The steps in planning a movement skill theme are discussed as well as sequencing the daily lesson, organizing facilities, equipment, instructional aids, and student helpers. Chapter 12, "Assessing Progress," centers on motor assessment, fitness, and physical activity assessment as the three primary evaluative responsibilities of the physical education teacher. The types and purposes of assessment are discussed along with a brief presentation of several motor, fitness, and physical activity assessment tests. Chapter 13, "Advocacy," concludes part II. This chapter is about educating others, communicating effectively with them, and motivating the various constituencies to actively support the continuing quest for both quality and daily physical education programs.

Part III, "The Developmental Program," combines what we know about the learner and the teacher and operationalizes it in a manner that is both developmentally appropriate and practical. Chapter 14, "The Developmental Curriculum," focuses on the sequential steps in planning the curriculum. Chapter 15 deals with "The Physical Education Content" and looks carefully at developmental games, dance, and gymnastics as the core content of the developmentally based program. Chapter 16, "Movement Skill Development Through Movement Concept Learning," focuses on the movement concepts of developmental physical education, namely effort, space, and relationship awareness. A solid grasp of this chapter will enable students to tackle part IV, "The Skill Themes," with a solid knowledge base. Chapter 17, "Safety Considerations and Legal Liability," concludes part III. This chapter centers on conditions that frequently result in a lawsuit and precautions to take to minimize legal liability. Teachers must recognize the risks involved in children's education and take positive steps to minimize children's exposure to harmful conditions, while at the same time maximizing their learning.

Part IV, "The Skill Themes," contains three chapters that form the core of the developmental movement skill theme approach. Chapters 18, 19, and 20, "Fundamental Stability Skill Themes," "Fundamental Locomotor and Non-Locomotor Skill Themes," and "Fundamental Manipulative Skill Themes," respectively, focus on the acquisition of mature patterns of fundamental movement. Each chapter outlines the recommended steps for developing a movement skill theme and describes a wide variety of fundamental movement skills. Each fundamental movement skill is also accompanied by a visual description and verbal description, common developmental difficulties that children encounter in progressing to the mature stage, and Teaching Tips for helping children overcome these developmental difficulties. This is followed by discussion of the concepts children should know, including a variety of skill concepts (how the body *should* move) and movement concepts (how the body *can* move). A variety of skill development activities are provided in the form of exploratory and guided-discovery experiences. This section will prove especially helpful to those new to the movement exploration and guided discovery teaching styles. Skill application activities conclude the chapter with a sampling of traditional game activities. This sampling of activities has been selected because they can be easily modified, promote inclusion, and are fun.

Part V, "The Content Areas," focuses on the three primary content areas of developmental physical education: developmental games, dance, and gymnastics. Chapter 21, "Developmental Games," presents a four-level developmental progression for including games in the curriculum. This is followed by discussions on how to assess the educational value of games, the dynamics of games teaching, and best practices for teaching games. Chapter 22, "Developmental Dance," examines the learning outcomes of dance, rhythmic fundamentals, and how to apply movement concepts to creative dance. This is followed by a discussion of the steps in developing a creative dance lesson, a four-level developmental progression for teaching dance, and lesson ideas that work. Chapter 23, "Developmental Gymnastics," provides the reader with a clear distinction between Olympic gymnastics and developmental gymnastics. This is followed with appropriate teaching methods and a four-level developmentally based teaching progression.

Part VI, "The Program Strands," concludes the text with three important chapters dealing with the active child, the thinking child, and the feeling child, respectively. Chapter 24, "Developing the Active Child," provides the reader with a wealth of aerobic endurance, muscular strength and endurance, and joint flexibility activities. The chapter concludes with a discussion of how to motivate children for increased physical activity involvement. Chapter 25, "Developing the Thinking Child," deals with critical thinking in the gymnasium and how to structure the learning environment to promote the development of critical thinking skills. Chapter 26, "Developing the Feeling Child," concludes the text. Although the last chapter, it is in many ways, particularly after the events of 9/11/01, one of the most important. This chapter focuses on the importance of addressing the affective domain, provides a developmental progression, and offers teaching strategies designed to promote personal and social responsibility.

The **Glossary** provides a concise definition for each term highlighted in the text that is listed in the Terms to Remember at the end of each chapter. The **References** list all of the resources cited throughout this text.

Please note that a variety of supplementary resources are available to help students and their instructors more effectively use this text. They include:

1. CD-ROM with lesson activities for developmental games, dance, and gymnastics

2. Electronic instructor guide including chapter lecture outlines and a test bank of multiple choice questions

3. Graphics package of the chapter lecture outlines in slide-show format

Acknowledgments

In the development of any project of this magnitude, many individuals deserve particular thanks. For preparation of the manuscript we are especially grateful to Edwina Johansen and Regina Graham for their typing of the manuscript. We are also grateful to the photographer of this edition of the text, Les Woodrum.

A long list of colleagues and former students deserve credit for helping us think through topics, for helping us crystallize our philosophy of developmental physical education, and for serving as models of excellence in teaching. There are too many to mention and they come from all over the world, but please be assured that we are forever grateful to each of you. We especially thank our dedicated colleagues from Australia, Brazil, Canada, Chile, China, Egypt, Finland, Great Britain, Hong Kong, Indonesia, Israel, Japan, Korea, Kuwait, Portugal, Singapore, Taiwan, Thailand, Turkey, and the United States who have become lifelong partners and friends in the quest for quality developmental physical education programs for *all* children. Our gratitude is also expressed to our editors at Human Kinetics, Scott Wikgren and Derek Campbell: Scott for his confidence in our abilities, and Derek for his helpful assistance in getting this edition in print.

Finally, we thank our God who sustains us, makes all things possible, and helps us see through new eyes.

The Learner

Here you are, about to embark on the delightful and critically important task of learning more about children in physical education and physical activity settings. Part I, "The Learner," will not only help you learn more about the developmental nature of children but will also enable you to couple this with the information that follows. As a result, with practice and experience you will be able to effectively teach children's physical education from a child-centered developmental perspective.

Chapter 1 sets the stage for the entire text. It provides an overview of developmental physical education and introduces you to the seven National Standards for Physical Education. **Chapter 2** provides you with a brief look at child growth and motor development. It is important to become knowledgeable about developmental change because as a teacher you will find that this influences all that you do. **Chapters 3 and 4** are critically important because enhanced movement skill, fitness acquisition, and increased physical activity are the core content areas of the developmental physical education program. **Chapters 5 and 6** focus on cognitive learning and affective growth, respectively. Developmental physical education teachers make many and varied contributions to children's development in both areas. **Chapter 7** introduces you to developmental disabilities among school-age children and offers you a wealth of teaching tips to help ensure your success.

Take time to read each of these chapters with care and to reflect on the tremendous potential that developmental physical education has in making real, lasting, and meaningful differences in the lives of children.

1

An Overview of Developmental Physical Education

Key Concept

▶ The National Standards for Physical Education provide a conceptual framework for achieving the aims of developmental physical education, namely learning to move and learning through movement, in a manner that is both individually appropriate and age appropriate.

As a college student you may be the product of a quality physical education program at both the elementary and the secondary school levels. On the other hand, you may have participated in physical education programs that were, at best, marginal in quality and quantity. Take a moment to reflect on your experiences in physical education during your elementary school years. Were these experiences enriching in terms of movement skill learning, physical activity and fitness enhancement, cognitive learning, and affective growth? Did your physical education program take place in an environment conducive to learning about the health benefits of physical activity, developing critical thinking skills, and enjoyment of learning? Were your experiences developmentally appropriate as well as age appropriate? If you answer yes to each of these questions, then you were one of those fortunate to be involved in a quality physical education program. If your answer is no to one or more of these questions, you were cheated out of a critically important educational experience.

This chapter will provide you with the tools to do the following:

▶ List and discuss the seven National Standards for Physical Education adopted by the National Association for Sport and Physical Education.

▶ Speculate on the need for quality physical education offered daily.

▶ Discuss what is meant by the terms *learning to move* and *learning through movement* as they relate to the aims and goals of developmentally appropriate physical activity.

▶ Define the term *developmental physical education* and illustrate how it incorporates the concepts of both individual appropriateness and age appropriateness.

▶ Distinguish between the skill themes and the program strands of the developmental physical education curriculum.

▶ Provide a generic definition for the term *physical fitness* and list the components of both health-related and performance-related fitness.

▶ Discuss the concept of general motor ability, or the "natural" athlete, in terms of movement skill acquisition.

▶ Discuss the role of developmental physical activity in children's cognitive learning.

▶ Explain how physical activity plays an important role in children's affective growth.

NATIONAL STANDARDS FOR PHYSICAL EDUCATION

The reasons for disparity among physical education programs are numerous and complex, but one of the most important reasons is that, until recently, national standards for physical education did not exist to help identify the essential characteristics of quality physical education programs. In 1995, however, the *National Standards for Physical Education* were adopted by the National Association for Sport and Physical Education (NASPE; **www.aahperd.org/naspe**). With almost 20,000 members, NASPE is the primary national professional organization charged with improving the quality and quantity of physical education programs in the United States. The National Standards are designed to provide guidance for teachers and educators who have responsibility for helping children meet the physical demands of the 21st century (Benham-Deal et al., 2002; Fay & Doolittle, 2002; Rink et al., 2002; Senne & Housner, 2002). The National Standards for Physical Education are the yardstick by which physical education programs in the United States are measured. There are seven content standards (goals). Together they describe the essential characteristics of the "physically educated individual." Each is referenced to specific benchmarks (objectives) for achievement in kindergarten and grades 2, 4, 6, 8, 10, and 12. As a teacher of physical education you should center your efforts on these standards. By doing so you will join a growing number of physical educators dedicated to children's learning to move and learning through movement. Figure 1.1 lists the seven Content Standards for Physical Education. Study them carefully. They form the framework for this text.

REALITY CHECK

What? National Standards?

Real-World Situation

You have accepted a position in a school district that for the first time has hired certified professional physical education teachers. Up to now, classroom teachers have been expected to include a "gym day" in their curriculum. Being well meaning, but not well informed, the school superintendent has authorized hiring "PE" teachers in order to meet the new union requirements of having a planning period for classroom teachers. As a result, the superintendent has few expectations of the new physical education program other than keeping children "quiet, happy, and good." As one of the new hires, with up-to-date knowledge of NASPE's National Standards for Physical Education, you have decided that it is critically important for the school district to adopt these standards as a means of ensuring consistency in the offering of quality physical education that is developmentally appropriate and consistent with national guidelines.

Critical Questions

Based on your knowledge of the National Standards for Physical Education and the critical importance of offering quality physical education programs that are developmentally based:

- How would you go about informing your superintendent of the National Standards and their importance?

- What would you do to convince your superintendent and building principal that the National Standards are relevant to the children in your school district?

- What will you say to counter the argument that "quiet, happy, and good is all that I am expecting out of the new physical education program"?

- How do you deal with the notion that some view your physical education class as little more than an opportunity for a mandated planning period for classroom teachers?

The physically educated person

I. demonstrates competency in many movement forms and proficiency in a few movement forms;

II. applies movement concepts and principles to the learning and development of motor skills;

III. exhibits a physically active lifestyle;

IV. achieves and maintains a health-enhancing level of physical fitness;

V. demonstrates responsible personal and social behavior in physical activity settings;

VI. demonstrates understanding and respect for differences among people in physical activity settings;

VII. understands that physical activity provides opportunities for enjoyment, challenge, self-expression, and social interaction.

FIGURE 1.1 The seven Content Standards for Physical Education.

The National Standards for Physical Education include Content Standards, Performance Standards, and Performance Benchmarks. **Content Standards** focus on what students should be able to do in terms of both movement skills and movement knowledge. Performance Standards key in on how good is good enough by specifying the degree of active achievement students should be able to reach in the Content Standards. **Performance Standards** specifically concern objective assessment of pupil progress, and are dealt with through Performance Benchmarks. **Performance Benchmarks** describe assessment guidelines for behaviors that objectively demonstrate progress toward a Performance Standard. Figure 1.2 depicts the relationships among Content Standards, Performance Standards, and Performance Benchmarks.

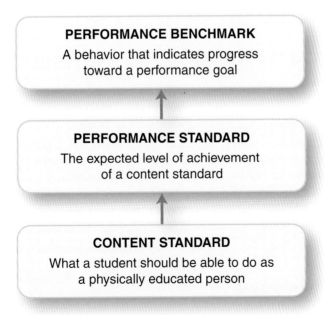

PERFORMANCE BENCHMARK
A behavior that indicates progress
toward a performance goal

PERFORMANCE STANDARD
The expected level of achievement
of a content standard

CONTENT STANDARD
What a student should be able to do as
a physically educated person

FIGURE 1.2 The relationship among a Content Standard, Performance Standard, and Performance Benchmark.

A CASE FOR QUALITY PHYSICAL EDUCATION OFFERED DAILY

Never before has the physical education profession been so strategically positioned and so vitally needed to make a difference in the lives of children. *Physical Activity and Health: A Report of the Surgeon General* (USDHHS, 1996), the two important publications from the Centers for Disease Control and Prevention titled "Guidelines for School and Community Programs to Promote Lifelong Physical Activity Among Young People" (CDC, 1997) and "Increasing Physical Activity: A Report on Recommendations of the Task Force on Community Preventative Services" (CDC, 2001), *Bright Futures in Practice: Physical Activity* (Patrick et al., 2001), and *Healthy People 2010* (USDHHS, 2000) all represent important government initiatives that clearly point to the need for increased physical activity and quality physical education programs (see text box 1.1). Each of these reports recognizes that physical education is one of the very few ways in which virtually all children can be reached: "Ensuring daily, quality physical education in all school grades is the first recommendation of the U.S. Surgeon General in his Call to Action to Prevent and Decrease Overweight and Obesity" (NASPE News, winter 2002, p. 8).

Quality physical education uses the gymnasium or playing field as a learning laboratory, has measurable objectives, and seeks to attain those objectives in a systematic manner. Quality physical education is within the reach of all teachers who are dedicated to children's learning. It is not a "throw out the ball" program or some form of glorified recess period. On the other hand, daily physical education is still an unfulfilled goal in the majority of schools in the United States. If children are to realize the full potential of physical education, then we must continue to strive for quality physical education programs offered daily.

Convincing evidence indicates that North American children are frequently unable to take advantage of the many benefits of vigorous physical activity because of

REALITY CHECK

Daily Physical Education: "Get Real"

Real-World Situation

For several years one of the goals of all those concerned with the physical activity of children has been quality physical education offered daily in our nation's schools. Periodically NASPE surveys the physical education requirements in all 50 states. Its most recent report, *Shape of the Nation Report* (NASPE, 2001), reveals that despite the efforts of many and the support of numerous federal agencies, only one state (Illinois) requires daily physical education among all students from kindergarten through grade 12.

Critical Questions

Based on your knowledge of the overwhelming support that exists for including physical education daily in the lives of children:

- Why, in your opinion, has daily physical education failed to become a reality in the vast majority of North American schools?

- Can you counter the argument that after-school activities offered through agencies such as the YMCA, Parks and Recreation, and Boys and Girls Clubs amply make up for what is not offered in the schools?

- Why is the quest for quality physical education offered daily realistic and of real merit?

- If daily physical education suddenly became a reality, what would be, in your opinion, the significant differences made in the lives of children?

The federal government of the United States is an important partner in promoting increased physical activity and quality physical education in the nation's schools:

Physical Activity and Health: A Report of the Surgeon General (1996)
U.S. Department of Health and Human Services
(www.surgeongeneral.gov)

This historic report examined the relationship between physical activity and health for all segments of society, including children and youth, setting the stage for all subsequent Surgeon Generals to strongly advocate for increased physical education time in America's schools.

"Guidelines for School and Community Programs to Promote Lifelong Physical Activity Among Young People" (1997)
Centers for Disease Control and Prevention (CDC)
(www.cdc.gov)

This publication clearly outlines the benefits of physical activity, exercise, and physical fitness during childhood by emphasizing that these activities have significant potential for reducing mortality and the development of many chronic diseases in adulthood. Recommendations regarding 10 aspects of school and community programs to promote lifelong physical activity among children and youth are discussed.

***Healthy People 2010* (2000)**
U.S. Department of Health and Human Services
(www.web.health.gov/healthypeople)

This is a major health promotion and disease prevention initiative that brings together many individuals and agencies to improve the health of all Americans. Physical activity and fitness is one of 28 focus areas. Key objectives in this area are to "increase the proportion of the nation's public and private schools that require daily physical education for all students."

"Increasing Physical Activity: A Report on Recommendations of the Task Force on Community Preventative Services" (2001)
Centers for Disease Control and Prevention (CDC)
(www.cdc.gov/mmwr/preview/mmwrhtml/rr5018a1.htm)

This important publication is the latest information available from the CDC and strongly recommends 5 of 13 community interventions reviewed. Physical education was one of the five that received the highest rating. Key research findings in support of school-based physical education provide scientific justification for quality programs.

***Bright Futures in Practice: Physical Activity* (2001)**
U.S. Department of Health and Human Services, Maternal Child Health Bureau
National Center for Education in Maternal and Child Health
(www.nmchc@circsol.com)

This practical, easy-to-use, and authoritative guide provides developmental guidelines for physical activity for infants, children, and adolescents. It is an excellent new resource for guidance in working in physical activity settings with children who have developmental disabilities.

**CONCEPT
1.1**

Quality physical education programs offered daily maximize the potential for children to adopt healthy lifestyles.

poor or nonexistent physical education programs, sedentary lifestyles, and the erroneous assumption that children—by the very nature of being children—get plenty of physical activity. As a result, low levels of physical fitness and movement skill attainment are all too common. Movement should be at the center of children's lives, permeating all facets of their development, whether in the motor, cognitive, or affective domains of behavior. To deny children the opportunity to reap the many benefits of regular physical activity is to deny them the opportunity to experience the joy of efficient movement, the health benefits of an active lifestyle, and a lifetime as a confident and competent mover.

Teachers in North America face three critical issues arising from the following facts:

1. Childhood obesity has been rising rapidly.
2. In-school and community violence among youth have alarmed us all.
3. Early puberty has important psychosocial ramifications.

Despite the vigorous attempts of professional organizations and state and federal agencies, **childhood obesity,** defined as being at or above the 95th percentile of weight for height, has reached alarming levels. Today's children are less active and have poorer diets than their counterparts of just 10 years ago. Today, almost 25% are considered to be overweight or obese, up from just 11% a decade ago. A survey by the American Obesity Association (2000; **www.obesity.org**) showed that 81% of parents of elementary, middle, or high school children are concerned with their children's getting adequate daily physical education.

Furthermore, obesity in childhood has a high positive correlation with obesity as an adult. The rapid increase in childhood obesity has produced a corresponding dramatic increase in the incidence of early markers of chronic health problems such as hypertension, type 2 diabetes, and elevated cholesterol. Despite no measurable generational change in height at all age levels since the 1960s, there has been a

REALITY CHECK

Three Big Concerns

Real-World Situation

Our world has changed. After the events of September 11, 2001, nothing seems the same. As a teacher you have a heightened awareness of three critical issues: in-school and community violence and student safety, childhood obesity, and precocious puberty among your students. Given these three big concerns and given the increased need to provide children with a safe, stable, and nurturing environment, you are determined to make a difference in the lives of the children you touch.

Critical Questions

Based on your knowledge of these critical issues and the potential impact of quality physical education that is developmentally appropriate:

- What can you do to make a difference?
- Why, in your opinion, are these three issues of such major importance?
- Who else in the school and in the community can assist you in effecting positive change in each of these areas?
- What about children's views on these three issues? Put yourself in their place: What do you think they are thinking?

definite generational increase in obesity at all ages in the United States. You will find the following Web sites on the topic of childhood obesity helpful:

- Centers for Disease Control and Prevention (**www.cdc.gov/health/obesity.htm**)
- National Institute of Child Health and Human Development (**www.nichd. nih.gov**)

The rise of in-school violence and community violence among children in North America has caused many educators and community leaders to rethink how we might use organized physical activity programs to promote the worthy use of the time spent after school through play, games, and sport. Physical education teachers can play an important role in reclaiming our schools and communities as places free from violence by promoting cooperative behavior and a renewed sense of community through physical activity. Check out the following Web sites for more information on school violence:

- Center for the Prevention of School Violence (**www.ncsu.edu/cpsv**)
- National School Safety Center (**www.nssc1.org**)
- National Resource Center for Safe Schools (**www.safetyzone.org**)

A recent trend toward early puberty, defined as beginning the preadolescent growth spurt and the development of secondary sex characteristics two or more years prior to one's age-mates, has become an area of increased concern among child development specialists. Although still a small proportion of the total population of elementary school age children, children in each school are entering puberty as young as seven or eight. The psychosocial ramifications are great, and the physical education teacher can play an important role in helping children through this difficult time. You can find additional information on the topic of puberty at the following Web sites:

- American Academy of Pediatrics (**www.aap.org/family/puberty.htm**)
- **www.keepkidshealthy.com/adolescent/puberty.html**

This chapter presents an overview of the many benefits of quality physical education that are sensitive to the needs and interests of children and that are based on the developmental level of the individual. But first, we must clearly outline the aims and goals of physical education and define the term "developmental physical education."

TEXT BOX 1.2

Now may be the best time ever to realize the tremendous potential for quality physical education to be an effective force in the lives of children. Never before has there been such a critical need for physical education programs taught by caring, concerned, and highly qualified adults. The tremendous rise in obesity, in-school violence, and early puberty among children, and the accompanying health risks have made it imperative that there be a resurgence of physical education programs throughout North America.

THE AIMS AND GOALS
OF PHYSICAL EDUCATION

An **aim** is the overarching purpose or intent of what we do. Many authors and leaders in the profession have stated the aims of physical education. Lofty ideals and flowery platitudes have often clouded the fact that the basic aim of physical education may be simply and succinctly stated as follows: to set aside daily a portion of the school day devoted to large-muscle activities that encourage and develop *learning to move* and *learning through movement.*

The **learning-to-move** aim of physical education is based on acquiring increased movement skills and enhancing physical fitness through increased physical activity. The **learning-through-movement** aim of physical education is based on the fact that effective physical education can positively influence both the cognitive and affective (social-emotional) development of children. Becoming physically educated by learning to move and learning through movement is an important aim of physical education. The National Association for Sport and Physical Education has defined the **physically educated** person in the following way:

- The physically educated person has learned skills necessary to perform a variety of physical activities.
- The person is physically fit.
- The person participates regularly in physical activity.
- The person knows the implications and the benefits of involvement in physical activities.
- The person values physical activity and its contributions to a healthful lifestyle.

A **goal** is a standard that we continually expend effort toward and strive to achieve. The seven Content Standards contained within the NASPE National Standards for Physical Education discussed earlier are in fact goals. In education, goals are long-term purposes measured through the attainment of a series of objectives. An **objective** is the means used to achieve a goal. Objectives are the observable, measurable, and quantifiable statements that guide the teacher in selecting appropriate educational strategies that help obtain the goals of the program. Quality physical education programs establish clearly defined objectives, and the content of the program reflects constant effort toward attainment of these objectives.

The acquisition of movement skills is a primary goal of developmental physical education for elementary school age children. This goal focuses on helping children become skillful movers, knowledgeable movers, and expressive movers in a wide variety of fundamental and specialized movement skills. The goal of physical activity and fitness enhancement focuses on activity for its health benefits. Therefore, emphasis includes, but goes beyond, helping children become fit movers. This goal also emphasizes helping children become informed movers and eager movers through promotion of an active way of life. The cognitive learning goals of developmental physical education center on helping children become more effective multisensory learners and active learners. Therefore, movement is a viable medium for both perceptual-motor and cognitive concept learning. Similarly, helping children achieve the behavior goals of becoming self-discovering learners and cooperative learners fosters affective development. By promoting these goals, knowledgeable teachers

CONCEPT 1.2

Learning to move and learning through movement are the broad-based aims of all quality physical education programs.

CONCEPT 1.3

The NASPE National Standards for Physical Education provide an important conceptual framework for the developmental physical education program.

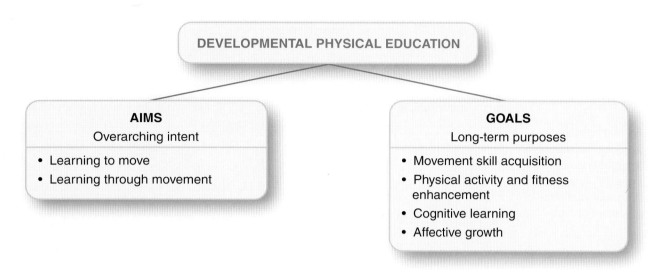

FIGURE 1.3   The aims and goals of developmental physical education.

use movement as an effective tool to enhance self-esteem, encourage positive socialization, and clarify values. Figure 1.3 diagrams the aims and goals of developmental physical education.

DEVELOPMENTAL PHYSICAL EDUCATION DEFINED

Children's development is frequently studied from a compartmentalized standpoint focusing on one domain (cognitive, affective, *or* motor) of human behavior to the exclusion of the others. This has led to an unbalanced view of the developmental process and resulting educational practice. It is crucial for those interested in developmental physical education not to compound the errors of compartmentalization and instead to view the child as a total integrated being (cognitive, affective, *and* motor). Compartmentalization is a root cause for the difficulty that the physical education profession has had historically in establishing itself as a legitimate aspect of the school curriculum. Only when educators in general, and school boards in particular, recognize and respect children as multifaceted individuals with a wide range of backgrounds—and that becoming physically educated involves complex interaction among the cognitive, affective, and motor domains—will physical education take its place in North American schools as a legitimate and respected force in the total school curriculum.

In addition to recognizing the vital interactive importance of each domain of human behavior, developmental physical education recognizes that there is a complex relationship among the individual's biological makeup, her own unique environmental circumstances, and the specific objective of the learning task she is engaging in. See figure 1.4 for a visual representation of this important concept. Because the three domains are interactive, it is critically important for teachers to have a strong conceptual grasp of motor development, movement skill learning, and the psychosocial aspects of human development, as well as the movement sciences of anatomy, physiology, and biomechanics.

Developmental physical education is physical education that emphasizes the acquisition of movement skills and increased physical competence based on the

FIGURE 1.4 Developmental physical education recognizes the relationship among the specific requirements of the movement task, the biology of the individual, and the conditions of the learning environment in promoting motor control and movement competence.

Motor Control and Movement Competence

Biology of the individual

Conditions of the learning environment

Requirements of the movement task

CONCEPT 1.4

Developmental physical education utilizes instructional strategies and learning experiences that are individually appropriate as well as age-group appropriate.

unique developmental level of the individual. It recognizes and incorporates the many contributions that systematic, sensitive teaching can make to both the cognitive and affective development of the individual. Developmental physical education encourages the uniqueness of the individual and is based on the fundamental proposition that, although motor development is age related, it is *not* age dependent. Consequently, teacher decisions concerning what to teach, when to teach it, and how to teach are based primarily on the appropriateness of the activity for the individual and only secondarily on the appropriateness of the activity for a particular age group.

Individual appropriateness, the key concept of developmental physical education, is based on the central proposition that each child has his unique timing and pattern of growth and development. Therefore, the movement activities children perform in developmentally based physical education programs are geared to their stage of motor development and level of movement skill learning (see chapter 3). Additionally, the inclusion of specific movement experiences is considerably influ-

Developmental physical education meets the needs of all children.

enced by personal levels of physical fitness (see chapter 4), cognitive development (see chapter 5), and affective growth (see chapter 6).

Age-group appropriateness is important in the developmental physical education program but is secondary to individual appropriateness. The developmental curriculum is *not* based on chronological age or grade level but is influenced by both. The process of development moves from simple to complex and from general to specific as individuals strive to increase their competence in the motor, cognitive, and affective domains of human behavior. As a result, patterns of behavior emerge that may help guide the selection of movement experiences that are typically appropriate for specific age groups. All children, however, diverge from typically expected age-group patterns of behavior at one time or another. Some have special needs that require significant modifications to the program (see chapter 7), whereas others can be successfully accommodated through careful attention to the concept of individual appropriateness.

Children are not miniature adults. Their needs, interests, and capabilities are quite different from those of adolescents and adults. Likewise, preschool, primary grade, and intermediate and upper elementary grade children vary considerably in their developmental capabilities, as should our expectations for them and the movement activities included in the physical education program. The developmental physical education program is not a recess or play period. Rather, it is a learning laboratory in which children learn to move, and learn through movement, by performing activities based on sound principles of child development and grounded in their own needs, interests, and unique abilities.

THE DOMAINS OF DEVELOPMENTAL PHYSICAL EDUCATION

Developmental physical education is sensitive to the motor, cognitive, and affective domains. These three domains of human behavior were first presented by leaders in curriculum and instruction in an attempt to develop a taxonomy of educational objectives. A taxonomy is a classification scheme—in this case, a scheme for sysatically classifying the objectives of education into motor, cognitive, and affective domains. Because it is a specific curricular content area, physical education should be viewed as a subject, like any other, that makes meaningful and measurable contributions to all three domains. In the following paragraphs we'll take a brief look at each of these domains.

Motor Domain

The motor domain is the basis for the movement skill themes of the developmental physical education program. Physical activity for health enhancement and cognitive and affective development form the important program strands that are woven throughout each skill theme (see figure 1.5).

The unique contribution of developmental physical education is in the motor domain through motor development. **Motor development** is progressive change in one's movement behavior brought about by interaction of the movement task with the biology of the individual and the conditions of the learning environment. In other words, one's unique hereditary makeup, along with specific environmental conditions (e.g., opportunities for practice, encouragement, and instruction), combines with the requirements of the movement task itself to determine the rate and extent of one's movement skill acquisition and fitness enhancement. Thus our job as physical educators is to help all children make adaptive change toward increased motor control and movement competence. We do this by involving them in movement activities that are both developmentally appropriate and age appropriate.

Movement Skill Acquisition

Movement skill acquisition is at the very core of the developmental physical education program. The term **movement skill** refers to the development of motor control,

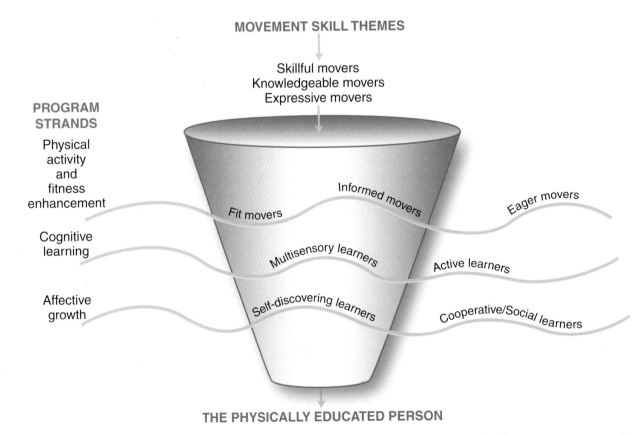

FIGURE 1.5 Movement skill themes are at the core of the developmental physical education program and their accompanying physical activity and fitness, cognitive, and affective strands.

precision, and accuracy in the performance of both fundamental and specialized movements. Movement skills are developed and refined to a point that children are capable of operating with considerable ease and efficiency within their environment. As children mature, the fundamental (or basic) movement skills developed when they were younger are applied as specialized (or complex) skills to a wide variety of games and to various sport, dance, and recreational activities. For example, the fundamental movement skill of striking an object in an underhand, sidearm, or overarm pattern is progressively refined and later applied in sport and recreational pursuits such as golf, tennis, and baseball.

We can also categorize movement skills into broad and sometimes overlapping categories (see figure 1.6). The movement categories of locomotion, manipulation,

SELECTED SPECIALIZED SPORT-RELATED MOVEMENT SKILLS

Football skills	Baseball skills
Basketball skills	Hockey skills
Tumbling skills	Apparatus skills
Track and field skills	Swimming skills
Wrestling skills	Racket-game skills
Dance skills	Etc.

SELECTED FUNDAMENTAL MOVEMENT SKILLS

Locomotion	Manipulation	Stability
1. Basic (one element)	1. Propulsive	1. Axial
a. Walking	a. Ball rolling	a. Bending
b. Running	b. Throwing	b. Stretching
c. Leaping	c. Kicking	c. Twisting
d. Jumping	d. Punting	d. Turning
e. Hopping	e. Striking	e. Swinging
	f. Volleying	
	g. Bouncing	
2. Combinations (two or more elements)	2. Absorptive	2. Static and dynamic postures
a. Climbing	a. Catching	a. Upright balances
b. Galloping	b. Trapping	b. Inverted balances
c. Sliding		c. Rolling
d. Skipping		d. Starting
		e. Stopping
		f. Dodging

FIGURE 1.6 Fundamental movement skills must be developed and refined prior to the introduction of specialized movement skills.

and stability represent the primary focus for movement skill theme development. Chapter 3, "Movement Skill Acquisition," examines these categories more closely in terms of movement skill development and movement skill learning.

Physical Activity and Fitness Enhancement

The critical fitness activities for achieving the health objectives of developmental physical education focus on enhancing the ability and motivation of children to function in an environment that both requires and promotes increased physical activity. Physical fitness can be viewed as a composite of health-related fitness and performance-related fitness. But it is often difficult for people to agree on a precise definition of physical fitness; and many use the term in a broad sense because the level of fitness required of one individual may not be the same as that required of another. A generic definition of **physical fitness** is the ability to perform daily tasks without fatigue and to have sufficient energy reserves for participation in additional physical activities, as well as to meet emergency needs. Muscular strength, muscular endurance, cardiovascular endurance, joint flexibility, and body composition are the **health-related fitness** components of fitness.

Children's aerobic fitness is enhanced during this locomotor activity. As these children share space, their directional (forward) and relationship (moving around a hoop) awareness is also developed.

Performance-related fitness (also known as *skill-related,* or *motor fitness*) is an elusive concept that has been studied extensively over the past several years and is classified by some experts as an aspect of physical fitness. Balance, coordination, agility, speed of movement, and power are among the most frequently cited components of performance-related fitness. For years, researchers have investigated and debated whether these components are general or specific, and the bulk of the evidence is in favor of their specificity. Proponents of the general nature of motor fitness (i.e., those who believed in the concept of the "natural" athlete) long believed that individuals who excelled in certain sports had corresponding abilities that automatically carried over to other activities. Although this often does occur, most now consider such carryover to be a result of the individual's personal motivation, partici-

"Cores, Strands, Developmentally Appropriate": What's All the Fuss?

Real-World Situation

On a visit home for the holidays, you share with family and friends your excitement about becoming a physical education teacher. You mention the tremendous potential of your chosen profession to make a real difference in the lives of children and are shocked to learn that your friends and family don't share your views and excitement. "What's this," they say, "about the 'core' of the physical education program focusing on movement skill acquisition and increased physical activity for health enhancement? And, what's all this about there being 'strands' in the developmentally based program that promote cognitive learning and affective growth?" They go on to quiz you: "Whatever happened to sweat and grunt gym classes like I had?" "Isn't PE just playing games?" They comment, "'Cores,' 'strands,' 'developmentally appropriate' sounds like a lot of fuss about nothing."

Critical Questions

Based on your knowledge of children and the importance of quality developmentally based physical education, take a stand (this will be your first of many):

- What, if anything, can you do or say to help counter these uninformed assertions?
- Why is quality developmentally appropriate physical education of real value to children?
- What do you see as the essential "core" and "strands" of your physical education program?
- Studying to be a physical education teacher: Is it worth the questions, the raised eyebrows, people constantly asking, "Why would you want to do that?"

pation in many fitness activities, and several specific sport aptitudes rather than a direct carryover of motor abilities from one activity to another. In other words, the components of performance-related fitness are "traits," not abilities, and the notion of general motorability—that is, the "natural" athlete—is not supported by the bulk of research on the topic (Burton & Rodgerson, 2001). Children's health-related fitness and performance-related fitness play important roles in the development of total fitness. Figure 1.7 provides an overview of the components of physical fitness. Chapter 4, "Physical Activity and Fitness Enhancement," discusses each in further detail.

```
                    PHYSICAL FITNESS
                   /                \
```

HEALTH-RELATED	PERFORMANCE-RELATED
• Muscular strength	• Balance
• Muscular endurance	• Coordination
• Cardiovascular endurance	• Agility
• Joint flexibility	• Speed
• Body composition	• Power

FIGURE 1.7 The health-related and performance-related components of physical fitness.

Cognitive Domain

Although developmental physical education contributes uniquely to the acquisition of movement skills and fitness enhancement, it also makes many important contributions to cognitive aspects of children's development. **Cognitive learning** is progressive change in the ability to think, reason, and act. Because children are both multisensory learners and active learners, an important strand of the developmental physical education program focuses on concept learning and perceptual-motor learning. Chapter 5, "Cognitive Learning," covers this topic in greater detail.

Concept Learning

Movement can be used to enhance the understanding and application of cognitive and academic learning. With regard to movement, **concept learning** is a permanent change in one's motor behavior brought about by experiences designed to foster understanding of the movement concepts, skill concepts, fitness concepts, and activity concepts of the developmental physical education program. Cognitive learning can, and does, occur in the gymnasium and on the playing field. Moreover, many important academic concepts traditionally taught in the classroom can be effectively learned in the gymnasium. In fact, authors have described how specific types of activities may reinforce concept learning of language arts competencies, basic mathematical operations, and social studies and science concepts.

Children observe the teacher's demonstration of putting two body parts inside of the hula hoop and two body parts outside of the hula hoop. This task enhances both the cognitive (mathematical) and motor (stability) domains of development.

There are many reasons why cognitive concept learning can be effectively taught through movement. One reason is that active participation is fun. Movement often meets the needs and interests of children more fully than classroom activities that are less active. When a child is actively participating in a game that is teaching academic concepts, her attention is not easily diverted by extraneous stimuli. Also, many of today's children undervalue academic achievement but have high regard for physical performance. Using active games as a learning medium pairs pleasurable and highly regarded play with less valued academic activity and thus increases children's interest in practicing the academic skill.

Active learning through movement activities enables children to deal with their world in concrete terms rather than in the abstract. Children generally think of movement as fun, not to be equated with the routine "work" of the classroom. But we should also note that not all children benefit academically through active participation in movement activities. And there is overwhelming evidence that the sedentary academic activities in traditional classrooms are quite effective for many individuals. What's the upshot of all this? Some children benefit greatly from a program that integrates movement activities with academic concept development, and most children will probably realize at least some improvement. Figure 1.8 illustrates the components of cognitive concept learning found in the developmental physical education program. Each is discussed further in chapter 5.

CONCEPT LEARNING

- Skill concepts
- Movement concepts
- Activity concepts
- Fitness concepts
- Academic concepts

FIGURE 1.8   The components of concept learning in the developmental physical education program.

Perceptual-Motor Learning

Learning is a process involving both maturation and experience. Not all children entering school are at the same ability level. Although little can be done to speed up the maturational component of this process, parents and teachers can influence the experiential component. **Perceptual-motor learning** involves the establishment and refinement of sensory sensitivity to one's world through movement. This sensory sensitivity entails developing and refining an adequate spatial and temporal world. All movement occurs in space and involves an element of time. Developing these concepts is basic to efficient functioning in a variety of other areas. It is possible to enhance children's knowledge of their spatial world by involving them in movement activities that contribute to their body awareness, directional awareness, and space awareness. Children's awareness of their temporal world may be increased through activities that focus on the synchrony, rhythm, and sequencing of movements. Selected visual, auditory, and tactile abilities may also be reinforced through movement in carefully selected activities.

Developers of many motor-training programs claim that such programs enhance the cognitive functioning of children. To date, there is little scientific research to support the hypothesis that certain movement activities directly impact the cognitive functioning of children. This does not mean that we cannot effectively use children's movement experiences during physical education programs as a medium for learning through movement. On the contrary, educators now recognize the importance of movement to enhance children's cognitive learning. In other words, through good teaching, movement becomes an effective way of increasing children's awareness of themselves and the world around them. The proper use of the

CONCEPT
1.7

Important cognitive and affective competencies can be effectively reinforced through the developmental physical education program.

"teachable moment" and an emphasis on developing the concepts of *why, what, how,* and *when* in relation to one's movement are important in helping children learn by reinforcing information acquired in the traditional setting of the classroom. Figure 1.9 outlines the perceptual-motor components that the developmental physical education program deals with. Chapter 5 discusses each in greater detail.

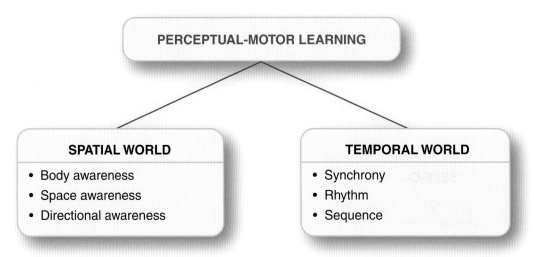

FIGURE 1.9   The perceptual-motor components in the developmental physical education program.

Affective Domain

An important outcome of any quality physical education program is enhancement in the affective domain. **Affective growth** is learning that increases the ability of children to act, interact, and react effectively with other people as well as with themselves. Affective growth is often referred to as "social-emotional development" and is vitally important to children. A good or poor parent, an affluent or culturally deprived environment, and the quality and quantity of stimulation largely determine whether children view their world as one that they can control or as one that controls them. When one has the sense that their hopes, dreams, and aspirations are not controlled by "fate" or "luck" but are, to a large extent, under one's own control, then there is an enhanced sense of self- and affective growth.

The movement experiences that children engage in play an important role in how they view themselves as individuals and how they relate to their peers and use their free time. Astute parents and teachers recognize the vital importance of balanced social-emotional development. They understand the affective development of children and use this knowledge to enhance children's self-esteem and positive socialization and to encourage and structure meaningful movement experiences that strengthen emotional and social development. Chapter 6, "Affective Growth," explores children's self-esteem and childhood socialization and examines how the developmental physical education program can incorporate this information.

Self-Concept Enhancement

Being good at games, sports, and vigorous physical activities contributes greatly to the development of a positive, stable self-concept in children. Although it is by no means the only way in which self-concept is established, movement plays an important role in most cases. **Self-concept** may be defined as an individual's personal perception of his competence in physical, cognitive, and social settings. It is a value-free description of self that impacts on all that we do. Children are active, energetic, emerging beings who use play and movement as ways to learn more about themselves and their bodies.

The beginnings of self-concept are formed during childhood. In their own eyes, children are often on one end of two extremes—good or bad—in all that they do. Because their egocentric nature does not permit them to view their particular strengths and weaknesses objectively, they frequently cannot fully grasp the concept that their abilities to act lie somewhere between these self-limiting poles. Since their world frequently centers on play and vigorous activity, the successes they experience in these areas are important in establishing their positive self-concept. Figure 1.10 provides an overview of the components of a positive self-concept. Chapter 6 explores each component in detail.

SELF-CONCEPT

- Belonging
- Perceived competence
- Worthiness
- Acceptance of self
- Uniqueness
- Virtue

FIGURE 1.10   Components of a positive self-concept.

Positive Socialization

Positive socialization in a physical education, recreation, or sport setting generally occurs in the form of fair play, cooperative behavior, and being a good sport—all indicators of positive moral behavior. Participation in physical activities usually occurs in a social setting, a setting that requires children to make decisions about both cooperative and competitive behaviors. Physical activity, then, has tremendous potential to foster positive moral behavior and to teach the virtues of honesty, teamwork, loyalty, self-control, and fair play. Responsible teachers can take advantage of the moral dilemmas—real or manufactured—that arise during play and games to foster moral growth among their students. In short, the child who is positively socialized into her culture is one who acts morally, is concerned about the welfare of others, and is willing to work cooperatively toward achieving common goals. Sport and movement activities offer teachers many opportunities to model and encourage positive socialization in children. Figure 1.11 illustrates the components of positive socialization. Each is discussed in further detail in chapter 6.

POSITIVE SOCIALIZATION

- Group affiliation
- Attitude formation
- Character education
- Moral growth

FIGURE 1.11   The components of positive socialization.

Summary

The National Standards for Physical Education, seven goals that together describe the essential characteristics of the "physically educated individual," are the framework within which virtually all developmentally appropriate physical education is taught. Quality physical education offered daily is more important today than ever before. Too many of today's children lead sedentary lives to allow us to assume that children, by virtue of being children, get sufficient physical activity. The dramatic increases in childhood obesity, school violence, and early puberty make a convincing case for quality physical education offered daily.

The terms *learning to move* and *moving to learn* embody the general aims and goals of physical education. Developmental physical education first and foremost is individually appropriate and secondarily is age-group appropriate. The potential outcomes of quality physical education experiences take form as the skill themes and program strands of the developmental physical education program.

Teachers must remember that the movement activities children engage in play an important role in their physical fitness as well as in movement skill learning. Generically defined, physical fitness is the ability to perform daily tasks without fatigue and to have the

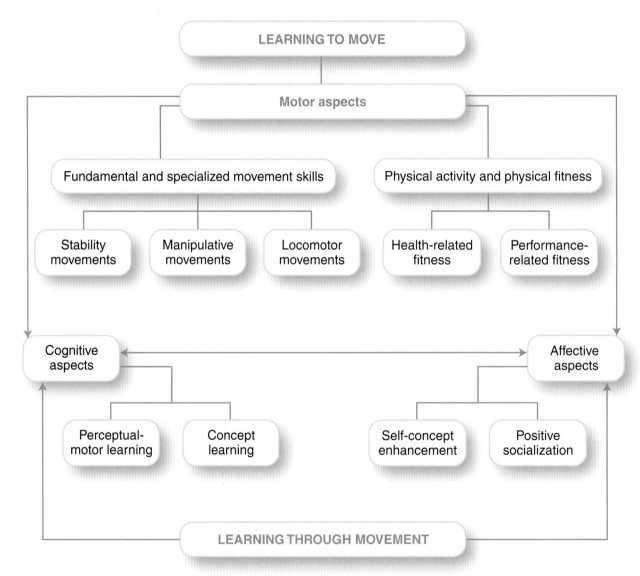

FIGURE 1.12   The aspects of the child's development dealt with in the developmental physical education program.

energy reserves needed to participate in additional physical activities as well as to meet emergency needs.

Little scientific support exists for the outdated concept of the "natural" athlete, making the role of the physical education teacher in skill development and enhancement critically important. Children are involved in the important and exciting task of learning to move effectively and efficiently throughout their world. They are developing a variety of fundamental and specialized movement skills and are enhancing their health through increased levels of physical activity. In short, they are learning to move with joy, efficiency, and control.

Children are also learning through movement. Movement is the vehicle by which they explore all that is around them. Movement enhances their perceptual-motor and cognitive concept learning, promotes the development of a positive self-concept, and promotes positive socialization. The interrelated nature of the motor, cognitive, and affective aspects of developmental physical education is readily apparent and is summarized in figure 1.12.

Terms to Remember

Excellent Readings

Boyce, B.A. (2000). School violence: The case of Jack the Knife. *JOPERD, 71* (7), 31-33, 40.

Bredenkamp, S. (1992). What is developmentally appropriate and why is it important? *JOPERD, 6* (3), 31-32.

Buschner, C.A. (1994). *Teaching children movement skills and concepts.* Champaign, IL: Human Kinetics.

Centers for Disease Control and Prevention. (1997). Guidelines for school and community programs to promote lifelong physical activity among young people. *MMWR, 46,* No. RR-6.

Daley, A.J. (2002). School based physical activity in the United Kingdom: Can it create physically active adults? *Quest, 54,* 21-33.

Lawson, H.A. (1998). Rejuvenating, reconstructing, and transforming physical education to meet the needs of vulnerable children, youth, and families. *JTPE, 18* (1), 2-25.

2

Childhood Growth and Motor Development

Key Concept

▶ The Performance Standards contained within the National Association for Sport and Physical Education's National Standards for Physical Education recognize that the process of growth and motor development proceeds in a predictable sequence but at varying rates among young learners.

In recent years there has been a surge of interest in the growth and motor development of children. No longer are educators content with the vague notion that children somehow magically increase their abilities to function as they advance in age. Physicians, psychologists, physiologists, physical educators, and coaches have become more aware of the need for accurate information about the process of growth and motor development and its influence on the developing child.

We must answer several questions before we can formulate sound developmental physical education programs. First, what is the normal, orderly process of growth? Second, what factors affect growth during childhood? Third, what are the influences of both maturation and experience on the process of motor development? Fourth, what are the typical motor, cognitive, and affective characteristics of children? This chapter provides some answers to these questions. The following Web sites will be helpful in pursuing advanced study:

- American Academy of Pediatrics (**www. aap.org**)
- American School Health Association (**www.ashaweb.org**)
- National Association for Sport and Physical Education (**www.aahperd.org/naspe**)
- National Center for Education in Maternal and Child Health (**www.ncemch.org**)

Chapter Objectives

This chapter will provide you with the tools to do the following:

▶ Describe the normal, orderly process of growth during the periods of early childhood and later childhood.

▶ Discuss the role of nutrition, exercise, chronic illness, and lifestyle factors in the process of childhood growth.

▶ Discuss what is meant by the self-regulatory process of growth.

▶ Distinguish between the cephalocaudal and proximodistal principles of development and demonstrate how they influence movement skill acquisition.

▶ Explain what is meant by the terms *differentiation* and *integration* with regard to the process of development.

▶ Speculate on the role of individual variability, readiness, and sensitive learning periods in the process of motor development.

▶ List and describe typical motor, cognitive, and affective characteristics of children during the early and later childhood periods.

▶ Propose specific implications for developmental teaching based on the typical characteristics of children.

There has been a surge of interest in the growth and motor development of children. No longer are educators content with the vague notion that children somehow "magically" increase their abilities to function as they advance in age. Physicians, psychologists, physiologists, educators, and coaches have become aware of the need for accurate information concerning the process of growth and motor development and its influence on the developing child.

PHYSICAL GROWTH

Physical growth, a process associated with increases in structural size, is marked by steady increases in height, weight, and muscle mass during childhood. Growth is not as rapid during childhood as during infancy, and it gradually decelerates throughout childhood until the preadolescent growth spurt. It is important for you to understand the process of physical growth throughout childhood and the factors that affect children's growth if you are to be effective in promoting movement skill acquisition and fitness enhancement. Figure 2.1, *a* and *b,* illustrates the weight-for-age, stature (height)-for-age, and body mass index-for-age percentiles for girls from 2 to 20 years. Figure 2.2, *a* and *b,* provides the same information for boys. Take time to study these charts. They represent the very latest information from the Centers for Disease Control and Prevention (CDC, 2000; **www.cdc.gov/nchs**) on the height and weight of American children and youth. Furthermore, they reveal a significant, pronounced upward shift in weight and body mass index since the last national sampling was published 25 years ago, but no significant changes in height. These charts will be helpful to you as a teacher in determining the growth status of your students and developing appropriate intervention programs.

CONCEPT 2.1

Growth occurs in an orderly and predictable sequence throughout childhood, but with considerable individual variation.

Early Childhood (Ages Three to Eight)

The annual height gain from the early childhood period to puberty is about 2 inches per year, with weight gains averaging 5 pounds per year. At this stage of growth, some differences may be seen between boys and girls in terms of height and weight, but these differences are minimal. The physiques of male and female preschoolers and primary grade children are remarkably similar when viewed from a posterior position, with boys being only slightly taller and heavier. Boys and girls have similar amounts of muscle and bone mass, and both boys and girls show a gradual decrease in fatty tissue as they progress through the early childhood period.

Body proportions change markedly during early childhood because of the various growth rates of the body. The chest gradually becomes larger than the abdomen, and the stomach gradually protrudes less. By the time children reach their sixth birthday, their body proportions more closely resemble those of older children in the elementary school.

Name_____

Record #_____

Mother's Stature_____		Father's Stature_____		
Date	Age	Weight	Stature	BMI*

*To Calculate BMI: Weight (kg) ÷ Stature (cm) ÷ Stature (cm) × 10,000 or Weight (lb) ÷ Stature (in) ÷ Stature (in) × 703

Revised and corrected November 28, 2000.

SOURCE: Developed by the National Center for Health Statistics in collaboration with the National Center for Chronic Disease Prevention and Health Promotion (2000).

http://www.cdc.gov/growthcharts

CDC

FIGURE 2.1a   For girls, ages 2 to 20 years: stature-for-age and weight-for-age percentiles.

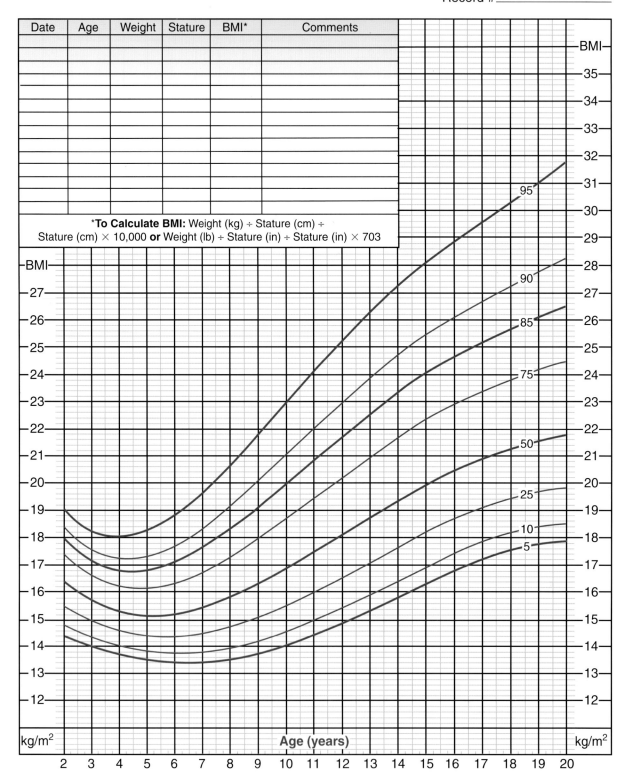

Name _____

Record # _____

Date	Age	Weight	Stature	BMI*	Comments

To Calculate BMI: Weight (kg) ÷ Stature (cm) ÷ Stature (cm) × 10,000 **or** Weight (lb) ÷ Stature (in) ÷ Stature (in) × 703

SOURCE: Developed by the National Center for Health Statistics in collaboration with the National Center for Chronic Disease Prevention and Health Promotion (2000).
http://www.cdc.gov/growthcharts

FIGURE 2.1b   For girls, ages 2 to 20 years: body mass index-for-age percentiles.

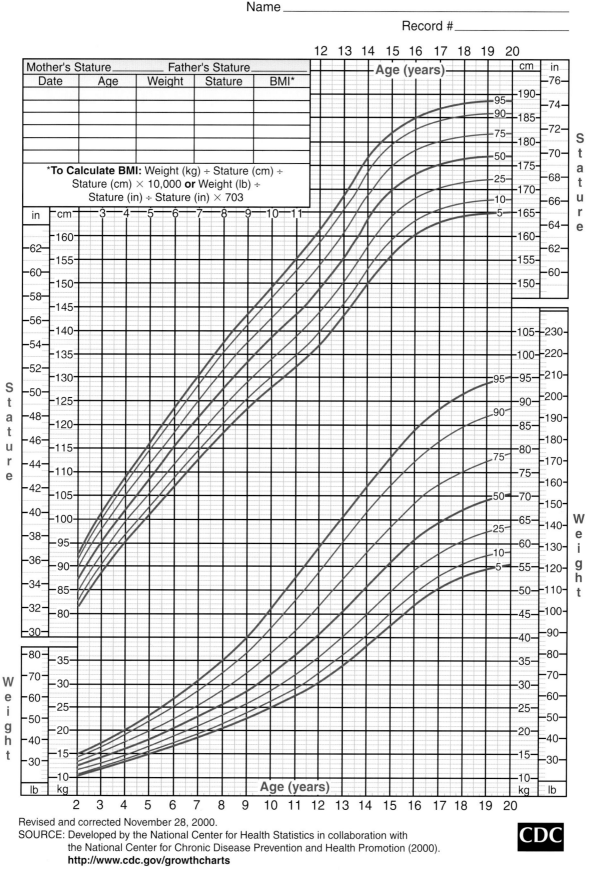

Name_____

Record #_____

Mother's Stature_____		Father's Stature_____		
Date	Age	Weight	Stature	BMI*

*To Calculate BMI: Weight (kg) ÷ Stature (cm) ÷ Stature (cm) × 10,000 or Weight (lb) ÷ Stature (in) ÷ Stature (in) × 703

Revised and corrected November 28, 2000.

SOURCE: Developed by the National Center for Health Statistics in collaboration with the National Center for Chronic Disease Prevention and Health Promotion (2000).
http://www.cdc.gov/growthcharts

CDC

FIGURE 2.2a   For boys, ages 2 to 20 years: stature-for-age and weight-for-age percentiles.

Name _____

Record # _____

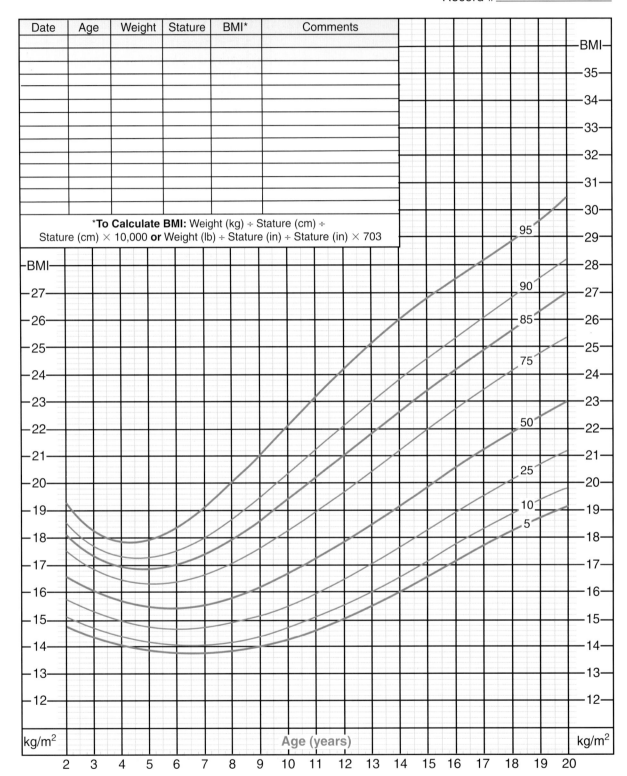

Date	Age	Weight	Stature	BMI*	Comments

*To Calculate BMI: Weight (kg) ÷ Stature (cm) ÷
Stature (cm) × 10,000 **or** Weight (lb) ÷ Stature (in) ÷ Stature (in) × 703

SOURCE: Developed by the National Center for Health Statistics in collaboration with
the National Center for Chronic Disease Prevention and Health Promotion (2000).
http://www.cdc.gov/growthcharts

FIGURE 2.2b   For boys, ages 2 to 20 years: body mass index-for-age percentiles.

Little People and Giants

Real-World Situation

As an elementary school physical education teacher, you intend to involve each of your three classes of fourth, fifth, and sixth graders in a series of lessons focused on enhancing their skills in the game of basketball. In each of the classes, the majority of students are 8, 9, and 10 years old, respectively. You recognize that they display increasing variation in height and weight both *between* the various age groups and *within* each age group. Additionally, many of the female students are both taller and heavier than the boys, particularly in grades four and five.

Critical Questions

When planning your physical education lessons and when setting up an after-school youth sport program:

- Should you attempt to equalize groups in terms of height and/or weight for the instructional portion of the class? Why or why not?
- Should steps be taken to equalize groups for height and/or weight during team play? Why or why not?
- Should boys and girls be combined for instruction and for team play? Why or why not?
- During the after-school program or in a local youth sport program, how should 8-, 9-, and 10-year-olds be grouped?
- What can be done to rectify these disparities if the situation involves American football, soccer, swimming, track and field, and so on?

Bone growth during early childhood is dynamic, and the skeletal system is particularly vulnerable to malnutrition, fatigue, and illness. The bones ossify (harden) rapidly during early childhood unless there has been severe, prolonged nutritional deprivation.

The development of **myelin,** a fatty substance around the neurons (commonly referred to as the process of myelination), permits the transmission of nerve impulses and is not complete at birth. At birth many nerves lack myelin, but with advancing age greater amounts of myelin encase the nerve fibers. Myelination is largely complete by the end of the early childhood period, thus allowing for efficient transference of nerve impulses throughout the nervous system. It is interesting to note that increased complexity in children's movement skills is possible following myelination. As the cortex matures and becomes progressively more organized, children are able to perform at higher levels in both a motor and a cognitive sense.

The sensory apparatus is still developing during the early childhood years. The eyeball does not reach its full size until about 12 years of age. The macula of the retina is not completely developed until the sixth year, and young children are generally farsighted. This is one important reason young children have difficulty fixating on and intercepting moving objects.

Young children have more taste buds than adults; and the taste buds are generously distributed throughout the insides of the throat and cheeks, as well as on the tongue, causing greater sensitivity to taste. This results in profound likes and dislikes for certain types of foods.

Because of the flat angle of the eustachian tube connecting the middle ear with the throat, young children are also more sensitive to infections of the ear. **Otitis media,** or inflammation of the inner ear, occurs commonly among young children and may influence their balancing abilities.

Later Childhood (Ages 8 to 12)

The period of later childhood, from about the 8th to the 12th year of life, is typified by slow but steady increases in height and weight and by progress toward greater organization of the sensory and motor systems. Changes in body build are slight during these years. Later childhood is more a time of lengthening and filling out prior to the prepubescent growth spurt that typically occurs around age 10 for girls and age 12 for boys. Children make rapid gains in learning during later childhood and are capable of functioning at increasingly sophisticated levels in the performance of movement skills. This period of continued slow growth in height and weight gives children time to get used to their growing body. This is an important factor in the typically dramatic improvement we see in coordination and motor control in the later childhood years. The gradual change in size and the close relationship maintained between bone and tissue growth are important factors in increased levels of motor functioning.

Differences between the growth patterns of boys and girls are minimal during later childhood. Both boys and girls have greater limb growth than trunk growth, but boys tend to have longer legs, arms, and standing height during this period. Likewise, girls tend to have greater hip width and thigh size during this period. Because relatively little difference in physique or weight is exhibited until the onset of the preadolescent period, girls and boys can participate effectively together in most activities.

During later childhood, very slow growth occurs in brain size. The size of the skull remains nearly the same, although there is a broadening and a lengthening of the head toward the end of this period.

CONCEPT 2.2

The rate and extent of growth are both influenced by a variety of environmental and genetic factors.

Fifth graders horizontally traverse a climbing wall. Physical characteristics and abilities between these particular 10- to 11-year-old boys and girls are more similar than different.

Perceptual abilities become increasingly refined. The sensorimotor apparatus works in greater harmony so that by the end of this period, children can perform numerous sophisticated skills. The ability to strike a pitched ball, for example, typically improves with age and practice because of improved visual acuity, tracking abilities, reaction time, movement time, and sensorimotor integration. A key to maximum

velopment of more mature growth patterns in children is utilization. In other words, if, through the normal process of maturation, children have improved perceptual abilities, these must be experimented with and integrated more completely with the motor structures through practice. The lack of abundant opportunities for practice, instruction, and encouragement during this period prevents many individuals from acquiring the perceptual and motor information needed to perform skillfully.

FACTORS AFFECTING CHILDHOOD GROWTH

Growth is not an independent process. Although heredity sets the limits of growth, environmental factors help determine whether someone reaches these limits. The degree to which these factors affect motor development is not entirely clear and needs further study. However, it is clear that factors such as nutrition, exercise, illness, and lifestyle play significant roles in the process of physical growth.

Nutrition

Numerous investigations have provided clear evidence that dietary deficiencies can delay growth during childhood. The extent of **growth retardation** depends on the severity, duration, and time of onset of undernourishment. For example, if severe, chronic malnutrition occurs during the first four years of life, there is little hope of catching up to one's age-mates in terms of mental development because the critical period of brain growth has passed.

Malnutrition can interrupt the physical growth process at any time between infancy and adolescence. Malnutrition may also contribute to the development of certain diseases that affect physical growth. For example, lack of vitamin D in the diet can result in rickets, vitamin B12 deficiencies may cause pellagra, and the chronic lack of vitamin C results in scurvy. These diseases are now relatively rare in our society, but the effects of kwashiorkor, a debilitating disease resulting from protein malnutrition that retards growth, are seen in many parts of the world where there is a general lack of food and good nutrition. Children suffering from chronic malnutrition, particularly during infancy and early childhood, may never completely reach the growth norms for their age level. Evidence of this comes from developing nations where adult height and weight norms are considerably lower than those for industrialized nations.

Dietary excesses may also affect the growth of children. In affluent countries, obesity is a major problem. The increased tendency toward obesity in our society is directly linked to lack of physical activity, combined with high-calorie, low-cost food. Each year, obesity is the direct cause of over 300,000 deaths in the United States, making it second only to smoking as the leading cause of preventable death (American Obesity Association, 2000; **www.obesity.org**). By definition, obesity is a failure in the body weight regulation processes that results in the excess accumulation of body fat. Obesity is now recognized by medical authorities to be a disease—one that has a strong familial component, influenced by both genetics and the environment. The causes of **childhood obesity** and its influences on motor development are of considerable concern. The constant barrage of television commercials extolling one junk food or another, the "fast food" addiction of millions, and the use of edibles as a pacifier or as bribery for good behavior may all affect the nutritional health of children. Because each child has her own unique biochemical composition, it is difficult to pinpoint where adequate nutrition ends and malnutrition or obesity begins.

Physical Activity

CONCEPT 2.3

Development proceeds in a predictable manner but varies greatly in rate and individual readiness.

One of the principles of physical activity relates to use and disuse. Stated simply, a muscle that is used will **hypertrophy** (increase in size) and a muscle that is not used will **atrophy** (decrease in size). In children, activity definitely promotes muscle development. Although the number of muscle fibers does not increase, the size of the fibers does, and muscles respond and adapt to increased amounts of stress. Maturation alone will not account for increases in muscle mass. An environment that promotes vigorous physical activity on the part of the child will do much to promote muscle development. Further, active children tend to have less body fat in proportion to lean body mass than children who are not active.

Although physical activity generally has positive effects on the growth of children, it can have negative effects if carried to an extreme. The popularity of youth sports and the intensity of training that often accompanies sport may be contributing to this problem, but the critical point separating harmful and beneficial activity is not clear. It seems reasonable to assume, however, that strenuous activity carried out over an extended period of time may injure children's muscle and bone tissue. "Swimmer's shoulder," "tennis elbow," and "runner's knees" are just a few of the ailments plaguing children who have exceeded their developmental limits. To help avoid such problems, teachers and parents should carefully supervise children's exercise and activity programs. Although exercise has great potential benefits to a child's growth, the limits of the individual must be carefully considered.

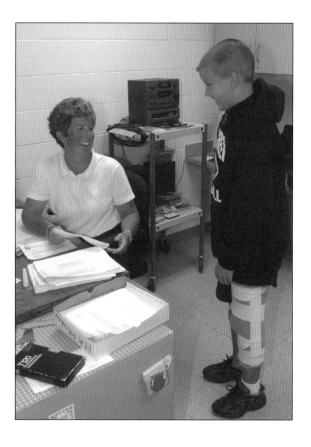

This fifth grade boy has a knee injury. The physical education teacher will need to modify lesson activities to accommodate this student.

Only the Strong Survive

Real-World Situation

For summer employment, you have accepted a position as an age-group swimming coach. The previous coach, who was highly successful, commonly required all swimmers in the 10 to 12 age group to swim as much as 7,000 to 10,000 meters per day. This was accomplished with "two-a-day" practices. Morning sessions were held from 5:30 to 7:30 A.M., and evening sessions were held from 5:30 to 7:30 P.M. Several parents question your level of commitment to maintain your predecessor's rigorous practice schedule. Several other parents are relieved that the "reign of terror" in terms of training demands is, in their view, about to end. Your continued employment over subsequent summers depends on your success with the team.

Critical Questions

Based on what you know about prepubescent children and the effects of exercise on their development:

- What are your major issues of concern?
- What is the potential for overuse injuries among your swimmers?
- How do you propose placating both groups of parents while at the same time respecting the developmental needs of your athletes?
- What is your position on the philosophy of "only the strong survive"?

Illness

While the standard acute childhood illnesses (chicken pox, colds, measles, and mumps) do not have a marked effect on growth, the extent to which other illnesses and diseases retard growth depends on their duration, severity, and timing. Often, the interaction of malnutrition and illnesses in children makes it difficult to determine accurately the specific cause of growth retardation. The combination of conditions, however, puts the child at risk and greatly enhances the probability of measurable growth deficits.

Interruption of the normal pace of growth is compensated for by a still unexplained **self-regulatory growth** process that helps children catch up to their age-mates. For example, although a severe illness may temporarily retard a child's gain in height and weight, there is a definite tendency to reach a parity with one's age-mates upon recovery from the illness. But although this self-regulatory process can compensate for minor deviations in the growth process, it cannot make up for major deviations. Restricted opportunities for movement and deprivation of experience have been shown to interfere with children's abilities to perform movement tasks that are characteristic of their age level. The extent to which children are able to catch up to their age-mates depends on the duration and severity of deprivation, the age of the child, and the level of motivation to make improvements.

Lifestyle

Secular trends are brought about by complex generational changes in lifestyle that result in the tendency for children today to be both taller and heavier, age for age, and to mature sexually at an earlier age than children several generations ago. The trend for secular increases is not universal, though. Although increases in growth, sexual maturation, and physical performance levels have been demonstrated in most developed countries, some developing nations have not shown secular increases

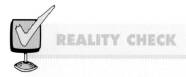

Secular Trends

Real-World Situation

It's in the news, it's on the television, it's in your professional journals: On the average, boys and girls are now significantly heavier than children of just 10 or 20 years ago. In fact, almost 12% of today's children are considered to be overweight or obese, whereas only 5% were classified as such a generation ago. Given this startling information, you are more determined than ever to make a difference in the lives of your children by adopting practices that promote increased physical activity.

Critical Questions

Based on what you know about physical inactivity among today's children:

- What specific proactive steps might you take to promote increased physical activity?
- What will you to do to help ensure long-term adherence to increased physical activity?
- What is your role and responsibility in terms of imparting relevant information related to diet and nutrition?
- What, if anything, can you do to eliminate the sale of junk food in school vending machines?
- What can you do to help break the dramatic trend toward overweight and obesity among all age groups?

and in some cases have even shown secular decreases. Most believe that secular trends are largely the result of changes in lifestyle and nutritional habits from one generation to another.

Secular trends in height in North America and other developed nations appear to have come to a halt. There has been little indication of secular increases in height and maturation in these countries in the past several years. But there has been a definite secular trend in weight increase among children and also in earlier sexual maturation. Recent studies have clearly revealed that today's children (and adults) are significantly fatter than their age-mates of just 10 years ago. Additionally, a distinct tendency toward early puberty among North American girls and boys has become an area of increasing concern among many child development experts.

DEVELOPMENT

Development is the continuous process of change over time beginning at conception and ceasing only at death. Motor development, therefore, may be viewed as progressive change in movement behavior throughout the life cycle. Motor development involves continuous adaptation to changes in one's movement capabilities in the continual effort to achieve and maintain motor control and movement competence. According to this perspective, development is not domain specific, and it is not necessarily stage-like or age dependent. Instead, according to this perspective, some aspects of an individual's development can be conceptualized into domains, or as being stage-like and age related, while others cannot. Furthermore, the concept of achieving and maintaining competence encompasses all developmental change—change that is both positive and negative throughout life.

Theories currently popular among many developmentalists offer hypothesized explanations for the processes of development. They address the critical question

"*Why* does developmental change occur as it does?" The aim of descriptive profiles of development is to describe what occurs in the developmental process by addressing the equally critical question "*What* are the typical markers of development in the normally developing individual?" The integration of both explanatory and descriptive models of development is depicted in figure 2.3. Take a few minutes to study this important figure and reflect on its implications for offering developmentally appropriate physical education—physical education that is both individually appropriate and age appropriate.

Both the processes and the products of motor development should constantly remind us of the individuality of the learner. Each individual has a unique timetable for the development and extent of acquisition of abilities. Although our "biological clock" is somewhat predictable when it comes to the sequence of movement skill acquisition during the preschool and elementary school years, the rate and extent of development are individually determined and dramatically influenced by the performance demands of the specific movement task itself.

CONCEPT
2.4

Human development is a complex phenomenon necessitating understanding of both its processes and products.

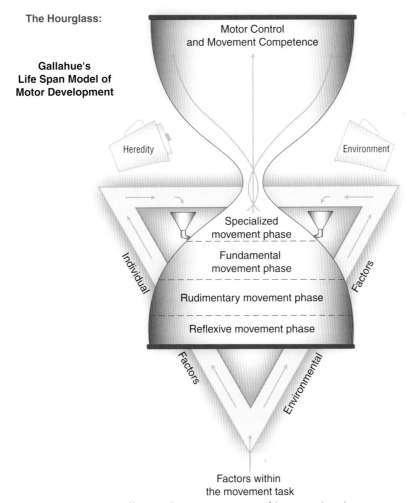

FIGURE 2.3 The hourglass offers a descriptive view of human development in terms of *what* the typical phases and stages of development are. The triangle offers a visual reference for asking *why* questions as to how heredity and the environment impact on the tasks of movement skill development.

Reprinted, by permission, from D.L. Gallahue and J.C. Ozmun, 2002, *Understanding motor development* (Boston: McGraw-Hill), 53.

Typical age periods of development are just that—typical, and nothing more. Age periods merely represent approximate time ranges during which certain behaviors are most frequently observed in normally developing children. Overreliance on these time periods would negate the concepts of continuity, specificity, and individuality in the developmental process and are of little practical value in work with children who have developmental disabilities.

FACTORS AFFECTING CHILDHOOD MOTOR DEVELOPMENT

Development brings about change in one's functional capabilities. We generally view development in children as an upward process leading toward increased capabilities. Development as a lifelong process, however, also encompasses the diminishing of capabilities in chronically ill children as well as the gradual regression in movement capabilities with advancing age. The process of motor development depends on a variety of developmental factors. As a teacher you will need to be aware of the tremendous complexity of the process of motor development and will need to take an objective view of your role as a catalyst for change in this process.

As children develop, gradual shifts or increments in the level of functioning occur in the stability, locomotor, and manipulative categories of movement behavior. During infancy, children gain the very simplest controls over their movements in order to survive at the lowest level of motor functioning. Preschool and primary grade children are involved in developing and refining their fundamental movement skills. The many complex movements found in the sport and dance activities of older children, adolescents, and adults are little more than highly elaborated forms of these fundamental movements.

The unique genetic inheritance that accounts for our individuality can also account for our similarity in many areas. One of these similarities is the trend for human development to proceed in an orderly, predictable fashion. A number of factors that affect motor development tend to emerge from this predictable pattern. Table 2.1 illustrates the typical sequence of emergence of selected locomotor, manipulative, and stability abilities during childhood.

CONCEPT 2.5

Several biological factors explain, in part, both the sequence and the rate of motor development in childhood.

TABLE 2.1—SEQUENCE OF EMERGENCE OF SELECTED LOCOMOTOR, MANIPULATIVE, AND STABILITY ABILITIES

Movement pattern	Selected abilities	Approximate age of onset
Walking		
Walking involves placing one foot in front of the other while maintaining contact with the supporting surface.	Rudimentary upright unaided	13 months
	Walks sideways	16 months
	Walks backward	17 months
	Walks upstairs with help	20 months
	Walks upstairs alone–follow step	24 months
	Walks downstairs alone–follow step	25 months

Movement pattern	Selected abilities	Approximate age of onset
Running		
Running involves a brief period of no contact with the supporting surface.	Hurried walk (maintains contact)	18 months
	First true run (nonsupport phase)	2-3 years
	Efficient and refined run	4-5 years
	Speed of run increases, mature run*	5 years
Jumping		
Jumping takes three forms: (1) jumping for distance, (2) jumping for height, and (3) jumping from a height. It involves a one- or two-foot takeoff and landing on both feet.	Steps down from low objects	18 months
	Jumps down from object with one-foot lead	2 years
	Jumps off floor with both feet	28 months
	Jumps for distance (about 3 feet)	5 years
	Jumps for height (about 1 foot)	5 years
	Mature jumping pattern*	6 years
Hopping		
Hopping involves a one-foot takeoff with a landing on the same foot.	Hops up to 3 times on preferred foot	3 years
	Hops from 4 to 6 times on same foot	4 years
	Hops from 8 to 10 times on same foot	5 years
	Hops distance of 50 feet in about 11 seconds	5 years
	Hops skillfully with rhythmical alterations, mature pattern*	6 years
Galloping		
The gallop combines a walk and a leap with the same foot leading throughout.	Basic but inefficient gallop	4 years
	Gallops skillfully, mature pattern*	6 years
Skipping		
Skipping combines a step and a hop in rhythmic alternation.	One-footed skip	4 years
	Skillful skipping (about 20%)	5 years
	Skillful skipping for most*	6 years
Reach, grasp, release		
Reaching, grasping, and releasing involves making successful contact with an object, retaining it in one's grasp, and releasing it at will.	Primitive reaching behaviors	2-4 months
	Corralling objects	2-4 months
	Palmer grasp	3-5 months
	Pincer grasp	8-10 months
	Controlled grasp	12-14 months
	Controlled releasing	14-18 months
Throwing		
Throwing involves imparting force to an object in the general direction of intent.	Body faces target, feet remain stationary, ball is thrown with forearm extension only	2-3 years
	Same but with body rotation added	3.6-5 years

(continued)

TABLE 2.1 — (continued)

Movement pattern	Selected abilities	Approximate age of onset
Throwing (continued)		
	Steps forward with leg on same side as the throwing arm	4-5 years
	Boys exhibit more mature pattern than girls	5 years and over
	Mature throwing pattern*	6 years
Catching		
Catching involves receiving force from an object with the hands, moving from large to progressively smaller balls.	Chases ball; does not respond to aerial ball	2 years
	Responds to aerial ball with delayed arm movements	2-3 years
	Needs to be told how to position arms	2-3 years
	Fear reaction (turns head away)	3-4 years
	Basket catch using the body	3 years
	Catches using the hands only with a small ball	5 years
	Mature catching pattern*	6 years
Kicking		
Kicking involves imparting force to an object with the foot.	Pushes against ball; does not actually kick it	18 months
	Kicks with the leg straight and little body movement (kicks at the ball)	2-3 years
	Flexes lower leg on backward lift	3-4 years
	Greater backward and forward swing with definite arm opposition	4-5 years
	Mature pattern (kicks *through* the ball)*	5-6 years
Striking		
Striking involves sudden contact to objects in an overarm, sidearm, or underhand pattern.	Faces object and swings in a vertical plane	2-3 years
	Swings in a horizontal plane and stands to the side of the object	4-5 years
	Rotates the trunk and hips and shifts body weight forward	5 years
	Mature horizontal pattern with stationary ball	5-7 years
Dynamic balance		
Dynamic balance involves maintaining one's equilibrium as the center of gravity shifts.	Walks 1-inch straight line	3 years
	Walks 1-inch circular line	4 years
	Stands on low balance beam	2 years
	Walks on 4-inch-wide beam for short distance	3 years

Movement pattern	Selected abilities	Approximate age of onset
Dynamic balance (continued)		
	Walks on same beam, alternating feet	3-4 years
	Walks on 2- or 3-inch beam	4 years
	Performs basic forward roll	3-4 years
	Performs mature forward roll*	6-7 years
Static balance		
Static balance involves maintaining one's equilibrium while the center of gravity remains stationary.	Pulls to standing position	10 months
	Stands without handholds	11 months
	Stands alone	12 months
	Balances on one foot 3 to 5 seconds	5 years
	Supports body in basic 3-point invert positions	6 years
Axial movements		
Axial movements are static postures that involve bending, stretching, twisting, turning, and the like.	Axial movement abilities begin to develop early in infancy and are progressively refined to a point where they are included in the emerging manipulative patterns of throwing, catching, kicking, striking, trapping, and other activities	2 months-6 years

*The child has the developmental *potential* to be at the mature stage. Actual attainment depends on environmental factors.

Reprinted, by permission, from D.L. Gallahue and J.C. Ozmun, 2002, *Understanding motor development* (Boston: McGraw-Hill), 183-185.

Developmental Sequence

Developmental sequence refers to the tendency for orderly, predictable sequence of motor control. **Cephalocaudal development** refers specifically to the gradual progression of increased control over the musculature, beginning with the head and moving to the feet. The tendency of young children to be clumsy and to exhibit poor control over their lower extremities may result from incomplete cephalocaudal development.

Proximodistal development refers specifically to progression in control of the musculature from the center of the body to its most distant parts. Young children, for example, are able to control the muscles of the trunk and shoulder girdle sooner than they can gain control over the muscles of the wrist, hand, and fingers. Teachers of primary grade children are recognizing this principle of development when they teach the less refined elements of manuscript printing before introducing the more complex and refined movements of cursive writing.

Developmental Variability and Readiness

Although children's development follows a characteristic sequence that is universal and resistant to major changes, the rate at which children acquire these traits and abilities is quite variable. **Developmental variability** refers to age variations in the rate of movement skill acquisition. For example, children progress at differing rates in attaining the mature fundamental manipulative skills of throwing and catching or the baseball skills of batting and fielding a ground ball. Such variability becomes entirely understandable when we consider the complex interaction among the cognitive, affective, and motor aspects of children's development. Compounding this variability are each child's unique hereditary makeup and specific environmental circumstances—all ensuring that children will develop at varying rates. Developmental variability is a critically important concept to consider in designing and implementing the developmental curriculum with an emphasis on individual appropriateness.

Readiness refers to conditions within both the individual and the environment that make a particular task appropriate for the child to master. As used today, the concept of readiness extends beyond biological maturation and includes environmental factors that can be modified or manipulated to encourage or promote learning. Some children simply are not ready for the experiences that we are prepared to provide them. For example, your students certainly will not be ready to learn how to do a handstand if they have not mastered the progression of skills leading from a tripod to a tip-up, a headstand, and finally a handstand. To ensure that we are on target with our instructional strategies and the content of our program, we need to be certain that children have the prerequisite skills.

It is important for us to recognize and respect the concepts of developmental variability and individual readiness both among groups of children and within individual children. We simply cannot consider children solely on the basis of their chronological age or grade level and expect to succeed in accomplishing movement skill acquisition and fitness enhancement.

Differentiation and Integration

A developing child's motor control is marked by the coordinated, progressive, and intricate interweaving of neural mechanisms of opposing muscle systems into an increasingly mature relationship. Two different but related processes are associated with this increase of functional complexity: differentiation and integration. **Differentiation** is the gradual progression from the gross global (overall) movement patterns of infants to the more refined and functional movements of children as they mature. **Integration** refers to the coordinated interaction of opposing muscle and sensory systems. For example, when attempting to grasp an object, the young child gradually progresses from ill-defined corralling movements to more mature and visually guided reaching and grasping behaviors. This differentiation of movements of the arms, hands, and fingers—followed by integration of the use of the eyes with the movements of the hand to perform rudimentary eye-hand coordination tasks—is crucial to normal development.

Sensitive Learning Periods

CONCEPT 2.6

Childhood represents an important sensitive period for movement skill acquisition.

Basically, a **sensitive period** is a broad time frame or window of opportunity when the learning of specific new skills is easier and quicker. For example, there appear to be sensitive periods for learning how to speak a foreign language, play a musical instrument, and perform a host of gross motor skills ranging from swimming and bicycle riding to gymnastics and baseball skills.

Children, especially young children, are generally fearless in terms of risking physical injury, personal failure, and peer ridicule. Additionally, they are eager learners unencumbered by a history of negative learning experiences, feelings of incompetence, and the fear of injury and rejection. We can view the entire period of childhood as a sensitive period for mastering fundamental movement skills and for being introduced to a wide variety of sport skills. Especially important is the period of early childhood—roughly from age three to eight. The development of mature fundamental movement skills is a prerequisite to the learning and mastery of sport skills. Failure to take advantage of this sensitive movement skill period of learning in childhood makes it difficult for the child to attain higher levels of skill later on.

Normal development in later periods may be hindered if children fail to receive proper stimulation during a sensitive period. For example, inadequate nutrition, prolonged stress, inconsistent caregiving, or lack of appropriate learning experiences early in life may have a more negative impact on development than would be the case if these factors were present at a later age.

The concept of sensitive periods does have a positive side. It suggests that appropriate intervention during a sensitive period tends to facilitate more positive forms of subsequent development than would be the case if the same intervention occurred later. The concept of sensitive periods rejects the notion that there are highly specific time frames in which one must develop movement skills. There are, however, broad periods during which a child can most easily develop certain skills.

EARLY CHILDHOOD DEVELOPMENT

Play is what young children do when they are not eating, sleeping, or complying with the wishes of adults. Occupying most of a child's hours, play may be viewed literally as the child's equivalent of work as performed by adults. Play is the primary means by which children learn about their bodies and movement capabilities. Play also facilitates cognitive and affective growth in young children and provides an important means of developing both fine and gross motor skills. Check out the excellent Web site from the National Center for Education in Maternal and Child health (**www.ncemch.org**) and the National Institute of Child Health and Human Development (**www.nichd.nih.gov**).

The preschool years are a period of important cognitive development. Preschool children are actively involved in enhancing their cognitive abilities in a variety of ways. During this time they develop cognitive functions that eventually result in logical thinking and concept formulation. Young children are incapable of thinking from any point of view other than their own. Their perceptions dominate their thinking, and what they experience at a given moment influences them strongly. During this preconceptual phase of cognitive development, seeing is literally believing. In the thinking and logic of preschool children, their conclusions need no justification. Even if they did, the children would be unable to reconstruct their thoughts and show others how they arrived at their conclusions.

Affective development is also dramatic during the preschool years. During this period children are involved in the two crucial social-emotional tasks of developing a sense of autonomy and developing a sense of initiative. Autonomy is expressed through a growing sense of independence, which may be seen in children's delight in responding with the word "no" to almost any direct question. The answer will often be "no" to a question such as "Do you want to play outside?" even when the child clearly would like to do so. We can view this behavior as the child's expression

TEACHING TIP 2.1

Implications for teaching developmental physical education based on typical *early childhood characteristics:*

- Emphasize the process (qualitative aspects) of movement prior to the product (quantitative aspects).

- Focus on fundamental movement skill learning, remembering that skill learning takes time, practice, and repetition.

- Teach fewer things well rather than doing a mediocre job with too many objectives.

- Provide plenty of opportunity for gross motor activities in both undirected and directed settings.

- Include plenty of positive reinforcement to encourage the establishment of a positive self-concept and to reduce the fear of failure.

- Stress developing a variety of fundamental stability, locomotor, and manipulative skills, first alone and then within movement phrases.

- Teach boys and girls together (it's the law); at this stage their interests and abilities are quite similar.

- Promote perceptual-motor learning through movement skill acquisition.

- Take advantage of the child's great imagination through the use of drama and imagery.

- Provide a wide variety of experiences that improve object-handling skills and promote eye-hand coordination.

- Incorporate bilateral skills such as skipping, galloping, and hopping with alternate foot leading after unilateral movements have been fairly well established.

- Encourage children to take an active part in the program by *showing and telling* what they can do to promote social interaction.

- Provide for individual differences and allow children to progress at their own rate.

- Establish standards for acceptable behavior and make sure children abide by them.

- Provide wise guidance in establishing a sense of doing what is right and proper for its own sake.

- Personalize instruction based on individual readiness.

of a newfound sense of independence and an ability to manipulate some factors in the environment, rather than always an expression of sheer disobedience. One way to avoid this natural autonomous reaction to a question is to form a positive statement instead, for example, "Let's go play outdoors." In this way the child is not confronted with a direct yes-or-no choice. But it is also important to make sure that there are many situations in which the expression of a child's autonomy is reasonable and proper.

We see young children's expanding sense of initiative in their curious exploring and their very active behavior. Children begin to engage in new experiences such as climbing, jumping, running, and throwing objects for their own sake and for the sheer joy of sensing and knowing what they are capable of doing. Failure to develop a sense of initiative and autonomy at this stage frequently leads to feelings of shame, worthlessness, and guilt. Establishing a stable self-concept in preschoolers is crucial to proper affective development because it directly affects both cognitive and psychomotor functions.

Through the medium of play, preschoolers develop a wide variety of fundamental stability, locomotor, and manipulative abilities. If they have a stable and positive self-concept, the gain in control over their musculature is a smooth one. The timid, cautious, and measured movements of the two- to three-year-old gradually give way to the confident, eager, and often reckless abandon of the four- and five-year-old. Preschoolers' vivid imaginations make it possible for them to jump from "great

CONCEPT 2.7

Children exhibit a variety of motor, cognitive, and affective characteristics that are, in a broad sense, age appropriate.

heights," climb "high mountains," leap over "raging rivers," and run "faster" than an assorted variety of "wild beasts."

Children of preschool age are rapidly expanding their horizons, asserting their individuality, developing their abilities, and testing their limits (as well as testing the limits of their family and others around them). In short, young children are pushing out into the world in many complex and wondrous ways. It is critical, though, to understand their developmental characteristics and their limitations as well as their potentials. Only in this way can we effectively structure movement experiences for young children that truly reflect their needs and interests and are within their level of ability.

Primary grade children take the first big step into their expanding world when they enter first grade. For most, first grade represents the first separation from the home for a regularly scheduled, extended block of academic time. It is the first venture out of the secure play environment of the home, day care center, or kindergarten and into the world of adults where systematic instruction occurs and learning is expected. For many children, entering a school represents the first time that they are placed in a group in which they are not the center of attention. It is a time when sharing, concern for others, and respect for the rights and responsibilities of others are established. Kindergarten is a readiness time in which children begin making the gradual transition from an egocentric, home-centered play world to the group-oriented world of adult concepts and logic. In the first grade, the first formal demands for cognitive understanding are made. The major cognitive milestone of the first and second grader is learning how to read at a reasonable level. The child is involved in developing the first real understanding of time and money and numerous other cognitive concepts. By the second grade, children should be well on their way to meeting and surmounting a broadening array of cognitive, affective, and motor tasks.

The following selected developmental characteristics represent a synthesis of findings from a wide variety of sources (Gallahue & Ozmun, 2002; Payne & Isaacs, 2001). We present them here to give you a more complete view of normally developing children during the early childhood years.

These kindergarteners and first and second graders are a multi-aged class. Here they play follow-the-leader with their teacher as they begin their physical education class. Their eagerness and enthusiasm are quite evident!

Motor Characteristics

- Growth proceeds at a slow but steady pace, with annual height gains of about 2 inches and annual weight gains of approximately 5 pounds.
- Perceptual-motor abilities are rapidly developing, but confusion often exists in body, directional, temporal, and spatial awareness.
- Good bladder and bowel control are generally established by the end of this period, but accidents sometimes occur with younger children.
- Children during this period are rapidly developing and refining fundamental movement abilities in a variety of skills. Cross-lateral movements such as skipping, however, often present more difficulty than unilateral movements.
- Children are active and energetic and would often rather run than walk.
- Gross motor control is developing rapidly and generally occurs sooner than fine motor control.
- Fine motor control develops to the point that children can dress themselves, color, stack blocks, and print with reasonable skill.
- The body functions and processes become well regulated. A state of physiological homeostasis (stability) becomes well established.
- The physiques of boys and girls are remarkably similar. A posterior view of boys and girls reveals no readily observable structural differences.
- Because children at this stage are farsighted, their eyes are not generally ready for extended periods of close work.

Cognitive Characteristics

- Children at this stage are increasingly able to express their thoughts and ideas verbally.
- A fantastic imagination enables children to imitate both actions and symbols with little concern for accuracy or the proper sequencing of events.
- Children continuously investigate and discover new symbols that have a primarily personal reference.
- Children learn the "how" and "why" of their actions through active play.
- Early childhood is a preoperational phase of development, resulting in a period of transition from self-satisfying behaviors to fundamental socialized behaviors.

Affective Characteristics

- During early childhood, children are generally egocentric and assume that everyone thinks the way they do. As a result, they often seem to be quarrelsome and exhibit difficulty in sharing and getting along with others.
- They are often fearful of new situations, shy, self-conscious, and unwilling to leave the security of what is familiar.
- They are learning to distinguish right from wrong and are beginning to develop a conscience.
- Children at the beginning of this period are often nonconforming and irregular in their behavior, whereas older children are often viewed as more stable and conforming.
- The self-concept is rapidly developing. Providing children with success-oriented experiences and positive reinforcement is especially important during these years. These experiences help to build children's sense of competence.

LATER CHILDHOOD DEVELOPMENT

Children in the middle and upper elementary grades are generally happy, stable, and able to assume responsibilities and cope with new situations. They are eager to learn more about themselves and their expanding world; they enthusiastically test their developing skills and typically have a wide range of interests.

The following are selected developmental characteristics typical of children during later childhood (Gallahue & Ozmun, 2002; Payne & Isaacs, 2001).

Motor Characteristics

- Growth is slow but steady, especially from age eight to the end of this period.

- The body begins to lengthen out, with an annual gain of only 1 to 2 inches and an annual weight gain of only 3 to 6 pounds.

- The cephalocaudal (head-to-toe) and proximodistal (center-to-periphery) principles of development are evident at this stage. Children's larger muscles are considerably better developed than their small muscles.

- Girls are generally about a year or more ahead of boys in physiological development. Separate interests between girls and boys begin to develop during this period.

- Hand preference is firmly established, with about 90% of children preferring the right hand and about 10% preferring the left.

- Reaction time improves. Difficulty with eye-hand and eye-foot coordination is evident at the beginning of this period, but by the end these types of coordination are generally well established.

- Both boys and girls are full of energy but often possess low endurance levels. Responsiveness to training, however, is great.

- Visual-perceptual abilities are generally fully developed by the end of this period.

- Fundamental movement skills should be well developed by the beginning of this period, and children are eager to be introduced to a variety of sport skills.

- Competence develops rapidly if children have ample opportunities for practice, quality individualized instruction, and positive encouragement.

Cognitive Characteristics

- Children's attention is often very focused, especially for activities that are of great personal interest. They are intellectually curious and are eager to know "why."

- Children are eager to learn and to please adults, but they need assistance and guidance in decision making.

- Children have good imaginations and display extremely creative minds, but self-consciousness often predominates.

- Children at the beginning of this period are limited in their abstract thinking abilities and learn best with concrete examples.

- More sophisticated abstract cognitive abilities are evident by the end of this period.

TEACHING TIP 2.2

Implications for teaching developmental physical education based on typical *later childhood characteristics:*

- Provide remedial opportunities for children to refine and combine fundamental movement skills to the point that their movements are fluid and efficient.
- Assure children that they are accepted and valued so that they know they have a stable and secure place in the school.
- Offer plenty of encouragement and positive reinforcement to promote continued development of a positive self-concept.
- To help promote self-reliance, expose children to experiences in which they have progressively greater amounts of responsibility.
- Help children adjust to the rougher ways of the school playground and neighborhood without being rough or crude themselves.
- Introduce children to individual, dual, and team activities as their competence develops.

- Children at this level often learn best through active participation. Integration of academic concepts with movement activities provides an effective way to reinforce concepts in science, mathematics, social studies, and the language arts.
- Discuss play situations involving such topics as taking turns, fair play, cheating, and being a good sport in an effort to establish a more complete sense of right or wrong.
- Encourage children to think before engaging in an activity. Help them recognize potential hazards as a means of reducing their sometimes reckless behavior.
- Children should have opportunities for participation in youth sport activities that are developmentally appropriate and geared to their needs and interests.

Affective Characteristics

- Interests of boys and girls are similar at the beginning of this period but soon begin to diverge. Both enjoy self-testing activities as a means of trying out and testing their developing skills.
- Large-group interaction and the concept of teamwork improve throughout this period.
- Children are often aggressive, boastful, self-critical, and overreactive; without effective adult interaction, they accept both victory and defeat poorly.
- Children are responsive to authority and are critically conscious of what is "fair."
- Children are adventurous and eager to be involved with friends in "dangerous" or "secret" activities.

Summary

The process of childhood growth and motor development is one that is predictable in terms of universal principles and sequential progressions as children develop higher levels of functioning. However, children show considerable individual variation due to a variety of environmental and hereditary factors, in both the rate and extent of acquisition of these higher levels of functioning. Several factors were discussed that influence growth and development and provide us with general cues to the maturational aspects of change throughout childhood. Consideration of these factors must be paramount as we select specific movement experiences and utilize specific teaching behaviors within the physical education program.

We must consider the individual appropriateness of the movement activities we employ in the developmental physical education program.

Teachers of developmentally appropriate physical education must learn about the typical motor, cognitive, and affective characteristics of early childhood (generally ages 3-7) and later childhood (generally ages 8-12). Among motor characteristics that change during each of these periods are the rate of growth, the development of movement abilities, and motor control.

Changes in cognitive characteristics relate to the ability to express thoughts and ideas and development of the ability to think abstractly, to cite two examples. Some important affective characteristics relate to the child's self-concept, sense of competence, and the ability to get along with and interact with others. Knowledge of these characteristics provides teachers with important guidelines for selecting movement experiences and applying teaching behaviors that are sensitive to the concept of age-group appropriateness.

Terms to Remember

Excellent Readings

Barnett, B.E., & Merriman, W. (1991). Misconceptions in motor development. *Strategies, 5* (3), 5-7.

Gabbard, C. (1998). Windows of opportunity for early brain and motor development. *JOPERD, 69* (8), 54-55, 61.

Hynes-Dusel, J. (2002). Motor development in elementary children. *Strategies, 15* (3), 30-34.

National Association for Sport and Physical Education. (2000). *Appropriate practice in movement programs for young children ages 3-5.* Reston, VA: AAHPERD.

National Association for Sport and Physical Education. (2000). *Appropriate practices for elementary school physical education (a position statement of NASPE).* Reston, VA: AAHPERD.

Patrick, K., Spear, B., Holt, K., and Sofka, D. (2001). *Bright futures in practice: Physical activity.* U.S. Department of Health and Human Services, Washington, DC: National Center for Education in Maternal and Child Health.

3

Movement Skill Acquisition

Key Concept

▶ A physically educated person demonstrates competency in many movement forms and proficiency in a few movement forms.

Content Standard #1: *National Standards for Physical Education:* National Association for Sport and Physical Education

Chapter Objectives

This chapter will provide you with the tools to do the following:

▶ List and distinguish among a variety of terms used to define movement skill acquisition.

▶ Provide examples of stability, locomotor, and manipulative movements at the fundamental and specialized movement skill phases.

▶ Describe and give examples of movement phrases using each category of movement.

▶ Discuss the importance of movement skill development during childhood.

▶ List and describe four primary environmental factors that influence movement skill development.

▶ Identify and discuss characteristics of the underlying stages of the fundamental movement phase and the specialized movement phase.

▶ Give examples of internally paced and externally paced; gross and fine; and discrete, serial, and continuous movement activities.

▶ List and discuss the three levels of learning a new movement skill and their accompanying six stages.

▶ Provide guidelines for teaching individuals at the beginning, intermediate, and advanced levels of movement skill learning.

▶ Propose means for incorporating movement skill homework into the physical education program.

The unique contribution of children's physical education is in the area of movement skill acquisition. In this chapter we look at how children become skillful movers. **Skillful movers** are individuals who move with control, efficiency, and coordination in the performance of fundamental or specialized movement tasks. Later chapters will deal separately with the topics of knowledgeable movers and expressive movers. In this chapter we first discuss the importance of developing children's movement skills, the categories of movement, the factors that influence how children acquire movement skills, and the phases and stages of motor development. After a brief discussion of the types of movement skills, we examine the levels and stages of learning a new movement skill. A discussion of movement skill homework and implications for teaching developmental physical education conclude the chapter.

THE IMPORTANCE OF DEVELOPING MOVEMENT SKILLS

Failure to develop and refine fundamental and specialized movement skills during the crucial preschool and elementary school years often leads children to frustration and failure during adolescence and adulthood. Failure to develop mature patterns in throwing, catching, and striking, for example, makes it difficult for children to succeed in and enjoy even a recreational game of softball. Children cannot take part, with success, in an activity if they have not learned the essential movement skills contained within that activity.

This does not mean that if people don't learn skills during childhood they cannot develop them later in life. But it is easiest to develop these skills during childhood. If a person does not develop the skills early, they too often remain unlearned. Several factors contribute to this situation. One is an accumulation of bad habits from improper learning. It is much more difficult to "unlearn" faulty movements than to learn to do them correctly in the first place. Self-consciousness and embarrassment are a second factor. "I have two left feet," "I'm all thumbs," and "What a klutz" are all self-derogatory phrases that children may use to comment on poor performance that lead to their reluctance to become active participants. A third factor is fear. Fear and anxiety about being injured and of being ridiculed by peers are very real feelings that often contribute markedly to difficulty in learning movement skills later in life. All of this means that it is crucial for children to fully develop their fundamental movement abilities and a variety of basic sport skills during childhood.

MOVEMENT SKILLS AND MOVEMENT PATTERNS

Although often used interchangeably, the terms *movement skill, fundamental movement skill, specialized movement skill,* and *movement pattern* have important distinctions. A movement skill, which may be either a fundamental movement skill or a specialized skill, is a series of movements performed with accuracy and precision. In a movement skill, control of movement is stressed and extraneous movement is therefore limited. Striking a ball with an implement is a movement skill.

A **fundamental movement skill** is an organized series of basic movements that involve the combination of movement patterns of two or more body segments. Fundamental movement skills may be categorized as stability, locomotor, or manipulative movements. Twisting and turning, running and jumping, and striking and throwing are examples of fundamental movement skills from each of these categories, respectively.

A **specialized movement skill** is a fundamental movement skill or combination of fundamental movement skills that have been applied to the performance of a specific sport-related activity. Thus the fundamental movement skills of twisting the body and striking an object may be applied, in their horizontal form, to batting in a game of baseball or, in their vertical forms, to playing golf or serving a tennis ball.

A **movement pattern** is an organized series of related movements. More specifically, a movement pattern involves the performance of an isolated movement that by itself is too restricted to be classified as a fundamental movement skill or a sport skill. For example, the sidearm, underarm, or overarm patterns of movement alone do not constitute the fundamental movement skills of throwing or striking or the sport skills of pitching or batting in baseball. They merely represent an organized series of movements in which movement is stressed but accuracy, control, and precision are limited.

CONCEPT 3.1

A variety of terms may be used to describe the various forms, levels, and types of movement skill.

Developmental physical education recognizes the need to focus on the process, or mechanics of movement skill acquisition, prior to the product, or performance aspects of movement skill development. It does so in a manner that promotes learning through exploration and self-discovery of the movement pattern whenever possible, before focusing on outcome measures such as "how far," "how fast," and "how many." Physical educators who recognize the validity of this developmental approach to movement skill learning concentrate their teaching efforts on helping children to become skillful movers by acquiring and mastering fundamental movement skills prior to sport skill specialization.

TEXT BOX 3.1

When asked about teaching basic skills to a new generation of players, Kareem Abdul-Jabbar, the NBA's all-time scoring leader, was quoted in *USA Today* as saying, "If you had asked me three years ago, I'd have said, 'Forget it. Are you out of your mind?' Now, it's not quite like that. There's a great need for people to teach the game. I don't think a lot of the young players, especially the front line players, are learning the fundamentals."

THE CATEGORIES OF MOVEMENT

Movement skills, whether fundamental movement skills or specialized movement skills, may be subdivided into categories. The three **categories of movement**—stability, locomotion, and manipulation—classify the intended function of one's movement (Gallahue & Ozmun, 2002). These three categories and resulting movement phrases can be further organized according to the sport skill themes (such as soccer or volleyball) in which these movement skills are most emphasized. Figure 3.1 summarizes these categories, and table 3.1 provides a list of selected sport skill themes from the developmental physical education curriculum.

Stability Movement Skills

Stability movement skills form the basis for all other locomotor and manipulative skills because all movement involves an element of stability. Stability movement skills, sometimes referred to as non-locomotor skills, are those in which the body remains in place but moves around its horizontal or vertical axis. In addition, there are dynamic balance tasks in which a premium is placed on gaining or maintaining one's equilibrium against the force of gravity. For example, dodging an opponent and the forward roll in tumbling are both considered stability skills because of the strong emphasis placed on maintaining equilibrium throughout each task. Axial movements such as reaching, twisting, turning, bending, and stretching are fundamental stability abilities, as are lifting, carrying, pushing, and pulling. Other fundamental stability skills involve a variety of positions that entail inverted support, such as the tripod and headstand. Still others involve transitional postures, such as body

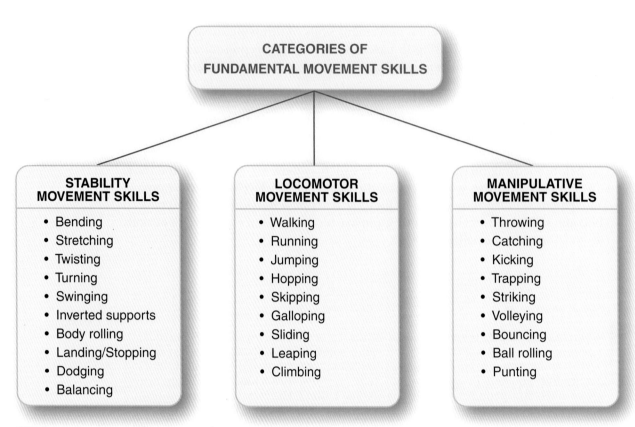

FIGURE 3.1   Selected fundamental movement skill themes.

TABLE 3.1—SELECTED SPORT SKILL THEMES AND THE MOVEMENT SKILLS EMPHASIZED IN EACH

Sport skill themes	Stability movement skills	Locomotor movement skills	Manipulative movement skills
Basketball skills	Selected axial movements Pivoting Dodging Guarding Picking Blocking Cutting Faking	Running Sliding Leaping Jumping	Passing Catching Shooting Dribbling Tipping Blocking Rebounding
Combative skills	All axial movement skills Dodging and feinting Static balance skills Dynamic balance skills	Stepping Sliding Hopping (karate)	Dexterity (fencing) Striking (kendo)
Dance skills	All axial movement skills Static balance postures Dynamic balance postures	Running Leaping Jumping Hopping Skipping Sliding Stepping	Tossing Catching

Sport skill themes	Stability movement skills	Locomotor movement skills	Manipulative movement skills
Disk sport skills	All axial movement skills Static balance postures Dynamic balance postures	Stepping Running Jumping	Tossing Catching
Football skills	Blocking Tackling Dodging Pivoting	Running Sliding Leaping Jumping	Passing Catching Carrying Kicking Punting Centering
Gymnastics skills	Inverted supports Rolling, landing All axial movement skills Static balance moves Dynamic balance moves	Running Jumping Skipping Leaping Hopping Landing	
Implement striking skills (tennis, squash, racketball, hockey, lacrosse, golf)	Dynamic balance skills Turning Twisting Stretching Bending Dodging Pivoting	Running Sliding Leaping Skating Walking	Forehand Backhand Striking Driving Putting Lobbying Smash Drop Throwing Trapping
Skiing skills	All axial movement skills Dynamic balance skills Static balance skills	Stepping Walking Running Sliding	Poling
Soccer skills	Tackling Marking Dodging Feinting Turning	Running Jumping Leaping	Kicking Trapping Juggling Sliding Throwing Blocking Passing Dribbling Catching Rolling
Softball/baseball skills	Selected axial movement skills Dynamic balance skills Dodging	Running Sliding Leaping Jumping	Throwing Catching Pitching Batting Bunting
Target sport skills	Static balance skills		Aiming Shooting

(continued)

TABLE 3.1 — (continued)

Sport skill themes	Stability movement skills	Locomotor movement skills	Manipulative movement skills
Track and field skills	All axial movement skills Dynamic balance skills	Running Hopping Vertical jumping Horizontal jumping Leaping Starting	Shot put Discus Javelin Hammer Pole vault Baton passing Throwing
Volleyball skills	Dynamic balance skills Selected axial movements	Running Sliding Jumping Diving Sprawling Rolling	Serving Volleying Bumping Digging Spiking Dinking Blocking

Children demonstrate dynamic balance as they travel across the tires in different ways.

rolling and springing movements. Stability skills emphasize static (stationary) balance or dynamic (moving) balance. Sport skill abilities in tumbling and gymnastics, as well as in diving and figure skating, all depend on stability.

Locomotor Movement Skills

Locomotor movement skills are those in which the body is transported in a horizontal or vertical direction from one point to another. Activities such as running, jumping, hopping, leaping, and skipping are considered fundamental locomotor move-

A first grader demonstrates a fundamental locomotor skill, jumping, over a hula hoop.

ments. When these fundamental skills become elaborated and further refined, they can be applied to specific sports. For example, the 50-yard dash, running the bases in softball, the high jump in track, and running a pass pattern in football are all specialized, sport-related locomotor skills.

Manipulative Movement Skills

Manipulative movement skills encompass either gross motor or fine motor movements. **Gross motor manipulation** refers to movements that involve giving force *to* objects or receiving force *from* objects. Throwing, catching, kicking, trapping, and striking are considered fundamental gross motor manipulative skills. Manipulative sport skills are an elaboration and further refinement of these basic skills. For example, hitting a tennis ball, throwing the javelin, catching a baseball, and playing the game of soccer all involve numerous manipulative skill abilities that are refinements of the fundamental tasks of striking, throwing, catching, and kicking, respectively.

The term **fine motor manipulation** refers to object-handling activities that emphasize motor control, precision, and accuracy of movement. Tying one's shoes, coloring, and cutting with scissors are all examples of fundamental fine motor manipulative skills. Target archery, violin playing, and the popular game of darts all have essential fine motor aspects and are considered to be fine motor, specialized movement skills. Physical educators are concerned primarily with the acquisition of gross motor manipulative skills and to a somewhat lesser extent with fine motor manipulative skills.

Movement Phrases

Movement phrases are combinations of stability, locomotor, and manipulative movements. They are introduced *after* children have mastered the basic elements of a single fundamental movement. For example, rather than being content with

CONCEPT 3.2

Stability, locomotor, and manipulative movements and the combination of these into movement phrases serve as the categories of movement into which fundamental and specialized movement skills may be classified.

Dribbling around an opponent is a specialized manipulative skill.

jumping off the springboard and landing in a bent-knee position, children now want to jump off, land, and do a forward roll. Or they may want to jump with a half turn followed by a backward roll. As their skills develop, these movement phrases become longer, more complex, and more refined.

Participating successfully in most games and sports involves the combination of movements into sequences. For example, striking and running are combined into a phrase in baseball batting and base running, as are running, reaching, catching, and throwing in a typical baseball fielding sequence. Movement skills, whether they are fundamental or specialized, are generally learned best when first focused on singly. However, after the skill has been reasonably well mastered, it should be combined with others and used in dynamic gamelike situations. Purposeful movement in the real world is a series of coordinated phrases, not isolated, unconnected movements.

ENVIRONMENTAL FACTORS AND MOVEMENT SKILL ACQUISITION

Historically, many educators erroneously assumed that children somehow "automatically" develop their movement skills as they mature. Therefore, the physical education period, particularly during the primary grades, was often viewed as little more than a glorified recess, in which an endless variety of games were played for little more reason than that they were fun or that they contributed to other social-emotional objectives. Little serious consideration was given to using the early grades as a time for helping children master their fundamental movement abilities or using the upper grades to introduce children to a wide variety of sport skills. Instead children's physical education was viewed as a time to get away from the confines of the classroom, to have fun, and to "blow off steam."

Most now recognize that environmental factors play an important role in movement skill acquisition and that children need encouragement, frequent opportunities for practice, and quality instruction in an ecologically sound environment to develop and refine their movement abilities. It is clear that the preschool and early elementary years are the critical time for mastering fundamental movement skills. Maturation alone will not account for this development. Children who have mastered these skills are ready to begin the exciting process of developing specialized skills and applying them to a wide variety of game, sport, dance, and recreational activities for a lifetime of vigorous movement.

CONCEPT 3.3

Environmental factors, including opportunities for practice, encouragement, instruction, and the environment setting itself, significantly influence the development of movement skills.

REALITY CHECK

We Just Want to Play the Game

Real-World Situation

Several of your students are on local youth sport teams. Invariably, some insist that because they play whatever sport skill theme you are focusing on, "We know all the skills. We just want to play the game." Being the excellent teacher that you are, you want to do your best to reach all of your students, including those who are unskilled as well as those who may be skillful.

Critical Questions

Based on the situation as presented and your knowledge of the importance of the environment in movement skill learning, think about how you should go about planning and conducting your lessons:

- You can't just ignore these vocal students and insist that they take part in the entire lesson with the rest of the class, but what can you do?

- If you give in, and instead of providing instruction in the skills of the particular sport, let the entire class play, what are the likely short- and long-term outcomes?

- You could let the more skillful play the game while you take time to instruct the rest of the class, but what are the ramifications of doing so?

- How might you use the skillful students as mini instructors to help you explain and demonstrate new skills to the rest of the class?

Opportunity for Practice

Three factors play a crucial role in children's opportunities to practice developing their movement skills—facilities, equipment, and time.

Many children live in congested cities in high-rise apartments, cramped housing complexes, or sprawling suburbs—all of which frequently lack sufficient facilities to meet their needs to move. The facilities to play ball, fly a kite, or play a game of tennis may be lacking. Even in areas where facilities have been set aside for public use, children must share their use with adolescents and adults. All too often, older children, and even adults, preempt the needs and interests of children. Consequently children are left to fend for themselves in the pursuit of vigorous movement experiences.

Opportunities for practice are also frequently limited by a lack of proper equipment. The cost of basketballs, baseball gloves, and hockey sticks, for example, is high. Parents and community centers often find it prohibitively expensive to purchase sufficient amounts and varieties of equipment for children to use.

A third factor, time, may be the most important determiner of opportunities for practice. Many children simply do not have the time to develop their movement skills. Their day is so highly programmed with school, television, computer games, and homework that little time is left for active movement.

Ample facilities, equipment, and time are all critical to fundamental movement skill development. Parents and teachers who fail to provide numerous opportunities for fundamental movement skill learning are substantially limiting children's developmental potential and their eventual success with the specialized sport skills of later childhood, adolescence, and adulthood.

Practice opportunities should be introduced under internally paced, or static, conditions. In this way, the learner can focus on one skill requirement at a time and therefore maximize opportunities for success. Then, as the child develops the skill, she should practice it, when appropriate to the skill, in externally paced, or dynamic, situations in which the environmental conditions are flexible and constantly changing. Such an approach to sequencing practice promotes a learning environment focused on adaptability, movement variability, and motor creativity. Please refer to the "Teaching Tip" sections throughout the book for specific ideas on how to structure opportunities for practice based on the type and level of movement skill being learned.

If children do in fact need ample opportunities for practice in order to develop their movement skills, then we must try to provide appropriate facilities, equipment, and time. The school physical education program offers the best avenue for ensuring learning opportunities for all children. The need first for *quality* and then for *daily* physical education is obvious. Quality physical education offered daily is essential if we are serious about the goals of increasing physical activity by developing skillful movers and providing ample practice opportunities for all.

Importance of Encouragement

Many children do not receive sufficient encouragement to develop their movement abilities. In many families today, both parents are employed outside the home. In other families a single parent is raising the children. A frequent result of such situations is that the time and energy required to involve children in physical activities are missing. Too often children are quick to imitate the adults in their lives

Here a parent helps her children practice in-line skating.

in their pursuit of the "good life"—in the "workaholic" ethic that leaves little time for family activities, leisure, and purposeful recreational pursuits. On the other hand, some children are part of a family in which the cares of the workday are left behind only to be replaced by a mind-dulling escape to the television, the computer, or other passive activities. This failure to stimulate, encourage, and motivate children to engage in physical activity because of a lack of time, energy, interest, or personal example results in the failure of many children to develop their movement abilities.

Quality of Instruction

The quality of the instruction given to children is perhaps the most crucial factor influencing development of their movement skills. Opportunities for practice and encouragement alone will not bring about the development of skillful movement in most children. You, the teacher, are the necessary ingredient. Without you, many children will never develop mature fundamental movement skills or acquire related sport skills. The school physical education program, whether at the preschool or elementary school level, is the *only* place where children can be guaranteed to receive the encouragement, opportunities for practice, and quality instruction so vital to movement skill acquisition.

Environmental Setting

The **environmental setting** refers to the immediate surroundings in which children are attempting to learn. It includes object props such as facilities, equipment, and supplies, and also behavior settings such as the number of students in the class and their ability to attend to the instructional cues that are provided by the instructor.

It will be important for you as a teacher to recognize that the ecological setting of the learning environment has a dramatic impact on movement skill learning. For example, ample numbers of balls are essential if we want children to be maximally active. But it is not enough simply to have the proper quantity. It is also critically

Ample opportunity for practice is demonstrated since all children are dribbling a soccer ball in this physical education class.

important to have a sufficient variety of balls—of different sizes, shapes, colors, and textures—if we are serious about helping children become skillful ball handlers.

Appropriate class size is equally important. The number of students in a class should be such that all children have ample opportunities for practice and for encouragement and instruction from a knowledgeable, caring teacher—a teacher who is able to cope realistically with the number of students present. This was not the case in a sixth grade physical education class that one of the authors had a daughter in—with 110 students and only one teacher! The teacher-to-student ratio in this case made it essentially impossible for the children to progress in their ball-handling skills. The teacher, under the circumstances, was able to do little else than maintain a semblance of order, resulting in lots of sitting, waiting, and watching while only a few students were active.

THE FUNDAMENTAL MOVEMENT SKILL PHASE

The phases of motor development are classified as the reflexive, rudimentary, fundamental, and specialized movement phases (see figure 3.2). The reflexive and rudimentary phases are characteristic of infancy and toddlerhood. They form critical building blocks for the fundamental and specialized phases of early childhood and beyond. Gallahue and Ozmun (2002) present a detailed discussion of each of these phases.

The period ranging from about two to seven years of age is generally considered to be the **fundamental movement phase** of movement skill acquisition. This young

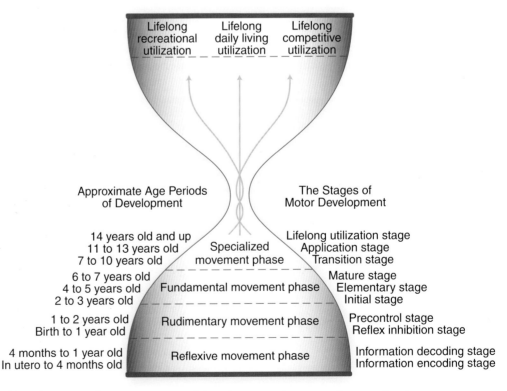

FIGURE 3.2 A descriptive view of the phases and stages of motor development.

Reprinted, by permission, from D.L. Gallahue and J.C. Ozmun, 2002, *Understanding motor development* (Boston: McGraw-Hill), 46.

age is the ideal time for children to master basic stability, locomotor, and manipulative skills. These movement skills may be viewed as developing along a continuum of stages within this phase, progressing from the initial to the elementary and finally to the mature stage (figure 3.2). A wide variety of fundamental stability, locomotor, and manipulative skills are described and pictured in chapters 18 through 20.

Initial Stage

At the initial stage of developing a fundamental skill, children make their first observable and purposeful attempts at performing the task. This is a stage characterized by relatively crude, uncoordinated movements. The child may make valid attempts at throwing, catching, kicking, or jumping; but major components of the mature pattern are missing, and movements are either grossly exaggerated or inhibited. Execution of the movement is not rhythmically coordinated. Two- and three-year-olds typically function at the initial stage.

Elementary Stage

The elementary stage of fundamental movement skill development is typical of the performance of three- to five-year-old children. The elementary stage of development appears to depend primarily on maturation. In this transitional period between the initial and mature stages, coordination and rhythmical performance improve, and children gain greater control over their movements. However, movements at this stage still appear somewhat awkward and lacking in fluidity.

Many adults are only at the elementary stage in such basic activities as throwing, striking, and catching. They have progressed to this stage primarily through maturation but, because of insufficient practice, encouragement, and instruction, they have failed to achieve the mature stage. The core of the developmental physical education program for preschool and primary grade children should focus on helping them progress from the elementary to the mature stage in a wide variety of fundamental movements.

Mature Stage

The mature stage of fundamental movement skill development is characterized by the integration of all the component parts of a pattern of movement into a well-coordinated, mechanically correct, and efficient act. From this stage, performance improves rapidly. For example, children are able to throw farther, run faster, and jump higher after attaining the mature stage. A mature fundamental skill may be continually refined, combined with other movement skills, and utilized in a variety of specialized movements.

CONCEPT 3.4

Movement skill development may be classified into a series of age-related, but not age-dependent, phases that in turn are made up of identifiable stages of movement skill acquisition.

Children can attain the mature stage in most fundamental movements by age six or seven. Frequently, however, they get there at varying rates. Some experience a delay or fail to achieve the mature stage in particular skills. Others are advanced and reach this stage more rapidly. If development is delayed over a period of years, certain skills may never be attained in their mature form without considerable effort and outside influence. Failure to develop mature patterns of fundamental movement will limit children in acquiring specialized sport skills in later childhood, adolescence, and adulthood. Mature fundamental movement skills form the basis for all sport skills, and they must be learned. If they are not learned, a cycle of frustration and failure results.

By the Numbers

Real-World Situation

Your building principal, who is well intentioned, believes that the primary function of the physical education class is to provide released time for group planning among the "real" teachers. Furthermore, your principal believes that children essentially develop their fundamental movement skills as a function of increased age and maturation—so your primary function is to keep them "quiet, happy, and good." As a result of this thinking, and in an attempt to be progressive and make decisions "by the numbers," the principal has proposed that you be assigned a first- through fifth-grade teaching schedule that collapses multiple classrooms for each grade into a single physical education class. Consequently you would have 60 to 100 students in each of your classes. This would enable the three "real" teachers for each of these grades to get together on a regular basis for joint curriculum planning.

As an inducement to gain your cooperation, your principal proposes that in place of the current schedule of 30 minutes of daily physical education for each class of 20 to 35 students, all classes will meet three times per week for a full 60 minutes. The principal points out that the new plan exceeds the old one by an extra 30 minutes of instruction per week, a full 20 hours per year.

Critical Questions

Based on the situation as presented, your knowledge of good teaching practice, and the phases and stages of motor development:

- What is your view of the principal's assumptions?
- If the principal's "by the numbers" reasoning is incorrect, how would you educate him or her?
- You know that children do not develop their movement skills primarily as a function of maturing and growing older, but how will you convince your principal?
- How might you go about convincing the principal that although movement skill development is age related, it is not age dependent?

THE SPECIALIZED MOVEMENT SKILL PHASE

The **specialized movement phase** typically begins around age seven. Most children begin to develop a keen interest in sport. Boys and girls alike select their favorite sport heroes, don football jerseys and baseball caps, choose the running shoe they like best, and frequently carry a basketball or a baseball glove to school. They are eager to learn new skills and apply them to a wide variety of sport activities. Efficient sport skill development is based on proper development of fundamental movement abilities. Although it begins in childhood, sport skill development frequently continues through adolescence and into adulthood. The specialized movement skill phase of development may be subdivided into three stages—transition, application, and lifelong utilization (figure 3.2).

Transition Stage

The **transition stage** of specialized movement skill development generally begins around age 7 and extends to about age 10. Children at this stage usually express a high degree of interest in many sports but possess little actual ability in any. If they have not developed mature skills during the fundamental movement phase, they will be hampered in sport skill acquisition. This has been termed a **proficiency barrier** and presents a very real dilemma for the individual (child or adult) interested in learning sport skills but possessing insufficient fundamental movement

Here two boys and two girls are playing a one-on-one lead-up game in soccer.

skills to do so. As a result, it is not too late to learn the fundamental movement skills, but to go back and learn them is much more difficult than it would have been earlier.

Children are eager to learn a variety of sports, and the physical education program should introduce sport skills and the basic elements of many sport-related activities—but only after children have reached the mature stage in corresponding fundamental movement skills. Children should have opportunities during the transition stage to further refine specific fundamental movements and to use them as sport skills in a variety of skill drills and lead-up activities. For example, the fundamental movement skill of kicking may be applied to the sport skill of using the instep kick in soccer. This skill may be practiced in drill situations and then applied to a lead-up activity such as multiple-goal soccer or other small-sided soccer games. At the transition stage, children should not play the official sport as part of the instructional physical education program. Rather, they should be exposed to the basic skills, rules, and strategies of several sports through skill drills and a variety of lead-up activities.

Application Stage

The application stage is typical of the middle school or junior high school student from about 11 to 13 years of age. However, with the surge of participation throughout North America in youth sport programs, this stage may actually begin much earlier for many. Many children are applying their movement skills to organized sport participation as early as age six or even sooner. The key element at the application stage is that children have developed sufficient skill and knowledge of the game to apply the activity meaningfully to competitive or recreational settings.

Children at the application stage have begun to select types of sports that they prefer. Preferences are based primarily on previously successful experiences; body type; geographic location; and emotional, social, and cultural factors. Some children prefer individual sports, whereas others prefer team sports. Some enjoy contact sports, whereas others prefer noncontact sports. Some particularly enjoy water sports; others, court sports; and still others, dance activities. The narrowing of interests at this stage is accompanied by an increased desire for competence. Form, precision, accuracy, and standards of good performance are all especially important to the learner at the application stage. Therefore, the child practices more complex skills, and strategies and rules take on greater importance.

Lifelong Utilization Stage

The **lifelong utilization stage**, the final stage within the specialized movement phase, is based on previous sport and fundamental skill stages and continues throughout life. Individuals select activities they particularly enjoy and pursue them throughout their lifetime for fun, fitness, and fulfillment. At this stage, high interest in specific activities is evidenced through active participation on a regular basis, whether on a competitive or a recreational level.

TYPES OF MOVEMENT PERFORMANCE

Movement may be classified in a variety of ways. One popular classification scheme uses the terms "externally paced movement" or "open motor skill" for movement skill performance that is governed by the conditions of the immediate environment, and "internally paced movement" or "closed motor skill" for a movement that takes place when the performer chooses. These terms (this text uses "externally paced" and "internally paced") serve as descriptors of both the nature of the movement and the intent of the activity. Movement may also be classified as gross motor or fine motor, and as either discrete, serial, or continuous. We'll take a brief look at each of these sets of definitions.

Externally and Internally Paced Movement

Externally paced movement activities involve making responses to constantly changing and unpredictable environmental cues—for example, bringing a soccer ball upfield or dribbling a basketball against a defensive player. Externally paced movements require rapidity and flexibility in decision making on the part of the performer. The racket sports and most aspects of the games of basketball, football, baseball, and soccer are externally paced. Physical education teachers as well as coaches need to recognize the nature of dynamic activities and to provide situations that promote rapid decision making and adaptive behaviors in a variety of gamelike conditions.

For both *internally* and *externally paced* movement activities:

- Identify whether the activity is externally or internally paced.
- Establish a learning and practice environment consistent with the dynamic or static nature of the activity.
- Introduce dynamic activities under static conditions first (that is, control the environment and conditions of practice).
- Introduce situations that require responses to

sudden and unpredictable cues in dynamic activities as the skill develops.
- Strive for greater consistency, duplication, and reduction of environmental cues for static activities as the skill develops.
- Encourage the learner to think through the activity in the early stages of learning.
- Encourage the learner to screen out unnecessary cues.

Internally paced movement activities require a fixed performance in a given set of environmental conditions. The performer has the luxury of moving at his own pace through the activity and has time to recognize and respond to the static conditions of the environment. Internally paced activities generally emphasize accuracy, consistency, and repetition of performance. Bowling, golf, archery, and weightlifting are considered internally paced activities, as are swimming, basketball free-throw shooting, and most track and field events. The teacher in these activities needs to provide ample opportunities for children to repeat the activity under conditions that duplicate as nearly as possible the actual performance environment.

CONCEPT 3.5

Initial learning of a new movement skill, whether gross or fine, or discrete, serial, or continuous, frequently occurs best under internally paced conditions.

Here a young learner demonstrates a free-throw shot in basketball, an internally paced activity.

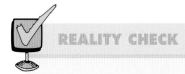

Internally Pacing Your Students

Real-World Situation

As part of a unit of instruction focusing on basketball skills, you are introducing driving to the basket for a layup shot, an internally paced skill. For your class of 30 fourth graders, you have available two 8-foot baskets and numerous basketballs. In order to maximize participation and to focus your instruction on learning the layup shot, you have decided to divide the class into five groups and assign them to various stations for practice on familiar basketball skills in addition to learning the layup shot.

Critical Questions

Based on the situation as presented, your knowledge of different types of movement skills, and the value of initial learning under internally paced conditions:

- How would you organize the class into five groups?
- What basketball skills would your students practice at each station?
- How would your students know if they were practicing correctly?
- How would you instruct students in the layup shot?
- How would you move from internally paced to externally paced skill instruction conditions?

Gross and Fine Movement

Although within the context of movement the line of demarcation between "gross" and "fine" is not a clear one, movements are often classified as one or the other. A gross motor movement involves the large muscles of the body. Most sport skills are classified as gross motor, with the exception perhaps of target shooting, archery, and a few others. Fine motor movements involve limited motion of parts of the body in the performance of activities requiring precision. The manipulative movements of sewing, writing, and typing are generally thought of as fine motor movements.

Discrete, Serial, and Continuous Movement

On the basis of its temporal aspects, movement may also be classified as discrete, serial, or continuous. A **discrete movement** has a very definite beginning and ending. Throwing, jumping, kicking, and striking a ball are examples of discrete movements. **Serial movements** are movements that are single and discrete and that are performed several times in rapid succession. Rhythmical hopping, basketball dribbling, and a soccer or volleyball volley are typical serial tasks. **Continuous movements** are movements that are repeated for a specified period of time. Running, swimming, and cycling are common continuous movements.

THE LEVELS OF MOVEMENT SKILL LEARNING

Research supports the concept that movement skill learning occurs in identifiable levels or stages (Gallahue & Ozmun, 2002; Magill, 2001). The terms you will encounter throughout this text to represent these levels are beginning (novice level), intermediate (practice level), and advanced (fine-tuning level). Each level refers to a pe-

CONCEPT
3.6

Characteristic levels of movement skill learning, independent of age, typify the learning of a new movement skill.

riod during which both the learner and the teacher have specific, identifiable tasks and responsibilities. In this section we look at the three levels of learning a movement skill. Figure 3.3 illustrates how these three levels correspond with the phases and stages of motor development. Keep in mind that in the real world you will encounter students at differing levels of skill development both within and between skills.

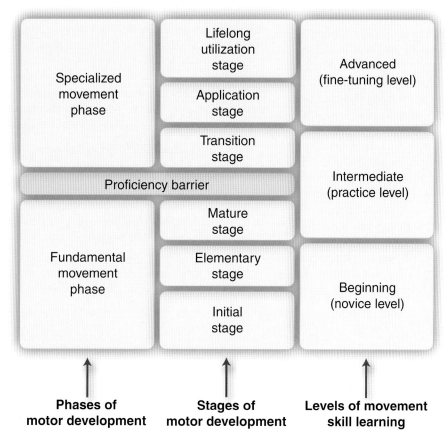

FIGURE 3.3 The interrelationship among the *phases* of motor development, *stages* of motor development, and the *levels* of movement skill learning.

Beginning/Novice Level

The **beginning/novice level** is the first level in the learning of a movement skill. At this level the movements of the learner are generally uncoordinated and jerky. The learner begins to construct a mental plan of the activity and is actively trying to understand the skill. Because of the conscious attention that the learner gives to every detail of the task itself, performance is poor. The learner may experience fatigue early in the activity, which is caused more by the mental requirements of the task than by the actual performance of the task. At this level the learner tends to pay attention to all the information that is available but is unable to screen out what is irrelevant. She is attracted as much by what is not important as by what is. Teachers of students at the beginning level of learning a movement skill need to be aware of the conscious cognitive requirements of this level and to understand that the instructional intent during this period should be only to provide the learner with a general idea of the skill or activity.

To Ski or Not to Ski: That Is the Question

Real-World Situation

Not too long ago, your senior author learned how to downhill ski. Having spent most of my life in the Midwest, I had almost no opportunity for practice, encouragement, or instruction in the skills involved in skiing. On a whim, my wife (Ellie) and I decided to take our two children to Montana for a skiing holiday with friends who happened to be excellent skiers and physical education teachers. Upon arrival at the ski resort our children (David Lee and Jennifer), who had previous skiing experience, headed off with their friends. Ellie and I proceeded to the top of the mountain with our friends. After a very brief lesson on starting, stopping, and changing direction, they bid us farewell and took off down the mountain. Here we were, two total novices, at the top of a major mountain with no idea of how to get down. We were at the beginning or novice level of learning a new movement skill. We were trying to first gain an *awareness* of what it was that we were trying to get our bodies to do. Next we were involved in the process of *exploration* and *self-discovery* of how to proceed down the mountain with a realistic chance of survival. Since then skiing has become a passion, but we will never forget those first four days in the mountains of beautiful Montana trying to learn how to ski.

Critical Questions

Using either the skiing example or a personal new movement skill learning situation, as well as your knowledge of the levels and stages of learning a new movement skill:

- What is the sequence of learning a new movement skill?
- What are the typical characteristics of the learner at each level and stage?
- If you had been our ski instructor, how would you have proceeded to help us become more skillful skiers? (If you are using a personal example, how would you go about helping yourself?)
- If motor development is age related, why is movement skill learning age independent?

This child practices an internally paced discrete manipulative skill and is at the beginning level of movement skill learning.

TEACHING TIP 3.2

For learners at the *beginning/novice level* of learning a new movement skill:

- Introduce the major aspects of the skill only. Be brief.
- Provide for a demonstration of the skill to help the learner form a mental picture.
- Permit the learner to try out the skill.
- Provide plenty of opportunity for exploration of the skill itself and self-discovery of general principles of the skill.
- Recognize that the beginning/novice level is primarily a cognitive phase and that the learner needs only to understand the general idea.
- When possible, compare the new skill to similar skills that the learner may be familiar with.
- Provide immediate, precise, and positive feedback concerning the skill.
- Avoid situations that emphasize the product of one's performance during this phase. Focus on the process.

Exploration Stage

Within the beginning/novice level of learning a new movement skill are two different stages. The first of these is the **exploration stage.** At this stage the child develops an awareness of the general characteristics of the movement task and begins to experiment with and explore it in relative isolation to other movement skills. At the exploratory stage of learning how to throw a ball, for example, a child lacks movement control but is forming a conscious mental plan and getting the general idea of what is required for a successful throw. Movement exploration techniques that permit the child to experiment with the many and varied ways of throwing a ball are especially beneficial in helping him get a general idea of how the body can move in the performance of the throwing task. (Refer to the section "Production Styles" in chapter 10, "Teaching Styles.")

These children are exploring and discovering ways to throw different objects into a large target created by gymnastics mats.

Discovery Stage

At the **discovery stage** of learning a new movement skill, the child begins to find more efficient means of performing the task. In ball throwing, a child's movement control and coordination begin to improve and become less consciously controlled. Guided discovery and problem-solving techniques are useful at this stage. These techniques help the child sort out the important from the unimportant in beginning to coordinate and control how the body should move in the performance of the overhand throwing pattern (once again, please refer to "Production Styles" in chapter 10, "Teaching Styles").

Intermediate/Practice Level

The **intermediate/practice level** of learning a new movement skill begins after the learner understands the skill in general and is able to perform it in a manner approximating the final skill. The learner at this level has a better understanding of the skill, and a mental plan for performing it becomes more fully developed. The skill at this level has utility and is practiced repeatedly. Conscious attention to the elements of the task diminishes. The learner begins to devote more attention to the goal or product of the skill than to the process. The poorly coordinated, jerky movements so evident at the beginning level gradually disappear. The learner gains a "feel" for the skill as kinesthetic sensitivity becomes more highly attuned. As a result, the learner relies less on verbal and visual cues and more on muscle sense. As with the beginning/novice level, the intermediate/practice level encompasses two different stages.

Teachers of students at the intermediate level recognize that students understand the skill and set up practice sessions that generally focus on refining the skill and maximizing learner feedback.

TEACHING TIP 3.3

For learners at the *intermediate/practice level* of learning a new movement skill:

- Provide numerous opportunities for practice and skill application.
- Provide opportunities for skill refinement in a supportive, nonthreatening environment.
- Devise practice situations that progressively focus on greater and greater skill refinement.
- Provide short, fast-paced practice sessions with frequent breaks before having longer sessions with few breaks.
- Be able to analyze skills and provide constructive criticism.

- Structure practice sessions that focus on quality performance (perfect practice makes perfect).
- Provide frequent, precise, immediate, and positive feedback.
- Allow for individual differences in the rate of skill learning.
- Focus attention on the whole skill whenever possible.
- Have learners practice a skill in the same way they will perform it in real life, and at the same rate.

Combination Stage

At the **combination stage** of learning a new movement skill, the child begins to join the actions of one movement skill with those of other movement skills. This is a practice time in which the child combines and integrates the new movement skill with previously learned skills and practices repeatedly in her first attempts to utilize the new skill in some activity form, such as a game, rhythm, or self-testing activity. For example, the child can now perform the overhand throw from a variety of positions instead of relying only on the classic overhand throwing preparatory stance. At the combination stage the child learns to throw on the run or to bend over and recover a ground ball immediately prior to throwing the ball to a partner.

Application Stage

When the child reaches the **application stage,** he pays more attention to refining the movement skill and applying it as a specialized movement skill to some form of recreational activity or introductory sport-related activity. He works on smoothing out the task through further practice and using the skill in an applied sense. Our ball thrower, for example, now applies his overhand throwing skills in a variety of throwing games.

Advanced/Fine-Tuning Level

The **advanced/fine-tuning level** is the third and final level in the learning of a movement skill. The learner at this level has a complete understanding of the skill. The mental plan for the skill is highly developed, and the learner pays very little attention to the cognitive aspects of the task. In fact, individuals at this level often have difficulty describing how they perform the activity. They often resort to a "Let me show you" or a "Do it like this" statement, then actually perform the skill. The learner at this level is refining and fine-tuning skills. In activities in which movement is the key element, it is smooth, fluid, and highly coordinated. In activities in which the absence of movement is most highly valued, there is a general appearance of ease, mastery, and control. The performer is able to ignore irrelevant information and is not bothered by distractions. The learner has excellent timing and anticipation of movements and appears to act automatically, although in reality the skill does require some minimal conscious control.

Among children in elementary school there are generally few performers at the advanced level of learning a movement skill. However, with the increased tendency to specialize in sport skill development at an early age, this may change. Teachers of students at the advanced level should focus on further refining and maintaining the skill and on providing selected feedback. Figure 3.4 illustrates the levels and stages of learning a new movement skill.

TEACHING TIP 3.4

For learners at the *advanced/fine-tuning level* of learning a new movement skill:

- Structure practice sessions that promote intensity and enthusiasm.
- Be available to provide encouragement, motivation, and positive support.
- Offer suggestions and tips on strategy.
- Structure practice sessions that duplicate gamelike situations.
- Help performers anticipate what they will do in specific gamelike situations.

- Know the performer as an individual and be able to adjust methods to meet individual needs.
- Provide feedback that focuses on specific aspects of the skill.
- Avoid requiring the performer to think about detailed execution of the skill, which may result in overattention to the cognitive elements of the task (sometimes referred to as analysis paralysis).

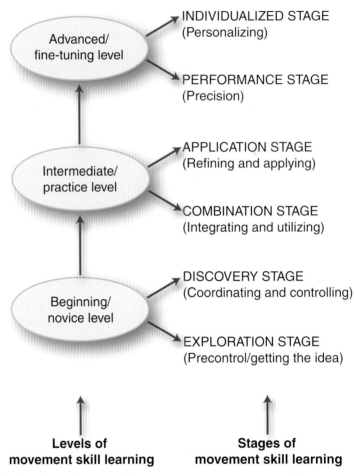

FIGURE 3.4   Levels and stages of learning a new movement skill.

Performance Stage

The advanced/fine-tuning level of learning a new movement skill also comprises two different stages—the performance stage and the individualized stage. At the **performance stage,** the learner is further involved in refining the elements of the movement task but with emphasis on utilizing it in a variety of performance situations. Precision and utilization of the skill in various settings, including youth sport activities, receive emphasis at this stage. Our ball thrower now combines his ball-throwing skills with catching, striking, and base running to play the game of baseball on a local youth sport team.

Individualized Stage

Although young children are seldom at this stage, learners at the **individualized stage** in the movement skill learning hierarchy are personalizing their performances. They make fine-tuning adjustments and modifications in the execution of the specific task in accordance with personal attributes or limitations.

Each level in the process of learning a new movement skill requires concerned, knowledgeable, and sensitive guidance by the teacher. It is imperative that as a teacher you understand the characteristics of the learner at each level so that you can structure the physical education period effectively for maximum learning and performance. Acquiring a movement skill is a process that takes time, so providing organized, quality instructional sessions geared to the learner's skill level and developmental level is crucial to helping children realize their full potential.

MOVEMENT SKILL HOMEWORK

On the basis of what we have just seen about the phases and stages of motor development and the levels of movement skill learning, it becomes important to consider the curricular reality that teachers often face. All too frequently, teachers have too many students and too little time to maximize learning. Movement skill homework is a partial answer to this situation. When children have tasks to work on at home, they can utilize the help of a parent or older sibling to practice the skills currently being stressed during the physical education period. Individual take-home sheets explaining the initial, elementary, and mature stages for several fundamental movement skills (see chapters 18-20) can be photocopied from this text and sent home with children to encourage further activity—for all children or just for those needing additional help. Each take-home sheet could contain appropriate information about the key elements of the particular skill, including teaching tips and suggested activities. Some Web sites provide teacher-designed homework activities that may be useful to you as a beginning teacher (check out **pecentral@vt.com**, or **www.PELinks4u.com**).

IMPLICATIONS FOR TEACHING DEVELOPMENTAL PHYSICAL EDUCATION

CONCEPT 3.7

Teaching for movement skill acquisition requires adoption of strategies that recognize the interaction among the requirements of the learning task, the biology of the individual, and the conditions of the environment, in a manner that is both individually appropriate and age group appropriate.

Our knowledge that fundamental and sport skill development depends on environmental factors such as practice, encouragement, and quality instruction has vital implications for the physical education of children. For the vast majority of children, personalized, developmentally appropriate instruction is essential. Teachers must allow for sufficient time to practice the skill and must use positive reinforcement techniques to continually encourage the learner.

As we said earlier, the development of movement skills is age related; it is not age dependent. Skill acquisition is highly individualized because of the unique hereditary characteristics and experiences of each child. Therefore, it is inappropriate to classify movement activities solely by age or by grade level; such a procedure violates the principle of individual appropriateness. Physical education teachers should select movement experiences based on the ability level of children and on their phase of movement skill development and level of movement skill learning. The use of approximate ages for the phases of motor development and their corresponding stages provides only age-appropriate guidelines to the functioning of most children. Many children may be significantly ahead of or behind this schedule.

Frequently there are differences in movement skill development within the same child. For example, it is entirely possible for an eight-year-old to be highly skilled and functioning at the application stage in swimming or gymnastics, and in two popular age-group sports, and still be only at the initial or elementary stage in fundamental manipulative skills such as throwing, catching, and running. Although we should continue to encourage accelerated behavior in one area, we should ensure that the individual develops at least an acceptable level of proficiency in all aspects of movement. The developmentally based physical education program provides for the balanced movement skill development of all children.

Summary

Movement skill acquisition is the core of the developmental physical education program. The term "movement skill" refers to a series of movements performed with accuracy and precision; a movement skill may be a fundamental movement skill or a specialized movement skill. A movement pattern is an organized series of related movements. One can categorize movement into the three functional categories of stability movements (such as the forward roll in tumbling), locomotor movements (such as running), and manipulative movements (such as throwing). Movement phrases are combinations of two or three of the categories of movements. The importance of movement skill learning during childhood is now recognized, as is the importance of environmental factors that significantly influence the acquisition of skillful movement.

The phases and stages of motor development relate to children's motor behavior in particular ways. Remember that although these stages tend to be sequential, predictable, and age related, they are neither age dependent nor determined by maturation. In other words, factors such as opportunities for practice, encouragement, quality instruction, and the environmental setting help determine the extent to which a child develops movement skills. It is important to take care to view the child both individu-ally and developmentally in the acquisition of movement skill.

We can categorize the types of movement skills on the basis of the context in which the movement occurs (externally and internally paced), the size or extent of the movement (gross and fine motor skills), or the time series in which the movement occurs (discrete, serial, and continuous).

The learning of a new movement skill occurs at predictable levels and stages, from the beginning or novice level, to the intermediate or practice level, and finally to the advanced or fine-tuning level. Again, remember that movement skill learning is age independent. All of us—children, adolescents, and adults—progress through these levels when learning a new movement skill. By carefully attending to the motor development and movement skill learning of children, first as individuals (individual appropriateness) and only secondarily as members of a group (age-group appropriateness), teachers can better provide effective instruction. Failure to do so will negate the foundations of developmental physical education.

Movement skill homework is a way to maximize learning. Teachers can incorporate movement skill homework into the physical education curriculum by enlisting parents or older siblings to help children practice at home, sending information sheets home to familiarize parents with the program and to encourage further activity, and assigning specific homework activities.

Terms to Remember

Excellent Readings

Anderson, A., Vogel, P., & Albrecht, R. (1999). The effect of instructional self-talk on the overhand throw. *The Physical Educator, 56* (4), 215-221.

Lidor, R., & Singer, R.N. (2000). Teaching performance routines to beginners. *JOPERD, 71* (7), 34-36.

McKenzie, T.L., Alcaraz, J.E., & Sallis, J.F. (1998). Effects of a physical education program on children's manipulative skills. *JTPE, 17* (3), 327-341.

Oslin, J.L., & Mitchell, S.A. (1998). Form follows function. *JOPERD, 69* (6), 46-49.

Sweeting, T., & Rink, J.E. (1999). Effects of direct instruction and environmentally designed instruction on the process and product characteristics of a fundamental skill. *JTPE 18* (2), 216-233.

Valentini, N.C., Rudisill, M.E., & Goodman, J.D. (1999). Incorporating a mastery climate into physical education: It's developmentally appropriate! *JOPERD, 69* (7), 28-32.

Wang, J., & Griffin, M. (1998). Early correction of movement errors can help student performance. *JOPERD, 69* (4), 50-52.

4

Physical Activity and Fitness Enhancement

Key Concepts

▶ A physically educated person exhibits a physically active lifestyle.

▶ A physically educated person achieves and maintains a health-enhancing level of physical fitness.

Content Standards #3 and #4: *National Standards for Physical Education:* National Association for Sport and Physical Education

Physical fitness is a topic of continuing interest throughout the world, as evidenced by the considerable coverage of the fitness status of children and youth in both the professional and lay literature. Studies comparing the physical fitness of youth over the past 30 years reveal that on average American boys and girls are less fit than their counterparts of 10, 20, or 30 years ago. Although the validity of these studies has been challenged in terms of the generalizations about youth fitness that have been derived from them, it is clear that much needs to be done to improve youth fitness and to heighten public awareness of the vital role of fitness in children's total development. The popular belief that children get plenty of regular, vigorous physical activity as a normal part of their everyday routine is no more than a myth for millions of youngsters. Although many adults have a heightened awareness of the benefits of vigorous physical activity, only a limited awareness of this has trickled down to children. We can eliminate this disgraceful situation if we make the improvement of youth fitness through increased physical activity and improved nutrition a national priority.

This chapter examines the challenge of helping children become *fit movers, informed movers*, and *eager movers*. We define the term *physical fitness* and discuss the importance of fitness development in children, the factors that influence the level of fitness, the idea of

This chapter will provide you with the tools to do the following:

▷ Discuss the current status of children's fitness.

▷ Provide a concise but specific definition of the term *physical fitness*.

▷ Distinguish between the terms *health-related fitness* and *performance-related fitness* and identify the components of each.

▷ Define and give specific examples of how each health-related component of physical fitness may be measured and enhanced.

▷ Define and give specific examples of how the performance-related components of physical fitness may be measured and enhanced.

▷ List and describe the basic principles of fitness development, and illustrate how each may be applied in a physical education setting.

▷ Discuss the concepts of fitness homework and fitness breaks, and illustrate how they may be successfully implemented.

▷ List several useful techniques for motivating children to be active movers.

fitness homework, and ways to motivate children to become physically active. A section on implications for developmental physical education concludes the chapter. The following Web sites will be especially helpful:

- Cooper Institute for Aerobic Research (**www.cooperinst.org**)
- President's Council on Physical Fitness and Sports (**www. fitness.gov**)
- American Council on Exercise (**www.acefitness.org**)
- National Association for Health and Fitness (**www. physicalfitness.org**)
- Shape Up America! (**www.shapeup.org**)

TEXT BOX 4.1

"Perhaps we should rethink the fitness objective for physical education. Obviously, the limitation in instructional time is a factor for consideration. Of greater importance is the question, 'What are we trying to accomplish with the fitness objective?' The primary objective is to equip children and youth with knowledge, attitudes, and skills for making healthy lifestyle choices—not only as children, but also as adults. . . . The most important fitness objective for physical education is to help students establish consistent exercise behavior patterns that will be maintained into adulthood."

Blair, S.N. (1992). Are American children and youth fit? The need for better data. *Research Quarterly for Exercise and Sport, 63* (1), 120-123.

THE CHALLENGE

Much of the news about children's fitness is not encouraging, but as parents become more concerned about healthful living and begin to improve their personal level of physical fitness, they tend to become more concerned about the fitness levels of their children. Additionally, considerable public attention is being drawn to children's fitness levels. Consequently there has been considerable grassroots action in communities across North America that has had a positive impact on raising fitness levels. Moreover, the American Alliance for Health, Physical Education, Recreation and Dance (AAHPERD), the National Association for Sport and Physical Education (Corbin & Pangrazi, 1998), and the President's Council on Physical Fitness and Sports (**www.fitness.gov**) are making a concerted effort to achieve the important goals of improving children and youth fitness levels and providing quality physical education offered daily. Most recently AAHPERD has collaborated with Human Kinetics Publishers and the Cooper Institute for Aerobics Research (**www.cooperinst.org**) to create the American Fitness Alliance (AFA). The AFA strives to educate children and youth about the importance of achieving and maintaining a healthy level of fitness. The AFA also advocates providing quality physical education offered daily. This may well be our best chance to truly make fitness and quality physical education a reality for all.

We need to be realistic, however, in the attempt to implement these objectives. To achieve the health-related objectives of enhancing aerobic endurance, muscular

CONCEPT 4.1

Adoption of long-term healthy lifestyle behaviors is the primary goal of the fitness portion of the developmental physical education program.

Smaller neighborhoods provide an opportunity for children to lead active lifestyles.

strength and endurance, and joint flexibility, 150 to 200 minutes of activity time per week would be required. Unfortunately, few North American elementary schools have that amount of time available to achieve fitness objectives, let alone the important skill objectives of physical education. It is time to critically reexamine what it is that we are trying to achieve in meeting the fitness objectives of physical education.

REALITY CHECK

"Whip" Them Into Shape

Real-World Situation

Your physical education classes meet three times per week for 30 minutes each. In addition to providing quality instruction in movement skill learning, you are anxious to promote positive fitness behaviors among your students. You are aware of the discouraging statistics showing the rapid rise in childhood obesity and have seen ample evidence of it in your community. Furthermore, several parents have expressed their dismay that the current physical education program seems to do little in terms of reducing obesity and increasing fitness levels. In fact, a petition is circulating among several concerned parents to adopt a curriculum geared to "whipping" kids into shape through an intense physical training program.

Critical Questions

Based on your knowledge of children's fitness and the differences implied between the terms *physical education* and *physical training*:

- Why is it difficult to significantly influence real and lasting fitness changes through this physical education program?

- How can the Stages of Change Model be applied to the adoption of healthy lifestyle behaviors?

- Given the situation presented, how might you promote positive fitness behaviors both during and after school hours?

- How would you respond to the petition for "whipping" kids into shape through an intense physical training program?

TEXT BOX 4.2

Appropriate Physical Activity for Children

Elementary school age children should accumulate at least 30 to 60 minutes of age- and developmentally appropriate physical activity from a variety of physical activities on all, or most, days of the week.

An accumulation of more than 60 minutes, and up to several hours per day, of age- and developmentally appropriate activity is encouraged for elementary school age children.

Some of the child's activity each day should be in periods lasting 10 to 15 minutes or more and including moderate to vigorous activity. This activity will typically be intermittent, involving moderate to vigorous activity with brief periods of rest and recovery.

Extended periods of inactivity are discouraged for children.

A variety of physical activities selected from the Physical Activity Pyramid (similar in concept to the Food Pyramid; see p. 93) are recommended for elementary school children.

Council on Physical Education for Children. (1998). *Physical activity for children: A statement of guidelines*. Reston, VA: National Association for Sport and Physical Education.

When we help children become knowledgeable movers and eager movers, as well as fit movers, we help them establish the basis for healthy lifestyle choices and for becoming active movers as adolescents and adults. Increased physical activity and fitness is an important objective of the developmentally based physical education curriculum. It is a strand throughout the entire curriculum, not just a unit or single theme. It is present in all that is done in the developmental movement program. Fitness is promoted through moderate to vigorous physical activity and participation in developmental games, developmental dance, and developmental gymnastics activities.

Perhaps a brief look at what has become known as the **Stages of Change Model** (Wright, Patterson, & Cardinal, 2000) will help you visualize what an individual goes through in changing a health behavior and how we may apply this important concept to children as we seek to increase their physical activity levels. According to the Stages of Change Model, an individual progresses through five identifiable stages on the way to becoming physically active. At the *precontemplation stage,* the person has not even considered the benefits of being active. When you work with children at this stage, it is important that you provide them with relevant and meaningful information about the benefits of physical activity and the risks of inactivity. At the *contemplation stage,* the individual is thinking about the possibility of becoming active in the near future. When children are at this stage, in addition to giving them relevant and meaningful information, teachers need to help them find ways to increase their physical activity that they consider fun, challenging, and enjoyable. At the *preparation stage,* the individual has decided to become active in the near future and may have even made small moves in that direction. Teachers of children at this stage need to be encouraging and to help them set realistic goals for increased physical activity. During the *action stage,* the individual consistently engages in a physically active lifestyle. The action stage most typically occurs during the first six months of an activity program. Teachers of children during the initial months of becoming more active need to be supportive of their students' efforts and help them realize that lapses in activity are to be expected and forgiven. The fifth and final stage, the *maintenance stage*, occurs when the individual maintains increased physical activity levels beyond the initial six-month period. Teachers of children at the maintenance stage should encourage them to explore alternative activities and to be sure that the activities they engage in are fun and enjoyable.

FIT MOVERS DEFINED

A generic definition of physical fitness was provided in chapter 1. Here we define **physical fitness** more specifically as a set of attributes related to the ability to perform physical activity coupled with one's genetic makeup, as well as the maintenance of nutritional adequacy.

CONCEPT 4.2

Physical fitness is a positive state of well-being influenced by regular vigorous physical activity, genetic makeup, and nutritional adequacy.

A child's personal level of physical activity coupled with his individual health status determines the upper and lower limits of physical fitness that can be reasonably expected. Nutritional status can also greatly inhibit or enhance one's level of physical functioning, and the person's genetic makeup influences the level of fitness that person can attain. All three factors play into the development and maintenance of children's fitness. **Fit movers** enhance their physical fitness in two broad areas: health-related fitness and performance-related fitness.

Health-Related Fitness

Health-related fitness is a relative state of being, not an ability, skill, or capacity. Health-related fitness is transient and not directly related to athletic skill. A high level of health-related fitness is associated with improved quality of life and lower risk of illness. The development and maintenance of the components of health-related fitness are a function of physiological adaptation to increased overload. Therefore, these components can be readily altered with use or disuse. Children who are fit movers strive for, obtain, and maintain personal standards of health-related fitness that are optimal for their individual level of development.

REALITY CHECK

Junk Food Junkies

Real-World Situation

In order to raise money for your annual physical education equipment budget and for playground apparatus, your school Parent Teacher Organization (PTO) has placed vending machines in the school that are filled with a variety of candy bars, chips, and cola drinks. Knowing that physical fitness is influenced, in part, by nutritional adequacy, you are presented with a dilemma. On the one hand, junk food certainly does not promote children's fitness; but on the other hand, the money raised through the vending machine program is invaluable to your program in paying for supplies and equipment.

Critical Questions

Based on your knowledge of children's fitness and the contribution of good nutrition to physical fitness:

- Would you try to remedy this situation?

- What would be your strategy for approaching the PTO?

- What alternative money-raising ideas would you present to the PTO?

- How do you counter the frequent argument, "They won't eat the good stuff. It will only go to waste"?

Performance-Related Fitness

Performance-related fitness, sometimes called skill-related fitness, is genetically dependent in terms of absolute potential, is relatively stable, and is closely related to athletic skill. The development and maintenance of performance-related fitness are a function of practice and skill development within broadly defined genetic limits. Children who are fit movers strive for, achieve, and maintain personal standards of performance-related fitness that are appropriate to their individual level of development.

HEALTH-RELATED FITNESS COMPONENTS

Muscular strength, muscular endurance, cardiovascular endurance, joint flexibility, and body composition are the health-related components of physical fitness. Important information about both the health-related and performance-related components of physical fitness is summarized in tables 4.1 and 4.2, respectively, and is discussed further in the following paragraphs.

Muscular Strength

Muscular strength is the ability of the body to exert a maximum force against an object external to the body. In its purest sense, it is the ability to exert one maximum effort. Children engaged in daily active play do much to enhance their leg strength by running and bicycling. Their arm strength is developed through such activities as lifting and carrying large objects, handling tools, and swinging on monkey bars.

Muscular strength may be increased through isotonic, isometric, and isokinetic means. **Isotonic strength** is the ability of a muscle or group of muscles to perform a maximal or near-maximal effort, once or for a limited number of repetitions, in which the muscles alternately shorten and lengthen. Free weights, pulley weights, sit-ups, and push-ups are commonly used to increase isotonic strength.

In this physical education class, a math problem was written on one side of a task card and an exercise was described on the opposite side. Children solved the math problem, and the answer determined the number of repetitions for the prescribed exercise. Here we see children exercising to enhance both muscular endurance and muscular strength.

TABLE 4.1 —COMMON MEASURES OF CHILDREN'S HEALTH-RELATED FITNESS AND A SYNTHESIS OF FINDINGS

Health-related fitness components	Common tests	Specific aspect measured	Synthesis of findings
Cardiovascular endurance	Step test	Physical work capacity	$\dot{V}O_2$max estimates are tenuous with young children. Children can achieve maximum $\dot{V}O_2$ values similar to those of adults when corrected for body weight. Maximal heart rates decrease with age. Trend for improved $\dot{V}O_2$max values in both boys and girls with age. Girls level off after age 12 or so. Boys continue to improve.
	Distance run	Aerobic endurance	
	Treadmill stress test	$\dot{V}O_2$max	
	Bicycle ergometer	$\dot{V}O_2$max	
	Heart rate monitors	Heart rate	
	Pedometers	Number of steps	
Muscular strength	Hand dynamometer	Isometric grip strength	Annual increase for boys from age 7 on. Girls tend to level off after age 12. Boys slow prior to puberty, then gain rapidly throughout adolescence. Boys superior to girls at all ages.
	Back and leg dynamometer	Isometric back and leg strength	
	Cable tensiometer	Isometric joint strength	
Muscular endurance	Push-ups	Isotonic upper body endurance	Similar abilities throughout childhood, slightly in favor of boys on most items. Lull in performance prior to age 12. Large increases in boys from ages 12 to 16, then a leveling off. Girls show no significant increases without special training after age 12.
	Sit-ups	Isotonic abdominal endurance	
	Flexed arm hang	Isometric upper body endurance	
	Pull-ups	Isometric upper body endurance	
Flexibility	Bend and reach	Hip joint flexibility	Flexibility is joint specific. Girls tend to be more flexible than boys at all ages. Flexibility decreases with reduced activity levels.
	Sit and reach	Hip joint flexibility	
Body composition	Hydrostatic weighing	Percent body fat	Children at all ages have higher percentages of fat than their age-mates of 20 years ago. Active children are leaner than obese children at all ages. Obese children are less active than non-obese children.
	Skinfold calipers	Estimate of percent body fat	
	Body mass index	Estimate of percent body fat	
	Electrical impedence	Estimate of percent body fat	

Reprinted, by permission, from D.L. Gallahue and J.C. Ozmun, 2002, *Understanding motor development* (Boston: McGraw-Hill), 248.

Isokinetic strength is the same as isotonic strength in that the muscles alternately shorten and lengthen, but they are also required to accommodate to variable resistance throughout the activity. In isokinetic strength activities the resistance is equal to the force applied throughout the range of motion. Variable resistance devices and Nautilus-type machines are commonly used to increase isokinetic strength.

Isometric strength is the ability of a muscle group to maintain a contracted state over a period of several seconds. An example of an isometric strength-building activity is a flexed arm hang or static push-up in which the arms are flexed to a 90° angle and the body weight is supported for 8 to 12 seconds. Isometric activities do not require special equipment but are generally viewed as less effective than either isotonic or isokinetic strength activities.

Muscular Endurance

Muscular endurance is the ability to exert force against an object external to the body for several repetitions without fatigue. Muscular endurance is similar to muscular strength in terms of the activities performed but differs in emphasis. Strength-building activities require overloading the muscle or group of muscles to a greater extent than endurance activities. Endurance-building activities require less of an overload on the muscles but require a greater number of repetitions. Boys and girls performing several sit-ups, pull-ups, or push-ups are performing muscular endurance activities.

When we speak of relative strength or relative endurance, we are referring to the child's fitness level adjusted for her body weight. It stands to reason that an adult's gross level of fitness is greater than that of a child; but when the body weight is divided into the total fitness score, the differences are much less pronounced.

Muscular endurance may be viewed as both a dynamic and a static phenomenon. Dynamic endurance is the muscle's ability to flex and extend repeatedly and is increased through progressive resistance training. This training should use light to moderate resistance with a moderate to high number of repetitions. On the other hand, static endurance is the muscle's ability to stay flexed for a long period of time. This type of endurance is also increased through progressive resistance training using light to moderate resistance, but the length of time the contracted muscle state is maintained is more crucial than the number of repetitions.

Cardiovascular Endurance

Cardiovascular endurance is specific to the ability of the heart, lungs, and vascular system to supply oxygen during sustained physical activity. It is generally considered the single most important aspect of fitness. Cardiovascular endurance refers to the ability to perform numerous repetitions of an activity requiring considerable use of the circulatory and respiratory systems. It is difficult to accurately measure the volume of oxygen used in aerobic activities by children without using sophisticated scientific equipment and causing considerable stress to the child. We do know, however, that children are generally not as active as they need to be to develop good cardiovascular endurance. Cardiovascular endurance is dependent, in large part, on the lifestyle of the individual child. The keys to developing cardiovascular endurance are frequency, duration, and intensity. The greater the frequency, the longer the duration, and the more intense the workout, the greater the impact will be on improving cardiovascular endurance. Activities such as running, pedaling a bicycle, and swimming are all aerobic and should be a part of children's daily life.

People can improve cardiovascular endurance by performing aerobic and anaerobic exercise. Aerobic exercise involves participation in vigorous physical activities in which the heart rate is elevated above a threshold level (approximately 140 to 180 beats per minute) and maintained at that level for an extended period of time (approximately 15 minutes or more). Distance running, cycling, and swimming are all aerobic activities. Anaerobic exercise, on the other hand, is high-intensity exer-

CONCEPT
4.3

Health-related fitness is multifaceted, is influenced by a variety of factors, and can be improved through vigorous physical activity.

These children's cardiovascular endurance is promoted as they perform various locomotor skills to music around a circle of cones.

cise of short duration that does not depend on the body's ability to supply oxygen. Sprint events in track and swimming are typical anaerobic activities. Children need to be involved in both aerobic and anaerobic exercise. Both contribute measurably to a healthy heart and healthy lungs and vascular system.

Joint Flexibility

Joint flexibility, another aspect of health-related fitness, is the ability of the various joints of the body to move through their full range of motion. Flexibility is joint specific and can be improved with practice. Most children are involved in numerous flexibility-developing activities. Their constant bending, twisting, turning, and

This physical education teacher leads stretching exercises prior to a developmental gymnastics lesson. The teacher can lead the exercises as well as encourage students to stretch on their own, like these boys who use soccer balls to stretch before a developmental games lesson.

stretching, along with the natural elasticity of their bodies, account for much of their flexibility. All you need to do is look at the contorted positions that children sit in while watching television or listening to a story to realize that they have a good deal of flexibility in the hip and knee joints. Too often, however, the range of motion diminishes in later childhood and adolescence because of lack of activity.

Body Composition

CONCEPT 4.4

Not only is reliable field assessment of body composition difficult, but some question whether body composition is a valid component of physical fitness.

Body composition is the proportion of lean body mass to fat body mass. It is a person's relative fatness or leanness adjusted for height. Although not universally agreed on as a component of health-related fitness because it is the only nonperformance measure among the components of health-related fitness, body composition is an important aspect of health-related physical fitness. Basically, those who oppose the inclusion of body composition as a measure assert that fitness is for *every body*—those that are slim and lean as well as those that are overweight and obese. Another objection is based on the idea that one's body type largely depends on heredity and as a result is very difficult to alter to any great extent. Moreover, there are problems in assessing body composition, which requires the use of fat assessment techniques that are frequently unreliable, embarrassing, and, to some people, socially objectionable.

On the other hand, proponents of body composition as a component of health-related fitness point out that it is an important aspect of overall health and fitness. They argue that being *overfat* is the issue, not being *overweight* as determined by traditional height-weight tables. Furthermore, they assert that obesity is at epidemic levels among children and youth and is measurably greater today than it was 20 or even 10 years ago. Moreover, they make the telling point that obesity contributes to degenerative diseases, health problems, and reduced longevity. For these reasons they advocate the inclusion of body composition as a component of health-related fitness.

Both sides of the issue present interesting arguments. Popular fitness tests include or exclude body composition as a health-related fitness component depending on the philosophy of the developer of the test. Our position is that body composition is an important component of health-related fitness—but the final decision is up to you.

PERFORMANCE-RELATED FITNESS COMPONENTS

CONCEPT 4.5

The components of performance-related fitness are closely related to the quantitative aspects of movement skill performance.

Performance-related fitness is an aspect of physical fitness related to the quality of one's movement skill, in terms of improved performance in play, games, and sport activities. The performance-related components of physical fitness are generally considered to be balance, coordination, agility, speed of movement, and power. Children who display skill in several activities such as bicycling, swimming, throwing, catching, and climbing are said to have good skill-related fitness. We emphasize the performance-related components of balance, coordination, agility, speed, and power in that order with children because of their developmental basis. In other words, we stress enhancing children's balance skills first, then promoting coordination and agility activities. Activities that promote speed and power are the last to be emphasized in the developmentally based physical education program. It is important to stress that movement control (balance, coordination, agility) should be developed prior to force production (speed, power). Table 4.2 summarizes key information about the performance-related components of fitness, which we discuss further in the following paragraphs.

TABLE 4.2—COMMON MEASURES OF CHILDREN'S PERFORMANCE-RELATED FITNESS AND A SYNTHESIS OF FINDINGS

Motor fitness components	Common tests	Specific aspect measured	Synthesis of findings
Coordination	Cable jump	Gross body coordination	Year-by-year improvement with age in gross body coordination. Boys superior from age 6 on in eye-hand and eye-foot coordination.
	Hopping for accuracy	Gross body coordination	
	Skipping	Gross body coordination	
	Ball dribble	Eye-hand coordination	
	Foot dribble	Eye-hand coordination	
Balance	Beam walk	Dynamic balance	Year-by-year improvement with age. Girls often outperform boys, especially in dynamic balance activities, until about age 8. Abilities similar thereafter.
	Stick balance	Static balance	
	One-foot stand	Static balance	
Speed	20-yard dash	Running speed	Year-by-year improvement with age. Boys and girls similar until age 6 or 7, at which time boys make more rapid improvements. Boys superior to girls at all ages.
	30-yard dash	Running speed	
Agility	Shuttle run	Running agility	Year-by-year improvement with age. Girls begin to level off after age 13. Boys continue to make improvements.
Power	Vertical jump	Leg strength and speed	Year-by-year improvement with age. Boys outperform girls at all age levels.
	Standing long jump	Leg strength and speed	
	Distance throw	Upper arm strength and speed	
	Velocity throw	Upper arm strength and speed	

Reprinted, by permission, from D.L. Gallahue and J.C. Ozmun, 2002, *Understanding motor development* (Boston: McGraw-Hill), 25.

Balance

Balance is a complex part of one's motor fitness that is influenced by vision; the inner ear; the cerebellum; the **proprioceptors** (nerve endings) in muscles, joints, and tendons; and the skeletal muscles. **Balance** is the ability to maintain one's equilibrium in relation to the force of gravity and to make minute alterations in the body when it is placed in various positions. We can subdivide balance into static and dynamic balance. **Static balance** is the ability to maintain one's equilibrium in a fixed position, such as when standing on one foot or on a balance board. **Dynamic balance** is the ability to maintain one's equilibrium while the body is in motion, such as when walking on a balance beam or bouncing on a trampoline. In actuality, all movement involves an element of either static or dynamic balance because balance is a basic aspect of all movement. For this reason it is important for children to begin developing their balancing abilities at an early age.

Balancing on three body parts, these girls demonstrate static balance.

Students have fun performing dynamic balancing as they circle around cones.

Coordination

Coordination is the ability to integrate separate motor systems with varying sensory modalities into efficient movement. The harmonious working together of the synchrony, rhythm, and sequencing aspects of one's movements is crucial to coordinated movement. Various parts of the body may be involved; for example, kicking a ball or walking upstairs entails eye-foot coordination. Eye-hand coordination is evident in fine motor activities such as bead stringing, tracing, and clay modeling or in gross motor activities such as catching, striking, or volleying a ball.

Agility

Agility is the ability to change direction of the entire body quickly and with accuracy while moving from one point to another. This ability may be enhanced in children through participation in chasing and fleeing games and through certain dodging activities. Working through mazes and obstacle courses also aids agility development.

Speed of Movement

Speed is the ability to move from one point to another in the shortest time possible. It is influenced by one's **reaction time** (the amount of time elapsed from the signal "go" to the first movement of the body) and **movement time** (the time elapsed from the initial movement to completion of the activity). Reaction time is generally considered to be innate, but movement time may be improved with practice. We can see children's speed of movement in activities such as running, climbing, and playing tag. We can improve children's speed of movement by providing ample opportunities for practice and open spaces to run and play.

Power

Power, the ability to perform one maximum effort in as short a time as possible, is sometimes referred to as *explosive strength* and represents the product of strength times speed. This combination of strength and speed is exhibited during jumping, striking, or throwing for distance. The speed of contraction of the muscles involved, as well as the strength and coordinated use of these muscles, determines the degree of power.

Explosive strength (power) is demonstrated as this boy jumps over a hula hoop.

INFORMED MOVERS DEFINED

Children need to be **informed movers**—that is, they need to know about and be able to apply fitness concepts to their own lives. Vigorous physical activity is important in childhood because exercise enhances the components of physical fitness. Exercise stimulates bone growth, develops lung capacity, aids in blood circulation, lowers blood pressure, and reduces cholesterol levels. Physical fitness also contributes to a heightened self-concept, improved body image, a sense of personal accomplishment, and self-discipline. It may further contribute indirectly to academic achievement; children are more alert and tend to pay more attention to their class work when they are physically fit. Furthermore, physical fitness helps children prepare for physical and emotional emergencies and aids in weight control.

Independent Exercisers

Children who are informed movers have the essential fitness knowledge and concepts to become independent exercisers. Although daily physical education and daily fitness breaks are a goal to strive for, the reality is that most North American children have an average of only two physical education lessons per week. Based on what we know about principles of fitness training (please refer to the FITT principle discussed in the following section), it is essentially impossible to make real fitness gains in such a limited amount of time. Therefore, it is important to adopt a philosophy of educating children in terms of physical fitness rather than simply training them. As they gain knowledge and come to value the outcomes of physical fitness, children have the tools to become independent and motivated exercisers.

One way of helping children become independent exercisers is through the use of activity calendars. Activity records are distributed to parents by letter or via a handout at a school-wide fitness fair. Explanations of requirements for various grade and developmental levels are provided. Personal activity records are posted on the refrigerator at home. Students, with parental assistance, maintain a log of their vigorous activities for the month. At the end of each month the activity records are submitted to the physical education teacher. Certificates of participation or other appropriate means of positive reinforcement may be given at the end of each semester.

Healthy Eaters

Obesity in children should concern parents and teachers. Because inactivity is a more relevant factor than overeating in childhood obesity, physical activity plays an important role in controlling weight. An obese child has less energy for vigorous activity and leads a more sedentary life than a child who is active. Although the total number of calories consumed by obese children may be no more (and may be even less) than the caloric intake of non-obese children, children who are obese actually gain weight because of their low level of physical activity. Children who are informed movers are also healthy eaters. They have the knowledge concepts embodied in the Food Pyramid that serves as America's guide to healthy eating (figure 4.1) and are able to translate this knowledge into action in their daily-life eating habits.

Nutrition records are an excellent means of helping children become more aware of the foods that they consume. Like activity records, daily food records may be sent home and, with parental assistance, may become a valuable means for educating children (and adults) on the essentials of healthful eating.

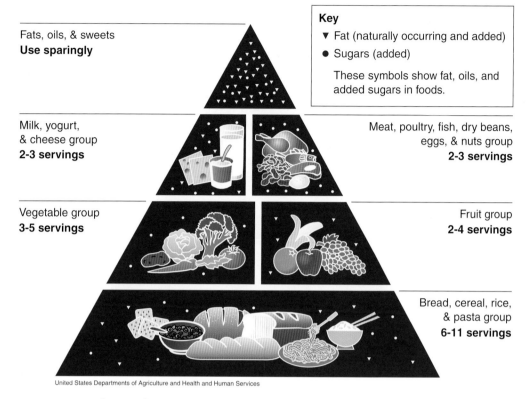

Fats, oils, & sweets
Use sparingly

Key
▼ Fat (naturally occurring and added)
● Sugars (added)

These symbols show fat, oils, and added sugars in foods.

Milk, yogurt,
& cheese group
2-3 servings

Meat, poultry, fish, dry beans,
eggs, & nuts group
2-3 servings

Vegetable group
3-5 servings

Fruit group
2-4 servings

Bread, cereal, rice,
& pasta group
6-11 servings

United States Departments of Agriculture and Health and Human Services

FIGURE 4.1   The Food Pyramid.

PRINCIPLES OF FITNESS DEVELOPMENT

Certain basic principles play a major role in the improvement and maintenance of physical fitness. As a teacher you should take the following factors into consideration when determining the type of fitness program to establish and the amount of activity for children to perform.

CONCEPT 4.6

Specific training principles play a crucial role in the development and maintenance of physical fitness.

REALITY CHECK

Getting Strong

Real-World Situation

Several of your older prepubescent students have expressed a strong desire to "get fit." One boy received a set of weights for his birthday and is eager to get started, along with his friends. The boy's parents come to you for advice. They are concerned that resistance training will "stunt his growth" and that there is little to be gained from training prior to puberty.

Critical Questions

Based on your knowledge of children's fitness development and principles of fitness training:

- What would be your advice to the parents and to the boys?

- How can the FITT principle be put to use in this situation?

- How would you respond to the concern that resistance training "stunts" growth?

- What, if any, are the real benefits to resistance training prior to puberty?

- What are the differences in the terms "resistance training," "weight training," and "weightlifting"?

Overload

The **principle of overload** is the basis for fitness enhancement. To increase fitness, a person must perform more work than he is generally accustomed to doing—either by increasing the volume of work done or by reducing the amount of time in which the same volume of work is accomplished. An overload of the specific system (muscular or cardiovascular) enhances one's level of fitness. The amount of overload must be progressively increased to promote continual fitness improvement.

Doing one's usual amount of physical activity will maintain a certain level of fitness. However, only when muscles are overloaded will strength, endurance (both muscular and cardiovascular), and joint flexibility be increased.

TEACHING TIP 4.1

Children need to understand and appreciate the *benefits of regular vigorous physical activity* if we are serious about their becoming both *informed movers* and *eager movers*:

Increased Muscular Strength and Muscular Endurance

- Stimulates bone growth
- Increases bone mineralization
- Reduces susceptibility to injury
- Enhances self-concept
- Improves body image
- Enhances physical appearance
- Improves cardiovascular endurance
- Improves lung capacity
- Strengthens the heart muscle
- Improves circulation
- Reduces cholesterol levels (low-density cholesterol)
- Lowers heart rate
- Increases oxygen-carrying capacity ($\dot{V}O_2max$)
- Aids in stress reduction and promotes relaxation
- May reduce susceptibility to the common cold

Greater Joint Flexibility

- Helps prevent injury
- Increases work and play efficiency
- Improves motor performance
- Increases range of motion
- Promotes fluidity of movement

Individually Optimum Body Composition

- Improves circulatory efficiency
- Reduces respiratory distress
- Reduces susceptibility to some diseases
- Enhances self-concept
- Improves performance-related fitness
- Improves game, sport, and dance performances
- Aids in weight control
- Provides the tools for enhancing health-related fitness
- Helps reduce number of injuries
- Encourages regular, active participation

Specificity

The **principle of specificity** deals with improvement in the various aspects of fitness specific to the type of training engaged in and to the muscles being exercised. Overload must be specific for the particular fitness component and muscle group being exercised. Even though the components of fitness and the systems of the body are related, specific types of training develop specific qualities of fitness and produce greater amounts of change in the parts exercised than in the parts not exercised. Strength activities, for example, do not have much influence on improving muscular or cardiovascular endurance. Coordination is not markedly improved through performance of push-ups, and running or playing soccer does not measurably strengthen shoulder girdle muscles. Because of the needs of the total child, the fitness program should contain several types of exercises.

Progression

The **principle of progression** is based on the concept that overload of a specific muscle group must be increased systematically over time. Too often children and some adults believe that they can begin to enhance their fitness at levels that far exceed their present capability. Progression is tied to concepts commonly known as the threshold of training and target zone.

The **threshold of training** is the minimum amount of exercise required to produce fitness gains. Those new to a fitness program can begin at or near the threshold level and gradually increase their activity in frequency, intensity, time, and type (FITT). The goal, therefore, is to gradually increase these components until the target zone is reached. The **target zone** is the point at which maximum benefits are obtained for one's individual level of fitness. Clearly, following the principle of progression is essential if real gains are to be made in fitness levels.

The FITT Principle

The **FITT principle** of frequency, intensity, time (duration), and type of exercise is closely associated with overload, specificity, and progression principles. The frequent use of a body part in vigorous physical activities will either improve the efficiency of that part (above threshold) or help it remain at about the same state. Failure to use the body part will diminish its efficiency. Muscles that are used regularly will hypertrophy, or increase in size, and the muscle tone will improve, whereas muscles that are not used regularly will atrophy, or decrease in size and tone. Exercise must be regular to be effective. Most experts agree that between three and six days per week are required for improvement.

Exercise intensity refers to the level of physical exertion, which must be beyond that required for daily living in order to produce fitness gains. The specific muscle or system must be overloaded above the threshold level, and the intensity must progressively approach the target zone.

To be effective, exercise time must be of sufficient duration. As a rule of thumb, 15 minutes is a minimum. Remember, however, that both the threshold of training and the individual's target zone increase as the person attains improved levels of fitness. Conversely, as fitness levels decline, the training threshold and target zone decrease.

Exercise type refers to the fact that many forms of exercise can yield the benefits of vigorous physical activity. Exercise type covers a full range of activities aimed at enhancing one or more of the components of fitness in a variety of play, game, and sport activities, as well as activities in traditional exercise settings such as calisthenics and jogging. Careful consideration of exercise type is vitally important when you are working with children. Most children are not sufficiently self-motivated to voluntarily take part in calisthenics or to run a mile on a regular basis. Turn the activity into a game, however, and it becomes much easier to motivate children to become active participants.

Individuality

The **principle of individuality** means that each person improves in level of fitness at her own rate. A number of factors, such as age, body type, nutritional status, body weight, health status, and level of motivation, determine one's individual level of fitness. No criteria exist for individual rates of trainability, and each child responds in a manner peculiar to her own particular environmental circumstances and hereditary characteristics. Therefore, overreliance on normative standards of fitness and comparison of children with one another are not advised. Remember that one of the primary goals of the fitness strand is to enhance fitness behaviors and to help children become eager movers—that is, to motivate children to be physically active and achieve personal standards of fitness.

WEAVING FITNESS INTO CHILDREN'S LIFESTYLES

It is important to recognize that given the principles of fitness training, the reality of making measurable contributions to children's fitness through the in-school physical education program is frequently limited. Why? Simply because of time. Insufficient time to attain a training effect from vigorous physical activity is the single greatest deterrent to children's fitness enhancement. Therefore, assigning **fitness homework** is a valid way to minimize the negative impact of insufficient time and to weave physical activity into children's lifestyle (Gabbei & Hamrick, 2001). Teachers can "assign" fitness homework for children to do during recess, after school with a parent or friend, at home while watching television, or before bedtime.

Fitness homework may take many forms. As a teacher you may simply assign students fitness tasks to complete during commercial breaks in their television watch-

REALITY CHECK

Fitting in Fitness

Real-World Situation

Your elementary school physical education program does not provide sufficient time for making a real difference in the fitness levels of your students. Because of the many constraints of the school day and the intense competition for more instructional minutes by all teachers, additional physical education time is not a realistic possibility. You are, however, determined to help children learn how to include fitness activities in their lifestyle independent of you and the physical education program.

Critical Questions

Based on your knowledge of children's fitness and the need for additional time to make a real difference in children's fitness levels:

- How would you involve your students in fitness homework?

- How could you promote fitness breaks among teachers, as well as among students, during the school day?

- What other motivational techniques might you include to help children become eager movers?

- How might you help parents become partners with their children in creating a playful fitness-enhancing home environment?

ing time. Later you may ask them to report to you informally on their progress and frequency of compliance. Fitness homework may also take the form of a home fitness chart sent to parents with an explanation of various fitness activities, their purpose, and supervisory hints. Parents can then help children with proper performance and exercise compliance, and perhaps even exercise with them.

Fitness homework is an effective motivational tool that assumes that children know how to work for higher levels of fitness and are eager to do so. Remember, the fitness strand of the developmental physical education program is intended not only to develop fit movers but also to create informed movers and motivate eager movers. The developmental program goes beyond fitness "training" and recognizes the importance of fitness "education." **Fitness training** can occur with little or no enthusiasm or cognitive comprehension of why it is essential or how to go about it. **Fitness education,** on the other hand, recognizes the following principles:

- It is essential for children to know why fitness enhancement is personally important.
- They must know how to go about increasing their fitness in a safe and healthful manner.
- They must be sufficiently motivated to participate with little or no outside prodding.

CONCEPT
4.7

Fitness homework and fitness breaks are valid means of weaving fitness into children's lifestyle.

EAGER MOVERS DEFINED

During their early years, children are usually **eager movers,** willing to participate in vigorous physical activity. As we have pointed out before, too often people assume that because children frequently participate in play activities during their spare time they do not need an instructional program of skill and fitness development. A teacher who takes this attitude often neglects to teach movement skills necessary for participation in physical activities that are vigorous. Children will participate in such activities only when they have developed sufficient skills to enjoy participation. By developing their movement skills, children acquire the tools for gaining and maintaining improved levels of fitness.

CONCEPT
4.8

A variety of motivational techniques must be used to sustain children's interest and participation in physical fitness activities.

In addition to providing challenging experiences, teachers need to provide a great range of activities. Curt Hinson, a nationally recognized elementary physical educator, has designed several unique and motivating fitness activities for children (Hinson, 1995). Hinson believes in the 4 C's: choice, challenge, curiosity, and creativity. The teacher should provide *choice*—or a variety of physical fitness activities. Activities should present a *challenge*—each activity should have varying degrees of difficulty to challenge varying fitness levels. Activities should be child centered and interesting enough to peak children's *curiosity.* And teachers should use *creativity*—should challenge themselves to design innovative and creative fitness games. Hinson, after teaching his students the prerequisite skills and concepts for a specific fitness game or activity, gives them a minimum of three fitness choices at the beginning of a class. He encourages children to be independent and to make their own choices about what fitness activity and how much of it to complete. This ultimately fosters children's intrinsic motivation and helps them to realize that they are personally responsible for their own fitness development.

TEACHING TIP 4.2

Techniques for *motivating children* to achieve greater fitness:

- Make it fun by giving the fitness activity a name and making it a game.
- Develop an all-school, 15- to 20-minute daily fitness break in addition to the instructional physical education program.
- Stress individual standards of achievement and personal progress.
- Emphasize the why and how of fitness.
- Avoid comparing children with one another and overreliance on norms.
- Add music to the workout session.
- Develop fitness bulletin boards.
- Vary distances, activities, repetitions, and time.
- Publish fitness information in the school newspaper.

- Develop graphs and charts of individual progress.
- Incorporate obstacle courses into the program.
- Try timed circuits, varying the circuit regularly.
- Try treasure hunts with younger children and orienteering skills with older students.
- Participate in the American Heart Association/ AAHPERD Jump Rope for Heart Program.
- Form a running club, jump rope club, or aerobics club for daily activities before school or during recess time.
- Get involved yourself and exercise with the children.

It is clear that by getting to know students and assessing their interests and abilities, you can plan activities that appeal to children, which is important in preventing experiences that are unsuccessful, frustrating, and not enjoyable. A positive attitude toward participation in vigorous physical activities is essential if children are to remain motivated toward an active way of life.

Children are generally positively motivated to engage in physical activity when they see someone they look up to being active. To this end, incorporating a "Principal's Weekly Fitness Walk" within your school may help children become more eager movers. Through good behavior, outstanding performance, or some other form of achievement, children earn the opportunity to take a power walk with the building principal. This is a novel and effective means of helping to convey the concept that fitness is for everybody. It also serves as a means of promoting habitual physical activity.

Active Movers

Physical fitness is accomplished through regular, systematic, intense participation in vigorous activities. Particular activities contribute more to one aspect of fitness than to others. Therefore, it is important to provide a variety of activities that interest children and motivate them to exercise regularly. Have a planned program and do not leave physical activity to chance. As you plan fitness-building activities that children can do at home, think about activities that require only a few minutes or an extended period of time that children can do with others or alone. It is helpful to give the children fitness challenges that they can practice or perform after school hours.

Playful Movers

With children, it is essential that you minimize the mind-dulling and often boring repetition of physical exercise. The more fun and gamelike the activities are, the easier it will be to motivate children. Remember, with children you can "give it a name and make it a game." In other words, modify the fitness activity to resemble a game or vigorous play activity to maximize participation and encourage compliance. For example, with younger children you may take advantage of their vivid imaginations and turn your fitness activities for the day into a story play such as a bear hunt, a trip to the moon, or a day at the circus. With older children you will be successful if you introduce personal record keeping, cooperative and vigorous gamelike fitness sessions, and aerobic dance activities (refer to Allsbrook, 1992).

Partners With Parents

Another area in which you can have an influence is parent education. Many parents are concerned when their child is not physically active, but frequently they do not know what to do to help. Also, many parents have lost or have never developed habits of regular, vigorous physical activity. A trained physical educator can establish a program of sessions to help parents learn more about children's physical development, ways to start a family fitness program, and helpful fitness-building activities. Operating alone, the school can have only limited success. Fitness is a year-round, lifelong objective. Thus there must be cooperative efforts between the home and the school to develop and maintain the physical fitness of children. The activity calendars and food records discussed earlier are effective means of involving parents in the fitness and nutrition education of their children. Your local Parent Teacher Organization (PTO) can also be very helpful (**www.pta.org**).

IMPLICATIONS FOR TEACHING DEVELOPMENTAL PHYSICAL EDUCATION

Lifelong habits of activity or inactivity are established during childhood. Creating positive attitudes toward gaining and maintaining an acceptable level of physical fitness, and providing opportunities to develop the components of fitness, are important objectives of the physical education program.

Traditionally, schools have placed children in environments that demand rigid conformity to inactivity. The scheduled physical education class and recess periods are frequently the only times children have an opportunity to be physically active during the school day. Although potentially helpful, the instructional physical education program generally is not capable of enhancing fitness levels to a significant degree because sessions are not long enough or frequent enough. Recess is often a time of inactivity or relatively sedentary play. Because of these problems, many schools are instituting daily **fitness breaks** of 15 to 20 minutes per day. The fitness break is an all-school activity, engaged in by students, faculty, and staff, that is in addition to the instructional physical education period. The emphasis is on continuous vigorous physical activity. Some schools use hallways, the gymnasium, the cafeteria, or outdoor facilities for mass participation. Other schools have self-contained breaks, led by the teacher in the classroom or on the playground.

Improved fitness results from participation in vigorous activities that require skill and that are interesting to children. As a teacher you will have the important responsibility of ensuring that children develop movement skills so that avenues open up for recreational pursuits. Schools must offer opportunities for children to develop and apply movement skills that are essential for self-direction in vigorous physical activities.

Summary

Fitness acquisition is important in helping children become fit movers, informed movers, and eager movers. Today's children live in the midst of a fitness boom that has permeated all facets of North American society. Unfortunately, however, only limited information has trickled down from this movement to children. The results of several recent national surveys of children's fitness clearly reveal that much more needs to be done. Recent encouraging signs point to a surge of interest in children's fitness, and there is hope for the future.

One can define *physical fitness* specifically as a positive state of being that is influenced by regular vigorous physical activity and also by genetic makeup and nutritional adequacy. We can divide physical fitness into the two broad areas of health-related fitness (consisting of muscular strength and endurance, cardiovascular endurance, joint flexibility, and perhaps body composition) and performance-related fitness (consisting of balance, coordination, agility, speed, and power). Basic principles of fitness enhancement include overload, specificity, and progression. To develop fitness gains, people should begin slowly and gradually increase their activity according to the FITT principle. It is essential that children understand these principles of training and adhere to them for balanced and healthful fitness attainment.

It is important, too, for teachers to convey these fitness concepts to children in developmentally appropriate ways so that children will possess the essential tools for their own fitness enhancement.

Fitness homework and fitness breaks are ways to extend and maximize the impact of fitness education among children. Time limitations placed on physical education teachers frequently make it exceedingly difficult, if not impossible, to demonstrate measurable improvements in children's fitness levels. Limitations in terms of insufficient frequency, intensity, and duration of training directly violate basic principles of fitness enhancement.

Physical education teachers need to devise techniques for motivating children to engage eagerly in positive fitness behaviors as part of their chosen lifestyle. Fun, variety, and peer group identification are important motivational tools that you will want to include in your fitness training programs.

The fitness strand of the developmental physical education program not only aims at fitness training to develop fit movers; it also includes fitness education and fitness motivation for developing informed movers and eager movers. Physical fitness is an important quality linked to a positive state of health and within the reach of all who are committed to the challenge and take seriously the message of increased physical activity. Developmental physical education has the opportunity to provide children with the essential tools to attain and maintain a healthy lifestyle that includes regular vigorous physical activity.

Terms to Remember

Excellent Readings

Corbin, C.B., Dale, D., & Pangrazi, R.P. (1999). Promoting physically active lifestyles among youth. *JOPERD, 70* (16), 26-28.

Corbin, C.B., & Pangrazi, R.P. (1998). *Physical activity for children: A statement of guidelines.* Reston, VA: NASPE.

Ernst, M.P., Pangrazi, R.P., & Corbin, C.B. (1998). Physical education: Making a transition toward activity. *JOPERD, 69* (9), 29-32.

Faigenbaum, A.D. (2001). Strength training children's health. *JOPERD, 72* (3), 24-30.

Hinson, C. (1994, January). Pulse-power—a heart physiology program for children. *JOPERD, 65,* 62-68.

Hopper, C., Fisher, B., & Munoz, K.D. (1997). *Health-related fitness for grades 1 and 2.* Champaign, IL: Human Kinetics. (Also available for grades 3 and 4, and 5 and 6)

Pangrazi, R.P., & Corbin, C.B. (1993). Physical fitness: Questions teachers ask. *JOPERD, 64,* 14-19.

Pangrazi, R.P., & Corbin, C.B. (1994). *Teaching strategies for improving youth fitness.* Reston, VA: AAHPERD.

Virgilio, S.J. (1997). *Fitness education for children.* Champaign, IL: Human Kinetics.

5

Cognitive Learning

Key Concept

////////

▶ A physically educated person applies movement concepts and principles to the learning and development of motor skills.

Content Standard #2: *National Standards for Physical Education:* National Association for Sport and Physical Education

Chapter Objectives

This chapter will provide you with the tools to do the following:

▶ Describe what is meant by the terms *cognitive map making*, *critical thinking*, and *divergent movement ability* and discuss how each may be facilitated through physical activity.

▶ List and describe the various components of cognitive concept learning.

▶ Demonstrate understanding of the concept that children become knowledgeable movers by being both active learners and multisensory learners.

▶ Define the term *perceptual-motor* and diagram the perceptual-motor process.

▶ List and describe the perceptual-motor components and give examples of each.

▶ Discuss the role of perceptual-motor learning in cognitive development.

▶ Distinguish between readiness and remediation in perceptual-motor learning and discuss the proposed role of each.

From the moment of birth, children begin to learn how to interact with their environment. This interaction is a cognitive as well as a motor process that is inseparable from movement. Voluntary, conscious thought and action are rooted in meanings derived from the environment. Although perceptual-motor learning is a spontaneous process in normally developing children, a significant number of children need assistance with this process.

The view taken in this chapter is that perceptual-motor learning and concept development are both aspects of cognitive learning that are especially important during the period of childhood. We therefore focus on the interactive nature of these processes. We discuss multisensory learning and its component parts, along with the importance of concept learning and perceptual-motor learning through movement.

You should note that the term *cognitive concept learning* is not to be confused with *academic concept learning*. Academic concept learning deals specifically with the traditional subject matter areas of math, language arts, science, and the like. Cognitive concept learning is a much more inclusive term that includes academic learning as only one of its several components.

ACTIVE LEARNERS DEFINED

Cognitive concept learning, through cognitive map making and critical thinking, is a viable outcome of the developmentally based physical education program. Developmental physical education takes into account children's levels of cognitive development, as well as their motor development, and recognizes that the motor and cognitive domains are indeed intertwined. **Cognitive concept learning** is, therefore, defined as the process by which information is organized, put into memory, and made available for recall and application to a variety of settings. Cognitive concept learning provides children with the tools for critical thinking. It uses movement activities to aid in retention, recall, decision making, and application.

Movement skill learning, whether it is the learning of fundamental or specialized movement skills, is an active learning process intricately interrelated with cognition. Movement skill learning cannot occur without the benefit of higher thought processes. All voluntary movement requires an element of cognition. The more complex the movement task, the more complicated the cognitive processing involved.

Cognitive Map Making

As movement skills are learned, **cognitive maps,** or mental images, are formed. These images are retained in memory, ready to be recalled and re-created on split-second notice. As skill continues to improve, performance appears to become almost automatic, involving little or no conscious thought. Although movement skill performance is not automatic in the true sense of the word, the skill has been so thoroughly learned that it looks that way. For example, when walking from place to place we give scant attention to how, when, and exactly where we place our feet. We do not consciously think about how our arms swing in opposition to our leg action or about the fact that we are striding forward in an alternating heel-to-toe fashion. All of these processes have been so thoroughly learned that they appear to be automatic because they do not require our conscious attention. But notice what happens when you walk on ice, in sand, or with a heavy backpack. The different set of conditions under which you are performing the task will cause you, for a short while, to attend consciously to the modified requirements of the task until you have formed a new cognitive map and put it into memory. So, too, is it with children. Because they are learning through exploration and discovery, it becomes critically important that we help them learn both the skill concepts and the movement concepts associated with how their body should move and how their body can move, respectively. By doing so, we materially aid them in forming cognitive maps of fundamental and specialized movement skills.

Critical Thinking

Lipman (1988) first defined **critical thinking** as "skillful, responsible thinking that facilitates good judgment because it (1) relies upon criteria, (2) is self-correcting, and (3) is sensitive to context" (p. 39). Critical thinking therefore is a form of cognitive accountability based on concept formation in which the learner notes relationships and makes conscious decisions based on established criteria. The constant knowledge explosion that today's children are immersed in demands that they become critical thinkers in order to be able to bring personal meaning and clarity to what is happening around them.

With regard to critical thinking in the motor domain, McBride (1992) was the first to define it as "reflective thinking that is used to make reasonable and defensible decisions about movement tasks and challenges" (p. 115). To link critical thinking with physical education, McBride proposed a four-phase model that includes the following steps:

1. The learner engages in cognitive organization.
2. The learner engages in cognitive action.
3. The process leads to cognitive outcomes.
4. The process leads to psychomotor outcomes.

CONCEPT 5.1

Cognitive concept learning in physical education involves children in the processes of critical thinking and cognitive map making.

REALITY CHECK

Stinkin' Thinkin'

Real-World Situation

As a new teacher, you are looking forward to incorporating teaching techniques that promote *critical thinking* and *cognitive map making* among students in your elementary school physical education program. The children at your new school do not have daily physical education. They do, however, have physical education twice a week for 30 minutes and daily recess for 20 minutes in the morning or the afternoon. During fall orientation, while you are sharing your plans with more experienced classroom teachers, two of these teachers—trying to be helpful—take you aside and recommend that you abandon your "lofty ideals" and get your head into the "real world." After all, they claim, "We teachers are the authorities on the subject matter, and no matter if we are in the classroom or the gymnasium, we are there to show and tell

students how to perform. Furthermore," they say, "you simply don't have enough time to engage your students in critical thinking in a meaningful way." The new school year is about to begin, and you have some decisions to make.

Critical Questions

Based on your knowledge about developing children's critical thinking and cognitive map making skills:

- Your plans for promoting critical thinking and cognitive map making among your students are under attack. How would you respond?

- Does learning occur from the outside in (the view of your two "helpful" colleagues) or from the inside out (a cognitive view of learning)?

- In your view, is learning a product or a process, or both? Why?

The use of indirect or production teaching styles (see chapter 10) that involve children in the important process of "learning to learn" has a positive impact on critical thinking skills in a physical education setting. When you use teaching behaviors in a ball-throwing skill theme, for example, you have students going through the following steps:

1. Students reflect on and make conscious decisions about essential aspects of throwing a ball for distance (cognitive organization).

2. They demonstrate implementation of these decisions in a variety of throwing activities (cognitive action).

3-4. They personally judge their success in terms of *why* the ball traveled as far and as accurately as it did (cognitive and psychomotor outcomes).

In this way you are promoting critical thinking skills among your students.

Here a student performs an underhand throw to a partner. You can facilitate critical thinking by asking questions about the throwing action—for example, "Why should you step forward on your opposite foot when you throw?"

By engaging children in critical thinking, the teacher relinquishes the role of sole authority and giver of information. Instead, the teacher becomes a facilitator who encourages students to ask questions, compare and contrast ideas, and create new solutions to movement problems presented to them. Research in the area of divergent movement ability (i.e., the ability to produce different fundamental movement skills when performing locomotor, manipulative, or stability tasks) has demonstrated that children's divergent movement abilities are the combined product of several critical thinking processes (Cleland & Gallahue, 1993; Cleland & Pearse, 1995).

TEXT BOX 5.1

Cognitive concept development is an integral part of all quality physical education programs. Helping children learn about and internalize movement concepts and skill concepts in a developmentally appropriate manner, consistent with NASPE's National Standards for Physical Education, makes important contributions to children's ability to function as critical thinkers and divergent movers. As a result, the potential to become physically fit and to maintain increased levels of physical activity is increased.

The famous developmentalist Jean Piaget (Peterson & Felton-Collins, 1986) was among the first to demonstrate a link between motor processes and cognitive learning. Piaget's work highlighted the important role that movement plays in the cognitive development of infants and young children. In Piaget's system, the **sensori-motor phase** of development involves coordination of the infant's and young child's motor activities and perceptions into a tenuous whole. This phase of development and the corresponding stages within that phase clearly illustrate the link between movement and cognition. The **preoperational phase** encompasses the early childhood years and is characterized by egocentric behaviors. The **concrete operations phase** is typical of the elementary school years and is typified by increasing curiosity. The achievement of competence within the preoperational and the concrete operations phases is considerably aided, according to Piaget, through the process of movement.

An important outgrowth of Piaget's work has been a cognitive theory of learning that emphasizes the *process* aspects of learning and not simply the product. Cognitive learning theory views learning as a process that involves experimentation, exploration, and individual decision making; it is a process that necessitates the reconstruction of incorrect events into a new, correct whole. A Piagetian view of learning, or, as it is often called, a cognitive or constructivist view of learning, lends considerable support to the importance of indirect, exploratory, guided discovery, and problem-solving approaches to learning, particularly for those at the beginning/novice level of learning a new movement skill.

THE COGNITIVE CONCEPT COMPONENTS

CONCEPT 5.2

It is essential for children to learn the skill concepts, movement concepts, activity concepts, and fitness concepts of developmental physical education if they are to be knowledgeable movers as well as skillful movers.

Several aspects of cognitive concept learning relate to movement (figure 5.1). In the following paragraphs we discuss each of these briefly and offer suggestions for using them in the developmentally based physical education curriculum.

Skill Concepts

Skill concept learning deals specifically with how the body *should* move. Teachers and coaches must recognize that problems associated with insufficient instructional time, large classes, the immaturity of some children, or simply the complexity of the task itself frequently make it difficult to attain the goal of developing skillful movers within the confines of the instructional class. For example, children are frequently unable to kick, throw, or dribble a ball at the mature stage. Therefore, it is essential that children learn about how their body is supposed to move in the performance of fundamental and specialized movement skills.

Unfortunately, the instructional portion of the school day fails, for one or more of the reasons just mentioned, to give children adequate help in becoming skillful in these fundamental movements. Similarly, older children often have trouble mastering many of the sport skills presented during the regular instructional portion of the class. But if we give these same children the vital skill concepts about how their body should move when kicking, throwing, dribbling a ball, or performing specific sport skills, they will have the necessary tools for learning outside the confines of the gymnasium—on the playground, at home, or on the youth sport team. Part IV of this book, "The Skill Themes," provides a wide variety of skill concepts for both fundamental and specialized movement skills.

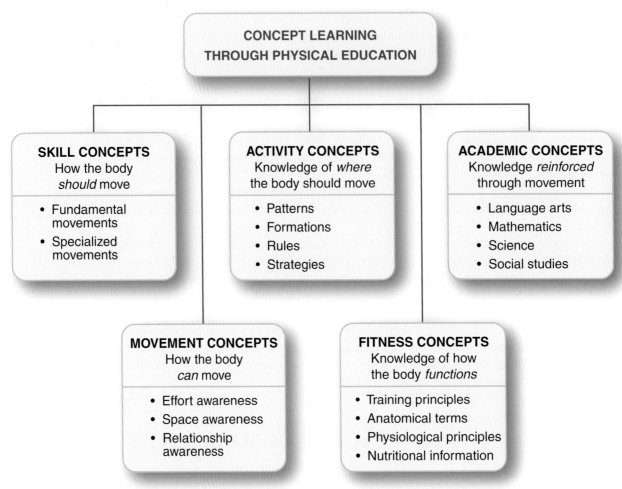

FIGURE 5.1 The components of cognitive concept learning.

Movement Concepts

Movement concept learning deals with how the body *can* move. Seldom in the real world does movement occur under the same conditions time after time. Most movement tasks in games, sport, and dance are dynamic in nature, mandating fluidity and flexibility in one's movement patterns. Furthermore, the ecology of the environment itself is dynamic. Changes in such things as the playing surface, facilities, equipment, and number of participants make it virtually impossible to address all of the possible ways in which the body can move. The dynamic nature of movement, the ever changing environment, and the situational requirements of the task make it absolutely essential for children to learn about how their body can move. Because in actuality, no two movements when repeated in a dynamic environment are ever exactly the same. As a result, we cannot teach each one but can only teach the concept of the movement for the person to apply in various circumstances.

Certainly, we should introduce a new movement skill first under static conditions, in which the environment and the task itself are maintained as nearly as possible in an invariant form. This procedure is essential at the beginning/novice level of new movement skill learning. But at the same time we must be mindful that this same movement skill will seldom be performed in isolation or under the same static conditions in which it was originally learned. This leads to the importance of movement concept learning as an essential aid to learning the many and varied ways in which the body is capable of moving in performing a single fundamental movement skill or a group of skills chained together as specialized sport skills.

Because our environment is constantly changing, we must develop plasticity (i.e., adaptability) of movement in order to move with control and efficiency. Therefore, to help young learners develop the ability to move in a variety of ways under a variety of circumstances, we need to ensure that they have ample opportunities to experiment with and explore the movement concepts of *effort awareness, space awareness,* and *relationship awareness* (see table 5.1). By experiencing how the body can move (effort), where the body can move (space), and with whom and with what the body can move (relationships), children become versatile dynamic movers—movers capable of responding with skill, precision, and plasticity to the variety of movement circumstances in which they move every day. Chapter 16, "Movement Skill Development Through Movement Concept Learning," provides an in-depth discussion. Part IV, "The Skill Themes," provides examples of numerous movement concepts for both fundamental and specialized movement skills.

TABLE 5.1—THE MOVEMENT CONCEPTS

Effort awareness (how the body can move)	Space awareness (where the body can move)	Relationship awareness (moving with objects/people)
Body movement with varying:	Body movement at varying:	Body movement in relation to:
Force Strong Light	**Levels** High/medium/low	**Objects** Over/under In/out Between/among In front of/behind Lead/follow Above/below
Time Fast Slow Medium Sustained Sudden	**Directions** Forward/backward Diagonally/sideward Up/down Various pathways (curved, straight, zigzag, etc.)	
Flow Free Bound	**Ranges** Body shapes (wide, narrow, curved, straight, etc.) Body spaces (self-space and general space) Body extensions (near/far, large/small, with and without implements)	**People** Mirroring Shadowing In unison Together/apart Alternating Simultaneously Partner/group

Activity Concepts

Activity concept learning deals with *where* the body should move. Activity concepts center on the learning of patterns, formations, rules, and strategies for effective participation in game, sport, and dance activities. Developmental physical education recognizes the importance of activity concept learning as a way to provide children with a knowledge base for effective participation—participation that will occur most frequently in recreational and competitive settings outside of the physical education class. Therefore, when we help children learn the activity concepts involved in games and sports and in rhythmic and dance activities, we are offering them the essential knowledge of where they should position themselves, how to respond to elements of the activity, and how to follow the rules and strategies for successful participation. Activity concepts must be geared to children's levels of motor, cognitive, and affective development. They must be both age group appropriate and individually appropriate.

As a teacher you will need to remember that although activity concepts can and should be taught systematically, they should not be the main focus of the lesson. The primary focus of the developmental lesson is on learning new movement skills and enhancing physical activity and fitness. Activity concepts should be included during the skill application portion of the lesson, but they should not serve as an excuse for promoting a physical education program that stresses "playing the game" rather than first learning the skills that enable a child to play the game successfully. Activity concepts are important in that they provide the learner with the tools for effective participation—participation that occurs primarily outside of the instructional physical education program.

Fitness Concepts

Fitness concept learning deals with *what* one needs to do to gain and maintain a healthy lifestyle. Because of the physiological requirements for achieving a training effect, fitness enhancement is not a reality in many physical education programs. Certainly, children's fitness enhancement is a laudable goal that should be sought. But it is an elusive goal in programs that do not provide sufficient frequency, intensity, and time for a training effect to occur. Children must, however, learn essential fitness concepts for healthful living and must be shown how they can incorporate these concepts into their daily lives.

It is essential that children learn about the principles of fitness training and have opportunities to apply them. They need to know not only the components of health-related and performance-related fitness but also how each may be enhanced. Children need to begin to learn and apply basic anatomical terms such as *abdominals, biceps,* and *triceps* and physiological terms such as *target heart rate, threshold of training,* and *static stretching.* They should also learn about the link between proper nutrition, fitness, and good health. Because of the stressful nature of many children's lives, it is becoming increasingly important to teach children about basic principles of relaxation and stress reduction.

Fitness concepts can be effectively integrated into the fitness strand of the developmental physical education program. But they must be integrated in a manner that is developmentally sound and also has curricular validity. In other words, it is important to recognize the cognitive comprehension level of your students and to tailor fitness concepts to that level of understanding. Also, it is important to adopt a curricular sequence that builds concept upon concept. This step avoids the trap of teaching children the same thing year after year with little or no consideration given to curricular progression.

Academic Concepts

Academic concept learning deals with using movement activities as a means of *reinforcing* knowledge concepts in language arts, mathematics, science, and social

School-Wide Olympic Games

Real-World Situation

Now that we have either the Winter or the Summer Olympics every two years, you have decided to propose to your building principal that the entire school faculty unite for a learning module coinciding with the Olympic Games. The idea is that your School Olympics will take advantage of a "teachable moment" by not only promoting the spirit of the Games but also using movement activities to *reinforce academic concepts* dealt with in art, music, science, reading, arithmetic, geography, and writing.

Critical Questions

Based on your knowledge of children's cognitive concept learning and the potential for reinforcing academic concepts in the gymnasium:

- How would you approach your building principal with your School Olympic Games idea?
- What important roles will the art and music teachers play in helping make the event a success?
- How will you involve the classroom teachers in your School Olympics?
- What are the specific academic concepts that could be effectively reinforced through this school-wide event?

CONCEPT 5.3

Movement can be used effectively to reinforce many of the academic concepts dealt with in the traditional classroom.

studies, concepts traditionally covered exclusively in the classroom. Movement activities have been shown repeatedly to be an effective way to help children grasp—through the use of additional sensory modalities (primarily the tactile and kinesthetic modes)—concepts that were once taught only in the two-dimensional, auditory-visual environment of the classroom (please refer to Purcell Cone, Werner, Cone, & Mays Woods, 1998).

If you are to make academic concept learning effective in the gymnasium, you need to do two things. First, you must take time to talk with classroom teachers and, when possible, visit classrooms. You can then see firsthand what is being taught, when it is being presented, and how the children respond. You will need to discuss with the classroom teacher in specific terms what you can do to supplement and reinforce the classroom curriculum. Such a procedure has an added bonus in garnering support for your program. Classroom teachers who know that you are interested in their instructional goals tend to be more receptive to *your* instructional goals. You will gain an ally in the support and promotion of your program when you show interest in the classroom teacher's program.

Second, you must teach for transfer of skills. In other words, you must help children link what is being taught in the classroom to its application in the gymnasium. You cannot assume that children will make this link themselves. When teaching for transfer it is important to use the gymnasium as a way to demonstrate the relevancy of academic concepts. For example, it is easy to demonstrate the importance of learning fractions when you are teaching how to compute batting averages or win-loss percentages. The ethnic heritage of cultures from around the world can be brought alive through games and folk dances characteristic of various cultures. Story writing can translate into small-group mini-plays that emphasize the movement components of the story. Academic concept learning that is integrated into the gymnasium should be a by-product of good teaching that is aware of and sensitive to the needs of the whole child (Garrahy, 2001). For more information, please refer to chapter 25, "Developing the Thinking Child."

MULTISENSORY LEARNERS DEFINED

CONCEPT 5.4

Because children are multisensory learners, all voluntary movement involves an element of perception.

Learning is a process that culminates in a relatively permanent change in behavior as a result of experience or practice. By its very nature, learning is a process that relies on both sensory and motor information. Learning is multisensory because it is dependent on what we see, hear, feel, taste, touch, and smell. Multisensory learning is a process of change brought about by the internalization and integration of sensory stimuli that result in a perception or a perceptual-motor response.

The word **perception**, which means awareness or interpretation of information, refers to the process of organizing and synthesizing information that we gather through the various sense organs with stored information or past data, a process that leads to a modified response pattern.

When we consider the term **perceptual-motor**, then, we know that the first part of the term signifies the dependency of voluntary movement activity on some form of sensory information. All voluntary movement involves an element of perceptual awareness resulting from sensory stimulation. The second part of the term *perceptual-motor* indicates that the development of one's perceptual abilities depends, in part, on movement. The reciprocal relationship between sensory input and motor output enables perceptual and motor abilities to develop in harmony.

CONCEPT 5.5

The quality of one's movement performance is significantly influenced by the accuracy of one's perceptions.

It has long been recognized that the quality of one's movement performance depends on the accuracy of perception and the ability to interpret these perceptions into a series of coordinated movement acts. The terms *eye-hand coordination* and *eye-foot coordination* have been used for years to express the dependency of efficient movement on the accuracy of one's sensory information. The individual in the process of shooting a basketball free throw has numerous forms of sensory input that must be sorted out and expressed in the final act of shooting the ball. If the perceptions are accurate and if they are expressed in a coordinated sequence, the shooter makes the basket. If not, the shot misses. All voluntary movement involves the use of one or more sensory modalities to a greater or lesser degree, depending on the movement act to be performed.

REALITY CHECK

Strike Three, You're Out

Real-World Situation

While engaging your students in a fundamental movement skill theme focusing on striking, you notice that several girls and boys have considerable difficulty making contact with a pitched ball. Many seem to be swinging "late" and others seem to be swinging wildly with little or no hope of making contact. You reflect on the fact that virtually all of these children are able to make good contact with the ball and use a mature striking pattern when hitting a stationary ball off a batting tee but that when it is tossed they consistently fail to hit the ball.

Critical Questions

Based on your knowledge of children's perceptual-motor development and your understanding that all voluntary movement involves an element of perception:

- What perceptual difficulties may these children be having that influence the motor outcome of the striking task?
- Why are some children successful with this task and others not?
- What modifications would you make in the equipment and surroundings that would promote greater success?
- What would be a developmentally appropriate teaching progression for improving children's striking skills?

As multisensory learners, children use their visual, auditory, tactile, and kinesthetic senses to learn about the spatial and temporal aspects of their expanding world. The **perceptual-motor process** is a process of attaining increased skill and improving the ability to function (figure 5.2). It involves the following steps:

1. *Sensory input:* receiving various forms of stimulation by way of specialized sensory receptors (visual, auditory, tactile, and kinesthetic) and transmitting this stimulation to the brain in the form of neural energy

2. *Sensory integration:* organizing incoming sensory stimuli and integrating this new information with past or stored information (memory)

3. *Motor interpretation:* making internal motor decisions (recalibration) based on the combinations of sensory (present) and long-term memory (past) information

4. *Movement activation:* executing the actual movement (observable act) itself

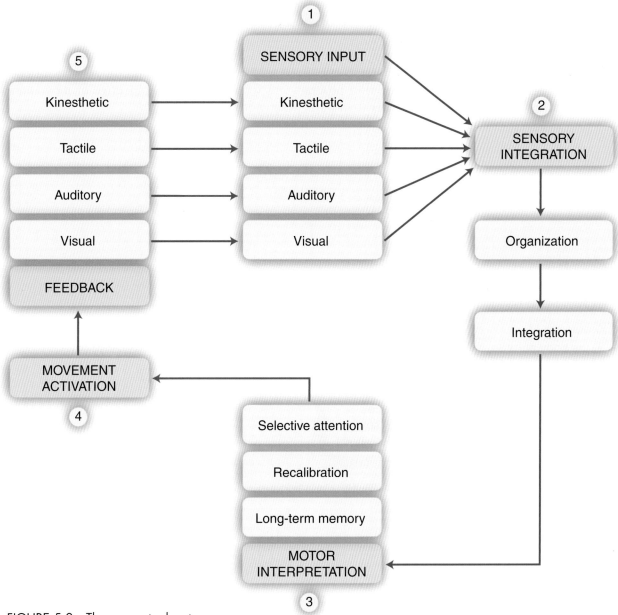

FIGURE 5.2   The perceptual-motor process.

5. *Feedback:* evaluating the movement act using various sensory modalities that feed back information into the sensory input aspect of the process, thus beginning the cycle again (KR, knowledge of results; and KP, knowledge of performance)

Figure 5.2 illustrates the perceptual-motor process. Take a few minutes to review this figure to fully appreciate the importance of perception in the process of movement.

THE PERCEPTUAL-MOTOR COMPONENTS

CONCEPT 5.6

The development of children's spatial and temporal world is aided through practice in perceptual-motor activities.

Although the movement experiences found in the regular physical education program are by definition perceptual-motor activities, some programs emphasize perceptual-motor quality rather than gross motor quality. In remedial and readiness training programs, for example, the emphasis is on improving specific perceptual-motor components. Therefore, movement activities are grouped according to the perceptual-motor qualities they enhance. One common grouping includes body awareness, spatial awareness, directional awareness, and temporal awareness (figure 5.3). Activities designed to enhance these qualities are used in the regular instructional physical education program but with the primary objective of movement skill acquisition rather than perceptual-motor learning.

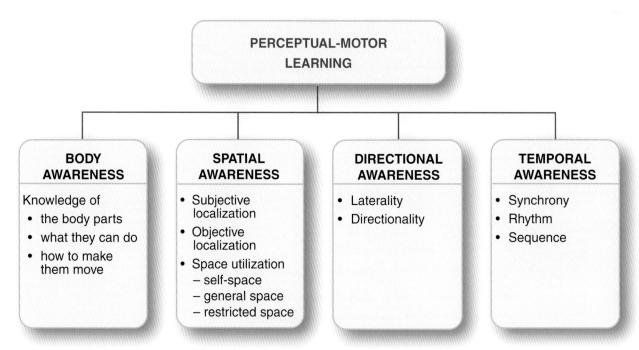

FIGURE 5.3   The components of perceptual-motor learning.

Body Awareness

Body awareness activities are designed to help children better understand the nature of their body and the functions of its parts. There are three aspects of body awareness: (1) knowledge of the body parts, (2) knowledge of what the parts can do, and (3) knowledge of how to make the parts move. Movement experiences that draw attention to one or more of these components contribute positively to the development of children's awareness of their bodies and movement capabilities.

Spatial Awareness

Spatial awareness activities are designed to enhance children's awareness of the orientation of their body in space and the amount of space that it occupies. Spatial awareness (not to be confused with *space awareness*) is developmentally based and progresses from subjective to objective localization as the child matures and gains new experiences. In the period of subjective localization, children are able to locate objects in space relative to themselves but frequently with an erroneous perception of the amount of space that their body occupies. In the period of objective localization, children are able to locate objects in space independently of themselves when making spatial and location judgments. Movement experiences that promote making spatial judgments relative to body location and how much space the body occupies may contribute positively to the child's awareness of space. "My body is to the left of the hoop" is a statement denoting subjective localization. "The hoop is in front of the cone" typifies the concept of objective localization.

Children need to understand that they can utilize the space about them in a variety of ways. Their self-space, or what we often call personal space, is the area immediately surrounding their body. General space is the total available space in the room, in the gymnasium, or on the playground. Restricted space is a specifically prescribed or limited area in which they may move. Additionally, movement serves as a primary means for children to learn how their body may take on different shapes, move at different levels, and move in a variety of pathways as it traverses space. Shape is formed as the body assumes positions such as ones that are wide, narrow, curved, or straight. Level is achieved by the body moving at a high, medium, or low position in relation to the ground. Pathways formed by the body moving through space can be curved, straight, zigzag, and so forth.

Directional Awareness

Directional awareness activities enhance awareness of the body as it is projected into space. Directional awareness gives dimension to objects in space and implies that one is moving in relationship to something else. The concept of relationship awareness as used in movement implies that one is moving in conjunction with other object props or people. You may, for example, move in relationship to the hoop, the rope, or the cones. You may also move in relationship to your partner, teammate, or opponent.

The concepts of left, right, up, and down take on meaning in a relationship context when the child has established directional awareness. A sense of laterality is an internal "feel" for direction in relation to one side of the body or the other. Simply "knowing" left from right, without having to give conscious attention to external cues such as the watch on your right wrist and the ring on your left hand, is evidence of a well-developed internal sense of laterality. A sense of directionality, which is the property signified by the *names* (i.e., *left* and *right*) given to directions, usually develops prior to the internal sense of laterality. Therefore, if you are aware that you have a left and a right hand but are not able to consistently and internally apply that concept, you have a sense of directionality *without* laterality. When we link movement activities to the verbal cues of in/out, up/down, over/under, left/right, between/among, and so forth, we help children develop a sense of directional awareness that encompasses both laterality and directionality.

Spatial awareness and directional awareness are enhanced in this ball-handling activity.

Temporal Awareness

Temporal awareness refers to the child's development of an internal time structure. Temporal awareness enables people to efficiently coordinate movements of the eyes and limbs. The terms *eye-hand coordination* and *eye-foot coordination* refer to the result of fully developed temporal awareness. Children who are developing their temporal awareness are in the process of learning how to synchronize movements in a rhythmical manner and to put them into the proper sequence. Rhythmical running, dancing, and juggling all require varying degrees of temporal awareness.

These children are developing eye-hand and eye-foot coordination as they perform a clapping and stepping rhythm dance with their teachers.

THE IMPORTANCE OF PERCEPTUAL-MOTOR LEARNING

The study of the influence of perceptual-motor development falls into two broad categories: (1) the influence of perceptual-motor experiences on nonimpaired children (**learning readiness**) and (2) the influence of perceptual-motor training among groups of individuals having some form of sensory, intellectual, physical, neurological, or emotional disability (**remediation**).

CONCEPT 5.7

There is little scientific support for the notion that practicing perceptual-motor activities has a direct effect on improving academic achievement.

For physical educators interested in the study of perceptual-motor behavior, the primary concern is the potential influence of planned programs of specific movement experiences on this behavior. Readiness programs are preventive and are geared toward preschool and primary grade children. Research supports the claim that practice in perceptual-motor activities does enhance children's abilities in this area.

Remedial training programs are directed at those children in the regular classroom who, for unexplained reasons, are failing to keep pace with their classmates. They do not have apparent physical, neurological, or intellectual disabilities, but they fail to reach their potential. Some of these children may have perceptually based learning difficulties. Although the idea is speculative, evidence suggests that perceptual-motor training programs may improve performance in the classroom for some of these children. In fact, though, the Association for Childhood Learning Disabilities (1987) has categorically denied the hypothesized benefits of perceptual-motor training on the remediation of learning disabilities and has encouraged its members, through a position paper, to refrain from making such claims.

REALITY CHECK

Come to My Gymnasium to Become a Better Reader!?

Real-World Situation

Over 40 years ago, many thought that practice in perceptual-motor activities had the potential for enhancing academic achievement, especially among children experiencing learning difficulties. Although sound scientific evidence is lacking, periodically individuals or groups still make claims that children with learning disabilities can be significantly helped to perform better in the classroom if, among other things, they take part in an organized program of perceptual-motor activities. This may include a variety of program types ranging from highly specific patterning activities to good-quality developmentally based physical education programs that focus on both the processes and products of movement skill learning. The speculation is that somehow these activities aid neurological organization, and as a result children enhance their abilities to function in the classroom.

Based on the information just presented, you have been asked to talk with two groups of parents who want your perspective on the impact of perceptual-motor training programs on (1) children's *readiness* for learning and (2) *remediation* of specific learning difficulties.

Critical Questions

Based on your knowledge of children's perceptual-motor development and the differences between perceptual-motor readiness and remediation:

- What is your response to parents concerning the potential of perceptual-motor activities to promote learning readiness?
- What do you say to the group of parents concerning the potential of perceptual-motor activities as a tool in the remediation of specific learning disabilities?
- If perceptual-motor training does not have a direct effect on academic achievement, does it have indirect effects that may be of benefit to the child?
- What, if anything, is the difference between a well-designed and well-taught "developmental physical education program" and a "perceptual-motor training program"?

CONCEPT
5.8

Practicing perceptual-motor activities *may* help improve some aspects of young children's learning readiness.

There are no panaceas in remedial or readiness training. We must view a physical education program that emphasizes perceptual-motor learning as only one avenue by which the perceptual abilities of children may be enhanced. We simply do not have sufficient evidence to support the claim that improved perceptual-motor abilities will directly affect children's academic performance. It could be argued, however, that one positive result of perceptual-motor-oriented physical education programs may be improved self-esteem for children. Improved perceptions of oneself as capable and competent may carry over to the classroom work of some children.

IMPLICATIONS FOR TEACHING DEVELOPMENTAL PHYSICAL EDUCATION

Developmental physical education enhances cognitive concept and perceptual-motor development by engaging children in gross motor activities that involve them in the decision-making processes of learning. Not all children are at the same level of cognitive development upon entering school. Cognition is a process influenced by both maturation and experience and, as such, proceeds at the child's individual rate. Because readiness is prerequisite to success in school, perceptual readiness is an important aspect of children's total readiness for learning.

The percentage of perceptually based learning difficulties is great enough to warrant readiness programs for some preschool and primary grade children. Even though the research is not conclusive that this training directly affects later learning, empirical evidence strongly supports the notion. Deprivation of experiences hinders learning, especially during the early formative years. Therefore, a well-planned developmentally based physical education program that incorporates a variety of movement activities provides many of the experiences that help children develop perceptual-motor and cognitive concept learning. As educators we need to continue to devise additional opportunities for movement experiences that are often absent from the lives of children. Providing supplementary experiences that children are unable to create, do not receive, or cannot fully utilize on their own will have a positive effect on the development of perceptual-motor and cognitive concept learning.

Summary

Children are both active learners and multisensory learners. Critical thinking, cognitive map making, and divergent movement abilities are important functions of the developmental physical education program. Cognitive concept learning dovetails with the idea that children are active learners; movement skill learning, whether of fundamental or specialized movement skills, is an active learning process intricately interrelated with cognition. Cognitive concepts, namely skill concepts, movement concepts, activity concepts, fitness concepts, and academic concepts, can be effectively taught in the gymnasium.

Movement has an obvious role in the perceptual-motor process, which is a process of attaining increased skill and improving the ability to function. The spatial and temporal aspects of perceptual-motor learning are body awareness, spatial awareness, directional awareness, and temporal awareness. While strong evidence is lacking that improved perceptual-motor abilities will directly affect children's academic performance, perceptual-motor learning may help improve learning readiness in young children. Although developmental physical education focuses primarily on movement skill learning and physical activity and fitness enhancement, it must remain open to and plan for opportunities to reinforce both perceptual-motor learning and cognitive concept learning.

Terms to Remember

Excellent Readings

Buschner, C.A. (1994). *Teaching children movement concepts and skills.* Champaign, IL: Human Kinetics.

Cleland, F.E. (1994). Young children's divergent movement ability: Study II. *JTPE, 13,* 228-241.

Cleland, F., & Gallahue, D.L. (1993). Young children's divergent movement ability. *Perceptual & Motor Skills, 77,* 535-544.

Cleland, F., Helion, J., & Fry, F. (1999). Modifying teaching behaviors to promote critical thinking in K-12. *JTPE, 18,* 199-215.

McBride, R., & Cleland, F. (1998). Critical thinking in physical education. *JOPERD, 68* (7), 42-46.

Mitchell, M., Barton, G.V., & Stannie, K. (2000). The role of homework in helping students meet physical education goals. *JOPERD, 71* (5), 30-34.

Nigles, L., & Usnick, V. (2000). The role of spatial ability in physical education and mathematics. *JOPERD, 71* (6), 29-33, 52.

Winnick, J.P. (2000). Perceptual-motor development. In J.P. Winnick (Ed.), *Adapted physical education and sport* (pp. 281-291). Champaign, IL: Human Kinetics.

Yongue, B. (1998). Relationship between cognitive and psychomotor development: Piaget in the gym. *Physical Educator, 55* (1), 19-23.

6

Affective Growth

Key Concepts

▶ A physically educated person demonstrates responsible personal and social behavior in physical activity settings.

▶ A physically educated person understands that physical activity provides opportunities for enjoyment, challenge, self-expression, and social interaction.

Content Standards #5 and #7: *National Standards for Physical Education:* National Association for Sport and Physical Education

This chapter will provide you with the tools to do the following:

▶ Define *self-concept* and *positive socialization* as they relate to children's becoming self-discovering learners and cooperative learners.

▶ List and discuss the components of a positive self-concept.

▶ Provide examples of how physical education experiences can help to enhance self-esteem.

▶ Discuss how improving children's sense of personal security and status can enhance self-concept.

▶ Discuss the influence of status, roles, and cultural norms on children's socialization into society.

▶ Speculate on how children's socialization into their culture is affected by group affiliation, character education, and moral growth.

▶ List a variety of factors that influence affective development.

▶ Describe how developmental physical education can make real and lasting contributions to children's affective development in terms of both "me" and "we."

▶ Discuss the implications of children's affective development for teaching developmental physical education.

Teachers play an important role in children's affective development by giving positive encouragement, helping with realistic goal setting and self-assessment, and using moral dilemmas as a positive learning medium. Learning in the affective domain is an important strand of the developmental physical education program. By their very nature, children are self-discovering learners and cooperative learners. They are intensely engaged in the process of learning about themselves and how to interact with others in their world. They are learning about their unique abilities and are forming the basis for their self-concept. They also are in the process of being socialized into a democratic society, a society that has certain behavioral requirements and expectations.

This chapter focuses on the twin affective topics of self-concept and positive socialization in and through the physical education setting. We discuss what is meant by the terms *self-concept* and *positive socialization* and examine the components of both. Factors influencing self-concept development and positive socialization are also covered, along with specific instructional implications for the developmentally based physical education program.

SELF-ESTEEM AND BECOMING
A SELF-DISCOVERING LEARNER

For children, as self-discovering learners, their sense of personal worth is at the very core of their existence. Children's self-concept is influenced by all aspects of their daily life and affects how they approach their world. Our self-perceptions may be quite accurate or quite different from reality. However, all self-perceptions are important because they determine whether our self-concept is positive or negative.

TEXT BOX 6.1

William James, one of the early students of self-concept, considered an individual's self-perceptions an important variable in understanding human behavior. He once remarked that when two people meet, there are really six persons present. There is each person as he or she is, each as the other sees him or her, and each as seen by himself or herself.

Self-concept is a personal assessment of worthiness that is expressed in the attitudes one holds toward oneself. It is a value-free description of self in that it does not make comparisons with others. On the other hand, the term **self-esteem,** although frequently used interchangeably with self-concept, is our self-description influenced by how we think others view us. Taken together, self-concept and self-esteem represent the total of our perceptions of our worthiness and competence. Our everyday experiences dictate whether we view ourselves as competent or incompetent, worthy or unworthy. However, in turn, our self-concept determines in large part how we act in and react to these views of self. Therefore, in many ways our self-concept determines what we expect to happen. People whose performances do not match their personal aspirations tend to evaluate themselves as inferior no matter how high their attainments may be. They are likely to feel inadequate, guilty, shameful, and even depressed.

Conditions that threaten to expose personal inadequacies are a major cause of anxiety. Belief in oneself and the conviction that we can impose order on a segment of our universe are basic prerequisites for a stable, positive self-concept. Both children and adults with low self-esteem tend to be more conforming than those who have high self-esteem. They may have suffered dominance, rejection, or severe punishment, all of which have a negative impact on self-esteem. But the result is often the same—neither children nor adults can function effectively as self-discovering and cooperative learners if they lack self-esteem and confidence.

CONCEPT 6.1

Self-concept and self-esteem are learned behaviors significantly influenced by children's experiences in physical activity.

COMPONENTS OF A POSITIVE SELF-CONCEPT

Positive self-concept has many components. Among the most important are a sense of belonging, the development of competence, a sense of worthiness, self-acceptance, recognizing and accepting one's uniqueness, and virtuous behavior (Gallahue & Ozmun, 2002). Figure 6.1 illustrates these components. Although no universal pattern or set of conditions seems to be absolutely required to produce a positive self-concept, research indicates that children must have the consistent, long-term presence of at least one significant person in their lives in order for this to happen. This significant person helps nurture the components that make up positive self-concept.

CONCEPT 6.2

Self-concept is influenced by many factors that can be manipulated through sensitive, caring teaching.

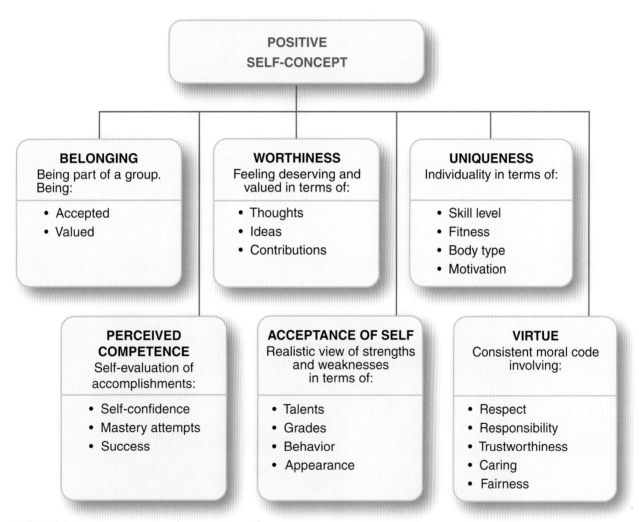

FIGURE 6.1   Components of a positive self-concept.

Belonging

Belonging is the positive feeling that an individual experiences when acting as part of a group and when feeling accepted and valued by the members of that group. Not only is it necessary for the group to regard the individual as belonging, it is also

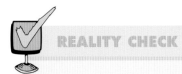

Teacher, I'm New

Real-World Situation

Well into the school year, a new family moves into your school district and the two children enter the local elementary school where you teach. When the first grade girl and third grade boy come to your physical education classes, you are quick to notice that they are new to the school and that they have yet to settle in, make friends, and feel comfortable in their new surroundings. Being familiar with the importance of children's self-concept and self-esteem to their total development, you make a special point of creating a welcoming environment for each child.

Critical Questions

Based on your knowledge of children's affective growth and the important role that physical activity plays in the development of self-concept and self-esteem:

- How would you go about creating a sense of *belonging* for each child?
- What steps would you take to enhance these children's perceptions of *perceived competence*?
- How would you promote their sense of *worthiness*?
- What could you do to promote their sense of *self-acceptance* and *uniqueness*?

essential that the individual regard herself as belonging. A sense of belonging is an important aspect of a positive self-concept. Teachers can do many things in the classroom to help children feel that they belong.

Learning and using each child's first name, as well as recognizing something unique about each child, is an excellent way to help children develop a sense of belonging. Being a contributing member of a class, club, or team also fosters a sense of belonging, as does wearing identity symbols such as T-shirts, "in" hairstyles, and particular types of gym shoes. As the teacher, you are in an excellent position to help children feel that they are an important part of what makes their class, group, or team "the greatest." Try to work constantly to include each student and to foster a group

Students are organized into small practice groups of three for playing a small-sided game of field hockey.

sense of "we" and "us." Reject the notion of exclusion and overidentification with the words "me" and "I" when encouraging a sense of belonging.

Insist that the number of students in physical education classes be no larger than the number of students in the classroom. Small classes foster a sense of belonging. Keep practice groups and teams as small as reasonably possible. Remember, it is generally better to have too few in a group activity than too many. Constantly work for group sizes that maximize the participation and contributions of all to the success of the activity.

Perceived Competence

Competence refers to how efficiently we accomplish a given task. **Perceived competence** is a personal self-evaluation of our competence in comparison to others and to previous personal experience. Perceived competence increases when one achieves personal goals or demonstrates individual improvement, and is situation specific. For example, you may perceive yourself as competent in baseball and basketball but incompetent in swimming and gymnastics. Additionally, perceived competence is relative to one's personal frame of reference. For instance, a Little League baseball player may perceive himself as an "all-star" player, his frame of reference being parents, coaches, teammates, and other players in the league. Seldom, however, does he extend his perception of baseball competence beyond this, to players in the Little League World Series, at the local high school, or at the professional level. Instead, he sees himself as being competent in the context of his world.

Competence is closely linked to **self-confidence**, which is an inner feeling of belief in oneself. When children have low self-confidence and perceived competence, it is likely that their feelings about the past are negative. It is the child's perception of these past experiences that a teacher may be most able to change. Potential for change is important for self-concept development. One of the steps teachers need to take to improve children's self-concept is to help them reinterpret the meaning of past experiences to put negative thoughts into their proper perspective.

Children need to see themselves as competent. Quality instruction in movement skill acquisition and fitness enhancement contributes greatly to a sense of perceived competence in children. Perceived competence tends to encourage increased mastery attempts and leads to higher levels of actual competence. Competence promotes self-confidence, which in turn leads to improved self-esteem and a more positive self-concept (figure 6.2).

Worthiness

A sense of **worthiness** develops out of seeing yourself as deserving and valued because of the kind of person you are, and because you see yourself as worthwhile in the estimation of others. To know that others value your thoughts, ideas, and contributions is to feel worthwhile. Too often, teachers convey the message that children's questions, answers, or performance levels are inadequate. Such behavior does not promote a sense of being valued. On the other hand, actions that are meant to express love and concern are not always pleasant (as in disciplining a child). It is therefore crucial for children's sense of worth that actions meant to express concern are perceived as such and are not viewed as an affront to the child's sense of worth as an individual.

The use of "magic words" such as "please," "thank you," "awesome," "good job," and "you can be proud of ..." convey the message to children that they are worthwhile and respected for who they are, not for what they are. Magic words encourage

FIGURE 6.2 A hierarchical view of self-concept enhancement through increased competence in the motor domain.

children to compliment each other during activities and promote socially appropriate responses and improved self-esteem. Also, taking photos or videotaping children involved in activities individually or as a group promotes personal and corporate identity, and the notion that "I am someone, and I count."

TEACHING TIP 6.1

Ten ways to avoid saying "no" or "wrong" to a child's answer:

1. "That's an interesting point of view."
2. "Perhaps I didn't make myself clear."
3. "Let me rephrase my question."
4. "You've got the general idea."
5. "That's part of the answer."
6. "Good thinking, but not quite what I was looking for."
7. "Are you saying that . . . ?"
8. "Now *there's* an interesting perspective."
9. "That's a good beginning—can anyone else help Jennifer finish the answer?"
10. "You sure have your thinking cap on, however. . . ."

The game of Beanbag Thank-You reinforces positive social behaviors. (See chapter 21 for an explanation of this game.)

Acceptance of Self

Self-acceptance involves recognizing and accepting that we have weaknesses as well as strengths, have limitations as well as abilities, and display incompetence as well as competence. To achieve self-acceptance it is crucial to view both these negative and positive aspects in their totality and to learn how to deal with them positively. For children, this is frequently a difficult process. Their right-wrong, good-bad view of the world (characteristic of the concrete operations level of cognitive development), as well as unrealistic expectations on the part of significant others, makes it hard for many children to accept themselves on the basis of who they are rather than what they have achieved. Acceptance of self has its roots in acceptance by others.

Accepting teachers are concerned about children and are willing to exert themselves on behalf of children. They are loyal sources of affection and support. They express their acceptance in a variety of ways, but perhaps the major underlying feature of the behaviors of accepting teachers is expression of interest and concern. Their actions convey an attitude of unconditional acceptance. For example, accepting teachers refrain from words or actions suggesting that a child's behavior, appearance, grades, or talents determine their view of the child. They instead accept each and every child for her uniqueness and innate value and worth. Accepting teachers make a clear distinction between the choices that a child makes and who the child is. For example, the choice of throwing the ball at another student was poor, but the teacher shows that she still cares for the thrower and trusts that he will learn from the situation.

One of the most potent ways of teaching children to be accepting of themselves is to demonstrate personal self-acceptance. Permitting children to see some of your weaknesses and some positive ways in which you deal with them can be a very useful technique. For example, when repeatedly missing a basketball free throw you may say, "I never was very good at making free throws, but I really love the game of basketball." Teachers are significant others in the lives of children, and their demonstration of personal self-acceptance serves as a positive role model for children to emulate. This can help children to view themselves in a more positive light.

Uniqueness

Recognizing, respecting, and celebrating one's personal **uniqueness** are a hallmark of a positive self-concept. The entire premise of developmental teaching—in the gymnasium or in the classroom—is based on the concept of individualization through developmentally appropriate experience. It is vitally important that we help children recognize and accept their unique qualities. Teachers who are attentive to students recognize children's uniqueness and structure their worlds appropriately. They allow for individual differences in experience, skill level, body type, fitness, and motivation.

Teachers are then able to permit relatively great freedom within the structure they have established because all children recognize that they have a legitimate place in the class or group. Limits need to be reasonable and appropriate to the developmental level of children, not inflexible or arbitrary. The uniqueness of the individual must be respected, encouraged, and celebrated.

Virtue

A frequently forgotten component of a positive self-concept is virtue. **Virtue** is the sense that you are operating with consistency in accordance with an established moral code—a moral code consistent with the expectations of your culture. In a physical education setting, that moral code may take the form of sharing, taking turns, being a good sport, fair play, and other forms of cooperative behavior. Children need to know that a basic requirement of a civilized society involves virtuous behavior. Teachers who both expect children to act accordingly and who help children see themselves as doing so are making an important contribution to positive self-concept development.

The group settings of the classroom, gymnasium, and playground are excellent places to foster children's sense of virtue. Clearly defined and fairly enforced rules for acceptable behavior provide children with a clear view of adult expectations. Catching children being good, rather than only catching them being bad, is an effective technique to foster a sense of virtue among children.

THE IMPORTANCE OF DEVELOPING CHILDREN'S SELF-CONCEPT

It is universally agreed that one's self-concept is learned. In the preschool and elementary school years, parents, teachers, and caregivers are the primary models for the developing behavior of children. They provide children's primary feedback; through them children learn how their behavior is influencing others. Parents and teachers are also the primary evaluators of behavior. They give "moral'" or "worth" meanings to the activities of children.

As the self-concept develops, children act in ways consistent with that concept. Significant others who serve as models and mediators in children's lives play a crucial role in determining the results of learning. Self-esteem develops only in the presence of others and is believed by many to be largely formed and stabilized by about age eight or nine. One of our tasks as adults working with children is to ensure that we nurture a profound sense of respect for the self through our teaching and that children develop a sense of both security and status through quality, sensitive, caring teaching.

CONCEPT 6.3

A positive view of self is vitally important in helping to provide children with a sense of security and status.

TEXT BOX 6.2

The Greatest Gift

As parents, teachers, and coaches we have the greatest gift to give children—a positive self-concept. We can do this by treating them as though they were already what they can only hope to become:

- Letting them, through our eyes, see themselves as competent, worthy, and in control of their destiny
- Giving them direction to their longings and leaving them with the conviction that their fate can be molded by their hopes and deeds, that their lives need not be shaped by accident, that their happiness does not depend on happenstance
- Introducing them to themselves
- Allowing them to learn who they are and what they can be

If this is accomplished, they will no longer be strangers to themselves. They will feel at home in the world. (David L. Gallahue)

Security

The security of children comes from their identification with significant others, primarily parents and teachers. **Security** also comes from knowing that you are loved, valued, and accepted unconditionally in spite of personal weaknesses, inadequacies, or limitations.

This fact has several important implications for self-concept development. First, identification provides a sense of belonging. Children begin to shape their self to become more like a revered adult. Second, having a sense of security provides an inner place where children know they are safe; they can operate from this safe base without fear of rejection. Third, security gives children a measure of what they perceive to be power since the wishes of parents and teachers tend to become the wishes that they adopt. Finally, security provides children with a sense of control

REALITY CHECK

Foul Mouth

Real-World Situation

While serving as a referee for a local youth sport league, you notice that a few of the coaches and several parents constantly yell at their players, berate them, and make sarcastic remarks. You have decided that it is your duty to address the situation during a coaches' meeting. In the middle of your remarks, one coach says, "Mind your own business. Stick to refereeing and let us coach. It's a cold cruel world out there. These kids need to learn how to take it and to deal with adversity now if they are going to survive." Several others nod in apparent agreement.

Critical Questions

Based on your knowledge of children's affective development and the importance of *security* and *status* in promoting a positive view of self:

- How do you respond to this comment?
- What steps could you take to remedy this abuse of power among some of the coaches?
- How would you approach the parents who are disrupting play with their negative comments and taunts?
- What items would you include in a Parent/Coach Code of Conduct?

over their environment. It provides them with the knowledge that their life is not shaped by fate or luck, that their destiny does not depend on happenstance. It provides children knowledge that they control their future and that they are unconditionally supported by parents, teachers, and coaches as they do so.

Status

Children are incompetent in most tasks in the early years of life; but considerable learning occurs during childhood, and a concept of personal status begins to emerge. **Status** refers to one's perceived position in a particular group—in the family, in the classroom, on the playing field, or with the peer group. The struggle throughout life is not so much between achieving competence and not achieving competence; it is more a matter of perceiving oneself in a positive way despite a lack of competence. Children seek status and must look at incompetence as an opportunity to learn rather than as a personal defect. The response of adults should be, "You may not be able to do it now, but with practice you will!"

Just as children receive considerable feedback about their incompetence, they need to receive positive feedback about their newly developing competencies. As school-age children spend more time with their peers, competencies are evaluated by age-mates. A child's perceived competence or perceived incompetence is likely to be enlarged or diminished by the peer group. This is a time when children frequently face harsh criticism from age-mates because their peers may not be mature enough to temper criticism on the basis of other people's feelings.

Competence frequently becomes enmeshed with competition during the elementary school years, and people begin to make judgments on the basis of how well children do in comparison with others rather than in comparison with past personal performances. The nature of our competitive society makes it difficult to avoid competition entirely, whether it is in games and sport or for good grades and personal recognition. As children venture more into the world, though, it is possible for their sense of competence to expand without overreliance on competition as the means.

As children develop, they have a larger set of evaluators and feedback agents, so there is the possibility of more negative as well as positive evaluations. They become increasingly aware of themselves as members of a group and enjoy their growing independence as they try to take care of their own needs in routine activities and in play. Their developing skills in gross motor activities help them play on equal terms with their peers. But when competition is used to measure competence, the increased possibility of failure becomes a reality. Failure may result in the lowering of one's status in the eyes of others and in one's personal self-evaluation. Success, on the other hand, tends to have the opposite effect and plays an important role in enhancing self-concept.

Teachers concerned with children's personal sense of status can devise ways for them to demonstrate competence through means other than competition. We recognize that the gymnasium, like the classroom, is a learning laboratory where the focus is on enhancing competence, not competing with one's peers. There are many opportunities for healthy competition in most communities, but competition should never be a focal point of the instructional physical education program if we are truly interested in promoting children's sense of security and status. In an article titled "If We Build It, They Will Come: Creating an Emotionally Safe Physical Education Environment," Helion (1996) presents six guidelines for doing just that:

1. In physical education classes, people should not be allowed to do or say anything that hurts others.
2. All students should be challenged at their own levels.
3. Teachers should follow the rules they create for their students.
4. Questions from students should never be treated as a sign of stupidity.
5. Teachers should never use sarcasm.
6. The enjoyment of games for their own sake should replace the need to win at all costs.

COOPERATIVE LEARNERS DEFINED

Simply stated, **cooperative learning** is a process of positive socialization that involves working with others to achieve a common goal. Commonly referred to by children as "working together," cooperative learning requires effective communication, mutual compromise, individual honesty, fair play, and teamwork. These values and skills can be taught effectively in the developmentally based physical education program and should be primary goals of the cooperative learning strand of the curriculum (see Grineski, 1995). Cooperative learning promotes children's positive socialization into their culture.

CONCEPT 6.4

Movement skill learning and fitness enhancement generally occur in a group setting requiring cooperative behaviors for successful participation.

In this cooperative activity, children become "human obstacles" for classmates to move under or around.

Working Together

Much of what children do occurs in the company of others, necessitating a variety of cooperative behaviors in both a cultural and a social context. This interaction takes many forms, and children adopt several social roles in their daily encounters with parents, caregivers, teachers, schoolmates, friends, teammates, and coaches. **Cultural socialization** is a process whereby the child modifies her behaviors to conform to the expectations of an individual or group. Through this process, children learn the rules and skills for functioning in their cultural milieu, which in turn enables them to be integrated into society and to participate as contributing members of society.

Children's socialization is largely dependent on three things: status, roles, and norms. Status refers to one's position in society as well as to one's position in a family or other group. Children have many positions. They have different levels of status conferred on them as sons or daughters, students, playmates, or athletes. As a result, they learn to play a role that is associated with the level of status identified for each position.

A **role** is an individual behavior used to carry out a particular status. For example, parents frequently remark on how much more mature their son or daughter acts at school than at home. Similarly, classroom teachers often observe vastly different behaviors on the playground or during the physical education class than in the classroom. In other words, the child's "job description" (status) in different social settings interacts with his "interpretation of the job" (role) and produces behaviors that frequently differ from one setting to another. These behaviors are governed by certain norms or standards of behavior.

Cultural norms are acceptable standards of behavior that are expected of all members of society regardless of their status or their perceived role in acting out that position. Cultural norms may, however, vary from one social setting to another. For example, commonly accepted behaviors in the gymnasium such as running, tagging, and throwing objects are not generally viewed as acceptable in the classroom. As children become socialized into their culture, they learn what is acceptable and unacceptable behavior in a variety of settings.

Social Decision Makers

Socialization is a process that goes beyond the mere internalization of status, roles, and norms in a nonthinking and conforming manner. It is a dynamic, interactive process between society and the individual—a process that depends on and requires both reasoning and decision making. One of the goals of developmental physical education, as well as of all good teaching, is to influence the process of children's socialization. Helping children learn about, experience, and adopt socially appropriate behaviors can do this. Cooperative behavior is not automatically conferred on children. It is learned behavior that can be modified and improved, especially during childhood.

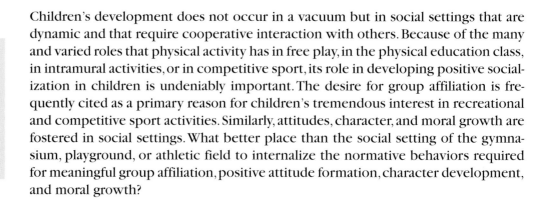

REASONS FOR FOSTERING POSITIVE SOCIALIZATION

CONCEPT 6.5

Positive socialization experiences contribute to improved group affiliation, positive attitude formation, character education, and moral growth.

Children's development does not occur in a vacuum but in social settings that are dynamic and that require cooperative interaction with others. Because of the many and varied roles that physical activity has in free play, in the physical education class, in intramural activities, or in competitive sport, its role in developing positive socialization in children is undeniably important. The desire for group affiliation is frequently cited as a primary reason for children's tremendous interest in recreational and competitive sport activities. Similarly, attitudes, character, and moral growth are fostered in social settings. What better place than the social setting of the gymnasium, playground, or athletic field to internalize the normative behaviors required for meaningful group affiliation, positive attitude formation, character development, and moral growth?

Bad Attitude

Real-World Situation

While sitting in the teachers' lounge at the beginning of the school year, several classroom teachers are sharing their "horror stories" of children they had the previous year who are about to enter the next grade. There is considerable animation among the group, and their remarks are frequently prefaced with statements like, "Last year I had _____ in my class. She/he was a real piece of work. What a bad attitude."

Critical Questions

Based on your knowledge of children's affective development, and the role that attitude formation and character education play in this process:

- What is your response to this conversation in terms of how it might influence your interaction with these students?
- Why are such discussions among teachers inappropriate?
- What can you do to promote positive attitude formation and character development in the gymnasium?
- What are some typical "bad" and "good" attitudes that you are likely to encounter in a physical education setting?

Group Affiliation

One of the most compelling forces of childhood is the need to belong. **Group affiliation,** the need to be accepted and identified as a member of a particular group, is quite powerful. In fact, the need for group affiliation tends to increase through the elementary years, peaking in the strong peer group influences of the junior high school and high school years. A sense of belonging, as discussed earlier, is an important component of a positive self-concept, and as a teacher you must not underestimate its value.

The importance of the peer group, youth sport, clubs, and even gangs is tied to the need for identity through peer group affiliation. Children who have developed their movement skills to the point where they are viewed by others (as well as by themselves) as competent are generally among the first to be included as part of the group. On the other hand, children who have failed to develop a reasonable level of movement competence in games and sports are frequently excluded from the group or at best only marginally tolerated.

Attitude Formation and Character Education

A major function of positive socialization is the transference of the attitudes and values of a culture from one generation to the next. Basically, **attitudes** are opinions about something or someone that result in a behavior. Therefore, an attitude is a learned behavior—based on knowledge or ignorance and positive or negative experiences—that results in a positive or negative value's being placed on something or someone.

Character refers to how we live in response to what we hold to be important, meaningful, and worthwhile. Our character tends to reflect the values that we hold and is an outgrowth of our attitudes. For example, children who do not like (value) physical activity and try to be excused from their physical education class are frequently accused of having a "bad attitude." For whatever reason, they have developed

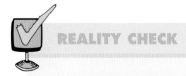

To Win the Championship

Real-World Situation

You are the coach of a local youth sport team. Last year the team had a losing record—in fact, they lost all but one game. Although a few got discouraged and quit, most of your players from the previous year have returned. Your coaching plan for this season includes sessions on individual and team goal setting at different points during the season. When asked what the team goals should be for the upcoming season, several of your players immediately shout, "To win the championship."

Critical Questions

Based on the situation as presented and your knowledge of children's affective development:

- How do you respond to the "win the championship" answer?
- How do you go about helping your players set *realistic goals*?
- How can your players become *authentic assessors* of themselves and others?
- How do you go about *encouraging* your players to do their very best and helping them learn how to encourage one another?

a negative attitude toward vigorous activity that has culminated in failure to value it as part of their lifestyle. As a result, they will go to great lengths to avoid active participation.

Attitudes and the positive or negative value attached to activities, places, events, and people are learned behaviors acquired in a social context. As a result, they may be shaped, modified, or changed. In order for someone to acquire an attitude that culminates in a value, three things must occur: compliance, identification, and internalization.

Compliance is associated with doing something in the hope that it will result in a favorable response from someone else. For example, a boy might share his jump rope with a playmate in the hope of getting a favorable response from the teacher. **Identification,** on the other hand, is a process that requires one to adopt the attitude or value of someone else. The boy might share his jump rope with a playmate because he knows that is what the teacher would do. Finally, **internalization** means taking on a particular behavior as part of one's own value system; the boy might share his jump rope because it is his own desire to do so. If this is the case, he has internalized what most of us would consider to be a positive character trait, sharing.

The developmental physical education program has both the opportunity and the responsibility to shape positive attitudes and help children value participation in vigorous physical activity. Of importance also is the responsibility, shared with all other teachers, of helping children internalize standards of proper behavior and conduct such as honesty, tolerance, acceptance, and empathy. It is important that you not shrink from these responsibilities under the misguided notion that it's not your job or on the assumption that someone else will teach these important lessons. You, the teacher, are often the only person in the lives of the children you work with who can take responsibility for helping them form wholesome attitudes and develop positive character traits.

In many communities, rich and poor, large and small, teachers are the only significant others left in the child's life who are capable of consistently imparting this information. The traditional triad of the home, the church, and the school has in many cases eroded to the point that the school is the only place where many of life's important lessons are taught in a planned and consistent manner. Forgive us if we appear to be preaching!—but it is essential to recognize the importance of positive attitude formation and character development as a daily function of all good teaching as we work toward the goal of positive socialization. Figure 6.3 depicts core traits for effective character education that cut across virtually all social strata. Take a few minutes to study each. Reflect on how you might infuse these in your teaching as you strive to build character in your students.

RESPECT	RESPONSIBILITY	TRUSTWORTHINESS	CARING
• Courteousness • Acceptance • Tolerance • Diversity	• Reliability • Commitment • Self-discipline • Dependability	• Honesty • Integrity • Truthfulness • Loyalty	• Thoughtfulness • Empathy • Compassion • Friendliness

FAIRNESS	CITIZENSHIP
• Leadership • Involvement • Tradition • Vision	• Equality • Harmony • Justice • Democracy

FIGURE 6.3 Core traits for character education and their related components that can be effectively integrated into the school curriculum.

Moral Growth

The concept of **moral growth** refers to the fact that the individual has both the potential and the need for higher levels of moral reasoning and moral behavior. **Moral reasoning** involves making intelligent decisions about what is right and wrong. **Moral behavior,** on the other hand, is living one's life consistently within a value system that has reasoned right from wrong. Most people believe that physical activity in the form of play, games, and sport participation has the potential for fostering moral growth. Why? Probably because of the variety of emotions raised and the unpredictable situations that come up in both cooperative and competitive activities. Free play, games, and sport participation provide ideal settings for teaching the qualities of honesty, loyalty, self-control, teamwork, fair play, and being a good sport. Refraining from lying, cheating, and intimidating opposing players involves moral decisions governed by concern for the physical and psychological welfare of others.

In most states, children under the age of nine are, by law, considered to be amoral and not responsible for their actions. That is, their sense of what is right and wrong has not been fully developed and internalized. Young children tend to be self-centered and to operate on the basis of "If it feels good, just do it." Therefore, they need to encounter social settings that provide them with opportunities for moral growth.

A way to encourage moral growth is to create moral dilemmas. A **moral dilemma** is a situation, real or manufactured, that offers an opportunity for moral reasoning and moral decision making under the careful supervision of the teacher. Group physical activities frequently give rise to moral dilemmas—in children's relay races, kick ball games, and self-report fitness scoring, for example. When such dilemmas do arise, the teacher has an excellent opportunity to call attention to them, thus promoting moral growth by helping students sort through what is good, right, and fair. Pay close attention to the Reality Checks throughout this chapter and to the later "Moral Dilemmas" section for how you might use moral dilemmas to promote moral growth.

Free play, physical education, and sport are ideal settings in which to observe and improve various levels of moral behavior. Remember, however, that unless children's thought processes are stimulated, moral dissonance is not likely to occur. And believe it or not, we want it to occur! **Moral dissonance** is personal questioning brought about by attention to moral dilemmas that arise out of situations involving good versus bad, right versus wrong, or fair versus unfair. If dissonance fails to occur, it is unlikely that moral reasoning, decision making, and moral growth will result. Figure 6.4 highlights the steps leading to moral behavior.

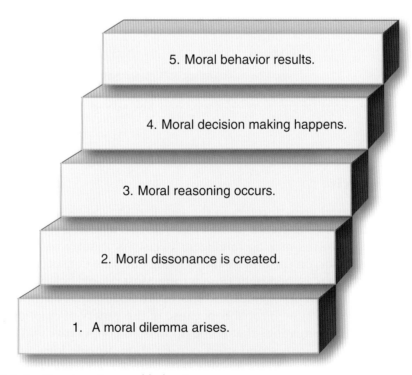

5. Moral behavior results.

4. Moral decision making happens.

3. Moral reasoning occurs.

2. Moral dissonance is created.

1. A moral dilemma arises.

FIGURE 6.4   Five steps to moral behavior.

Children need to clearly understand the definitions of the following terms and how a player manifests them through *being a good sport*:

- **Fair play:** Playing according to the rules and applying them equally to all
- **Teamwork:** Working cooperatively with one or more persons toward a common goal
- **Loyalty:** Consistent fidelity to an individual, group, or team
- **Self-control:** Being in control of and taking responsibility for one's actions
- **Being a good sport:** The combined result of fair play, teamwork, loyalty, and self-control in both victory and defeat

FACTORS THAT INFLUENCE AFFECTIVE DEVELOPMENT

Many factors contribute to affective development of children. Among them are giving praise and encouragement, setting realistic goals, encouraging realistic self-assessment, and using moral dilemmas to teach fair play.

Encouragement

Encouragement takes many forms and ranges from self-encouragement to encouraging others. It is often difficult for adults to say nice things about themselves, but children must learn that it is all right to feel good about oneself. Children learn from models and from imitation. To teach **self-encouragement**, teachers can encourage themselves verbally in front of students. This is difficult to do because most of us have learned not to "brag" or to draw attention to ourselves for fear of being considered conceited or prideful. You can begin self-encouragement by expressing self-satisfaction in minor accomplishments. You might, for example, say how you feel about something you have done or made like, "I really felt good when I made that foul shot," or "It made me feel good to know that I made that bulletin board display." If someone in the class responds with, "I don't think it's so great," it is appropriate to say, "I didn't say it was great, but things don't have to be perfect for us to feel good about them." Teachers should regard self-reinforcement and positive self-referent language such as this as a teaching activity.

Try the *sandwich approach* when encouraging children:

- *First,* find something good about the effort or the performance and tell the child. ("Your windup and arm action are looking much better.")
- *Second,* provide an instructional cue. ("Remember, follow through in the direction that you want the ball to go.")
- *Third,* encourage the performer with a positive statement. ("Keep up the good work: you're making real progress.")

The purpose of self-encouragement is not to enhance your self-concept but to teach children that it is okay to feel good about themselves. You can begin by praising your own work and then move to praising personal qualities. Begin with things that are not highly personal. It might be easier to use group encouragement first, for instance by saying, "The team did a great job" or "Our class can do it," before using individual self-praise. Question-asking is one of the tools that you can use to get children to praise themselves. A question such as "Don't you think you did well on that?" gives children a chance to say something positive about themselves. But it is important at some point to move into more personal qualities so that children begin to see that it is okay to say nice things about themselves as individuals. It may be helpful to tell your students what you are doing. This helps them to know it is all right to say nice things when they feel good about what they have done and that one of the joys of life is to share our good feelings with one another.

Self-encouragement and **encouraging others** are positively related. Learning to encourage is a skill that is applied to others as well as to oneself. Learning how to encourage others permits each child to become a reinforcer for other children. Both children and teachers need to be taught how to encourage others and how to receive encouragement from others.

Teachers should give positive reinforcement in specific small areas of good and poor performance. Children need to hear statements that cushion failure with success—"You will do better next time"; "You didn't get a hit this time, but you probably will next time up"; "Wow! What a super effort, you're really getting the idea." This helps to connect the failure with hope for the future.

Goal Setting

Goal setting must be individual, must be done in relation to past performance, and must have an end in view. If children are to have a commitment to reach a goal, it is important that they have some part in setting the goal. The goal should be slightly higher than that reached in previous performance. This may be far below the eventual performance toward which the child is striving or toward which you are aiming, but the lower level is reasonable in the sense that it is attainable. This gives positive reinforcement for the achievement of a near goal on the way to achieving a larger goal.

Self-Assessment

Teaching children **self-assessment,** or how to evaluate themselves realistically, is an important factor influencing affective development that people sometimes ignore. Children do not have a natural basis for realistic evaluation and self-assessment. They tend to be overly harsh with themselves and give themselves fewer "strokes" than adults would deem appropriate. Our goal here, then, should be to help children evaluate themselves both accurately and realistically. If you are dealing with true failure, help your students or team look at it from the standpoint of learning. Improvement and learning extend the possibility of turning the experience of personal or team failure into one that can build up the individual's self-concept and the group's sense of identity and cohesiveness. It is true that failure is a fact of life, and it is something that we all must face. But is it really necessary for failure to be such a big part of the lives of so many children? We must help to minimize failure and to put it into its proper perspective if we are serious about using physical activity as a way to enhance self-concept and promote positive socialization.

Every child should be able to find some degree of success and accomplishment in the physical activities of the gymnasium or athletic field. As teachers we must structure experiences in such a way that each individual can succeed at some level. For some, success may simply be getting into the game, making a hit, or catching a fly ball. For others, it may be hitting a home run, making a double play, or being on the all-star team. Success should never be measured solely by one's win-loss record or coming in first place. We must help children to make realistic assessments of their efforts and to find additional means of measuring success. This is a difficult process, but we need to help children learn how to evaluate their success on the basis of personal improvement and learning and not simply being the "best."

Authentic assessment accomplishes this by providing children opportunities to appraise their own progress, describe their feelings about an activity or physical education class, or evaluate their own cognitive understanding. Authentic assessment is defined as the child's demonstration of the desired behavior under real-life conditions rather than in artificial or contrived settings (Melograno, 1998). According to Schiemer (2000), "In physical education, we need to look toward developing authentic assessment that allows each student to apply their skills and knowledge in a way that is personally meaningful" (p. 3) (refer to the section on alternative assessment in chapter 12, "Assessing Progress").

Students complete a self-check task card (the self-check teaching style; see chapter 10) in the content area of soccer. Personal acknowledgment of their accomplishments in physical education class is enhanced with use of this type of assessment tool.

Unrealistic evaluations by self and others only compound the problems of real failure. The purpose of realistic assessment is not to have children completely avoid negative evaluations. Some realistic assessments may be negative. However, a negative evaluation that is realistic provides a basis for change that will allow positive performance and therefore positive self-assessment.

Moral Dilemmas

As mentioned earlier, a moral dilemma is a behavior situation, real or manufactured, that requires moral reasoning and moral decision making based on that reasoning. Moral behavior in the physical education setting goes beyond the socially accepted conventions of shaking hands or congratulating an opponent. It involves making decisions about one's personal code of conduct—decisions that look out for the rights of others—in play, game, and sport settings. Physical education teachers and coaches are in unique positions to foster real moral growth. The demands for cooperation, sharing, turn-taking, courteous behavior, fair play, and being a good sport must all be expected of the participants and modeled at all times by teachers and coaches.

TEACHING TIP 6.4

Steps that lead to *moral growth* include the following:

- Create or take advantage of an existing moral dilemma. (For example, discuss student cheating in self-reporting scores on a standardized fitness test.)

- Ask those involved to *describe* the dilemma. ("What happened?" "Why did it happen?" "How did it happen?")

- Help students *focus* on the specific word or term describing the dilemma. ("This is an issue involving _____." The term might be honesty, fair play, communication, cooperation, teamwork, or being a good sport.)

- Work with students to *define* the meaning of the word and the consequences if the issue is ignored. ("Honesty is being truthful, trustworthy, and fair. Failure to be honest leads to, or results in, _____.")

- *Operationalize* the meaning of the word and its importance to the current situation. ("Why is it important to be honest when recording our fitness scores?")

- *Apply* the concept implied by the word first to other relevant topics in the same setting and then to other areas. ("What are other areas in games and sports where honesty is very important?" Then: "Why is honesty important in all that we do?")

- *Reinforce* positive moral behaviors whenever possible. ("I'm sure pleased with the accurate and honest reporting of your fitness scores.")

TEXT BOX 6.3

Successful participation implies that the "bottom line" is more than winning or losing; it concerns giving your all while at the same time giving others the respect and dignity that they deserve. Placing children in contrived situations in which they have to think about, make decisions about, and act on moral issues provides a training environment for moral growth. Another way teachers can enhance moral growth is by taking advantage of "teachable moments"—spontaneously arising situations that provide an opportunity for moral decision making. Additionally, the behaviors that you, the teacher, model for children play a vital role in children's learning to recognize and respond to moral issues.

Structuring moral dilemmas in the gymnasium and encouraging children to work through them in both a thinking and a caring manner promote a sense of moral virtue. For example, in a competitive ball game in which the score is tied, time is running out, and one team must get the ball in order to have a chance of winning, you might stop the activity, sit the class down, and present the dilemma: Is it okay to intentionally foul your opponent or fake an injury in order to have a time-out called? This will elicit a variety of responses, both for and against intentional fouling and feigning injury, and provide you with the opportunity to promote moral reasoning and moral growth.

IMPLICATIONS FOR TEACHING DEVELOPMENTAL PHYSICAL EDUCATION

Considerable speculation, theory, and research have revealed the unique contribution of physical activity to the affective development of children. Because the number of variables influencing such research is formidable, it is difficult to know for certain whether the relationship between physical activity and improvements in self-concept and positive socialization is causal or only casual. In other words, do specific types of experiences in physical activity measurably affect specific aspects of affective development (i.e., a causal relationship)? Or, does physical activity in general influence, among other things, one's affective development (i.e., a casual relationship)?

The fact that we don't know the answer does not mean that quality developmental physical education programs cannot or do not have a significant impact on self-concept development and positive socialization. It simply means that at this time a precise measurement of the specific variables and the extent of this influence is not possible. Child development specialists, psychologists, and educators are quick to recognize that affective development is difficult to measure objectively. It is, however, relatively easy to subjectively observe positive changes in children who have been involved in a quality physical education program that is success oriented, developmentally appropriate, geared toward reasonable goals, challenging, individualized in instruction, and full of positive reinforcement.

The movement skill levels of children are often controlled by factors outside of their influence. Things such as physical stature, health-related conditions, lack of experience, and poor instruction make it impossible for many children to meet their own personal standards of performance or those of the peer group. Movement is not the only influence on children's affective development, but it is an important one.

If movement skills are poorly developed, the chances are good that this will negatively affect children's perceived movement competence. If children begin to feel they are not able to do things, they tend to become less willing to participate. Also, if other children show that they do not regard someone highly because of lack of ability, that child is more apt to feel negative and to encounter problems of group affiliation and positive socialization.

It is important that children develop a proper perspective on success and failure. Children must experience success. Using teaching approaches that emphasize the individuality of the learner is an excellent way to help all children find a measure of achievement. Using exploratory, guided discovery, and problem-solving approaches to learning—especially during the beginning/novice level of learning a new movement skill—is an excellent way of permitting a variety of "correct" solutions and helping to ensure success. It is critical that children feel they are making progress, especially at the early stages of learning a new movement skill. Success has a tendency to increase effort and the number of mastery attempts. Perceptions of failure, however, tend to discourage the learner, heighten anxiety, reduce effort, and decrease the number of attempts at learning the new skill.

The ratio of success to failure that children experience should emphasize success to the point that they are conditioned to expect further and greater success. Persons with low self-esteem wish for success just as much as others, but they do not believe they have the necessary qualities or the "right stuff" to achieve success. Children will gain little by repeating a task for which their responses are inappropriate, their ability inadequate, or their information insufficient. Children need to have

141

some sense that eventually they will be able to master the task; otherwise, they will not be willing to continue trying. This suggests the importance of analyzing the movement situations children are engaged in and the resources at their disposal for accomplishing movement tasks successfully.

You should always remember that individualizing instruction is important in programming for success. Try to design individualized activities in accordance with each child's motor, cognitive, and affective level of functioning. There will be some stretching and growing, but the steps forward are small enough and individualized enough that the child can be assured of finding success. Individually appropriate movement experiences are necessary for the balanced and wholesome development of all children.

Because children often respond to scary or daring challenges, adventure activities may lure them into performing new and more challenging feats. You will need to consider what is developmentally appropriate in the challenge and to sequence the task according to difficulty. This is crucially important in determining a child's sense of success or failure. Competition should not be introduced until children have developed a sufficient degree of movement competence and can appreciate cooperative behavior in a competitive setting.

Adults working with children need to be accepting. There is no place for teasing, scaring, or criticizing. All these ways of treating children have a negative affect on self-concept and positive socialization. The person who works with children in movement skill acquisition and fitness enhancement needs to be a warm, caring adult because children need more than anything else the trust and endorsement of significant others. Caring teachers who are interested in helping children develop to their fullest potential should look seriously at the levels of movement skill and fitness children have attained. Although developmental physical education is not a panacea for all educational problems, it can, through good teaching, make positive contributions to a stable, positive self-concept and the components of positive cultural socialization.

Summary

The child is both a self-discovering learner and a cooperative learner. Components important to the child's developing self are *self-concept, self-esteem,* and *self-confidence.* Physical education teachers can enhance the several components of positive self-concept in children by helping them develop a sense of both security and status through quality, sensitive, caring teaching. All good teachers, parents, and coaches make positive contributions to children's self-esteem; and all can help to enhance children's sense of belonging, competence, worthiness, self-acceptance, appreciation for personal uniqueness, and virtue. Teachers of physical education, as well as coaches, are frequently in an especially good position to influence the development of the self because of the high positive value that most children place on being good at games, sports, and other physical activities and because of the social settings in which most physical activities occur.

Because children are also cooperative learners, their positive socialization, or cooperative interaction with others in both social and cultural settings, is particularly important. Reasons for encouraging positive socialization include group affiliation, positive attitude formation, character development, and moral growth. Physical education teachers can contribute to children's affective development by giving praise and encouragement, setting realistic goals, encouraging realistic self-assessment, and using moral dilemmas to teach fair play. Self-concept enhancement and positive socialization have a number of important implications for the developmental physical education program.

Terms to Remember

Excellent Readings

Anderson, A. (1999). The moral dimensions of teaching physical education. *The Physical Educator, 46* (1), 49-56.

Butler, L.F. (2000). Fair play: Respect for all. *JOPERD, 71* (2), 32-35.

Carlson, T. (1995). We hate gym: Student alienation from physical education. *JTPE, 14,* 467-471.

Fisher, S. (1998). Character development: Developing and implementing a K-12 character education program. *JOPERD, 69* (2), 21-23.

Gibbons, S.L., & Ebbeck, V. (1997). The effect of different strategies on the moral development of physical education students. *JTPE, 17* (1), 85-98.

Goodwin, S.C. (1999). Developing self-esteem in physical education. *The Physical Educator, 56* (4), 210-214.

Gough, R.W. (1998). Character development: A practical strategy for emphasizing character development in sport and physical education. *JOPERD, 69* (2), 18-23.

Halliday, N. (1999). Developing self-esteem through challenge education experiences. *JOPERD, 70* (6), 51-58.

Hellison, D. (1995). *Teaching responsibility through physical education.* Champaign, IL: Human Kinetics.

Martinek, T., & Hellison, D. (1998). Values and goal-setting with underserved youth. *JOPERD, 69* (7), 47-52.

Martinek, T., McLaughlin, D., & Schilling, T. (1999). Project effort: Teaching responsibility beyond the gym. *JOPERD, 70* (6), 59-65.

O'Sullivan, M., & Henninger, M. (2000). *Assessing student responsibility and teamwork.* Reston, VA: NASPE.

Parker, M., Kallusky, J., & Hellison, D. (1999). High impact, low risk: Ten strategies to teach responsibility. *JOPERD, 40* (2), 26-28.

Patrick, C.A., Ward, P., & Crouch, D.W. (1998). Effects of holding students accountable for social behaviors during volleyball games in elementary physical education. *JTPE, 17,* 143-156.

Children With Disabilities

Key Concept

▶ A physically educated person demonstrates understanding of and respect for differences among people in physical activity settings.

Content Standard #6: *National Standards for Physical Education:* National Association for Sport and Physical Education

The Education for All Handicapped Children Act of 1975 (Public Law 94-142) ensures that all children from ages 3 to 21 are provided an "appropriate education." Additionally, the Education of the Handicapped Amendments Act of 1986 (Public Law 99-457), which became effective in 1991, extends previous legislation to include infants, toddlers, and preschoolers from birth to age five (Dunn, 1991). These important federal laws, which have dramatically influenced how individuals with disabilities are treated in the United States, are especially important to physical educators. Physical education is the only subject area specifically identified in the definition of a "special education." Physical education as defined by the Individuals with Disabilities Act (U.S. Department of Education, 1998) is "the development of (a) physical and motor fitness; (b) fundamental motor skills and patterns; and (c) skills in aquatics, dance, and individual and group games and sports (including intramural and lifetime sports)" (p. 18).

The provisions of Public Law 105-17, better known as the Individuals with Disabilities Education Act (IDEA), mandates that all children with diagnosed disabilities must be provided with an appropriate physical education program and that this program must be offered in the "least restrictive environment" (Kozub, 1998). Therefore, children with special

This chapter will provide you with the tools to do the following:

▶ Identify essential aspects of federal laws targeted at individuals with disabilities and discuss their implications for teaching physical education.

▶ Distinguish among various types of programs designed to physically educate children with disabilities.

▶ Identify and discuss the basic elements of a variety of physical, mental, emotional, and learning disabilities.

▶ Suggest ways that a physical education program might be modified to accommodate children with various physical, mental, emotional, and learning disabilities.

▶ Identify and discuss the unique social and personal needs of children with disabilities.

▶ Recognize the many and varied roles that physical education plays in the lives of children with disabilities.

CONCEPT
7.1

All children have a right to an education appropriate to their motor, cognitive, and affective level of development.

physical, mental, or emotional needs must be given the opportunity to take part in the regular physical education program unless their needs can be met only through a specially designed program as prescribed by their **Individualized Education Program (IEP)**. Physical education contributes to the growth and development of children with disabilities through the medium of movement. This fact has been wisely recognized in IDEA, which mandates a policy of inclusion (i.e., "mainstreaming") whenever and wherever possible.

REALITY CHECK

You May Be Excused: Or Can You?

Real-World Situation

Before you assumed your new teaching position, the previous teacher had excused children with disabilities from participation in the physical education program. Although they came to the class and were permitted to "assist" the teacher with taking roll, setting out equipment, and keeping score, they were not required or encouraged to actively participate. As the new physical education teacher, you had planned on including all children in your classes as active participants.

Critical Questions

Based on your knowledge of children with disabilities and the provisions of the Individuals with Disabilities Education Act (IDEA; U.S. Department of Education, 1998):

- Why isn't it permissible to exclude most children with disabilities from participation in the regular instructional physical education program?
- What should you do if your building principal says, "It's okay to exclude them, don't worry about it"?
- When is it permissible to exclude children with disabilities from the regular instructional physical education program?
- What is meant by the IDEA term *inclusion?*

In this chapter we examine the role of physical education in the education of children with disabilities. The chapter also considers the challenges of social adjustment faced by children with disabilities. Furthermore, the "Teaching Tip" boxes throughout the chapter provide practical teaching strategies for the regular physical education program that includes children with disabilities. The following Web sites will be especially helpful:

- American Association on Mental Retardation (**www.aamr.org**)
- Disabled Sports USA (**www.dsusa.org**)
- March of Dimes (**www.modimes.org**)
- National Information Center for Children and Youth With Disabilities (**www.nichcy.org**)
- Special Olympics International (**www.specialolympics.org**)

Although Public Laws 94-142 and 99-457 frequently use the term *handicapped,* many view this term as degrading. The terms *disabil-*

ity, *challenged*, *special needs*, and *limiting condition* are generally regarded as more appropriate and are strongly encouraged. In fact, IDEA officially replaced the term *handicapped* with the term *disability*.

TEXT BOX 7.1

Classrooms in today's schools are diverse in many ways. Children from various cultures, age groups, family structures, socioeconomic backgrounds, and ethnic groups together form unique communities of learners. These heterogeneous student communities also include students with a range of cognitive, affective, and motor abilities. Inclusive classrooms embrace *all* students, including those who have diagnosed disabilities.

THE PHYSICAL EDUCATION PROGRAM

CONCEPT 7.2

In public schools, children with disabilities must be integrated into the developmental physical education program in the least restrictive manner.

Children cannot be excluded from a physical education program because of a disability, whether temporary or permanent, mild or severe, single or multiple. Whenever possible, they must be included in the regular physical education class (Rizzo & Lavey, 2000). When the disability prohibits participation in the regular physical education class, as determined by the child's IEP, by law a specialized program must be offered.

Children need to be included in the regular physical education program whenever possible to learn how to interact effectively with their environment, develop

---

REALITY CHECK

You and Me and the IEP

Real-World Situation

In many school districts, a trained adapted physical education specialist or physical therapist is not available. As a result, the regular physical education teacher is frequently asked to take part in determining the IEP and the least restrictive environment for children with disabilities. This frequently includes making informed judgments or using a battery of motor assessment tests to help in the decision-making process. Recommendations are then made to the head of the IEP team.

Critical Questions

Based on your knowledge of children with disabilities and motor assessment techniques:

- What would you include in your motor assessment of children diagnosed with specific physical disabilities, sensory impairments, cardiovascular limitations, or neuromuscular limitations?

- What would be your primary points of consideration for inclusion of children with mental retardation?

- What would be your primary markers for recommending inclusion in regular group activities for children diagnosed with emotional disabilities?

- How would you evaluate the potential for inclusion among children with distractibility, impulsivity, and hyperactivity?

movement skills, and enhance fitness levels. Children who do not have a disability gain an opportunity to learn tolerance and acceptance and to become unencumbered by the notion that someone is "different."

Teaching children with different abilities is a challenge, particularly to the beginning teacher. Modifications of activities, equipment, and teaching methodology require teachers to make careful and informed choices. Many children with diagnosed disabilities have instructional aides, and learning how to take effective advantage of the expertise of aides is also a challenge to many physical educators. The needs of children with disabilities may be met through one or more of several types of physical education programs: the adapted program, the remedial program, and the developmental program (see figure 7.1).

THE ADAPTED PROGRAM

A modified program of movement activities that maximizes the potential of persons with disabilities through an individualized education program (IEP).

THE REMEDIAL PROGRAM

A program of specific exercises and activities for correcting errors in body mechanics and perceptual-motor functioning.

THE DEVELOPMENTAL PROGRAM

An individualized program of movement activities based on personal needs and designed to enhance movement, fitness, physical activity, and social/emotional skills.

FIGURE 7.1 The relationship among adapted, remedial, and developmental physical education programs.

Children with developmental disabilities can be included in regular physical education activities. Modified equipment and assistance from a trained aide or adapted physical educator are often required to provide a least restrictive environment.

The Adapted Program

The **adapted physical education** program provides for physical activities that are modified according to the physical, mental, and emotional needs of children with a diagnosed disability in compliance with the Adapted Physical Education National Standards (National Consortium, 1995). In this sense, regular physical education programs that make real and constant efforts at individualizing instruction are in fact "adapting" their instruction to the needs of all children. These teachers are constantly modifying the learning goals and movement experiences based on the unique needs and current abilities of the children they teach.

The Remedial Program

The **remedial physical education** program differs from the adapted program in that its aim is corrective and it includes specific exercises and physical activities designed to improve body mechanics. Improvements in such basic movement tasks as standing, sitting, and moving through space are important learning goals of the remedial program, as is improvement in perceptual-motor functioning.

Specialized training is required in the area of remedial physical education. The remedial program should be conducted under the supervision of a physician and may incorporate suggestions from a physical therapist, occupational therapist, or school psychologist.

Most elementary schools do not have the physical facilities and specialized equipment often recommended for carrying out an effective remedial program. Consequently, teachers frequently must improvise and use what is available in the school and community. Furthermore, remedial programs that do exist frequently promote exclusion and separate classes for children with disabilities, thereby undermining the important concepts embodied in mainstreaming and inclusion. In any case, it is necessary to keep complete records for each child in the program. These records should include a health history, IEP, and an updated physician's report with a clear description of appropriate physical activities to be engaged in by the child. It is worth reemphasizing that specialized training is necessary to conduct an effective remedial physical education program and that these programs require the supervision of a physician.

The Developmental Program

The **developmental physical education** program, because it is based on what is individually appropriate for the child as well as what is age appropriate, actually contains elements of both the adapted and the remedial programs. It is concerned specifically with individual improvement in movement skill acquisition, physical activity, fitness enhancement, cognitive learning, and affective growth. The developmental physical education program is concerned with *all* children, those with disabilities and those without. The developmental program is similar to the adapted program in that it strives to individualize learning and modify movement experiences based on the unique physical, mental, and emotional abilities of each child. The developmental program is similar to the remedial physical education program in that it shares the goals of improved body mechanics and perceptual-motor functioning.

The developmental physical education program can be implemented effectively with all children. Assessment of movement abilities is required, however, before a

CONCEPT
7.3

An essential tenet of developmental physical education is the need for individual appropriateness in the selection of movement experiences for all children.

specific program of activities is planned. Assessment may take many forms. It may be subjective or objective, process based or product based, individual or group. But it must be regular and systematic and must occur before children begin a program of activities, as well as after. Chapter 12 deals with assessment of progress in motor skills, physical fitness, and physical activity.

Inclusion

The philosophy of **inclusion** of children with mild to severe disabilities is currently very popular in the United States and is an outgrowth of IDEA. Basically, full inclusion refers to fully integrating children with severe disabilities, as well as those with lesser disabilities, into regular and physical education classes with their peers who do not have a diagnosed disability. Schools that practice a philosophy of full inclusion involve children with a wide range of severe disabilities in all aspects of the class, not just as special visitors at certain times during the day. Full inclusion places special demands on the physical education teacher and is viewed by some as a difficult task.

Inclusion is possible if your curriculum is developmentally based in more than name only. If your curriculum is developmental, it should be able to incorporate the broad range of abilities that today's children have. Careful analysis of the learning tasks contained in a lesson makes it possible, with practice, to devise appropriate learning outcomes for all students. Inclusion is possible if you have additional help—in fact, the use of a teacher's aide, parent helpers, and peer student helpers is essential. Inclusion is possible if you have the active support of parents, school administration, and other school personnel. Doubtless the job of the physical education teacher becomes more demanding because of the focus on inclusion. But the program can succeed if it is developmentally based, has a realistic student-to-teacher ratio, and receives active support.

CONCEPT 7.4

A philosophy of inclusion of children with mild to severe disabilities in all aspects of the educational process has been adopted by many school systems and is supported by law.

In this physical education class, students from a local college serve as instructional assistants. Also, a lowered basketball hoop and smaller ball contribute to this student's success in shooting.

REALITY CHECK

Go for It: Full Inclusion

Real-World Situation

As a seven-year-old, Brad is bright and outgoing and makes friends easily. He is interested in all kinds of sports, even horseback riding. Brad has severe spastic cerebral palsy, has great difficulty sitting erect, uses a wheelchair, and is prone to seizures. Previously, his IEP permitted him to be excluded from the regular physical education class, but a new policy of full inclusion in the school district has resulted in Brad's being placed in your class. You are highly competent in delivering a developmentally based physical education program to your regular students but have only minimal background and training in working with individuals who have disabilities as severe as Brad's.

Critical Questions

Based on your knowledge of individuals with disabilities and the situation as presented:

- What are the legal and ethical consequences of refusing to accept Brad into your class?
- By law, what forms of assistance are available to Brad?
- What forms of assistance may be available to you?
- How would you go about including Brad in your regular physical education program?

CATEGORIES OF DEVELOPMENTAL DISABILITIES

Children with developmental disabilities are generally classified into four broad and sometimes overlapping categories of disabilities: physical disabilities, mental disabilities, emotional disabilities, and learning disabilities. In this section we take a brief look at several specific conditions that are frequently encountered in children in the public schools.

Children With Physical Disabilities

A **physical disability** is any physical condition that interferes with the child's educational performance and includes disabilities resulting from disease, congenital factors, and other unspecified causes. About 3% of the school-age population have physical impairments. Children with physical disabilities are characterized by one or more disabling conditions, resulting from faulty functioning of their sensory receptors or their musculature, that in some manner limit or restrict their ability to function. Children with a physical impairment may have one or more disabling conditions. These conditions restrict the children's movement and mandate modifications in the physical activities they engage in. For purposes of our discussion, physical disabilities are subdivided into sensory impairments, cardiovascular limitations, neuromuscular limitations, pulmonary limitations, and musculoskeletal limitations (see figure 7.2).

CONCEPT 7.5

Children with physical disabilities may exhibit sensory, cardiovascular, neurological, or orthopedic limitations that can be successfully compensated for through developmentally appropriate physical education.

Sensory Impairments

A **sensory impairment** is a condition in which the sensory receptors are unable to transmit or interpret stimuli in a manner conducive to educational performance. By far the most common sensory impairments are visual limitations and auditory limitations.

SENSORY IMPAIRMENTS	CARDIOVASCULAR LIMITATIONS	NEUROMUSCULAR LIMITATIONS	MUSCULOSKELETAL LIMITATIONS
• Visual • Auditory	• Congenital heart disease • Rheumatic heart disease • Coronary heart disease • Hypertension	• Cerebral palsy • Epilepsy	• Osgood-Schlatter condition • Arthritis • Postural deviations

FIGURE 7.2 Common physically limiting conditions found among children.

TEACHING TIP 7.1

Children with *visual impairments* may range from the legally blind to the partially sighted:

- Use a whistle or verbal cue to signal the class to move or stop.
- Clearly mark field dimensions and safety hazards in bright colors.
- Use a "buddy system" for all activities.
- Use many auditory cues to help the student gain a quicker understanding of space and distances.

- Set definite goals and objectives to be reached.
- Use music often, both for relaxation and for motivation.
- Include strenuous big-muscle activities.
- Modify activities that require quick directional changes.
- Provide structure, routine, and consistency.

The child with a **visual impairment** is defined as one whose educational performance is adversely affected even when corrective lenses are worn. Public Law 94-142 specifically states that the child does not have to be blind or even severely sight limited to qualify as having a visual limitation. The physical education program for visually impaired children may be modified to provide additional tactile, kinesthetic, and auditory stimulation for less severe impairments. Severe visual impairments may require substitution of other sensory modalities for sight. Verbal directional guidance, tactile stimulation, and the use of specialized sound-emitting devices can all be very helpful in the physical education program for children with a visual impairment.

Children with a **hearing impairment** have difficulty processing verbal information with or without amplification, and this interferes with their educational performance. Hearing impairments are among the most common limiting conditions found in children and adults. Hearing loss may range from partial to complete. Frequently people form mistaken judgments about a child with a hearing impairment that has gone unattended, thinking that the child has mental retardation, is a slow learner, or has behavioral problems. The following are possible signs of hearing impairment:

- Faulty speech patterns; faulty pitch, tone, or volume
- Holding the head to one side, inattentiveness, excessive daydreaming, and inability to follow directions

- Inability to detect who is speaking and what is being said
- Emotional instability; hostility or extreme withdrawal
- Failure in school
- Difficulty in maintaining balance
- Inability to join class discussions and group games
- Feelings of social inferiority

TEACHING TIP 7.2

Children with *auditory impairments* range from those who are hard-of-hearing to those who are totally deaf:

- Establish and maintain good eye contact.
- Place students where they can easily see the teacher.
- Use visual cues in conjunction with auditory cues whenever possible.
- Speak clearly and concisely.
- Encourage working with a "buddy" to aid learning.
- Make liberal use of visual aids.
- Be aware that children with auditory impair-

ments frequently have problems with balance and require extra spotting in many balance-based activities.

- Do not yell in an attempt to make yourself heard. Instead, speak slowly and clearly, using visual prompts, demonstration, or signing when possible.
- Be consistent and patient, and be sure to follow through.
- Do not take failure to respond or apparent disinterest as a personal affront.

Children with auditory impairments that can be corrected through the use of hearing aids should be able to take part in most of the activities of the regular physical education program. In activities that necessitate removal of the aids (such as swimming and gymnastics), the student should be accompanied by a "buddy"; and teachers should be certain that they speak clearly, distinctly, and directly toward the student. Children with severe auditory impairments that cannot be corrected (deafness) require special attention. People working with these children need to give attention to providing more visual input than verbal input. Demonstrations, written descriptions, wall charts, and videotape replays with closed captions are all effective teaching tools for use with many deaf children.

Cardiovascular Limitations

Cardiovascular limitations include congenital heart disease, rheumatic heart disease, coronary heart disease, and hypertensive heart disease. Although often thought of as a major health problem only in adults, cardiovascular disorders are also prevalent in children.

Depending on the specific nature of the disorder, children may be severely or only moderately restricted in the type, amount, and duration of physical activity they may take part in. It is of the utmost importance for teachers to work closely with the child's physician so that they know what degree of involvement is permitted and to be alert for signs of undue physical stress. Most children with cardiovascular disabilities can benefit from a modified physical education program that works within the limits of their abilities and is sensitive to their special needs.

TEACHING TIP 7.3

Cardiovascular limitations require special attention and careful monitoring of the amount of vigorous physical activity. The following guidelines will be helpful:

- Work within the guidelines clearly established by the child's physician.
- Watch closely for signs of undue stress and fatigue.
- Provide frequent rest periods.
- Incorporate mild to moderate physical activities into the program, including archery, golf, and bowling for older children.
- Provide opportunities for less strenuous activities such as dance, low-level games, and basic tumbling skills for younger children.

- Work for increased fitness and skill levels at a slower, more relaxed pace than with non-impaired children.
- Require a periodic medical clearance for participation.
- Listen to students and be sensitive to their requests to rest.
- Use lightweight equipment when possible.
- Require a physician's clearance after the student has been absent due to illness.

Neuromuscular Limitations

Children with **neuromuscular limitations** have damage to the brain or spinal cord. Cerebral palsy and epilepsy are the most common neurological disorders.

Cerebral palsy is a nonprogressive, permanent condition caused by damage to the motor area of the cortex. It results in a kind of paralysis, weakness, tremor, or

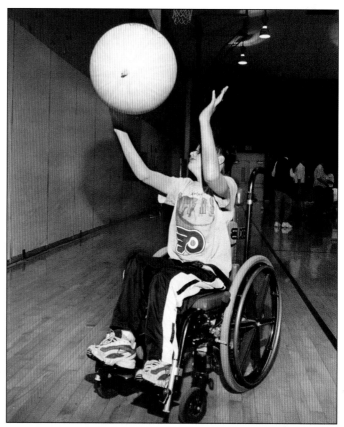

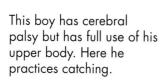
This boy has cerebral palsy but has full use of his upper body. Here he practices catching.

TEACHING TIP 7.4

Children with *cerebral palsy* present a special challenge to the physical education teacher:

- Work in conjunction with the physical therapist to provide appropriate activities.
- Stress socialization and acceptance by peers rather than skill perfection.
- Focus on movement skills that have a high carryover value for later life and for present leisure-time activities.
- Concentrate on throwing balls to promote controlled releasing.
- Have students practice catching bounced balls rather than ones that are tossed. Have them kick or strike stationary balls. These movements are easier and promote greater success.
- Encourage rhythmic activities to promote increased motor control.
- Encourage aquatic activities as an excellent way to promote relaxation.
- Initiate sustained, flowing-movement activities for children with spasticity.
- Give students with athetosis extra help with relaxation.
- Avoid balance and fine motor coordination activities with children who have ataxia.

uncoordinated movement, depending on the severity and location of the brain damage. Cerebral palsy is classified into five categories. You are most likely to encounter the first three of these:

1. **Spasticity** is typified by limited voluntary control of movement as a result of hypertonia of the muscles. An exaggerated stretch reflex causes the arms and legs to contract rapidly when passively stretched and results in an inability to perform precise movements. The legs are often rotated inward, the arms stiff and flexed at the elbows. Body movements are characteristically jerky and uncertain. Spasticity is the most common form of cerebral palsy, occurring in about 60% of all cases. Mental retardation, speech disorders, and perceptual problems are also frequently associated with spastic cerebral palsy.

2. **Athetosis** accounts for approximately 25% of all cerebral palsy and is characterized by involuntary, jerky, wormlike movements. Movement is uncontrollable, random, and almost constant. Facial grimaces are common, as are hearing, speech, and visual impairments.

3. **Ataxia** represents about 10% of all cerebral palsy and is typified by very poor balance and coordination. Movements are deliberate but awkward and wobbly. Perceptual abilities are generally diminished, especially in the proprioceptive and vestibular areas. Speech disorders are common.

4. **Rigidity** is characterized by extreme body stiffness and by absence of the stretch reflex. Mental retardation is common with this condition, as are restricted movement and hyperextension. About 3% of all cases of cerebral palsy are classified as rigidity.

5. **Tremor** is the least common form of cerebral palsy, occurring in only about 2% of the cerebral palsy population. A primary characteristic of tremor is rhythmic and involuntary movements. When voluntary movement is attempted, the tremor tends to increase. Tremors are often mixed with muscle rigidity. Mental retardation is common.

The degree of involvement of cerebral palsy and other neurological impairments may be classified by location:

- *Monoplegia*—involvement of only one limb (rare)
- *Paraplegia*—involvement of both legs only
- *Hemiplegia*—involvement of one arm and one leg on the same side of the body
- *Triplegia*—involvement of three limbs (rare)
- *Quadriplegia*—involvement of all four limbs

In all cases of cerebral palsy—whether mild, moderate, or severe—the individual will benefit from a program of modified physical activities. The physical educator can do much, working in conjunction with the physician, to improve the child's level of physical functioning. Social integration with peers is of special importance for the child with cerebral palsy.

Epilepsy, a condition caused by an electrochemical imbalance in the brain, is typified by seizures that may be mild or severe. Seizures may, in many cases, be effectively controlled with a variety of drugs. Persons with epilepsy may exhibit one or more of the following types of seizures, which range from generalized nonconvulsive seizures to generalized convulsive seizures, when uncontrolled by medication.

- **Grand mal seizures** are convulsive seizures accompanied by an aura phase, which is characterized by a sinking feeling or a vague feeling of uneasiness. This is followed by a tonic phase in which there is a loss of consciousness and rapid, involuntary, writhing contraction of the muscles. The clonic phase follows, typified by intermittent contractions. This is followed by a deep, relaxed sleep phase.

- **Jacksonian seizures** are convulsive seizures similar to grand mal but without the aura and tonic phases. They are characterized by intermittent contraction and relaxation of the muscles beginning in one part of the body and spreading outward. The seizures are also accompanied by loss of consciousness.

- **Petit mal seizures** are nonconvulsive seizures characterized by a momentary loss of consciousness. The child suddenly stops all activity, appears dazed, and then resumes regular activity.

- **Psychomotor seizures** are nonconvulsive seizures characterized by short-term changes in normal behavior; the person has no memory of the atypical behavior. Temper tantrums, incoherent speech, and aggressive behaviors are frequent symptoms.

Most children with epilepsy should be encouraged to take part in the regular physical education program. However, because excessive sensory stimulation or trauma to the head may trigger seizures, care should be taken to avoid both situations.

Pulmonary Limitations

Elementary school teachers encounter two primary pulmonary limitations: asthma and cystic fibrosis. Here we look briefly at both of these.

Asthma, a pulmonary condition affecting the bronchial tubes, for some unexplained reason has shown a dramatic increase over the last several years. A significant number of children in all regions of the country have asthma. Asthma interferes with normal breathing and may range from mild to severe. Physical activity can be beneficial for children with asthma. Low fitness is not inherent to the disease. In fact, fitness levels range from those seen in Olympic athletes to the very poor levels found in sedentary children. Fitness levels do, however, decrease as the severity and number of asthma attacks increase. In designing programs for individuals with asthma it is important to find activities that do not provoke an exercise-

Children with *epilepsy* frequently take part in the regular program with few restrictions. Be certain, however, to follow these guidelines:

- Work with the child's physician to outline a program of physical activities.

- Remember that children with epilepsy are in all other ways like their peers except for occasional seizures, and these seizures are generally controlled effectively through medication.

- In the event of a seizure, remain calm and administer appropriate first aid. Help the other children to understand what is happening and to be accepting of the condition.

- Focus on activities requiring concentration, such as rhythmic activities.

- Promote inclusion rather than exclusion.

- Request that the classroom teacher alert you to any abnormal behavior the child may have displayed prior to the physical education class.

- Avoid climbing activities when the child's condition is doubtful.

induced asthma attack. A warm-up period is especially important prior to vigorous activity in order to accustom the air passage to exercise. Activities such as swimming, team games that permit brief rest and recovery periods, and circuit training are generally recommended. People with asthma should avoid exercise in cold and dry air whenever possible.

Cystic fibrosis is a progressive noncurable disease in which the lungs fill with mucus over time, causing difficulty in breathing and eventually death. The primary limiting factor in children with cystic fibrosis is ventilation, thereby limiting aerobic endurance. Instructors must seek the written advice of the child's physician before the child begins an activity program. Activities that permit frequent rest periods such as swimming, circuit training, walking, and team sports with short bouts of exercise are generally recommended.

Musculoskeletal Limitations

Physical education classes commonly include children with a wide variety of musculoskeletal limiting conditions, including Osgood-Schlatter condition, arthritis, and postural deviations. A **musculoskeletal limitation** is a disease or condition of the bones or muscles that limits the child's ability to move effectively and efficiently.

Osgood-Schlatter condition is common in prepubescent boys and girls and is typified by pain and swelling around the knee joint. It is completely curable with medical treatment and frequently disappears after a few years without medical intervention. The cause of the condition is separation of the patellar ligament from the tibia, frequently as a result of undue tendon strain, improper alignment of the leg, or direct injury to the knee. Repeated jarring activities, such as improper running technique or landing heavily, seem to contribute to this condition.

For treatment, some authorities recommend complete immobilization of the leg for a minimum of six weeks, followed by restricted physical activity for up to one year. Others recommend a continued program of regular physical activities limited only by the individual's pain tolerance. Teachers at the upper elementary and junior high school levels encounter frequent cases of Osgood-Schlatter condition. Be prepared to modify or restrict activities as required by the child's physician.

Arthritis is frequently thought of as a disease of the aged, but a significant number of children also have the disease; currently it has no cure. Basically, **arthritis** is a painful condition caused by inflammation of the joints. Rheumatoid arthritis, the most common form of arthritis found in children, attacks the entire skeletal system and results in inflammation, stiffness, and acute pain in the joints. **Juvenile rheumatoid arthritis** varies greatly in severity, but in all cases, movement of the affected joints is recommended.

Children with arthritis should be included in the regular physical education program whenever possible. They should be encouraged to take part in sustained stretching activities to promote joint flexibility. Some activities may need to be modified during periods when the condition is particularly painful.

Postural deviations are common among elementary school age children. They may be classified as either functional or structural. Functional **postural deviations** are the result of faulty muscular development, frequently caused by habitual postures and overdevelopment of certain muscle groups. Children who habitually carry their books on one side of the body or who consistently sit on the floor with their knees forward and their feet behind are likely to develop functional postural deviations.

Structural postural deviations involve structural abnormalities of the skeletal system itself. These abnormalities may be caused by congenital defects, uncorrected functional deviations, or skeletal injuries that have not healed properly. Structural impairments require surgery for correction, whereas functional impairments are correctable through a program of proper activities to strengthen identified muscle groups.

Postural problems are common among school-age children. Among the most widespread are scoliosis, lordosis, and kyphosis.

- **Scoliosis,** or lateral curvature of the spine, may be structural but is most often functional. If left untreated, the characteristic "C" curve of the spine may develop into an "S" curve. If scoliosis is detected in the young child, a program of corrective exercises should begin immediately. If it is not detected until late adolescence, little can be done, but the condition will probably not develop further if the individual wears a back brace or corset for several years.

- **Lordosis,** or swayback as it is sometimes called, is typified by an exaggerated curve of the lower back. This exaggerated lumbar curve results in a forward tilt of the pelvis and weak abdominal muscles. Corrective measures at the early stages of lordosis include making the individual aware of her posture and helping her to develop the habit of consciously tucking the hips under the spine. Activities designed to strengthen the abdominal muscles and to stretch the muscles of the lower back are also helpful.

- **Kyphosis,** which is frequently called hunchback, is a condition characterized by an exaggerated curve in the thoracic region of the spine. Round shoulders, winged scapula, and a forward head tilt frequently accompany kyphosis. A program of exercises designed to stretch the chest muscles and strengthen the back muscles helps alleviate the condition.

Children With Mental Retardation

Mental retardation is a condition that generally results in significant subaverage intellectual functioning, affecting motor development as well as intellectual development. The lag in motor development results, in part, from problems that children with mental retardation have with cognition (an intrinsic condition) and often from a lack of opportunity for activity (an extrinsic condition). This statement should not be viewed as simply another means of demonstrating the vast differences between these children and their chronological peers. Rather the intent is to point out that, to a large degree, the lag in motor development often apparent in children with mental retardation results from the gross neglect that individuals in this population have experienced for years in terms of environmental factors such as opportunity for practice, encouragement, and instruction.

What can we expect if a person's life is spent in endless hours of boredom ensuing from continuous inactivity? Human beings need physical activity to continue functioning at their optimum level, regardless of their intellectual capabilities. We cannot expect children with mental retardation to approach their chronological counterparts in terms of physical functioning if they do not have sufficient movement experiences and sound guidance in their motor development. Although the ability of the

TEACHING TIP 7.7

Children with *mild mental retardation* will benefit from the following suggestions:

- Stress gross motor activities, focusing on fundamental stability, locomotor, and manipulative skills.
- Work for higher levels of fitness in a consistent and progressive manner.
- Be sure all instruction builds skill upon skill and is success oriented.
- Show more and explain less.
- Include routine and structure in each session.
- Keep rules simple.
- Provide for many kinds of rhythmical activities.
- Stress the element of fun in physical activity.
- Provide manual assistance in certain activities for the children as needed.

- Reduce skills to their simplest components.
- Name the movement or skill being taught to help develop a movement vocabulary.
- Be sure that practice periods are short, with frequent changes in activities to reduce frustration.
- Let children repeat their successes several times to enjoy the feeling of accomplishment.
- Reward approximation of the skill with frequent verbal praise.
- Avoid activities in which individuals are eliminated.
- Set standards of acceptable behavior by praising good behavior rather than focusing on the negative.

The needs of children with mental, emotional, and learning disabilities can be served effectively, at some level, through the developmental physical education program.

child's mind to function establishes outer limits on the potential functioning of his body, we must not let this distract us from striving for maximal performance.

Physical education programs can aid greatly in reducing the "halo" of physical inadequacies that contributes negatively to an individual's mental retardation. An ever expanding circle of artificial disability forms around the original and unalterable mental disability. Just look at the performance scores on numerous tests of physical status by children with mental retardation. A well-planned program of movement activities will help. Physical education is not a "cure" for mental retardation, but a quality physical education program can significantly reduce the halo effect. In fact, even if children with mental retardation may be unable to perform at the same level as children without, they can often progress at a similar rate.

Children with mental retardation do well in modified games, dance, and gymnastics activities, and also in such sports as track and field, soccer, basketball, swimming, and bowling. Physical educators can do much to help children with mental retardation approach their chronological peers in terms of skill mastery by providing them with a well-planned, individualized program of activities that gradually increase in complexity and require greater movement control. Modified games and skills, when mastered, should be continually replaced by others that are fun, challenging, and satisfying.

Mental retardation is typified by faulty development of intelligence to the point of interference with the ability to learn. In 1992 the American Association on Mental Retardation adopted a classification system for mental retardation that did away with the traditional four-levels approach, which relied heavily on the results of intelligence

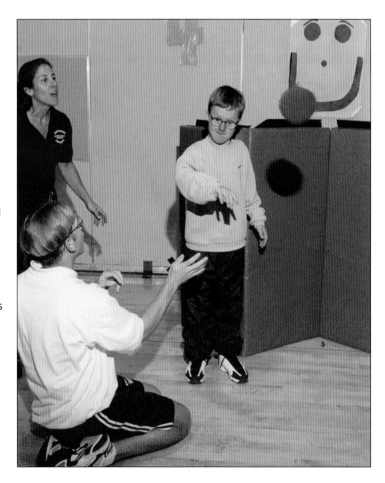

This boy, who has Down syndrome, is practicing overhand throwing and catching skills with a partner. The gymnastics mat serves as a "catcher" so that the student does not have to run after balls that he does not successfully catch.

TEACHING TIP 7.8

Children with *mild mental retardation* will benefit from the following suggestions:

- Permit ample time for learning to occur.
- Shorten sentences, using few verbal cues and more visual and tactile cues.
- Teach only one skill at a time.
- Reinforce and praise all accomplishments, no matter how small.
- Praise attempts as well as accomplishments.
- Simplify instructions and repeat them frequently.

- Use frequent demonstrations of the task to be learned and actual hands-on physical manipulation through the skill as necessary.
- Use visual prompts and color coding as necessary.
- Stress compliance with basic rules of safety.
- Treat each individual with dignity, respect, and a sincere display of caring.

tests. Today, individuals are classified by the degree of limitation, either mild or severe. Children with **mild retardation** need only intermittent or limited support and are generally included in the regular physical education class. Those with **severe retardation** need extensive long-term or even constant support and are generally not part of the regular physical education program. Children with mild mental retardation may be expected to take part in the developmental physical education program and will benefit most from a specially designed instructional program adapted to their particular needs.

It is generally assumed that roughly 3% of the total population meet the criteria for mental retardation. Among this 3%, approximately 95% are in the mild range. Only about 5% of the entire population with mental retardation are in the severe range.

The causes of mental retardation are numerous and varied. The vast majority of cases of retardation are caused by brain damage that occurs prior to, during, or relatively soon after birth; environmental factors, namely infections or drugs; or genetic factors (i.e., chromosomal abnormalities) (figure 7.3).

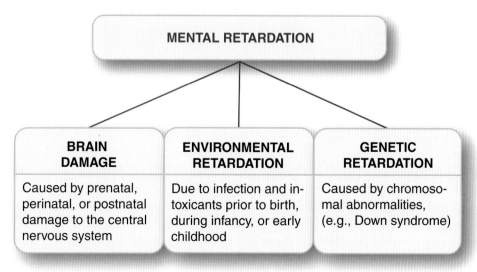

FIGURE 7.3   Three primary causes of mental retardation.

Traumatic Brain Injury

Traumatic brain injury, the primary cause of mental retardation, is characterized by damage to the central nervous system before birth (prenatal), during birth (perinatal), or after birth (postnatal). Prenatal factors that have been linked with mental retardation include poor maternal nutrition, the use of chemical agents (drugs, alcohol, and tobacco), and maternal illnesses. Perinatal factors include the use of drugs to aid in the birth process itself and the manner and type of delivery. Postnatal factors range from infant accidents and injuries to infant nutrition and chemical imbalances.

Environmental Retardation

Factors such as infections and intoxicants in the system of the expectant mother, the infant, or the young child are a secondary cause of mental retardation, which in this case is termed **environmental retardation.** For example, the expectant mother who contracts rubella (German measles) during the first trimester of her pregnancy or who uses crack cocaine or other mind-altering drugs, runs the risk of damaging her unborn child. A mother with syphilis transmits the condition to her child, and retardation frequently results. Rh incompatibility, infant poisoning, and a variety of diseases that occur during infancy also contribute to mental retardation.

Genetic Retardation

Genetic retardation is the third and least common type of mental retardation. Genetic retardation is brought about by chromosomal abnormalities. Deviations in the structure or number of chromosomes are related to gene mutations or the effects of certain drugs, viruses, and ionizing radiation. Down syndrome, one of the most frequently encountered forms of genetic retardation, is caused by chromosomal damage. It is frequently characterized by cardiovascular impairments in addition to mental retardation.

Children With Emotional Disabilities

Children with emotional disorders are characterized by behavior patterns that have a detrimental effect on their adjustment and that interfere with the lives of others. The causes of emotional disorders are not completely understood, nor is it clear why some individuals react in a negative emotional way while others with equivalent backgrounds do not. For example, a child living in a dysfunctional family in which there are various forms of abuse and neglect may, as expected, react in a negative emotional way. But another, living in similar conditions, may not. Emotional disorders are generally classified as either classic emotional disturbance or autism. We look briefly at both here.

Emotional Disturbance

As defined by Public Law 94-142, a child with an **emotional disorder** is one who has an inability to learn that cannot be explained by sensory problems, health factors, or intellectual deficits; is unable to make and maintain satisfactory interpersonal relationships with peers and adults; demonstrates inappropriate behaviors; is generally unhappy or depressed; or develops physical symptoms in response to school or personal problems. Any one of these five indicators is not sufficient to classify a child as having an emotional disorder. But, as a rule of thumb, three or more would be sufficient cause for concern.

A child with an emotional disorder may be characterized by extremes in behavior, chronic unacceptable behavior, or persistent problems at home or school. Estimates of the number of children with classic emotional disorders have ranged from only 2% to over 20% of the total population, with boys outnumbering girls 4 to 1. Even the conservative figure of 2% equates to a school-age population of over 1 million children who are considered to have serious emotional disorders, a fact that warrants the attention of all educators.

TEACHING TIP 7.9

Although the behaviors displayed by children with *emotional disorders* range from prolonged withdrawal to extreme disruption and hostility, these guidelines will be helpful:

- Understand that children with an emotional disorder need someone stable and orderly to serve as an example of steadiness.
- Structure the learning environment so that the child knows exactly what is expected. Using a teacher-centered teaching approach often works best.
- Learn to expect the unexpected. You can count on children with emotional disorders to overreact to new or potentially threatening situations.
- Set limits on what the child can and cannot do. Clearly define what is acceptable and unacceptable behavior. The process of limit-setting should be done in the spirit of helpful authority. Children feel safer when they know the boundaries in which they may operate.
- Set limits in such a way that they raise little resentment.
- Limits should be phrased in language that does not challenge the child's self-respect. For example, say "Time to put the balls away" instead of "Don't shoot another time, John. Put the ball away immediately!"
- Accept the fact that children with emotional disorders may progress little in the first month or two. Their progress will depend on the severity of their disturbance. A sense of trust and rapport must develop between teacher and child.
- Nonverbal reactions and facial expressions often give away your thoughts. The child with an emotional disability may depend a great deal on nonverbal clues to acceptance, resignation, disappointment, pride, and so forth.
- Learn to attend to the signs you communicate

to the child as well as to the signs conveyed to you.
- Help the child express feelings and vent hostilities through socially acceptable channels.
- Be firm and consistent in your discipline, but discipline in a manner that conveys an attitude of helpfulness, not authority.
- Learn and use each child's name and let the children know yours.
- Structure activities for success. All children should be able to achieve an element of success to help them overcome a sense of failure and lack of confidence.
- Immediately reinforce and praise the child for desired behavior.
- Avoid imposing standards or limits that are not within the child's capabilities.
- Be cognizant of individual differences and modify activities to meet these needs.
- Avoid elimination activities that exclude children from even part of the lesson.
- Use competitive activities sparingly, and ease children into competitive situations very carefully.
- Activities should be within the individual's capabilities but must be challenging. If they are too easy, the child will not perform. If they are too hard, the child will not perform or will quit.
- Do not let small incidents snowball. The child must know who is in charge and respect that position.
- Be thoroughly prepared and try to anticipate problems before they occur.
- Be patient, understanding, and quick to forgive.

Severe, prolonged emotional disorders are linked to a variety of psychological, sociological, and physiological factors. Psychological factors result from constant frustration and arise from the child's inability to cope with the real or imagined pressures of society. The consequence is feelings of anxiety, fear, hostility, or insecurity, which are manifested in inappropriate behavior patterns. Sociological factors include early home experiences such as abuse and neglect, and socioeconomic aspects of the home environment such as poverty and homelessness. Child abuse, ranging from physical and verbal abuse to sexual abuse and neglect, is an important sociological contributor to severe emotional disturbances. Likewise, physiological factors such as heredity, neurological disorders, and chemical imbalances may contribute to emotional disabilities. Figure 7.4 lists a variety of classic emotional disturbances that you are likely to encounter in your teaching career.

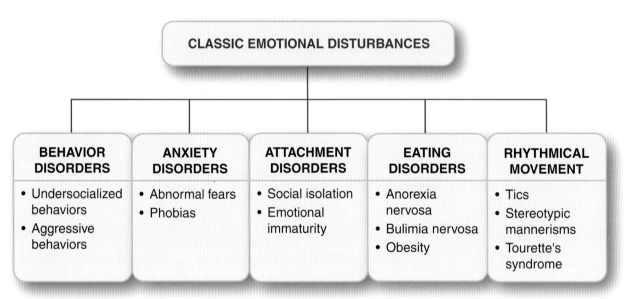

FIGURE 7.4   Common emotional disorders and typical associated behaviors found among children.

Children with emotional disorders may exhibit unusual anxiety reactions, atypical frustrations, fears and phobias, and impulsive behaviors. The following signs and symptoms may help in identifying these children in the classroom:

- A tendency to have accidents
- Hyperactivity
- Imaginary fears and phobias
- Regressive, immature behavior
- Aggressive, hostile behavior
- Withdrawal into a fantasy world
- Abnormal fear of failure and criticism
- Unexplained poor school achievement
- Frequent disciplinary visits to the principal's office
- Inability to relate appropriately with the peer group

Autism

Officially, autism is no longer considered a form of emotional disturbance. The Individuals with Disabilities Education Act (U.S. Department of Education 1998) calls for autism to be recognized as a separate diagnostic category. The fact is, however, that children with autism are generally grouped with those who are classified as having an emotional disability and those who have significant problems requiring behavior management.

Autism is a pervasive developmental disability that manifests itself prior to age three, persists throughout life, and is characterized by significant delays in both language and social development. The disorder of autism affects the central nervous system. Although its origin is unknown, some of the factors it may be associated with are chemical exposure during the fetal period, nutritional imbalances, or untreated phenylketonuria (PKU, a condition associated with an individual's inability to biochemically process phenylalanine, which can result in mild to severe retardation if left untreated). There is little support for claims that autism is psychological in character and associated with poor parenting.

Individuals with autism range in intelligence from severely retarded to above average, although most have some degree of retardation. Children with autism are frequently included in the regular physical education program even though they may have a tendency to exhibit peculiar speech patterns, bizarre behaviors, lack of social responsiveness and withdrawal, unusual **rhythmical stereotypes** (i.e., rocking and head banging), and **echolalia** (i.e., involuntary repetition of the words of others).

Children With Learning Disabilities

Learning disabilities are the fourth classification of disabilities in children. Public Law 94-142 defines the child with a **learning disability** as one who is restricted in the ability to read, write, think, speak, spell, or do mathematical operations due to the

TEACHING TIP 7.10

In working with children who have *learning disabilities,* the following guidelines will be helpful:

- Know and understand the specific nature of the child's learning difficulty.
- Structure personalized activities that work within the child's present level of abilities.
- Help the child find an element of success during each lesson.
- Progress from simple to more complex activities in small increments, being sure to use positive encouragement.
- Provide numerous opportunities for reinforcing academic concepts through movements that are normally dealt with in a classroom setting.
- Remember that children with specific learning disabilities have generally experienced a great deal of frustration and failure. Therefore it is very important to create an atmosphere of challenge and success.
- Promote a "yes I can" attitude.
- Help the child gain a better understanding of his body, the space it occupies, and how it can move.
- Help the child establish a sense of feel for direction through carefully sequenced movement activities.
- Make frequent use of rhythmic activities and stress the rhythmical element in all coordinated movement.

inability to fully utilize basic psychological processes involved in using spoken or written language. The term *learning disability* excludes problems in learning that may be traced to physical (visual, auditory, or motor) disabilities and mental retardation. It also excludes learning disabilities brought about primarily by cultural, economic, or environmental conditions. Children with a specific learning disability are sometimes referred to as ATLO children, an acronym for "All Those Left Over."

When a child has a specific learning disability, it is often difficult to detect. Such children often appear typical in their physical, social, and mental development, but for some unexplained reason they fail to achieve at an acceptable level in school. The discrepancy between potential and performance often results in peer-related problems and considerable emotional upheaval. The learning impairment itself may be relatively minor and specific to motor, perceptual, writing, or speaking difficulties; or it may be complex and involve the intricate interaction of several or all of these processes. Although perceptual-motor training programs have been advocated for years as an effective way to remediate learning disabilities, the area is too diverse and too complex to merit such simple solutions.

The effects of perceptual-motor programs on the academic achievement and cognitive processes of children with learning disabilities are highly speculative. The fact is that quality physical education programs do produce positive changes in personal, social, and motivational response patterns of children. It may be that these factors have an indirect influence on the acquisition of skills and abilities necessary for academic success (figure 7.5).

FIGURE 7.5 Two common learning disabilities encountered in the regular physical education process.

ATTENTION DEFICIT DISORDER (ADD)	HYPERACTIVITY
• Distractibility • Impulsivity	• Constant movement • Fidgeting • Short attention span

Distractibility and Impulsivity

Many children with learning disabilities have problems with **distractibility** and **impulsivity.** Characteristic displays of distractibility include not paying attention, failing to finish things, finding it difficult to concentrate on schoolwork, and finding it difficult to stick with play activities. Impulsivity is characterized by acting before thinking, having trouble getting organized, needing lots of supervision, frequent calling out in class, and impatience in waiting one's turn in game and group situations.

Hyperactivity

Children with **hyperactivity** typically have extreme difficulty in sitting still long enough to complete a task. They may or may not also display characteristics of distractibility and impulsivity. Hyperactive children are always on the move, fidgeting, moving their feet, tapping their fingers, constantly talking, and in perpetual motion. They tend to wear teachers out because there is seldom a pause in their constant movement. This is frequently reflected in poor behavior reports, failing grades, and exhausted parents and teachers.

Children with hyperactivity are frequently bright and outgoing but need patient, understanding help in slowing down, calming down, and simply relaxing. Although medications can be prescribed, a supportive, calm, caring, and structured environment can be of significant benefit. The physical education teacher can help by providing ample opportunities for vigorous physical activity in a structured setting.

Other Disabilities

The category of "other disabilities" includes a variety of health restrictions that may not be as easily observed as those discussed earlier but that adversely affect the child's educational performance. These conditions may result from health problems such as asthma, diabetes, obesity, hemophilia, anemia, tuberculosis, or leukemia. In each case it is important for the physical education teacher to work closely with the physician, parents, rehabilitation specialists, and other school officials to provide appropriate educational opportunities in the least restrictive environment.

THE INDIVIDUALIZED EDUCATION PROGRAM

Appropriate identification, assessment, programming, and evaluation of the child's progress must be a team approach. Identification is the procedure by which children with special needs are located. Assessment is the means by which they are examined and their present status is determined. Motor assessment includes the initial screening, frequently by the regular physical education teacher, and a more extensive evaluation by the adapted physical education teacher. Once the child has been identified and her present level of abilities has been determined, it is possible to program appropriate learning activities.

Programming involves development of an IEP, which is individualized and need based and which must be implemented in the least restrictive environment. In a team approach, the physical education teacher should participate in formulating the IEP, because it is he who will be responsible for its implementation and evaluation. The final aspect of the team process, evaluation, refers to the procedures used to determine the degree to which the objectives established in the IEP have been met.

SPECIAL NEEDS OF CHILDREN WITH DISABILITIES

The needs and interests of children with physical, mental, or emotional disabilities are essentially the same as for all other children. Children with disabilities generally profit most when included in the regular physical education program. They need to be accepted for who they are and treated with respect as contributors to the group, class, and society as a whole. They need challenging movement experiences that are within the limits of their abilities. They need ample opportunities to solve problems for themselves and to develop a greater sense of independence rather than dependence. Children with physical, mental, or emotional disabilities need to experience a wide variety of movement activities designed to break down the

CONCEPT
7.7

Children with disabilities often face body image and social adjustment problems that can be dealt with through developmentally appropriate physical education.

The Blind Guy: A Real Champion

Real-World Situation

Recently your senior author was in Minnesota evaluating the physical education curriculum at one of the state's fine universities. One of the faculty members, Jim, an acquaintance from an earlier meeting, offered to give me a tour of the building. I was somewhat surprised by his offer because he is blind. I almost politely refused but then remembered an incident from our first meeting a few years earlier in which he had challenged me to a game of darts.

I remembered reluctantly accepting my colleague's challenge, not wanting to embarrass him in front of his many friends, and being fully confident in my ability to beat the "blind guy." Oh my! After three tries I had yet to win a game. It was then I learned that in addition to his many other physical accomplishments, he was a national blind dart champion.

So I accepted his invitation of a tour. As you have probably already guessed, he gave me a flawless tour throughout the entire building, pointing out all major facilities and discussing particular nuances of equipment in both the laboratory and activity spaces. This is a socially well-adjusted individual with a superb body image.

Critical Questions

Based on your knowledge of individuals with disabilities and the situation as presented:

- How do you account for this man's excellent body image?
- Speculating, what do you think may be the reasons for his abilities to perform so well in activities that we usually think of as requiring sight?
- What would you do to contribute to the social adjustment of individuals with various disabilities?
- The word "abilities" is embedded in the frequently used term "disabilities." With reference to the "blind guy," what does this mean to you? In other words, can you reconcile these apparent polar opposite terms?

artificial limitations that are often built up around their disability. Like all children, they need ample opportunities for practice, sincere encouragement, and skilled instruction if we are to expect them to improve their movement competence and level of fitness. Children need especially to adjust socially to their disability and to establish a realistic body image.

Social Adjustment

A major problem that children with disabilities encounter is social adjustment. This problem often results from external or societal factors. Historical attitudes relating to the treatment of exceptional individuals have had a tremendous negative impact on modern society and its attitudes. Only relatively recently has emphasis shifted from people's disabilities to their abilities. This more enlightened view has had a great effect on education of people with disabilities, as reflected in federal and state legislation, and has vastly improved their self-acceptance and social integration.

The physical education program that includes children with disabilities makes a profound positive impact on the social adjustment of both those with disabilities and those without. The physical education program that is developmentally based, individualized, and personalized is geared to the needs and abilities of all children. As such, it influences the acceptance of these children by society and hence the individual's acceptance of herself. The nondisabled population must understand that persons with disabilities are not looking for concessions or sympathy but want to be treated like others within their individual limits. Inclusion leads to acceptance. Inclusion promotes understanding, encourages favorable attitudes, and leads to both public acceptance and self-acceptance.

Body Image Enhancement

We all possess an awareness of our own body and its possibilities for movement and performance. This quality, or body image as it is commonly called, is a learned concept that results from observation of how the parts of our body move and how these various parts relate to each other and to external objects in space.

A well-developed body image is important because of its potential impact on self-concept. If children fail to form a reasonably satisfactory body image, their self-concept is likely to be distorted, and they will be limited in their emotional and social development. The extent to which our body image is developed depends largely on movement experiences. Both the quality and the quantity of these movement activities are important. Movement experiences lead to a better orientation in space and provide information about the body that we would be unable to obtain otherwise. Movement enables us to gain sensory information concerning changes in muscle tone. The more information received and the better the quality of the information, the more developed the body image is. The movement experiences and diverse gross motor activities inherent in a well-planned physical education program contribute a great deal to the development of a stable body image, which in turn influences self-esteem.

When children with disabilities are restricted from taking part in vigorous activities or when their performance is atypical, they fail to form a complete body image or may develop one that is distorted. This imperfect image further affects their perceptions of themselves and their external world. Distorted perceptions tend to undermine self-assurance and often lead to social and psychological difficulties.

Being able to perform a movement task in an acceptable manner contributes to one's confidence and self-assurance. When children with disabilities have an opportunity to develop their movement abilities and to improve their body image, their confidence and self-assurance increase. Then the personality is reinforced and the likelihood of problems of social adjustment is diminished. Working as a team, parents, teachers, and rehabilitation workers can contribute to children's physical and psychological development.

IMPLICATION FOR TEACHING DEVELOPMENTAL PHYSICAL EDUCATION

The aim of the special program of physical education is to help each child reach that child's potential physical, social, and emotional level of functioning in a well-planned, progressive program built around the child's own unique needs, interests, and abilities. Teachers of children with disabilities must realize that the objectives they set and the outcomes they seek are often different from those sought by the child. Avoid the pitfall of selecting activities to satisfy program objectives based on your own abilities, interests, and feelings.

Success in teaching children with disabilities depends on the teacher's positive acceptance of each child and a genuine willingness to assimilate children with disabilities into the regular physical education program. The ability to individualize and personalize instruction to meet children's unique needs and interests is also essential for long-term success. It is the teacher's responsibility to establish a climate conducive to learning, a climate in which children feel free to learn, to probe, and to explore. The key to success is in establishing freedom within limits. These limits should serve as guidelines rather than restraints. They should also produce a nonthreatening environment that enables the teacher to accept children at whatever level they are functioning encourage their enjoyment of movement activities, and motivate them to become as skilled as they can be within their special situations.

Summary

Individuals with disabilities are covered by several important federal laws. All children with diagnosed disabilities must be provided an appropriate physical education program, and this program must be offered in the least restrictive environment. Children with disabilities must be given the opportunity to take part in the regular physical education program unless their needs can be met only through a specially designed program as prescribed by their Individualized Education Program (IEP). Adapted programs, remedial programs, and developmental programs are the types of specialized programs designed to offer physical education to children with disabilities.

Developmental disabilities are classified into four broad and sometimes overlapping categories—physical, mental, emotional, and learning disabilities. Physical education programs can be modified in many specific ways to accommodate children with particular disabilities—for example, using a buddy system for a child with auditory impairment, modifying physical activity for a child with cerebral palsy, selecting activities that include frequent rest periods for a child with cystic fibrosis. Although the needs and interests of children with disabilities are essentially the same as for all other children, children with disabilities also tend to have special needs in relation to social adjustment and body image enhancement. Physical education can be a powerful force in the lives of children with disabilities by helping to meet these needs.

Terms to Remember

Excellent Readings

Block, M.E., & Garcia, C. (Eds.). (1995). *Including students with disabilities in regular physical education.* Reston, VA: AAHPERD Publications.

Block, M. (1998). Don't forget the social aspects of inclusion. *Strategies, 12* (2), 30-34.

Block, M.E., Lieberman, L.J., & Connor-Kuntz, F. (1998). Authentic assessment in adapted physical education. *JOPERD, 69* (3), 48-55.

Doolittle, S., & Demas, K. (2001). Fostering respect through physical activity. *JOPERD, 72* (9), 28-33.

Hamill, J. (Ed.). (1992). The physically challenged child. *Pediatric Exercise Science, 4.* (Series of articles)

Kassler, S.L. (1995). *Inclusive games.* Champaign, IL: Human Kinetics.

Lieberman, L.J., & Cowart, J.F. (1996). *Games for people with sensory impairments.* Champaign, IL: Human Kinetics.

Murata, N.M. (2000). Speech-language strategies for physical educators. *JOPERD, 71* (2), 36-38.

National Association for Sport and Physical Education. (1995). *Including students with disabilities in physical education: A position statement of NASPE.* Reston, VA: AAHPERD.

Thompson, D., Hudson, S.D., & Bowers, L. (2002). Play areas and the ADA: Providing access and opportunities. *JOPERD, 73* (2), 37-41.

Webb, D., & Pope, C.C. (1999). Inclusive context: Going beyond labels and categories. *JOPERD, 70* (7), 41-47.

Wilson, S. (2000). Disability case studies: Learning to include all students. *JOPERD, 71* (2), 37-41.

Winnick, J.P. (Ed.). (2000). *Adapted physical education and sport.* Champaign, IL: Human Kinetics.

The Teacher

Part II focuses on you, the teacher. Although we, the authors, are university professors, we both continue to be actively involved with public and private school physical education. We are in the "trenches" with real students and effective teachers who daily apply the concepts contained in part II. The information contained here is the result of our collective experiences as well as the experiences of our many valued colleagues in the field. It is intended to be practical, realistic, and doable, as well as theoretically sound and research-based.

Chapter 8 provides an in-depth look at what it takes to be an effective teacher. The essential skills, varied responsibilities, and important decisions you will make on your journey to effective teaching are discussed. **Chapter 9** provides a wealth of practical information to help you get started right when it comes to positive discipline and classroom-management skills. Both teacher-centered and child-centered approaches to discipline are discussed. **Chapter 10** serves as the basis for the various teaching styles that you will use as an effective teacher. Varying your teaching styles to fit the appropriateness of the teaching-learning situation will help you connect with students. **Chapter 11** gets down to the nitty-gritty of curriculum planning. Developing skill themes and lesson plans highlights this chapter. **Chapter 12** provides the essentials for assessing student progress. Emphasis is placed on the core content areas of the developmental program: movement skill, fitness, and physical activity assessment. **Chapter 13** concludes part II with an important discussion of your responsibilities for physical education advocacy. Educating and communicating with fellow teachers, parents, and community leaders about the values of physical activity are ongoing responsibilities. Selling your program and motivating others to take responsibility for their physical activity are musts.

8

Effective Teaching: Skills, Responsibilities, Choices

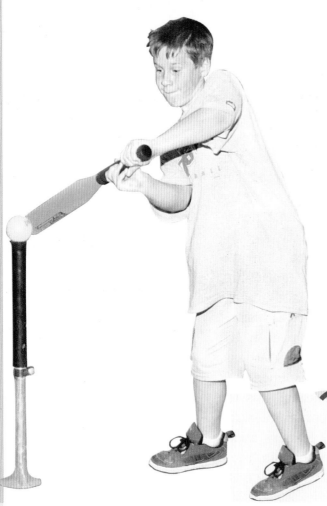

Key Concept

▶ Effective teaching is a dynamic, interactive process between student and instructor requiring communication and commitment to individual learning and enjoyment of the content.

Teaching children physical education is a rewarding and challenging job requiring knowledgeable, committed teachers. Physical educators must be able to create a highly positive atmosphere between themselves and the children they teach. As a teacher you must understand children's developmental characteristics, recognize their individual differences, and plan activities that are meaningful to them and that also achieve your learning objectives. The Web site PE Central (**www.pecentral.org**) is an excellent resource for those committed to being effective teachers.

Effective teaching in physical education has been described as teaching that results in more intended learning than does less effective teaching. To be an effective teacher and achieve intended learning outcomes, physical educators must perform specific *teaching functions*. Rink (1993) has characterized these functions as follows:

- Identifying intended outcomes for learning
- Planning learning experiences to accomplish those outcomes
- Presenting tasks to learners
- Organizing and managing the learning environment
- Monitoring the learning environment
- Developing the content
- Evaluating the effectiveness of the instructional/curricular process

In addition to these recognized teaching functions, the Content Standards for Physical Education developed by the National Association for Sport and Physical Education (NASPE) serve as a curricular framework or guide for physical

Chapter Objectives

This chapter will provide you with the tools to do the following:

- ▶ Identify the many and varied responsibilities of the teacher.
- ▶ Identify the typical stages of concern that teachers experience in their profession.
- ▶ List and discuss several personal, classroom, and assessment qualities of successful teachers.
- ▶ Describe specific techniques for getting and maintaining children's attention.
- ▶ Discuss the importance of clarity in communicating with children and list several specific techniques.
- ▶ List the various forms of feedback and describe how they may be effectively used.
- ▶ Discuss problems associated with changing a well-learned but incorrectly performed movement skill.
- ▶ Identify a variety of common nonverbal postures, gestures, and facial expressions used by teachers.
- ▶ Speculate on the use of nonverbal communication techniques in effective teaching.
- ▶ Demonstrate techniques of conveying enthusiasm.
- ▶ Identify the role that physical distance plays in effective communication.
- ▶ Analyze the messages received from children's verbal and nonverbal communication.

education programming and instruction. As discussed in chapter 1, the seven Content Standards address movement skill development, fitness, and physical activity, as well as cognitive and affective development.

To fully implement the developmental physical education model advocated throughout this text and to fully address the NASPE Content

---

TEXT BOX 8.1

"Outstanding teachers engage youngsters, interact with them, draw energy and direction from them, and find ways to give them a reason to follow along" (Ayers, 1993, p. 127).

Standards for Physical Education, teachers must fulfill varied responsibilities and employ an array of skills. For example, they must use clear verbal communication, effective classroom management, and relevant feedback. In addition, teachers must make choices about what to teach and how to teach. Mosston and Ashworth (2001) present several questions (i.e., choices) that may persist in the mind of every teacher—novice or veteran—when preparing to enter a classroom:

- What do I want my students to accomplish? What are the objectives of my lesson?
- What methodology will I choose in order to reach the objectives of the lesson? What will be my teaching behavior?
- What is the sequence of the lesson? How do I arrange the materials?
- How do I organize the class for optimal learning? In pairs? By providing individual activities?
- How do I motivate my class? How do I offer appropriate feedback?
- How do I create a climate conducive to thinking, social interaction, and good feelings?
- How do I know that my students and I have reached the objectives? Have we reached all of them? Some?

YOUR RESPONSIBILITIES AS A TEACHER

CONCEPT 8.1

Teachers have a variety of important responsibilities that go well beyond classroom instruction.

Physical education teachers assume many responsibilities in carrying out their duties. They must take on the tasks of planning the curriculum, organizing the program, planning and implementing the lesson, and assessing student progress. Additionally, teachers accept the seldom mentioned responsibilities of counseling students, acting as a community representative, and providing for their own long-term professional growth.

Planning the Curriculum

The physical education teacher is entirely responsible for developing the overall curriculum, an important task that is crucial to a successful program. Planning the curriculum takes time and requires careful analysis of students' needs and interests as well as a survey of available facilities, equipment, and time allotments. Successful curriculum planning requires input from many sources and coordination with fellow teachers and administrators. Please refer to chapter 14 for a complete discussion of the developmental physical education curriculum.

TEXT BOX 8.2

The ingredients of effective teaching in physical education are not unlike those for teaching in any other subject area. To do a thorough job you must have specialized training, interest in and enthusiasm for your subject matter, a sound grasp of teaching techniques, the ability to communicate effectively with children, and a continuing desire to understand the developing child.

Organizing the Learning Environment

Along with planning the overall curriculum, as a physical education teacher you will be responsible for organizing the learning environment. Physical education teachers are generally responsible for ordering, taking inventory of, and maintaining gymnasium and playground equipment. They assume responsibility for periodic safety checks of gymnasium apparatus and outdoor play equipment. In addition, they are frequently responsible for escorting children to the gymnasium and back to the classroom. As the physical education teacher, you will have to work hard to carry out these obligations and make maximum effective use of your time and the time you have with your students. Please refer to chapter 11 for a complete discussion on creating an exciting and developmentally appropriate learning environment.

Planning and Implementing the Lesson

Developing the overall curriculum and organizing the learning environment are important, but they precede the teacher's most vital work: actually planning and implementing the lesson. Physical education teachers primarily instruct students in how to acquire movement skills, attain and maintain physical fitness, and understand movement. A lesson may be implemented in many ways, but the goal is the same: for children to become skillful movers, to develop an understanding of and appreciation for the "why" of physical activity, and to incorporate it into their daily lives. You may use a variety of teaching approaches and motivational techniques; but your selection and use of them will depend on your philosophy of learning, educational background, personality, and expertise as a teacher. Chapter 10 presents a complete discussion of teaching styles.

Teachers must serve as evaluators or assessors to determine whether the objectives of their instruction have been met. Assessment may be subjective or objective, formal or informal, process oriented or product oriented. Assessment of children should stress the positive aspects of their performance, focusing on personal

Careful storage of equipment facilitates efficient and appropriate selection of equipment for the physical education lesson.

improvement and the discovery of their individual potential. Child-centered assessment should help promote an "I believe in you; you must believe in you!" attitude between teacher and student. Assessment should serve as an important form of feedback to students, parents, and the teacher. Please refer to chapter 12 for a complete discussion on assessing student progress.

Counseling Students

A role that physical education teachers frequently play—although generally this is not spelled out—is that of counselor. For years physical educators and coaches have informally assumed this important but often underappreciated role. Because of the very nature of physical activity and the rapport generated through sensitive, caring instruction, physical education teachers often have numerous opportunities to serve effectively as counselors on a wide range of issues. Routine counseling opportunities may range from helping children adjust to school, home, and peer situations to providing techniques for healthful living and helping students understand and cope with their changing body.

Your role as a counselor needs to be recognized and taken seriously. But remember that unless you have special training, your ability to deal with major problems and your effectiveness in this regard are limited. Child abuse, school violence, drug and alcohol use, sexual activity, gender orientation, homelessness, and coping with the effects of divorce are serious topics that require trained professional assistance. With children who have these issues, it is perfectly appropriate to be supportive, but by all means be certain to seek out professional counseling and advice. Spring Independent School District in Houston, Texas, initiated a program to train Teachers as Counselors (TAC). Frequently there are too few trained counselors in public schools to directly provide sufficient services for children. Teachers who receive specific training and ample counselor support may provide students with effective group experiences. The TAC program is one viable alternative for providing teachers with the knowledge and leadership skills needed to supplement a school's counseling services (Wasielewski & Scruggs, 1997).

Johnson and Johnson (1995) offer guiding principles aimed at enabling schools to become orderly and peaceful places where high-quality education can take place. Their research demonstrates that students must be trained to manage conflicts constructively without physical or verbal violence. Their Peacemakers Program provides negotiation and mediation procedures that can be implemented within schools. Negotiation procedures are highlighted in figure 8.1.

For students in conflict, help them:
1. Define what they want
2. Describe their feelings
3. Explain the reasons underlying those wants and feelings
4. Reverse their perspectives in order to view the conflict from both sides
5. Generate at least three optional agreements with maximum benefits for both parties, and
6. Agree on wisest course of action

FIGURE 8.1   Conflict resolution.

From: Johnson, D.W., & Johnson, R.T. (1995). Why violence prevention programs don't work—and what does. *Educational Leadership, 52* (5), 63–70.

According to many experts, today's children are in a crisis of identity and moral decision making. As a physical education teacher, you'll find that the impact you have as a counselor will often be equal to your impact as an instructor. But don't make the mistake of *telling* the child what she *should* do. Instead, present all sides of the issue, helping the student find her own solution. Teachers can guide students in values education and positive moral decision making, but they should not impose their particular value system on others unless specifically asked to do so. When in doubt about how to respond to a sensitive counseling issue, check first with your immediate supervisor or the building principal. The worst thing you can do is to provide no guidance at all, claiming that it is not part of your job description. Remember, you may be the only one in that particular child's life trusted enough to provide guidance.

Acting As Community Representative

As a professional educator, you'll find that people ask you about your views concerning the education of children. You'll be expected to be knowledgeable about a variety of educational issues and to have formulated rational, intelligent positions. For example, people will value your views on youth sport, weight training for children, diet and exercise, and childhood obesity. Furthermore, your views will reflect on the school system or agency of which you are a representative.

As an educator you have a tremendous opportunity to serve as an effective community representative. You have training and knowledge about a variety of issues that are important to the public. This knowledge can enable you to serve as an effective voice in the community.

Continued Professional Growth

Continued professional growth is an important responsibility of all educators. This may take many forms, but it is generally accomplished through graduate study, continuing education, professional reading, and involvement in professional organizations and societies.

To continually grow as an effective teacher, the professional educator must be committed to advanced education beyond the undergraduate degree. Most states require teachers to pursue a master's degree or some form of continuing education to maintain a valid teaching license. Check with your state department of education to be certain of the requirements in the area where you will work. Continued professional growth may also be fostered through subscribing to and reading professional journals. Many professional journals and newsletters are especially valuable for elementary physical education teachers and youth sport coaches. If you are serious about continued professional growth, you should subscribe to and read at least one of these.

Involvement in professional organizations or societies at the local, state, and/or national level is another long-term responsibility of the professional physical educator. This may take the form of attending professional workshops and special meetings, serving on committees and in action groups, or even making professional presentations. The American Alliance for Health, Physical Education, Recreation and Dance (AAHPERD) is the professional association to which most physical educators in the United States belong. There are local AAHPERD organizations in each state and region of the country. The National Association for Sport and Physical Education (NASPE) is an association within AAHPERD with over 20,000 members; NASPE is the primary advocate for physical education in the United States. The Canadian Association for Health, Physical Education and Recreation (CAPHER) has affiliates in each province, and the International Congress for Health, Physical Education, Recreation-Sport and Dance (ICHPER-SD) is the association that many physical educators from around the world belong to. Professional societies such as Delta Psi Kappa, Phi Delta Phi, and Phi Epsilon Kappa also provide a means for continual professional growth.

TEXT BOX 8.3

Successful teachers are effective in both communicating with children and listening to them. They are good planners, organizers, and implementers of meaningful learning experiences. Successful teachers consistently demonstrate genuine concern for the welfare of their students.

CONCEPT 8.2

On their way to becoming master teachers, teachers typically go through identifiable stages of concern, for their personal success, their self-interests, and finally genuine concern for others.

DEVELOPING AS A TEACHER

No one becomes an effective teacher overnight. But just what is "effective" teaching? Effective teaching is both an art and a science that takes considerable time, effort, and practice. It is a dynamic, interactive process between instructor and student that requires mutual communication and commitment to individual learning and enjoyment of the content. Effective teachers have a genuine concern for their students and manifest this concern in their teaching behavior.

Professional journals and newsletters help you keep informed and up to date:

Adapted Physical Activity Quarterly
Human Kinetics Publishers
P.O. Box 5076
Champaign, IL 61825-5076
www.HumanKinetics.com

Journal of ICHPER-SD
1900 Association Drive
Reston, VA 20191
ichper@aahperd.org

International Journal of Physical Education
c/o Verlag Karl Hofmann
D-7060 Schorndorf,
Postfac 1360
Federal Republic of Germany
www.hofmann-verlag.de

Journal of Health Education
American Association of Health Education
AAHPERD Circulation Department
1900 Association Drive
Reston, VA 20191
www.aahperd.org/aahe

Journal of Physical Education, Recreation and Dance (JOPERD)
AAHPERD Circulation Department
1900 Association Drive
Reston, VA 22091
joperd@aahperd.org

Journal of School Health
American School Health Association
7263 State Route 43,
P.O. Box 708
Kent, OH 44240
330-678-1601

Journal of Teaching in Physical Education
Human Kinetics Publishers
P.O. Box 5076
Champaign, IL 61825-5076
www.HumanKinetics.com

Physical Education Index
Ben Oak Publishing Co.
P.O. Box 474
Cape Girardeau, MO 63702-0474
573-334-8789

Palestra
Challenge Publications Ltd.
P.O. Box 508
Macomb, IL 61455
www.palestra.com

The Physical Educator
901 W. New York Street
Indianapolis, IN 46202
www2.Truman.edu/pel

Quest
Human Kinetics Publishers
P.O. Box 5076
Champaign, IL 61825-5076
www.HumanKinetics.com

The Research Quarterly for Exercise and Sport
AAHPERD Circulation Department
1900 Association Drive
Reston, VA 22091
800-213-7183, ext. 490

The Right Moves (Newsletter)
NASPE
Council on Physical Education for Children
1900 Association Drive
Reston, VA 22091

Spotlight on Youth Sports (Newsletter)
Youth Sports Institute
213 IM Sports Circle Building
Michigan State University
East Lansing, MI 48824-1049
ythsprts@mscu.edu

Strategies
NASPE
1900 Association Drive
Reston, VA 22091
strategies@aahperd.org

Teaching Elementary Physical Education
Human Kinetics Publishers
P.O. Box 5076
Champaign, IL 61825-5076
www.HumanKinetics.com

Pediatric Exercise Science
Human Kinetics Publishers
P.O. Box 5076
Champaign, IL 61825-5076
www.HumanKinetics.com

You Can Do It All: Or Can You?

Real-World Situation

It's your first professional teaching position at Youcan Doitall Elementary School. Naturally, you're excited about the opportunity to start using the skills you have learned during your college days and to begin teaching what you love best: elementary school children. Your lofty ideals and plans are somewhat tempered when you learn that there is more, much more, to your responsibilities than planning the curriculum, organizing the learning environment, and implementing your program in a developmentally appropriate manner consistent with the NASPE Standards for Physical Education. For the first time you are confronted with the reality that your job involves a host of additional responsibilities, ranging from informally counseling students, acting as a community representative on a variety of issues, and (of course) continued professional growth, to other activities that may seem mundane, such as taking lunchroom duty and supervising recess. You also have to deal with frequently giving up your gymnasium or outdoor activity space for "really important" school activities. Additionally, you are expected to teach 10 back-to-back 30-minute classes per day with little more than 20 minutes for lunch and no planning period. Last, you learn that it will be your yearly responsibility to plan and conduct an all-school student performance that highlights your program. Sure, you can do it all—or can you?

Critical Questions

Based on the reality of what it takes to be an effective teacher:

- If this is a realistic depiction of what may be waiting for you "out there," what may you be able to do to help remedy this situation?
- On your journey to becoming a "wise" teacher, how would you put the situation as presented into perspective?

You might be interested in knowing that on the road to becoming an effective teacher, most people go through a series of predictable stages. The following are three stages of concern that you can expect to go through as you strive to become a master teacher.

Concern for Personal Success

No matter how well prepared you are as you complete your education or how many practice-teaching experiences you have had, your first concern as a new teacher is most likely to be personal success: personal success in the school and particularly in the gymnasium and on the playground.

Concern for success in the school at large takes many forms. Adjusting to the policies—both unwritten and written—of your new place of employment is important to success, as is learning the names, roles, and expectations of your fellow teachers and supervisors. Remember, you are "the new kid on the block," and you will have to make adjustments to the structure and roles already in place. Finding your way around the school, locating equipment and supplies, and becoming acquainted with the school custodian and secretary are important to your personal success as a teacher. Often these people can help you maintain facilities and equipment and order needed items; and they can often help you adjust to the community mores and the character of the faculty, administration, and students.

Personal success in the gymnasium and on the playground is often a more immediate concern. What happens between you and your students during the early days, weeks, and months will do much to set the stage for the students' later behavior. Too frequently, new teachers enter a school totally unprepared for gaining and maintaining control of their classes. Too often, their teaching diminishes to a "tug-of-war" over who will be in control. Your success as a teacher depends on your ability to win this battle by commanding the respect of your students, gaining and maintaining their attention, and ensuring class control. Refer to chapter 9 for a complete discussion of management strategies and positive discipline. The physical environment of the gymnasium and playground is quite different from that of the classroom. Children often exhibit a different set of behaviors in these environments. Therefore, it is of utmost importance to have a plan of action for ensuring your personal success in this setting.

Concern for Self

Once teachers have mastered the basic elements required for success and survival, concern often becomes more inwardly focused. Teachers at this stage tend to ask questions such as "What's in it for me?" and "How can I make this easier on me?" and "Why me?" At this stage of concern, teachers tend to feel overworked and underpaid. Consequently, if you are like most, you may feel misunderstood and unappreciated by your peers as well as your students. Although this stage is self-centered and appears to violate the ideals of "dedicated" teaching, it is a phase that most teachers go through. It does, however, have its benefits. Teachers with an acute concern for self have done much to cause local school boards to reexamine pay scales, workloads, and extracurricular expectations. Therefore, this stage, when viewed in its proper perspective, has contributed much to making the teaching profession a more attractive place to seek employment in the past few years.

Teachers frequently demonstrate a healthy concern for self at the beginning of the school year by establishing basic rules and routines that are teacher centered. Rule making, however, should ultimately be a collaborative process between teacher and students. Such a process provides students with input and ownership. Individuals at the third stage of becoming effective teachers have this type of mutually cooperative relationship with students.

Concern for Students

Genuine concern for the learning and welfare of students is the essence of successful teaching. Teachers at this stage are not encumbered by anxiety about personal success—they have demonstrated their capability in this arena—nor are they preoccupied with a "What's in it for me?" attitude. They recognize the benefits and liabilities inherent in their profession in general and their own situation in particular, and they have chosen to get on with the business of educating children to the best of their ability. During this stage, a teacher gains a sense of "wisdom." This wisdom has a number of components:

- Solid factual knowledge about teaching and about the subject matter
- Rich procedural knowledge about teaching strategies and practical knowledge of how and when to use them
- A sense of the context of instruction and the context in which the students are being instructed
- An awareness of variations in values and priorities of both their peers and their students
- An uncertainty about the effects of specific teaching decisions, coupled with a willingness to take risks and to try a variety of ways to actively participate with the students in the learning process (Arlin, 1999)

In summary, wise teachers are reflective practitioners who question how their curricular and pedagogical choices affect their students' learning and feelings about their educational experiences.

No teacher progresses through these stages at a set rate. Some teachers are early casualties and never get beyond the stage of quest for personal success. Some never advance beyond the concern-for-self stage and continue their careers looking for little beyond a paycheck. Most successful teachers, however, have reached the third stage and demonstrate a genuine, lasting interest in their children, both as students and as individuals. We certainly hope you too will reach this third stage!

CONCEPT 8.3

The characteristics of effective teachers are observable, predictable, and obtainable through practice and hard work.

BEING AN EFFECTIVE TEACHER

Effective teachers are those who, through planned instruction, are able to bring about positive changes in the learner. Such changes occur in an environment that is meaningful and nonthreatening, one that aids in developing a thinking and acting individual. The following personal, classroom, and assessment qualities contribute to successful teaching.

REALITY CHECK

Oh Gee, Look at Me—Am I Effective As I Can Be?

Real-World Situation

Finally, you're a "real" teacher. On your own, expected to be on the job at 7:30 A.M. and not to leave before 4:30 P.M. Students, and even some of your new colleagues, call you "Ms." or "Mr." It sounds so strange—and it feels so strange not to be wearing your ball cap or blue jeans to school each day. Naturally, you want very much to be an "effective" teacher, one who is able to consistently bring about positive changes in your students. But this is all so new, so surreal. Not even your practicum and student teaching experiences prepared you for this. You're on your own, without that comfortable "safety net" of a professor or supervising teacher.

Critical Questions

Based on what you know about what it takes to be an effective teacher:

- What personal traits will you display to maximize your potential for connecting with students and your fellow teachers?
- What will you wear now that you are a teacher and not a student?
- How can you use "magic words" to help you connect with your students?
- What can you do to ensure that you remain current in your content and delivery?
- What qualities will you display in your classroom in order to maximize your effectiveness as a teacher?

Your Personal Traits

On entering the classroom or gymnasium, the student sees the teacher. A variety of personal characteristics display the teacher's attitude toward the subject matter, individual students, and the class itself. We can describe effective teachers in the following ways:

• **Interested.** Effective teachers display an interest in students as individuals while refraining from being overly friendly to the point that they cannot act as a disciplinarian if necessary. This interest indicates to students that the teacher cares about them not only as students but also as people. Teachers do a number of things to display a genuine interest in students:

- Provide positive and specific feedback
- Speak personally to as many students as possible and call them by name
- Give students responsibilities (equipment distribution; choices in modifying games)
- Deal with students equitably—that is, provide feedback to all skill levels and to both boys and girls
- Build students' self-esteem by acknowledging their birthdays, likes and dislikes, and personal interests

• **Honest.** Effective teachers are honest with themselves and their students. Their lack of condescension and their willingness to admit to a mistake or lack of knowledge show students that they can be trusted.

• **Enthusiastic.** They are alive with enthusiasm about the subject matter and are eager to share this knowledge. This tends to help students want to learn rather than feeling that they have to learn. Enthusiasm can be directly conveyed through voice intonation or through participation with the children during physical education activities. It may be indirectly conveyed within the learning environment through the use of stimulating decorations or music during class.

A teacher's enthusiasm can often be displayed through participation with students as demonstrated in this small-sided game.

• **Human.** Effective teachers smile, have an aura of warmth, and show a sense of humor. Students want to believe that teachers are human; only by acting human can teachers display true concern for the class.

• **Courteous.** They respect students as innately worthwhile human beings and demonstrate their respect by consistently using *magic words* such as "please," "thank you," "keep trying," and "you're awesome!" (Magic words can be displayed on a large poster board on gymnasium walls.) Furthermore, effective teachers insist that students respect one another and treat others with courtesy. They encourage students in a positive manner and help students learn to do the same with their peers.

- **Effective at speaking.** Successful teachers have a clear voice and a vocabulary geared to the students' level. They do not talk down to children or at them but talk to them in language the children can understand. It is a pleasure to listen to teachers who speak well and are easily understood.

- **Confident.** They are confident in their abilities and do not find it necessary to enhance their egos at the students' expense. They are able to be leaders and are sensitive to the needs of the group. This enables students to find comfort in the teacher's leadership without feeling threatened.

- **Properly dressed.** They recognize that personal appearance does affect how students view a teacher. They dress neatly and appropriately for their age, which creates a positive image of the teacher and enhances the enjoyment of the class.

- **Knowledgeable.** They are in command of their subject matter. They are well read and up to date in their knowledge. Today teachers have many resources to assist them in staying "with it." The National Association for Sport and Physical Education has published a resource we have referred to throughout this text, whose full title is *Moving Into the Future: National Standards for Physical Education* (NASPE, 1995). This document now represents the major curriculum planning resource for physical educators in the United States. Internet resources also provide a vehicle through which teachers can communicate with one another and share teaching ideas (**www.pecentral.com**, monitored by Virginia Tech University, is one such Internet site). Involvement in professional associations (e.g., AAHPERD) is an excellent way to continue the quest for learning what and how to teach children in physical education. Being up to date and "with it" helps teachers ensure that the students will receive high-quality, current, and correct information.

Your Conduct in the Classroom

As the teacher enters the classroom or gymnasium, the process of rigorous scrutiny by students begins. Many factors related to the teacher's actual conduct of the class play an important role in the teacher's success. Students often regard as excellent teachers those who use up-to-date teaching methods, clearly state their objectives, and strive for clarity and personalized instruction. The following are things effective teachers do in the classroom or gymnasium:

- **Maximize participation.** Effective teachers are able to maximize participation on the part of all students. They devise strategies for eliminating long lines and avoiding the need for students to sit, wait, and watch while others perform. This helps students get the most time-on-task and learning enjoyment possible. An effective teacher minimizes management time (15% or less) and maximizes participation time (80% or more).

- **Teach by objectives.** They have clearly stated objectives for each lesson that are reflected in the activities selected, teaching styles used, and behavioral outcomes sought. This helps students know what is expected of them and relates the content of the lesson to these expectations. (Please refer to chapter 11 for more on writing learning objectives.)

- **Arrive promptly.** Effective teachers are early or on time for classes. This illustrates enthusiasm and interest in and respect for the students. It also permits time for questions, comments, or informal conversation.

- **Prepare.** They carefully plan each class period so that all of the time allotted is used wisely. This makes students feel that their time in class is well spent and the content important. Effective teachers do not drag out a class period simply to fill in the time.

- **Use resources.** They take advantage of a variety of outside resources, when applicable, to enhance learning and vary the normal class routine. This broadens the students' scope of knowledge and enhances interest in the class.

- **Review and preview.** They provide a brief verbal or visual review of the previous lesson and a preview of the material to be covered during the current class period. This enables students to link previous information with new information and to follow the day's lesson more closely. A simple means of presenting review/preview information is to use a chalkboard where the focus (objectives) of the previous lesson is listed along with the objectives of the current one. Using colored chalk, trivia questions, and cartoon characters promotes attention to and interest in the chalkboard display.

- **Check for understanding.** They do not assume that students automatically understand what they have been instructed to do. Effective teachers constantly check for understanding by asking strategic questions. For example, prior to having a skill drill, the effective teacher asks specific questions about key aspects of the drill in order to ensure that all are clear on the procedure.

- **Stress practicality.** Effective teachers recognize the necessity for practical application of ideas and concepts to everyday life. They illustrate the relevancy of the material for students and enable students to accurately and personally apply the information.

- **Think realistically.** They are consistent and realistic in their expectations of students. This provides students with clearly stated boundaries of acceptable behavior and standards of performance. Furthermore, effective teachers are realistic about what can be learned in the amount of time available. They prefer to have students learn fewer things well than to learn many things at only a mediocre level.

- **Remain open.** They are open to student questions and comments and create a forum for the exchange of ideas. This encourages thinking and synthesizing of knowledge on the part of students.

- **Speak clearly.** They clearly state the objectives of the lesson in language that students understand. They do not overload students with verbiage. This helps students focus on what is important.

- **Stay in control.** Effective teachers are objective, consistent, and constructive in applying disciplinary measures. They recognize the individuality of each student, which assures students that they will be dealt with fairly.

Your Assessment Process

All teachers face the responsibility of assessing students' progress toward meeting lesson objectives. Teacher, peer, and self-assessment are the three main types of assessment used in physical education. Assessment tools designed for use by students must be "user friendly" and developmentally appropriate. (Please refer to chapter 12 for a complete discussion on assessing progress.) In relation to performing assessment, effectiveness means doing the following:

- **Assess by objectives.** Take the time to develop objectives for your students and for yourself. Because students need to know what is expected of them and how they will be evaluated, teachers must identify what goals they want their students to reach and must specify how they are going to help students achieve those goals.

- **Use valid instruments.** Employ valid measures to assess students' mastery of the subject matter. Each assessment should be based on a testing situation relevant to that particular subject matter.

- **Vary techniques.** Do not assess students by totally objective or totally subjective means. Teachers should employ both objectivity and subjectivity in testing situations to make the evaluation more meaningful.

- **Respond in a timely manner.** Provide meaningful feedback to students as quickly as possible. Use assessment of knowledge and of performance as a consistent and positive form of feedback. This helps students focus on their strengths and upgrade their weaknesses. Teachers need to correct assignments and tests and return them as soon as possible, with meaningful comments to indicate to students their strong and weak points.

- **Show understanding.** Understand that people perceive things differently. A teacher who exhibits this understanding is letting students know that he is interested enough in them to listen to their interpretations of questions and the reasons for their answers.

- **Stay informed.** Recognize that external factors may affect student performance. Teachers should take the time to learn about their students as individuals and to find out what they are involved in outside of school as well as during the school day.

- **Treat students fairly.** Steadfastly refuse to let personal prejudice, bias, or preference interfere with fair and honest assessment. This assures students that they will be evaluated on what they know or can do, not on artificial criteria such as hair length, style of dress, or likeability.

YOUR VERBAL COMMUNICATION SKILLS

CONCEPT 8.4

Communication skills must be mastered for effective teaching.

Verbal communication is a crucially important tool for teachers, for both explanations and presentations of movement challenges. No matter what teaching styles and techniques you use in a lesson, it is essential that you be able to get and maintain the students' attention and provide clarity in your instruction.

Getting Attention

Getting the attention of a group of children requires a variety of communication skills. First, it is important to stand where you can be seen by all of the class. Standing at the edge of a circle formation or far enough back from a straight-line formation ensures that all students can see. It is much easier to get the attention of the group if you can see and make eye contact with every child. One easy way to ensure that you can maintain eye contact is to have the students seated when you talk to them as a group. In this way, you can more easily see children at the back of the group, and students in the front will not block your line of sight.

The teacher in this lesson familiarizes students with the task cards that will be used during their physical education class. Each student will be given a task card, and the teacher will read through it, provide any necessary demonstrations, and then check for students' understanding.

REALITY CHECK

"Listen Up"

Real-World Situation

It's a beautiful day and you have decided to take your class of 30 students outside for their lesson. The skill theme is throwing and catching. You have sufficient equipment for one ball for every two children and have decided to use a peer teaching technique in which one student is the performer and the second the peer teacher. Sounds like a plan—but oh my, how even the best of plans can go so wrong.

As soon as the class exits the school building they scatter in all directions. When you try to gather them for instruction you soon realize that because of competing noises, many children can't hear you. Furthermore, because of the many new stimuli in the outdoor teaching environment, you are quick to notice that it is difficult to get and maintain attention. With all that is going on, you're not certain your students understand what they are to do in implementing peer teaching.

At the end of the skill theme you're not sure they have retained anything from lesson to lesson.

Critical Questions

Based on the situation as presented and what you know about communication skills as a requirement for effective teaching:

- What can you do to minimize scattering of students to all points of the school yard upon exiting the building?
- How can you get your students' attention and ensure that they can hear you?
- What will you do to help keep their attention?
- How can you check for understanding?
- How can you check for retention?
- What else can you do to maximize your communication skills under the conditions as presented?

The easiest way to get children's attention is to use a predetermined signal. You should use the selected cue consistently and only as a signal for the class to stop all activity, face toward you, and listen carefully for the next instructions. Traditionally, physical education teachers have used a whistle for getting attention. This is the most effective way to get attention outdoors or when the class is spread out over a large area. However, using a whistle is not always practical, particularly when you are indoors with classrooms located nearby. Instead, some teachers use a drum or tambourine. Others merely clap their hands or silently raise a hand overhead. Still others use a verbal command such as "Freeze." Whatever technique you select, the key is consistency. Be consistent in using cues and consistent in your expectation that all students are to cease what they are doing and focus their attention on you.

Maintaining Attention

Once you have succeeded in getting the attention of the group, it is important to be able to maintain it with a minimum of distractions. Children, like adults, need to be talked "to," not "at." Therefore, it is important not to be condescending. A monosyllabic, "singsong" way of speaking seems not only condescending to most children but also offensive. You can talk to children effectively without resorting to this type of verbal behavior. You may have to modify your vocabulary to suit the level of understanding of the children you are dealing with, but remember, they are not babies and should not be treated as such.

The way you project your voice is important when you are trying to maintain children's attention in a physical education setting. Because gymnasiums are large spaces, often with poor acoustics, and because playgrounds are open, it is necessary to project your voice so that all can hear. In no case, however, should you attempt to shout over the din of noise that is characteristic of groups of children. If you are unable to project your voice so that everyone can hear you clearly, then use your attention-getting command along with a second cue to gather the group to you.

Vocal intonation is also an issue. If you're like most people, you've had teachers who lulled students to sleep with a constant drone. Maintaining a steady pitch in your speech is important, but altering it with inflections where appropriate creates a more interesting speech pattern and makes you easier to listen to. Avoid a speech pattern that trails off to a whisper. This is very distracting to children and makes it difficult for them to maintain their attention.

Providing Clarity

Another important element of effective verbal communication is **verbal clarity.** As teachers, we are usually keenly interested in our subject matter and enthusiastic about conveying our interest to others. Therefore, we may frequently tend to oververbalize and to provide too much information. Keep verbal instruction to a minimum. Try to be concise in explanations, taking into account the maturity and skill level of the students. Rather than long instructions, it is often more effective to give only a short explanation on the basic elements of the skill or game, then have children become immediately involved in the activity. In this way, you can easily observe their level of understanding and ability and can adjust subsequent explanations to fit individual needs.

When you speak, use good grammar and pronounce words correctly. Classroom teachers are constantly concerned with children's grammar; therefore, it is important for the physical education teacher to set a good example for appropriate use of the English language. Improper use of tenses and terms, and failure to pronounce the "ing" at the end of words such as "going," "doing," "something," and "nothing," are unacceptable. Avoid using slang and colloquialisms. It is unnecessary to demonstrate that you are "one of the group." Avoid distracting verbal hitches such as "okay," "listen up," and "uh," as well as overuse of favorite words or phrases. Listeners soon focus on these habits of speech and tend to concentrate on them rather than on the message itself.

To foster clarity, try to summarize using key words or phrases. This helps children understand the information and provides a brief review of the key points of your presentation. It works well to use key phrases to reinforce instructions or to organize students quickly. For example, you may summarize three important classroom management concepts with the words "be quick, quiet, and courteous" rather than rambling on about the virtues of each behavior. Providing frequent opportunities for questions about specific aspects of your verbal instruction is also important. When you explain an activity, stop from time to time to ask if students have specific questions about that portion of the explanation. At all costs, avoid giving a complete, detailed explanation of an activity or task and then asking, "Are there any questions?" This typically results in a rush of questions that could have been dealt with more easily during the explanation. Furthermore, when children have a question but have to wait until the end for an answer, they tend to shut down all other thought processes and concentrate only on their question. Consequently, much of your explanation is not absorbed, and you are often forced to repeat yourself a second or even a third time. You can easily avoid much of this by giving students frequent opportunities to ask questions about specifics as you go along.

Demonstrations

Providing a visual model of a motor skill or sequence of skills is also a part of the communication process. Rink (1996) summarizes three main points about effective demonstrations, or modeling:

1. Models should be accurate and of the same gender as the learner (whenever possible, use both girls and boys to demonstrate).
2. If the task needs to be broken down, it should be demonstrated in sequence.
3. Complex tasks need to be seen more than one time by a learner; and whereas the expert model (i.e., proficient student or the teacher) produces "learning by imitation," the "learner" model (i.e., a student demonstrator) is more likely to promote more cognitive processing of the skill by the learner (pp. 184-185).

Verbal cues or words and phrases that describe the critical features of a skill also help the learner sort out and attend to what is relevant. For example, the term "round" might refer to keeping the chin tucked and knees bent and close to the chest during a forward roll. "Give in" might refer to bending the knees upon landing from a jump.

Research on how to present motor tasks has suggested that the use of full demonstration, summary cues, and student verbal rehearsal enables students to achieve higher product results (i.e., how fast, how far, how high), achieve higher process scores (i.e., correct form in relation to how the skill is actually executed), and better verbalize how to perform skills (Kwak, 1993).

Checking for Understanding and Retention

It is essential that you check to be sure that children understand what is expected of them, have internalized the concepts you are trying to convey, or can perform the skills being taught. **Checking for understanding** involves asking recall-type questions or asking for brief demonstrations of the material taught. Questioning and demonstrations of competency not only hold students accountable for their learning but also provide you with both a sequential and an ongoing evaluation of the effectiveness of your teaching. Check for understanding throughout the lesson and especially during the lesson summary (Rauchenbach, 1994). For example, before having students do a skill drill, it is appropriate to ask specific questions about key aspects of the drill in order to ensure that everyone is clear on the procedure. Asking questions about key elements of the lesson during the lesson summary is another effective means of checking for understanding.

You will also find it helpful to check for retention from the previous lesson. **Checking for retention** involves asking questions about the previous lesson and asking for student demonstrations of previously taught content. You can do this effectively during the review portion of the previous lesson prior to the introduction of new information in the current lesson. Checking for understanding promotes children's **set-to-learn,** which involves the students' preparation for, and expectation of, learning to occur. Children frequently associate the open space and informal setting of the gymnasium and playground with free play, recess, and reckless abandon, and not with the learning that goes on in the classroom. The gymnasium and playground are

1. Clarify goals and main points
   a. State goals and objectives of the presentation.
   b. Focus on one thought, point, or direction at a time.
   c. Avoid digression.
   d. Avoid ambiguous phrases and pronouns.
2. Step-by-step presentation
   a. Present the material in small steps.
   b. Organize and present the material so that one point is mastered before the next point is given.
   c. Give explicit step-by-step direction (when possible).
   d. Present an outline when the material is complex.
3. Specific and concrete procedures
   a. Model the skill or process (when appropriate).
   b. Give detailed and redundant information for difficult points.
   c. Provide students with concrete and varied examples.
4. Check the students' understanding
   a. Be sure that the students understand one point before proceeding to the next point.
   b. Ask the students questions to monitor their comprehension of what has been presented.
   c. Have students summarize the main points in their own words.
   d. Reteach the parts of the presentation that the students have difficulty comprehending, either by further teacher explanation or by students tutoring other students.

FIGURE 8.2   Rosenshine and Stevens' aspects of clear presentations.

From B. Rosenshine and R. Stevens, "Teaching Functions." In *Handbook of Research on Teaching,* 3rd ed., edited by M.C. Wittrock. Copyright, 1986, by the American Educational Research Association. Reprinted with permission of the publisher.

classrooms too. They are learning laboratories, and children soon understand this when you hold them accountable for learning. (See figure 8.2 for more about clear presentations [Rosenshine & Stevens, 1986].)

Providing Feedback

Sometimes known as **knowledge of results (KR)** and **knowledge of performance (KP)**, feedback is necessary for effective and efficient learning. Teachers and coaches frequently rate their effectiveness and that of others on their ability to provide the learner with meaningful information during an activity (KP) and after its completion (KR). Although several factors influence the efficiency of learning a movement skill, the type, quality, duration, and frequency of feedback are among the most critical.

TEACHING TIP 8.2

Feedback is one of the most critical elements in effective communication. Consequently it is important to follow these guidelines:

- Identify the type of skill being learned and the level of movement skill learning.
- Determine the cause of the learner's errors.
- Use feedback during and immediately following performance.
- Tell the learner the cause of the error (be concise).
- Tell the learner how to correct the error (be precise).
- Check to see that the learner understands the information given.
- Focus on correcting one error at a time.
- Use positive feedback techniques that encourage the performer.
- Correct errors by beginning with a positive statement, then giving an instructional hint, and finishing with a compliment (the "sandwich approach").
- Be certain to reward approximations with sincere praise and encouragement.

- Use feedback frequently to minimize practice errors, but don't overload the learner with too much information at one time.
- Encourage the performer to improve by continuing to practice outside of class.
- Be certain that your praise is genuine and freely given and that it rewards individual progress and improvement.
- Provide ample opportunities for knowledge of results.
- Encourage personal skill analysis during the beginning and intermediate levels of learning the skill so that the learner can use internal feedback.
- Discourage verbal skill analysis during the advanced level of learning the skill.
- Recognize the individuality of each learner and vary the types and degrees of feedback accordingly.

Basically, **feedback** is the information that the performer receives as the result of some form of response. This information may be provided through internal or external sources, may occur during performance (concurrent feedback) or after performance (terminal feedback), or involve knowledge of performance or knowledge of results.

Internal feedback, sometimes called intrinsic feedback, is obtained by the learner as a result of the task itself. In performing a movement task, internal feedback is received in the form of visual, tactile, and kinesthetic cues. For example, in preparing

CONCEPT 8.5

Providing the learner with meaningful feedback is at the very heart of effective teaching.

to do a forward roll, the learner receives internal feedback concerning hand and foot placement and body position throughout the roll. Learners who are at the beginning/novice level of learning a new movement skill are generally ineffective in their use of internal feedback. Those at the intermediate/practice or advanced/fine-tuning levels benefit much more.

External feedback, or augmented feedback as it is often called, takes the form of verbal cues from an instructor or from the use of some mechanical device. The internal feedback that occurs while the person is doing the forward roll may be augmented by external feedback through teacher comments about positioning and body alignment. A videotaped replay of the forward roll could provide additional external feedback.

Feedback that is supplied during the performance of a task is called **concurrent feedback.** Athletes who say that they are in a "zone" or have the "feel" of an activity are using internal cues about their body while performing the task. Feedback provided by the instructor during the activity may focus on the process. For example, a teacher might caution our forward roller to push off with the hands and stay tucked as the performer prepares to roll forward.

Feedback that is provided after performance of a task is called **terminal feedback.** Terminal feedback focuses on the product of one's actions. What occurs as a normal result of the performer's actions is called internal terminal feedback. For example, the forward roller remains tucked and achieves almost enough momentum to complete the roll back to a squat position. The tumbler than evaluates the margin of error and corrects for it. Instructors can augment terminal feedback through comments to the performer or by using videotaped replays.

Manual assistance is given by this teacher, providing an intermediate-level learner with kinesthetic feedback.

Basically, feedback gives learners information about the correctness of their actions. It serves three major functions. First, it provides the performer with terminal information (knowledge of results) or concurrent information (knowledge of performance) that leads to error correction and the desired response. Second, it reinforces the performer in ways that may be either positive (encouragement) or negative (criticism). Positive reinforcement tends to preserve, augment, or enhance the

TEACHING TIP 8.3

Sequential steps for *changing a well-learned skill* that is incorrectly performed:

- Determine whether there is sufficient time to make the change (think in terms of weeks and months, not hours or days).
- Determine whether the learner really wants to make the change.
- Be certain that the learner understands why the change is being made.

- Be certain that the learner realizes that performance will probably regress before it improves.
- Provide a supportive, encouraging environment.
- Structure practice sessions that will gradually bring the learner from the beginning to the intermediate level and finally back to the advanced level of learning the skill.

desired behavior. Negative reinforcement tends to decrease or inhibit the behavior. Corrective feedback should, whenever possible, be positive. Third, feedback motivates the learner. Although it is not completely understood how feedback influences motivation, it is known that feedback of some sort is necessary to heighten the motivational level of the performer. Teacher feedback is also used in large-group instruction to motivate and keep practice focused.

Changing Well-Learned Techniques

Teachers frequently have children come to them with a well-learned but incorrect technique of performing a fundamental or sport skill. The child may be experiencing some success with the technique, but proper execution would be more efficient and would lead to even greater success. The teacher needs to decide whether to make an **error correction** in the form of changing the individual's habitual performance peculiarities or to leave the performer alone. It is often difficult and time-consuming to change a well-learned technique. Any new learning requires returning a learned behavior to a conscious cognitive level (i.e., bringing it back to the beginning skill level). Under stress and under conditions in which decisions have to be rapid, the performer is likely to revert to the first or most well-learned response. Only after considerable practice can the performer consistently replace the incorrect response with the correct action. Both you (the teacher) and the learner (your student) need to mutually agree that there is ample time and desire to change a well-learned but incorrectly performed movement pattern.

CONCEPT 8.6

Changing a well-learned but incorrectly performed technique is a process that requires time, effort, and communication between student and teacher.

YOUR NONVERBAL COMMUNICATION SKILLS

Nonverbal communication, or body language, is the projection of messages through subtle and often unconscious changes in our posture, gestures, and facial expressions. It has been estimated that our verbal vocabulary ranges from about 28,000 to 40,000 words—but our nonverbal "vocabulary" is endless. It is important to be aware of the subtleties in our nonverbal communication and to recognize the messages that we are transmitting. In fact, we are often more apt to convey these messages in their true form through body expression than through verbal expression. It is important, then, for your body language to convey to children that they matter and are valued and that you are pleased to be with them. The following discussion focuses

CONCEPT 8.7

Teachers' nonverbal messages are frequently as meaningful and powerful as their verbal messages.

on the use of various postures, gestures, and facial expressions and the messages that they tend to convey.

Postures

The **postures** that you take when standing before a class convey a variety of nonspoken messages. If you stand erect with your weight evenly distributed on your feet, you tend to convey confidence and assuredness. Standing with the body weight on one foot portrays an image of being relaxed, easygoing, and at ease. On the other hand, shifting your body weight from foot to foot is often an indication of uneasiness, nervousness, or boredom. Placing your hands in your pockets may also convey a lack of interest or attention on the part of a teacher.

The use of your arms also conveys messages to students. For example, the arms folded tightly across the chest may convey a variety of messages. If you assume this position with an erect body posture and with the weight distributed evenly over your feet, the message is one of determination and steadfastness. On the other hand, if your arms are folded and the body weight shifts from foot to foot, you tend to convey a need for comfort, security, and assurance. Placing the hands on the hips or keeping them clasped behind the back are postures frequently assumed by teachers who convey authority or being in control.

Think for a moment of some of your habitual postures, or take time to observe the body postures of one or more of your instructors. What messages are your instructors giving you? For example, what message is being conveyed to you by your instructor standing on one or both feet, or by leaning up against the wall or sitting on the desk? What messages are you picking up from placement of the hands on the hips or behind the back? It is important to note, though, that a person's postures do not necessarily provide accurate nonverbal messages. The point is that they do send a message; and it is this message, accurate or not, to which students react.

Gestures

Most of us use a variety of gestures in our daily communication with others. **Gestures** are movements of the body, head, arms, hands, or face that express an idea, opinion, or emotion. Teachers are often masters of the use of gestures that communicate meaning in very specific terms. In fact, it is often joked that many elementary school teachers would be unable to talk if their hands were tied to their sides. They often use gestures consciously to supplement the spoken word. For example, when saying "big," "small," "high," or "low," teachers commonly make corresponding gestures. For young children this is often appropriate and provides visual reinforcement of basic verbal concepts. On the other hand, older children often find the mannerism distracting and condescending when overused.

The use of pointing gestures often conveys a clear and undeniable message. Pointing the index finger forcefully at a student tends to be viewed as threatening. It singles the student out from the rest of the group and creates an uncomfortable feeling. Pointing the index finger forcefully downward conveys the message of reinforcing a point, while pointing it upward serves as a message of appeal from a higher authority. Steepling the fingers often conveys the message of "I have the advantage." Rubbing the hands together conveys a sense of expectation, and twiddling the thumbs is often viewed as a sign of boredom. Tapping the fingers or playing with paper clips, rubber bands, or similar objects conveys restlessness or nervousness. Habitual gestures such as persistent tugging on an ear, rubbing your chin, hiking up your pants, or clearing your throat not only convey a feeling of being ill at ease but also distract students from your real message.

Take a few moments to analyze the gestures that you and others characteristically use. What messages are you conveying? What messages are being conveyed to you? Do any of your gestures send the wrong message, or are any of them distracting mannerisms? If so, it's a good idea to make a conscious effort to modify or eliminate these habitual forms of nonverbal communication.

Facial Expressions

As the saying goes, a picture is worth a thousand words. Our **facial expressions** are often just that. Although we verbally say one thing, others may often interpret it as something else. This can happen because of the multitude of facial expressions that we use when communicating. Raising the eyebrows conveys a message of surprise. Squinting one eye tells others that we are suspicious. Wrinkling the brow suggests distaste. Standing with the mouth open displays awe or surprise, and thrusting the jaw forward gives a message of defiance.

People use the eyes as a potent nonverbal form of communication. Staring out the window or glancing frequently at your watch tells people you're bored. Rolling the eyes conveys exasperation or seems to say "How could you be so stupid?" An eye roll followed by mutual glances with another person sends the same message and invites others to share in your nonverbal criticism of an offender. The tendency to focus on and talk to one segment of the class conveys to the others that they don't really count.

These are only a few of the facial expressions that people use. Each of us has an almost limitless number of expressions that we use every day. It is important to remember and fully understand the messages that you are giving to others in this way. Often what people "hear" us say is completely different from what we are saying with words because the words do not match the facial expressions, gestures, and postures. Our actions truly do speak louder than our words.

CONVEYING YOUR ENTHUSIASM

CONCEPT 8.8

Demonstrating real interest in their subject matter and their students is an important quality of effective teachers.

One of the most important but frequently overlooked aspects of successful interaction with children is the ability to convey enthusiasm for the subject matter and for the children themselves. Your verbal and nonverbal communication skills may be above reproach, but if you show little genuine enthusiasm in your teaching, you will have little success. Children are remarkably perceptive in their assessment of teachers. If they sense that you have little interest in them or in your subject matter, they will be quick to "turn you off." Let's look briefly at what you can actively do to convey your enthusiasm.

Interest in Your Subject Matter

Children are quick to pick up on your interest or lack of interest in various aspects of the curriculum. If they see that you are hesitant to get involved in certain activities, this will negatively affect their attitude. Trouble will manifest first in a series of groans and moans. It may advance to outright refusal to take part and other forms of belligerent behavior. On the other hand, a display of active, eager involvement by the teacher conveys an attitude of acceptance and eagerness to participate.

Well-planned and executed lessons that move along quickly with a minimum of disruption also communicate a sense of enthusiasm. Children do not look for constant effervescent behavior on the part of teachers as a measure of enthusiasm. On the contrary, you may have a quiet and reserved manner and still be viewed by children as enthusiastic. The display of a genuine interest in students' learning and your creation of an environment that maximizes their potential for improvement are more important to children than a surface show of energy.

Interest in Your Students

Successful teachers can express their interest in their students in numerous ways. One basic way is to learn their names. This is often difficult, especially for the physical education teacher, who sees several different classes a day. The tendency is to learn only the names of those students who stand out in some way. Then you know by name only the students who have persistent behavioral problems or are exceptionally good or poor in physical activities. Unfortunately, the majority of children may often go nameless. One way to learn names is to use group cards, with a Polaroid picture of the members of each group. Another is to have the children wear name tags (although this may interfere with certain activities) that they make and decorate themselves during art class. Still another technique is to try to associate the child's name with some outstanding trait, characteristic, or ability. Once you have learned names, try to avoid using only the child's last name. Using the child's given name is much more personal and conveys a message of warmth and interest in the child as a person. Having class photos displayed on a physical education bulletin board also brings attention to children and may contribute to their feelings of positive self-worth.

Children judge a teacher to be interested in them if the teacher shows a genuine interest in their learning and sets high but realistic goals for achievement. Teachers show their interest in children by recognizing and respecting the individuality of the learner.

Successful teachers convey their interest in children by establishing acceptable standards for behavior and adhering to these standards consistently. Displaying genuine interest in children and enthusiasm for teaching them is difficult if you are constantly reprimanding, scolding, and disciplining. Whether your boundaries are narrow or broad is not as crucial as your consistent adherence to whatever boundaries you have established and the impartial manner in which you deal with unacceptable behavior.

CONCEPT 8.9

Teachers can improve their communication skills with practice, and should view development of these skills as a continuing process.

IMPROVING YOUR COMMUNICATION SKILLS

Understanding the various messages conveyed through physical distance, observing children in different settings, and self-study can do much to improve your ability to communicate with children.

Respect Physical Distance

Distance messages are the messages you give to children and adults based on the physical distance between you and them. How close you stand to those you are talking to has a marked effect on what they hear, attend to, and retain. The closer you

TEACHING TIP 8.4

PHYSICAL DISTANCES AND THEIR NONVERBAL MESSAGES

Feet	Distance	Nonverbal message
1 to 3	Intimate	"You are too close and threatening." (This is a personal space reserved for special people and occasions.)
4 to 6	Near friendly	"I feel more comfortable."
7 to 10	Far friendly	"We can still communicate but on less friendly terms."
11 to 15	Formal	"I can move into or out of immediate contact with the situation at will."
16 to 20	Remote	"I am removed from the situation and out of contact."

are to the learner, the greater the attention the learner will give you, up to a point. The greater the distance between you and the learner, the less able you are to attend to each other.

In general, distances from 4 to 10 feet are the most appropriate for effective teaching and learning. Distances of 1 to 3 feet tend to be too close and to invade one's "personal space." Use of this space is generally reserved for special people or special occasions. Invasion of personal space tends to make people feel ill at ease. Distances greater than 10 feet tend to make the learner feel less involved in the learning situation. A distance between teacher and student of about 4 to 15 feet is generally considered to be a formal distance, allowing the individual to psychologically move into or out of the learning environment at will. Distances over 15 feet are considered remote distances. In education, teachers use physical distance as an effective teaching technique, constantly varying their distance from the students to achieve the desired effect.

Observe Children

Another way to improve communication skills with children is through naturalistic observation. **Naturalistic observation** refers to observation in an unobtrusive manner in a variety of settings. Successful physical education teachers frequently visit the classroom or spend time observing children during recess or at after-school activities. Occasional visits to the classroom serve two important functions. First, they enable you to observe children's behavior and interaction patterns with the classroom teacher, with whom they spend the bulk of the school day. This can provide you with valuable information about the child's behavior as well as specific techniques of class management and control. Second, your visit communicates to children that you are interested in them and in what they do when they are not with you.

If you sit in on and take part in the activities of a reading circle or a science lesson, you'll find not only that the experience is enlightening but also that it helps establish positive communication between you and the children, as well as between you and the classroom teacher. Observing and interacting with children in a variety of settings is a positive step in improving your communication skills. It takes extra time but is well worth the effort.

LISTENING TO CHILDREN

CONCEPT 8.10

Taking the time to know children through active listening to their verbal and nonverbal messages is essential to effective teaching.

An important aspect of effective communication that is sometimes overlooked is actively listening to children. **Active listening** means simply taking the time to stop what you are doing, face directly toward the speaker, make direct eye contact, and give both nonverbal and verbal feedback indicating that you are paying attention. All teachers need to cultivate active listening skills. Teachers often are so busy with what they have to say and how they are saying it that they forget that the children are also giving messages to them. These messages take many forms, verbal and nonverbal. The way we pick up on and respond to these explicit and implicit messages plays a significant role in our success in effective, two-way communication with children.

REALITY CHECK

Your Body Language Tells Me So Much

Real-World Situation

Students quickly learn to read teachers' nonverbal messages of interest, boredom, surprise, disapproval, and so forth through our many postures and gestures, but what about our reading of their nonverbal messages? Experienced teachers are constantly reading the nonverbal messages that students are either intentionally or nonintentionally communicating. Teachers take in this information and make on-the-spot adjustments to their lessons.

Critical Questions

Based on what you know about nonverbal communica-

tion and your experiences with communicating nonverbally:

- How do students nonverbally communicate boredom, disinterest, ridicule, and disrespect?
- What other messages are communicated with various postures and gestures?
- Based on specific student postures and/or gestures, what might be their nonverbal messages, and what, if anything, will you do to counteract messages of inattention, boredom, confusion, anger, or surprise?
- Why is "reading" one's nonverbal communication so important?

Children's Verbal Messages

Listen carefully to what children are saying to you and how they say it. Try to be alert to the meaning behind their words and the message they are giving you with their speech patterns. Children who speak loudly or tend to mumble may be giving you a message that they have a hearing problem. Boisterous children often speak aggressively, whereas timid children tend to speak with a barely audible voice. Confident children tend to give complete answers or explanations to inquiries and are not hesitant to acknowledge their failure to understand or comprehend. On the other hand, timid children are often slow to speak up if they do not understand or have questions. Furthermore, when forced to respond verbally, they tend to offer shorter replies or explanations and to speak more softly. Children who chatter almost constantly and need to be reminded to be silent are often displaying a need for acceptance or approval. The speech patterns of children can provide meaningful messages and help you to adjust your responses accordingly.

Children's Nonverbal Messages

Alert teachers "listen" to children's nonverbal messages as well as the verbal ones. Often, their nonverbal messages provide clear insights into their many moods. For example, the child who is fidgeting communicates a message of "Let's get moving." Children who do not sit up in an attentive posture are indicating that they are not interested in the lesson. Persistent head nodding is often used as approval-seeking behavior.

TEXT BOX 8.4

Children convey nonverbal messages in numerous and unique ways. Remember, these messages may be indicators of things as they actually are, or they may express what the child wants you to think things are. In either case, it is important that you "listen" to these messages and respond to them accordingly.

How children raise their hands in response to a question is also revealing. Hesitant hand raising tends to communicate, "I think I know the answer, but I'm not quite sure." Wild hand waving says, "Teacher, teacher, call on me!" Holding the hand high above the head conveys assurance and confidence about knowing the answer. Holding a raised hand in a propped-up position conveys a message of "Please take pity on me and let me answer your question."

Being sensitive to how children use their eyes and the messages they are trying to communicate is important. Avoiding eye contact is a way of saying "I'm not here; don't call on me." Staring out the window or off into space is often a sign of boredom. Rolling the eyes undeniably conveys the message of "Teacher, how could you be so dumb?" Doing a double take after making an error or a mistake in a game or sport activity (such as dropping a ball) serves as a common means of telling people, "It wasn't really my fault; some outside force caused me to do it."

Children send nonverbal messages in numerous and unique ways. Remember, these messages may be actual indicators of things as they are, or they may be what the child wants you to think they are. In either case, it is important that you "listen" to these messages and respond to them accordingly.

Knowing the Learner

It is vitally important that you as the teacher know your students and recognize that each comes to you with a different set of motor, cognitive, and affective characteristics. You are confronted with a huge number of individual differences, and you need to consider as many of them as possible when planning the lesson. Some individual differences are easy to detect; others are not and may remain hidden. But it will surely be to your advantage to recognize and adjust to as many factors as possible.

TEACHING TIP 8.5

Successful teachers recognize the following facts about *individual differences:*

- Children learn at different rates.
- Children's potential for performance excellence varies.
- Requisite fundamental movement skills must be mastered prior to sport skills.
- Responses to instructional approaches vary among individuals.
- Responses to winning and losing vary among individuals.
- Responses to encouragement, criticism, reward, and punishment vary among individuals.
- The background of related experiences varies from child to child.

- Differences in home-life experiences influence children differently.
- Attention span and ability to concentrate vary greatly among individuals.
- The developmental level of children varies, resulting in dissimilar potentials for learning and performance.
- Children display greater or lesser degrees of movement skill depending on a combination of environmental and hereditary factors.
- The ability to analyze, conceptualize, and problem-solve—all important in movement skill learning and sport participation—varies among individuals.

Summary

Although the teacher's roles are many and varied, teaching itself—effective teaching—is the one that counts the most. It can be said that there is really no teaching if learning does not occur. If physical education teachers are to be viewed seriously as important contributors to the school curriculum, they must take their responsibility to be an effective teacher seriously. In striving to become effective teachers, people typically go through a series of predictable stages in which concern for personal success evolves into concern for self and finally into deep concern for the learning and welfare of students.

Characteristics of effective teachers include personal traits—for example, teachers must be enthusiastic and knowledgeable. Effective teachers tend to display certain key characteristics and behaviors in the classroom and in assessing students. For example, in the classroom it is essential for teachers to be prepared, to be realistic, and to stay in control; and in making assessments teachers must use valid testing measures and must be fair. Developing the skills of the master teacher takes time and considerable practice but is within your grasp if you are genuine in your commitment to effective teaching and have a real interest in children.

Techniques for effective verbal and nonverbal communication are basic requirements for good teaching. Verbal communication skills are important in getting and maintaining attention, providing clarity and feedback, and helping children relearn incorrectly performed skills. Effective nonverbal communication is a subtle, but critically important, means of providing children with messages about their performance.

Conveying enthusiasm and communicating effectively are both essential aspects of good teaching and are important to students in many ways. By demonstrating genuine interest in your subject matter and in your students' learning, you can convey the important message of enthusiasm. Teachers can improve skills in communicating with children through a variety of techniques, ranging from observation of children and self-study to respecting physical distance and actively listening to what children have to say. The verbal and nonverbal messages that children give are also important clues to knowing the learner. Take time to observe and listen to children. Their messages are generally quite clear and unmistakable.

Terms to Remember

Excellent Readings

Ayers, W. (1993). *To teach: The journey of a teacher.* New York: Teachers College Press.

Gage, N.L. (1978, November). The yield of research on teaching. *Phi Delta Kappan,* 230-235.

Magill, R.A. (2001). *Motor learning: Concepts and applications.* Boston: McGraw-Hill.

Mandigo, J.L., & Holt, N.T. (2000). Putting theory into practice: How cognitive evaluation theory can help us motivate children in physical activity environments. *JOPERD, 71* (1), 44-49.

Rink, J. (1993). *Teaching physical education for learning.* St. Louis: Mosby Year Book.

Rolan, C.B., & Neitzschman, L. (1996). Groups in schools: A model for training middle school teachers. *Journal for Specialists in Group Work, 21,* 18-25.

Stevens-Smith, D.A. (2000). Help! It's my first year of teaching, and I don't know where to start! *JOPERD, 71* (4), 50-54.

9

Facilitating Learning: Positive Discipline and Classroom Management

Key Concept

▶ Positive discipline is a learning process effectively guided by competent teachers, culminating in the establishment of student self-control.

Chapter Objectives

This chapter will provide you with the tools to do the following:

- ▶ Discuss the concept of discipline from a variety of perspectives.

- ▶ Define and identify *classroom management strategies*.

- ▶ Formulate strategies to promote positive discipline.

- ▶ Describe the importance of consistency in helping children develop self-control.

- ▶ Discuss alternative discipline models.

- ▶ Distinguish between an aggressive and an assertive authority style.

- ▶ List several techniques for being an effective role model for children.

- ▶ Discuss the importance of self-assessment in determining personal strengths and weaknesses and in gaining and maintaining class control.

As new teachers enter the gymnasium, their concerns often include personal survival, lesson design, effective management of equipment, achieving high time-on-task, organizing students efficiently, motivating students to participate, and helping students demonstrate responsible, caring behaviors. Although this may seem like an overwhelming set of tasks, teachers can accomplish them when they establish effective and developmentally appropriate discipline and class management strategies. Discipline and class management are two important aspects of creating a positive learning environment in physical education. These are the central topics of this chapter.

DISCIPLINE DEFINED

**CONCEPT
9.1**

People interpret the goals of discipline in a variety of ways, resulting in considerable variation in the techniques used and outcomes achieved.

Some teachers define discipline as the way a teacher responds to students' misbehavior. To some, the term discipline refers to the level of teacher control existing in one's classroom—"I have effective discipline." To others it signifies a form of punishment—"I had to discipline them." Teachers may also think of discipline as a form of self-control—"She certainly is disciplined." The fact is, discipline can mean all of these things! We define **discipline** as a way of enabling students to use their time effectively to meet learning objectives without inhibiting others from attempting to achieve the goals of the lesson.

Without discipline in the gymnasium or classroom, effective learning may be difficult to achieve. Therefore, one of the first responsibilities of the teacher is creating and fostering an atmosphere of positive discipline.

TEXT BOX 9.1

"The purpose of discipline in the classroom is to reduce the need for teacher intervention over time by encouraging students to develop self-control over their own behavior. When teachers understand and apply appropriate models of discipline, the hope is that students will internalize the need for self-discipline not only in the classroom but beyond its walls. The lessons learned will have long-range consequences for students, and ultimately for the world in which we all must live" (Charles, 1992, p. vii).

Teachers who use **positive discipline** are generally viewed as confident, competent adults who are in charge of their classrooms or gymnasiums and who are leaders and role models for children. They can and are willing to assume authority in molding and shaping children's behavior. Teachers with positive discipline do not have to nag or intimidate children to make them behave. On the contrary, teachers who can discipline effectively typically take a series of positive steps to set the boundaries for acceptable behavior and gain the respect and trust of their students.

**CONCEPT
9.2**

One of the most critical elements of effective teaching is the ability to help children move toward a consistent state of positive self-control.

Positive discipline does not depend solely on externally imposed standards for behavior. Positive discipline requires self-control and assumption of responsibility for one's actions on the part of students. Positive discipline does not require that every student be in rigid lines or formations, responding on command. Such a setting does little to promote self-control or ensure long-lasting positive behavior. Overuse of rigidity and structure, when not essential to the lesson, tends to stifle learning and provides little opportunity for children to become self-disciplined. For maximum learning to take place, children must be actively involved in the learning process, and the teacher must serve as a helpful guide and a motivator of desirable responses. In the gymnasium and on the playground, learning is often a noisy process with plenty of activity and with children engaged in a variety of related but often different tasks.

Discipline has not failed if children overtly express enthusiasm or excitement in exploring the movement potential of their bodies. It has not failed if the gymnasium is humming with task-related conversation or when eight eager youngsters simultaneously burst out with an idea, suggestion, or solution. Discipline has failed, however, if one or more disruptive children infringe on the rights of the class or of individuals within the class. It has failed if the specific objectives of the lesson cannot be effectively met because of the climate of the classroom or if one or more disruptive individuals curb the interests, initiative, or individuality of any person.

REQUIREMENTS FOR POSITIVE DISCIPLINE

CONCEPT 9.3

Positive discipline tends to be mastered by teachers who are good role models and effective communicators and who accept responsibility for thorough planning and continual self-assessment.

Teachers with positive discipline exhibit remarkable similarity in their **authority style.** Although there is not a universal formula or set of specific behaviors that will guarantee effective discipline, teachers who are successful in terms of class control tend to develop their authority style in three ways that we consider next: by being positive role models, efficient planners, and positive shapers of student self-control.

REALITY CHECK

What Goes Around Comes Around

Real-World Situation

Sometimes teachers, especially new teachers, assume that their position of authority assures that students will be respectful of them and fellow classmates. Not so: What goes around comes around. In other words, if you treat students with respect and are a good role model of positive behaviors, your students will tend to reflect many of the same behaviors. Unfortunately, we have observed teachers who show little respect for their students and in turn receive little respect from them. Sarcastic remarks such as "How stupid," "You never listen," and "You've got to be kidding" have no place in the vocabulary of teachers intent on being good role models. So too, demands such as "Get over here" and "Shut up" are without justification. Children and adults alike have a tendency to treat others simi-

larly to how they are treated. Being a positive role model in your actions and being respectful of students in your words will rub off on students.

Critical Questions

Based on your experiences and how you intend to behave as a teacher:

- As you reflect on teachers you have had throughout your educational career, what specific behaviors did they exhibit that demonstrated respect or disrespect of you and others?

- What specific verbal behaviors will you try to exhibit as a positive role model for students?

- What specific actions, other than your verbal behavior, will you try to exhibit as a positive role model for students?

Be a Positive Role Model

Communicating genuine interest in your subject matter, enthusiasm for learning, and a willingness to participate with the class do much to create a positive atmosphere. Displaying interest in your pupils as people by establishing high but reasonable expectations for them and helping them reach these goals are keys to being a positive role model.

Teachers who are effective role models display confidence and willingness to accept their role of authority, are personable and fair, and react appropriately and consistently when children misbehave. They clearly communicate the boundaries of acceptable behavior and are impartial in using their authority when these boundaries are overstepped. Teachers who set positive examples for children are doing much to provide a role model for self-discipline. Failure to establish your role model as a positive one will inhibit your effectiveness in gaining and maintaining class control.

Plan Efficiently

Teachers with good discipline are generally good planners. They take the time to plan their lessons carefully, are well organized, and make maximum effective use of their time. Thorough planning enables you to be properly prepared. Physical education teachers need to pay particular attention to this because of the size of their teaching environment, the necessity of moving groups of children from place to place, the need for frequent changes in formation, and the nature of the physical activity itself. Teachers with effective class control have taken the time to plan their lessons thoroughly in a manner that is responsive to the needs, interests, and ability levels of their students; and they are organized in their approach to learning.

TEACHING TIP 9.1

Suggestions for *efficient planning:*

- Carefully prepare each lesson.
- Overplan for each lesson.
- Develop lessons around individual and group needs.
- Take into consideration the space to be used.
- Plan to minimize formation changes.
- Establish and be consistent in the use of common class management techniques.
- Have ample equipment available, in good repair, and quickly obtainable for use.
- Plan for maximum activity and minimum inactivity.
- Create a physical environment that is pleasant and safe.
- Promote an atmosphere of learning enjoyment.

Lessons that make the best use of the allotted time are those that provide for a maximum of active involvement by all of the students. Poor lesson planning, failure to organize the class efficiently, and inactivity (brought about by lack of equipment, waiting in line, or long, detailed explanations) do little to create an atmosphere conducive to positive discipline.

Encourage Students' Self-Control

The highest form of positive discipline is **self-control.** Children are active, energetic beings in the process of developing self-discipline. The following guidelines have proven helpful to teachers attempting to instill self-control in children.

- **Be reasonable.** Don't invariably demand the desirable or prohibit the undesirable. We have often heard adults complain, "Everything I want to do is either unhealthy, illegal, or fattening." If we, who have had years to reconcile ourselves to society's restraints and curbs on our primitive drives, still have these feelings, how much more do children resent the restrictions and taboos that have been conceived by adults and that they understand only vaguely, at best?

CONCEPT
9.4

Teachers can effectively promote student self-control by consistently applying a variety of developmentally appropriate behavior-shaping techniques.

- **Follow through.** Immediate follow-up is essential for prompt compliance by students and avoidance of a "scene." Don't wait until you are provoked, exasperated, or desperate. You cannot give an important instruction while attention is diverted elsewhere. Remember, you are helping to teach children good habits of listening, attending, and promptness. You do not teach these things by scolding or punishing. If you follow through, the child will know you mean business, and few warnings will be necessary.

This teacher uses proximity control (standing near students) to effectively monitor their behavior.

- **Be consistent.** Perhaps only complete rejection disturbs children's security more than inconsistency. If you expect to get consistency in response to direction, you must provide a consistent stimulus and a consistent expectation of performance from day to day. A recent cartoon pinpointed the position that many children find themselves in. The child says, "When you wanna do somethin' scary, you're a little tiny boy, but when they want you to do somethin' scary, you're a great big boy." Always let the children know what they can expect from you, and expect their best of them.

- **Use praise.** Praise more than you administer discipline. It is important also to praise effort as well as performance because trying hard shows responsibility, even when the results are not perfect. But be sure that your praise is sincere. Children quickly sense lack of sincerity. Under no circumstances should you ever resort to bribes. They backfire, they can cause great harm, and they suggest the opposite of good behavior by encouraging deals and the placing of a price tag on being good and responsible. Avoid expecting perfection, and don't be afraid to admit that even you make mistakes.

- **Be assertive.** It is important to distinguish between the terms *assertive* and *aggressive* as applied to behavioral control. Teachers who nag, accuse, argue, speak in anger, get into power struggles, and use harsh punishment are displaying aggressive behavior. Assertive behavior, on the other hand, is apparent in teachers who make clear, direct requests; reveal honest feelings; persist; listen to children's point of view; give brief reasons; and carry out reasonable consequences for misbehavior.

TEACHING TIP 9.2

Consider the following tips on the *value of consistency:*

- To survive in society, children must learn to function in their reality. Ignoring their reality or manipulating it does not help them learn how to cope.

- Children must relate to a number of different people during the course of the day (parents, classroom teachers, physical education teacher, coach). Therefore, a single set of expectations makes life easier and increases the probability of acceptable behavior.

- Children respond positively to the security of a consistent routine. Knowing what to expect enables them to function more freely and puts them at ease.

- Specific statements and directions, used consistently, are much easier for the child to respond to than general comments. Specifics help reduce ambiguity. For example, it is better to say, "Put the ball in the bag" than "Don't play with the ball."

- Life without limits is unrealistic. Life with inconsistent limits is scary. Clarifying acceptable limits of behavior, as well as consistently applying the consequences of violating these limits, promotes security and self-control.

- Self-control develops gradually. The more consistent our treatment of children, the more consistent will be their development of an acceptable level of self-control.

- Children pattern their behavior after significant others. Teachers are significant others; therefore, the role model you provide enables children to act more consistently.

When children view you as assertive in your discipline, they will treat you with respect and will attempt to take responsibility for their actions. Teachers whom children view as aggressive tend to establish control based on fear and do little to help children develop self-control.

• **Demonstrate trust.** Show children that you have faith in them through the responsibility that you give them. If you believe in them and expect their best, you are more likely to get their best. Don't be afraid of losing their love. Children can understand that it is precisely because you do care for them that you provide redirection, restraint, and reprimands when warranted. On the other hand, don't be afraid of "spoiling" children through the generous use of kindness, affection, and consideration. These ways of treating children don't spoil them, but lack of direction, inconsistency, and indecision do.

EFFECTIVE CLASSROOM MANAGEMENT STRATEGIES

Organization is important to the planning process and is a key element in maintaining good class control in the physical education setting. The consistent use of a variety of class management techniques contributes to class organization. **Classroom management** involves the way a teacher organizes students for learning (e.g., formation of groups, partnering techniques), the distribution and collection of equipment, and the allocation of class time. Class protocols (routines and procedures) and rules for good behavior are two components of effective class management. Effective classroom management maximizes learning time. Students must actually practice protocols in order to be able to clearly understand and consistently demonstrate them. As a rule of thumb, no more than 20% of class time should be devoted to classroom management tasks. The following discussion focuses on creating protocols, developing rules for good behavior, establishing a stimulating learning environment, communicating effectively, and self-assessment.

REALITY CHECK

Developing Protocols and Rules for Good Behavior

Real-World Situation

A new school year has begun. You are excited about the many plans you have and want to start out on the right foot. The previous year was one of constant battles with several of your classes—just "little things," but such a waste of everyone's time. Whispering, talking out of turn, not paying attention, pushing, shoving, disrespecting others—you know, little things, but such a nuisance. Fortunately, yelling at students is not your style; in fact, whenever you have resorted to it you have been quick to notice how it puts a damper both on the class and on your enthusiasm for the lesson. Something has to be done if all students are to have a fair shot at learning, but what? When you talk to some of your colleagues, they offer a variety of suggestions ranging from using exercise as punishment to excluding students from class and paddling. None of these are attractive approaches to you, and you have decided to develop both *class protocols* and *rules for good behavior* for your gymnasium and outdoor activity space.

Critical Questions

Based on your knowledge about class protocols and rules for good behavior:

- What are several set protocols that you could implement to help classes run smoothly?

- How would you go about engaging your students in helping you develop rules for good behavior?

- What five rules would you post in your gymnasium and outdoor activity space?

- What are the advantages and disadvantages of having rules for good behavior in your gymnasium and outdoor activity space?

Create Class Protocols

Class protocols involve "predetermined ways of handling situations that frequently occur in the physical education setting" (Lavay, French, & Henderson, 1997, p. 25), for example:

- Students follow a set procedure when they need to use the rest room (e.g., take a brightly painted stick that is kept in a particular location).

- Teachers follow a procedure for taking attendance (e.g., scan the class during an instant activity).

- Students follow a procedure for getting drinks from a water fountain located in the gymnasium or in a nearby hallway.

- Students know where to place clothing that they take off during activity.

- There is a procedure for handling minor and major injuries.

- There is a procedure for starting and stopping activity.

- Teachers follow a procedure for establishing partners or small groups (teams).

Sample physical education behavior code:

1. During directions:
   a. Quiet, eyes on teacher, equipment still.
   b. Raise your hand to ask a question.
2. Moving signals:
   a. Move when you hear the signal.
   b. Stop quickly on signal.
   c. Follow instructions (the first time).
3. Equipment:
   a. Get it out/put it away.
   b. Move equipment quickly, cooperatively, directly.
4. Positive behaviors:
   a. Cooperate with classmates and teachers.
   b. Follow the school thinking rules.

From a gymnasium wall in Winnipeg, Canada

Consequences for violating the code:

1. Warning
2. Time-out
3. Mini-class (i.e., meet with the teacher to work out a plan for positive behavior)
4. Contact home (plus above)
5. Office detention (plus above)

Develop Rules for Good Behavior

Rules for good behavior are guidelines for behaviors that you expect students to display. Children are generally more secure when they know what is expected of them and what comes next. Having a regular sequence of activities in the gymnasium and having a limited number of clearly understood classroom and gymnasium thinking rules do much to provide children with a framework for acceptable behavior. The rules should be clear and concise and should outline the consequences for misbehavior. The rules should be posted on a wall where everyone can see them and should be sent home with students. Communicating the rules in these ways ensures that students, fellow teachers, and parents are all familiar with the requirements for positive discipline in the gymnasium.

If the rules of the gymnasium have been clearly explained and posted where they can be easily seen, children are less likely to overstep these boundaries. One effec-

TEXT BOX 9.2

Guidelines for Creating Rules

- Involve students in the process. This will foster ownership.
- State rules in positive terms.
- Make no more than five to six rules.
- Develop general rules that are flexible, covering various class situations.
- State consequences clearly.
- Be sure students understand rules and consequences.

Pat's (the new PE teacher)
3 P's: Proactive Protocol Plan
✓ Stopping and starting signals!
✓ Distribution of equipment!
✓ Getting drinks!
✓ Going to the rest room!
✓ Taking attendance!

tive technique in setting rules is to request that students help generate the rules and help determine the consequences for violating them. Such a technique involves students in the decision-making process and promotes self-discipline.

It is important to remember that you must teach your students what the rules for acceptable behavior are. You cannot expect that they will know or willingly accept these rules unless you help them learn and understand. If children can expect that the routine of the lesson will follow a consistent format, they tend to be more at ease and less disruptive.

Here the teachers discuss guidelines for behavior with first and second grade students.

When establishing guidelines for acceptable behavior, it is wise to limit the number of "don'ts" because the word reinforces unacceptable behavior. State rules from a positive standpoint rather than a negative one. For example, rather than saying "Don't run," "Don't talk," or "Don't get out of line," it is usually better to say, "Walk quietly," "Remain silent," or "Stay in line." Emphasizing the positive often has a correspondingly positive influence. You will, of course, need to make exceptions if a child's safety is at stake or if you need to protect property. But avoid a long list of "don'ts" if the primary purpose is for your convenience or comfort.

TEXT BOX 9.3

Guidelines for Implementing Rules

- Post rules in an area where all students can see them.
- Use pictures and colorful graphics to illustrate rules for nonreaders.
- Practice and review rules periodically.
- Inform administrators, classroom teachers, and parents of the rules.
- Modify rules if necessary, and involve students in this process.

Establish a Stimulating Environment

The physical appearance of the gymnasium is also important. An atmosphere that is bright, cheery, and generally appealing is conducive to positive behavior. Neat bulletin boards, posters, painted murals, activity charts, or photographs of students—which should be changed frequently—promote interest and give students a sense that you care.

TEXT BOX 9.4

Create a stimulating environment by posting "magic words" on the walls. Encourage students to use them to praise and encourage others!

"YOU'RE AWESOME!"

"KEEP PRACTICING!"

"NICE TRY!"

"THANKS!"

"WAY TO GO!"

Communicate Effectively

Teachers who can minimize and deal effectively with behavioral problems tend to be good communicators. Those who recognize the power of both the spoken word and the unspoken word and who systematically work at interacting positively with children generally have fewer behavior problems. The use of positive reinforcement techniques rather than negative or criticizing behaviors has been shown to be effective in winning the respect and attention of children. Giving attention to all students (not just those who are gifted or those who need extra attention) and reinforcing their positive behaviors both verbally and nonverbally are techniques used by teachers with good class control.

TEACHING TIP 9.4

Techniques for *effective communication:*

- Develop effective verbal and nonverbal communication skills.
- Strive for meaningful interaction with children.
- Work for maximum communication with children.
- Use positive reinforcement techniques.
- Work toward giving each child some form of positive reinforcement in each lesson.

- Provide positive feedback to children's attempts to behave in a positive manner.
- Avoid nagging, teasing, shaming, belittling, and other aggressive forms of communication.
- Be consistent in what you say and how you use verbal and nonverbal forms of communication.

Assess Yourself

Teachers who periodically assess their own teaching behavior and the learning styles of their students generally have fewer behavior problems with their classes. The process of self-assessment enables teachers to stop for a moment, look the situation over, and chart a new course, if necessary, in a more positive direction. Minor changes in modeling, planning, or communication techniques can often result in dramatically improved behavior on the part of the class. Self-assessment is most effective with the aid of videotaped replays of lessons and peer evaluations of your teaching.

It is a common mistake for physical education teachers to neglect assessing their students' behavior and to assume that it will work to use identical methods with each class during the course of the day. Remember, as a physical education teacher, your job in maintaining class control and promoting self-control is considerably more complex than that of the classroom teacher. First, you don't deal with one class for the entire day but with many classes for only a portion of the day. Second, the physical environment of the gymnasium or playground tends to evoke a different set of behaviors than those seen in the classroom. Last, and most important, each class that comes to your program tends to be a direct reflection of the standards for behavior established by the particular classroom teacher. Therefore, you may need to modify your methods for gaining and maintaining control for each class. Requesting constructive feedback from individual teachers and observing in the classroom will help you make any necessary adjustments. Do not assume that, because a certain set of techniques worked well the previous year with the third grade (or any other grade), this year's third graders will respond in the same way. You will be the one who needs to make the adjustments if you are going to be successful in your discipline.

Guidelines for *self-assessment:*

- Focus on regular, systematic review of your teaching techniques.
- Take stock of the directions your class control techniques are taking and chart a new direction if warranted.
- Observe children in a variety of settings.

- Observe classrooms in a variety of settings.
- Modify your techniques as needed to fit the specific children you are dealing with.
- Do not assume that teaching the same way as last year will be appropriate for this year!

YOUR PHILOSOPHY AS A GUIDE

There are different philosophical foundations that may guide an educator's approach to discipline. Your approach may be based on your own personal philosophy of teaching. For example, what are your values and beliefs? What do you believe your role as a physical educator is? What is the student's role in the learning process? Does your role go beyond the established physical education curriculum? What do you want your students to learn? What are your goals for your students in terms of their behavior? What is your role in the management of their behavior? What is the students' role?

Behavior-Shaping Discipline Techniques

Our instructional practices, including those related to discipline and class management, are based on our assumptions about children. If you adopt a **behavioral approach to discipline**, you believe that children's behavior can be modified by sys-

REALITY CHECK

You WILL Behave!

Real-World Situation

Unruly children often view student teachers and substitute teachers as "bait" to be toyed with and challenged. These students seem to take great joy in disrupting classes and seeing how far they can push before getting a reaction from the teacher. To make matters worse, a "ripple effect" often occurs and even the generally well-behaved children begin acting up. Soon the entire class is out of control. As a new teacher you are determined not to let this happen to you. Even though you have heard stories of how over 50% of new teachers never complete their third year as teachers largely because of behavioral problems from disruptive students, you have made up your mind this will not happen in your case.

Critical Questions

Based on your reality and what you know about teacher-centered discipline techniques:

- What will you do to avoid being caught in this downward spiral of disintegrating classroom behavior?
- What nonverbal behaviors could you use to help reduce disruptive behaviors?
- What verbal techniques would you use to reduce disruptive behaviors?
- How would you use time-out as a behavior-shaping tool?
- How could you use positive practice overcorrection as a behavior-shaping tool?

tematically changing the environment in order to develop, increase, decrease, or maintain a behavior. Behavioral theories assert the following ideas:

- External control is necessary, and without it, students are not as likely to learn or to act appropriately.
- Students must be told exactly how to behave and what will happen if they don't do what they're told.
- Positive reinforcement must be given to a child who does something nice if you want the child to keep acting that way.
- Teachers need to help students control their impulses.

Through the use of a behavioral approach, you link the behavior to be changed to actions occurring before the behavior, called **antecedents,** and to the consequences that will occur after the behavior. Lavay et al. (1997) provide the example of a teacher who states: "Line up and get ready for physical education class [antecedent]. The first student to be ready at his space and quiet [desired behavior] will be the leader for today [consequence]" (p. 36). Antecedents stimulate a behavior to occur, and consequences follow the behavior and affect the probability they will increase or decrease in the future.

Subscribing to a behavioral approach, a physical educator may choose to use positive reinforcement for rewarding appropriate behavior. Many physical educators commonly use social reinforcement. A smile, an approving nod, a "high five," an arm around a student's shoulder, and an approving verbal statement about a student's behavior or actual performance are all examples of social reinforcement. Positive verbal reinforcement is most effective when it includes a comment about the desired behavior—for example, "Good running with your knees high!" (Lavay et al., 1997, p. 47).

Lavay and colleagues also describe tangible activity reinforcement. Tangible reinforcers might include stickers, charts, or adding a marble to the "classroom marble jar" for good class behavior. Physical activity reinforcers may include the use of specific equipment, students' being chosen to demonstrate a skill, or students' being allowed to choose an activity.

Teacher-Centered Discipline Techniques

As a teacher you must also strive to decrease persistent inappropriate behavior. The best method of handling behavior problems is a program designed to prevent them from occurring. However, once problems do occur, there are several remedial actions that you can take. Remember, though, to apply teacher-imposed discipline with the dignity of the student in mind. It is crucial to respect the innate rights of the individual as a human being and not strip the student of dignity through humiliation or ridicule.

CONCEPT 9.5

Most of the techniques used to impose teacher control over students fail to solve the underlying cause of the discipline problem.

Each of the following techniques—nonverbal, verbal, and time-out responses—has been found to be successful in helping teachers establish and maintain class control. It is important, however, to remember that no method of control gets to the heart of the issue—knowing why the problem occurred or how to prevent it from occurring again.

Nonverbal Responses

Teachers can use a number of nonverbal responses to acknowledge children's misbehavior. Often these quiet forms of control can do much to improve individual behavior and the behavior of the class in general. Your eyes are a valuable tool. Disapproving glances or a fixed gaze on the misbehaving child frequently stops the misconduct. Stationing yourself close to the area where misbehaving students are located is also helpful. A gentle hand on the shoulder of a child who may be off-task is often enough to show that you are displeased with the student's behavior.

Verbal Responses

Your voice can also be a powerful tool. Use it wisely because your choice of words, pitch, and tone can convey a very clear message of intent. Remember that to discipline with dignity you must avoid, at all costs, yelling, screaming, sarcasm, and belittling children for their behavior. If the infraction is minor, treat it as such. Too often teachers who overreact to small disruptions find themselves exhausted and their children conditioned to their overreaction. As a result, the teacher has little emotion or voice to cope with the major problems that are sure to occur. General comments to the class with a brief explanation of acceptable behavior are more appropriate.

If you fail to establish control in this manner, you may need to use sterner techniques. Singling out by name those who are misbehaving, with a brief comment on what is acceptable behavior, is often effective. As an example, you might say, "Daniel and Jennifer, it's important for everyone to have their eyes focused up here and to be listening carefully to the lesson. Do you understand?" Be certain to check for understanding by getting a verbal response to the question at the end of your statement. This helps break the pattern of misbehavior and cause a refocusing of attention.

TEXT BOX 9.5

The manner in which we respond to children's behavior is an aspect of communication that people sometimes overlook. Remember, good behavior is not suddenly or magically achieved by most children. It is a learned process that is shaped over time. This learning process is rooted in the teacher's responses to the students' attempts to improve their behavior. Responses that focus on the positive aspects of behavior rather than on the negative aspects have repeatedly been shown to result in better behavior. In no case should teasing, belittling, or condescending statements be used as a method of responding to students' poor behavior.

Time-Out

If you are unable to bring disruptive students under control with nonverbal and verbal techniques, it is sometimes appropriate to provide a time-out space. This should be a predesignated spot in the gymnasium or on the playground that is removed from the class but in clear view of the teacher at all times. Henderson, French, Fritsch, and Lerner (2000) define using a **time-out** as "sending a student to a safe, easy-to-monitor, non-reinforcing area each time he or she exhibits an undesirable behavior" (p. 31).

Removing a disruptive child from the class for a portion of the lesson gives both the student and the teacher time to regroup and refocus. Be sure, however, not to overuse this technique or to exclude the child for too long. Exclusion for longer than 5 minutes tends to be less effective than shorter periods (French, Silliman, &

Henderson, 1990). Also, be certain to talk privately with the child before it's time to reenter the class, asking, "What did you do to cause me to remove you from class?" and "How should you have behaved, or how can we prevent this from happening again?" and "Are you ready to rejoin the class on your best behavior?" If the problem is between two students, as in name-calling, pushing and shoving, or fighting, and they have been removed for time-out, be certain that they talk over the problem and work it out together before returning to class.

One advantage of using time-out is that it is simple and quick to implement. But there are several disadvantages of using time-out:

- When used exclusively, time-out teaches the student which behaviors are unacceptable but not which behaviors are desirable.
- Opportunity to learn is taken away during the time-out period.
- Students may purposefully try to misbehave in order to be assigned to time-out.

It is important, therefore, for teachers to document their use of time-out with students.

When possible, avoid excluding students from an entire class or sending them to the principal's office. Handling your own discipline problems whenever possible conveys a message to the children of being in control. Teachers who constantly send disruptive students to the principal's office are actually inviting further difficulties because they are viewed by students and fellow teachers as ineffective leaders, unable to manage their own classrooms. It is less likely that a third party will effectively solve a behavioral problem. Of course, there are situations in which delegating your authority to another is appropriate and useful, but, as a rule of thumb, avoid it whenever possible.

TEACHING TIP 9.6

Steps in maximizing the effectiveness of *time-out:*

- Provide a specific designated spot for the child to go to.
- Place gymnasium thinking rules close by for the child to read.
- Ask the child to reflect on the behaviors that resulted in the time-out.
- After a period of 5 minutes or less, try the following:
  - Establishing good eye contact, talk quietly to the child out of the hearing range of the rest of the class.
  - Be certain that the child knows why she was required to take a time-out.
- Ask the child if she is ready to return.
- If the answer is "yes" check for understanding by asking the child to reiterate the acceptable behavior required for reentry.
- If the answer is "no" or is unacceptable, provide additional time for the student to "cool off" and consider the consequences of the poor behavior before you again begin the procedure just described.
- Once the student is back in class, observe for compliance and compliment positive behaviors.

Positive Practice Overcorrection

In positive practice **overcorrection**, students who exhibit inappropriate behaviors are required to repeatedly practice a positive, desired behavior (see Henderson et al., 2000). For example, if a student is speaking or "talking out" without permission, the teacher asks her what she should do before speaking and has her practice this behavior—that is, raising her hand first and waiting to be called on. Although the technique of positive practice overcorrection is effective, a disadvantage may be the need for one-on-one supervision of the student while she practices the desired behavior. Another disadvantage is that a beginning teacher may not be able to keep the rest of the class productively involved while monitoring one or two students—and in addition, students may refuse to do what you ask them to do. Finally, it may be difficult, on the spot, to think of an appropriate overcorrection activity for the student to actually perform.

TEACHING TIP 9.7

Techniques for being a *positive role model:*

- Be assertive.
- Be proactive.
- Act in proportion to the need.
- Be consistent.

- Clearly communicate expectations.
- Convey interest and enthusiasm.
- Set reasonable individual and group goals.

Child-Centered Approaches to Discipline

Alfie Kohn (1996, p. 11), a prominent educator and theorist, suggests that teachers take a positive view of children. Kohn believes that compared to a less positive view, an optimistic view is more accurate and more likely to generate practices that work; he also recommends that our attention should be directed toward what children require for optimal functioning. Kohn doesn't ask, "How can we control students?" Instead he asks, "What can we do to help them flourish?"

The discipline and management practices described by Kohn go beyond traditional disciplinary programs and are based on the assumption that children have an innate disposition to be socially responsive. The National Institute of Mental Health confirms what several research studies have found: Even children as young as two years old have the cognitive capacity to interpret the physical and psychological states of others, the emotional capacity to affectively experience the other's state, and the behavioral repertoire that permits the possibility of trying to alleviate discomfort in others. These are the capabilities that, we believe, underlie children's caring behavior in the presence of another person's distress. Young children seem to show patterns of moral internalization that are not simply fear based or solely responsive to parental commands. Rather, there are signs that children feel responsible for (as well as connected to and dependent on) others at a very young age (Zahn-Waxler & Radke-Yarrow, 1992, pp. 127, 135).

Strategies and practices in Kohn's model are based on psychological theories and research demonstrating that humans all possess basic needs. Deci and Ryan (2000) suggest that humans have three universal needs: autonomy, relatedness, and competence (ARC). *Autonomy* refers not to privacy but to self-determination, the experience of oneself as the origin of decisions rather than as the victim of things outside one's control. *Relatedness* refers to connection to others, a need for belonging and love and affirmation. Finally, *competence* suggests that all of us take pleasure from learning new things, from acquiring skills and putting them to use. A developmentally based physical education program offers many rich opportunities for these basic human needs to be met.

Constructivist Approaches

Schools and classrooms that address the three basic human needs and that operate on the belief that children can be socially responsible view discipline and classroom management from a cognitive perspective. A cognitive perspective to discipline is represented by a constructivist approach that enables children to attach personal meaning to actions and deeds. Use of a **constructivist approach to discipline** provides opportunities for students to construct and actively invent ethical meaning; in other words, they have an opportunity to figure out for themselves and with each other how one ought to act. The constructivist approach is child centered. Teaching strategies are dictated by children's needs, not by the teacher's beliefs and preferences. Teachers share their control with students, and students are expected to control themselves. Two of the aims of teaching practices in this type of physical education program are the following:

- Maximizing opportunity for students to make choices, to discover, and to learn for themselves
- Creating a caring community in the classroom so that students have the opportunity to do these things together

Kohn believes that if the objectives of educators are to promote depth of understanding, continuing motivation to learn, and concern for others, then it is necessary to go beyond the traditional premises (i.e., student compliance to the teacher's rules or demands) underlying the need to discipline students as well as effective classroom management.

Classrooms As Communities

Every classroom has the potential to be a "community." In a community, students feel cared about and are encouraged to care about each other. They experience a sense of being valued and respected; the children matter to one another and to the teacher. They have come to think in the plural: they feel connected to each other; they are part of an "us." As a result of all this, they feel safe in their classes, not only physically but also emotionally.

To create a community, one must establish student-teacher relationships. Without positive relationships with students, teachers are limited in the ways they can interact with students and often resort to methods of control within the classroom. Positive relationships are characterized by trust, respect, and understanding. Dollard and Christensen (1996) suggest that relinquishing hierarchical power structures (teachers controlling students) will result in a more "manageable" classroom. Teachers must take the lead in building caring relationships. One method of accomplishing this is through entering into dialogue with students. Dialogue involves understanding students' perspectives, sharing understandings, and allowing for mutual decision making about the issues at hand. Noddings (1991) describes the features of dialogue this way:

- **Caring attitude.** When the attitude is caring and solicitous, students and teachers feel safe in expressing perceptions and needs without fear of coercion or manipulation.

- **Flexibility.** Outcomes are not planned; rather participants explore multiple possibilities as they arise in the dialogue.
- **Attention.** Each participant is committed to listening to and understanding the other party.
- **Search for a response.** Those engaged in the dialogue are searching for an appropriate response. There is mutual identification and analysis of a range of possibilities that would address the situation or problem being discussed.

Noddings (1992) says, "Schools should become places in which teachers and students live together, talk to each other, reason together, take delight in each other's company" (p. 169). Noddings provides several intervention strategies that help teachers to dialogue with their students. Problem-solving is a cognitive intervention in which the child shares his perceptions of a difficult situation. The child must be able to recognize that a problem exists and decide what he wants to happen in the situation. Second, the child must be able to generate a number of possible solutions to the problem and select the best solution. Finally, the child must be able to plan a strategy to carry out the solution and then look at the consequence of the actions.

Self-Management

Self-management, including self-assessment, is another technique for an individual student to employ. This technique helps move the child's locus of control from one that is external to one that is internal (or from the teacher to the student). It teaches students skills that a person can use throughout life. Through self-assessment, children learn to observe and record their own behavior and then compare their behavior to a predetermined standard. For example, a child is being punished frequently for talking out without raising her hand. The teacher talks with the child to be certain that she understands why she should not call out in a classroom where the students are trying to focus on a movement task. If the student agrees that she wants to change this behavior, the teacher teaches her how to keep track of the number of times she talks out during a set time period. A standard is then set—for example, two "talk-outs" per time period. The goal is for the student to reduce the number of "talk-outs" to that number or below. Next the teacher teaches the child to self-monitor, using internal dialogue to remind herself to stay on task and to raise her hand to speak or ask for help.

Conflict Resolution

Conflict resolution is a specific problem-solving technique. It entails a process of communication and problem-solving that leads to resolution among two or more students. Conflict resolution helps turn conflicts into win-win situations for students. The steps of the process look like this:

- Participants gather information about the conflict.
- They work to clarify the conflict as seen from each person's point of view.
- They identify common interests among the people involved.
- They brainstorm options for a solution to the conflict.
- Students may write out an agreement or a contract (or a form can be designed by the teacher and completed by the students).
- The contract is "sealed" with a "high five" or a handshake.

Contingency Contracts

Contingency contracts are yet another method of promoting positive social behaviors and building students' self-esteem. Both teachers and students can design individual or group contracts. Group contracts give children a sense of being in charge of their classroom and of themselves, and can facilitate important social skills such as problem-solving and negotiation. Epanchin, Townsend, and Stoddard (1994) propose the following five steps in developing contingency contracts.

1. The teacher and the student explore the reasons(s) and rationale(s) for targeting a given behavior and agree on the importance of selecting that behavior.
2. The parties to the contract negotiate a precise definition of the behavior and the circumstances under which it is to occur.
3. The parties discuss the consequences of living up to or failing to live up to the contract until they are mutually satisfied with these consequences.
4. The parties draw up a contract outlining the behavior of interest and the contingencies.
5. All parties sign the contract.

Contingency contracts focus on children's strengths rather than on their shortcomings. Behavioral techniques such as contracting empower students since all members of the classroom (i.e., teachers and students) have a voice in what transpires.

At the heart of all constructivist strategies is a nonjudgmental way of thinking that puts understanding and empathizing with children at the center. Through a caring relationship embedded in a constructivist philosophy of learning, teachers can give their students lifelong skills for getting along in school, at work, and in interpersonal relationships.

TEACHING SOCIAL SKILLS IN PHYSICAL EDUCATION

The National Association for Sport and Physical Education's (NASPE, 1995) National Standards for Physical Education state that students should be able to demonstrate responsible personal and social behavior and an understanding of and respect for differences among people in physical activity settings. The physical education setting is one of the best places to effectively teach positive social skills because it is a learning environment where students can explore the many dimensions of social behavior. According to Solomon (1997), three principles have been identified for helping children build social skills.

1. Children must have opportunities to engage in self-direction (e.g., help to create class rules).
2. They must perceive tasks as meaningful and important (e.g., developmentally appropriate activities).
3. They must feel they are valued members of the class community (e.g., must have opportunities to share their ideas and feelings).

These three factors form the foundation for teaching social skills within the physical education context. Teaching social skills is also a process, involving identification of the social skill to be addressed in class (e.g., encouragement, caring, courtesy), defining the targeted skill, and brainstorming with students what they would see and hear when they are demonstrating the skill during physical education class. From there a lesson plan, or individual learning activity that fosters the social skill for that lesson, can be created.

Using a T-chart can facilitate brainstorming. The "skill for the day" is written at the top of the chart. For the left side of the chart, students provide behaviors they would see when the skill is being demonstrated. For the right side of the chart, students provide phrases they would hear when the skill is being demonstrated. The chart is then posted where it can be easily seen (Kerby, 1997, p. 9).

TEACHING TIP 9.8

CHILDREN SEE YOUR NONVERBAL MESSAGES AND "hEAR" THE MESSAGE YOU CONVEY

Children see	Children "hear"
Nodding	"Good work!"
Clapping	"That's great!"
Thumbs-up	"Keep trying!"
High five	"You're doing terrific!"
Cheering	"Don't give up!"
Waving	"All right!"
Pat on the back	"Way to go!"

Adapted, by permission, from S.D. Kerby, 1997, "Making the case for teaching social skills," *Teaching Elementary Physical Education,* 8 (5), 8-9.

Additional suggestions (Vigil, 1997) are that either teachers or the students themselves monitor students' use of the targeted social skill during the lesson and that lesson closure include a discussion in which the students evaluate what occurred during the activity. For example, the teacher may ask, "What were some encouraging things you saw or heard?" "How did it feel to have someone encourage you?" "How did it feel to encourage others?" "What can you do the next time to make your group more successful?" (Vigil, 1997, p. 4).

Focusing on social skills is an important facet of a successful physical education learning experience for young children. If you emphasize social skills in your physical education class, you are addressing the three basic universal needs of humans for autonomy, relatedness, and competency. Such a focus is consistent with a constructivist model of discipline in that it involves students in the process and recognizes the worth of their ideas and contributions.

Summary

Positive discipline is a learning process guided by competent teachers. Successful teaching means that we help children move from teacher-controlled behaviors toward greater self-control. Overreliance on teacher-imposed standards of control and punishment not only fails to provide children with opportunities but also fails to give them responsibility for their own behavior.

Effective teachers use many techniques for helping children develop the long-term goal of increased self-control. Among the features of a positive discipline model are establishing rules and routines, being reasonable, being consistent, following through, being assertive, and demonstrating trust in children. Additionally, teachers with positive authority styles are positive role models, effective communicators, efficient planners, and critical self-assessors of their personal teaching behaviors.

Teacher-centered strategies for establishing and maintaining class control include nonverbal responses, verbal responses, and time-out. Child-centered or constructivist discipline strategies include self-monitoring, contingency contracts, and conflict resolution. Physical education teachers should be mindful of the importance of teaching social skills and the process involved in helping children acquire useful social skills.

Terms to Remember

Excellent Readings

Belka, D.E. (1991). Let's manage to have some order. *JOPERD, 62,* 21–23.

Boyce, B.A. (1998). When push comes to shove: A behavior management case. *JOPERD, 69* (7), 53–55.

Boyce, B.A., & Walker, P. (1991). Establishing structure in the elementary school. *Strategies, 5,* 20–23.

Hill, K.L. (1991). Pay attention. *JOPERD, 62,* 18–20.

Johnson, R. (1999). Time out: Can it control misbehavior? *JOPERD, 70* (8), 32–34.

Miller, S., & McCormick, J. (Eds.). (1991). Stress: Teaching children to cope. *JOPERD, 62,* 53–70.

Spark, W.G. (1993). Promoting self-responsibility and decision making with at-risk students. *JOPERD, 64,* 74–78.

Vogler, E.W., & Bishop, P. (1990). Management of disruptive behavior in physical education. *The Physical Educator, 47,* 16–26.

10

Teaching Styles: Connecting With the Learner

Key Concept

▶ Effective teachers modify their teaching behaviors based on the developmental characteristics and needs of their students and the specific learning objectives of the lesson.

This chapter will provide you with the tools to do the following:

- Identify what is meant by the term *teaching style*.
- Understand the purpose of learning how to use different teaching styles.
- Distinguish between reproduction (direct) and production (indirect) teaching styles and their appropriate use.
- Briefly describe main teaching styles within the spectrum of teaching styles.
- Discuss how different teaching styles can be employed within a lesson.
- Discuss how a child's motor development and level of movement skill learning influence the selection and use of various teaching styles.
- Discuss the role of student comprehension and compliance in the selection and use of different teaching styles.
- Speculate about the impact of various teaching styles on the learner.

Teaching is a learned behavior, but what exactly is it? Mosston and Ashworth (2001) characterize teaching as the ability to be aware of and utilize possible connections with the learner in all domains of human behavior (i.e., cognitive, affective, and motor). As learned skills, teaching behaviors can be modified and changed. Skilled teachers are thoroughly versed in a variety of teaching styles that they use on the basis of the needs of their students and the specific objectives of the lesson. This chapter presents a variety of teaching styles, commonly called the **spectrum of teaching styles,** to enable you to appreciate the vast array of teaching behaviors available, as well as integrate these styles into what we know about the processes of motor development and movement skill learning. We finish the chapter with a discussion of student comprehension and compliance factors that directly affect your ability to select from among the spectrum of teaching styles.

A *teaching style* is a specific set of decisions made by the instructor to achieve the learning objectives of the lesson; these decisions result in identifiable behaviors on the part of the teacher.

WHY MULTIPLE TEACHING STYLES?

As discussed in chapter 8, we have many questions to answer and decisions to make when we are preparing to teach a physical education lesson. How do we manage the time, space, and equipment available to us? How should we organize our students? How should we interact with our students? How do we create a climate that promotes critical thinking, positive social behaviors, and positive feelings toward self and others? How will the unique characteristics of our students affect the lesson? How much responsibility do we want them to assume? Clearly, these and many other questions can and should be asked. Moreover, decisions based on these questions must be made.

The structure of the *spectrum of teaching styles* reflects two basic human capacities: the capacity for reproduction and the capacity for production. All human beings have, in varying degrees, the capability to reproduce known knowledge, replicate models, and practice skills. All human beings have the capacity to produce a range of ideas and a range of things; all have the capacity to venture into the new and tap the yet unknown (Mosston & Ashworth, 2001, p. 5).

Mosston and Ashworth (2001) emphasize that every act of "deliberate teaching is a consequence of a prior decision" (p. 8). The relationship between teachers and students varies depending on who makes the decisions. These decision patterns are called **teaching styles,** and the framework that holds them together is the *spectrum of teaching styles,* or the *Spectrum* for short. The Spectrum identifies the structure of each teaching style by delineating the decisions that are made by the teacher and those that are made by the learner before, during, and after the lesson. The Spectrum outlines how to shift appropriate decisions from the teacher to the learner as both move from one teaching style to another. It also describes the influence of each style on the learner in the cognitive, affective, and motor domains.

You may ask, "Why do I need to learn how to use different teaching styles?" There are four major purposes for selecting from the Spectrum: (1) personal choice, (2) tradition, (3) the diversity of today's student population, and (4) multiple objectives of the lesson. We'll consider each of these briefly.

TEXT BOX 10.3

The act of teaching is governed by decision making about the learner, the task, and the environment. According to Mosston and Ashworth (2001, p. 3), "The entire structure of the Spectrum stems from the initial premise that teaching behavior is a chain of decision making. Every deliberate act of teaching is a result of a previously made decision."

TEXT BOX 10.4

The Spectrum of Teaching Styles: Why Should We Use It?

- Our natural teaching tendencies may limit our options and potential contributions to students' learning.
- The Spectrum provides options for both the teacher and the learner.
- The Spectrum, by providing options, makes it possible for teachers to reach more students and to create conditions that foster inclusion.
- Multiple objectives in education demand that we address different domains of learning, including the motor, cognitive, and affective.

REALITY CHECK

Decisions, Decisions: So Many Decisions

Real-World Situation

Well here you are, enrolled in yet another "methods class." In your preparation to become a teacher, you are most likely being exposed to many such classes intended to make you a better teacher. This one is no different in that sense, but it is different in that you are being asked to learn more about and implement a variety of teaching styles in physical activity settings. You may be thinking, "What's all the fuss, teaching is teaching." You may have even decided to use the teaching styles of a favorite teacher from high school. But, with all that you know about developmentally based physical education, does it really make sense

to select on this basis? You may say "of course not"— but that is exactly what a significant number of new teachers do.

Critical Questions

Based on your knowledge of the reasons for selecting a teaching style:

- What teaching styles are your favorite and least favorite to use? Why?
- On what basis would you select one teaching style over another?
- What teacher decisions are of critical importance in selecting a teaching style?

Personal Choice

Personal choice plays an important role in selecting a teaching style. Every teacher brings a different set of personality traits to the "teaching table." As Mosston and Ashworth explain, "Our personal style reflects a unique combination of who we are, how we do things, and what we believe about our relationship with students" (2001, p. 16). Your personal style may not be instrumental in meeting specific learning objectives. Your natural teaching tendencies, or idiosyncratic style, may limit your options and potential contributions to students' learning. Therefore, it is critically important to be well versed in a variety of teaching styles if your objective is to maximize student learning.

Tradition

Traditionally, many physical educators have thought of teaching as best accomplished through the use of a particular set of teaching behaviors and sequence of learning tasks. It is common to hear an experienced teacher say, "I usually do this and it works, so why change?" A traditional approach to teaching a physical education lesson generally includes a teacher explanation of the task or lesson objective(s) followed by a teacher or student demonstration. Practice time, for individual or small groups of students, is then provided. The duration of practice, as well as the pacing of practice, is determined by the teacher. Next, the teacher provides feedback (i.e., usually direct and corrective) to the whole class and to individual students. Finally, the teacher conducts lesson closure (i.e., a review and question/answer period). In other words, the teacher makes all the decisions. This traditional, teacher-centered style is not a wrong way; it simply accomplishes one set of learning objectives and meets specific student needs. The spectrum of teaching styles, on the other hand, provides options to both the teacher and the learner.

Student Diversity

Today's classrooms often have a significant amount of diversity in the student population. Students frequently represent different cultural backgrounds; learning styles (i.e., auditory, visual, tactile, etc.); and abilities in the social, motor, and cognitive domains. Selecting teaching styles from the Spectrum provides you with options and makes it possible for you to reach more students and to create conditions that foster inclusion.

Multiple Objectives

Teachers of physical education often have multiple objectives in their lessons. As discussed in part I, the National Standards for Physical Education of the National Association for Sport and Physical Education (NASPE) address the three domains of learning. For example, Content Standards #5 and #6 address the affective domain; Content Standard #2 addresses the cognitive domain; and Content Standards #1, #3, #4, and #6 primarily address the motor domain. These Content Standards serve as guides for the development of physical education curricula and for using varied teaching methods.

Using multiple teaching methods facilitates multiple learning outcomes. For example, if one of your objectives was to develop higher-order thinking skills among your students, you would want to use teaching methods that foster students' ability to analyze, synthesize, and apply their knowledge rather than methods that relate to lower-order thinking skills such as recall, recognition, or identification. Accomplishing higher-order thinking would require a different set of teaching behaviors.

CONCEPT 10.1

A teaching style is a specific set of decisions made by the teacher to achieve the learning objectives of the lesson; these decisions result in identifiable behaviors on the part of both the teacher and the learner.

THE SPECTRUM OF TEACHING STYLES

Mosston and Ashworth (2001) grouped teaching styles into two clusters (figure 10.1). The first cluster represents teaching options that foster reproduction of past knowledge. The second cluster represents options that invite the production of new knowledge—that is, knowledge new to the learner, not the teacher.

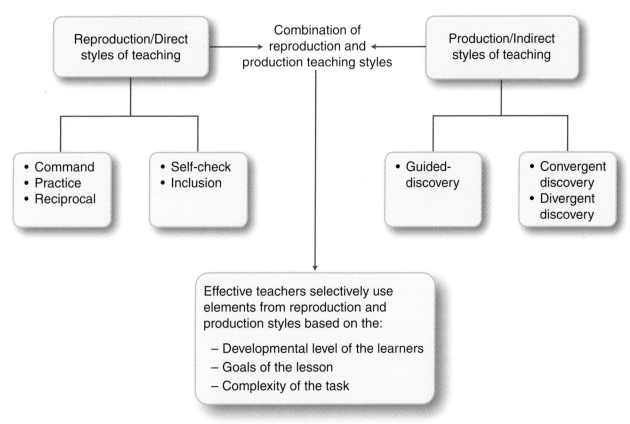

FIGURE 10.1 The spectrum of teaching styles and their link between direct and indirect teaching styles.

The **reproduction cluster** engages students in lower-order thinking processes such as memory, recall, identification, and sorting or cognitive operations that deal with past and present knowledge. The **production cluster** facilitates the discovery of concepts as well as the development of alternatives and new concepts.

Teachers in the developmental physical education program may use a variety of teaching styles effectively. The following paragraphs deal with both the reproduction teaching styles and the production teaching styles.

CONCEPT
10.2

No one style of teaching in the spectrum of teaching styles is better or best; each style is best for the objectives it can achieve.

Reproduction Teaching Styles

Reproduction teaching styles are the traditional teaching approaches that have been used by many physical educators and classroom teachers over the years. These styles are **teacher-centered methods** in that the teacher makes all or most of the decisions concerning what, how, and when the student is to perform. The use of teacher-centered approaches is based on **behavioral learning theory,** which contends that

Muska Mosston's Spectrum of Teaching Styles and the Art and Science of Teaching

Real-World Situation

Shortly before his death, Muska Mosston, the dynamic creator of the spectrum of teaching styles, and your senior author were keynote speakers at a major national conference sponsored by NASPE. The conference focused on the topic of developmental physical education, and Professor Mosston was in the audience during my presentation linking the *phases of motor development* and *levels movement skill learning* with the use of varying styles of teaching. At the conclusion of the talk, he came to the podium and with his characteristic enthusiasm exclaimed, "David, marvelous, you have linked the art of teaching (the spectrum of teaching styles) with the science of teaching (the phases of motor development and levels of movement skill learning)—we need

to work together to bring our message to more people." Unfortunately, that opportunity never materialized because of Mosston's untimely death.

Critical Questions

Based on your knowledge of Mosston's spectrum of teaching styles:

- What was Professor Mosston talking about?
- What does the term "spectrum" as used by Professor Mosston signify?
- How would you combine what we know about human development and learning with Professor Mosston's spectrum of teaching styles?

---

learning occurs from the outside in through the correct reproduction of events. Accordingly, proponents of the behaviorist viewpoint hold that because we, the teachers, already know how a movement skill should be performed, it is our responsibility to help children model or learn these "correct" techniques in the most expedient manner possible. Additionally, because time is at a premium and "incorrect" learning will only slow down and interfere with correct learning, those who favor the behaviorist theory advocate direct styles.

Reproduction styles, or *direct teaching styles* as they are often called, have many advantages. They are efficient and focused, and they leave little chance for misunderstanding or misinterpretation. The structured learning environment associated with direct styles is conducive to good class control, and direct styles are easy to use with individuals or with large groups of children. They get right to the point: learning the mechanically correct technique for the skillful performance of a movement task. The various types of reproduction styles include the command, practice, reciprocal, self-check, and inclusion styles.

Command Style

The **command style** of teaching is the time-honored method of teaching movement skills. Its primary purpose is to have the student learn the task quickly and accurately, in compliance with the decisions made by the teacher. The essence of this style is the immediate response to a stimulus. It is a process of replication, reproduction, and duplication of the "correct" performance. Command teaching consists of the following steps:

- The instructor gives a short explanation and demonstration of the skill to be performed.

- Students practice before the instructor gives further directions or points out specific errors.
- The instructor offers general comments to the class about their performance.
- The instructor gives further explanation and demonstration if necessary.
- Students practice, and the instructor gives coaching hints to individuals or groups having difficulty.
- Students implement the skill in an appropriate activity.

The command method makes all or most of the pre-performance and performance decisions for the learner. The teacher controls what is to be practiced, how it is to be done, and when the activity should begin and end. Uniformity, conformity, and replication are emphasized. A folk dance step, the correct overhand throwing technique, and a forward roll can all be effectively taught using the command style.

Command style teaching is being used here as the teacher demonstrates part of an "urban folk dance" for students to replicate. Here the students practice the dance as they replicate the dance movements in synchrony with the teachers.

Practice Style

The **practice style** is similar to the command method in that the teacher still determines what is to be practiced. This style is appropriate for teaching a fixed task that must be performed according to a specific model. When using the practice style, though, the teacher permits a greater degree of decision making on the part of the children. Students are asked to decide the order of the task(s); starting and stopping time; interval of practice; pace and rhythm; and location, or where they practice. Children are also encouraged to ask questions for clarification. In the practice style, the learner has more time to practice the skill individually and privately and receives more individual feedback from the teacher. When a teacher uses the practice style, the sequence looks like this:

1. The teacher explains and demonstrates the task, perhaps using a task sheet in written or pictorial form.
2. Students have a period of time to practice the designated task.
3. The teacher offers corrective feedback to learners and stays with learners to verify the corrected behavior.
4. The teacher visits, observes, and offers feedback to those who perform correctly and make the decisions appropriately.
5. The activity ends with a closure.

The task sheet in this style becomes the source of information, puts the focus on the learner, and holds the learner responsible for using the information on the task sheet (figure 10.2).

Reciprocal Style

The **reciprocal style** of teaching, sometimes referred to as "peer teaching," permits individual students to work with a partner in learning a new skill. Small-group teaching is similar except that a third person is involved. With both reciprocal and small-group instruction, the learner receives immediate partner or observer feedback that is based on specific criteria established by the teacher. Reciprocal teaching and small-group teaching are both excellent means of involving the entire class, focusing on error correction, and promoting positive socialization. In essence, reciprocal teaching establishes one student as the "mini teacher" and the other as the learner or performer. When circulating through the class, the instructor needs to be careful to reinforce the role of the mini teacher by speaking only to that person—not the learner—to obtain information about the learner's performance. Speaking directly to the learner will undermine the role and responsibilities of the mini teacher (i.e., observer). In small-group instruction, which works exactly the same, the third person serves as a tosser or retriever or takes some other specified role.

For catching, as an example, one student may serve as the performer, a second as the observer, and the third as the tosser or feeder. The performer executes the specific task of catching an 8-inch playground ball from a specified trajectory and distance. The observer watches to see if the performer moves to get "square" or behind the ball, extends arms out, reaches for the ball, uses only the hands to catch, and bends elbows upon catching to absorb force. The specific criteria have been determined by the teacher and are written on a developmentally appropriate task card (figure 10.3). The observer records the learner's performance. Meanwhile, the teacher

Student's Name: _____

Classroom Teacher's Name: _____

Date: _____

To the student:

Practice each of the jumps described below. Each jump can be performed

  1. On a mat

  2. Off of a low foam shape

  3. Off of a high foam shape

Place a ✓ next to the completed task.

Jumps	Check ✓ when completed
A. Stretched jump from two to two feet	_____ 1. On a mat _____ 2. Off a low foam shape _____ 3. Off a high foam shape
B. Jump from two to two feet, bring knees up toward chest (tuck)	_____ 1. On a mat _____ 2. Off a low foam shape _____ 3. Off a high foam shape
C. Jump from two to two feet with arms and legs wide (star jump)	_____ 1. On a mat _____ 2. Off a low foam shape _____ 3. Off a high foam shape

Teacher's Comments:

FIGURE 10.2 Practice style task sheet for jumping variations.

From *Developmental Physical Education for All Children* (4 ed.) by David L. Gallahue and Frances Cleland Donnelly, 2003, Champaign, IL: Human Kinetics.

Performer: Throw several times using the tennis balls toward the target on the wall.

Observer: Watch the thrower and give "help" when needed. Check YES ✓ if the thrower demonstrates the part of the throw you are watching, and NO ✓ if the thrower does not.

Remind them to:
Begin with their side toward the target
Begin with their throwing hand behind their ear
Step forward onto their opposite foot
Follow through across their body

Parts of the Throw to Watch:	Throws

Watch step #1 on throws #1-3

Step 1

Side toward target and throwing

Hand behind ear

1. Yes _____ No _____
2. Yes _____ No _____
3. Yes _____ No _____

Watch for step #2 during throws #4-6

Step 2

Steps forward onto opposite foot

1. Yes _____ No _____
2. Yes _____ No _____
3. Yes _____ No _____

Watch for step #3 during throws #7-9

Step 3

Follows through across body

1. Yes _____ No _____
2. Yes _____ No _____
3. Yes _____ No _____

Teacher's Comments:

FIGURE 10.3 Reciprocal style task card for the overhand throw.

From *Developmental Physical Education for All Children* (4 ed.) by David L. Gallahue and Frances Cleland Donnelly, 2003, Champaign, IL: Human Kinetics.

circulates among the class, speaking directly to the mini teacher, or the observer, about specific aspects of each learner's performance.

Self-Check Style

In the **self-check style,** more decisions are shifted to the learner. This challenges students to assume more responsibility. In self-checking, learners are expected to develop an awareness of their performance. Learning to observe one's own performance and then making a self-assessment based on specific criteria lead to kinesthetic awareness. However, individuals (children and adults) at the initial stage of fundamental movement skill development or at the beginning/novice level of movement skill learning will not benefit measurably from kinesthetic feedback. The teacher, therefore, must design a developmentally appropriate task sheet. On this type of task sheet children may simply check off the order in which they perform a task, or parts of a task they have completed, or the number of tasks they have completed. Regardless of the type of task sheet used in self-check style, learners must be honest and objective about their performance and must be able to accept their limitations. The teacher's role is to observe the learners' performance of the task and their use of the criteria sheet for self-check. The teacher should also communicate with the learners about their proficiency and accuracy in the self-checking process. Finally, the teacher should offer feedback at the end of the lesson to the whole class, in the form of general statements, about their performance of the role.

A group of boys completes a self-check task card in soccer.

Inclusion Style

The **inclusion style** introduces a different concept of task design—multiple levels of performance in the same task. This shifts a major decision to children, one that they cannot make in the other styles: at what level of performance does one begin?

The teacher still decides on the content of the lesson and the levels of performance available to the learner. The levels of the task to be practiced can be presented on a task sheet, on a chalkboard, or even verbally. For example, in an educational gymnastics lesson based on jumping and landing, the teacher may say, "Boys and girls. I would like you to practice jumping from one to two feet. You may jump on a mat, off the low foam shape (12 inches) onto a mat, or from the higher foam shape (24 inches) onto a mat." The children then decide which of the three jumping tasks they practice. The teacher should still provide a model of correct performance. When using the inclusion style, the teacher needs to consider the children's level of cognitive understanding. They cannot be expected to make abstract decisions about the levels of a task to be performed.

Production Styles

The second cluster of teaching styles, the production cluster, invites the learner to participate in discovering new movements and engaging in cognitive operations other than memory and recall. Children may be challenged to problem-solve, create, compare/contrast, or categorize. The discovery process can result in convergent thinking (guided discovery style and convergent discovery style) or divergent thinking (divergent production style). Production styles, or *indirect teaching styles* as they are often called, focus on the use of child-centered methods of teaching. **Child-centered methods** put the child at the center of the learning process. These methods are based on the philosophy that learning is more than the reproduction and modeling of mechanically "correct" movement behaviors. The belief behind child-centered methods is that *learning to learn* through experimentation, problem-solving, and self-discovery is essential to any "real" learning. Indirect teaching styles are grounded in **cognitive learning theory**, which holds that learning is an internal process that occurs from the inside out through incorrect mastery attempts and that the process of learning is just as important as the product.

CONCEPT 10.3

Learning how to learn is an important objective of indirect or production styles of teaching.

TEXT BOX 10.5

Child-centered teaching methods are based on the philosophy that learning is more than the reproduction and modeling of mechanically "correct" movement behaviors. Teachers using child-centered methods believe that *learning to learn* through experimentation, problem-solving, and self-discovery is essential to any "real" learning. Indirect or production teaching styles are grounded in *cognitive learning theory*, which holds that learning is an internal process that occurs from the inside out through incorrect mastery attempts and that the importance of the process of learning is equal to the importance of the product.

One advantage of production teaching styles is that they help children become more involved in the learning process itself. This happens because children have opportunities and receive encouragement to explore and experiment with movement in a variety of ways. Another important advantage of production or indirect styles of teaching is that they allow for individual differences between learners. All students are able to find a degree of success at their particular level of ability.

Indirect teaching styles have disadvantages, though. One major disadvantage is that they are time-consuming. Another is that teachers unfamiliar with these styles frequently find them difficult to use productively. Production styles require practice and patience on the part of the teacher. Students must have plenty of time for experimentation, trial and error, and question-asking. Teachers who have not been trained in these techniques sometimes find indirect styles difficult to use. They often have trouble in maintaining class control, structuring challenging movement problems, and providing for continuity both within and between lessons. These disadvantages, however, do not mean that production styles are inferior to reproduction styles of teaching movement. On the contrary, indirect styles play an important role in movement skill learning, particularly at the early stages of learning a skill.

Guided Discovery Style

The teacher using the **guided discovery style** designs a sequence of questions, each intended to help the learner make a small discovery. The teacher presents these questions to students in a sequence. Each question elicits a single, correct response by the learner. During the discovery process, the teacher provides periodic feedback to students and acknowledges their discovery of the concept. For example, a guided discovery lesson episode might help children discover the purpose of a follow-through in throwing or discover a principle; it could subsequently address NASPE Content Standard #2. Such a lesson might include the following set of questions:

- "Boys and girls, when you practice your overhand throw, where does your arm begin when throwing?"
- "Where should your arm finish, or follow through, at the end of your throwing pattern?"
- "Try throwing several times, stopping in the middle of your throw, and then several times completely finishing your throwing action. What is the main difference or result of your throw when you stop in the middle and when you stop at the finish or end of your throw?"

This sequence of questions invites students to solve a problem and to compare and contrast two different ending positions when throwing. The purpose of the questions is to lead children in discovering the purpose of a follow-through in the overhand throw—that is, achieving greater force.

Convergent Discovery Style

In the **convergent discovery style,** children are challenged to proceed through the discovery process without any guiding clues or questions from the teacher. They must still strive to find one correct solution to the movement task presented by the teacher. The teacher offers feedback or clues (if necessary) without providing the solution. Mosston and Ashworth (2001) present this example: "Design and perform a smooth, flowing 'movement sentence' by combining three of the following words: grow, spin, creep, pounce, explode or shrink" (p. 194). The key is in asking students to design only one sentence describing a movement that must be smoothly performed. "Students must make decisions about which three words to choose, the order of the words in the sentence, the movement that will represent each word, and the way of performing the movements, thus each will discover his or her own single solution to the problem" (Mosston & Ashworth, 2001, p. 194). When engaged in convergent discovery, children need to function physically, emotionally, and cognitively at a higher level than in any of the previous styles.

Divergent Production Style

When learning new motor skills, young children should explore the range of possibilities. The **divergent production style** engages children in discovering and producing new movement responses. The teacher decides the subject matter and designs the movement problems. It is important to design developmentally appropriate problems, taking into account children's level of skill proficiency, cognitive understanding, emotional maturity, and ultimately their safety. Time needs to be allotted so that children can inquire, explore, and design movement solutions. The teacher's role during the discovery process is to accept the students' responses and to verify that they are indeed solving the problem.

Feedback should be neutral and should be provided to the entire group, acknowledging that the process of discovery and divergent production is going well. The teacher should not focus on any particular solution by an individual student. These are some examples of movement problems:

- "How many ways can you send the playground ball toward the wall?"
- "How many different ways can you balance on three body parts?"
- "How many ways can you use the playground ball in your own personal space?"

It is important to remember that what may be new to children may not be novel to the teacher.

Two boys are exploring different ways to balance the hula hoop on various body parts at different levels. Exploration is prompted by using the divergent production style and by framing questions to foster exploration: "Boys and girls how many different ways can you and your partner balance the hula hoop on different body parts?"

These second graders discover different ways to support the body or balance on three different body parts. Using the divergent production style prompts students to find multiple solutions to a problem.

The key to effective use of any production teaching style is the thoughtful construction and use of movement challenges that allow for a variety of interpretations but still remain within the confines of the stated objectives of the lesson. Although reasonable solutions to movement challenges are considered correct, if you use this style you should not infer that the lesson will take its own course simply because you pose one or two questions to the class. You must constantly rephrase and restructure questions in an effort to probe and challenge each student. At the end of the process of attempting solutions to the movement problem, the children have an opportunity to evaluate their interpretations in light of the solutions of others.

Combining Reproduction and Production Styles

No one style is better than any other style. The lesson objectives should guide us in selecting one or more teaching styles for any lesson. For example, we can proceed from general to specific instruction within the same lesson. You might begin a lesson using the divergent production style by asking, "How many different ways can you position your body and feet when you throw?" After a period of discovery, you might continually formulate and reformulate questions that are progressively narrower in scope. By limiting students' options (e.g., asking them to select a stance in which they can shift their weight from their back to front foot), you are now using the convergent discovery style. You might then select the correct stance, demonstrate it, have the children replicate and practice this stance, and provide individual feedback to students; now you are using the practice style. Many students will be able to perform the skill correctly at this point. You might group those students with others who are experiencing difficulty and instruct the students to work on the overhand throw using group or peer tutoring (reciprocal style). Those

CONCEPT
10.4

A teacher can utilize reproduction (direct) and production (indirect) teaching styles within the same lesson.

241

So Many Teaching Styles, So Little Time

Real-World Situation

Your physical education classes will comprise boys and girls from a variety of home and educational backgrounds, and with a variety of learning styles. Some will respond brilliantly to "production" styles, whereas others will seem to respond best to "reproduction" styles. This, coupled with your learning goals for students, will make it difficult for you to settle on one preferred style.

Critical Questions

Based on your knowledge of reproduction and production teaching styles and the individuality of learners:

- Why may it be appropriate to combine various teaching styles within a single lesson?
- What will you use as your guide for moving from one teaching style to another within a particular lesson?
- When might it be inappropriate to use any one of the reproduction and production teaching styles?
- Why is it important to be concerned about when and how to use different teaching styles?

still having difficulty might observe other students or the teacher perform the desired skill and then work on it under progressively more direct supervision (command style).

HOW DO I CHOOSE TEACHING STYLES?

Up to this point we've discussed why multiple teaching styles exist in the first place and what the various teaching styles in the Spectrum are. We've also seen that many factors, such as the teacher's personality, expertise, values, and learning objectives, influence the choice of styles. Teachers must also consider student factors such as their level of maturity, behavior, and interest, as well as the available facilities, equipment, time, and safety.

The following considerations deal with characteristics of the learner and can guide you in selecting the teaching style that is appropriate for a particular movement skill theme:

- Ability to handle the task complexity (see chapter 2)
- Phase and stage of motor development (see chapter 3)
- Level of movement skill learning (see chapter 3)
- Comprehension of the task (see chapter 5)
- Behavioral ability to comply (see chapter 6)

Declaring that one style of teaching is superior to another is not correct. Teachers who are sensitive to the needs, interests, and developmental level of their students and who have considered both the environmental conditions and task complexity select carefully from a variety of teaching styles.

In the following paragraphs we consider three specific student factors that play into a teacher's choice of a teaching style: student movement skill learning factors, student comprehension, and compliance.

CONCEPT 10.5

Use of a particular teaching style may be determined by specific student factors of motor development and movement skill learning.

TEACHING TIP 10.1

FACTORS TO CONSIDER IN SELECTING AN APPROPRIATE TEACHING STYLE

Learner factors	Environmental factors	Task factors	Teacher factors
Stage of motor development	Facilities	Task complexity	Philosophy
Level of movement skill learning	Available equipment	Task difficulty	Personality
Level of cognitive comprehension	Time allotted	Risk of injury	Lesson objectives
Fitness level	Safety considerations	Movement pattern formation	Ability to adapt
Self-control	Class size		Class control
Interest			Self-confidence

TEACHING TIP 10.2

The developmental approach to teaching physical education recognizes the following concepts:

- All children learn differently.
- Children are learning how to learn.
- Motor development and movement skill learning factors should be primary determiners of the use of specific teaching styles.

- Teachers must carefully consider student comprehension and compliance factors before selecting a teaching style.
- Factors within the task, the individual, and environment itself may dramatically influence the selection of one style over another.

Movement Skill Learning Factors

When children and adults learn a new movement skill, they tend to go through a series of learning levels, as discussed in chapter 3 ("Movement Skill Acquisition") and recapped briefly here. As we said in chapter 3, the three learning levels are based on two important developmental concepts: first, that the acquisition of movement skills progresses from the simple to the complex and, second, that people proceed gradually from general to specific as they develop and refine movement skills. Recognition of the learner's place in this skill-learning hierarchy is important because it helps to determine both the teaching styles and movement activities we select.

Beginning/Novice Level

Whether children or adults, individuals at the beginning/novice level of acquiring a new movement skill first develop an awareness of just what the skill actually entails.

They begin to form a mental picture (cognitive map) and then explore the skill itself. Exploration of the skill generally occurs as a single unit; it is broken down into its simplest elements and practiced alone rather than being combined with other skills. At this level the learner does not have good control of the skill but gradually gets used to it and forms a gross general idea of how the body can move (the movement concept). During this first level, the learner forms a mental picture of how the body should move and attempts to bring it under conscious control.

As the learner becomes familiar with the elements of the skill, the process of discovery begins. The learner discovers ways of performing the skill through problem-solving and other indirect means, such as observing others and studying photos, film, or textual information. The learner gradually gains greater control and begins to coordinate the movements involved in executing the skill. During this period, basic performance of the skill tends to be under less conscious control than during the exploratory stage.

Individuals at the beginning level of learning a movement skill benefit from production teaching styles that help them develop an awareness of the skill and that foster freedom of movement exploration and guided discovery. These styles permit the learner to explore the movement task in its many forms and to develop a conscious mental image of the task. These same individuals tend to be at the initial and elementary stages within the fundamental movement phase of motor development. They are typically younger children of preschool and primary grade age but may be older children, adolescents, or adults. Again, remember that although development is age influenced, it is not age dependent. Therefore, individuals at the early stages of learning a new movement skill, whether children or adults, benefit greatly from production styles of teaching that help them get a general idea of how to execute the task. Reproduction styles of teaching are also appropriate to use at the beginning level of movement skill learning; however, the time to use them is after children have had an opportunity to explore and discover a range of movement possibilities.

TEXT BOX 10.6

Recognition of the learner's place in the movement skill learning hierarchy is important because it helps to determine both the teaching styles and movement activities selected for use.

Intermediate/Practice Level

Once the learner has gotten a general idea of how to perform a skill, it is practiced and combined with other movement skills. At the intermediate/practice level of learning a movement skill, the individual experiments with movement phrases. Skills are combined, elaborated on, and practiced in a variety of ways. Reproduction or production teaching styles may be used, with emphasis on practice through application of the skill to a variety of game, dance, and gymnastics activities.

The use of production teaching styles during the intermediate level is a logical extension of using the styles emphasized during the beginning stage of learning a skill. The learning experiences differ only in that the learner combines various movement skills rather than dealing with them in isolation. Individuals at the mature stage within the fundamental movement phase, and at the transitional stage within the specialized sport skill phase of motor development, benefit from movement experiences fostered by both reproduction and production styles of teaching. Individuals combining numerous movement skills are typically children who have mastered their fundamental stability, locomotor, and manipulative skills. They tend to benefit from movement activities that use combinations of different movement skills.

Advanced/Fine-Tuning Level

The advanced/fine-tuning level of learning a movement skill is characterized by a high degree of skill refinement. The combined skills that were selected at the intermediate level are further practiced and refined. The skills are frequently incorporated into more dynamic activities (i.e., involve unanticipated variables such as catching on the move, offensive and defensive playing) and often competitive sport and game activities. Individuals at the advanced level focus on improved accuracy, precision, and economy of movement. At this level, performance appears to be automatic, with little conscious attention given to the elements of the task as it is being performed. Often when a skilled performer reaches the advanced level, unique, personalized modifications begin to appear in the skill.

Generally speaking, the teacher in the regularly scheduled elementary school physical education program does not have a great number of children at the advanced level of learning movement skills. Although some children may be at this level in some areas, most are at the beginning or intermediate level. But appropriate experiences should be provided for children at all levels of ability.

The teaching styles you select and the movement activities you include in your program will be determined by where your students are in their phase and stage of motor development and the level of movement skill learning they are in. Figure 10.4 illustrates the interaction between the phases and stages of motor development, the levels of movement skill learning, and the appropriate teaching focus.

Student Comprehension and Compliance Factors

Students' comprehension, or ability to understand, and their ability and willingness to comply with instructions play an important role in selection of a teaching style. The ability to comply may vary according to the complexity of the movement task, the ability level of the children, and their level of self-control. You must adjust your teaching behavior to the needs of your students and determine whether you "invite" the learner to perform, "direct" the learner to perform, or "manipulate" the learner's performance.

Inviting to Perform

The first level of teacher intervention in the learning process involves inviting the learner to perform. If the movement tasks that make up the lesson are easy to understand and the children are capable of and willing to comply with your instructions, then it is appropriate to extend an invitation to perform. In other words, **inviting the learner** to perform frees you to select production teaching styles to satisfy the skill objectives of the lesson. Styles that are child centered and that incorporate

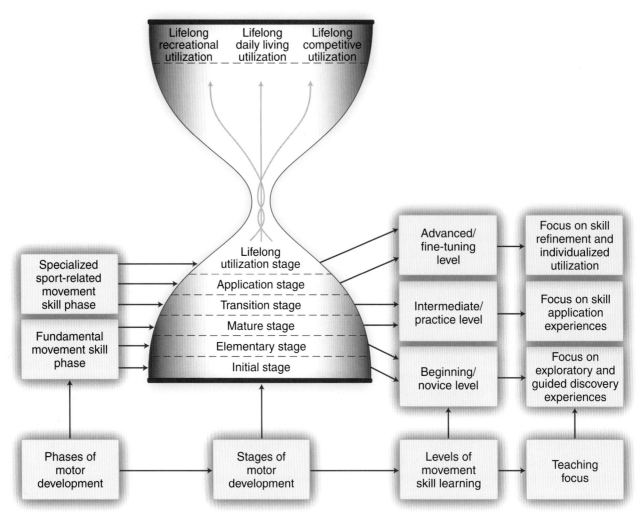

FIGURE 10.4   The interrelationship among the phases and stages of motor development, levels of movement skill learning, and teaching focus in movement skill acquisition.

movement exploration and guided discovery approaches are appropriate when you are inviting performance. These indirect styles of teaching are particularly effective during the early stages of the fundamental movement phase and at the beginning level of learning a new movement skill.

Directing to Perform

When the individual progresses to higher skill levels or is required to combine two or more movement skills, experienced teachers frequently modify their instructional approach by **directing the learner** to perform. The complexity of the movement task may hinder the learner's ability to comprehend how to actually perform the skill. Safety factors involved in performance of the task and available time, equipment, and facilities all have to be considered. Students at the mature and transitional stages of motor development and at the intermediate level in learning a new skill tend to benefit from direct styles of teaching as well as indirect styles. Using the command, practice, or reciprocal styles is effective for learners at this level.

Manipulating Through Performance

Sometimes, if a movement task is too cognitively complex for the performer, if the requirements are very exacting, or if safety is a major consideration, it becomes advisable to manipulate the learner through the task. **Manipulating the learner** has two aspects: manipulating the environment or physically manipulating the learner. You may, for example, manipulate the environment when teaching the mature over-hand throwing pattern by using props or learning devices that help the learner get the idea of stepping forward on the opposite foot or using good hip rotation. On the other hand, when teaching a back handspring, you'll want, at first, to physically manipulate the learner through the task several times at reduced speed. Both types of manipulation are used to help give the learner a "feel" for the skill.

The teacher in this developmental gymnastics lesson is physically assisting (or manipulating) a student, thus helping the student learn how to support her body weight while in a straddle position.

Physical manipulation is frequently used with individuals who have a cognitive disability. Actual patterning through a specific movement task is used to reinforce verbal commands. In this way the learner not only receives auditory and visual cues about the task but also receives tactile and kinesthetic cues. The use of several sensory modalities assists slow learners in grasping the essentials of the task at hand.

Whether you invite, direct, or manipulate children through performance of a movement skill depends on your students. Being sensitive to their individual needs and the needs of the class as a whole can help you incorporate appropriate teaching techniques at the appropriate time. It is altogether possible that within a single lesson you will do all three. You may invite performance by providing the class with movement challenges and other indirect forms of instruction. You may direct performance by providing specific instructional cues, teacher and student demonstrations, and other direct forms of instruction. You may even manipulate individual children by assisting them through various movement tasks.

CONCEPT
10.7

Indirect and direct teaching styles may be effectively combined for effective movement skill learning.

Summary

Effective teachers carefully select and use various teaching styles. Teaching styles should be selected based on a combination of the degree of decision making our students are developmentally prepared for and the desired objectives or the products of learning.

It is important to develop our students' decision-making, socialization, cognitive, and psychomotor skills. The NASPE National Content Standards for Physical Education address the importance of targeting all domains (i.e., cognitive, social, and motor) of learning. The literature also clearly supports engaging students in critical thinking. To accomplish this, teachers should use styles from both the reproduction and production clusters of teaching styles.

Developmental physical education recognizes that movement skill learning is an individual process that culminates in a product. Children must learn how to learn (the process), but it is equally important for them to become skillful movers (the product). Teachers of developmental physical education thus recognize the potential value of both direct and indirect teaching styles and reject the notion that a single teaching style is universally appropriate. The selection and use of teaching styles should be based on what we know about the learner's phase and stage of motor development, the level of movement skill learning, and the ability to comprehend and comply with the requirements of the task. Effective teachers are well versed in a variety of indirect and direct styles of teaching and use a variety of methods to maximize student learning and retention based on the needs of the learner.

Terms to Remember

Excellent Readings

Byra, M. (2000). A review of spectrum research: The contributions of two eras. *Quest, 52,* 229-245.

Byra, M., & Jenkins, J. (2000). Matching instructional tasks to learner ability—the inclusion style of teaching. *JOPERD, 71* (3), 26-30.

Cleland, F. (2002). The spectrum connection—assessment, social responsibility, and critical thinking. *TEPE, 13* (4), 10-13.

Ernst, M., & Byra, M. (1998). Pairing learners in the reciprocal style of teaching: Influence of student skill, knowledge, and socialization. *The Physical Educator, 55* (1), 24-37.

Franks, B.D. (Ed.). (1992). The spectrum of teaching styles: A silver anniversary in physical education. *JOPERD, 63* (1), 25-56. (Series of articles)

Hopple, C. (1993). Making a change: Three veteran teachers share their experiences. *TEPE, 4,* 1-11.

Lidor, R., & Singer, R.N. (2000). Teaching performance routines to beginners. *JOPERD, 71* (7), 34-36, 52.

McBride, R., & Cleland, F. (1998). Putting the theory where it belongs: In the gymnasium: Critical thinking in K-12 physical education. *JOPERD, 69* (7), 42–46.

Mosston, M. (1992). Tug-o-war no more: Meeting teaching-learning objectives using the spectrum of teaching styles. *JOPERD, 63* (1), 27–31.

Mueller, R., & Mueller, S. (1992). The spectrum of teaching styles and its role in conscious deliberate teaching. *JOPERD, 63* (1), 48–53.

Rink, J. (1993). *Teaching physical education for learning.* St. Louis: Mosby.

Siedentop, D., & Tannehill, D. (2000). *Developing teaching skills in physical education.* Mountain View, CA: Mayfield.

11

Planning for Success: Skill Themes and Lesson Planning

Key Concept

▶ Successful lessons are the result of systematic planning and careful organization geared to both age-group and individual appropriateness.

The thematic approach to teaching has become popular in recent years. A **developmental skill theme** is a movement skill or group of related movement skills that a lesson or unit of study is based on in order to achieve the aims of learning to move and learning through movement. Developmental skill themes center on specific movement skills (either fundamental or specialized skills) that are to be developed and refined as the major focus of the lesson. What makes them developmental is that they incorporate what we know about children's motor development (see chapter 2, "Childhood Growth and Motor Development"), the phases and stages of motor development and levels of movement skill learning (see chapter 3, "Movement Skill Acquisition"), children's health-related and performance-related fitness (see chapter 4, "Physical Activity and Fitness Enhancement"), and their cognitive and affective development (see chapters 5 and 6, "Cognitive Learning" and "Affective Growth") in the planning and implementing of lessons that are individually appropriate, meaningful, and fun. Activities from the content areas of physical education (developmental games, dance, and gymnastics) are incorporated into the skill theme approach as a means of achieving these curricular objectives. For example, children who are at the fundamental movement phase of development take part in lessons designed to advance them to a more mature stage in running, jumping,

Chapter Objectives

This chapter will provide you with the tools to do the following:

▶ Describe the steps in planning a skill theme.

▶ List several examples of preplanning that should occur prior to developing the lesson.

▶ Provide examples of techniques for pre-assessing student entry levels for a skill theme.

▶ Distinguish among and give examples of the yearly plan, unit plan, and lesson plan as applied to movement skill themes.

▶ Outline and describe the anatomy of the daily lesson plan.

▶ Discuss several factors to take into consideration when implementing the daily lesson.

▶ Provide examples of various techniques for evaluating the lesson.

▶ Discuss the concept of "moving on" to a new skill theme, and list factors to consider.

▶ Discuss the concept of "revisiting" a skill theme and factors to be considered.

▶ List several suggestions for organizing indoor and outdoor facilities and equipment.

▶ Discuss the importance of planning ahead in terms of placing equipment and its use.

▶ Provide examples of several instructional aids that may help implement the lesson.

▶ Describe how student helpers can be an asset to the lesson.

▶ Illustrate a variety of activity formations and discuss the purpose and advantages of each.

throwing, or catching. Those within the specialized phase take part in skill themes that enhance combinations of skills and concepts used in developmentally appropriate modifications of sport forms (i.e., basketball, softball, soccer, etc.). The central intent of a developmental skill theme approach is to enable children to achieve the curricular goals of becoming skillful movers, knowledgeable movers, and expressive movers. The developmental skill themes covered in part IV, "The Skill Themes," focus on fundamental movement skill learning.

> **TEXT BOX 11.1**
>
> The central intent of the developmental skill theme approach is to help children achieve the curricular goals of becoming *skillful movers*, *knowledgeable movers*, and *expressive movers*.

CONCEPT 11.1

Teachers must plan specifically for learning to occur and avoid the trap of simply keeping children "busy, happy, and good."

In this chapter we examine the actual steps involved in planning the developmental physical education program at the grassroots level. We discuss planning the daily lesson, formatting the lesson, evaluating its effectiveness, deciding when to move on, and revisiting a skill theme. The chapter also includes suggestions for organizing facilities, equipment, and classes and gives you guidelines for preparing instructional aids.

PLANNING A MOVEMENT SKILL THEME

CONCEPT 11.2

Planning involves a number of specific steps that must be followed to maximize the impact of the physical education curriculum.

Planning is a crucial element in the success of any educational program. Without careful planning, the physical education class ends up being little more than a glorified recess period. Experience has shown that teachers who fail to plan are really in essence planning to fail. They delude themselves with the notion that they are too competent, too busy, or somehow above planning. As a result, they invariably run into difficulties and unwittingly encourage a series of disasters that are unnecessary, unfulfilling, and educationally unsound. Here we discuss a better approach—an effective approach—to planning and implementing developmental movement skill themes.

Preplanning

Once the basic parameters of the physical education curriculum have been established, you may begin the important and challenging process of **program preplanning** for your unique teaching situation. A first step in preplanning is to inventory the facilities, equipment, and supplies that you'll have. You will need to know the teaching schedule, including the number of times classes meet per week and the length of each class, and also whether or not the children "dress" for gym.

Planning, Planning, Planning—Why All the Planning?

Real-World Situation

You have recently accepted a position as a physical education teacher at a local elementary school. Being a recent college graduate, you are filled with knowledge and with enthusiasm for your new job. You realize that you don't know anything specific about the students you will be teaching in terms of their movement skill levels, but you do know what age-appropriate activities should be included. Your plans are many and your ideas are sound—you think. But you don't know where to begin. You ask yourself, "Will I be expecting too much?" and "Will I be expecting too little?" and "Do they have the skill level they should have?" You can probably get by on the strength of your personality and your ability to keep children "quiet, happy, and good," but you know that this is not enough if you are to effect real learning among your students.

Critical Questions

Based on what you know about the steps in planning a movement skill theme:

- Why bother integrating your preplanning ideas with the reality of entry-level assessment?
- What information is critical during your preplanning process?
- How will you go about doing entry-level assessments without taking up too much time and still get valid information?
- If we know our students' age and grade level, why not simply develop lessons that are age appropriate?

This important general information, along with other considerations such as class size, alternative facilities during inclement weather, and community mores, comprises basic facts about the actual teaching-learning environment.

The exact amount of time to be spent on any skill theme should remain somewhat flexible. With younger children, two to four class periods on some themes is appropriate, with the themes revisited later on in the school year. With older children you may wish to spend as long as three or four weeks on a specific unit of instruction. Although it is suggested that near-equal balance be given to skill themes during the course of the school year, the specific amount of time you spend on particular skill themes will change as the abilities of individuals or the class change. For example, it may be helpful to children to focus more heavily on stability skill themes during the early periods of learning and gradually reduce this amount as they progress to more mature stages of ability. Emphasis on some skill themes, particularly in the manipulative areas, should increase from year to year. Emphasis on others may remain constant.

Assessing Entry Levels

After the initial preplanning, observe your students and informally assess their current movement abilities. This is known as **entry-level assessment.** (The chapters in part IV, "The Skill Themes," describe the characteristics of numerous fundamental movement skills. Read these chapters carefully and study the accompanying illustrations for each stage.)

To assess your students' present abilities in the movement skills you intend to focus on, use simple checklists. (Keep in mind, too, that it is virtually impossible to conduct detailed formal assessments in a timely manner without the assistance of a trained teacher's aide.) On the basis of this observational assessment, you can then classify your students or the group according to their level of movement skill

The manipulative skill themes of throwing and catching are facilitated by using a station lesson format in this primary grade lesson.

learning *(beginning/novice, intermediate/practice,* or *advanced/fine-tuning).* With this information, you can then make specific plans for lessons, taking care to use methods and techniques designed to move the class on to more skillful performance.

It is crucial to the concept of developmentally appropriate teaching that you observe and assess students before beginning the specific planning and implementing phase. Teachers have often been guilty of planning and implementing lessons and entire programs on age-related criteria alone. Diagnostic teaching requires that we carefully observe and assess the entry level of children before formulating and implementing specific strategies to advance them to the next stage of development.

Specific Planning

Once you have completed the preplanning and observational assessment of the entry level of ability, specific planning may begin. In **specific planning,** the teacher develops an age-appropriate scope and sequence chart (figure 11.1). The **scope and sequence chart** will provide you with an overview of the content of the curriculum in terms of age-group appropriateness. On the basis of the outline of the scope and sequence chart, preplanning information, and the observed performance of the children, you can begin to formulate more detailed yearly plans, unit plans, and daily lesson plans.

CONCEPT 11.3

Entry-level assessment is an essential aspect of planning the developmentally appropriate physical education lesson.

CONCEPT 11.4

Specific planning starts with the scope and sequence chart and ends with the daily lesson plan.

REALITY CHECK

Yearly Plans, Unit Plans, Lesson Plans: Who's Got the Time?

Real-World Situation

For years the physical education profession has suffered the skepticism of others because of the tendency of some among us to do little or no serious planning for learning among our students. The temptation is great to do just enough to get by. After all, you are the teacher who will have these students from grade to grade, so there is little internal accountability. You, along with the art and music teachers, are the anomaly among the teachers in the school, and as a result few principals have a real grasp of what a quality physical education program should look like. And you are the one who is often hired more as an afterthought for providing a planning period for the "real teachers." Consequently, the temptation is to "roll out the ball" and to occupy children's time without any real scope,

sequence, or breadth to your program—to get by, but to give little.

Critical Questions

Based on what you know about planning for success:

- What reasons might there be for poor, insufficient, or nonexistent planning among some teachers?

- What might you be able to do to encourage a colleague who lacks planning skills or initiative to "get with it" and be a credit to the profession?

- How will you go about developing your yearly, unit, and lesson plans?

- What resources can you make use of to facilitate the time-consuming task of planning?

The Yearly Plan

The **yearly plan** represents the scope of activities to be included in the curriculum at any grade for an entire school year. It is more detailed than the total curriculum outline and often reflects a seasonal influence that is based either on climatic

Number of lessons	Primary grades			Number of lessons	Intermediate grades		
	Kindergarten	First grade	Second grade		Third grade	Fourth grade	Fifth grade
5	Organization and pre-assessment	Organization and pre-assessment	Organization and pre-assessment	5	Organization and pre-assessment	Organization and pre-assessment	Organization and pre-assessment
5	Skill/fitness testing	Skill/fitness testing	Skill/fitness testing	5	Skill/fitness testing	Skill/fitness testing	Skill/fitness testing
5	Introduction to body awareness	Beginning body awareness	Intermediate body awareness	20	Beginning ball skills I	Beginning soccer skills	Intermediate soccer skills
15	Introduction to locomotor skills I	Beginning locomotor skills I	Intermediate locomotor skills I				
15	Introduction to upper limb manipulative skills	Beginning upper limb manipulative skills	Intermediate upper limb manipulative skills	15	Beginning strength training	Intermediate strength training	Beginning football skills
10	Introduction to body handling skills I	Beginning body handling skills I	Intermediate body handling skills I	20	Beginning ball skills II	Beginning basketball skills	Intermediate basketball skills
10	Introduction to lower limb manipulative skills I	Beginning lower limb manipulative skills I	Intermediate lower limb manipulative skills I				
15	Introduction to rhythmics	Beginning creative rhythmic skills	Intermediate creative rhythmic skills	15	Advanced creative rhythmic skills	Beginning folk and square dance	Intermediate folk and square dance
10	Introduction to flexibility and body control	Beginning flexibility and body control	Intermediate flexibility and body control	20	Beginning ball skills III	Beginning volleyball skills	Intermediate volleyball skills
10	Introduction to upper body propelling skills	Beginning upper body propelling skills	Intermediate upper body propelling skills				
10	Introduction to body handling skills II	Beginning body handling skills II	Intermediate body handling skills II	20	Upper and lower limb striking skills	Beginning field hockey skills	Intermediate field hockey skills
10	Introduction to locomotor skills II	Beginning locomotor skills II	Intermediate locomotor skills II				
15	Introduction to upper limb manipulative skills II	Beginning upper limb manipulative skills II	Intermediate manipulative skills II	15	Advanced rhythmic skills	Beginning rhythmic aerobics	Intermediate rhythmic aerobics
15	Introductory dance	Beginning rhythmic skills	Intermediate rhythmic skills	15	Introduction to lifetime skills I	Beginning disc sport skills	Intermediate disc sport skills
15	Introduction to upper limb striking skills	Beginning upper limb striking skills	Beginning track and field skills	15	Introduction to lifetime skills II	Beginning softball skills	Intermediate softball skills
15	Introduction to lower limb manipulative skills II and post-assessment	Beginning lower limb manipulative skills II and post-assessment	Intermediate lower limb manipulative skills II and post-assessment	15	Beginning track skills and fitness testing	Individual track and field skills and fitness testing	Advanced individual track and field skills and fitness testing

FIGURE 11.1   A sample scope and sequence chart (K-5) geared to age-group appropriateness.

Here all elementary physical education teachers meet with the district supervisor of physical education to discuss yearly curricular goals.

conditions, which may permit or prevent conducting classes outdoors, or on the time of year for particular activities. The yearly plan should provide an outline of the skills the class is to perform in each unit of instruction and is geared closely to developmental appropriateness (figure 11.2).

The Unit Plan

A **unit plan** is developed after the yearly plan has been outlined. Unit plans should reflect the National Content Standards for Physical Education developed by the National Association for Sport and Physical Education (NASPE). The unit plan also represents the themes of instruction (such as fundamental throwing and catching skills: *developmental games;* jumping and landing, transfer of weight: *developmental gymnastics;* or shape and level, locomotor patterns and pathways, strong and light movements: *developmental dance*). The unit plan is broken down into the specific skill themes that will be covered each week and the activities that will be used to develop these skills.

TEACHING TIP 11.1

Unit plans can be organized in numerous ways but should contain the following information:

- Title of the unit
- Specific objectives to be achieved by the learner
- Skills to be taught, in the appropriate sequence
- Specific activities to be used to develop these skills

- The equipment needed
- The method of evaluating the students' achievement of the objectives
- Sources of information for teachers and students

GRADE 1

Weeks	1-2	3-6	7-10	11-14	15-18
Unit	Class preplanning and assessment	Fundamental locomotor skills I	Fundamental manipulative skills I	Fundamental stability skills I	Fundamental rhythmic skills

Specific skill themes to be stressed	Skill and fitness testing
	
	Review of skills from previous year
		Running
		Starting
		Stopping
		Changing direction
		Tagging
		Dodging
		Pivoting
			Overhand throw
			Underhand throw
			Catching
			Vertical toss
			Object manipulation
				Static balance
				Dynamic balance
				Body rolling
					Movement to varying:
					  Accents
					  Tempos
					  Intensities
					  Rhythmic patterns
					Application of rhythmic fundamentals

	19-22	23-26	27-30	31-34	35-36
	Fundamental locomotor skills II	Fundamental stability skills II	Creative dance skills	Fundamental manipulative skills II	Review, evaluation, and summary
	Hopping Skipping Galloping Leaping Jumping	Static balance Dynamic balance Body rolling Body supports Inverted supports	Singing dances Simple dance forms	Kicking Bouncing Ball rolling Striking Dribbling	Skill and fitness testing Review of skills taught during the year

GRADE 5

Weeks	1-2	3-6	7-10	11-14	15-18
Unit	Class preplanning	Touch football skills	Soccer skills	Dance skills	Gymnastics skills
Specific skill themes to be stressed	Skill and fitness testing Review of skills from previous year	Passing Catching Centering Blocking Defense Rules Strategy	Kicking Trapping Dribbling Passing Tackling Rules Strategy	Creative dance Dances without partners Folk dances Square dance	Apparatus Tumbling Weight transfer Vaulting

	19-22	23-26	27-30	31-34	35-36
	Basketball skills	Volleyball skills	Softball skills	Track and field skills	Review, evaluation, and summary
	Dribbling Shooting Pivoting Passing Rules Strategy	Serving Bumping Setting Rotating Rules Strategy	Batting Pitching Throwing Fielding Catching Rules Strategy	Long jump High jump Dashes Distance run Hurdles Relays	Skill and fitness testing Review of skills taught during the year

FIGURE 11.2   A sample yearly plan for a first grade and a fifth grade class, based on developmental appropriateness.

The Lesson Plan

A **daily lesson plan** enables teachers to make the best use of each class period, saves energy and time, and assures progression in the program. Each lesson should be a meaningful experience through which the pupils learn something new and refine previously learned materials and skills.

Maximum active participation by all should be the goal of every lesson. A way to accomplish this is to provide, when possible, individual pieces of equipment for each child. When this is not feasible, you may want to use a station concept in which children rotate in small groups from one activity station to another. Using reciprocal style teaching also accommodates several students when equipment for each child is not available (please refer to chapter 10, "Teaching Styles"). Another key to maximum activity is to predetermine the smallest number of participants that are needed for success of the activity, forming several small groups instead of one or two large groups. Lesson plans enable teachers to review and relate to the overall program objectives. They help in the preparation of the coming lesson, provide an organized and progressive procedure that aids in keeping class interest and building individual motivation, and often help prevent disciplinary problems. Lesson plans help the teacher emphasize important points and skill elements. And they aid in evaluating teacher as well as pupil progress.

CONCEPT 11.5

Use of a daily lesson plan is the critical point at which the planning process and *real* children meet.

The lesson plan is more specific than the unit plan and is the primary means of clarifying exactly what you intend to do during a specific lesson with "your" children. Lesson planning, which is essential for success in any curricular area, helps to ensure that the teacher devises specific strategies for implementing the objectives of the lesson that are geared to the children being taught. In developmental physical education, lesson planning is essential because it is the focal point of planning for individual appropriateness.

TEACHING TIP 11.2

When planning the lesson, be sure to plan for:

- Maximum participation in meaningful activities for all
- Opportunities for each class member to acquire new skills in accordance with the stated objectives
- Participation in, appreciation of, and enthusiasm for vigorous physical activity
- A variety of carefully selected activities that have motor, cognitive, and affective value
- Opportunities to correlate and integrate physical education with other subject areas in the curriculum
- Opportunities for personal and social growth
- Opportunity for self-evaluation of daily accomplishments

The primary purpose of the lesson plan is to help you think through your lesson so that it is maximally efficient in terms of the children you teach. You can keep lesson plans in a file for easy reference for the following year when you may wish to use parts of the lesson again. You can make notations concerning the effectiveness of the lesson and include suggestions for modifications. Figure 11.3 presents a sample lesson plan outline.

Lesson Objectives	Introduction	Review Activity	Lesson Focus		Summary/ Dismissal
			Skill Development	Skill Application	Review:
Motor:					
Cognitive:					Preview:
					Homework:
Affective:					Dismissal:

Unit: _____ Skill Theme: _____
Grade: _____ Class: _____ Day/Week/Month: _____

a

Equipment Needed:	
Resources:	
Class Evaluation	Self-Evaluation
Safety Considerations:	

b

FIGURE 11.3   Sample format for a daily lesson plan on a 5-by-8-inch index card: *(a)* front, *(b)* back.

SEQUENCING THE DAILY LESSON

Once you figure out the objectives of the lesson, you will need to focus on the actual content of the lesson. The lesson generally consists of four parts when there is ample time for all these components to be included: introduction, review, body, and lesson summary or closure (figure 11.4).

Introduction (Set induction)

Begin the lesson with an easy-to-organize, active, maximum-participation activity to be used as a warmup activity or as a lead-in to the body of the lesson. | 5-10 minutes

Review (Cognitive set)

Briefly go over the main points of the previous lesson, using a specific activity and key teaching phrases. | 5-10 minutes

Body (Lesson focus)

A. *Skill development:* Focus on new skill learning through practice in a variety of exploratory, guided discovery, or skill-drill activities that focus on improvement. | 10-15 minutes

B. *Skill application:* Use new skills in developmentally appropriate game, dance, or gymnastic activities. | 5-10 minutes

Summary

A. *Review:* Briefly review the highlights of the day's lesson | 3 minutes

B. *Preview:* Briefly state the objectives for the next lesson.

C. *Homework:* Assign movement skill and/or fitness homework. | 2 minutes

D. *Dismissal:* Rather than letting the children run to the doors, provide a fun, novel, and challenging dismissal activity.

_____

30-50 minutes total

FIGURE 11.4   Suggested format and time frame for implementing the lesson.

Sometimes teachers are required to implement a lesson as short as 15 to 20 minutes. If this is the case, meticulous planning is absolutely essential. You cannot afford to waste even a minute. Furthermore, the review portion and skill development portion of the body of the lesson should remain intact, as much as possible. You may be able to incorporate the introductory portion of the lesson into the review, and you may need to sharply curtail or eliminate the skill application portion of the body of the lesson. With encouragement, children can apply the skill themselves during recess, at the noon hour, or after school. The lesson summary will have to be brief, perhaps occurring on the way back to the classroom.

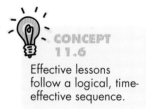

CONCEPT
11.6
Effective lessons follow a logical, time-effective sequence.

The number of learning objectives for a lesson depends on the duration of the class and the number of times a class meets per week. It may also depend on children's level of movement skill learning (i.e., beginning/novice, intermediate/practice, advanced/fine-tuning), as well as their social and cognitive maturity. Adoption of an attitude of doing fewer things, but doing them well, is advised. Avoid "throwing in the towel" and resorting to endless game playing with the excuse that "there just isn't enough time to teach." We must make maximum quality use of the time we do have, while making a real effort to increase the frequency and number of minutes for each lesson. Our goal should be at least 30 minutes of daily instructional physical education for all. Remember, you are not alone in trying to achieve this goal. This is also the expressed goal of the United States Congress, the American Medical Association, the United States Department of Health and Human Services, the American Academy of Pediatrics, NASPE, and the President's Council on Physical Fitness and Sports.

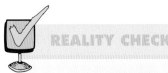

The Daily Lesson: "Where the Rubber Meets the Road"

Real-World Situation

The daily lesson has several parts, all sequenced so as to make maximum effective use of limited time. As a new teacher your tendency will be to overplan in some aspects of the lesson and to underplan in others. As a result, you may find yourself in the not-so-envious situation of being only halfway through the lesson when the bell rings and it's time for the students to go back to their classroom. Worse yet, you may find yourself finished with the lesson with several minutes to go before the bell rings. Whatever the case, there is no excuse for not sequencing lessons so as to make maximum effective use of time *and* maximize student learning and retention.

Critical Questions

Based on what you know about the importance of sequencing the daily lesson:

- Why is more time given to some parts of the lesson and less time to others?
- Why is the beginning of the lesson so important to its success?
- What purposes does the review portion of the lesson serve?
- What function does the body of the lesson serve?
- Why is setting aside time for a lesson summary important?

Lesson Introduction

The **lesson introduction** is sometimes referred to as **set induction**, **anticipatory set**, or **cognitive set** because it *sets* the stage for the lesson to come and provokes students' interest and enthusiasm. It is short, lasting only about 5 minutes. It is closely related to the focus of the day's lesson, designed to get the children organized and quickly involved, and frequently has a vigorous fitness component. You can also think of the introductory activity as an *instant activity,* one that may serve as a warm-up or as a lead-in activity for the lesson to follow. Ideally, it will be all of these. The keys to successful introductory activities are total participation, vigorous participation, and ease of organization. The introductory activity is often an important way to prepare children to focus their attention on the lesson to come and to understand its purpose.

The introduction can be designed in a number of different ways. For example, children might read the directions for an instant activity from among those displayed on a chalkboard. The class would then engage in the activity and dissect the activity, with the teacher's guidance, to complete the set induction. Another method might be to provide children with individual task cards designed to prompt activity. Regardless of the type of warm-up, lead-in, or instant activity, the equipment should be set up beforehand so that the activity can proceed quickly and efficiently. The following are three examples of set induction.

- **Example 1.** "When you're playing basketball with your friends, do you sometimes have trouble dribbling the ball up court without getting it stolen from an opposing player? Well, today we're going to learn two ways to prevent that from happening. First I would like you to find your own personal space. When the music begins you will move through general space, speeding up and slowing down as the music speeds up and slows down. Use the locomotor skills of jogging and sliding sideways. Be sure to change directions quickly and sharply."

- **Example 2.** "Have you ever tried putting three simple locomotor movements together: a hop, a step, and a jump? Today, we're going to begin doing just that by learning how to do what is called the triple jump. But first let's get with a partner and see how far we can do each one separately."

- **Example 3.** Play *four corners.* Four (or more) tall cones are positioned at each of the corners of a rectangular or square space. Posters are displayed on each cone. Approximately four locomotor skills are written in sequence on these posters, each one in a different color. Children, divided into four groups, begin at a specified cone. As music plays, the children perform the first locomotor skill written on the poster displayed on their cone. They change the locomotor skill when they come to a new cone. Thus on the first trip around the cones, children execute the first locomotor skill written on each poster; on the second time around they perform the second locomotor skill, and so forth, until they have completed all 16 locomotor skills.

Lesson Review

The **lesson review** comes after the introduction. It generally lasts from 5 to 10 minutes or less and focuses on the highlights of the previous lesson. Lengthy explanations and discussions of the previous lesson should be avoided. Rather, an appropriate activity, coupled with strategic teacher comments, should be the major aspect of this portion of the lesson. Remember, the reason for review is to help the child make the link between the material that was covered in the previous lesson and what will be presented as new material in the present lesson. One way to do a review is to use a previously made videotape of the students practicing a skill or playing a small-sided game. Another technique is to ask a student volunteer or two to demonstrate a skill as you highlight critical movement cues. The following are two examples of the review portion of the lesson:

- **Example 1.** "Remember in our last lesson when we practiced striking patterns? What cue did we emphasize? That's right, side-to-target! Today, we are going to continue practicing this striking skill; however, we will be hitting the shuttlecock over a net and thinking about 'racket back' and 'low to high'!"

- **Example 2.** "Last lesson we worked on individual movement phrases on the mats using rolls, turns, and springs. What were three important things that we learned about each? What kinds of rolls, turns, and springs did you use in your routine? Let's take a few minutes to try them again. Now, today, we are going to discover two new ways to travel down the mat using rolls, turns, and springs, and we're also going to add one more element to our personal movement phrases."

Body of the Lesson

The **body of the lesson** is the central focus of the daily lesson—this is the part of the lesson you'll devote the greatest amount of time to. It may range from 15 to 25 minutes long, depending on the total time allotted for class. The body of the lesson contains two sections: skill development and skill application. **Skill development** is the single most important part of the entire lesson and may be divided into one or more teaching episodes. A **teaching episode** is a segment that focuses on a particular aspect of skill development and incorporates the use of a particular teaching style (please refer to chapter 10, "Teaching Styles," for a detailed discussion). In the skill development portion of the lesson there may be more than one teaching episode as skill upon skill is built and you move from one teaching style to another in your quest to maximize learning. It is in this part of the lesson that you teach the new material to be learned that day. **Skill application** follows skill development and enables students to use newly learned skills in appropriate game, dance, or gymnastics activities.

Teachers need to take care to focus on the developmental aspect of the skill, concentrating efforts on progressing to higher levels of ability rather than playing games for their own sake. Remember, only after children have mastered the skill reasonably well should it be incorporated into gamelike activities.

The body of the lesson centers on skill development through practice, using a variety of teaching approaches that you select depending on the objectives of the lesson. Children at the fundamental movement skill phase benefit from a variety of exploratory, guided discovery, and basic skill development activities. Boys and girls at the sport skill phase benefit more from activities that stress application of these skills, focusing on improved performance.

The body of the lesson has also been described as a "task system" including managerial and instructional tasks (figure 11.4). "Students will enter the gymnasium or need to move to an outdoor space (managerial-transition task). They will have to be informed as to what content will be practiced for the lesson (informing, refining, extending, and applying instructional tasks). They may have to be organized differently for different instructional tasks (managerial-transitional tasks)" (Siedentop & Tannehill, 2000, p. 259). Managerial tasks are "noninstructional" and include tasks such as setting up equipment, changing group formations, or moving students from one area to another. Instructional tasks include the following four, in order of their appearance in the lesson:

1. **Initial or introductory tasks.** An initial task is a movement task that is used to begin a teaching episode or lesson. All subsequent tasks are based on this initial task.

2. **Extending tasks.** The lesson is developed, or progressions are created, by applying the movement concepts to develop or modify a skill theme. Changes of speed, direction, pathway, or relationship to a partner are all movement concepts that could be used to vary an initial task, hence creating a progression of tasks. These extending tasks are often *within-task progressions*. In within-task progressions the movement skill does not change; instead it is modified or developed using one or more movement concepts.

3. **Refining tasks.** Through refining tasks, students become more aware of the technical components or proper form of a skill. Refining tasks cannot always be preplanned or anticipated. Teachers must observe their students' performance and subsequently utilize this information to provide relevant refining tasks (Siedentop & Tannehill, 2000, p. 218).

4. **Application tasks.** An application task establishes a challenge for students. You might say, for example, "Can you bounce the ball in and out of the hula hoop 10 times without losing control?" An application task may also offer students the opportunity to use the movement skill or skills in an authentic, applied way, such as in a developmentally appropriate game situation. This may also be the time when students put movement phrases together to create a dance or gymnastics movement sentence. Application tasks can be presented to students at any time during the body of a lesson; they are not used only at the end of a teaching episode or lesson.

Lesson Summary

The **lesson summary**, which includes the lesson review and class dismissal, is the last portion of the lesson, and is an important part of the lesson even though it may last only 2 or 3 minutes. Authentic assessment of students' motor, social, or cognitive understandings often takes place during the lesson closure (please refer to chapter 12, "Assessing Progress," for a more detailed discussion of authentic assessment). The summary gives the instructor an opportunity to bring closure to the lesson by helping the children review what was stressed during the lesson and why they took part in certain activities. The summary portion of the lesson also permits time to highlight what will be presented in the next lesson, assign fitness and skill practice "homework," and arrange for orderly dismissal.

TEXT BOX 11.3

Effective teachers recognize the need for a scope and sequence chart that provides an age-appropriate blueprint for their program. As an effective teacher you must also recognize the vital need for developmental appropriateness achieved through observational assessment and detailed, but flexible, individual planning. A constant process of evaluating and reassessing student progress, interest, and needs will enable you to be flexible and to refocus and revisit lessons to create the most effective learning environment.

IMPLEMENTING YOUR DAILY LESSON

It is easy to read about a variety of teaching styles and to gain textbook knowledge of how and when it is appropriate to apply each method. But as you undoubtedly realize, such textbook knowledge is no substitute for actual experience and will not make you a good teacher. Nevertheless, our purpose in this section is to help by offering practical suggestions for implementing the movement lesson. You must couple this knowledge with frequent practice with children and critical self-analysis if it is to have real and lasting benefit.

Putting It All Together

The primary objectives of the developmental physical education lesson exist to help children acquire movement skills and enhance fitness. Additional objectives in a variety of cognitive and affective competencies are also an important part of the total curriculum. These objectives may be simply stated in terms of expected learner outcomes, but it is important that these outcomes be suitable for the child's developmental level. For example, the lesson objective may be "to improve jumping ability in the jump for distance" or "to be able to catch a small ball with greater efficiency."

Once the learning outcome has been established, the teacher proceeds to formulate the movement challenges or instructional tasks to be presented in the lesson. Initially, the tasks may be open ended and exploratory; guided discovery and then progressive problem-solving may follow. The progressive problem-solving or limitation portion of the lesson should lead to refinement of the desired skill by ensuring that each succeeding challenge or question given the learner is more narrowly defined. You should attempt to anticipate a broad range of possible responses before presenting the challenges in the lesson. It takes practice to structure meaningful movement challenges that lead to progressive skill refinement. Be prepared for solutions other than those you anticipate, and recognize the necessity for restructuring problems that the students do not clearly understand at first.

You will need to consider whether and at what point to intervene with more direct styles of teaching. Following the movement challenge portion of the lesson, you may decide to select from the reproduction cluster of teaching styles, including the command, practice, reciprocal, self-check, and inclusion styles.

You must next determine what specific developmental game, dance, or gymnastics activities to use. These activities should use the movement skills that earlier were incorporated into the lesson. You may decide, for example, to have the children play a circle or tag game to reinforce the running skills worked on in the lesson; or you may select a rhythmical activity with a fast tempo to permit rhythmical running.

The last part of lesson planning concerns the summary and review. It is important for you to sit down for a few minutes with your students at the end of the lesson to review the movement skills that were stressed. In this way you reinforce the lesson's concepts and crystallize them in the children's thinking and action. The lesson summary is an excellent time to encourage students to do skill or fitness "homework" at home or with their friends.

Achieving Successful Lessons

To implement a successful movement lesson, the teacher needs to keep five basic principles in mind:

1. **Students must be given maximum active learning time.** The teacher must be certain that children are in fact making progress toward accomplishing the specifically stated objectives of the lesson. It is not enough that each child is active—the children must achieve **active learning time** in physical education (ALT-PE). The definition of ALT-PE is "the amount of time a student spends engaged successfully in activities related to lesson objectives" (Siedentop & Tannehill, 2000, p. 24). Activities, therefore, must be designed to achieve the lesson objectives; and objectives must be clearly stated in terms of their intended motor (movement skill acquisition; physical activity and fitness enhancement), cognitive (perceptual-motor and concept learning), and affective (personal and social) outcomes. Remember, it is your responsibility to actively teach toward the stated objectives of your lesson. It is not enough to assume that learning occurs simply through participation in physical activities.

2. **Instructors must understand and be able to apply basic body mechanics.** It is important to understand the basic body mechanics of each skill. To foster efficient development of movement skills, you must understand the principles of movement involved and how to apply them. As a result, you should provide general corrective feedback to the whole class and individual corrective feedback to individual students. State your feedback in positive terms. Positive general feedback might be "Good job, class, everyone was moving to open spaces!" or "Excellent, everyone was bending their knees as they landed from their jump!" Positive individual specific feedback might be "Good job, Stacey, you stepped forward with your

TEACHING TIP 11.3

These hints will help you implement *successful lessons:*

- Be thoroughly prepared; overplan.
- Maximize activity time and time-on-task for all.
- Insist on complete attention from the class at all times.
- Have all necessary equipment and supplies readily available prior to the lesson.
- Stand where everyone can see and hear you.
- Do not "talk down" to students, but use a vocabulary that is warm, friendly, and understandable to them.
- Begin class with a vigorous warm-up activity focusing on the fitness strand of the lesson.
- Teach by objectives; center your lesson on a specific movement skill theme geared to the developmental level of your students.
- Constantly observe and informally assess pupil progress; modify the lesson content accordingly.
- Be certain to incorporate the cognitive and affective strands into the lesson.

- Summarize, using key words or phrases.
- When asking for questions from the class, be specific.
- Emphasize the process aspects of movement skill learning (form, style, mechanics) prior to the product aspects (how far, how fast, how many).
- Never let an activity drag. Change activities *before* children lose interest.
- Be observant of individual differences; structure the lesson so that all feel challenged and can find a measure of success.
- Use the final few minutes for reviewing the lesson, self-evaluation, and assigning "homework" in preparation for the next lesson.
- Incorporate dismissal techniques that are novel, fun, and orderly.
- Evaluate each lesson in terms of achievement of the objectives.

opposite foot during your throw!" or "John, your follow-through across your body was effective!" Feedback like this also works for refinement tasks provided during the body of the lesson.

3. **A safe learning environment is essential.** A successful lesson is a safe lesson. The teacher must constantly anticipate potential dangers and ensure that proper safety precautions are being followed. For example, a return to more direct teaching approaches may be necessary during certain portions of the lesson to remedy an unsafe situation quickly and efficiently.

4. **Teachers must challenge all to do their best.** It is important that you circulate throughout the class during the lesson and structure movement challenges in a variety of ways. Challenges may take the form of questions, problems, discussions, or verbal cues and should be varied so that none are used to the exclusion of the others. Examples of helpful phrases are "Who can . . . ?" "How can you . . . ?" "Let's try . . ." "Find a way to . . ." "Let's see if . . ." and "Is there another way to . . . ?" It's important not to oververbalize at the expense of active involvement on the part of the children.

5. **Teachers must maximize time-on-task.** Successful lessons maximize *time-on-task* and the amount of activity itself. Children have a great need to be active. Thus the lesson should be one of active learning, not learning with little or no activity. Similarly, the amount of actual learning time spent on the objectives of the lesson is critical to the lesson's success. Time spent on class control problems, getting equipment, reorganizing groups, or taking attendance is time wasted because it detracts measurably from achieving the objectives of the lesson.

The physical education teacher circulates among students engaged in an instant activity so that he can motivate and challenge the students to do their best!

Successful lessons depend on careful adherence to the five factors just discussed. In addition, your genuine interest, enthusiasm, experience, ingenuity, and imaginative use of teaching approaches are also essential to the successful lesson.

Evaluating the Daily Lesson

Each aspect of the daily lesson we have outlined is important to successful teaching of the physical education lesson. Carefully plan all aspects of the lesson to maximize its impact. You should evaluate the effectiveness of your lessons periodically and make adjustments in the methods, techniques, and approaches used. Without periodic evaluation, it is impossible to know whether students have improved their abilities or how to plan effectively for subsequent lessons. Therefore, it is advisable for teachers to assess the children's progress regularly. At the preschool and elementary school levels, the key to successful evaluation is simplicity. As long as you are familiar with the developmental characteristics of both fundamental and specialized skills, simple observational assessment (process assessment) will generally suffice. On the basis of your informal evaluation of progress, you will need to modify your lessons. Constant monitoring of pupil progress will provide you with information necessary to plan effective, challenging, and developmentally appropriate lessons. Chapter 12, "Assessing Progress," deals with both process assessment and product assessment of movement skill learning and physical fitness in both traditional and alternative environments.

Moving On

Probably the most crucial but least scientific aspect of the entire planning process is knowing when to move on to another skill theme. It is impossible to provide anything more than general guidelines on how much time should be spent on a

TEACHING TIP 11.4

Moving on to a new skill theme is appropriate under these conditions:

- A high percentage of students have achieved the objectives of the skill theme.
- A high percentage of children have shown a reasonable degree of improvement beyond their entry level.

- Active interest in the lesson has decreased and the amount of time the children spend on task has decreased.

particular skill theme. No two groups, classes, or individuals are exactly alike. Experienced teachers, however, sense when it is time to move on to another theme.

Ideally, every teacher wants all children to achieve a 100% success rate throughout the entire curriculum. This of course is not possible given the normal variation in natural abilities, learning styles, and other factors. Experienced teachers, however, continue to strive for 100% success, being fully aware that they will have to individualize their teaching to try to reach this elusive goal. Don't be discouraged about achieving less than perfection. It is important to adopt an attitude that success is equal to improvement and that improvement is relative to the individual's entry level. For example, if you determine at the onset of the unit that children are at the initial stage in volleying and striking and they have "only" achieved the elementary stage after several lessons, there has been improvement, even though the mature stage has not yet been reached. To maximize success, the movement challenges must be just that, challenges, but they should not be overwhelming. Therefore, you need to carefully and continually observe and refocus the lesson to achieve a balance between success, challenge, and failure.

CONCEPT 11.7

Knowing when to move on to another skill theme, and when to revisit a previous skill theme, is based on developmental considerations frequently masked in behavioral indicators.

Revisiting Skill Themes

Revisiting, which is based on developmental principles of physical and cognitive maturation, refers to coming back to skill themes at different times throughout the school year. Subtle clues of frustration, boredom, inattention, and general off-task behavior are good indicators that it is time to refocus your lessons or move on to another skill theme. As a rule of thumb, it is better to spend two or three lessons on a skill theme with preschool and primary grade children and revisit it once or twice during the school year than it is to focus all your attention on that skill theme at one time. Children in the upper elementary grades tend to benefit from longer periods of time on a particular skill theme but also benefit from revisiting. You probably should not spend more than a maximum of 8 to 10 lessons on any one unit of instruction at one time. Remember, however, to be flexible and responsive to the needs of your students and to revisit when appropriate.

Effective teachers recognize the need for a scope and sequence chart that provides an age-appropriate blueprint for their physical education program. As an effective teacher you must also recognize the vital need for developmental appropriateness through observational assessment and detailed, but flexible, individual planning. A constant process of evaluating and reassessing pupil progress, interest, and needs enables you to be flexible and to refocus and revisit lessons to create the most effective learning environment. Figure 11.5 provides an overview of the nature of the steps in planning and implementing the lesson.

FIGURE 11.5   Steps in planning and implementing the lesson.

ORGANIZING FACILITIES

Physical education teachers need to pay particular attention to the facilities that serve as teaching stations. Indoor facilities should be clean and free of safety hazards and should have proper flooring, lighting, and acoustics. Outdoor facilities need to be free of safety hazards, to be located away from occupied classrooms, and to have clearly defined physical boundaries.

Indoor Facilities

The gymnasium is a classroom, a learning laboratory in which children use their entire bodies in the process of learning. It is of utmost importance that the gymnasium be free of potential safety hazards. In many elementary schools the gymnasium also serves as the school cafeteria or as a multipurpose room. Lunch tables are often stored against walls or shoved into a corner. Instead, every effort should be made to store tables and other equipment elsewhere. If this is not possible, it is important that such items be secured and that the boundaries of the gymnasium be clearly redefined to exclude the storage area. The space that is used by your students must be free of obstacles if it is to be safe.

The physical education teacher prepares equipment for a lesson to be conducted outside.

The flooring used for the indoor learning environment is also important. Tiled, wooden, or carpeted floors all have important implications for the types of activities that are safe to include in the lesson and the type of footwear children should wear. You should give careful attention to the way the floor is marked. It is easy to apply pressure-sensitive tape for temporary markings, but you need to be sure to remove it when you are finished. If pressure-sensitive tape remains on the floor for several months, it often becomes difficult to remove. Masking tape should not be used for floor markings unless it is removed weekly—masking tape dries out quickly and becomes extremely difficult to remove. The number of permanent markings for the gym floor should be limited. Too many lines tend to be confusing to children.

The acoustics of gymnasiums are often difficult for teachers to deal with. The large size of the gymnasium, the use of equipment, and a lack of sound-baffling materials such as carpeting or ceiling tile often result in poor acoustics. Be sure that you are familiar with the acoustics of your indoor teaching station. If the acoustics are bad, you will need to adjust your voice and use nonverbal cues accordingly. Failure to do so will result in considerable frustration and voice strain.

The gymnasium should be well lighted and free of shadows. All lights should be covered with protective grids to prevent breakage. The ceiling height and location of the lights will determine whether certain activities can be included or excluded. Volleyball, for example, should be prohibited if the lights are not covered or if the ceiling is too low to permit proper play.

Gymnasium floors should be cleaned at least twice each day. Remember, much of the children's time is spent on the floor, so it needs to be free of dirt and debris. A large push broom or mop should be kept close by for frequent use. Gymnasium mats should be neatly stored and periodically cleaned with mild soap and water. Blindfolds, bandannas, and other cloth items should be laundered frequently and stored properly.

Outdoor Facilities

You should inspect the outdoor physical education facility daily for potential safety hazards. Be certain that the area is free of obstacles, broken glass, and holes. Frequently, non-school groups use outdoor facilities after school hours. Therefore it is important to perform the daily inspection immediately before you conduct classes. This takes only a few minutes and helps reduce potential hazards.

The surface of the outdoor physical education area should be level, dry, and free of stones and other debris. The facility should be far enough away from classrooms that physical education classes do not interfere with other classes. It should be located on school property as far from parking lots and city streets as possible, but at the same time should be close enough to the school to permit easy access to equipment and shelter in case of a sudden change in the weather.

The boundaries of the outdoor instructional area must be clearly defined and enforced. The feeling of freedom that often comes with being outdoors must not hamper conduct of the class. It is important to be able to maintain visual and verbal contact with each member of the class at all times when outdoors. Defining, clearly marking, and enforcing boundaries will make your outdoor teaching job much easier. For more information on this topic please refer to *Guidelines for Facilities, Equipment and Instructional Materials in Elementary Physical Education* (2001), a resource guide published by the American Alliance for Health, Physical Education, Recreation and Dance through the NASPE Council on Physical Education for Children.

CONCEPT 11.8

Effective lessons make maximum use of the time available through careful organization of facilities, equipment, instructional aids, and student helpers.

This outdoor area illustrates the importance of a flat, grassy area for teaching games. It is important to take care of outdoor facilities, to check for debris, water, or other unsafe conditions.

ORGANIZING EQUIPMENT

The selection, placement, and use of equipment are important aspects of effective organization of the lesson. To encourage maximum class participation and minimize disruptive behavior, teachers need to see that all members of the class are actively

The 3 S's: Safe, Secure, Sanitary Conditions

Real-World Situation

Many of today's schools are used by a host of groups, some invited and others not. In the real world you may find that your teaching facility is the home of weekly bingo games, adult basketball leagues, PTO meetings, and so forth. Unfortunately, many schools now find it necessary to have metal detectors that students must pass through and police officers on duty throughout the school day and at extracurricular activities. Furthermore, you may also see that the playground space is a gathering spot for all sorts of activities, both authorized and unauthorized, after school and throughout the night. As a consequence, your facilities and equipment may be in less-than-desirable condition at the start of each school day. Because your first responsibility is to maintain safety and security for your students and to conduct your program under sanitary conditions, you will have to take an active role in ensuring that these necessary conditions are met. Failure to do so not only endangers your students, it also undermines the credibility of your program.

Critical Questions

Based on what you know about the requirement for a safe, secure, and sanitary environment in which all children can achieve their individual potential:

- What are the basic requirements for safe and clean facilities and equipment?
- What role can you play in ensuring the safety and security of students?
- What should your role be in ordering, maintaining, and discarding equipment?

involved throughout the lesson. Waiting in long lines or sharing equipment among several children can invite restlessness, boredom, and behavioral problems. On the other hand, if gymnasium equipment is properly selected, placed, and used, the learning objectives of the lesson can be maximized.

A well-organized equipment closet aids the instructional program through ready availability of items.

Selection

When purchasing equipment, it is wise to buy quality items. Although quality equipment often costs more to begin with, it is generally less expensive to maintain in the long run. Purchasing quality equipment through reputable companies often affords longer, more effective use of the equipment and an opportunity for returns or exchanges when necessary.

It is helpful to keep a complete inventory of all gymnasium equipment. A listing of all bats, balls, beanbags, hoops, mats, and gymnastics apparatus is a must. The condition of the equipment should be noted on the inventory checklist, and faulty or broken equipment should be immediately repaired or replaced. An equipment inventory should be conducted at least twice a year—once at the beginning of the school year and again at the end. This will provide a complete accounting of the equipment that is available for use and an indication of what is needed. A copy of the inventory and list of defective or missing equipment should be given to the building principal or other appropriate school officials.

Placement and Use

The placement and use of equipment have a dramatic effect on the lesson. Whenever possible, provide for maximum participation by all members of the class. When using small apparatus such as balls, hoops, beanbags, and wands, it helps to have an implement for each child. It's worthwhile to give attention to the way this equipment is distributed to the class and returned to its proper place. Simply giving the command "Get a ball" will not do. To minimize confusion, pushing, and other disruptive behavior, a predetermined system must be in place. Equipment can be passed out to students by the teacher, or it can be handed out by squad leaders, or it can be obtained by students in small groups. Whatever methods you choose, be sure that they are quick and efficient and that they cause a minimum of disruption.

A staff employee lays mulch on a playground. Twelve inches of mulch is the minimum depth to ensure safe landings from jumping off of playground equipment.

When large apparatus is being used, the physical layout should be such that each piece of equipment is free of obstacles and can be easily viewed by the teacher from any part of the room. Mats should be placed under each piece of apparatus, and the equipment itself must be safe. The equipment should be visually inspected and tested before use. Safety hazards must be immediately corrected or repaired. Never continue to use a piece of equipment that you know to be defective.

To make maximum effective use of the allotted class time, inspect all equipment and have it ready for distribution prior to class. Small equipment that is neatly stored on racks, in utility bags, or in containers can be quickly and easily put to use. Be certain, however, that after the equipment has been used it is returned immediately to its proper location. This will ensure easy access for the next class and a minimum of loss.

The use of large apparatus sometimes poses another problem. Setting up climbers, mats, balance beams, and the like is time-consuming. For this reason it is generally advisable to have as few large-equipment changes as possible from class to class. Be certain, though, to have all the equipment out in its proper place, inspected, and ready to use before the class enters the gymnasium. Failure to do so only wastes time and creates unnecessary confusion. If equipment changes are necessary, students can be taught how to move certain pieces of apparatus under direct supervision.

Remember, the balls, bats, hoops, mats, and other equipment available to you represent the "tools" of your profession. It's important to take the time to make sure these items are in ample supply and good condition. There is little excuse for a physical education program with minimal or no equipment. Just as children cannot be expected to learn to read without books, they cannot be expected to develop their movement abilities without the proper equipment. The physical education program must have an annual budget that provides for equipment purchase, replacement, and repair. Insufficient funds can be supplemented, to a degree, through the use of homemade equipment. However, teachers cannot be expected to develop and implement first-rate programs using only homemade equipment. Money-raising projects sponsored by the PTO or other interested groups can supplement the equipment budget. Much of the gymnasium and playground equipment in elementary schools is obtained through fund-raising projects and donations by parent and teacher organizations.

PREPARING INSTRUCTIONAL AIDS

Another aspect of organizing the learning environment is the preparation and use of instructional aids. Successful teachers use various types of items to enhance understanding and appreciation of the subject and to clarify instructions. The use of task cards, bulletin boards, and other visual aids can be an important aspect of the lesson.

Task Cards

A **task card** is a written description of a skill or movement activity to be performed. It clearly indicates acceptable individual levels of achievement and may include a verbal and or visual description of the task. Task cards are an effective visual technique to use with station teaching, as well as with several teaching styles. They give students information about what is to be done, how it is to be done, and what the standards of acceptable performance are. Task cards enable members of the class to work on one or more activities at the same time. They permit maximum participation and promote individual standards of achievement.

Students gather around to review a task card designed for a station activity.

Bulletin Boards

Don't overlook the value of bulletin boards in the elementary school physical education program. You can use the **bulletin board** to create interest, impart knowledge, and record information. Whether they are located in the gymnasium or in the hallway, bulletin boards should be neat and attractive and should reflect your creative talents. To be most effective, they should be changed frequently during the school year.

Bulletin boards featuring upcoming units of work can heighten interest. Using magazine photos and drawings that show outstanding performers executing the same skills that you will be focusing on tends to create an atmosphere of anticipation for the lessons to come.

Bulletin boards can also be an effective way to impart knowledge. Use a bulletin board, for example, to display illustrations of the major muscle groups of the body throughout the school year, one group at a time, highlighting their locations and appropriate activities for strengthening them. Set up a nutrition bulletin board to depict the Food Guide Pyramid. You might post a list of all students who have achieved a certain standard on a skills test. Or you might make the various components of health-related fitness the theme of a bulletin board.

A sample bulletin board is used to stimulate students' interest in physical education.

Visual Aids

Videotaped performances can be used effectively in the physical education program to provide children a visual model of the skills or sports they will be learning. A videotape of outstanding performers in gymnastics or soccer, for example, helps to create a mental image of the level of skill that is possible. At the same time, when using this technique teachers need to be careful to remind children that attaining such high levels of skill takes considerable time, effort, and practice. The approach should be "You may not be able to do this now, but if you work hard you will be able to do many of these skills later." Using videotapes of skilled athletes helps motivate students to learn and do their best, and communicates a purpose for skill learning and practice. Don't overlook the opportunity to videotape your own students. This will provide you and them with a useful learning tool and is also fun and highly motivational.

Skill charts, another effective visual aid used by many teachers, may be purchased commercially or may be homemade. The major advantage of a skill chart is that it gives students a visual representation of the various elements of a particular skill. For example, the key elements in a soccer kick, an overhand throw, or a forward roll may be illustrated in photos, line drawings, or even stick figures. This is particularly important during the early stages of skill learning when the child is attempting to form a conscious mental image of the task.

ORGANIZING STUDENT HELPERS

The very nature of the physical education program lends itself to the use of helpers. Large classes, varying facilities, and the use of many different types and amounts of equipment all highlight the importance of helpers in the physical education program. Also, the teacher is sometimes unable to demonstrate certain tasks or needs several extra hands to assist with spotting. Squad leaders and gym helpers can contribute greatly to a program.

Squads and Squad Leaders

Squads are a useful technique for organizing groups of children. It is generally advisable to have an even number of squads so that they may be easily combined for various activities. There should be an even number of students per squad, and squads should be as small as possible to ensure maximum participation. Small squad sizes of 6 or 8 students are preferable to larger groups of 10 or more. To ensure balance in ability levels, it should be the teacher who directs placement of students into squads. Squads should never be chosen in a manner that is embarrassing or humiliating to children.

Once the class has been divided into squads, have them select an appropriate squad name. Naming, numbering, or color coding squads makes organization and regrouping throughout the lesson easier. It also helps to create group identity and promote group pride. A designated location for each squad to go to upon entering the gymnasium is a helpful organizational technique.

Squad leaders should be selected for each group. The honor and responsibility of being a squad leader should be given to all children sometime during the course of the school year. Squad leaders should be changed frequently, generally at the beginning of a new unit of work. The composition of the squads themselves should be changed at least three or four times during the school year. Squad leaders can perform many valuable functions such as taking roll, obtaining equipment, keeping records, moving their group, or leading exercises. Squad leaders should be praised for a job well done. Be sure to encourage them to have pride in the responsibilities of being a leader.

Physical Education Helpers

Physical education teachers are often permitted to incorporate helpers into their programs. **Physical education helpers** may be older students interested in working with youngsters. They may be high school students considering a career in physical education. Some school systems provide funds for hiring adult paraprofessionals to serve as physical education helpers. In any case, their presence in the program can be invaluable. Physical education helpers can be assigned many of the routine chores of the physical education program such as organizing equipment, assisting with record keeping, officiating, leading activities, and helping with assessment. Remember, the use of gymnasium helpers is intended to give you more time for personalized instruction; be sure to make maximum effective use of your time. Physical education helpers should never be left in charge of the entire class. They should always be used in a professional manner to assist in providing the best program possible.

Summary

Skill themes, the approach advocated in this text, are a popular and effective means of helping children become more skillful movers. A three-step approach to planning a skill theme includes preplanning, assessing entry levels, and specific planning. Careful planning, organizing, and implementing of the lesson are the very core of the teacher's responsibilities. Preplanning and entry-level assessment set the stage for the progressively more specific steps in the planning process, namely developing yearly plans, unit plans, and daily lesson plans.

The sequence of presentation of the daily lesson

In *organizing groups of children,* remember that each formation used in the gymnasium and on the playground is used for specific purposes; avoid selecting activities that require frequent formation changes.

Single-circle formation

- This formation is frequently used for circle games and dances.
- The single circle is used for activities using a parachute.
- This is a good formation for discussions.
- Keep groups small for maximum participation (six to eight maximum).
- Stand at the edge of the circle when talking, never in the center.

File formation

- The file formation is frequently used for locomotor and ball-dribbling activities.
- It is used for numerous skill drills.
- Keep groups small (no more than eight to a group).
- Be sure the number of students in a group is an even number.
- Clearly explain and enforce rules.

Double-circle formation

- The double circle is often used for circle partner activities.
- It is used for numerous circle dances and mixers.
- It is used for some circle games.
- Use floor markings to designate places.
- Change partners often.

Shuttle formation

- This formation is used for numerous locomotor, throwing, and catching activities.
- It is used for some skill drills.
- Explain and enforce a definite travel procedure.
- Stand where all can see you.
- Be sure that students wait behind the restraining line until their turn.

Scatter formation

- The scatter formation is used for movement exploration and problem-solving activities.
- It is a great formation for creative expression activities.

- Be sure to set geographical boundaries before the class scatters.
- Be sure that each child has ample personal space for moving.
- Do not stand in one place; move throughout the class.

Parallel line formation

- This formation is used for throwing, catching, and kicking skills.
- It is used for basketball skill relays.
- Provide a restraining line to keep lines straight.
- Keep groups small, with a maximum of six to eight per line.
- Be sure that lines are sufficiently far apart to promote proper execution of the skill.

Half-circle formation

- The half circle is frequently used for leader demonstrations.
- Use existing circle markings whenever possible.
- Avoid joining of hands for extended periods when forming a half circle.
- The leader stands slightly outside the half circle so that all can see.

Station formation

- This is an excellent formation for promoting maximum participation and lesson variety.
- It permits the teacher to be at the point of greatest need.
- Often there is a task card for each station that details the activity to be practiced.
- Various attainment levels (Level I, Level II, Level III) can be posted at each station to promote time-on-task and personalized mastery attempts.

Checkerboard formation

- This is an excellent formation for structured activities and with large groups.
- The checkerboard provides maximum use of space.
- Avoid standing at one end of the formation for long periods; move around its perimeter.

is important if the teacher is to make maximum effective use of the time available. The lesson begins with a brief introductory activity followed by a review of the previous lesson. After that, the bulk of the allotted time is spent on the body of the lesson and skill development (i.e., with informing tasks, extending tasks, and/or refining tasks), followed by skill application (i.e., application tasks). The lesson concludes with a brief summary of the lesson, a novel dismissal activity, or both.

Ways to implement successful lessons range from practical techniques for pulling the lesson together to evaluating the effectiveness of the lesson and determining when to move on to a new skill theme. Physical education teachers must use efficient and effective techniques for organizing equipment and facilities. Using instructional aids such as task cards, bulletin boards, and visual aids, and organizing facilities and equipment maximize your potential for success. Organizing student helpers in the form of squad leaders and older physical education student aids is an important aspect of implementing the lesson successfully.

Terms to Remember

Excellent Readings

Barney, D., & Lynn, S. (2000). Classroom and practice routines: Starting the year off right. *Strategies, 13* (6), 8-11.

Brown, S., & Brown, D. (2000). Making the most of a 30-minute class. *Strategies, 13* (1), 3-36.

Conkell, C.S., & Askins, J. (2000). Integrating fitness into a skill themes program. *TEPE, 11* (1), 22-25.

Lottes, C., & Garman, J.F. (1999). Time management: An easy four-step process. *Strategies, 12* (6), 13-15.

Neide, J. (2000). Active learning strategies for HPER. *JOPERD, 71* (5), 26-29.

Ryan, C. (2000). Moving with a theme. *Strategies, 14* (1), 20-22.

Yongue, B., & Kelly, K. (2000). The five-step approach to teaching for skill acquisition. *TEPE, 11* (2), 15-16, 25.

12

Assessing Progress: Motor, Fitness, and Physical Activity Assessment

Key Concept

▶ Individualized entry-level and exit-level assessments of movement skills and fitness levels are important aspects of the developmental physical education program.

This chapter will provide you with the tools to do the following:

▶ Discuss the importance of entry-level and exit-level assessment in the developmental skill theme approach.

▶ Distinguish between process assessment and product assessment.

▶ List and discuss specific characteristics of several observational assessment devices.

▶ Describe appropriate techniques for observational assessment.

▶ Define and give examples of an assessment that is valid, reliable, objective, and administratively feasible.

▶ Distinguish among within-individual assessment, group comparisons, and between-individual assessment.

▶ Discuss the role of total-body observational assessment and segmental analysis and the steps in performing these assessments.

▶ Describe what norms are, how they may be used, and their advantages and disadvantages.

▶ List and then discuss the role of physical fitness testing in the developmental physical education program.

▶ Discuss considerations regarding what to assess and when to assess in relation to children's physical fitness.

▶ List the test items of the most popular field-based fitness tests used in North America today, and describe the merits and limitations of each.

▶ Become familiar with current software packages available to aid in various aspects of both motor and fitness assessment.

▶ Discuss why alternative assessment strategies have gained popularity as ways of performing children's motor and fitness assessment.

Assessment is an important aspect of any sound physical education program because it helps teachers measure students' current levels of ability, students' progress, and their own teaching effectiveness. Motor assessment, fitness assessment, and physical activity assessment refer to the collection of relevant information for the purpose of making reliable curricular decisions and discriminations among students. These topics are the primary focus of this chapter, along with alternative assessment strategies that have become increasingly popular in recent years. The following Web sites will be of additional assistance:

CONCEPT 12.1

Entry-level assessment prior to instruction in a skill theme is a critical component of the developmental approach to children's physical education.

CONCEPT 12.2

Exit-level assessment coupled with entry-level assessment permits the learner to check on individual progress.

- Fitnessgram (**www.americanfitness.net**)
- President's Challenge (**www.indiana.edu/~preschal**)
- Cooper Institute for Aerobic Research (**www.cooperinst.org**)
- American College of Sports Medicine (**www.acsm.org**)

FORMATIVE AND SUMMATIVE ASSESSMENT

By assessing the students' current level of performance, you can obtain a baseline or yardstick by which to measure progress. This form of assessment, frequently termed formative or **entry-level assessment,** can be easily and quickly done at the very beginning of a unit of instruction. With this information in hand, you can develop an instructional unit based on where students are rather than where they should be. Entry-level assessment permits you to fit the program to the needs of the student rather than fitting the student to a predetermined program.

> **TEXT BOX 12.1**
>
> *Assessment* is an important aspect of any sound physical education program because it helps teachers measure students' current levels of ability, students' progress, and their own teaching effectiveness. Motor, fitness, and physical activity assessment is the collection of relevant information for the purpose of making reliable curricular decisions and discriminations among students.

CONCEPT 12.3

Motor assessment and fitness assessment must both be directly related to the objectives of the program.

Assessment is also used to measure pupils' progress over time. Evaluation of progress at the end of a unit of instruction is frequently called summative or **exit-level assessment.** If your operational philosophy centers on the goal of individual improvement, you will want to combine exit-level assessment ratings with entry-level assessment. For example, you could re-administer a basketball skills test at the end of a unit of instruction to determine whether a student has made progress. This method of comparing individual entry and exit levels of achievement is frequently called **self-referenced assessment.** This approach differs from the normative or standards approach, in which students are compared by age against previously established class standards or group norms.

Self-referenced assessment is the preferred method of assessment in the developmentally based physical education program. This type of assessment reinforces the concept of individual differences that forms the cornerstone of developmental physical education. Norm-referenced assessment, on the other hand, is based on age-group appropriateness and is of only secondary importance to developmental physical education. Teachers can further use assessment to measure their own effectiveness. By determining students' level of ability and rate of progress, teachers can estimate how successful they have been in teaching movement skill acquisition and fitness enhancement. If, for example, you are able to show significant progress by your students in their level of basketball skill acquisition, then you can assume that learning has taken place and that you were instrumental in that progress. If, however, you see little or no progress, you may question your effectiveness in presenting that unit of instruction.

With regard to movement skill acquisition and fitness enhancement, self-referenced assessment at both the beginning and the end of a unit of instruction is highly recommended. Part IV of this text, "The Skill Themes," contains specific information for practical self-referenced entry- and exit-level assessment.

CONCEPT 12.4

Assessment may take many forms, but it must be administratively feasible and reliable and must yield valid estimates of one's present level of functioning.

REALITY CHECK

Who's Got the Time?

Real-World Situation

You've heard all about it, and conceptually it makes sense to use some form of formative (entry-level) assessment before planning the specific content of your lessons and summative (exit-level) assessment to check on individual and group progress. Sounds nice, makes sense, but "Get real—who's got the time?" Don't the experts realize that you along with the majority of physical education teachers barely have enough time to teach anything of substance as it is? Assessment? It can't be done, or can it?

Critical Questions

Based on what you know about curricular planning and assessing of student progress:

- How might you incorporate formative and summative assessment given the limited time most physical education teachers have with their students?

- Is formative and summative assessment of any real value? Why or why not?

- What role can this thing called "self-referenced" play?

- Bottom line: Why does it make a difference if we assess or not?

MOTOR ASSESSMENT

Master teachers continually assess their students through both informal and formal means. They constantly adjust and revise their lessons to facilitate learning. At the elementary school level, two forms of assessment are appropriate: process assessment and product assessment. Both may be used—the choice depending on the level of student ability, the specific needs of the students and the teacher, and the amount of available time.

Motor assessment is a primary means of assessment in the developmental physical education curriculum. Motor assessment takes two primary forms: process, or observational, assessment, which is qualitative and therefore subjective, and product, or performance, assessment, which is quantitative and therefore objective. Both process and product assessments have a place in the developmental curriculum. As students are learning new skills, process assessment is of particular relevance. Once they have mastered skills, product assessment may have greater value.

CONCEPT 12.5

Process assessment focuses on the qualitative aspects of movement. Product assessment focuses on its quantitative aspects.

Process Assessment

Process assessment is the observational approach to assessment that has to do with the form, style, or observed qualitative performance of a fundamental movement or sport skill. When focusing on the movement process, teachers are little concerned with the product of the act, such as how far the ball travels, how many baskets the

Process or Product: That Is the Question

Real-World Situation

Who ran the fastest? Who jumped the highest? Who made the most baskets? In other words, "Who's best?" These are the types of questions that you will be asked by students after any form of product assessment. How fast? How high? How many? These make up the critical quantitative components of product assessment in the motor domain. But what about process assessment? What about form, style, and body mechanics? What about the qualitative aspects of movement?

Critical Questions

Based on your knowledge of quantitative and qualitative assessment and the differences between these techniques:

- When assessing the motor behavior of elementary school children, when and why is one form of assessment (quantitative or qualitative) better than the other?
- When is it most appropriate to use qualitative (observational) assessment techniques?
- When is it most appropriate to use quantitative (performance) assessment techniques?
- What guidelines will you incorporate in your teaching when using quantitative and qualitative assessment?

child makes, or how fast the child runs the 50-yard dash. Instead, they are concerned primarily with the body mechanics used to throw the ball, make the basket, or run the dash. Observational assessment is an effective subjective technique for knowledgeable teachers to use; it is an important technique when you consider that in physical education one of our primary goals is to help children learn movement skills. We must focus on efficient body mechanics, or the process of movement, before focusing on the product. According to the approach we discuss throughout the skill theme chapters, when children are at the fundamental phase of movement skill development we assess whether they are at the initial, elementary, mature, or sport skill stage. For children at the specialized movement phase, we must determine whether they are at the transitional, application, or lifelong utilization stage of skill development.

TEXT BOX 12.2

Observational assessment is an effective subjective technique for knowledgeable teachers to use and is an important technique when you consider that your primary goal is to teach movement skills. Concern for the proper mechanics, or the process of movement, must come before focusing on the product.

It is not enough to assume that all 5- and 6-year-olds will be at one stage, 7- and 8-year-olds at another stage, and 9- and 10-year-olds at yet another stage. Because of the varying opportunities and experiences the children have had in terms of practice, encouragement, and previous instruction, a rigidly graded or age-based approach to movement skill acquisition and fitness enhancement is not acceptable as a valid means for curricular planning. Therefore, observational assessment of the process of children's movement becomes basic to effective use of the developmental approach.

TEACHING TIP 12.1

When *observing and assessing* children's movement patterns:

- *Be unobtrusive.* This is especially important with young children, who often alter their pattern of movement if they are aware that they are being observed.

- *Stress maximum effort.* Instructing children to throw as far, run as fast, or jump as high as they can encourages best performances.

- *Stand where you can clearly view performance.* Stand far enough away that you can observe the entire task.

- *First, observe the total-body action.* Try to look at the entire action to get a general impression of individual and group performance lev-

- els (i.e., initial, elementary, mature, or sport skill stage).

- *Second, observe segmentally.* For individuals assessed to be at less than the mature stage, do a segmental analysis of each body part involved in the action. This will help you pinpoint specific problems.

- *Compare.* Occasionally ask another trained individual to observe and assess several children. Compare ratings for objectivity.

- *Be consistent.* Strive for consistency in your observations to maximize the reliability of your process assessments.

Guidelines for Observational Assessment

Observational assessment, because it is qualitative and subjective, requires the teacher to know the proper mechanics of a wide variety of movement skills. To help with this, the stability, locomotor, and manipulative skill theme chapters (chapters 18 through 20) present verbal and visual descriptions of children performing at the initial, elementary, and mature stages in over 20 fundamental movements. The purpose of this information is to familiarize you with the basic body mechanics and techniques used in executing the fundamental movement skills that children should acquire during the childhood years.

Meaningful assessment often involves providing learners with feedback about the qualitative aspects or the process of their performance. For example, it would be helpful to tell this student that her legs are fully extended and straight, that her arms are in opposition and stretched out, and that her focus is down versus up and out.

Product Assessment

Product assessment is quantitative and therefore deals with how far, how fast, how high, or how many. In other words, it deals with the end results of one's movement, as measured by elapsed time, as in the 100-yard dash; distance covered, as with the standing long jump or shot put; accuracy, as in basketball goal shooting or target archery; or the number of repetitions, as with chin-ups or push-ups. Performance assessment is an effective objective technique to use in skill assessment after learners have mastered the mechanics of a task. After students have advanced to the mature stage of a skill, they are ready to begin applying the skill to specific sport-related activities. For example, the mature throwing pattern can now be further developed and applied to throwing a football or pitching a baseball. Remember, in terms of mechanics, a sport skill is often little different from the fundamental movement skill. The goal has changed in terms of the speed, accuracy, or distance required for success in the sport activity; but the basic mechanics are essentially the same, only adapted to the specific demands of the task.

CONCEPT 12.6

One can obtain estimates of children's present level of motor performance in fundamental movement skills and specialized sport skills through product assessment.

TEXT BOX 12.3

Performance assessment is an effective objective technique to use in skill assessment *after* the mechanics of a task have been relatively well mastered. Once students have advanced to the mature stage of a skill, they are ready to begin applying the skill to specific sport-related activities.

Guidelines for Performance Assessment

Form (process) does have some influence on performance (product), but we really don't know the extent to which performance is related to correct form. The fitness tests discussed in the following section represent three different performance assessments of children's physical fitness.

TEACHING TIP 12.2

To maximize the usefulness of *performance evaluations*, consider the following questions:

- *Validity.* Does the performance measure what it claims to measure?
- *Reliability.* Does the performance measure whatever it is measuring consistently?
- *Objectivity.* Does the performance measure yield highly similar results when administered by others?

- *Feasibility.* Is the performance measure straightforward and easy to set up and administer? Can it be self- or partner administered, or must it be teacher administered?
- *Utility.* Can the results be used for valid educational purposes such as self-appraisal, program planning, or reporting progress?

Motor Assessment Tools

The motor assessment devices discussed in this section are observational assessment-based devices. The Fundamental Movement Pattern Assessment Instrument, originally developed by McClenaghan and Gallahue (1978) and expanded here, is an informal observational assessment instrument for making within-individual comparisons, as is the Developmental Sequence of Fundamental Motor Skills Inventory (Seefeldt & Haubenstricker, 1976). Neither is intended for making comparisons between individuals. Both, however, provide the teacher with valuable information for making important curricular decisions.

The Test of Gross Motor Development (Ulrich, 2000) is noteworthy in that it has been standardized and has both observational and performance assessment components. Also, it can be used for between-individual and between-group comparisons, as well as for detecting within-individual changes. Therefore this test can be used as an effective research tool, whereas in their present form the two previously mentioned observational assessment instruments cannot be used for research.

CONCEPT 12.7

Observational assessment instruments can aid the teacher in making important curricular decisions about children's fundamental movement abilities.

Fundamental Movement Pattern Assessment Instrument

The FMPAI (Fundamental Movement Pattern Assessment Instrument) was first published in 1978 (McClenaghan & Gallahue). The expanded version included here has been revised to form the observational assessment basis for the fundamental movement skill themes covered in chapters 18 through 20. The expanded FMPAI is a carefully developed informal assessment instrument used to classify individuals at the initial, elementary, or mature stage of development in several fundamental movement skills.

The FMPAI has proven to be highly reliable among trained observers. Content validity has been established for most of the fundamental movements. The original version included five fundamental movements (overhand throwing, catching, kicking, running, and horizontal jumping); the expanded version has several additional items. The developmental sequence for each of the original five movement skills was based on an exhaustive review of the biomechanical literature. The literature was also reviewed (Gallahue & Ozmun, 2002) for the additional items, and proposed developmental sequences were established for walking, vertical jumping, hopping, galloping and sliding, striking, body rolling, dodging, and one-foot balancing. The authors' hypothesized, and therefore not validated, developmental sequences were formulated for jumping from a height, dribbling, ball rolling, volleying, trapping, and beam walking. Sufficient literature is not available at this time to validate the developmental sequences of these fundamental movement skills.

The expanded FMPAI is an efficient, easy-to-use tool designed to help you assess the present status of groups of children or a single child and to assess change over time in the process of moving. The FMPAI does not, however, give you a quantitative score, nor can you use it to compare one child or group of children to another child or group (i.e., *between-individual* or *between-group* comparisons). Instead, this instrument is intended to assess developmental changes over time within individuals (*within-individual* comparisons). It uses observational assessment as a valid and reliable way to collect data and compare within individuals. Figures 12.1 and 12.2 provide samples of both total-body and segmental group observational assessment charts. Feel free to photocopy these for your personal use.

A **total-body assessment** chart is best used with groups of children in an informal setting where you are able to observe body mechanics in the performance of any one of the stability, locomotor, or manipulative movements mentioned earlier in this section. A total-body assessment helps you get a general picture of the group's level of ability and to identify children who are experiencing difficulty.

The **segmental assessment** chart allows you to pinpoint exactly where the problem lies. By segmentally observing the leg, trunk, and arm action, you will gain a

Mark the proper stage (I, E, M, S)* for each skill. Then give an overall rating in the space provided.	Stability Skills								Locomotor Skills										Manipulative Skills						
	Static balance	Dynamic balance	Body rolling	Dodging	Springing/Landing	Axial movements	Inverted supports	Transitional supports	Running	Jump for distance	Jump for height	Jump from height	Hopping	Skipping	Sliding	Galloping	Leaping	Climbing	Throwing	Catching	Kicking	Trapping	Dribbling	Volleying	Striking	Ball rolling
Name																										

**Fundamental Movement Skills
Total Body/Group Observation Chart**

Class _____ Grade _____ Observer _____

*I = initial stage, E = elementary stage, M = mature stage, S = sport skill stage

FIGURE 12.1   Sample total-body/group observational assessment chart.

From *Developmental Physical Education for All Children* (4 ed.) by David L. Gallahue and Frances Cleland Donnelly, 2003, Champaign, IL: Human Kinetics.

**CONCEPT
12.8**

Observational assessment of the qualitative aspects of children's movement should incorporate both *total-body* and *segmental* analysis techniques.

more complete picture of the individual and his specific needs. An **individualized assessment** form (figure 12.3) is a personalized progress report that you may send home periodically so that parents can keep abreast of their children's progress in the developmental physical education program.

The FMPAI is most effectively used with preschool and primary grade children who are generally at the fundamental movement phase of development. But it may also be used with older individuals who are delayed in their motor development because of specific limiting conditions such as early sport specialization, poor or nonexistent physical education programs, or physical or mental disabilities. For individuals at the specialized movement phase of development, sport skill observational assessment charts are effective diagnostic tools. These charts follow the same principles as the FMPAI and can be an effective tool for determining whether students are at the beginning, intermediate, or advanced stage in learning a specific sport skill.

Developmental Sequence of Fundamental Motor Skills Inventory

The DSFMSI (Developmental Sequence of Fundamental Motor Skills Inventory) was developed by Seefeldt and Haubenstricker (1976). The DSFMSI categorizes each of 10 fundamental movement skills into four or five stages. The fundamental movements of walking, skipping, hopping, running, striking, kicking, catching, throwing,

Fundamental Locomotor Skills
Segmental Group Observation Chart

Class _____ Grade _____ Observer _____

Mark the proper stage (I, E, M, S)* for each body segment. Then give an overall rating in the space provided. Name	Leg action	Trunk action	Arm action	Overall rating	Leg action	Trunk action	Arm action	Overall rating	Leg action	Trunk action	Arm action	Overall rating	Leg action	Trunk action	Arm action	Overall rating	Leg action	Trunk action	Arm action	Overall rating

*I = initial stage, E = elementary stage, M = mature stage, S = sport skill stage

FIGURE 12.2 Sample segmental group observational assessment chart for selected fundamental locomotor skills.

From *Developmental Physical Education for All Children* (4 ed.) by David L. Gallahue and Frances Cleland Donnelly, 2003, Champaign, IL: Human Kinetics.

jumping, and punting have been studied. These developmental sequences are based on data obtained from exhaustive film analyses. Children are observed and matched to both visual and verbal descriptions of each stage and are classified along a continuum from stage one (immature) to stage five (mature). Although reliability scores have not been reported, personal communication with the developers has indicated that, with training using specially designed films and a stop-action projector, interrater reliability is high.

Test of Gross Motor Development II

The TGMD-II (Test of Gross Motor Development) developed by Ulrich (2000) uses principles from both the FMPAI and the DSFMSI as a means of assessing fundamental movement skills in children from 3 to 10 years of age. Selected locomotor and manipulative skills make up the 12-item test. The locomotor skills include running, galloping, hopping, leaping, horizontal jumping, and sliding. The manipulative skills include striking, ball bouncing, catching, kicking, overhand throwing, and underhand rolling.

Administration of the TGMD takes about 15 minutes per child. A manual with a clear set of test instructions is available. Both test-retest reliability and interrater reliability scores are high. Additionally, the validity of each item has been

		Physical Education Progress Report															

Dear Parent:

The skills checked have been assessed for this 9-week period. More than one check in a row indicates progress from one stage to another.

Physical Education Progress Report

Child's name _____ Grade _____ Observer _____

	1st 9 wks.				2nd 9 wks.				3rd 9 wks.				4th 9 wks.				Stage of Development
	Initial stage	Elementary stage	Mature stage	Sport skill stage	Initial stage	Elementary stage	Mature stage	Sport skill stage	Initial stage	Elementary stage	Mature stage	Sport skill stage	Initial stage	Elementary stage	Mature stage	Sport skill stage	**I** Initial stage **E** Elementary stage **M** Mature stage **S** Sport skill stage

Stability skills: Maintaining balance in static and dynamic situations — Comments

One-foot balance																	
Beam walk																	
Body rolling																	
Dodging																	
Landing																	

Locomotor skills: Giving force to the body through space — Comments

Running																	
Jumping																	
Hopping																	
Skipping																	
Leaping																	

Manipulative skills: Giving force to and receiving force from objects — Comments

Throwing																	
Catching																	
Kicking																	
Dribbling																	
Striking																	

Parent Comments

_____   _____
Parent Signature   Date

_____   _____
Parent Signature   Date

_____   _____
Parent Signature   Date

FIGURE 12.3　Sample progress report for fundamental movement skills.

From *Developmental Physical Education for All Children* (4 ed.) by David L. Gallahue and Frances Cleland Donnelly, 2003, Champaign, IL: Human Kinetics.

established. The TGMD is easy to administer and can be used effectively with a minimum amount of special training. It provides both *norm-referenced* (i.e., scores compared to a statistical sample) and *criterion-referenced* (i.e., scores compared to a preestablished standard) interpretations for each fundamental movement skill and can be used as a device for between-individual and between-group comparisons, as well as for within-individual comparisons.

FITNESS ASSESSMENT

Fitness testing is common in most schools. The results of fitness tests are used for several purposes:

- Determining the physical status of children
- Identifying those who are deficient in certain areas and need special help
- Classifying students
- Measuring progress
- Aiding in activity selection and program planning

CONCEPT 12.9

A variety of published instruments are available for assessing children's physical fitness and enhancing their fitness education.

The results of each child's performance on tests of fitness should be placed in the cumulative record and made available to parents. Parents should be encouraged to promote activities for their children that will help overcome deficiencies in fitness levels. Many parents are eager to do whatever they can to help improve their child's physical functioning. Therefore, we strongly urge that, for each child, teachers send fitness test results and recommendations home to parents for review and comment.

When selecting a fitness test to include in the physical education program, you must be certain that it suits your purposes and meets certain criteria. As you select,

---

REALITY CHECK

Fitness Assessment: What, When, and How?

Real-World Situation

Before you assumed your new position at RU-FIT Elementary School, the previous physical education program centered on enhancing children's physical fitness and participation levels in moderate to vigorous physical activity through movement skill development. You want to continue to emphasize physical fitness and physical activity enhancement through movement skill development but are unsure about *what* to assess, *when* to assess, and *how* to assess in a manner that yields valid information and maximizes achievement of your program objectives.

Critical Questions

Based on what you know about physical fitness and physical activity assessment:

- In your view, when are the best times during the school year to assess children's physical fitness?
- What fitness components will you choose to assess and why?
- How will you go about organizing your classes for fitness assessment?
- What, if any, published fitness assessment test will you administer, and why?
- How will you go about assessing your students' levels of physical activity?
- How do you see heart rate monitors and pedometers being incorporated into your program?

you will need to consider information about reliability, objectivity, validity, norms, utility, and ease of administration.

When to Assess

Fitness testing can play an important role in the total program if the results of these measures are used to aid the teacher, pupil, and parent in improving children's fitness levels, their attitudes toward the value of fitness, and their knowledge of how to improve their personal level of fitness. Fitness testing can be of real value for determining students' present level of functioning and identifying areas that need special attention. It can be an effective motivator and an excellent way to reinforce the value of personal improvement in fitness. But you will not be able to achieve any of this if you wait until the end of the school year to assess your students. To be of real value, fitness testing needs to be a systematic and regular part of the program, both early in the school year and at the end.

Be careful not to expect too much from children immediately after they return from summer vacation. Hold off on the initial school fitness testing until four to six weeks after school has begun. By then, children will have had an opportunity to regain conditioning levels they may have lost over the summer.

TEXT BOX 12.4

When selecting a fitness test for inclusion in the physical program, be certain that it suits your purposes and meets certain criteria. In the selection process you will need to consider information concerning reliability, objectivity, validity, norms, utility, and ease of administration.

What to Assess

CONCEPT 12.10

Selection of specific physical fitness measures should be based on the goals and objectives of the program.

A debate has raged in the professional literature and among professional societies and organizations over what we should measure in children's fitness testing. Some claim that we should assess only the health-related components of physical fitness. Others insist that we should include performance-related components along with the health-related ones. The decision is yours. Your decision, however, should be based on the curricular goals and physical activity and fitness objectives of your program. A number of published fitness tests are available, each somewhat different in the items assessed and the support materials available. Careful examination of the content of each will enable you to select the one that is most compatible with your needs. If none suits the purposes of your program, then it is perfectly appropriate to develop a fitness assessment device tailored to your particular situation.

For both of the published fitness assessment batteries described in the sections that follow, norms, recognition awards, and educational materials are available. Be certain to review both these assessments in relation to your curricular objectives and the needs of your students.

Norms are standards of performance that have been established so that comparisons may be made within groups of children and between groups of children. Published norms are generally national in scope. However, they may also be established on a school, city, or state basis. Norms permit the teacher to compare pupils' performance to other students' performances. Although norms are helpful only in terms of comparing children against one another, they do rely on age-group appropriateness for their validity. In reality they are of little practical value in the developmental physical education program because of its emphasis on individual appropriateness.

Fitness awards are intended to serve both as extrinsic motivators and as recognition for achieving a predetermined standard of fitness excellence. They typically take the form of patches, pins, or certificates that honor children for their level of achievement in comparison to established norms. Although popular, these awards may convey the wrong message about individual fitness achievement. The very fact that only those with the highest scores receive awards may significantly reduce motivation on the part of the majority of the class because of their inability to achieve in the top percentiles on normed tests of fitness. You may want to consider using fitness awards to recognize positive personal fitness behaviors—behaviors that everybody has an opportunity to achieve. Using fitness awards in this way can motivate a far greater number of children because the reward is for positive fitness behaviors (the process) rather than scores on a battery of tests (the product). The two fitness tests described in the next section (the President's Challenge and Fitnessgram) provide for a variety of educationally sound incentives and fitness education materials.

Fitness education materials range from comic books and videotapes to Web sites and CD-ROMs, from educational posters and wall charts to lesson plans and entire fitness education curricula. The intent of these materials is not only to motivate children but also to educate them in the essential knowledge and concepts governing fitness attainment, maintenance, and enhancement.

CONCEPT 12.11

Children's fitness education is essential for long-term exercise adherence, motivation, and concept learning.

Fitness Assessment Tests

The two tests of physical fitness that are used most frequently in U.S. public schools are the President's Challenge Physical Fitness Test, published by the President's Council on Physical Fitness and Sports (PCPFS, 2002-03), and Fitnessgram, published by the American Fitness Alliance (2002b). The President's Challenge is the oldest and most widely used and is highly respected in the United States. It is based on national norms, whereas Fitnessgram, a newer fitness test endorsed by a consortium of highly respected organizations (American Alliance for Health, Physical Education, Recreation and Dance; the Cooper Institute for Aerobics Research; and Human Kinetics Publishers), compares scores to carefully researched health standards rather than national averages. Thus the focus and support materials for these tests differ somewhat and serve varying needs of fitness educators. Select the test that best suits your needs. Better yet, devise your own battery of tests and use that as your own personalized physical fitness assessment device. Table 12.1 provides an overview of these two popular fitness assessment tests.

CONCEPT 12.12

Published physical fitness tests may be used to supplement and support sound fitness education programs.

The President's Challenge

The President's Challenge Physical Fitness Program is sponsored by PCPFS (2002-03). The President's Challenge is by far the most frequently administered fitness test in the United States, used in approximately 28,000 schools nationwide. The test is designed for children and youth from ages 6 through 17, who may strive for the *Presidential Physical Fitness Award* (scoring above the 85th percentile on all five tests) or the *National Physical Fitness Award* (scoring above the 50th percentile on all five tests). A *Participation Physical Fitness Award* recognizes those who attempt all five tests but score below the 50th percentile on one or more of the items. A *State Champion Award* recognizes the top schools in each state that have

TABLE 12.1—TWO POPULAR TESTS OF PHYSICAL FITNESS

Fitness test	Test items	Fitness component
The President's Challenge	Curl-ups	Abdominal strength/endurance
	Shuttle run	Speed
	Mile run/walk	Heart/Lung endurance
	Pull-ups	Upper body strength/endurance
	Flexed-arm hang	(Pull-up alternate)
	V-sit reach	Flexibility
	Sit and reach	(Option to V-sit)
Fitnessgram	Mile walk/run	Aerobic endurance
	Skinfold/Body mass index	Body composition
	Back saver, sit and reach	Joint flexibility
	Curl-ups	Abdominal strength/endurance
	Push-ups	Upper body strength/endurance
	Trunk lift	Trunk extension
		Strength and flexibility

the highest percentage of students qualifying for the Presidential Award. The *Health Fitness Award* is designed for students who achieve a healthy level of fitness, defined as meeting or exceeding certain minimum health criteria on the following five test items:

1. Partial curl-ups
2. One-mile run/walk
3. V-sit reach (or sit and reach option)
4. Right angle push-ups (or pull-ups option)
5. Body mass index

Published standards for both the Presidential Award and the less demanding National Award were most recently validated in 1998 by means of comparison with a large nationwide sampling. A unique feature of the President's Challenge is the inclusion of children with disabilities as potential qualifiers for all of the awards.

The President's Challenge test battery includes five items required of both males and females:

1. Number of curl-ups completed in 60 seconds (option: partial curl-ups)
2. Thirty-foot shuttle run for time
3. One-mile run/walk for time (6-7-year-old option: 1/4 mile; 8-9-year-old option: 2 miles)
4. Maximum number of pull-ups (option: right angle push-ups; or for the National and Participant Physical Fitness Awards only, flexed arm hang)
5. V-sit reach for distance (option: sit and reach)

The PCPFS recommends testing fitness at least twice a year. An additional recommendation is to supplement the President's Challenge with other health and fitness measures such as body composition, blood pressure, and posture checks.

Fitnessgram

Fitnessgram (American Fitness Alliance, 2002b), a physical fitness program originally developed by the Cooper Institute for Aerobics Research, is based on the latest research on children's physical fitness. Its primary objective is to provide teachers with all they need to know to accurately assess student fitness levels and develop individualized approaches to improving students' physical fitness. Fitnessgram strives to accurately assess the components of health-related fitness from kindergarten through college. A key feature of Fitnessgram is that participants are not compared to each other or to national averages but to minimal health fitness standards that have been established for each age and gender. Therefore, norms are not used for comparison of one child or group to another. Instead, each child strives to reach or exceed the minimal health fitness standards, called *Healthy Fitness Zones.*

The following are the six items on the Fitnessgram test:

1. A one-mile walk/run for time, or the "pacer" test for aerobic endurance
2. Percent body fat assessed through triceps skinfold thickness
3. Sixty-second curl-ups test
4. Maximum number of push-ups (alternatives: pull-ups, flexed arm hang, or modified pull-ups)
5. Shoulder stretch
6. A trunk extension test measured in inches

Once you have conducted the initial fitness assessments, you can print out a Fitnessgram report for each student. The report contains recommendations for physical activity program options to help students make it into the Healthy Fitness Zones for those areas in which they need to improve. The Fitnessgram report also includes a section for parents that explains the value of physical activity.

An important addition to Fitnessgram, one that makes it a complete testing and educational package, is *Physical Best* (American Alliance for Health, Physical Education, Recreation and Dance [AAHPERD], 2002a). As the educational component of Fitnessgram, Physical Best provides valuable information about implementing a health-related fitness education program. Activity guides are available for both the elementary and secondary levels. These include a wealth of instructional activities that are developmentally appropriate as well as educationally sound, fun, and relevant to today's students. All Physical Best materials meet the requirements of the National Association for Sport and Physical Education's National Standards for Physical Education. A teacher's guide (*Physical Education for Lifelong Fitness: The Physical Best Teacher's Guide,* AAHPERD, 2002b) is also available. This guide should be an important addition to your personal professional library.

Brockport Physical Fitness Test

The Brockport Physical Fitness Test is a unique health-related criterion fitness test for children from 10 to 17 years of age with various disabilities. The test consists of 27 potential items—potential in that you can customize a test battery for individuals or groups depending on their particular needs. Additionally, it is designed to work in conjunction with the Physical Best educational resources once you have determined your students' level of fitness and identified their fitness goals. Consequently the computer software can be used in conjunction with the Fitnessgram software. The Brockport Physical Fitness Test is adaptable to, and provides fitness parameters for, individuals with mild mental retardation, visual impairments, spinal cord injuries, cerebral palsy, congenital anomalies, and amputations.

PHYSICAL ACTIVITY ASSESSMENT

CONCEPT 12.13

Physical activity assessment is a form of authentic assessment that is sensitive to the real world of today's children.

In recent years the assessment of children's physical activity and the impact of physical activity on health have become topics of considerable interest to physical educators. Today, the consensus among health professionals is that people can derive significant health benefits through moderate amounts of physical activity. This is in sharp contrast to the long-standing view that vigorous physical activity is essential to improving one's health status. The Surgeon General's report (U.S. Department of Health and Human Services, 1996) stresses the importance of accumulating at least 30 minutes of moderate physical activity on most days of the week. Although increased levels of physical fitness remain an obvious goal of physical education, the National Association for Sport and Physical Education in its definition of the physically educated person (see chapter 1) focuses more on behavioral outcomes than performance outcomes. As Welk and Wood (2000) note, "In addition to having good skills and reasonable levels of fitness, a physically educated person is considered to be someone who participates in regular physical activity, knows the benefits of participation, and values the contribution that activity can make to a healthy lifestyle" (p. 30).

Teachers assess physical activity using a variety of formats. Heart rate monitors, pedometers, and student self-reports are among the most popular. In this section we consider both of these methods.

Heart Rate Monitors

Heart rate monitors have become popular in many schools across North America. They are an easy and accurate means of measuring physical activity in the school setting. Although relatively expensive and difficult to use effectively outside of the school and with large numbers of children, heart rate monitors have proven to be an excellent in-class educational and motivational device. These devices enable you to monitor children's in-class activity, make adjustments as students progress, and document individual performance. Of equal importance, however, they enable students to monitor their own activity levels. Thus students can take responsibility for bringing their heart rate up and maintaining a threshold training level in order to obtain maximal benefit from their physical activity. The heart rate monitor is also an excellent educational and motivational tool, helping children to learn important lessons about the value of physical activity and to chart their own progress. Heart rate monitors are wireless and are easy to use, and when used properly they provide continuous accurate feedback.

Pedometers

Pedometers are becoming increasingly popular as a means of measuring physical activity. Pedometers are seen by many professionals as an excellent means for promoting physical activity (Beighle, Pangrazi, & Vincent, 2001). Basically, a pedometer is a small device usually worn on the hip and calibrated to one's average step length.

The total number of steps over a given period of time is recorded. Pedometers are inexpensive motivational devices as well as informal assessment tools. Some teachers even permit students to take the devices home from school so that they can get a 24-hour step count. Ten thousand steps a day is generally seen as the threshold for receiving a fitness benefit.

Self-Report Instruments

Although physical activity monitoring devices are now available along with heart rate monitors and pedometers, probably the simplest form of activity assessment is the physical activity self-report. Self-reports are inexpensive paper-pencil surveys that can be used by a large number of children at one time and can provide a wide range of information from the very general to the very specific. Self-reports are limited, though, by the ability of your students to understand and recall their daily activities and by the bias often associated with self-reporting, which is a subjective method. Here we describe three self-report instruments suitable for elementary school children.

Previous Day Physical Activity Recall

The PDPAR (Previous Day Physical Activity Recall) developed by Weston, Petosa, and Pate (1997) is designed for after-school use. The PDPAR requires children to report on their after-school activity in 30-minute increments. A numbered list of common activities is presented, and children rate their intensity level in each that they take part in as *very light, light, medium,* or *hard* (figure 12.4). The results can be used to determine the type and amount of physical activity children get during the after-school hours. Results can also point out to children the need for increased amounts of physical activity and can provide the teacher and parents with valuable prescriptive information.

Self-Administered Physical Activity Checklist

The SAPAC (Self-Administered Physical Activity Checklist) (Sallis et al., 1996) is a self-administered survey instrument that lists 21 activities in which children commonly participate. The SAPAC gives students an opportunity to rate their activity levels from the previous day and estimate their minutes of actual participation. They are asked to rate the intensity of their activity levels by indicating whether the activity made them breathe hard or feel tired *none, some,* or *most of the time.* For their minutes of activity they are asked to estimate *before, during,* and *after-school* minutes in active participation (figure 12.5).

The Child/Adolescent Activity Log

The CAAL (Child/Adolescent Activity Log) (Garcia et al., 1995) uses an activity grid to chart the duration and variety of common physical activities that children and youth take part in (figure 12.6). With this grid you are able to determine the variety of activities a child engages in, the number of bouts of those activities, and their duration. As a subjective assessment device, the CAAL—like the other self-report instruments we have discussed—is subject to student recall, honesty, and comprehension. For all these self-report measures it is recommended that children fill them out over at least three days during a typical week, including one day on the weekend.

Name_____ Teacher_____ Grade_____ Date_____

Think back to yesterday after you finished school. For each of the 30-minute periods, select a primary activity that you performed and put the number in the Activity Number box. For each activity, then check how hard the activity was in terms of physical effort. Use the terms "Very Light," "Light," "Medium," or "Hard" to estimate the intensity. Light is like slow walking, medium is like fast walking, and hard is like running.

		Activity Number	Very Light	Light	Medium	Hard
Afternoon	3:00					
	3:30					
	4:00					
	4:30					
Supper	5:00					
	5:30					
	6:00					
	6:30					
Evening	7:00					
	7:30					
	8:00					
	8:30					
	9:00					
Night	9:30					
	10:00					
	10:30					
	11:00					

Activity Numbers

Eating	Spare Time	Physical Activities
1. Meal/Snack	10. Watch TV	18. Walk
Sleep/Bathing	11. Go to movie/concert	19. Jog/Run
2. Sleeping	12. Listen to music	20. Dance (for fun)
3. Resting	13. Talk on phone	21. Swim (for fun)
4. Shower/Bath	14. Other (list) _____	22. Swim laps
Transportation	15. _____	23. Ride bicycle
5. Ride in car, bus	16. _____	24. Lift weights
6. Travel by walking	17. _____	25. Use skateboard
7. Travel by bike		26. Play organized sport
Work/School		27. Did individual exercises
8. Homework		28. Did active game outside
9. House chores		29. Other (list) _____

FIGURE 12.4   The Previous Day Physical Activity Recall (PDPAR) self-report is designed for after-school use (Weston, Petosa, & Pate, 1997).

From *Developmental Physical Education for All Children* (4 ed.) by David L. Gallahue and Frances Cleland Donnelly, 2003, Champaign, IL: Human Kinetics.

Name_____ Teacher_____ Grade_____ Date_____

Write the number of minutes you performed each of the activities you did for more than 5 minutes. Did it make you breathe hard or feel tired none (N), some (S), most of the time (M)? Indicate the intensity level with the letters N, S, or M to correspond to these intensities.

Activity	Before School		During School		After School	
	Minutes	Intensity (N S M)	Minutes	Intensity (N S M)	Minutes	Intensity (N S M)
1. Bicycling						
2. Swimming laps						
3. Gymnastics						
4. Exercise (push-ups, sit-ups)						
5. Basketball						
6. Baseball/Softball						
7. Football						
8. Soccer						
9. Volleyball						
10. Racket sports (badminton, tennis)						
11. Ball playing (four square, kickball)						
12. Games (chase, tag, hopscotch)						
13. Outdoor play (climbing trees, hide and seek)						
14. Water play (swimming pool, ocean, lake)						
15. Jump rope						
16. Dance						
17. Outdoor chores (mowing, raking, gardening)						
18. Indoor chores (mopping, vacuuming)						
19. Mixed walking/running						
20. Walking						
21. Running						
22. Other _____						

FIGURE 12.5   The Self-Administered Physical Activity Checklist (SAPAC) is a previous-day physical activity recall device (Sallis et al., 1996).

From *Developmental Physical Education for All Children* (4 ed.) by David L. Gallahue and Frances Cleland Donnelly, 2003, Champaign, IL: Human Kinetics.

Name_____ Teacher_____ Grade_____ Date_____

Yesterday was: (circle one)   Sun.   Mon.   Tues.   Wed.   Thurs.   Fri.   Sat.

Put a checkmark (✔) by each activity that you did yesterday and a checkmark in the box to show the total number of minutes.

Activity	✔	1-10 minutes	11-20 minutes	21-30 minutes	31-40 minutes	41-60 minutes	2+ hours
1. Walking							
2. Jog/Run							
3. Ice/rollerskating							
4. Swimming for fun							
5. Swimming laps							
6. Bicycling							
7. Aerobic/Dance							
8. Volleyball							
9. Football							
10. Softball/Baseball							
11. Soccer							
12. Tennis/Racketball							
13. Basketball							
14. Gymnastics							
15. Ice hockey							
16. Jump rope, tag, Frisbee							
17. Sledding (in the snow)							
18. Exercise to music							
19. Martial arts (karate, judo)							
20. Weightlifting							
21. Wrestling							
22. Other _____							

FIGURE 12.6   The Child/Adolescent Activity Log (CAAL) charts the duration and variety of common physical activities (Garcia et al., 1995).

From *Developmental Physical Education for All Children* (4 ed.) by David L. Gallahue and Frances Cleland Donnelly, 2003, Champaign, IL: Human Kinetics.

COMPUTER APPLICATIONS FOR ASSESSMENT

Computers have become a primary aid to the assessment process. They save time, allow convenient storage of information, and are excellent for multi-entry assessments and comparisons. The good news on this is in the area of fitness assessment. Computer software packages are available for the President's Challenge and Fitnessgram. They are easy to work with, inexpensive, used successfully by thousands of teachers each year, and PC and Macintosh compatible. The not-so-good news is in the area of motor assessment. Although some software packages are available, none have been tested and used as extensively as have the fitness test packages.

The software available for computer-assisted assessment and instruction is changing rapidly. In fact, by the time this text appears in print, the software products we are about to mention will probably be out of date. We therefore recommend that you contact one or more of the software vendors mentioned in this chapter for an up-to-date list of programs suitable for use with your students. If you're serious about motor and fitness assessment but have limited time for testing and large numbers of students to evaluate, then you need to seriously consider purchasing and using one or more of the following software packages.

CONCEPT 12.14

Computer applications for assessment are widely available, user friendly, and developing rapidly in both quality and quantity.

REALITY CHECK

Computers in the Gymnasium? You Must Be Kidding!

Real-World Situation

Being relatively computer literate along with your students, you think that now is the time to begin utilizing computers in your physical education program. On approaching your building principal with a request, you are somewhat dismayed when the principal exclaims, "Computers in the gymnasium—you must be kidding." Of course you're not, and you're entirely serious in your contention that computers will be a great aid to both you and your students. But you will have to convince your principal before funds are appropriated.

Critical Questions

Based on what you know about computer-assisted instruction and computer applications for assessment:

- How will you go about convincing your principal that computers do in fact have a place in the gymnasium?

- What forms of instruction and assessment can be enhanced through computer applications?

- How will you incorporate the use of computers, once you have them, in a manner that promotes maximum student involvement?

Computerized Motor Assessment

To date, there are no commercially prepared software packages available for use with the motor assessment tests discussed earlier. The two that we describe here, however, may be used in a variety of ways to suit your motor skill assessment needs.

Physical Skills Manager

Physical Skills Manager (CompTech Systems Design) is a software program that allows analysis of up to 15 motor skills of your choice. Raw scores are converted to a scale of 0 to 10 and permit the charting of improvement in performance over time.

Physical Education Record Keeper

The Physical Education Record Keeper (Richard Hurwitz) is a Macintosh-compatible software package that enables you to record student progress over time. This software also allows you to record biographic and class data, tests and objectives, target goals for each objective, objectives yet to be met, and an activity prescription to meet program goals.

Computerized Fitness Assessment

A number of computer software packages are available to aid you with the results of your fitness assessment. Programs can assist you with class record keeping, individual reports, tracking individuals over time, and reporting and prescribing personalized fitness profiles.

President's Challenge Software

Fitness Tracker is the official software of the President's Challenge Physical Fitness Test. It automatically calculates award levels for each student and helps you keep track of your students from year to year at all age and grade levels. Additionally, you can print out the scores for each student and provide the student with valuable information on how to improve. You can also print out charts depicting current standards for both girls and boys, using either the fitness award criteria (President's Award, National Award, Participant Award) or the Health Fitness Award option. Fitness Tracker (PCPFS, 2002-03) is available on CD-ROM, and to date is PC compatible only (**www.msfitnesstracker.com**).

Fitnessgram Software

Fitnessgram also offers a sophisticated teacher's software package. Version 6.0 is currently available on CD-ROM (American Fitness Alliance, 2002b) and is capable of generating personalized printed reports for each participant, as well as class reports. Levels of achievement are compared with Healthy Fitness standards, and suggestions for improvement can be provided to each student. The software package is designed to be a time saver that helps with administrative tasks such as moving students to new classes or teachers and assigning student passwords. Student Fitnessgram software is an extension of the teacher's version. It is available on the same CD-ROM and is a great motivational device allowing students to record their own test scores and daily physical activities. It is user friendly and visually appealing, and serves and promotes individual responsibility. Fitnessgram software can be downloaded to a variety of other spreadsheet formats and is easily exportable. Contact **www.americanfitness.net** for additional information.

Brockport Physical Fitness Test Software

Sophisticated, easy-to-use computer software is available for the Brockport Physical Fitness Test. It prints out goals, results, and fitness plans for each student as an individual. Separate reports can be generated for parents and teachers. The software package permits you to select a personalized battery of tests from any of the 27 available. Contact **www.americanfitness.net** for additional information.

Physical Activity Software

To date, the software for physical activity assessment is limited. One device, however, currently leads the industry—Activitygram physical activity assessment. Activitygram is an extension of the student version of the Fitnessgram physical fitness test that includes a computerized assessment of physical activity (American Fitness Alliance, 2002a). It is designed so that students can enter their own data on a computer in the gymnasium or in the school computer lab. Activitygram is user friendly and can take the form of a paper-pencil test if appropriate computer hardware is not available (figure 12.7). Two features set it apart from other physical

Practice Logging Form

Name _____ Teacher _____ Grade _____ Date _____

Record the *primary* activity you did during each 30-minute interval during the day using the list at the bottom of the page. Use the numbers and letters from the chart to indicate the activity. For example, walking would be activity 1A. You may have done several things in each 30-minute time period, but try to pick the activity you did for the most time. Choose an intensity level that best describes how it felt (Light: *"easy"*; Moderate: *"not too tiring"*; Vigorous: *"very tiring"*). Note all Rest activities should have Rest checked for the intensity.

Time	Activity category	Rest	Intensity Level			Time	Activity category	Rest	Intensity Level		
			Light	Mod	Vig				Light	Mod	Vig
7:00						3:00					
7:30						3:30					
8:00						4:00					
8:30						4:30					
9:00						5:00					
9:30						5:30					
10:00						6:00					
10:30						6:30					
11:00						7:00					
11:30						7:30					
12:00						8:00					
12:30						8:30					
1:00						9:00					
1:30						9:30					
2:00						10:00					
2:30						10:30					

Categories of Physical Activity

	1	2	3	4	5	6
	Lifestyle Activity	Active Aerobics	Active Sports	Muscle Fitness Activities	Flexibility Exercises	Rest and Inactivity
	"Activities that I do as part of my normal day"	"Activities that I do for aerobic fitness"	"Activities that I do for sport and recreation"	"Activities that I do for muscular fitness"	"Activities that I do for flexibility and fun"	"Things I do when I am not active"
A	Walking, bicycling, or skateboarding	Aerobic dance	Field sports (baseball, softball, football, soccer, etc.)	Gymnastics or cheer, dance, or drill teams	Martial arts (tai chi)	Schoolwork, homework, or reading
B	Housework or yardwork	Gym equipment (stairclimber, treadmill, rowing machine, etc.)	Court sports (basketball, volleyball, soccer, hockey, etc.)	Track and field sports	Stretching	Computer games or TV/video
C	Playing active games or dancing	Aerobic activity (bicycling, running, skating, etc.)	Racket sports (tennis, ping pong, badminton, and racketball)	Weight lifting or resistance exercise (push-ups, sit-ups)	Yoga	Eating or resting
D	Work-active job	Aerobic activity (physical education)	Sports (physical education)	Wrestling or martial arts (karate, aikido)	Ballet/Dance	Sleeping
E	Other	Other	Other	Other	Other	Other

Figure 12.7 The Activitygram paper-pencil assessment can be used if appropriate computer software is not available (American Fitness Alliance, 2002a).

From *Developmental Physical Education for All Children* (4 ed.) by David L. Gallahue and Frances Cleland Donnelly, 2003, Champaign, IL: Human Kinetics.

activity assessment devices: it accommodates weekend as well as in-school activity assessment and uses a physical activity pyramid as a guide for physical activity inclusion into one's daily life much like the Food Guide Pyramid does for daily food intake.

ALTERNATIVE ASSESSMENT

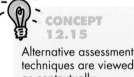

CONCEPT 12.15

Alternative assessment techniques are viewed as contextually relevant to "real-world" movement and fitness situations.

Recently, many have shifted away from more traditional forms of motor and fitness assessment toward alternative forms of assessment. As discussed earlier, in traditional motor skill assessment, students are asked to demonstrate their current ability to perform a designated skill such as a run, throw, or jump for its own sake, and are assessed by the teacher on the qualitative (process assessment) or quantitative (product assessment) merits of this performance. So, too, in traditional fitness assessment, students perform a battery of fitness tests; teachers then compare their performances to either established standards of performance (norm-referenced testing) or individual standards of achievement (self-referenced testing). Physical activity assessments using heart rate monitors or self-report inventories, however, are viewed as more contextually relevant to the real world of children and youth.

In alternative assessment techniques, assessment scenarios are designed around more real-life situations; the context of the testing environment more closely matches the context in which the movement skill or fitness component will actually be used. For example, rather than simply observing children perform a variety of fundamental movement skills in isolation from one another, you might devise a game activity that utilizes several of the skills that your students have been working on in

Using a task sheet designed to assess specific aspects of game play in this "real-life" small-sided hockey game is an alternative and appropriate practice for assessing students' game-playing performance.

class. Then, while observing your students playing the game, you are assessing how they actually incorporate these skills into a real-life situation. In other words, the game context makes the activity more like real life than performing the skill in isolation is.

Alternative assessment techniques also place greater emphasis on learner outcomes in the form of higher-order cognitive skills and integrated learning. Although it is important for children to be able to perform fundamental movement skills at the mature or sport skill stages, and to be able to demonstrate a certain standard of physical fitness, alternative assessment techniques are different in that they are more contextually relevant. That is, they more closely relate to how the skill will actually be used in real-life situations rather than artificial testing environments. As a result, alternative assessment has come to be known as **authentic assessment.** Its proponents argue that authentic assessment facilitates teaching, enhances learning, and results in greater student achievement. Moreover, it actively engages students in using their movement skill and fitness knowledge to solve "real-life" problems. Heart rate monitors and physical activity self-report surveys are excellent examples of forms of alternative or authentic assessment.

According to Lund (1997), authentic assessment has five characteristics:

1. Authentic assessment requires the "presentation of worthwhile and/or meaningful tasks that are designed to be representative of performance in the field" (p. 25). With elementary school children we can do this by putting children in lifelike situations in which they must use the skills learned in class in developmental game, dance, or gymnastics activities, or must demonstrate knowledge of the fitness components required for successful performance in an activity.

2. "Authentic assessments emphasize 'higher level' thinking and more complex learning" (p. 26). In other words, authentic assessment is designed to determine how children use the new knowledge and skills that they have been taught. After children learn how to dribble, pass, and shoot a basketball, for example, observing, recording, and responding to their basketball skills in the context of a basketball lead-up game is a typical means of helping students utilize higher-order thinking and more complex skills.

3. "The criteria used in authentic assessment are articulated in advance so that students know how they will be evaluated" (p. 26). The teacher must clarify the objectives of the lesson by clearly indicating why and how students are to be evaluated. In our basketball skills example, the teacher would clearly state what she was looking for in terms of the use of movement skills and team play. The students would then be clear on how they were being evaluated.

4. Lund says that "authentic assessments are so firmly embedded in the curriculum that they are practically indistinguishable from instruction" (p. 26). In other words, authentic assessment is viewed as continuous and formative rather than simply a summative experience at the end of a semester or unit of work. Our basketball skill learners and teacher would continuously work together in the rhythmical "dance" of teaching, learning, and assessing.

5. Lund holds that "the role of the teacher from adversary to ally is changed through authentic assessment" (p. 26). As such, authentic assessment is ongoing and continuous. The learner has multiple opportunities to demonstrate his abilities, and the teacher likewise has multiple opportunities to provide feedback.

Types of Alternative Assessment

Assessments can be designed to gather formative information about students' cognitive, affective, and psychomotor progress. Teachers, peers, or students (i.e., self-assessment) can administer the assessment. Authentic assessment, "unlike traditional assessment, which uses one-dimensional measurements based on a single setting" (Schiemer, 2000, p. 4), provides an ongoing individual view of children as they participate in physical education class activities—thus it is *formative*. This ongoing information, often recorded on worksheets, is scored and entered into an individual student portfolio. Teachers can also provide feedback to their students by writing comments or suggestions on an assessment worksheet before returning it to the student. Progress across the three domains of learning can be documented through collecting a variety of assessments within a student portfolio. Three sample assessments are provided in figures 12.8, 12.9, and 12.10.

Student's Name: _____

Class Time: _____ Classroom Teacher: _____

Date of Administration: _____

Type of Small-Sided Game: _____

Game Criteria to Observe	Beginning	Intermediate	Advanced
Moves to open spaces to receive object			
Uses body feints to dodge an opponent when in possession of object			
Can speed up and slow down with control when in possession of object			
Supports other players during game play			

Beginning – Inconsistently demonstrates strategy of motor skill; performed infrequently during a 10-minute small-sided game (only 1 or 2 times)

Intermediate – Demonstrates strategy or skill more consistently (3-5 times); body timing and coordination of movement are average

Advanced – Frequently demonstrates the strategy or motor skill (6 or more times during play); body coordination and rhythmical timing create "smooth and controlled" performance

Teacher's Comments:

Figure 12.8 Game-playing assessment tool—teacher assessment.

Managing Alternative Assessment

Teachers often question how they will "fit in" authentic assessment, especially when students have physical education only once or twice per week. Schiemer (2000) highlights issues that teachers must confront when implementing authentic assessment and provides several strategies for dealing with these frustrations. Schiemer offers a 2-minute assessment strategy and emphasizes that careful preplanning is the key. The following are suggested protocols for managing assessment:

Name: _____ **Date:** _____

BLUE   GREEN   RED   YELLOW

Draw a smile face for True. Draw a frown face for False.

☺ Use a dodge to keep from bumping into other students.

☺ You move slowly when you dodge.

☺ When you dodge, you change directions.

☺ Are you good at dodging?

Critical elements of dodging: _____ (quick, change direction, look)
Full name _____
Concept quiz _____
Independent working skills _____

Alternative Assessment Objective:

The child will demonstrate the ability to identify some of the critical elements of dodging.

Teacher Tips

- Make sure the students know that a smile face means "true" and a frown face means "false"

Extensions

- Review the critical elements of dodging:
  - ✓ Stay balanced
  - ✓ Change directions and speeds quickly
  - ✓ Move away from an object or a person
  - ✓ Dodging can be stationary or on the move
  - ✓ Dodging helps us move safely
- Brainstorm a list of activities, games, and sports that use the skill of dodging. Some examples to get you started include:
  - ✓ Football   ✓ Tag   ✓ Soccer
  - ✓ Fencing   ✓ Wrestling
- List other action words that describe dodging. Some examples to get you started include:
  - ✓ Keep away   ✓ Fake, move quickly and change direction

Teacher's Comments:

Figure 12.9 Critical elements of dodging—self-assessment.

Adapted, by permission, from Suzann Schiemer, 2000, *Assessment strategies for elementary physical education* (Champaign, IL: Human Kinetics), 84-85.

Name: _____   **Date:** _____

VOLLEYBALL ASSESSMENT

1. When you perform a forearm pass (bump) should you swing your arms above your shoulders?
   Yes _____   No _____

2. What part of your body bends and extends to provide force for a forearm pass?
   Shoulders _____   Legs _____   Stomach _____

3. Forearm passes are used for what purpose? Describe one:
   _____
   _____
   _____

Teacher's Comments:

Figure 12.10 Volleyball self-assessment.

"(1) using color coding as a means to facilitate the distribution and collection of assessment equipment and materials, (2) utilizing student/class aides to check assessment sheets for names and dates and (3) the use of low-end technology (e.g., tape recorder) in meeting the various learning support adaptations for students" (p. 10).

Summary

Motor assessment, fitness assessment, and physical activity assessment are important aspects of the developmental physical education program. Entry-level assessment, done at the beginning of a unit of instruction, helps the teacher develop instruction based on where students actually are. Exit-level assessment, in combination with entry-level assessment, provides information about the progress of individual learners. Assessment may be process based or product based. Process, or observational, assessment focuses on the body mechanics of fundamental movement skills or sport skills. Product, or performance, assessment focuses on the outcome of the movement in terms of time elapsed, distance traveled, or number of repetitions accomplished. Both process and product assessments yield information that is useful for determining a student's present status, measuring progress, and helping teachers plan the program for movement skill acquisition and fitness enhancement. All must be valid, reliable, objective, and administratively feasible. Some, however, are more or less useful depending on their intent of being used for within-individual, between-individual, or group comparisons.

Three motor assessment tests that teachers use are the Fundamental Movement Pattern Assessment Instrument, the Developmental Sequence of Fundamental Motor Skills Inventory, and the Test of Gross Motor Development. The Fundamental Movement Pattern Assessment Instrument serves as an informal means of within-individual comparison for developmentally appropriate program planning in the skill theme chapters that follow. Fitness assessment is an additional important means of determining status and measuring progress, and the results are an important aid in planning programs. Among the many published fitness assessment tests, the two most popular are the President's Challenge, which is norm referenced, and Fitnessgram, which is criterion referenced. These tests are philosophically sound and scientifically based, and they yield valid and reliable results.

Many physical education teachers use computer-assisted assessment devices. The rapid growth of the computer software industry and the continual updating and expanding of existing software make it difficult to provide a critical overview of the most current materials. Popular motor and fitness assessment packages save a great deal of time, store large amounts of information, and make many aspects of assessment more efficient than in the past.

Authentic assessment is alternative assessment that many view as more relevant to "real-world" movement and fitness situations than traditional forms of assessment and can serve as a valuable tool in the elementary physical education program. Alternative assessment differs from traditional assessment in that the activities take place within a more lifelike context rather than in isolation and so seem more relevant. Authentic assessment is a continuous, ongoing process.

Terms to Remember

Excellent Resources

American Fitness Alliance. (2002). *Fitnessgram 6.0* [CD-ROM]. Champaign, IL: Human Kinetics. **www.americanfitness.net**

Beighle, A., Pangrazi, R.P., & Vincent, S.D. (2001). Pedometers, physical activity, and accountability. *JOPERD, 72* (9), 16-19, 36.

Burton, A.W., & Rodgerson, R.W. (2001). New perspectives on the assessment of movement skills and motor abilities. *Adapted Physical Activity Quarterly, 18,* 347-365.

CompTech Systems Design. *Fit America and physical skills manager* [Computer software]. P.O. Box 516, Hastings, MN 55033. (CompTech offers a wide variety of computer software appropriate for children's physical education.)

Connaughton, D., & Poor, L. (2000). Assessing and promoting physical fitness in a school setting. *Strategies, 13* (3), 8-12, 29.

Cooper Institute for Aerobics Research. (1999). *Fitnessgram: Test administration manual.* Champaign, IL: Human Kinetics.

Cooper Institute for Aerobics Research. (1999). *Fitnessgram test kit.* Champaign, IL: Human Kinetics.

Gallahue, D.L., & Ozmun, J.C. (2002). *Understanding motor development: Infants, children, adolescents, adults* (chapter 12). Boston: McGraw-Hill.

Garcia, A.W., Broda, M.A.N., Frenn, M., Coviak, C., Pender, N.J., & Ronis, D.L. (1995). Gender and developmental differences in exercise beliefs among youth and prediction of their exercise behavior. *Journal of School Health, 65,* 213-219.

Hensley, L.D. (1997). Alternative assessment for physical education. *JOPERD, 68* (7), 19-24.

Hodges, P., Kulinna, W.Z., Behnke, M., Johnson, R., McMullen, D., Turner, M.E., & Wolff, G. (1999). Six steps in developing and using fitness portfolios. *TEPE, 10* (5), 15-17.

Holt/Hale, S. (1999). *Assessing and improving fitness in elementary physical education.* Reston, VA: AAHPERD.

Holt/Hale, S. (1999). *Assessing motor skills in elementary physical education.* Reston, VA: AAHPERD.

Kirk, M.F. (1997). Using portfolios to enhance student learning & assessment. *JOPERD, 68* (7), 29-33.

Knudson, D. (2000). What can professionals qualitatively analyze? *JOPERD, 71* (2), 19-23.

Lund, J. (2000). *Creating rubrics in physical education.* Reston, VA: AAHPERD.

McClenaghan, B.A., & Gallahue, D.L. (1978). *Fundamental movement: A developmental and remedial approach.* Philadelphia: Saunders. (Original five-item version)

Morrison, C.S. (2000). Why don't you analyze the way I analyze? *JOPERD, 71* (1), 22-25.

O'Sullivan, M., & Henninger, M. (2000). *Assessing social responsibility and teamwork.* Reston, VA: AAHPERD.

Pinheiro, V. (1994). Diagnosing motor skills—a practical approach. *JOPERD, 63,* 49-54.

Pinheiro, V.E.D. (2000). Qualitative analysis for the elementary grades. *JOPERD, 71* (1), 18-20, 25.

President's Council on Physical Fitness and Sports. (2000). *Fitness Tracker* [President's Challenge Physical Fitness Test software]. Micro Services, 14 Harmony Lane, Danville, NJ 07834. (943-627-1781)

President's Council on Physical Fitness and Sports. (2002-03). *The President's Challenge: Physical fitness program packet.* 400 East 7th Street, Bloomington, IN 47405. (800-258-8146) **www.indiana.edu/~preschal**

Sallis, J.F., Strikemiller, P.K., Harsha, D.W., Feldman, H.A., Ehlinger, S., Stone, E.J., Williston, J., & Woods, S. (1996). Validation of interviewer- and self-administered physical activity checklists for fifth-grade students. *Medicine and Science in Sports and Exercise, 28* (7), 840–851.

Strand, B., Walswick, P., & Sommer, C. (2000). Tracking children's caloric expenditure in physical education. *JOPERD, 71* (5), 35–39.

Ulrich, D.A. (2000). *Test of gross motor development.* PRO-ED, 5341 Industrial Oaks Blvd., Austin, TX 78735. (512-892-3142)

Weston, A.T., Petosa, R., & Pate, R.R. (1997). Validation of an instrument for measurement of physical activity in youth. *Medicine and Science in Sports and Exercise, 29* (1), 138–143.

Wilkinson, C., Pennington, T.R., & Padfield, G. (2000). Student perceptions of using skills software in physical education. *JOPERD, 71* (6), 37–40, 53.

Winnick, J.P., & Short, F.X. (2001). *The Brockport physical fitness test kit.* Champaign, IL: Human Kinetics. (Contains CD-ROM computer software) **www.americanfitness.net**

Winnick, J.P., & Short, F.X. (2001). *The Brockport physical fitness test manual.* Champaign, IL: Human Kinetics.

13

Advocacy: Educating, Communicating, Motivating

Key Concept

▶ Advocacy is your responsibility and an essential component of the physical education curriculum.

Chapter Objectives

This chapter will provide you with the tools to do the following:

▶ Define *advocacy*.

▶ Become familiar with national trends on the status of physical education in schools.

▶ Understand the what and why of physical education and the how of advocacy.

▶ Become more knowledgeable about professional publications designed to inform the public of the importance and benefits of daily, quality physical education.

▶ Become familiar with a variety of advocacy activities at the national, district, state, and local levels.

Teaching physical education the way it should be taught requires an exceptional individual. This individual is committed to renewing and expanding her knowledge base; involved in school and professional associations; dedicated to the needs and interests of children; and willing to promote, and inform others about, the importance of daily, quality physical education for all children. It is the last dimension that we concentrate on in this chapter—that is, advocating for your physical education program.

Advocacy has been described as a behavior. "It is the art of making one's own views count within a group's decision-making process. **Advocacy** is the process by which we inform

The sky is the limit! Photos such as this one, depicting the practice of fundamental movement tossing and catching skills, are a part of Chester County Family Academy's physical education program. Eye-catching photos speak volumes about a well-designed physical education program.

CONCEPT 13.1

Advocacy is the art of making one's own views count within a group's decision-making process.

others of the benefits of our profession, and it necessitates communication with a clear purpose . . ." (Watson & Hildebrand, 2000, p. 46). Advocacy, also frequently described as **public relations**, is telling people what you are doing, why you are doing it, and what the benefits are for your students (Scantling, Lackey, Strand, & Johnson, 1998, p. 13). Advocacy is a part of pursuing excellence. Simply stated, it is the right thing to do as a committed professional deeply interested in the value of physical activity for all children and youth.

WHY ADVOCACY IS IMPORTANT TO YOU

As a young professional or preservice teacher, you will no doubt sometimes find many aspects of your role as a physical educator overwhelming. Curricular planning, assessment, scheduling, and budgeting are just a few of the "teacher tasks" that can become monumental challenges. You may ask, "Who has time for promoting their program?" The answer should be "You do!" If you do not have the support of your school colleagues, administrators, parents, and community, you may not have a program to plan or budget for.

Yes, the existence of and support for physical education programs have been threatened in several states. As Gabbard (2000) notes, "Many programs have taken back seats to more 'substantive classes' as school board members, administrators, and education leaders sharpen their focus on courses they believe will help meet state standards" (p. 6). Currently only 25% of U.S. children participate in any type of daily physical education, and nearly one-quarter of U.S. children are considered to be over-weight or obese. This constitutes a 20% increase in obesity among children during the decade of the 1990s. In 1999, California conducted one of the largest statewide physical fitness testing programs, involving more than a million students. Only 20% of these students (grades five, seven, and nine) met the minimum fitness standards.

The **Surgeon General's report** (USDHHS, 1996) for the first time recognized that physical activity is a significant factor in improving an individual's overall health, but the report also indicated nearly a 16% decline (41.6% in 1991 to 25.4% in 1995) in high school programs requiring daily physical education. Another national project, *Healthy People 2000,* released in 1990, proposed an agenda targeting the preven-tion of disease. The document contained 310 objectives organized into 22 priority areas. Two school-related objectives, associated with physical activity and fitness and directly linked to providing daily school physical education, were included. Objective 1.8 reads: "Increase to at least 50 percent the proportion of children and adolescents in first through 12th grade who participate in daily school physical education." Objective 1.9 states: "Increase to at least 50 percent the proportion of school physical education class time that students spend being physically active, preferably engaged in lifetime physical activities" (National Association for Sport and Physical Education [NASPE], 1999, Part II, p. 5). First released by NASPE, the *Shape of the Nation Report* in 1997 coincidentally revealed how most states had failed to achieve the recommendations made in the Surgeon General's report and in *Healthy People 2000.* In 1997, only four states required daily physical education (Illinois, Hawaii, Kentucky, and Rhode Island). By 2001, the most recent *Shape of the*

CONCEPT 13.2

Only 25% of children in the United States participate in any type of daily physical education instruction.

REALITY CHECK

Physical Education: A Place at the Table?

Real-World Situation

Tonight, your second author talked with a friend who is a teacher in an elementary school with 650 students. Mary Lou informed me that despite the fact that her school district is known for producing fine athletes, some even going on to play at the college and professional levels, elementary physical education has always been taught by classroom teachers. Mary Lou and her class of 21 second graders go to the gymnasium once a week for 30 minutes. Knowing the value of physical education, she engages students in a variety of planned activities. Currently they are in a six-week dance unit. Mary Lou told me, though, "Not all of the teachers take PE seriously. Some even skip it all together." Even though the district she teaches in is considered above average in terms of funding, the most commonly ac-cepted reasons for this lack of attention to physical education are (1) "We don't have enough money to hire professional physical education teachers" and (2) "I never had PE in grade school, why is it so important

now?" Although both art and music teachers are em-ployed in the school, physical education teachers still do not have a "place at the table."

This case as presented is true and, unfortunately, not unusual. Physical education taught by trained pro-fessionals is still not a reality for many children.

Critical Questions

Based on what you know about advocacy and your role as an advocate for quality programs:

- What do you see as your responsibility for promot-ing quality physical education?

- How do you counter arguments such as "We don't have sufficient funds" or "The measurable benefits of physical education are negligible"?

- Why has this problem persisted for so many years in this school district?

- In the absence of professional physical education teachers in this school district, what could you or should you do as a fellow teacher to offer support?

Nation Report revealed that only one state, Illinois, has kept the requirement of daily physical education, although waivers may be obtained. Because of these declines and an accompanying lack of status that physical education may have within a school district or state, we must strive to maintain physical education's place in our schools and to enhance its effectiveness.

ADVOCACY: THE "WHAT" AND "WHY" OF PHYSICAL EDUCATION

The public relations manual developed by NASPE, titled *SPEAK II (Sport and Physical Education Advocacy Kit II)*, highlights what we as physical educators know and understand:

- Schools are the most efficient vehicle for providing physical activity and fitness instruction because they reach most children and adolescents.
- Quality physical education contributes to students' health-related fitness, physical competence, and cognitive understanding about physical activity.
- Quality physical education programs endow students with the knowledge, attitudes, and skills they need to lead a healthy and active lifestyle.
- Every student in our nation's schools, from kindergarten through grade 12, should have the opportunity to participate in quality physical education (NASPE, 1999, Part III).

REALITY CHECK

We Just Don't Have Enough Time for More PE

Real-World Situation

Recently, your senior author served as an external consultant to a school district in Illinois that was undergoing review. As you read in this chapter, Illinois is the only one of our 50 states to require daily physical education of all students from kindergarten through grade 12. In my review of the elementary physical education curriculum and in my discussions with teachers, I learned that physical education was in fact not offered daily. Physical education was, and still is, only offered two to three times per week for a maximum of 30 minutes each time. When I brought this disparity between what should be and what actually was to the attention of the superintendent, I was quickly informed that it was a simple matter to request a variance from the state statute. Furthermore, I was informed, "As soon as the state authorizes six-day-a-week schools, I will be happy to comply with the statute and offer physical education daily. We simply don't have enough time to offer daily physical education with all the other requirements that we are faced with."

Critical Questions

Based on what you know about the benefits of quality physical education programs offered daily:

- What is your argument for offering physical education daily?
- How would you go about advocating for daily physical education in this school district?
- Is requesting a variance from a state education statute ethical?
- If we have been just "tilting at windmills" when we promote the cause for quality physical education programs offered daily, how might we generate sufficient public support to change the status quo?
- If the school day is in fact so crowded with other required activities, why not just eliminate physical education altogether and let children get their instruction through outside agencies such as the YMCA, Boys and Girls Clubs, or various youth sport organizations?

Defining Physical Education

In communicating with, educating, and motivating others about the importance of quality daily physical education, we must explain what it is as well as why it is important. "Physical education assures a minimum amount of physical activity by children and provides a forum to teach skills and knowledge to support lifelong physical activity" (NASPE, 1999, Part II, p. 6). *SPEAK II* outlines how to achieve the "critical content" (i.e., skills and knowledge) of physical education (Part I, p. 7). First, the physical education curriculum must facilitate achieving the National Content Standards for Physical Education (please refer to chapter 1). To accomplish this, the curriculum should include these elements:

- Fitness education and assessment to help children understand, improve, and/ or maintain their physical well-being
- Instruction in a variety of motor skills that are designed to enhance the physical, mental, and social-emotional development of every child
- Development of cognitive concepts about motor skills and health-enhancing levels of fitness
- Opportunities to develop social and cooperative skills and gain a multicultural perspective
- Involvement for all children in activities that provide maximum amounts of appropriate physical activity

In addition to these curricular components, the following guidelines ensure a high-quality physical education program:

- Elementary school children should receive 150 minutes per week of instructional physical education; middle and high school students should receive 225 minutes per week of instructional physical education.
- Teachers who have baccalaureate degrees that license them as physical education specialists should teach kindergarten through grade 12 physical education.
- The physical education specialist needs to stay abreast of the latest research, issues, and trends in the field through ongoing professional development.
- Equipment and facilities must be adequate to allow all children to maximize fitness and skill development.
- Physical education classes should contain numbers of students similar to those for other classrooms—about 25 students per class.

Several NASPE publications are helpful in conveying the message about what quality physical education should include. The following pamphlets (by NASPE and the Council on Physical Education for Children [COPEC]) may help you inform others about the what, why, and how of elementary physical education:

- *Appropriate Practices for Elementary School Physical Education* (NASPE-COPEC, 2000a)
- *Opportunity to Learn—Standards for Elementary Physical Education* (NASPE-COPEC, 2000c)
- *Appropriate Practices in Movement Programs for Young Children Ages 3-5* (NASPE-COPEC, 2000b)

- *Guidelines for Facilities, Equipment and Instructional Materials in Elementary Physical Education* (NASPE-COPEC, 2001b)
- *Physical Activity Guidelines for Infants and Toddlers* (NASPE, 2002).

You can obtain these pamphlets by contacting NASPE at the American Alliance for Health, Physical Education, Recreation and Dance headquarters in Reston, Virginia, or by ordering online at **www.aahperd.org**.

The Importance of Physical Education

Another common question asked by parents, administrators, and community members is "Why do children need physical education?" Depending on their previous educational experiences, people may or may not think of physical education as a valuable component of the total school curriculum. As NASPE summarizes the "why" of physical education for children, "Physical education is an integral part of the total education of a child. Quality physical education programs are needed to increase the physical competence, health-related fitness, self-esteem and enjoyment of physical activity for all students so that they can be physically active for a lifetime" (1999, Part III, p. 1).

A well-planned and well-implemented program provides a number of benefits:

- Enhancement of health-related fitness—increases muscular strength, flexibility, muscular endurance, cardiovascular endurance, and body composition
- Support for other subject areas—reinforces knowledge learned across the curriculum
- Self-discipline—facilitates development of student responsibility and respect for individual differences
- Skill development—develops motor skills and movement concepts that allow for safe, successful, and satisfying participation in physical activities

Here's a captivating photo with a catchy caption to help "sell" your program: Children love to move at Chester County Family Academy! Here students learn about personal space and general space as they practice locomotor skills and develop cardiovascular endurance!

- Experience with goal setting—gives children the opportunity to set and strive for personal, achievable goals
- Regular, healthful physical activity—provides a wide range of developmentally appropriate activities for all children
- Improved judgment—can influence moral development by giving students the opportunity to assume leadership roles, cooperate with others, question their own actions, and accept responsibility for their own behavior
- Improved self-confidence and self-esteem—instills in children a stronger sense of self-worth, enabling them to become more confident, assertive, emotionally secure, independent, and self-controlled
- Stress reduction—through physical activity, provides an outlet for releasing tension and anxiety
- Strengthened peer relationships—helps children learn to socialize more successfully (NASPE, 1999, Part III, p. 1)

The program at Hillside Elementary School in West Chester, Pennsylvania, strives to actively engage all children in purposeful skill-building activities.

The Council on Physical Education for Children and the Middle and Secondary School Physical Education Council, both structures within NASPE, recently collaborated on a position paper, *Benefits and Importance of Physical Education in the K-12 Curricula* (2001a). This is an important document to provide to administrators, school board, and parents.

THE "HOW" OF ADVOCACY

You are the best advocate for quality physical education programs. Your professional demeanor accounts for much of how others perceive and ultimately feel about the physical education program at your school. Personal characteristics such as the way you dress and your promptness, dependability, and enthusiasm about your program directly influence what others note about your physical education program. As a teacher you will be on display at all times. Advocating for your program involves telling others what your children are doing in physical education. Bulletin boards, based on a variety of themes, are a great way to promote your program, motivate your students, and share curricular information with your colleagues. Newsletters are also great advocacy tools. Some teachers publish their own newspapers. The school may copy and distribute newspapers for a teacher. Other teachers may include updates on the physical education program within the regularly circulated school newsletter. Newsletters are a substantial and very professional way to promote your program. A wide variety of Web resources are also available.

Physical education at Mary C. Howse Elementary School is "Jumpin' for Joy!" A photo like this one excites parents and children. A photo in a newsletter or Web page is a great advocacy tool.

Scantling et al. (1998) describe what should be included in an action plan for physical education, ranging from nationally and state-sponsored activities to a selection of locally developed public relations activities. Additionally, they provide month-by-month action plans, beginning with a staff meeting in September to plan the advocacy activities for the year. As the first activity of the year, the authors recommend sending a newsletter home to educate parents on the benefits of physical education (figure 13.1). The physical education public relations action plan should be a team effort on the part of all staff members, with specific responsibilities assigned to one or more teachers.

In *SPEAK II* (NASPE, 1999), the following guidelines describe the advocacy process:

- Create a curriculum that supports the achievement of your goals and objectives.
- Provide a clear understanding about the difference among physical education, athletics, and physical activity.

Web Resources for Child and Youth Physical Activity

- American Academy of Pediatrics (AAP): **www.aap.org**
- American Alliance for Health, Physical Education, Recreation and Dance (AAHPERD): **www.aahperd.org**
- American Association for Health Education (AAHE): **www.aahperd.org/aahe**
- American Association for Leisure and Recreation (AALR): **www.aahperd.org/aalr-main.html**
- American Association of Mental Retardation (AAMR): **www.aamr.org**
- American College of Sports Medicine (ACSM): **www.acsm.org**
- American Medical Association (AMA): **www.ama.assn.org**
- American Obesity Association (AOA): **www.obesity.org**
- American Public Health Association (APHA): **www.apha.org**
- American School Health Association (ASHA): **www.ashaweb.org**
- Boys and Girls Clubs of America: **www.bgca.org**
- Boy Scouts of America: **www.bsa.scouting.org**
- Campfire Boys and Girls: **www.campfire.org**
- Centers for Disease Control and Prevention (CDC): **www.cdc.gov/nchs**
- Cooper Institute for Aerobics Research: **www.cooperinst.org**
- Disabled Sports USA: **www.dsusa.org**
- Girl Scouts of America: **www.girlscouts.org**
- Girls Incorporated: **www.girlsinc.org**
- March of Dimes: **www.modimes.org**
- National Association for Girls and Women in Sport (NAGWS): **www.aahperd.org/nagws**
- National Association for Health and Fitness: **www.physicalfitness.org**
- National Association for Sport and Physical Education (NASPE): **www.aahperd.org/naspe**
- National Association of Pediatric Nurse Associates and Practitioners: **www.napnap.org**
- National Athletic Trainers Association (NATA): **www.nata.org**
- National Center for Education in Maternal and Child Health (NCEMCH): **www.ncemch.org**
- National Education Association: **www.nea.org**
- National Information Center for Children and Youth with Disabilities: **www.nichcy.org**
- National Institutes of Health—Child Health and Human Development Clearinghouse: **www.nichd.nih.gov**
- National Institutes of Health—National Heart, Lung, and Blood Institute: **www.nhlbi.nih.gov**
- National Intramural-Recreation Sports Association (NIRSA): **www.nirsa.org**
- National Maternal and Child Health Clearinghouse: **www.nmchc.org**
- National Parent Teacher Association: **www.pta.org**
- National Park Service: **www.nps.gov**
- National Program for Playground Safety: **www.uni.edu/playground**
- National Recreation and Park Association: **www.activeparks.org**
- National Safety Council: **www.nsc.org**
- National Strength and Conditioning Association: **www.nsca.org**
- Office of Disease Prevention and Health Promotion: **www.odphp.osophs.dhhs.gov**
- President's Council on Physical Fitness and Sports: **www.fitness.gov**
- U.S. Consumer Product Safety Commission: **www.cpsc.gov**
- Women's Sports Foundation: **www.womenssportsfoundation.org**
- YMCA of the USA: **www.ymca.net**

Dribble From the Gym

Physical Education Newsletter
Exton Elementary 2001-2002

Physical Education Instructors

Mr. Jackson/Mrs. Sider

We would like to welcome all parents and students to the 2001-2002 school year. As you know Mr. "Y" is Exton's Intern Assistant Principal and we wish him the best in his new position. I have had a wonderful start here at Exton Elementary School; everyone has been very welcoming. I am slowly getting to know the students one-by-one.

If you have any questions concerning physical education please feel free to contact me. I am looking forward to a great school year here at Exton.

~~ Important ~~

Please take note of your child's physical education days and remind him or her to wear sneakers. Not only is being prepared important, we are also concerned with your student's safety during physical activities.

~~ Activity Promotes ~~
~~ Wellness ~~

Physical Education Rules

1. Be prepared–must wear sneakers
2. Behave appropriately
3. Be safe
4. Respect yourself, others, and equipment
5. Enter and exit gym quietly

Important Dates to Write on Your Calendar!

Fun Runs–East High School
Fri., Sept 17th and Oct 12th

Jump Rope for Heart
TBA–February 2002

4/5th District Track Meet
April 30th, 2002

Field Day
May 23rd, 2002

Roller Skating: Caln Rink
2001: Tues 10/9, Wed 11/7, Wed 12/5, 2002: Tues 1/8, Wed 2/6, Mon 3/18.

PTO Physical Education Meeting
7 p.m., May 9th, 2002

5th Grade After School Sports
Girls most Mondays
Boys most Thursdays
Oct. 1st–Jan. 31st

4th Grade After School Sports
Girls most Mondays
Boys most Thursdays
Feb. 2nd–May 23rd
More information will follow

School picnic
June 5th

Exton's Physical Education Program

Physical education at Exton is based on two concepts. The first is the NASPE (National Association for Sport and Physical Education) standards. These standards are part of the WCASD curriculum. They are in place for the sole purpose of monitoring each individual child's progress according to National Standards. The second concept is HAL or Healthy Active Living. It is important that students understand that they must be healthy and active for a **lifetime.**

This is accomplished through Physical Education class, and by providing extra-curricular activities for the students to participate in. Parents can also help by encouraging their children to play games at home. Exton's physical education program uses these two concepts as its backbone for teaching physical skills, as well as personal and social skills.

Making period grades are based upon four categories:

1. Physical education skills
2. Listening and following directions
3. Individual effort
4. Understanding physical education concepts

Illness or Injury

If your child is attending school but may not take Physical Education class because of injury or illness please send me an excuse signed by you or a doctor.

REMEMBER: EXERCISE IS MEDICINE!!!
BE FIT FOR LIFE!!!

FIGURE 13.1 Sample newsletter.

Adapted, by permission, from C. Jackson, 2001, "Dribble from the gym"—Physical education newsletter (Exton, PA: Exton Elementary School).

- Assess students to see the extent to which they are achieving the stated goals and objectives of your program.

- Inform parents and community of student achievements.

- Publicize new initiatives taking place in your program.

- Be sure that children know how well they are achieving objectives and that they can share their expertise with their parents.

The unique aspect of the process we have outlined relates to assessment of your students and communicating with parents about assessment. Many schools do not have separate "report cards" for physical education. But report cards are an excellent way to communicate student achievement in physical education. Please refer to figure 13.2 for a sample physical education report card. You can also convey student achievement through poster displays, bulletin boards, newsletters, and school announcements and by sending home authentic assessments completed in physical education.

You will need to tailor your public relations activities to meet your program needs and to fit your own schedule. The following activities are ideas for promoting your program:

- Celebrate National Heart Month (February) with a Jump Rope for Heart event.

- Celebrate National Girls and Women in Sports Day (first Thursday of February) by inviting successful female high school athletes to talk to your students or at a parents' night.

- Organize your classes to participate in a Jump Rope and Hoops for Heart Project, and donate the funds raised to the American Heart Association.

- Take part in Project ACES (All Children Exercise Simultaneously) with a mass school-wide exercise session. Invite fellow teachers, administrators, staff, and parents to help organize and join the mass activity session.

- Celebrate National Physical Education Day (May 1) with a family fun night or an all-school demonstration event highlighting your program.

- Participate in Bike to Work and School Day (during the third week in May) by organizing a safe and fun bike-to-school event. Work with parents and local police officers to ensure that children are supervised when crossing busy streets. Sponsor a bike rodeo in the gymnasium or outdoor play area.

- Invite the media to visit and take pictures of your students in action. A picture does say a thousand words, and photos accompanied by a brief article highlighting aspects of your physical education program can work wonders in garnering support. The community newspaper sometimes wants to do a "human interest" story or an article about an innovative educational project. If you are planning an interesting back-to-school event, the community newspaper may provide coverage.

- Have an Olympic Celebration or Field Day in which the community can participate.

- On Back to School Night, have parents participate in a physical education class with their children; distribute pamphlets such as *Tips for Family Fitness Fun, Shape Up America,* and *Is Your Child Being Physically Educated?*

- Videotape or take pictures of your students and make a physical education scrapbook or, better yet, a Web page.

Smith Elementary School
Physical Education Progress Report – Primary Grades (K-3)
Academic Year Fall - _____ to Spring - _____

Student's Name: *Ryan King*

Grade: *1st*   **Classroom Teacher:** *Mrs. Jones*

Grading Period: (1)   2   3   4

The physical education program at Smith Elementary School provides:

✔ A curriculum based on teaching motor skills and movement concepts.

✔ Developmentally appropriate activities in games, dance, and gymnastics.

✔ Individualized instruction helping all children succeed and be challenged.

✔ The inclusion of health-related fitness activities throughout the curriculum.

✔ Frequent and ongoing assessment.

✔ Building children's social skills and problem solving abilities.

Social Skills:

O (Outstanding) – 100% of the time

G (Good) – 75-85% of the time

NI (Needs Improvement) – less than 75% of the time

Grading Period:	(1)	2	3	4
Shares With Others	*O*			
Negotiates Well With Others	*G*			
Assists Peers	*G*			
Stays On Task	*O*			

Primary Grade Children's Motor Skills Are Assessed Using the Following Stages:

Initial – Skill is just being learned, parts of the skill are missing (preparation, execution, follow-through), timing and coordination developing, skill sometimes exaggerated (too small, too big)

Elementary – All parts of the skill are present but not consistently performed, rhythmical coordination and timing improving, accuracy and force control continuing to develop

Mature – All parts of the skill present and rhythmically coordinated, accuracy and force can be controlled

Skill Themes

Skill Themes	Grading Period 1	Movement Concepts	Grading Period 1
Kicking	*I*	Direction	*I*
Running	*E*	Force	*E*
Throwing	*E*	Trajectory	*E*
Catching	*I*	Relationship to a partner	*I*

Teacher's Comments: *Ryan is very enthusiastic in physical education. He is developing his fundamental movement skills and with continued practice & encouragement he will develop mature skills by the end of the semester!*

FIGURE 13.2   Sample report card.

- Send items about physical education home with students on a frequent basis (physical education homework, certificates, "happygrams")
- Develop bumper sticker slogans. Better yet, have a school-wide contest to select each year's bumper sticker slogan (e.g., Physical Education—For Life; Physical Education—Nature's Medication)
- Collaborate with classroom teachers by integrating thematic units of instruction.
- Invite administrators, school board members, parents, and the community to attend your physical education classes.

You may also capitalize on National Sport and Physical Education Week (an annual event that takes place during the first week in May) by hosting a variety of public relations activities. Schiemer (1996) provides a detailed description of daily activities specially designed to celebrate this week. T-shirts, sneaker days, and guest speakers are just a few of the ideas suggested. "Fit Kits" can be given to each student, faculty, and staff member who participates in selected activities during the week. These kits might contain several items that promote physical activity and may be contributed by local agencies and businesses.

At Brown Elementary School in Newburyport, Massachusetts, teacher Cathy Hill collaborates with the administration, classroom teachers, parents, and grandparents to conduct a thematic field day event each spring. The theme corresponds to the interdisciplinary theme for the entire school year. "Recycling," "Cultures," and "The Future" are three sample themes for field day activities.

There are many more ideas that you can add to your advocacy agenda. A novel idea initiated by teacher Curt Hinson in Wilmington, Delaware, is the "grocery bag project." In this project, children decorate hundreds of grocery bags with messages or pictures about their physical education program. They then return the grocery bags to the store for use.

Fund-raisers also provide opportunities to advocate for your program and obtain needed financial support. Turner and Turner (1998, p. 5) describe a "jog-a-thon" fund-raiser. The following components ensure success of this fund-raiser:

- Staff "buy-in"
- A letter to parents requesting volunteers
- Written student guidelines
- An informational letter to fellow faculty and staff members
- Pledge envelopes and lap sheets
- An event timeline
- Incentives (prizes)
- A benefits sheet

The jog-a-thon prize information sheet is described in figure 13.3.

Another tactic is to request parent or staff donations. Your request for donations should be minimal; it should be approved beforehand by your building principal, and the monies should be collected by someone other than yourself or by a school-sponsored group. The proceeds can be used to purchase big-ticket items, preferably items that will be of benefit to all. In one fund-raiser of this type, families purchased "rocks" for a vertical climbing wall. A banner streaming from an airplane printed above the climbing wall displayed the names of all families who made a contribution, no matter how large or small.

JOG-A-THON

Prizes **Prizes** Prizes **Prizes** Prizes **Prizes** Prizes

10 Individual Prizes:

There will be five cash prizes awarded to the students who collect the most money, and five cash prizes awarded to students who collect the most pledges (minimum $1 pledge).

Most Money		Most Pledges	
1st Prize	$25	1st Prize	$25
2nd Prize	$20	2nd Prize	$20
3rd Prize	$15	3rd Prize	$15
4th Prize	$10	4th Prize	$10
5th Prize	$5	5th Prize	$5

Class Prizes: The two classes that bring in the most money will get a make-your-own sundae party.

All-School Drawing: If you collect money for at least five pledges, your name will be entered in a drawing to win one of many great prizes.

Don't miss the chance to join in the fun of celebrating our school's spirit!

FIGURE 13.3 Jog-a-thon fund-raiser information sheet.

No matter how you promote your physical education program, the purpose of the advocacy project should be to communicate with, educate, and motivate the public about the benefits of including a quality physical education program in our schools. Remember, you are the most important ingredient in any program of advocacy. Remember also that advocacy in physical education is an ongoing process vitally important to the health of your program and the profession in general.

TEXT BOX 13.2

Perhaps we are turning the corner and making progress. In 2002, the State of Texas enacted legislation that mandates 30 minutes per day or 135 minutes per week of standards-based structured physical activity for elementary school children.

Summary

Advocacy begins with you. The status of physical education across the nation has been threatened. *Shape of the Nation Report* (2001c) substantiates the need to defend the inclusion of daily, quality physical education in our schools. Advocacy can be defined as making one's views count within a group's decision-making process. Advocacy involves informing administrators, colleagues, parents, school boards, and community members about the what and why of physical education for children, as well as about the benefits of teaching children physical education. To become effective advocates for their programs, teachers can and should become familiar with professional publications designed to inform the public of the importance and benefits of daily, quality physical education.

Advocacy is an ongoing process that is part of the responsibility of physical education teachers, and there are many types of advocacy ideas that teachers can implement. These include local public relations activities, such as communicating with and educating parents about the physical education program, and state-sponsored and nationally sponsored activities.

Terms to Remember

Excellent Readings

Docheff, D.M., Feltmann, K., & Rothenberger, T. (2001). Family fun night: Ideas to promote family and fitness. *Strategies, 15* (2), 15-18.

Grenier, M. (1996). Pump up your public relations. *TEPE, 7* (5), 9.

National Association for Sport and Physical Education. (2002). *99 tips for family fitness fun.* Reston, VA: Author.

Human Kinetics Video. (2002). *P.E. 4 Life: Active body active mind.* Champaign, IL: Human Kinetics (video and CD-ROM).

Tipton, J.S., & Tucker, S.L. (1998). Fundraising can be fun! Bumper stickers anyone? *TEPE, 9* (3), 14.

Wood, S.L., & Lynn, S. (2000). Web gym—Getting your physical education program on-line. *TEPE, 11* (5), 28-30.

The Developmental Program

Part III will give you a solid grasp of what it takes to put the developmentally based physical education program into action. This is where the "rubber meets the road." In the chapters that follow, we provide you with the essential tools for curriculum building, determining appropriate content, movement concept learning, and providing a safe learning environment for all children. **Chapter 14,** "The Developmental Curriculum," provides a step-by-step approach to curriculum planning. We, the authors, use this approach whether planning a children's physical education program or developing a new college-level course for learners such as you. It has proven to be a highly useful and valuable approach to program building. It's difficult to overemphasize the importance of the information in this chapter for helping you to get organized and put your curriculum on paper. **Chapter 15,** "The Physical Education Content," centers on the tools of our profession—developmental games, developmental dance, and developmental gymnastics—and on ways to select appropriate activities based on the individual needs of children. **Chapter 16,** "Movement Skill Development Through Movement Concept Learning," is of central importance to the developmental physical education program in that it emphasizes the movement concepts of effort, space, and relationship awareness that are essential to knowledge about how the body can move. **Chapter 17,** "Safety Considerations and Legal Liability," concludes part III by briefly overviewing the necessary conditions of legal liability, situations that lead to legal action, and practical ways to minimize your exposure to legal liability.

14

The Developmental Curriculum

Key Concept

▶ Curriculum is an organized process of bringing meaning, scope, sequence, and balance to the goals and objectives of the program so that it reflects the values and mission of those charged with its implementation.

The elementary school physical education curriculum is an integral part of the total school program. As such, it incorporates a broad series of movement experiences that help children acquire movement skills and that promote physical activity and fitness enhancement, as well as promoting cognitive and affective growth. An elementary school physical education curriculum that is well planned, well taught, and based on the developmental level of children is not a frill or appendage to the school program. It is a positive force in the education of the total child.

To achieve the goals of physical education, teachers use many movement activities from the various content areas of physical education (see chapter 15, "The Physical Education Content") to accomplish program objectives. The specific activities from each content area are viewed as activity tools and not as ends in themselves. The teacher's role is to teach children through activities. The focal point must always be the child, not the activity. If the goals of physical education are to have any real meaning, then curricular models must be congruent with these goals. Curricular models serve as "blueprints" for action; they make up the basic structure around which the daily lesson is planned and carried out by the teacher in the gymnasium or on the playing field.

The information presented in the preceding chapters is of little value if you cannot organize it and practically apply it to the lives of children. The value of theory and research that fail to foster models for implementation is limited at best. Conversely, curricular models not based on both sound research and sound theory are also of limited value. So, this chapter outlines the steps in constructing a curriculum and

Chapter Objectives

This chapter will provide you with the tools to do the following:

▹ Outline the steps in curriculum construction.

▹ Discuss the ingredients of an effective mission statement.

▹ Succinctly state your philosophy of physical education.

▹ Distinguish among aims, goals, general objectives, and specific objectives.

▹ Discuss what is meant by the term *conceptual framework* and outline the conceptual framework for the developmental curriculum.

▹ Discuss the merits and characteristics of behavioral objectives.

▹ List and describe a variety of teaching conditions that will influence the content of your curriculum.

▹ Demonstrate knowledge of what is meant by *scope*, *sequence*, and *balance* in terms of curriculum construction.

▹ Develop a scope and sequence chart for a real or proposed physical education program.

▹ Discuss the role of assessment in the total curricular process.

▹ Diagram the anatomy of the developmental physical education curriculum.

▹ Discuss the many and varied aspects of the extended curriculum.

▹ Describe special programs that frequently serve as an extension of the physical education curriculum.

proposes a developmentally based curricular model for implementing the physical education program during the preschool and elementary school years. We also discuss recess and noon-hour programs, daily fitness programs, intramural and club sport programs, and interscholastic programs as part of the extended curriculum.

STEPS IN CURRICULUM PLANNING

You should follow six basic steps in developing a curriculum in any subject area, whether that subject is math, science, physical education, or basketball coaching.

1. Establish a value base for the program.
2. Develop a conceptual framework.
3. Determine the program objectives.
4. Design the program.
5. Establish assessment procedures.
6. Implement the program.

These six steps have been used in business and industry as well as in education for the past several years and are a commonly accepted way of doing what has come to be known as "strategic planning." Strategic planning models are simply a means of organizing a new program and putting it into action. It matters little what the program is; the organizational steps are the same. We ourselves have used these six steps in countless situations, ranging from curriculum building for elementary schools and Olympic development programs to strategic planning models for colleges and universities. From much personal experience we know that if properly applied, these six steps really do work (figure 14.1). In the following paragraphs we discuss each step.

REALITY CHECK

Curricular Choices That Really Matter

Real-World Situation

Hopefully, you will soon be assuming your first professional teaching position. As a physical education teacher, you will be required, as are all other teachers, to plan your curriculum. Unfortunately, unlike other teachers, you will probably be on your own. Consequently you will have to get down to the nitty-gritty of putting your program on paper—a daunting task. Basically, you have four choices: (1) adopt someone else's curriculum, (2) adapt an existing curriculum to fit your needs, (3) start from scratch and devise your own curriculum, or (4) just "wing it" (after all, who will know?). In fact, as a new teacher filled with lots of new ideas, you will be able to get by for the first year or so. But soon you will begin to question yourself. You will probably ask, "Did I teach that last year?" "Am I repeating myself" "Why do I feel inferior to my fellow teachers?" and "Why don't I get the respect that I deserve from my principal and the other teachers?"

Critical Questions

Based on what you know about curricular planning:

- Which of the four choices will you make and why?
- Why is it so difficult for some physical education teachers to devise written curricula?
- What are the advantages and disadvantages of adopting another's curriculum?
- How will you avoid the trap of "winging it?"

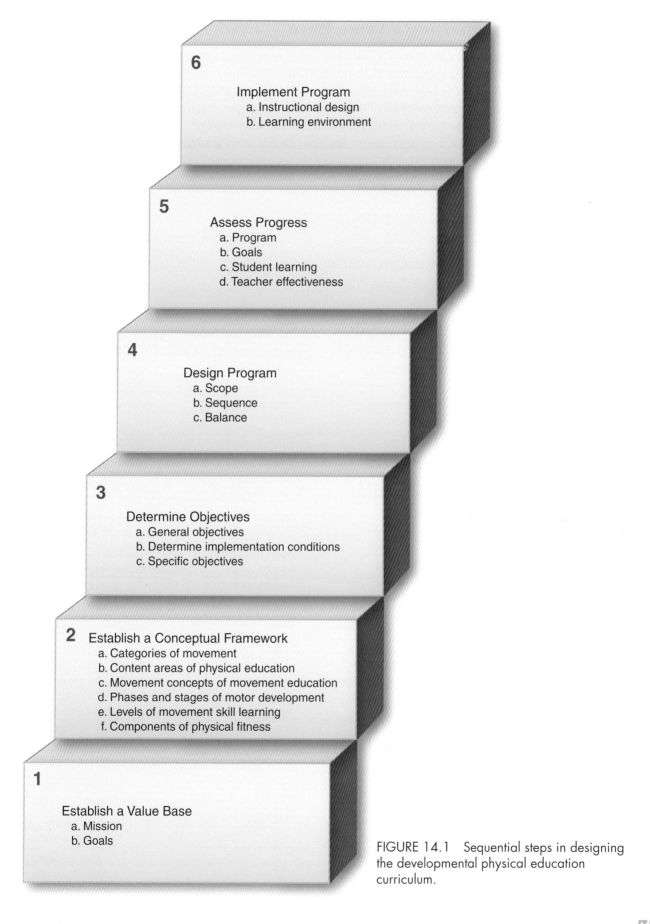

FIGURE 14.1 Sequential steps in designing the developmental physical education curriculum.

Establishing a Value Base

A necessary first step in all curricular planning is to establish the value base on which the curriculum is to be built. Your **values** represent, in list form, what you hold near and dear with regard to children's physical education. You may value things such as movement skill learning, developmentally appropriate activities, co-operative behavior, critical thinking skills, increased physical activity, and so forth. Your values form a working framework for an organizing center and for development of your mission statement.

TEACHING TIP 14.1

The physically educated person *has, is, does, knows,* and *values* the following:

Has learned skills necessary to perform a variety of physical activities:

- Moves using concepts of effort awareness, space awareness, and relationship awareness.
- Demonstrates competence in a variety of manipulative, locomotor, and stability skills.
- Demonstrates competence in combinations of manipulative, locomotor, and stability skills performed individually and with others.
- Demonstrates competence in many different forms of physical activity.
- Demonstrates proficiency in a few forms of physical activity.
- Has learned how to learn new skills.

Is physically fit:

- Assesses, achieves, and maintains physical fitness.
- Designs safe personal fitness programs in accordance with principles of training and conditioning.

Does participate regularly in physical activity:

- Participates in health-enhancing physical activity at least three times a week.
- Selects and regularly participates in lifetime physical activities.

Knows the implications and benefits of involvement in physical activities:

- Identifies the benefits, costs, and obligations associated with regular participation in physical activity.
- Recognizes the risk and safety factors associated with regular participation in physical activity.
- Applies concepts and principles to the development of motor skills.
- Understands that wellness involves more than being physically fit.
- Knows the rules, strategies, and appropriate behaviors for selected physical activities.
- Recognizes that participation in physical activity can lead to multicultural and international understanding.
- Understands that physical activity provides the opportunity for enjoyment, self-expression, and communication.

Values physical activity and its contributions to a healthful lifestyle:

- Appreciates the relationships with others that result from participation in physical activity.
- Respects the role that regular physical activity plays in the pursuit of lifelong health and well-being.
- Cherishes the feelings that result from regular participation in physical activity.

Source: From *The Physically Educated Person*, National Association for Sport and Physical Education, 1992, Reston, VA: NASPE

Your Mission Statement

The **mission statement** represents what your curriculum attempts to do. The mission statement should be clear and concise, and it should be an outgrowth of your working list of values. The statement should be broadly based and should represent the best thinking of the curriculum committee. Hammering out a mission statement as a group effort is often difficult. But it is a necessary first step in establishing the intent of your program by setting the stage for all that follows. Your mission statement will serve as the cornerstone for outlining the broad goals of the curriculum.

The mission statement should be brief, typically consisting of one short paragraph. In the first few sentences, introduce the reader to the broad, general aims of the program (e.g., learning to move, moving to learn). In the next several sentences, state the overall goals of the curriculum (e.g., the seven Content Standards of the NASPE National Standards for Physical Education). In the final sentence, summarize what has been stated and reemphasize the value of the program to the individual, community, or society. Please refer to figure 14.2 for a sample school-wide mission statement.

CONCEPT 14.2

The content of the curriculum should directly reflect the values, mission, and goals of the curriculum.

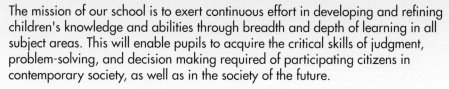

The mission of our school is to exert continuous effort in developing and refining children's knowledge and abilities through breadth and depth of learning in all subject areas. This will enable pupils to acquire the critical skills of judgment, problem-solving, and decision making required of participating citizens in contemporary society, as well as in the society of the future.

Social, physical, and emotional development must be emphasized to give pupils opportunities to gain experience and develop a positive sense of value concerning themselves and their place in society.

Our teachers' role is to facilitate, nurture, and advance learning. As educators, we are committed to better understanding the process of learning and the nature of children's development. As new methods and techniques of organization and instruction emerge, it is essential for our teachers to promote and implement innovations that reflect new knowledge.

In achieving its goals, the elementary school must foster cooperative efforts and share responsibility among all participants in the educational process—learners, parents, teachers, administrators, and the community.

FIGURE 14.2 Sample school-wide mission statement.

Your Curricular Goals

Your list of curricular goals for the program follows the mission statement. Usually **curricular goals** are broad areas of continuing interest and importance. Goals have also been defined as statements of intent that describe large blocks of subject matter found in a unit or course of study (Melograno, 1996). For example, in the cognitive domain, problem-solving might be a content goal. In the affective domain, learning to make responsible decisions could be a content goal. In the psychomotor

TEACHING TIP 14.2

A sample *mission statement* for a developmental physical education curriculum might read like this:

The mission of our physical education curriculum is to involve students in culturally relevant and developmentally appropriate movement experiences that focus on learning to move and learning through movement. Movement skills and fitness levels, thinking and reasoning abilities, and social-emotional skills are all enhanced by engaging children in a comprehensive program of fundamental movement, sport skill, physical fitness, and dance experiences.

In our physical education program, the principles and values behind movement skills and lifetime fitness are taught in an atmosphere that promotes student understanding and appreciation. Through child-centered developmentally based approaches to teaching that are responsive to the safety and welfare of students, our physical education curriculum contributes to self-esteem enhancement, responsible behavior, creative expression, and group cooperation.

We do this in an environment that both values and provides opportunities for social growth, increased emotional maturity, and responsible citizenship. In our physical education program, the value of each child is recognized as we strive for individual excellence in a caring and nurturing environment—an environment that promotes learning to move and learning through movement for all children.

domain, developing fundamental movement skills is a goal. All goals in your program should directly reflect your values and mission statement.

Developing a Conceptual Framework

A conceptual framework should undergird any curriculum. The **conceptual framework** is a basic but often overlooked aspect of curriculum building. It represents

TEACHING TIP 14.3

The *goals* of the developmental physical education curriculum include the following:

Motor development goals

- To assist children in becoming *skillful movers*
- To aid children in becoming *knowledgeable movers*
- To promote children's development as *expressive movers*
- To provide children with opportunities to become *fit movers*
- To educate children with the fitness knowledge to be *informed movers*
- To create an environment that encourages children to be *eager movers*

Cognitive development goals

- To foster an environment that encourages children to be *multisensory learners*
- To stimulate children's interest in being *active learners*

Affective development goals

- To assist children in becoming positive *self-discovering learners*
- To create an environment that helps children become *cooperative learners*

CONCEPT 14.3

Establishing the conceptual framework is an important but frequently overlooked step in the curricular process.

the essential concepts on which your curriculum is based. It is the necessary link between your values, mission, and goals and the actual design of the program. Your conceptual framework clarifies, defines, and classifies terms and concepts as they are used in the curriculum.

In the developmental physical education curriculum, the conceptual framework is composed of the following areas:

- Categories of movement
- Content areas of physical education
- Movement concepts of movement education
- Phases and stages of motor development
- Levels and stages of movement skill learning
- Components of physical fitness
- Styles of teaching

All areas are central to the design and implementation of the developmentally based program. Take a few minutes to study Teaching Tip 14.4, which outlines the conceptual framework of the developmental physical education curriculum.

TEACHING TIP 14.4

All curricula require a conceptual framework to establish common ground and terminology for implementing the program. The *conceptual framework* of the developmentally based physical education curriculum includes these areas:

1. Categories of movement
   a. Stability movements
   b. Locomotor movements
   c. Manipulative movements
   d. Movement phrases
2. Content areas of physical education
   a. Developmental games
   b. Developmental dance
   c. Developmental gymnastics
3. Movement concepts
   a. Effort awareness (i.e., force, time, and flow)
   b. Space awareness (i.e., level, direction, and range)
   c. Relationship awareness (i.e., objects and people)
4. Phases and stages of motor development
   a. Fundamental phase (initial, elementary, and mature stages)
   b. Specialized phase (transition, application, and lifelong utilization stages).

5. Levels and stages of movement skill learning
   a. Beginning/novice level (awareness, exploration, and discovery stages)
   b. Intermediate/practice level (combination and application stages)
   c. Advanced/fine-tuning level (performance and individualized stages)
6. Components of physical fitness
   a. Health-related components (muscular strength, muscular endurance, cardiovascular endurance, joint flexibility, and body composition)
   b. Performance-related components (balance, coordination, agility, speed, and power)
7. Styles of teaching
   a. Reproduction styles (direct, teacher-centered methods)
   b. Production styles (indirect, learner-centered methods)
   c. Combination of teaching styles (production and reproduction styles)

Determining Program Objectives

Once you have determined the value base of your curriculum and the conceptual framework that will govern its structure, you can state your general objectives for the program. General objectives begin to flesh out the goals of the program in descriptive terms. Once you have decided on the general objectives, it is critically important to clearly describe the conditions under which your program is to be implemented. For example, be sure to indicate the number of days per week the children are to have physical education instruction, the average number of students per class, facilities and equipment that are readily available, and anything else that is likely to affect the content of your program. Be certain to go through this step before determining the specific objectives of your program.

Create General Objectives

General objectives are broad, desired outcomes that are established for the learner to achieve. These objectives may well be stated in terms of the motor, cognitive, and affective areas of development. The physical education program that is developmentally based, properly planned, and carefully implemented can achieve a variety of general objectives. The degree to which your program achieves them will depend on the developmental level of your students, your philosophy and expertise, and the teaching styles that you use.

TEACHING TIP 14.5

A sampling of *general objectives* from the developmental curriculum includes the following:

I. Motor area (skillful mover and fit mover goals translated into general objectives)

  1. Movement skill objectives

    a. To achieve mature levels in a variety of fundamental stability skills

    b. To develop mature patterns in a variety of fundamental locomotor skills

    c. To attain mature skill development in a variety of fundamental manipulative skills

    d. To develop an acceptable level of skill in a variety of individual, dual, and team sports

    e. To enhance skillful rhythmic movement in a variety of fundamental, creative, and folk and square dance activities

  2. Physical fitness objectives

    a. To foster improved levels of health-related fitness

    b. To promote improved performance-related fitness

II. Cognitive area (knowledgeable mover, active learner, and multisensory learner goals translated into general objectives)

  1. To improve perceptual-motor learning in body, spatial, directional, and temporal awareness

  2. To develop knowledge and understanding in a variety of activities, including rules, strategies, fitness concepts, healthful living, and responsible decision making

  3. To reinforce a variety of academic concepts in mathematics, science, social studies, and language arts

III. Affective area (expressive mover, self-discovering learner, and cooperative learner goals translated into general objectives)

  1. To encourage self-expression, motor creativity, and aesthetic appreciation of movement

  2. To contribute to a positive self-concept, self-confidence, and perceived physical competence

  3. To develop positive socialization skills through cooperative play

Determine Conditions for Implementation

Before establishing the specific objectives of the program, you must conduct a thorough survey of factors that may affect the program's content. The **conditions for implementation** that will affect the specific design of the program, such as available facilities and equipment, class sizes, length and number of class periods, and so forth, should be concisely stated to assess the boundaries within which the program must be conducted. This will give you a good idea of what is possible and what you can even try to do. If, for example, one of your general objectives is "to develop a variety of team sport skills," you will need to determine if you have ample space, sufficient equipment, and high enough ceilings before translating this general objective into the specific volleyball skill objective of "to be able to perform the overhead pass to a partner." Space, time, equipment, and facilities will play an important role in determining the specific objectives of your program. Other factors that will influence your specific objectives are the size and experience level of your classes, the number of times you meet per week, and the length of lessons.

TEXT BOX 14.1

Only you know the conditions under which you must try to achieve the objectives of your program. Therefore, only you can determine what the specific objectives should be. The conditions under which physical educators are required to implement their programs vary greatly. In fact, there is frequently tremendous variation among schools in the same school district. Taking the time to realistically assess the teaching and learning environment will enable you to establish specific objectives that are reasonable and obtainable. Not taking the time to do this will only lead to considerable frustration and failure.

Only you know the conditions under which you will be trying to achieve the general objectives of your program. Therefore, only you can determine what the specific objectives of the program should be. The conditions that physical education programs operate under vary greatly throughout North America. In fact, there is frequently tremendous variation among schools in the same school district. Taking the time to assess the teaching and learning environment realistically will enable you to establish specific objectives that are reasonable and obtainable. Not doing so will lead to considerable frustration and failure.

Create Specific Objectives

CONCEPT
14.5

Specific objectives may be stated as behavioral objectives, terminal objectives, or benchmark objectives.

Once you have established the general objectives and listed the conditions under which the curriculum will be carried out, it will be possible for you to determine the **specific objectives** of the program. The specific objectives that you establish may be stated in process terms (i.e., behavioral objectives) or in product terms (terminal objectives), both of which may be reflected in benchmark (marker) objectives throughout the program.

Each of the *specific objectives* in the examples that follow is directly related to the *general objectives* of "developing mature patterns in a variety of fundamental locomotor (as well as manipulative and stability) skills." This general objective is in turn directly related to the *curricular goal:* "to assist children in becoming skillful movers." Moreover, this goal is also directly related to the *mission* of the program, which includes "learning to move"—which in turn links directly with one of the *values* of the developmental physical education program, namely "increased movement competency."

TEACHING TIP 14.6

Before determining the *specific objectives* of *your* program, you must have the following information:

- Facilities available (both school and community)
- Equipment available
- Number of class periods per week
- Length of class periods
- Average number of pupils per class

- Pupils' entry-level assessment
- Geographic location
- Typical weather conditions
- Community mores
- Educational goals of the school system and community

Behavioral objectives are a form of specific objectives. They have three important characteristics:

1. They are observable.
2. They are measurable.
3. They establish the criteria for performance.

Behavioral objectives are valuable and worthwhile, but they are time-consuming to write and are frequently of limited value when the three characteristics are commonly understood by trained professionals. They are valuable, however, in that they clearly identify what is to be learned and how it is to be assessed. The following is a sample of specific objectives stated in behavioral terms that may be appropriate for elementary school children.

The student will:

- Perform a tuck forward roll down an incline mat, beginning from a squat position and finishing in a squat position.
- Catch a playground ball with two hands, standing a distance of 15 or more feet away from a partner.
- Distinguish the difference between an even and an uneven beat in a musical composition and demonstrate both using two different locomotor movements.
- Make 7 of 10 basketball free throws, using correct form, toward an eight-foot basket and from a chosen distance from the basket.

Physical education teachers frequently use **terminal objectives** rather than writing out each objective in behavioral terms. In stating terminal objectives, teachers simply list the specific motor, cognitive, and affective objectives to be achieved in the program. The list is not sequenced by age or grade level but rather from simple to complex and from general to specific. It's a good idea for you to become familiar with writing behavioral objectives before using terminal objectives to state lesson objectives. The following are examples of terminal objectives.

This young lady completes a forward roll on an incline mat with her knees tucked into the chest and arms extended, both criteria for success. Behavioral objectives should include the "conditions" of the task (i.e., "on an incline mat"; this should refer to the objective on the facing page).

Here a Hillsdale Elementary School student demonstrates correct form by catching a playground ball with two hands only. Behavioral objectives must include criteria for success.

Students will increase competency in:

Stunts and Tumbling Skills
- Log roll
- Forward roll
- Backward roll
- Tripod
- Headstand
- Handstand

Soccer Skills
- Instep kick
- Push pass
- Outside-of-foot pass
- Punting

Rhythmic Skills
- Accent
- Tempo
- Intensity
- Rhythmic pattern

Benchmark objectives are a sampling of specific marker objectives intended to be achieved by a certain time. The National Association for Sport and Physical Education's National Standards for Physical Education use grades 2, 4, 6, 8, 10, and 12 as marker years for determining which specific objectives have been achieved in each of the seven Content Standards. Figure 14.3 provides an example of benchmarks to be achieved by the end of the second grade.

Standard I:

Demonstrates competency in many movement forms and proficiency in a few movement forms.

Sample Benchmark Objectives:

1. Demonstrates skills of chasing, fleeing, and dodging to avoid others.
2. Combines locomotor patterns in time to music.
3. Balances, demonstrating momentary stillness, in symmetrical and nonsymmetrical shapes on a variety of body parts.
4. Receives and sends an object in a continuous motion.
5. Strikes a ball repeatedly with a paddle.

Standard II:

Applies movement concepts and principles to the learning and development of motor skills.

Sample Benchmark Objectives:

1. Identifies four characteristics of a mature throw.
2. Uses concepts of space awareness and movement control to run, hop, and skip in different ways in a large group without bumping into others or falling.
3. Identifies and demonstrates the major characteristics of mature walking, running, hopping, and skipping.

Standard III:

Exhibits a physically active lifestyle.

Sample Benchmark Objectives:

1. Seeks participation in gross motor activity of a moderate to vigorous nature.
2. Participates in a wide variety of activities that involve locomotion, nonlocomotion, and manipulation of objects outside of the physical education class.
3. Willingly completes physical education activity "homework" assignments.

Standard IV:

Achieves and maintains a health-enhancing level of physical fitness.

Sample Benchmark Objectives:

1. Sustains activity for longer periods of time while participating in chasing or fleeing, traveling activities in physical education, and/or on the playground.
2. Identifies changes in the body during vigorous physical activity.
3. Supports body weight for climbing, hanging, and momentarily taking weight on hands.
4. Moves each joint through a full range of motion.

Standard V:

Demonstrates responsible personal and social behavior in physical activity settings.

Sample Benchmark Objectives:

1. Uses equipment and space safely and properly.
2. Responds positively to an occasional reminder about rule infraction.
3. Practices specific skills as assigned until the teacher signals the end of practice.
4. Stops activity immediately at the signal to do so.
5. Honestly reports the results of work.
6. Assists partner by sharing observations about skill performance and practice.

Standard VI:

Demonstrates understanding and respect for differences among people in physical activity settings.

Sample Benchmark Objectives:

1. Appreciates the benefits that accompany cooperation and sharing.
2. Displays consideration of others in physical activity settings.
3. Demonstrates the elements of socially acceptable conflict resolution.

Standard VII:

Understands that physical activity provides the opportunity for enjoyment, challenge, self-expression, and social interaction.

Sample Benchmark Objectives:

1. Appreciates the benefits that accompany cooperation and sharing.
2. Accepts the feelings resulting from challenges, successes, and failures in physical activity.
3. Willingly tries new activities.

FIGURE 14.3 Sample benchmark objectives to be achieved in the second grade for each of the seven Content Standards.

Reprinted from *Moving Into the Future: National Standards for Physical Education* (1995) with permission from the National Association for Sport and Physical Education (NASPE), 1900 Association Drive, Reston, VA 20191-1599.

Design the Program

Once you have determined the objectives of the program, it's time to make a **scope and sequence chart,** which outlines the scope, sequence, and curricular balance necessary to satisfy the specific objectives of the program from unit to unit and from year to year. In this section we discuss each of these aspects of the program design. Figure 14.4 presents a sample scope and sequence chart. It provides a general view of the objectives throughout the school year (scope) for each grade level (sequence), reflecting a broad range of activities (curricular balance).

CONCEPT 14.6

Actual design of the curriculum is reflected in a scope and sequence chart that is both balanced in content and age appropriate.

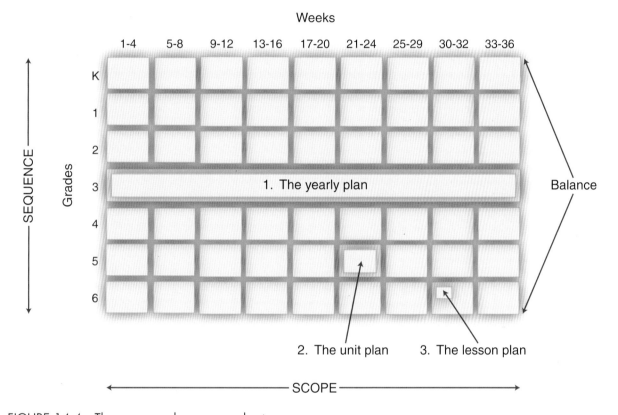

FIGURE 14.4   The scope and sequence chart.

In the developmental curriculum, the scope and sequence chart is the point of contact between the program goals, the general and specific objectives, and the actual learning activities of the program. The scope and sequence chart is constructed to reflect content that is age-group or grade appropriate, but what actually determines the developmental appropriateness of the program is the specific learning activities that are taken from these content areas and applied to the children being taught.

Communicate the Program Scope and Sequence

The term **program scope** as used in curriculum building refers to the content of the program in terms of its breadth or range throughout the academic year. The actual variety of units of work and skill through the year at any grade level represents the scope of the program for that grade level. For a curriculum to be effective, it must demonstrate sufficient scope. It should be broad enough to encompass a multitude of skills, activities, and ability levels.

TEACHING TIP 14.7

Criteria for selecting appropriate learning experiences:

- Select activities that match the development level of the participants.
- Select activities that are both physically and psychologically safe and that emphasize learning and cooperative participation instead of winning and making value judgments of comparative worth.

- Select activities that promote real learning, active participation, and learning enjoyment rather than activities that require little challenge or require waiting, watching, and general inactivity.
- Select activities that are relevant to the lives of the children and that have the potential of being applied to lifelong activities.

When using the term **program sequence**, we are referring to progression in terms of the year-to-year ordering of skills taught in the curriculum. In other words, the sequence of the program reflects the timing and depth of the program from grade to grade. For the curriculum to be effective, there must be clear evidence of progressive skill development from year to year. This is reflected in the sequence of the curriculum.

TEXT BOX 14.2

In the developmental curriculum the scope and sequence chart is the point of contact between the program goals, general and specific objectives, and the actual learning activities of the program. The scope and sequence chart is constructed in such a way that it reflects content that is age-group or grade appropriate. But it is the specific learning activities taken from these content areas and applied to the particular children being taught that determine the developmental appropriateness of the program.

Establish Curricular Balance

The term **curricular balance** refers to the relative emphasis of the curriculum in terms of the time spent on specific content areas and the variety inherent in the program. Figure 14.5 presents suggested approximate yearly time percentages for the various content areas of the physical education program based on age-group appropriateness. More importantly, though, the "Teaching Tip" boxes that follow list specific criteria for selecting or designing learning experiences that are developmentally appropriate.

Any physical education curriculum that is to have real value for children must endeavor to achieve harmony among scope, sequence, and curricular balance. This harmony helps to ensure that the activities the children engage in will be broad based (scope), age-group appropriate (sequence), and of continuing interest (curricular balance).

Establishing Assessment Procedures

Assessment, the fifth step in planning the curriculum, is an important part of the total process because only through assessment can you determine whether or not

CONCEPT 14.7

Assessment is the primary means of determining whether or not the objectives of the curriculum have been achieved; assessment serves as a basis for curricular revision.

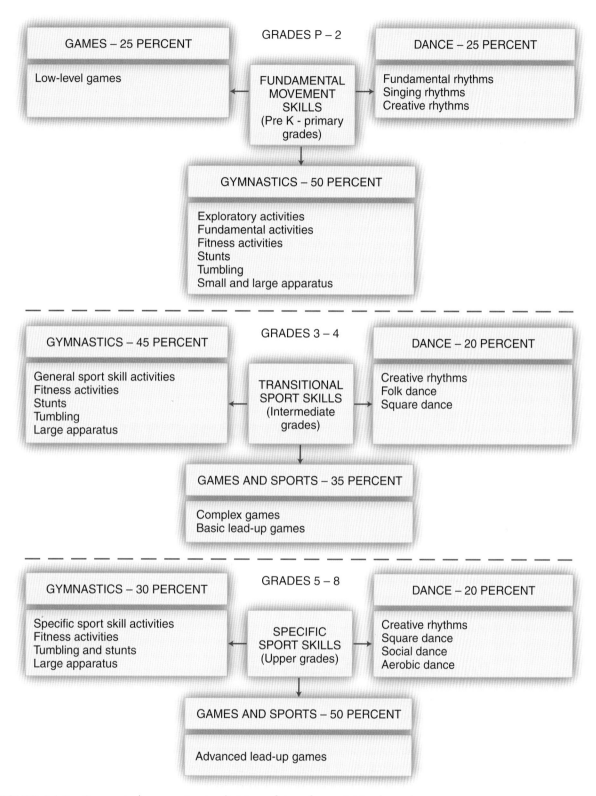

FIGURE 14.5 Suggested approximate division of time for activities based on age-group appropriateness.

your students have achieved the objectives of the program. Evaluation is a method of determining the strong and weak points of your program and your teaching. It may take many forms and may be either subjective (process) or objective (product). Chapter 12, "Assessing Progress," covers both process and product assessment.

Implementing the Program

Implementing the program is the sixth and final step in the curricular process. Implementation is the critical transition between planning and action (a.k.a.: "where the rubber meets the road"). A careful reading of the six planning steps should alert you to the extent and scope of planning that goes into the curricular process. Failure to go through this planning process will result in considerable frustration on your part, and on the part of your students, as you attempt to implement your program. The important things to remember are that each step is directly related to the preceding one and that curricular building is a sequential, orderly process. It is vitally important for you to follow the following four steps as you prepare to implement a skill theme:

1. Preplan.
2. Observe and assess.
3. Plan and implement.
4. Evaluate and revise your lessons.

At the beginning of each chapter in part IV, "The Skill Themes," is a "Teaching Tip" box that will help you with this process.

THE DEVELOPMENTAL CURRICULAR MODEL

CONCEPT 14.8

Developmental curricular models incorporate into their conceptual framework an emphasis on understanding the learner as an individual.

The **developmental curricular model** for children's physical education is based on the concept that the development of one's movement abilities occurs in distinct but often overlapping phases of motor development in each of the categories of movement. This is achieved through participation in activities that are applied to the traditional content areas of physical education and the movement concepts of movement education. These activities are geared to the learner's level of movement skill learning and level of physical fitness, and the activities are implemented through a variety of teaching styles (Gallahue & Ozmun, 2002). See figure 14.6 for an illustration of this conceptual framework.

Preschool and Primary Grades

Developmental teaching recognizes that preschool and primary grade children are generally involved in developing and refining their fundamental movement skills. These skills serve as the themes of the curriculum and the basis for the formation of units of instruction at this level. During this period, teachers usually emphasize indirect styles of teaching more than direct styles because children tend to be at the beginning level of learning many movement skills. Types of activities that facilitate the use, practice, and mature development of fundamental movement skills include guided discovery activities that permit plenty of movement exploration; problem-solving experiences involving the movement concepts of effort, space, and relationship awareness; and developmental games, dance, and gymnastic activities (figure 14.7).

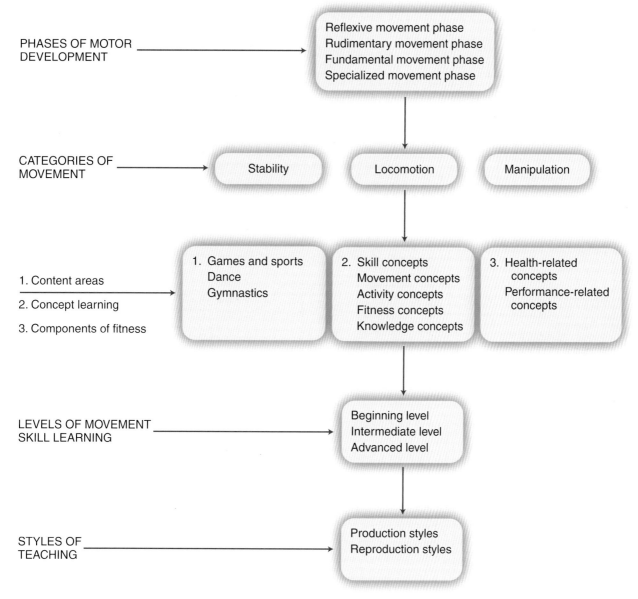

FIGURE 14.6   Outline of the conceptual framework for the developmental physical education program.

Intermediate and Upper Elementary Grades

When the developmental model is applied to the intermediate and upper elementary grades, the focus of the curriculum changes from the fundamental movement phase to the specialized movement phase of development. During this phase, children are typically combining and using stability, locomotor, and manipulative skills in a wide variety of sport-related activities. At this phase, we view units of instruction in the context of the activity to which they are being applied. The game of softball, for example, becomes a sport skill unit and involves combinations and elaborations of fundamental stability abilities (twisting, turning, and stretching), locomotor abilities (base running and sliding), and manipulative skills (throwing, catching, striking). Teachers now focus their attention on developing

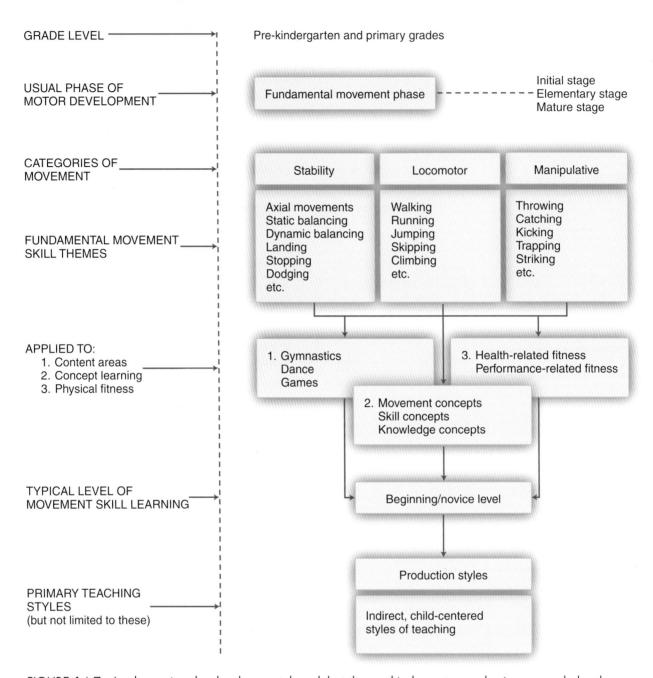

GRADE LEVEL → Pre-kindergarten and primary grades

USUAL PHASE OF MOTOR DEVELOPMENT → Fundamental movement phase --- Initial stage / Elementary stage / Mature stage

CATEGORIES OF MOVEMENT →

Stability	Locomotor	Manipulative

FUNDAMENTAL MOVEMENT SKILL THEMES →

Axial movements Static balancing Dynamic balancing Landing Stopping Dodging etc.	Walking Running Jumping Skipping Climbing etc.	Throwing Catching Kicking Trapping Striking etc.

APPLIED TO:
1. Content areas
2. Concept learning
3. Physical fitness

1. Gymnastics
Dance
Games

2. Movement concepts
Skill concepts
Knowledge concepts

3. Health-related fitness
Performance-related fitness

TYPICAL LEVEL OF MOVEMENT SKILL LEARNING → Beginning/novice level

PRIMARY TEACHING STYLES
(but not limited to these) → Production styles

Indirect, child-centered styles of teaching

FIGURE 14.7   Implementing the developmental model at the pre-kindergarten and primary grade level.

the movement skills related to particular sport activities. These skills serve as the lesson themes within any given unit of instruction and are applied to the various content areas and knowledge concepts (rules, strategies, understandings, and appreciations) of physical education. Children's characteristic level of movement skill learning at this phase is the intermediate level. Therefore, emphasis is on combining skills and practicing them in a variety of static activities and dynamic games. As a result, emphasis is typically on more direct teaching approaches (see figure 14.8).

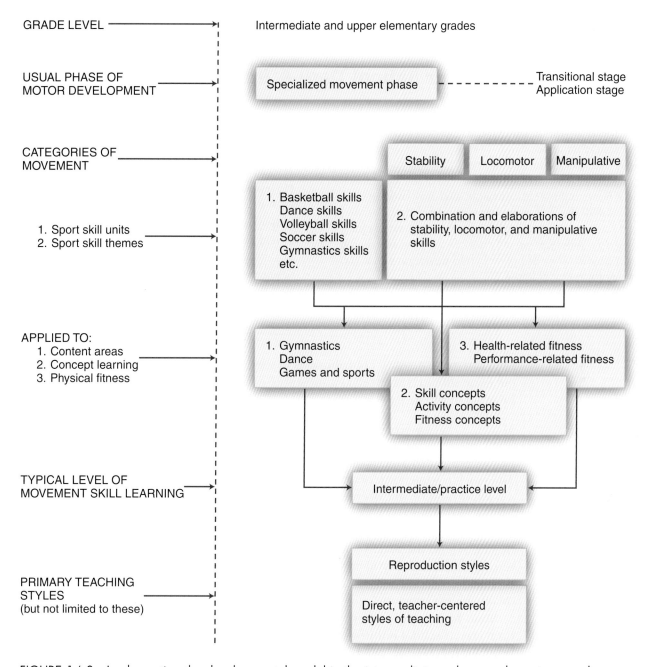

GRADE LEVEL → Intermediate and upper elementary grades

USUAL PHASE OF MOTOR DEVELOPMENT → Specialized movement phase --- Transitional stage / Application stage

CATEGORIES OF MOVEMENT → Stability | Locomotor | Manipulative

1. Sport skill units
2. Sport skill themes →

1. Basketball skills
Dance skills
Volleyball skills
Soccer skills
Gymnastics skills
etc.

2. Combination and elaborations of stability, locomotor, and manipulative skills

APPLIED TO:
1. Content areas
2. Concept learning
3. Physical fitness

1. Gymnastics
Dance
Games and sports

3. Health-related fitness
Performance-related fitness

2. Skill concepts
Activity concepts
Fitness concepts

TYPICAL LEVEL OF MOVEMENT SKILL LEARNING → Intermediate/practice level

PRIMARY TEACHING STYLES (but not limited to these) →

Reproduction styles

Direct, teacher-centered styles of teaching

FIGURE 14.8 Implementing the developmental model in the intermediate and upper elementary grades.

THE EXTENDED CURRICULUM

The physical education teacher is frequently responsible for conducting programs in addition to the basic instructional program. Such additional programs are commonly referred to as the **extended curriculum,** or the hidden curriculum. Recess and noon-hour programs, daily fitness programs, intramural and club sport programs, and interscholastic programs are all logical extensions of the instructional program.

CONCEPT
14.9
The extended curriculum is potentially an important addition to instructional physical education.

The 12-Hour School Day: A Reality for Many

Real-World Situation

The rapid growth in extended-school-day programs for children is mind-boggling. These programs were originally established to accommodate the needs of working parents. Children frequently arrive at school as much as 2 hours before classes begin and stay as long as 3 hours after the end of the regular school day. Arriving at 6 A.M. and not leaving school until 6 P.M. makes for a long day. Although we may debate the merits of such a long day in terms of optimal child development, it is a reality for many children.

Critical Questions

Based on what you know about the extended curriculum and the need for increased physical activity among children:

- How would you organize the before- and after-school care programs at your school?
- What types of activities would you incorporate that would be both fun and educationally sound?
- How could you link the activities of your physical education curriculum with the activities of the extended-day program?

Each can make positive contributions to various aspects of children's development, but none should be viewed as a substitute or replacement for a quality instructional program in physical education.

Recess and Noon-Hour Programs

Recess is a North American tradition. Just about every elementary school in North America has some form of daily recess. The recess period typically takes the form of a midmorning or midafternoon break from the normal academic routine. Recess usually lasts from 10 to 20 minutes and is held outdoors whenever possible so that children can play and have an opportunity to "let off steam" in acceptable ways. The theory behind the recess period is that this break from the relatively inactive routine of the classroom will enable children to refocus their energies and attention on their schoolwork. There is enough empirical evidence to warrant continuation of quality recess programs.

Noon-hour programs are an outgrowth of busing. In many school systems, children stay at school rather than going home during the lunch hour. The noon-hour program follows the lunch period and allows children to take part in free-choice activities on the playground or in the gymnasium. Children should not be permitted to gulp down their lunch in an effort to get more time on the playground or in the gymnasium. Approximately 20 minutes should be set aside for eating lunch, and early finishers should be required to wait the full 20 minutes.

Both the recess and the noon-hour programs are, by tradition, loosely structured. Children are generally allowed free choice in their activity selection. Most children select vigorous play activities, but some choose more quiet and sedentary activities. The keys to a successful recess or noon-hour program are proper facilities, ample equipment, and adequate supervision. The physical education teacher is frequently assigned responsibility for ensuring all three. Contact the Council on Physical Education for Children (COPEC; NASPE Position Papers at **aahperd.org**) for the "position paper" outlining guidelines for recess in the elementary school.

The facilities, whether indoors or out, are important to the success of the program. They should be free of safety hazards and should be regularly checked for unsafe conditions, which must be eliminated. The outdoor area should have ample space so that primary grade children may play in areas separate from older children. The play area should contain hanging and climbing apparatus when possible. Large grassy and asphalt areas for a variety of activities are ideal. Markings for line and circle games such as four-square and hopscotch are helpful stimulators of purposeful, vigorous activity. Similarly, the indoor facility, whether the gymnasium or a multipurpose room, should be set up to allow for free choice and encourage vigorous activity.

The availability of equipment for the recess and noon-hour program is the second key to success. There should be enough equipment (balls, Frisbees®, ropes, and so forth) so that all who want to play may do so. In many schools, classroom teachers keep a "fun box" with equipment to be used for recess. Children check out the equipment and are responsible for returning it to the box at the end of their play period.

Supervision is the third key to a successful recess or noon-hour program. Teachers frequently dread recess duty because of the mass chaos that often seems to occur in this situation. Certain conditions do much to minimize such chaos:

- One teacher is assigned to supervise no more than two classes at one time.
- The supervisor can see all children at all times.
- There is ample space and equipment for meaningful activity.
- The children are given instruction in appropriate playground activities.

The physical education teacher can play an important role in helping make the recess and noon-hour programs worthwhile to children and easy for classroom teachers to supervise. Taking the time to instruct children in how to organize a game of kick ball, soccer, or four-square works wonders. Ensuring that the supervising teacher knows the basic rules of several appropriate games and has the proper equipment to help get them started is helpful. Finally, a behavior code for play on the playground or in the gymnasium will help reduce problems and maximize the educational potential of the recess and noon-hour programs.

Daily Fitness Programs

In recent years, many school districts in Canada and the United States have introduced **daily fitness programs** into the total school program. Daily fitness programs frequently replace a recess period or take place during the last 20 minutes of the school day. Fitness programs are an addition to the instructional physical education program, and often the entire student body, faculty, and staff participate.

Because of the sedentary nature of our society, many children do not get sufficient regular, vigorous physical activity. The instructional physical education program generally does not have adequate amounts of time or the regularity of a daily program to positively influence fitness levels to a significant degree. The realization that children are not as physically active as they need to be, coupled with the results of recent research linking the positive benefits of vigorous physical activity to human wellness, has caused many educators to add daily fitness activities to the total school curriculum.

Often a specific 15- to 20-minute portion of the day is set aside for the daily fitness program, with the entire school population taking part. Hallways may be used for stationary jogging or aerobic exercise to music. The gymnasium or multi-purpose room may serve as a station for rope-jumping activities, and the classroom may be used for flexibility and vigorous strength- and endurance-building exercises. Trained students and teachers can act as fitness leaders. Daily fitness programs strive for total, active involvement for the entire time that has been set aside. People perform at their individual level of ability and are encouraged to do their best.

As the physical education teacher, you may be responsible for the daily fitness program. In schools where it does not yet exist, it will be your responsibility to develop a solid rationale to convince the administration, faculty, and students of the need for such a program. Once they are convinced, you will need to train teachers and students as fitness leaders. It will be important to keep interest in the program high and to demonstrate improved levels of fitness.

Intramural Programs

The intramural sports program is a logical extension of a quality physical education program, but it should never be a substitute for physical education. **Intramurals** are physical activity programs conducted between groups of students within the same school. Intramurals generally take place before school, during the noon hour, or after school. The intramural program should include all students who desire to participate, regardless of their skill level. In the elementary school, intramurals are special-interest programs for boys and girls who want to use the skills they have learned in the physical education class. The intramural program places greater emphasis on playing the game than on instruction, although there is often an instructional component relating to rules and the application of strategies.

The physical education teacher is frequently responsible for conducting a varied intramural program throughout the school year. Activities may be seasonal and may last four to six weeks. Popular intramural activities with elementary students include dance (urban folk dance or "stepping"), step-aerobics, roller blading, jump rope, biking, and a variety of team sports such as floor hockey. Players may be grouped into teams in a variety of ways. Regardless of the procedure, the teacher's primary consideration should be the equalization of teams. All players should have as near an equal chance to play and contribute to the team's success. Remember, emphasis in the intramural program should be on skill application and fun in a wholesome recreational

TEACHING TIP 14.8

Bill of Rights for Young Athletes: All young athletes have the right to

- participate in sports,
- participate at a level commensurate with their own maturity and ability,
- have qualified adult leadership,
- play as a child and not as an adult,
- share in the leadership and decision making of their sport participation,

- participate in a safe and healthy environment,
- have proper preparation for participation in sport,
- have an equal opportunity to strive for success,
- be treated with dignity, and
- have fun in sports.

From R. Martens and V. Seefeldt, *Guidelines for Children's Sports* (Reston, VA: AAHPERD, 1979).

setting. For the intramural program to be successful, written policies regarding parental approval, eligibility, first aid, medical care, and awards should be available to all participants. The program should be evaluated regularly in relation to its stated goals and objectives. Because participation is voluntary, the number of participants is often a good barometer of the program's success in terms of student interest.

Club Programs

Club programs are similar to intramural programs in that they are held before, during, or after school. However, the emphasis of the club program is on further instruction in specific activities, and competing against one's classmates is of little concern. Elementary school children frequently enjoy being members of a gymnastics club, fitness club, bicycle club, or leaders club.

Club programs are an extension of the regular physical education class in that they permit children with specific activity interests to get additional practice and instruction. They are especially enjoyable for the teacher because they permit work with small groups of students who are highly motivated to learn more about the activity.

Club participants frequently make good gym helpers. With training, they can be given some special responsibilities in the regular physical education class. This not only provides leadership experiences for these students but also gives the teacher much-needed assistance and freedom to work with others who require additional instruction.

Interscholastic Programs

The extramural or **interscholastic program** provides children an opportunity to compete against boys and girls from other schools. The interscholastic program can be of great value to the children it serves, but it should be included in the curriculum only after both quality physical education and intramural sports programs are in place. Interscholastic activities should never replace or disrupt these basic but critically important programs.

The aim of interscholastic athletic programs is to provide children with opportunities to develop into more complete and competent individuals. These programs are not intended to be an entertainment medium for parents, and they do not exist for the glorification of the coach. A win-at-all-cost attitude in any youth sport program should not be tolerated. Giving individuals the opportunity to pit their skills against others is the lifeblood of sport. Winning is important, but it must not be regarded as the primary reason for competition in the elementary school youth sport program.

SPECIAL PROGRAMS

CONCEPT 14.10

A number of special events that heighten interest and add variety may be incorporated into the physical education curriculum.

The physical education teacher is often asked to conduct various special programs. In contrast to extended curricular activities, special programs typically last anywhere from less than an hour to a full day. Whether they are long or short, special programs usually involve extensive planning and preparation. Special activities in the form of play days, sports days, and field days, along with gym shows and public demonstrations, are common at the elementary school level.

"Ladies and Gentlemen—in the Center Ring"

Real-World Situation

Count on it, it's going to happen. Either your building principal or the PTO president will come to you with a "simple" request to conduct an all-school event, hold a gym show, or take part with your students in some form of public demonstration. Think about it: organizing, preparing, and presenting a special program that may involve 100 or more students in a public display of what they have learned in your class. Sounds enticing—a great way to highlight your program, and a wonderful opportunity for your students to display their skills.

Critical Questions

Based on what you know about planning special programs:

- Where will you find time to practice?
- Is it fair to focus your regularly scheduled physical education program on preparing for the special program? Why?
- How will you go about getting help from fellow teachers and parents?
- Can you, should you, require students to participate?

Special Days

At the elementary school level there are three main types of special-day activities: the play day, the sports day, and the field day.

The **play day** is a special day of activities in which children from different classes in the same school or from two or more schools play together on the same team. Play days among schools are frequently held at a central location in the community. Activities might include softball, soccer, basketball, and volleyball games. Children are randomly assigned to teams, and they do not compete as a class or as a school.

The **sports day** is similar to the play day except that classes or schools compete as a team against others in a tournament-like atmosphere. There is more emphasis on competition and awards. Sports days should emphasize participation by everyone. All children should have an opportunity to play on a team representing their class or school.

The **field day** focuses on a variety of activities and is generally held within a single school, usually near the end of the school year. Track and field days are popular in many elementary schools. The field day is usually held during school hours, and all children from each class compete against one another. Cooperative field days are also exciting. Cathy Hill at Brown Elementary School in Newburyport, Massachusetts has designed several cooperative and interdisciplinary field days. Cathy is the 2002 Massachusetts Elementary Physical Education Teacher of the Year. Field day themes at Brown Elementary School have included "recycling," "multicultural awareness," and the most recent field day was based on the school's "Year of Science" theme. Each field day station featured a different science concept, such as angular momentum or friction. Cathy Hill can be contacted at **chill@newburyport.k12.ma.us**.

Gym Shows and Public Demonstrations

Many experienced physical education teachers promote their program with an annual gym show or public demonstration. These special programs may be held after school, during the early evening hours, or on a weekend. They frequently take place

a

b

(a) The student from Brown Elementary School in Newburyport, Massachusetts, discovers the principle of angular momentum during the "Year of Science" field day. *(b)* These students choose a piece of material to use as they prepare to go down the slide. They will compare and contrast how different materials affect friction during sliding.

Photos courtesy of Cathy Hill.

in conjunction with a PTO meeting or a local service club program, or as a special event at a shopping mall.

Gym shows often focus on the highlights of the year's program, but this should not be the goal. The goal of the gym show is to give children an opportunity to demonstrate what they have learned in physical education class. These shows may also serve as a subtle means of getting maximum attendance at a PTO meeting or parents' night. In any case, the gym show can effectively showcase your program and build faculty and community support. Be certain to take advantage of the opportunity to conduct an annual gym show. Although it takes extra time, the dividends will be well worth the effort.

TEACHING TIP 14.9

Guidelines for a successful *gym show:*

- Involve all grades and every child in the show.
- Keep the program short. Forty-five minutes to one hour should be sufficient.
- Select activities that are part of the regular physical education program.
- Select activities that can be easily learned and performed by all.
- Do not worry about polished performances. Work for an acceptable standard.
- Do not use physical education class time for extended practices.
- Provide the audience with a printed program that outlines the sequence of performances and the objectives they achieve in the program.

- Use scarves, sashes, or hats as simple costumes to enhance the general appearance of a performance.
- Use appropriate musical accompaniment whenever possible to add to the general effect.
- Props such as parachutes, flashlights, streamers, and hoops also enhance the performance.
- Send an announcement home concerning the gym show along with a permission slip allowing participation.
- Allow for a complete run-through of the program before the big night.
- Take photos for use in a bulletin board display.
- Enlist the help of classroom teachers for supervision on the night of the performance.

The **public demonstration** is different from the gym show in that it commonly involves a smaller number of students and is sponsored by service organizations and shopping malls. A public demonstration might involve members from one or more of the club sport programs sponsored by the school. The gymnastics club, for example, may be asked to demonstrate their skills. Public demonstrations are usually polished performances; children have time to practice outside of the physical education period, and those who participate have special interests and abilities in the activity. When planning a public demonstration, follow the same guidelines as for the gym show. But be certain to arrange for transportation to and from the demonstration site and to provide for ample adult supervision at all times.

Gym shows and public demonstrations are excellent promotional devices for the physical education program. Although they are time-consuming and often nerve-racking, they are an important part of the extracurricular program because they inform the public about physical education and broaden the base of support for quality programs.

Summary

Curricular planning is essential if you are planning for success as a teacher. A broad-based, six-step procedure applies to all subject areas, including physical education: (1) establish your value base; (2) develop a conceptual framework; (3) determine your program objectives; (4) design the program; (5) establish your assessment procedures; and (6)

implement the program. You should be sure to update your curriculum continually to maximize the effectiveness and relevancy of your program. When actually implementing the program you must (1) preplan, (2) observe and assess, (3) plan and implement, and (4) evaluate and revise your lessons. Careful attention to the details of the curriculum will contribute greatly to your success.

A curriculum is a blueprint for action geared to age-group appropriateness and subject to modification based on its individual appropriateness. The developmental physical education curriculum model takes into consideration both age-group appropriateness and individual appropriateness in the formation of specific objectives and individualized assessment procedures.

A frequently "hidden" aspect of the physical education curriculum is the extended program, which includes recess and noon-hour programs, fitness programs, intramurals, activity clubs, special programs, and interscholastic athletics. It is important to plan these programs carefully so that they complement but do not overshadow the instructional physical education program. Special programs such as play days, field days, gym shows, and public demonstrations are also part of the extended curriculum in physical education.

Terms to Remember

Excellent Readings

Bain, L.S. (1988). Curriculum for critical reflection in physical education. In R.S. Brandt (Ed.), *Content of the curriculum, 1988 ASCD yearbook.* Washington, DC: Association for Supervision and Curriculum Development.

Graham, G. (2001). *Teaching children physical education: Becoming a master teacher.* Champaign, IL: Human Kinetics.

Hellison, D. (1985). *Goals and strategies for teaching physical education.* Champaign, IL: Human Kinetics.

Hellison, D.R., & Templin, T.J. (1991). *A reflective approach to teaching physical education.* Champaign, IL: Human Kinetics.

Hopple, C. (1995). *Teaching for outcomes in elementary physical education: A guide for curriculum and assessment.* Champaign, IL: Human Kinetics.

15

The Physical Education Content

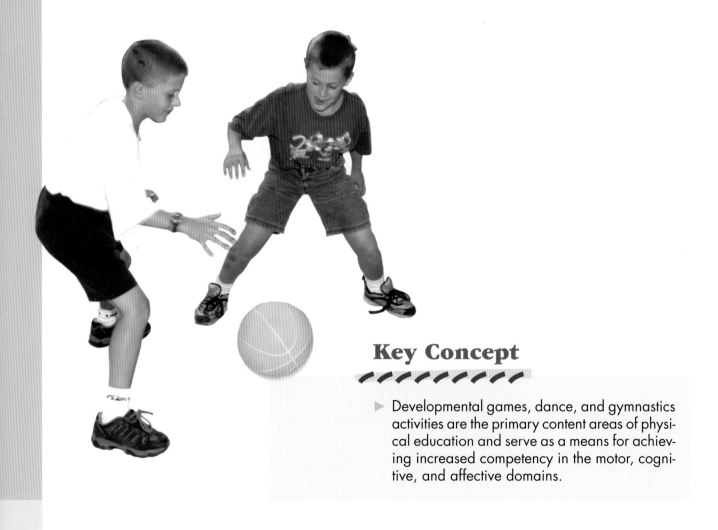

Key Concept

▶ Developmental games, dance, and gymnastics activities are the primary content areas of physical education and serve as a means for achieving increased competency in the motor, cognitive, and affective domains.

Chapter Objectives

This chapter will provide you with the tools to do the following:

▶ Discuss the role of developmental games, dance, and gymnastics activities in the process of becoming a physically educated individual.

▶ List and give examples of each of the content areas and their subdivisions.

▶ Demonstrate how the content areas of physical education can and should be related to the specific objectives of the developmental curriculum.

▶ Provide guidelines for selecting appropriate activities for students.

Game, dance, and gymnastics activities are part of the cultural heritage of all children. Although environmental conditions and standards of living change, the urge to play games, dance dances, and test one's skills remains a constant characteristic of every culture. Geographic location does not alter the age-old urges to run, jump, hop, chase and flee, hide and seek, hunt, guess, and dodge. We may find hundreds of variations on these themes, with as many different names, but the original theme remains the same.

Game, dance, and gymnastics activities can be of value in preschool and elementary school physical education if they are developmentally appropriate and are incorporated into the curriculum for the right reasons. However, some physical education programs have become little more than play periods in which activities are engaged in simply for fun. Although fun is a worthy by-product of any good educational program, it should not be the primary purpose of the physical education program. Game, dance, and gymnastics activities are a means to an end rather than an end in themselves.

This chapter focuses on developmentally appropriate game, dance, and gymnastics activities as the three primary content areas of

CONCEPT 15.1

Developmental game, dance, and gymnastics activities may serve many purposes, but all go beyond the basic objective of fun and extend to defensible educational objectives.

CONCEPT 15.2

In the developmental approach to teaching physical education, developmental games are a means of reinforcing and applying the results of movement skill learning.

the developmental physical education curriculum. We look at the subdivisions of each content area and suggest ways to include effective activities in the physical education program. This chapter sets the stage for part V, "The Content Areas." Individual chapters in part V are devoted to developmental games (chapter 21), developmental dance (chapter 22), and developmental gymnastics (chapter 23) within the physical education curriculum.

DEVELOPMENTAL GAMES

When used properly, games are an important educational tool of the physical education program. Games may be static, dynamic, predesigned, teacher designed, or student designed. The predesigned games you'll read about in the following chapters are merely sample activities to help get you started. You can easily modify these activities to suit your needs. Designing your own games is also a worthwhile task. After all, who knows your students' needs and interests better than you? Furthermore, it can be of significant value to have students design games themselves, although this generally takes additional time and a gymnasium atmosphere conducive to creative problem-solving. The activities you select and the methods you use to teach games will depend on several factors: the objectives of the lesson, the ability of your students, the size of the class, available time, equipment, and facilities.

REALITY CHECK

Developmental Games: Your Toolbox for Learning

Real-World Situation

With the course that you are currently taking in conjunction with the use of this textbook, and perhaps in additional courses, you will probably take part in a variety of games typically enjoyed by young children. Although you are aware that these games are an important part of the teacher's "toolbox," you feel somewhat uncomfortable playing these games with your fellow students. After all, you are adults. You are further mortified when others peek into the gymnasium and see you and your classmates "just playing kiddies' games" as part of your educational experience.

Critical Questions

Based on what you know about games and their place in the developmental curriculum:

- How do you justify the playing of children's games by adults as part of a valid educational experience for college students?

- What role do educational games play in the developmental physical education program?

- What are the four types of games, and when are they most appropriately incorporated into the developmental curriculum?

- How do you respond to friends and family who may think of this course as "just playing kiddies' games"?

Types of Games

Games may be classified in a variety of ways depending on their purpose and nature. In the developmental approach to teaching children's physical education, we view educational games primarily as a tool for applying, reinforcing, and implementing a variety of fundamental movement and sport skills. Games are not viewed as a primary means of learning new movement skills. Although movement skill acquisition is a primary objective of the movement lesson, games serve mainly as a means for applying and utilizing present skill levels. But it is still possible to achieve other important objectives through proper game selection and good teaching. Games are frequently classified as low-level types of games, cooperative games, lead-up games, and official sports (please refer to figure 15.1).

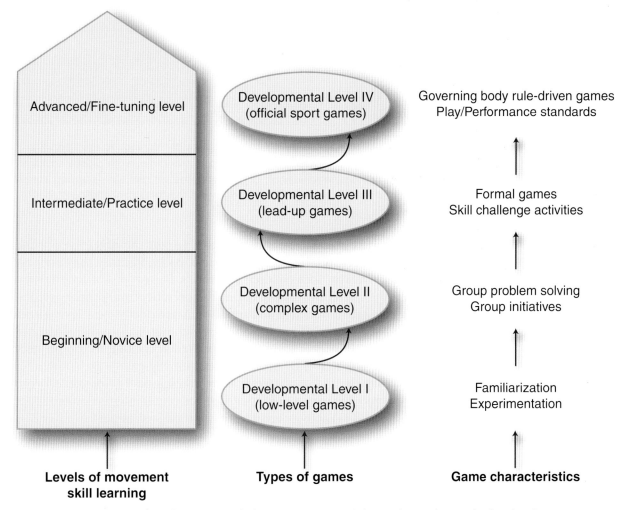

FIGURE 15.1 Game classifications and characteristics, and their relationship to the levels of movement skill learning.

Low-Level Games

Low-level games, or Developmental Level I games, are activities that are easy to play, have few and simple rules, require little or no equipment, and may be varied in many ways. Low-level games may be viewed as **familiarization games**—that is, games that help the learner become acquainted with the basic skills involved in an activity. They may also be viewed as **discovery games** because in playing them the learner is establishing an awareness of the spatial requirements of the game while at the same time experimenting with how the game is played. These games are particularly appropriate for learners who are at the beginning/novice level of learning the skills that are used in the game.

These Hillsdale Elementary students play a low-level game of "tossing" to the "popcorn pot" (the gymnastic mat target). Inside the "popcorn pot" are cones with plastic saucers on top. If the beanbag knocks the saucer off of the cone, the student has "popped some corn!" Emphasis is on proper execution of the underhand toss and challenging students to increase their distance from the target.

Low-level game activities may be easily modified to suit the objectives of the lesson, the size of the space, and the number of participants. Because they are easy to learn and can be enjoyed by both children and adults, these types of activities are often used as an educational tool, primarily during the preschool and primary grades. When viewed from a skill reinforcement and application perspective, low-level games are classified as fundamental stability, fundamental locomotor, or fundamental manipulative games. That is, low-level games are classified according to the primary category of movement skill that they promote. Additionally, games are sometimes classified according to their (1) theme (tag; holiday and seasonal games), (2) formation (scattered, circle, and line games), (3) special space requirements (limited-space and classroom games), and (4) activity level (active and passive games).

Cooperative Games

Cooperative games have become popular in recent years because they emphasize group interaction and positive socialization in a cooperative setting that de-emphasizes competition. They are more complex than low-level games and are viewed by us, the authors, as Developmental Level II games. Cooperative game activities are frequently classified as group initiatives, group problem-solving activities, and trust activities.

Group initiatives center on working cooperatively to accomplish a given task. For example, the lap sit is a popular group initiative for children and adults alike. Participants line up very close behind one another and, on a signal, sit down lightly on the lap of the person directly behind them.

Group problem-solving activities are similar to group initiatives except that they involve an element of creative problem-solving on the part of the participants, with possible alternative solutions to the problem posed by the instructor. For example, you may ask a group of four or five to get from point A to point B in contact with one another but without their feet ever touching the ground. The several possible solutions to the problem all require the group to work cooperatively.

These girls at Hillsdale Elementary School play a cooperative game over the "alligator swamp" involving the underhand toss and two-hand catch. The object of the game is to increase the width of the alligator swamp, thereby increasing the distance of the toss.

   Trust activities are activities that require the participants to work cooperatively to overcome a challenge involving an element of danger. Trust falls and body passing are typical trust activities. Trust activities, do, however, involve an element of risk and should only be used in small groups with older children who are sufficiently mature and ready to take on the responsibility. They must always be carefully spotted and used only with the approval of your immediate supervisor.

Lead-Up Games

Lead-up games, or Developmental Level III games, are active games that include the use of two or more of the sport skills, rules, or procedures involved in playing the official sport. Lead-up games may be relatively simple or complex. On their simplest

Mary C. Howse fifth grade students play a small-sided or lead-up game of basketball.

level they take the form of skill challenge games in which the individual has an opportunity to test his developing skills. Formal games represent the more complex aspects of lead-up games. In **skill challenge games** the rules are few and simple, and the focus is on "how far," "how fast," or "how many." The game of horse is a basketball shooting skill challenge game. Circle soccer is a soccer kicking and trapping skill challenge game.

Formal games are lead-up games in their more complex form. In these activities the rules and strategies of the game are more significant, and players must make meaningful use of the skills. Half-court basketball and six-a-side soccer are formal lead-up games with a generally accepted set of rules and strategies.

We can view lead-up games as a means to an end or as an end in themselves. As a means to an end, they are preparatory to playing the official sport and are a way of further developing one's ability to master the skills, rules, and strategies of the official sport. As an end in themselves, they represent a less complex version of the official sport that is more suited to the intermediate/practice level of skill learning and to the available facilities and equipment.

Lead-up games play an important role among upper elementary and junior high school students, and they are frequently more fun to play than the official sport itself. These games allow students to practice and perfect sport skills in a modified environment. Most youngsters are not thrilled with the repetitive practice of skill drills. They are, however, interested when these same skills are used in gamelike situations. Therefore it's an excellent idea, after students have mastered a skill reasonably well, to modify skill drills to take on game form: give it a name and make it a game. As students gain proficiency, you can make the lead-up games more complex by incorporating a greater number of skill elements and more involved strategies, and by requiring a closer approximation of the regulations of the official sport.

Official Sport Games

Official sport games, or Developmental Level IV games, are many and varied. They are most frequently classified as team sports, dual sports, and individual sports. Sometimes, however, they are classified according to other characteristics:

- The facilities used (court sports, aquatic sports)
- The type of team interaction (contact sports, noncontact sports, combative sports)
- The equipment used (racket sports, ball sports)

An **official sport game** is one governed by a set of rules and regulations that are recognized and interpreted by an official governing body as the standard for performance and play.

Official sports have no place in the instructional elementary school physical education program. Official sport games are particularly appropriate for individuals at the advanced/fine-tuning level of movement skill learning. Few elementary school students are at this level; instead, these children need considerable instruction and practice in movement skill learning. Official sports may, however, be a part of the intramural program, the interscholastic sport program, or the agency-sponsored youth sport program. The physical education period is a learning laboratory—for learning, practicing, and putting new skills to use in a variety of movement situations.

Selecting Appropriate Game Activities

The inclusion of games in the physical education lesson typically begins during the preschool and primary grade years. Astute teachers use games as an educational tool. Every game a teacher selects should be chosen for specific reasons that depend on the elements of the lesson; these may range from practicing specific movement skills and enhancing various components of physical fitness to promoting social learning and academic concept development. If the teacher has clearly defined objectives for the use of one or more particular games in a lesson, then we may be sure that games will serve an educational purpose. If, however, the objective is primarily fun with only remote consideration given to skill, fitness, social, or academic objectives, then this part of the lesson has "missed the boat" entirely and is making little or no contribution to the physical education of children.

When choosing a game for inclusion in the lesson, do not limit selection to the "appropriate" grade-level placement you so often see in textbooks and card files of games. Children with a sound movement background can easily play and master games graded one or two levels above the level generally expected of their age. The list of active games is almost endless. Textbooks and card files are filled with thousands of different activities. But you don't need to be familiar with all or even most of these games if you adhere to the principles of game selection and modification we just discussed. Remember, a game is only a vehicle used to achieve an end. It is not, and should not be, an end in itself in the developmentally based physical education program.

TEACHING TIP 15.1

The following process is recommended for *selecting developmentally appropriate game activities* for inclusion in the lesson:

- Determine the specific objectives of your lesson and select games that will help reinforce these objectives.
- Determine the ability level of your students in terms of skill, comprehension, and interest.
- Modify games to fit the specific objectives of the lesson, the ability of the class, and the movement skills used.

Determining Ability Levels

Once you have clearly determined the objectives of your lesson, you must assess the general ability level of the class. You will also need to know your students' ability to understand and comply with the rules of the game. Finally, you will need to have a feel for the potential level and duration of students' interest in the activity.

If the skill requirements of the game are beyond the children, they will soon lose interest and quit. If the game is so complex that only a few are able to comply with the rules, there will be mass confusion and little benefit to be derived from the activity. If the game involves long waiting for a turn, is an elimination type of game, or provides little chance for meaningful participation by everyone, then all but the most highly skilled students will soon lose interest.

Knowing your students' abilities is the easiest way to determine which games should be modified. The rules are not chiseled in granite. It is important to change games to suit the ability of your students and not the mythical students addressed in this or any other text.

Modifying Games

You can modify the game activities that you select for your lesson to better suit the objectives of the lesson, the ability of your students, and the specific movement skills involved. You do this simply by carefully reading the description of the game and then altering the game as needed.

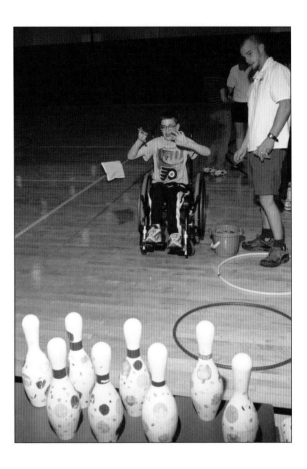

Games should be modified to meet the needs of all students. This participant in the West Chester University Adapted Physical Education program demonstrates a toss toward a set of bowling pins.

Once you know how to modify games, it is possible—even if you have only a limited number of resources—to devise an endless variety of meaningful and educationally sound games. A solid grasp of the lesson objectives, a good imagination, and a willingness to experiment will help you incorporate games into the lesson successfully.

DEVELOPMENTAL DANCE

Responding to rhythm is one of the strongest and most basic urges of childhood. It is basic to the life process itself, as evidenced by the rhythmical functions of the

TEACHING TIP 15.2

Games may be modified in a variety of ways:

- Change or add to the movement skills used to play the game.
- Alter the rules to more closely suit the objectives of the lesson.
- Modify the equipment used.
- Change the duration of the game.
- Alter the number playing in a group.
- Change the formations or boundaries used.
- Intensify the game by stepping up the pace of the activity.

- Alter the game to encourage problem-solving.
- Modify the game to stimulate creativity in making up new games.
- Redesign the game to promote maximum active participation of all students.
- Redistribute teams during the game.
- Modify the game to represent a special holiday or event.

body, as in breathing, in the heartbeat, and in the performance of any movement in a coordinated manner. We can define **rhythm** as the result of measured releases of energy over repeated units of time.

CONCEPT 15.3

Developmental dance is an important element of the physical education curriculum and should be incorporated throughout the curriculum.

Dance is an extension of rhythmical movement into creative, expressive, interpretative, and joyful activity. It is important that children be exposed to a wide variety of rhythmical experiences. The rhythm and dance offering in the school must be presented in a meaningful and purposeful manner to meet the individual developmental needs of all the children.

Children begin developing their rhythmic abilities during infancy, as seen in the infant's cooing response to the soft, rhythmical sounds of a lullaby and in the infant's repeated attempts to make pleasurable rhythmic sounds and sensations last longer. As children develop, they continue to explore their environment. An internalized time structure is established and refined. Because this ability to respond rhythmically is developed through practice and experience, rhythmic activities play an important role in the lives of children.

Movement is one important avenue by which rhythmic abilities may be developed and refined. Since rhythm is a basic component of all coordinated movement, the two may be effectively combined to enhance both of these interdependent areas.

Rhythm and Types of Dance

Rhythm is a distinctive and essential quality inherent in all coordinated movement and dance. For motion, sound, or design to be rhythmic, a formed pattern must be present. Music and dance must possess three qualities to be rhythmic. First, there must be a regulated flow of energy that is organized in both duration and intensity. Second, the time succession of events must result in balance and harmony. Third, there must be sufficient repetition of regular groupings of motion, sound, or design.

Because rhythmic structure in music is allied with rhythmic structure in movement, children generally love both. They enjoy the melodic, rhythmic succession of beats characteristic of music and the opportunity to express this through movement. As children listen to music, they respond to its rhythm in a variety of ways. They kick and laugh, jump and clap. They wiggle and giggle, twirl and skip.

Dance: "Do We Have To?"

Real-World Situation

As a physical education teacher, you know that developmental dance is one of the three primary content areas of the curriculum and that it has a legitimate place in the education of children. However, even though you have had a course or two designed to prepare you for using music with movement, you feel uncomfortable and ill prepared. Furthermore, you know that some children will moan and groan when they learn that they will be dancing. Last, because of their religious beliefs, some parents will insist that their child be excused from all dance activities. With these three impediments to incorporating developmental dance activities into your program, you are tempted to simply remove it from your curriculum.

Critical Questions

Based on what you know about developmental dance and its value:

- Why should you include dance in the curriculum?
- What can you do to enhance your comfort level about teaching dance?
- What can you do to counter the familiar refrains you'll hear from some students: "Do we have to?" or "Dance is for sissies"?
- How might you be able to accommodate the religious views of parents and their children concerning dance in the curriculum?

Sometimes they listen and relax, and sometimes they simply burst into song and dance. They begin, in their own crude way, to make their own music. They hum, sing, and play a variety of improvised instruments. The formation of a rhythm band using a variety of homemade pieces of rhythmic equipment is an important first opportunity for children to organize their efforts into an expressive whole.

All children have music as a part of their being, and it is the teacher's job to help them bring out their interests and explore their potential. Rhythmical music and movement should be a vital part of the school program. You may not feel particularly adept at singing or playing a piano, but you can play chords on a guitar or use a tape recorder, records, a small xylophone, a set of simple bells, or a drum. In any case, you need to find some way of using music to accompany rhythmic activities within your lesson. Rhythmic activities may be classified into six general and sometimes overlapping areas: fundamental rhythms, singing rhythms, creative rhythms, folk dance, social dance, and aerobic dance.

Fundamental Rhythms

Rhythmic fundamentals are the first and most basic form of understanding and interpreting rhythmic movement. **Rhythmic fundamentals** involve developing an awareness of the various elements of rhythm and being able to express these elements through movement. The teacher who wants to develop fundamental rhythmic abilities needs to keep the following **elements of rhythm** in mind:

- **Underlying beat**—the steady, continuous sound of any rhythmical sequence
- **Tempo**—the speed of the movement, music, or accompaniment
- **Accent**—the emphasis given to any one beat (usually the first beat of every measure)
- **Intensity**—the loudness or softness of the movement or music
- **Rhythmic pattern**—a group of beats related to the underlying beat

Each of the elements of rhythm may be expressed through movement that varies in effort, space, and relationships. Hence, an endless variety of movement activities may be devised to develop an increased awareness of both the elements of rhythm and the qualities of movement. A thorough knowledge of the fundamentals of rhythm is prerequisite to adequate performance in any form of rhythmical endeavor such as dance, instrumental music, or vocal music. The child should be able to "feel" the elements of rhythm and be able to express them through coordinated (rhythmic) movement. Remember, participation in stability, locomotor, and manipulative activities that stress the elements of rhythm also helps to improve students' performance in a variety of fundamental movement skills while learning about the elements of rhythm. For example, practice with running, jumping, and skipping to different tempos, intensities, and accents can enhance knowledge of the fundamental elements of rhythm as well as promoting increased skill development in the movements themselves.

Singing Rhythms

Singing rhythms are another form of rhythmic expression that provide children with an opportunity to develop a better understanding of phrasing. Performing the movements required of a particular activity plus singing the words to the rhythm helps children develop a keener sense of rhythmic movement in a variety of gross motor and fine motor activities. **Singing rhythms** include rhymes and poems, finger plays, and singing dances. Each may progress from the very simple to the complex. The activities you select will depend on the ability level, maturity, and interests of your students. Singing rhythms are appealing to children because they do one or more of the following:

- Tell a story
- Develop an idea
- Have a pleasing rhythmic pattern
- Stimulate use of the imagination
- Have dramatic possibilities

Singing plays an important role in the life of young children. Children love repetition, and they sing the songs they know over and over again. They like to respond to songs through movement. When responding to active songs, they usually join in the singing. This singing is important because it helps to internalize the rhythm of the song. When simple songs are used, children are given a variety of opportunities for repetition of movement as well as a chance to be creative and express themselves dramatically.

Creative Dance

Creative dance, a third way of expressing rhythm through movement, is generally considered an extension of rhythmic fundamentals and should become part of the elementary school curriculum after the children have a basic grasp of the fundamentals of rhythm. Creativity is a major objective of modern education; therefore, creative dance can and should be included in the physical education curriculum. Creative rhythmic movement allows children to express ideas, emotions, feelings, and interpretations and may take a variety of forms, including exploration, improvisation, rhythmic problem-solving, and simple compositions. We need only look at

In this creative dance lesson students were jumping on an imaginary springboard and projecting their partner into space. Here you see the young lady springing her partner into the air. This activity was part of a lesson on flying.

TEACHING TIP 15.3

Some practical suggestions for teaching *creative dance* include the following:

- Begin early. Waiting too long when children are more inhibited will only result in frustration for the teacher.
- Keep activities relatively simple during the early years.
- Stress rhythmic fundamentals first.
- Focus on imitative rhythms at the primary level.
- Emphasize creative rhythmic activities during the middle grades.
- For older children, use plenty of vigorous activities and work in small groups.
- Be positive and accepting.

- Dance with the children. This will help remove many apprehensions.
- Use more interpretive activities and few imitative activities with older children.
- Be sensitive to what children's interests are (e.g., sports, space, contemporary music).
- Develop lesson themes around the children's interests as well as their needs.
- Include plenty of rhythmic problem-solving in the upper grades.
- Permit children to devise simple group compositions.

the inhibited, stereotypical movements to music of the average fourth or fifth grader to realize that we have not adequately fostered creative expression in many children.

Folk Dance

Folk dances are a fourth form of rhythmic expression through movement. **Folk dances** are structured dances characteristic of the cultural heritage of peoples throughout the world. In fact, one purpose for including folk dance in the elementary school curriculum is to enhance children's appreciation for other cultures. Furthermore, folk dances encourage social interaction within the peer group and provide oppor-

The following are suggestions for teaching *folk dance* in the elementary school:

- Name the dance, tell about its origin, and give other interesting facts.
- Teach new material first.
- Have children listen to the music.
- Demonstrate the dance (or its parts) using a partner or a small group of children.
- Permit the entire class to try the whole dance or parts of it (depending on its complexity), first without the music and then with music.
- Unify the parts into the whole dance using the music.

- Select activities that promote skill development prior to emphasizing social development.
- Focus on dances without partners prior to dances with partners.
- Avoid activities that compromise one's gender identification.
- Focus on vigorous activities, particularly during the early stages of learning folk and square dances.

tunities for combining patterns of movement into an integrated whole with the benefit of musical accompaniment.

Country and western dances are peculiarly North American and reflect the culture of the early settlers. Both line dances and square dances are composed of a wide variety of movements that range from the very simple to the highly complex.

Social Dance

Social dance, a fifth medium through which rhythm may be expressed by movement, is performed with a partner and reflects the mores of the culture at the time of their popularity. The very nature of social dance is constantly changing as our culture changes. For example, a few years ago, break dancing was popular; before that it was disco dancing; and before that, the twist and swing dancing. Often when preparing to include social dance in the curriculum, we fail to recognize and include these nontraditional forms of social dance. People frequently assume that social dance automatically implies the waltz, the fox-trot, the tango, and other more traditional forms.

The need for including traditional social dance in the elementary curriculum is questionable. For most schools and communities, it is recommended that traditional

Practical pointers for *selecting partners:*

- Have a prearranged system that does not permit random choosing of partners.
- Switch partners often.
- Modify activities that require boys and girls to assume a closed dance position or skater's waltz position. An elbow turn or hand clasp will do.

- Do not require boys to take girls' parts or girls to take boys' parts.
- If the class is all one gender, avoid describing roles as "the girl's part" or "the boy's part." Instead, designate roles by the position of "lead" and "follow."

social dances not be included in the curriculum until the children are ready socially. The resistance and immaturity of many fourth, fifth, and sixth graders frequently make it exceedingly difficult to teach traditional social dances. But because children often express interest in learning more modern or nontraditional forms of social dance, it's a good idea for teachers to consider including these in the curriculum.

Aerobic Dance

In recent years aerobic dance activities have become very popular among both adults and children. **Aerobic dance** is simply exercise to music led by an instructor who cues the participants on the proper exercise for each phrase of music. Aerobic dance activities have many benefits. First, they add fun to what many people may otherwise view as "boring" exercises. Second, they provide a social environment of group participation that encourages exercise compliance. Third, they reinforce children's ability to listen to and respond rhythmically to a piece of music. Finally, aerobic dance activities are for males and females, young and old, fit and unfit, able and disabled. All can participate in a manner individually suited to them.

With children, limiting aerobic dance activities to low-impact aerobics is strongly recommended. **Low-impact aerobics** avoids wear and tear and constant banging on young bodies and bones. Low-impact aerobics also helps decrease exercise-induced injuries such as stress fractures and growth plate and joint injuries.

Besides being fun, aerobic dance enhances fitness and contributes markedly to understanding and applying the elements of rhythm discussed earlier. Children love the opportunity to bring in contemporary music, design exercise routines to their music, and try out routines with classmates. Aerobic dance has great potential for reaching and teaching children and youth in terms of fitness enhancement and the application of fundamental rhythm concepts.

Selecting Appropriate Dance Activities

The inclusion of dance activities in the physical education program usually begins during the early years with fundamental rhythmic activities and a variety of singing rhythms and finger plays. After mastering the fundamentals of rhythm, children generally enjoy expressing their rhythmic abilities through imitative activities, creative rhythmic activities, and simple folk dances. Older children enjoy creative activities that permit them to interpret ideas, moods, holidays, and sporting events through movement. They benefit from more complex folk dances and a few simple square dances. They benefit from creative activities that permit rhythmic problem-solving and the formation of basic dance compositions; and they enjoy more complex square dances and an introduction to aerobic dance activities.

Once you have settled on your objectives for including rhythmic activities in the lesson, you must determine the level of rhythmic abilities of the class. You will need to have a general idea of their level of competence in listening and responding to various forms of musical accompaniment, ranging from the sound of a drum or the clap of your hands to piano music or a symphonic recording. You will need to be keenly aware of the social maturity of the class. These factors greatly influence children's ability and willingness to comply with the requirements of the rhythmic activities you select. Remember to focus on the *skill element* involved in dance prior to the *social element*. Introducing dances with partners will be of limited success if the children are not yet sufficiently skillful or are socially immature.

DEVELOPMENTAL GYMNASTICS

Developmental gymnastics, or *educational gymnastics* as it is often called, offers opportunities to develop fitness, body awareness, and greater movement. Nilges (2000) notes that the "joy of mastering one's body weight and taking 'head over heels' is a unique movement sensation that all children have a right to experience" (p. 6). The content of educational gymnastics is based on these fundamental movement skill themes:

- Jumping and landing
- Rolling
- Steplike actions
- Balance
- Hanging/swinging/climbing
- Transfer of weight

Educational gymnastics predominately uses a problem-solving teaching approach. By presenting students with open-ended problems or individualized movement challenges, educational gymnastics develops skill within the ability and understanding of the individual student (Nilges, 1997). Perceptual-motor abilities are also enhanced through developmentally appropriate gymnastics content.

This Mary C. Howse Elementary School student practices dynamic balance as she travels across the wooden plank.

The equipment used for educational gymnastics instruction differs from that for Olympic-style gymnastics. Small apparatus may include the following:

- Hula hoops
- Wands
- Balls
- Foam shapes (to move over, under, around, or through)
- Ropes

Larger apparatus may include these items:

- Jumping boxes or foam shapes
- Benches
- Climbing frames (bridges, trestles, cargo nets)
- Hanging ropes

Developmental gymnastics has been categorized as a self-testing activity because it permits a student to perform as an individual and to establish personal standards of achievement. Children may also perform educational gymnastics activities with partners or in small groups. The key is for all students or groups to create their own gymnastics movement sentences based on the lesson constructs.

Developmental gymnastics activities may be classified in a variety of ways depending on their nature and purpose. In the developmental approach to physical education, educational gymnastics is viewed as a tool for enhancing a variety of movement, fitness, and perceptual-motor skills. Therefore, the gymnastics content area may be classified into individualized movement challenges, perceptual-motor activities, apparatus activities, and fitness activities.

CONCEPT 15.4

Developmental gymnastics activities are an essential aspect of the developmental physical education curriculum because they permit individual levels of practice, participation, and performance.

TEACHING TIP 15.6

Practical suggestions for presenting *developmental gymnastics activities:*

- Stress total participation.
- Stress individual standards of achievement.
- Encourage children to learn from one another.
- View yourself as a facilitator of learning.
- Emphasize the positive aspects of each child's performance.
- Encourage alternate solutions to movement challenges.
- De-emphasize competition and provide a relaxed atmosphere for learning.
- Use informal group organizational techniques (avoid line and circle formations).
- Present activities that offer challenges for all children.
- Practice skills under static conditions prior to dynamic conditions.

- Build skill upon skill.
- Help children understand the "why" of their movement as well as the "how."
- Encourage an awareness of individual capabilities and limitations.
- Emphasize safety at all times.
- Encourage children to attempt progressively more challenging activities.
- Focus on exploration and guided discovery experiences during the beginning/novice level of skill learning.
- Focus on combining movement skills and skill application at the intermediate/practice level of skill learning.

Olympic Gymnastics, Developmental Gymnastics: What's the Difference?

Real-World Situation

As part of the curricular plan that you submit to your building principal, you indicate that one of the content areas of your program will be "gymnastics." Not knowing the difference between Olympic gymnastics and developmental gymnastics, the principal asks you to come to the office and explain yourself. After all, she says, "We don't have any gymnastics equipment and only a few mats. Furthermore," she continues, "we are not in the business of developing gymnasts. Children can go to the local gymnastics center if they want to become gymnasts." Last, she says, "We are responsible for children's safety, and this looks to me to be much too dangerous to include in the curriculum."

Critical Questions

Based on what you know about developmental gymnastics:

- What is the difference between Olympic gymnastics and developmental gymnastics?
- How do you counter the principal's argument about not having gymnastics equipment?
- How do you respond to the principal's well-intentioned concern that the school is not in the business of developing gymnasts?
- With regard to the safety issue, how can you minimize the chance of injury in developmental gymnastics?

Individualized Movement Challenges

Throughout this text we have stressed the importance of fundamental movement and sport skill development. A *fundamental movement* is an organized series of basic movements such as running, jumping, throwing, catching, twisting, or turning. A *sport skill* is a fundamental skill that has been combined with other skills, refined, and applied to a variety of sport-related tasks, such as batting and base running in softball or the 100-meter dash and high jump in track and field. Both fundamental and sport skills can be further developed and refined through the use of **movement challenges.** Teachers using individual movement challenges to develop and refine movement skills frequently introduce a challenge with phrases such as "Who can," "Let's try," or "See if you can." The skill theme chapters on fundamental skill development (chapters 18-20) present an abundance of movement challenge activities.

Perceptual-Motor Activities

Perceptual-motor activities may consist of gross or fine motor movements that are intended to develop and refine specific perceptual-motor abilities and selected perceptual skills. The perceptual-motor skills most influenced by quality movement programs are body awareness, spatial awareness, directional awareness, and temporal awareness. Likewise, the perceptual skills most susceptible to influence through movement activities are visual perception (depth, form, and figure-ground perception), auditory perception (listening skills, auditory discrimination, and auditory memory), and tactile/kinesthetic perception (tactile/kinesthetic discrimination and tactile/kinesthetic memory).

All voluntary movement entails an element of perception. From the standpoint of perception, movement differs only in the type and amount of sensory and motor interpretation required. Therefore, by definition, all voluntary movement is actually perceptual-motor in character. Hence, from the standpoint of teaching, the difference between a motor activity and a perceptual-motor activity lies in the primary objective of the movement task. If the primary objective is skill or fitness enhancement, the activity is not classified as a perceptual-motor experience. If, on the other hand, the primary objective is perceptual enhancement, the activity is classified as perceptual-motor. Remember, however, that these same activities may also serve equally well to improve movement skill and fitness levels.

Apparatus Activities

Because of expense and storage problems, many schools are not equipped with **large apparatus** such as parallel bars, balance beam, indoor climbers, and cargo nets. This is not the case with **small apparatus** such as hoops, wands, beanbags, balls, balance boards, homemade rackets, and coffee-can stilts. The primary concept behind small-apparatus activities is that there should be sufficient equipment for every child to take part without waiting for a turn. Individualized equipment not only maximizes participation; it also heightens learning and enjoyment. A further benefit tends to be the reduction of boredom and discipline problems.

Fitness Activities

Activities designed with the objective of enhancing specific components of fitness are frequently considered to be self-testing. Although many games, sports, and rhythmic activities may contribute to one's level of fitness, the primary objective of fitness activities is to improve one's level of fitness. Fitness activities focus on improved aerobic capacity, greater muscular strength and endurance, increased joint flexibility, and improved motor fitness. Therefore, activities such as calisthenics, weight training, jogging, rope jumping, and distance swimming are all considered fitness development activities.

Summary

Three primary content areas of physical education are developmental games, developmental dance, and developmental gymnastics. Each content area makes a different kind of contribution to the curriculum and is appropriate to incorporate into the curriculum as an aid to learning depending on the objectives of the lesson. Developmental games are fun; they also add a dimension of group interaction to the lesson and help promote movement skill development. However, using games as "filler" for a lesson without clearly stated objectives is educationally indefensible. Competitive games do not teach new skills; they merely reinforce the present skill level of the individual and provide a way to apply newly learned movement skills.

Developmental dance activities are also fun, and they add an exciting dimension to the physical education program. However, rather than lumping the rhythmic experiences for the school year into one three- or four-week unit, it is advisable for teachers to use rhythmic activities throughout the curriculum as a means to many ends or as ends in themselves.

Developmental gymnastics activities permit children to test and improve their movement abilities without undue concern for group goals or teamwork. By virtue of being self-testing, individualized movement activities permit students to concentrate on the movement task itself.

Teaching by objectives is essential for all sound educational endeavors. The objectives of developmental games, dance, and gymnastics activities all center around one or more of the following:

Movement Skill Acquisition

1. To enhance fundamental movement skills (basic stability, locomotor, and manipulative skills)
2. To enhance sport skill performance (individual, dual, and team sports)

Physical Activity and Fitness Enhancement

1. To promote improved health-related physical fitness (muscular strength and endurance, joint flexibility, cardiovascular endurance, and improved body composition)
2. To promote improved motor performance (balance, coordination, agility, speed, and power)

Affective Growth

1. To promote cooperative group interaction with others (group spirit, fair play, teamwork, and being a good sport)
2. To promote positive self-growth (self-concept, self-esteem, and self-confidence)

Cognitive Learning

1. To promote learning readiness skills (learning to listen and following directions)
2. To reinforce academic concepts taught in the classroom (science, mathematics, language arts, and social studies)
3. To stimulate critical thinking (strategy, knowledge, and application of rules)
4. To promote perceptual-motor learning (body, spatial, directional, and temporal awareness)

The content areas of the physical education program represent the "tools" of your profession. They are not an end in themselves but a means to an end. They are the means by which children become more skillful movers and fit movers. Additionally, they serve as a vehicle for helping children become more effective cognitive and affective learners. Clear delineation of the specific objectives of playing games, dancing dances, and performing educational gymnastics activities is absolutely essential if physical educators expect to be understood and accepted in the educational community.

Terms to Remember

Excellent Readings

Games

Belka, D.E. (1994). *Teaching children games: Becoming a master teacher.* Champaign, IL: Human Kinetics.

Belka, D. (2000). Developing competent games players. *TEPE, 11* (3), 6-7.

Butler, J. (1997). How would Socrates teach games? A constructivist approach. *JOPERD, 68* (9), 42-47.

Curtner-Smith, M.D. (1996). Teaching for understanding: Using games invention with elementary children. *JOPERD, 67* (3), 33-37.

Howarth, K. (2000). What makes games an educational tool? *Strategies, 13* (1), 29-31.

Marin, E., Stork, S., & Sanders, S. (1998). Creating games for the physical education learning center. *JOPERD, 69* (4), 9-11.

Mauldon, E., & Redfern, H.B. (1981). *Games teaching.* Great Britain: Macdonald and Evans.

Morris, G.S.D., & Stiehl, J. (1999). *Changing kids' games.* Champaign, IL: Human Kinetics.

Parker, M. (1998). Tell me, show me, but most of all involve me! *JOPERD, 69* (1), 7-9.

Tyson-Martin, L. (1999). The "four R's" of enhancing elementary games instruction: Refocus, recycle, reorganize, restructure. *JOPERD, 70* (7), 36-40, 51.

Dance

Frye-Mason, J., & Miko, P. (2002). Critter dance. *JOPERD, 73* (3), 49-52.

National Dance Association. (1997). *National Standards for Dance Education.* Reston, VA: Author.

Purcell, T.M. (1994). *Teaching children dance: Becoming a master teacher.* Champaign, IL: Human Kinetics.

Willis, C.M. (1995). Creative dance education—establishing a positive learning environment. *JOPERD, 66* (6), 16-20.

Willis, C.M. (1995). Creative dance—how to increase parent and teacher awareness. *JOPERD, 66* (5), 48-53.

Wirszyla, C., & Gorecki, J. (1998). Teaching dance in physical education. *Strategies, 12* (1), 13-16.

Gymnastics

Nilges, L.M. (1997). Educational gymnastics—stages of content development. *JOPERD, 68* (3), 50-55.

Nilges, L.M. (1998). Refining skills in educational gymnastics. *JOPERD, 70* (3), 43-48.

Nilges, L.M. (2000). Teaching educational gymnastics: Feature introduction. *TEPE, 11* (4), 6-10. (Series of articles)

Rikard, G.L. (1992). Developmentally appropriate gymnastics for children. *JOPERD, 63,* 44-46.

Werner, P.H. (1994). *Teaching children gymnastics: Becoming a master teacher.* Champaign, IL: Human Kinetics.

16

Movement Skill Development Through Movement Concept Learning

Key Concept

▶ Children become more skillful movers and knowledgeable movers when their physical education experiences are based on movement skill development through movement concept learning.

This chapter will provide you with the tools to do the following:

▶ Justify the importance of using movement concepts to teach children's physical education.

▶ Explain what is meant by the "language" of movement in children's physical education.

▶ Describe the four components of the movement framework.

▶ List and describe the elements within each of the four components of the movement framework.

Using a developmental approach to teaching children's physical education—focusing on movement skills and movement concepts—is a challenging task. You may be thinking, what are the movement skills and movement concepts that I should be teaching? Where do they belong in the curriculum? Do I teach individual skills or combinations of movement skills and movement concepts? What do movement skills and movement concepts have to do with teaching games or dance? We address each of these questions in this chapter first by examining the "language" of developmental physical education.

THE MOVEMENT CONCEPTS OF DEVELOPMENTAL PHYSICAL EDUCATION

For a better understanding of movement concepts, you may want to think of these concepts as the special *language* of movement. As Allison and Barrett (2000) state, "Physical education teachers need a detailed and clear language to both observe and describe movement so that their mental images of students' movement responses are as complete as possible. Helping children improve their movement skills is much easier when the teacher has such a rich descriptive language to use when observing and talking about those skills" (p. 46). Seeing the core content of developmental games, dance, and gymnastics as analogous to a language is helpful because a language has its own vocabulary (figure 16.1). The success of the developmental physical education program depends on teachers who are knowledgeable about this vocabulary of movement.

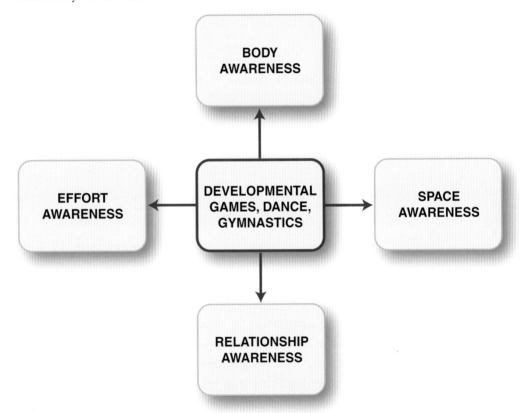

FIGURE 16.1 The movement framework is the "language" of elementary physical education.

The vocabulary that makes up the language of movement consists of four components of awareness: *body awareness, space awareness, effort awareness,* and *relationship awareness.*

- **Body awareness**—a sense of *what* the body can do
- **Space awareness**—knowledge of *where* the body can move
- **Effort awareness**—knowing *how* the body can move

- **Relationship awareness**—a sense of *with whom* and *with what* the body can move

These four movement concepts are based on the work of Rudolf Laban (1879-1958) and are frequently called a **movement framework.** Laban's students and others, including us, have modified his descriptive analysis of human movement for use in educational settings. We use this framework extensively throughout part IV, "The Skill Themes" (chapters 18-20), and in part V, "The Content Areas" (chapters 21-23).

Locomotor, manipulative, and stability skills can be developed and refined using the movement framework. So, too, can the content areas of developmental games, dance, and gymnastics be structured to incorporate this movement framework in such a way that it promotes both movement skill development and movement concept learning.

The traditional physical education program based on games, folk and square dances, and Olympic-style gymnastics generally does not use a movement framework as the basis for constructing learning experiences. Let's look at a sample game activity typical of the traditional physical education program:

> The students are playing the game of *stopper ball*, a lead-up game to basketball. The object of the game is the same as in basketball, to score by shooting your team's ball through the opponent's basketball hoop. Each team, however, has a ball, so play is with two balls (playground ball or basketball). The game begins with a jump ball using a large beach ball (the two balls used for scoring are placed in a hula hoop along the sideline). The opposing team attempts to prevent scoring by throwing the beach ball on top of the opponent's basketball hoop. This prevents a team from scoring (or shooting their ball through the hoop). Players use dribbling and passing to move their team's ball down the court. If the beach ball is on top of their basketball hoop, preventing them from scoring, they must toss their ball at the beach ball to dislodge it from the rim before they can score. Teams therefore need to strategize in order to get the beach ball on top of their opposition's basketball hoop, as well as to get it off.

It is clear that students must consider several variables when playing this game. Because of the game modifications, they need to communicate with each other and think while playing the game. If you are thinking of using this game in a lesson, these should be your first two questions:

1. Is the game developmentally appropriate for the particular children being taught?
2. Are there movement skills that are being reinforced through this game?

Two important additional questions are the following:

3. Is the game based on a movement framework?
4. Is the game being used to develop aspects of body awareness, space awareness, effort awareness, and relationship awareness?

Of course, the answer can be "yes" to all four questions, but questions 3 and 4 can be answered with a "yes" *only* if the teacher intentionally presents the game from a perspective that incorporates instruction in the movement concepts of the activity as well as its skill concepts. In other words, the task progressions and game content must consider elements of the movement framework *prior* to playing the game and use them *while* playing the game.

CONCEPT 16.1

The movement framework provides a way to conceptualize movement and constitutes the "language" of the developmental physical education program.

CONCEPT 16.2

Movement concepts are intentionally taught in the developmental physical education program incorporating use of the movement framework.

In the case of *stopper ball,* you would have to have the children practice several instructional tasks, focusing on movement skills and movement concepts, in order to teach them the language and accompanying vocabulary of the game. Some of these skills and concepts may include the following:

- Dribbling (a manipulative skill requiring body awareness) along different pathways (requires space awareness)
- Changing speeds while dribbling along different pathways (requires effort awareness)
- Dodging (a stability skill requiring body awareness) opponents (requires relationship awareness) while dribbling along different pathways (requires space awareness)
- Passing (a manipulative skill requiring body awareness) with varying force (requires effort awareness) to a partner or teammate (requires relationship awareness)
- Passing to open spaces (requires space awareness)
- Moving to an open space to receive a pass (requires space awareness)

Generally, a curriculum based on games does not use a movement approach because the game rules and game play are the instructional focus rather than the movement skills and movement concepts that constitute the game. Although valuable for its own sake, this type of curricular approach does not foster children's acquisition of a movement vocabulary and does little to enhance their movement skill and movement concept development.

Likewise when teaching developmental gymnastics, if you state, "Today we are going to learn to do a cartwheel," are you teaching children from a movement perspective if the focus is on movement skill learning *alone*? The answer is a simple but emphatic no! In a lesson using a movement perspective, children must *also* be learning about the movement vocabulary (i.e., the movement concepts of effort, space, body, and relationship awareness) of developmental gymnastics. In order to be using a movement approach to the lesson, the teacher must also include information about transfer of weight from the hands to the feet (body awareness). Additionally, she must help the children understand that a cartwheel is only one of several ways to transfer weight from the hands to the feet—one in which the head is at a low level while the body travels along a straight pathway (space awareness). The children should also practice other movement tasks that incorporate bearing weight on the hands and feet.

Developmental physical education incorporates a movement framework by focusing on important movement concepts (i.e., how the body *can* move) as well as skill concepts (i.e., how the body *should* move). This helps children become more skillful movers, knowledgeable movers, and expressive movers.

Body Awareness—What the Body Can Do

The movement skills are the "what" of educational games, dance, and gymnastics and are included within the category of body awareness (figure 16.2). Body awareness involves knowledge of the following:

- The body parts
- What the body parts can do
- How they can do it

CONCEPT 16.3

Traditional physical education programs have not emphasized the importance of acquiring a movement vocabulary.

CONCEPT 16.4

An awareness of what the body can do is an important component of readiness for learning.

Movement Concept Learning: What, Where, How, and With Whom the Body Moves

Real-World Situation

As a teacher deeply committed to quality developmentally appropriate physical education experiences, you are frustrated by the lack of time that you have with your students. Although you know that daily physical education would be in the best interests of your students, you recognize that it simply is not, for the foreseeable future, going to be a reality in your school. Therefore, you are more intrigued than ever by the notion that teachers can in fact enhance movement skill learning by equipping their students with the movement concepts of body, space, effort, and relationship awareness. You recognize, however, that movement concept learning is new to your students and is different from what is expected by some of your fellow teachers. In your view, movement concept learning equips learners with the tools for self-learning and is essential if physical education instruction is to have a lasting impact.

Critical Questions

Based on what you know about movement skill development through movement concept learning:

- What will you say to your colleagues as a way of convincing them that concept learning in your gymnasium is indeed necessary and appropriate?

- What will you say to your students and their parents as a way of helping them understand and apply movement concept learning in their everyday life?

- How do you justify taking additional time from the limited time you have with students to incorporate movement concept learning into your program?

Body awareness includes awareness of the movements that the human body can perform, including locomotor movements (e.g., walking, running, galloping, jumping, skipping, hopping, leaping, sliding, rolling), stabilizing movements (e.g., bending, stretching, twisting, curling, dodging, turning, balancing, pushing, pulling), and manipulative movements (e.g., throwing, catching, striking, bouncing, kicking). Each of these locomotor, stability, and manipulative skills can also be described by one or more of the following four actions, or intended functions of the movement:

1. Giving force to the body or an object
2. Receiving force from the body or an object
3. Bearing weight on the body in static and dynamic balance situations
4. Gesturing (Allison & Barrett, 2000; Gallahue & Ozmun, 2002)

For example, when jumping, you are giving force to the body on the takeoff and receiving force when landing. When throwing and catching a ball, you are imparting or giving force to the ball when throwing and receiving force when catching. When you are balancing on one foot, emphasis is on bearing weight and maintaining static balance. So too when you are doing a headstand or handstand. When rolling, you are applying forward and downward force with the feet and hands, and bearing weight on the back of your head, upper back, and feet while balancing in a dynamic setting. Gesturing could be incorporated into all of these movements on both the preparatory and follow-through actions through distinct flourishes of the head, trunk, arms, or legs. As developmental physical educators it is important that we incorporate this terminology into our teaching and that we help children learn more about this aspect of the vocabulary of movement.

CONCEPT 16.5

Being familiar with where the body can move in space is an important aspect of the child's movement vocabulary.

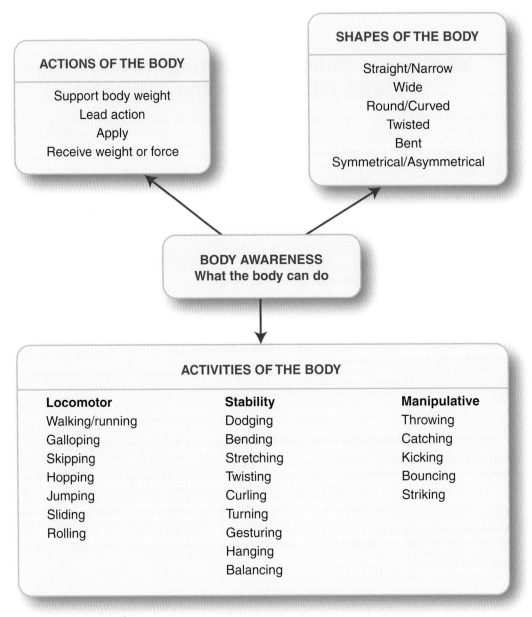

ACTIONS OF THE BODY

Support body weight
Lead action
Apply
Receive weight or force

SHAPES OF THE BODY

Straight/Narrow
Wide
Round/Curved
Twisted
Bent
Symmetrical/Asymmetrical

BODY AWARENESS
What the body can do

ACTIVITIES OF THE BODY

Locomotor	Stability	Manipulative
Walking/running	Dodging	Throwing
Galloping	Bending	Catching
Skipping	Stretching	Kicking
Hopping	Twisting	Bouncing
Jumping	Curling	Striking
Sliding	Turning	
Rolling	Gesturing	
	Hanging	
	Balancing	

FIGURE 16.2 Body awareness.

Space Awareness—Where the Body Can Move

Developing space awareness is an essential movement task for beginning movers who are at the fundamental movement phase of development and at the beginning or novice level of movement skill learning. Space awareness is composed of the elements of *pathways, range, level,* and *direction* of movement (figure 16.3). Each is briefly discussed in the following paragraphs.

The body may move in *straight, curved, zigzag,* or *diagonal* **pathways of movement.** These pathways may be on a variety of surface areas and in the air. Children need to explore the various pathways in which their bodies can move and discover for themselves the many possibilities. Exploring the various pathway possibilities of a variety of locomotor skills is an experiment in learning more about where the body can move.

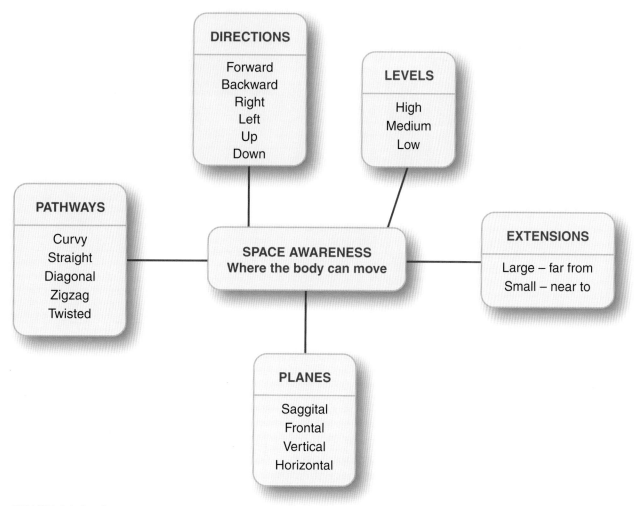

FIGURE 16.3   Space awareness.

Range of movement refers to the size of the movement and the extent to which the body may reach. The size of a movement may range from *big* to *small,* and children need to learn about and make distinctions between the size possibilities of their movements. Bringing attention to the size of someone's movements when the person is throwing a ball for distance and then for accuracy is an experiment in range, an experiment that focuses on the necessity of modifying the size of the movement based on the goal of the activity. Range of movement may also occur at the *far extension* of the body or *very close* to the body. Experimenting with one's personal space at a near range and a far range helps enhance one's sense of space awareness.

The **level of movement** refers to the body or its parts being in a *high, medium,* or *low* position. Exploring and discovering the myriad of movement possibilities at different levels enhance space awareness. For example, children can throw, run, jump, balance, and roll at varying levels.

Going from one point to another represents the **direction of movement.** These directions include *forward* and *backward, to the right* and *to the left, up* or *down, in to* or *out of, diagonally,* and so forth. The concept of direction is a component of readiness for learning and an important one for young children to internalize.

These Mary C. Howse students demonstrate different shapes at varying levels as they participate in a dance lesson.

Each of these elements of space awareness occurs with reference to either one's personal space or general space. **Personal space** is the immediate area in all directions around one's body at its furthest possible span. **General space** is the larger movement area including the space of other movers. Children can practice being aware of the amount of space their own body occupies and how far they can extend the body in all directions within a variety of educational game, dance, and gymnastics activities. For example, think about a games lesson in which children are walking and then jogging around hula hoops, scattered throughout the general space (i.e., the gymnasium), and stopping in a bent-knee, wide base-of-support ready position in response to the stopping and starting of music. This activity involves awareness of personal and general space, and it also involves relationship awareness as children must maneuver their body around other movers and around the hula hoops on the floor. So too, in a dance lesson children can learn more about space awareness as they travel along different pathways, at different levels, to an imposed rhythmical beat. Or you may ask students to make a big and wide shape versus a small and narrow shape. A developmental gymnastics lesson may emphasize space awareness as students move through general space performing a gymnastics movement "sentence" along a curvy pathway.

All fundamental movement skills can be practiced alone and in combination with one another and may be modified by the elements of space awareness. In this way children explore and discover the range of movement possibilities and develop an extensive movement repertoire as they practice locomotor, stability, and manipulative movement skills that are varied using these elements.

Effort Awareness—How the Body Can Move

Effort awareness is often difficult for the beginning teacher to understand and intentionally "teach for" within a lesson plan. The human body, however, simply can-

CONCEPT 16.6

Knowing the appropriate amount of effort expended in movement situations is an important movement concept for children to obtain.

Children learn about personal and general space as they move around a hula hoop.

not move if physical effort is not applied. Effort awareness emphasizes the *dynamics* and *qualities* of movement. Consequently it includes the elements of *time, weight,* and *flow.*

The **timing of movement** refers to the speed at which a movement occurs. A movement can be performed at a *fast, medium,* or *slow speed.* A sustained movement is considered a slow effort. A quick and sudden movement is a fast effort.

The **weight of movement** refers to the strength or force with which a movement is performed. *Strong* and *light* are the movement descriptors for the element of weight. A strong movement in a games context might be to block an oncoming soccer kick-on-goal. Defending a soccer goal kick (i.e., a movement incorporating the locomotor skill of jumping and the stability skill of stretching) would also be quick and could be at a high, medium, or low level. In gymnastics, transferring weight from hands to feet while "vaulting" over a foam shape could be described as a strong movement.

This boy exerts a strong amount of force as he transfers weight onto his hands in order to propel his body over the foam vault.

The **flow of movement** refers to the continuity of movement. In terms of flow, movements are either *free* or *bound*. Movement that is ongoing and unstoppable is a *free movement*. A curvy, wiggly, and loose movement like "cooked spaghetti" is a free movement. A leap is also a free movement—once you take off, you cannot stop the movement until you have executed the landing. A kick or a throwing action is bound because it can be stopped while it is being performed.

This student at Hillsdale Elementary School demonstrates a bound movement, striking a stationary ball.

Relationship Awareness—With Whom/What the Body Moves

CONCEPT 16.7

All movement occurs in relationship to someone or something else, making relationship awareness a fundamental concept of successful movement through space.

Relationship awareness has to do with interactions with objects and/or other people (figure 16.4). Moving with other players and the ball in the game of soccer or field hockey is an experience in relationship awareness. Using music and props in performing a creative dance activity involves the movement concept of relationship awareness. Conforming to the rules of the game also entails interactions that emphasize relationship awareness. All of these interactions occur during game play or during performance or creation of a dance or a gymnastics sentence. There are many different relationships and combinations of relationships possible in every movement context. Try to structure learning activities so that relationship awareness is reinforced. Here we overview the main elements of relationship awareness, which are *moving with equipment, moving with others, moving with props,* and *moving to rules*.

Moving with equipment occurs when a child moves on top of a gymnastics bench or around an obstacle. It also occurs when someone jumps off a foam shape, hops in and out of a hula hoop, or catches a ball thrown to an open space.

Moving with others occurs when children dance alongside a partner, meet and part, or follow a partner in a dance or gymnastics learning activity. In a games lesson, children might focus on supporting or moving behind a teammate, or moving along-

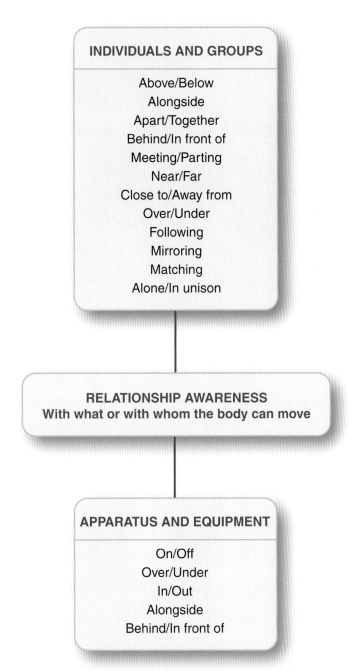

FIGURE 16.4   Relationship awareness. Note: The diagrams of the movement framework are based on Logsdon, Alleman, Straits, Belka, and Clark's (1997) depiction of the movement framework.

side a teammate to become "open for a pass." Game players need to learn to "cover space" and to "create space" for themselves and others.

Children learn another form of relationship awareness in **moving with props** such as elastic bands, body socks, hoops, scarves, music, and so forth. Performing locomotor skills individually or in combination across the floor to a rhythmical beat also fosters children's relationship awareness.

Relationship awareness may also involve **moving to rules** of a game, dance, or gymnastics activity. Movement skills, therefore, are performed within the rules of

These fifth-grade students at Mary C. Howse are playing a small-sided game of basketball. The two offensive players demonstrate the relationship of "meeting to receive a pass" while the defensive player attempts to move between the offensive players to intercept the ball.

These students are participating in a dance lesson. One student (partner A) jumps on an imaginary springboard as the other student (partner B) is simultaneously projected into the air. This represents an action-reaction relationship.

the specific activity. For example, a boundary line constrains the movement of a game player. Players must become aware of and control their movement in relationship to a boundary line. Children may also perform a combination of locomotor and stability movements to musical accompaniment or perform specific movement skills based on the "rules" of the activity or movement form.

Summary

Developmental physical education focuses on the learning of movement skills and movement concepts as the core of the curriculum. Children are more likely to acquire a rich movement repertoire when their learning experiences are organized purposefully around movement skill learning and the internalization of important movement concepts. The movement vocabulary originally created by Rudolf Laban provides a movement framework for organizing and describing the concepts of human movement. The movement framework consists of the movement concepts of body awareness, space awareness, effort awareness, and relationship awareness. Lessons in movement skill acquisition (part IV, "The Skill Themes") and lessons in developmental games, dance, and gymnastics (part V, "The Content Areas") should include one or more elements of body, space, effort, and relationship awareness. When teachers utilize the movement framework as an organizing principle of their instruction, they are making meaningful contributions to helping children learn more about the *why, what, where,* and *how* of their movement.

Skill concepts (i.e., knowing how the body *should* move) and movement concepts (i.e., knowing how the body *can* move) form the foundation of the developmental physical education curriculum. They are also the core ingredients of the skill themes (i.e., fundamental stability, locomotor, and manipulative skills) and content areas (i.e., developmental games, dance, and gymnastics) of the curriculum. Helping children become more skillful movers, knowledgeable movers, and expressive movers is enhanced when teachers focus on one of the movement skills and movement concepts within a specific learning experience. In addition, children's movement repertoire is expanded as they acquire movement skills and learn how to modify and vary them using the movement concepts.

Terms to Remember

Excellent Readings

Allison, P.C., & Barrett, K.R. (2000). *Constructing children's physical education experiences: Understanding the content for teaching.* Needham Heights, MA: Allyn and Bacon.

Gallahue, D.L., & Ozmun, J.C. (2002). *Understanding motor development: Infants, children, adolescents, adults.* Boston: McGraw-Hill.

Logsdon, B.J., Alleman, L.M., Straits, S.A., Belka, D., & Clark, D. (1997). *Physical education unit plans for grades 3-4. Learning experiences in games, gymnastics, and dance.* Champaign, IL: Human Kinetics.

Wall, J., & Murray, N. (1990). *Children and movement.* Dubuque, IA: Brown.

17

Safety Considerations and Legal Liability

Key Concept

► Teachers must be aware of the conditions for legal liability and understand that they can reduce the possibility of legal action by prudent behavior, adherence to written policies, and risk management procedures.

This chapter will provide you with the tools to do the following:

▶ List and discuss the conditions required for proving negligence in a court of law.

▶ Discuss and give examples of three forms of negligence.

▶ Describe what is meant by an *attractive nuisance* and provide examples of how this risk may be reduced or eliminated.

▶ Describe what is meant by the term *malpractice* in an educational setting.

▶ List and discuss possible defenses against a claim of legal liability.

▶ Describe common types of lawsuits brought against physical education teachers and list ways to minimize these risks.

The very nature of physical education classes, which take place in the gymnasium, swimming pool, or playground, exposes the teacher to greater liability for accidents and injuries than in any other area of the school curriculum. Although being aware of this liability is critical, physical education teachers should not be unduly anxious about the issue. A clear understanding of what constitutes legal liability, what conditions may lead to legal action, and how such problems may be minimized or avoided will do much to relieve the anxiety. Such understanding will also help promote a safe and healthful environment in which children can participate with reasonable assurance that proper precautions have been taken. This chapter provides information about some of the legal responsibilities assumed by teachers. Teachers should also become familiar with guidelines and statutes as they apply to states, provinces, and school districts.

CONDITIONS OF LEGAL LIABILITY

Tort liability, or **legal liability,** is a term meaning that someone is at fault, that this fault has caused injury or loss to another, and that someone is legally responsible. A physical education teacher may incur legal liability through three means: negligence, contributing to an attractive nuisance, and malpractice (Carpenter, 2000; Dougherty, 2002; Dougherty, Auxter, Goldberger, & Heinzmann, 2002).

REALITY CHECK

A Teacher's Playground Nightmare

Real-World Situation

You and two other teachers have been assigned lunch-time recess duty on the playground, where all students in the school take part in free-play activities for 20 minutes each day following lunch. While on duty, one teacher leaves to make an emergency trip to the bathroom, and the other is busy taking two children to the principal's office after breaking up a routine scuffle. You are all alone supervising several hundred children when a child is seriously injured.

Critical Questions

Based on what you know about your responsibility to provide a safe and healthful environment and the conditions of legal liability:

- How would you characterize supervision on the playground with three teachers present? With one?
- What is your responsibility to the injured child?
- What is your responsibility to the remaining children on the playground?
- Was there a breach of duty on your part or on the part of your two colleagues?
- Could an attorney make a case of legal liability for the child's injuries?
- In the future, what steps would you recommend be taken to maximize children's safety and minimize exposure to a claim of legal liability?

Negligence

Legally, **negligence** is considered to be failure on the part of an individual to act in a manner judged to be reasonable, careful, and prudent that one would expect of someone with essentially equal training or status. The physical education teacher who exposes children to unreasonable risks or who fails to supervise activities properly may be considered negligent. Negligence may be claimed but must be proven in a court of law. Four factors must all be present to establish negligence: established duty, breach of duty, proximate cause, and damage.

Established duty must be determined. In order for a teacher to be held negligent, it must first be established that the teacher has a duty to follow certain standards of behavior that protect the student from unreasonable risks. For example, the physical education teacher has the established duty of actively supervising all activities during the regularly scheduled physical education class period.

Breach of duty must be proven. Once an established duty has been determined, it must be shown that the teacher actually failed to conform to these standards of behavior. For example, our teacher decides to make a quick trip to the rest room, leaving the class unsupervised.

Proximate cause must be established. If a breach of duty has been proven, it must then be shown that there is a reasonable relationship between the teacher's breach

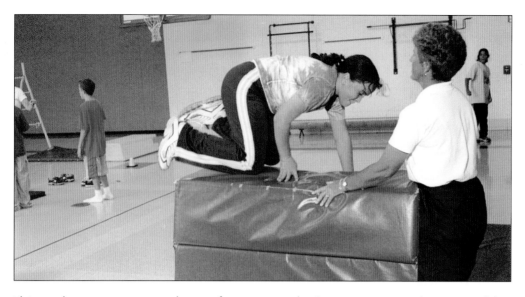

This teacher is spotting a student performing a vault. Correct spotting techniques and the ability to see all students (i.e., "back to the wall") are important responsibilities of a teacher and would be a preventive measure guarding against negligence.

breach of duty and the injury received. For example, while unsupervised, a student falls from the top of the climbing ropes. If proximate cause is established, damage must be determined.

Damage refers to actual injury or loss. Proven injury or loss entitles the plaintiff to compensation for physical discomfort and financial loss and may place certain

If students were left unsupervised while climbing ropes and an injury occurred, proximate cause could be established. In this photo, students are safely using the climbing ropes, and a landing mat, 12 inches in thickness, is provided for dismounts.

legal restraints on the defendant. Our student who fell from the climbing ropes receives injuries, requiring several days of missed school and several thousand dollars in medical expenses. At this point, if all four of the conditions for negligence are proven, it could be determined that the teacher is liable due to negligence for the damages that occurred and thus is required to make restitution.

The best defense against being declared liable for an injury or loss due to negligence is to prove that at least one of the four aspects of negligence is not present. A key to establishing negligence is first determining whether or not an individual acted in a manner to avoid foreseeable injury or harm. The law is clear in stating that the duty of the physical education teacher is to attempt to anticipate the dangers involved in the program and to guard against negligence. If, in fact, negligence is proven, it will be declared negligence due to malfeasance, misfeasance, or nonfeasance.

Malfeasance refers to committing an illegal act. For example, failure to comply with and implement the requirements of Public Law (P.L.) 94-142 (the Education for All Handicapped Children Act of 1975), those of P.L. 99-457 (Education of the Handicapped Amendments Act of 1986), or those of Title IX (the Educational Amendments Act of 1972) leaves a teacher liable for negligence due to malfeasance. Similarly, violations of student rights—such as denying students due process of law, using unauthorized corporal punishment, or discriminating against children for hair length and clothing choices—may expose teachers to negligence by malfeasance.

Misfeasance is defined as improper performance of a lawful act. In other words, the teacher may operate within the law but not up to the standards deemed to be reasonable. For example, our teacher who left the class unsupervised to use the rest room could be shown to be negligent through misfeasance. The use of improper first aid techniques in treating an injury that results in permanent disability or death also falls under the category of misfeasance. Misfeasance has occurred when you have been trained to do something but do it incorrectly.

Nonfeasance is defined as failure to perform a required act deemed appropriate under the circumstances. For example, failure to administer emergency first aid when a student's life is in danger could result in liability due to negligence by nonfeasance. In other words, nonfeasance has occurred when you have been trained to do something but fail to act.

Contributing to an Attractive Nuisance

A second way in which an individual may incur legal liability for injury or harm to students is by contributing to an attractive nuisance. An **attractive nuisance** is a place or thing (e.g., a piece of equipment, supplies, or a facility) that poses a danger but is appealing or enticing. For example, a swimming pool or weight-training facility may be considered to be an attractive nuisance if left unattended or unsupervised. It is not enough to claim that students were told not to use the facility or that warning signs were posted. If the facility permits easy though uninvited or illegal access, the defendant in a legal suit may be found guilty by reason of contributing to an attractive nuisance. Similarly, gymnastics equipment, boxing gloves, and fencing equipment may all be considered to be attractive nuisances if they are used by students while unsupervised. Suppose, for example, the gymnastics equipment is set up in the gymnasium and the teacher is enjoying a well-deserved planning period or lunch across the hall. A student who peeks into the unattended gym, sees the equipment, and subsequently sustains an injury may have ample grounds for a lawsuit.

CONCEPT 17.2

Negligence may take three forms: malfeasance, misfeasance, and nonfeasance.

CONCEPT 17.3

In physical education and athletics, legal liability is often caused by contributing to an attractive nuisance.

Gymnastics equipment should be checked for proper placement and to make sure it is in good condition before it is used. Equipment, especially for gymnastics, should never be left unsupervised in an open or unlocked gymnasium, or it potentially becomes an attractive nuisance.

The best way to avoid charges of contributing to an attractive nuisance is to store all equipment and supplies properly under lock and key, to arrange for proper supervision of facilities at all times, and to lock all facilities when they are not in use. Remember, children love to explore and experiment with their ever expanding world. It is perfectly natural for them to be attracted to the physical education facilities and equipment. Your duty as a teacher is to ensure that the facilities and equipment are properly supervised and secured at all times.

Malpractice

Malpractice is a legal concept that has only relatively recently been applied to the teaching profession. Basically, **malpractice** is negligent behavior, improper behavior, or unethical behavior on the part of an individual that results in injury or damage to the student. Injury or damage may be mental, social, or emotional as well as physical. In recent years, for example, entire school districts have been sued for malpractice by individuals who were passed on from grade to grade without the basic skills and who were granted a high school diploma without the minimal competencies expected for graduation. Physical education classes, intramural programs, and athletic programs may be liable for charges of malpractice if they use grossly improper teaching techniques (e.g., using corporal punishment), inappropriate activities (e.g., playing "murder ball" with fully inflated volleyballs or soccer balls), faulty or nonexistent spotting procedures (e.g., requiring students to climb on climbing ropes without prior conditioning or without mats underneath), or archaic training methods (e.g., failing to provide sufficient water and rest breaks during training in hot or humid conditions). Also, physical education programs that base grades on nonrelevant criteria may be accused of malpractice. Using criteria for grades such as attitude, hair length, and cleanliness could result in a claim of malpractice.

Students have a right to assume that they will receive proper instruction, training, and care. If these rights are violated, they may have grounds for claiming liability on

CONCEPT 17.4

The number of lawsuits claiming malpractice may be significantly reduced through continuing education and careful adherence to the stated objectives of the school curriculum.

the part of the individual teacher, administrator, or the school district. In any such lawsuit, negligence must be proven. The best way to prevent a lawsuit is to exercise reasonable and proper care at all times.

DEFENSES AGAINST NEGLIGENCE

In the defense of a teacher charged with negligence, several negating factors may need to be considered. These are generally referred to as contributory negligence, assumption of risk, and acts of nature.

Contributory Negligence

Contributory negligence refers to the plaintiff's being held partially or wholly at fault for the injury received. Before contributory negligence is determined, the child's age, capabilities (both physical and mental), and prior training are considered. For example, during a supervised class field trip, a sixth grader sneaks away from the group, sustains an injury, and isn't discovered to be missing for almost an hour. Such a situation may result in a case of contributory negligence if it is determined that the child was old enough to comply, and capable of complying, with the requirement of staying with the class (age of reason) and it is also determined that the supervising teacher was negligent in his supervision and inability to locate the missing child sooner. The **age of reason** in most states is considered to be age 12. If the plaintiff shares the fault, then she may be compensated in part or may not be compensated at all for damages.

In some regions, however, the concept of **shared negligence** has been broadened to include comparative negligence. In these states the plaintiff may be compensated on a proportionally reduced basis according to the actual percentage of shared negligence. For example, the wandering student may be found to be 50% at fault, and thus the extent of the supervising teacher's liability is limited to one-half of the total dollar amount of the verdict.

Assumption of Risk

Assumption of risk is a legal term indicating that in certain situations people assume responsibility for their own safety. Individuals who participate in nonrequired intramural and athletic activities and are aware of the risks involved are generally considered by the court to have assumed the risk for their own safety and well-being. This is not the case, though, for students in a required physical education class. A claim of negligence due to injury occurring through participation in required physical activities is usually not considered to fall under the defense of assumption of risk. This is an important concept that has numerous legal implications for the incorporation of stress challenge and risk activities into the required physical education program. The age, experience, and maturity of the students, as well as their awareness of the risks involved and the degree to which they are required to take part in these activities or are given equal opportunity for participation in alternative activities, all need to be carefully considered.

Act of Nature

An **act of nature** refers to something completely unexpected and unforeseen that is *totally* beyond the control of the defendant. It might be considered an act of

CONCEPT 17.5

Legal defenses based on contributory or shared negligence or assumption of risk are frequently difficult to prove with young children because of the concept of age of reason.

nature if, for example, a tree is struck by lightning on a clear day and the children playing under that tree are injured or killed. Acts of nature, however, are very difficult to prove in a court of law even under the most favorable of legal circumstances.

Proximate Cause

Proximate cause is a legal defense claiming that an accident and resultant injury were not caused by the negligence of the individual in charge because the incident and injury would have occurred regardless of whether or not the individual had been present. Suppose, for example, a child falls and breaks an arm while running down a gently rolling grassy slope on the playground during a regularly scheduled and properly supervised recess period. Running is generally considered an appropriate behavior on playgrounds; and running up and down hills is also appropriate and even encouraged. Furthermore, children do occasionally fall while running, and no amount of teacher supervision could be reasonably expected to prevent all such accidents. Therefore, if sued for negligence due to improper supervision, the supervising teacher could mount a defense based on proximate cause.

CONDITIONS LEADING TO LEGAL ACTION

A number of potential danger spots exist that may leave you, the physical education teacher, open to legal action. Being aware of these conditions and taking appropriate preventive measures will greatly reduce exposure to charges of legal liability. Among the conditions that most frequently lead to charges of legal liability are ignoring mandated legislation, providing improper instruction, providing inadequate supervision, and failing to provide a safe environment.

REALITY CHECK

Equal Time for All

Real-World Situation

You are scheduled to have the gymnasium for basketball practice for your middle school's girls' team for 2 hours after school each day. Because of limited facilities, you and the boys' basketball team have worked out a compromise—an agreement regarding use of the conditioning facilities and the gymnasium. When the boys are in the gym, your girls are in the conditioning room, and vice versa. Although not an ideal situation, it has worked out for both groups until now. The boys' team, however, is nearing the end of the season, and a few more victories will ensure a position in the district-wide play-offs. The boys' coach has asked for your "cooperation" in permitting the boys

to have the gymnasium for the full 2 hours of practice until the end of the season. If you agree, the girls' team won't have a place to practice.

Critical Questions

Based on what you know about frequent conditions leading to legal action and the provisions of Title IX:

- What is your response to the boys' coach?
- What is your response to the building principal, who supports the other coach's request that you "cooperate"?
- What, if any, grounds might there be for legal action based on the provisions of Title IX?

Teachers should be aware of and abide by prevailing federal, state, and local laws as a primary means of minimizing legal liability.

Ignoring Mandated Legislation

Federal and state laws have contained **mandated legislation** concerning certain procedures in the design and implementation of educational programs. The three pieces of mandated legislation that have had the greatest impact on physical education and athletic programs are the Educational Amendments Act of 1972 (Title IX), the Education for All Handicapped Children Act of 1975 (P.L. 94-142), and Education of the Handicapped Amendments Act of 1986 (P.L. 99-457).

Title IX makes it illegal to discriminate among students in matters of education on the basis of gender. This law has had vast implications and ramifications within the physical education profession. Considerable progress has been made in implementing Title IX over the last several years, but educators still need to be reminded occasionally of their responsibility. The majority of accusations of discrimination have charged that female students were not given the same opportunities to participate as their male counterparts. Failure to comply with the requirements of Title IX has resulted in numerous lawsuits. Following the guidelines outlined in numerous publications will help you avoid legal action. In fact, an excellent resource for case reviews that may affect the physical educator can be found as a regular feature in the *Journal of Physical Education, Recreation and Dance*. Several of these case reviews are cited at the end of this chapter in the "Excellent Readings" section.

P.L. 94-142 and its updated "cousin" **P.L. 99-457** require that all children with disabilities be provided a free and appropriate public education. The law further mandates that school systems provide means to protect the rights of these children. Most important, they provide that students with a limiting condition be mainstreamed (educated in the regular classroom) as much as possible and that an Individualized

Students with disabilities must have an IEP including specific learning objectives for physical education. Here we see a young boy with Down syndrome practice striking.

Educational Program (IEP) be prepared and implemented. Furthermore, children with special needs must now be placed in the least restrictive environment, and parents must be involved in the educational decisions that affect their child. This sweeping legislation has dramatically changed how children with disabilities are educated in the public schools (see chapter 7).

These laws are particularly important to the physical education profession because physical education was the only curricular area targeted as a specific focus of concern within these laws. Physical education has been mandated as a direct service that must be provided to all children unless their counterparts without disabilities do not receive physical education. The law does not permit the substitution of services or the use of related services in place of physical education. Failure to implement the provisions of P.L. 94-142 and P.L. 99-457 within the school district and within individual schools leaves both administrators and physical education teachers liable for legal action (Thompson, Hudson, & Bowers, 2002).

Improper Instruction

A frequent cause of legal action against physical education teachers is negligence due to inadequate or **improper instruction.** The very nature of many physical education activities involves an element of risk. Activities in the swimming pool, on the gymnastics apparatus, and on the athletic field all involve risk. The job of the teacher is to reduce this risk through proper instructional techniques and supervision.

CONCEPT 17.7

Teachers of physical education are obligated by law, as well as by ethical considerations, at all times to provide adequate supervision and appropriate instructional techniques in a safe and healthful environment.

Progressive instruction builds skill upon skill, follows established teaching procedures, emphasizes safety, and provides for the needs of the individual. Among the most frequently filed types of lawsuits are those claiming that the instruction that was provided for an activity was inappropriate or nonexistent. It is crucial to have written lesson plans and an approved written curriculum to document the scope and sequence of your instruction. Teachers are left open to legal action through failure to follow an established curriculum; nonexistent lesson planning; use of outmoded instructional strategies and questionable activities such as murder ball, circle dodgeball, and certain combative activities; and failure to follow reasonable safety precautions and spotting techniques.

Inadequate Supervision

A claim of improper or **inadequate supervision** is another frequent cause of legal action against teachers. As a general rule, the teacher should never leave an individual or class unsupervised, even for a brief period of time. The very nature of most physical education activities and of the equipment used makes it imperative that supervision be adequate at all times.

Supervision is an active process that may be conducted by the teacher or other approved personnel. Supervision extends to the playground, lunchroom, after-school activities, and school-sponsored events. If an injury does occur while children are being supervised, a number of factors will need to be considered. One is the ratio of students to supervisors; others are whether a written supervisory policy was available and followed and whether the injury was caused by improper supervision. For example, if a teacher is required to supervise several hundred children alone, it is not only the teacher who is exposed to liability; it's also the school principal and the school district. Proper supervision extends to conduct in the physical education class and on the athletic field. It is the teacher's responsibility to maintain good class

The teacher in this primary grade physical education class is demonstrating active supervision of his students.

control and to ensure that all activities are carefully supervised. Supervision by adult volunteers or other students is not acceptable unless it is expressly permitted by the school district as determined by state law.

Failure to Provide a Safe Environment

Teachers are open to the possibility of legal action when they fail to establish a safe and healthful environment by ensuring the proper condition of supplies, equipment, and facilities. A safe and healthful environment extends further to planning for safe use of locker room and shower facilities.

It is the duty of the physical education teacher to routinely inventory the physical condition of the supplies, equipment, and facilities for which she is responsible and to keep an accurate record of the dates and results of these inspections. Any defects or potential safety hazards should be eliminated on the spot, when possible, or reported immediately in writing to the building principal. Continued use of defective equipment or continued participation in a hazardous environment is morally indefensible. There is no defensible reason for using defective or broken equipment such as a cracked bat or a brick for second base. All efforts should be made to bring existing facilities and equipment into compliance with acceptable standards of health and safety.

Locker rooms and shower areas are potential danger areas that hold unusual hazards. They are frequently small, overcrowded, and slippery, presenting numerous opportunities for injury due to falls, bumps, and burns. A written policy for the use and supervision of locker room and shower facilities should be developed. Traffic patterns, time limits, and a code of acceptable behaviors should be established and enforced.

MINIMIZING YOUR LEGAL LIABILITY

An obvious way to avoid exposure to claims of legal liability and negligence is to eliminate the pitfalls already discussed in this chapter. Implementing mandated legislation, requiring proper instruction and supervision, and providing for a safe and healthful environment are all basic to quality education. However, schools and teachers may reduce liability further by keeping good records, having and enforcing written policies for emergency care and extracurricular activities, heeding legitimate excuses, and having liability insurance coverage.

CONCEPT 17.8

Record keeping and risk management procedures reduce both the likelihood of injury and the probability of successful lawsuits.

REALITY CHECK

The Fifth Grade Field Trip: A Potential Mess

Real-World Situation

As a highlight of the end-of-the-year school program for fifth graders, who are about to graduate and go on to the middle school, your principal has authorized a daylong field trip to a theme park located 3 hours by bus from the school. You have been given the responsibility for organizing and supervising this event involving up to 80 students. Naturally, your first concern is for the safety and well-being of all those who participate. For starters, you have scheduled two school buses to depart from the school at 7:00 A.M. on a Saturday morning and to return by 11:00 P.M. that same day. The fifth graders are excited about the upcoming event, as are the classroom teachers who have agreed to accompany you on the field trip.

Critical Questions

Based on what you know about the importance of supervising students, minimizing legal liability, and having a written extracurricular activity policy:

- What are the steps that you will take to make sure that this event is properly conducted and supervised?

- How would you handle unforeseen situations that might arise, such as a bus breakdown, a lost or injured child, or failure of a parent to pick up a child at the designated time?

- How would you deal with these and other such situations?

- What minimum requirement would you impose in terms of adult supervision throughout the field trip?

Record Keeping

An excellent way to avoid or minimize the effects of a lawsuit is to keep accurate, up-to-date records. There should be a written record of all accidents, no matter how minor, and of all periodic inventories of the condition of all supplies, equipment, and facilities under your jurisdiction.

Accident Reports

If an injury does occur, it is essential that an accident report be filled out and filed with the principal's office no later than the close of the school day. Many school districts use a standard accident report form. If such a form is not readily available, we invite you to use the sample form shown in figure 17.1.

Basically, the **accident report** should contain the name, address, phone number, age, and grade of the injured child. The location where the injury took place, the person responsible for supervision, the time of day, and a brief description of the activity leading up to the accident are essential. This information should be followed

Student Accident Report

This form should be completed in triplicate and signed by the building principal, school nurse, and supervising teacher. The original will be forwarded to the superintendent's office. The second copy will be kept in the principal's office, and the third copy will be retained by the supervising teacher.

Name of Injured _____

Age _____ Grade _____ Home _____

Home Address _____

Date of Accident _____ Time of Accident _____

Specific Location of Accident _____

_____

Staff Person(s) Supervising _____

Address _____

Description of the Activity Leading to the Accident _____

_____

_____

Nature of the Injury _____

_____

Description of Emergency Care Given _____

_____

_____

Emergency Care Given by _____

Address _____ Phone _____

Medical Treatment Recommended _____ Yes _____ No

Medical Official Providing Treatment _____

Address _____ Phone _____

Specify Where Taken After Accident _____

_____ First Aid Room _____ Home _____ Hospital _____ Other

Out-of-School Transportation Provided by _____

Address _____

Parent/Guardian Name _____

Parent/Guardiam Contacted _____ Yes _____ No _____ Time

Additional Comments _____

_____

_____

Name of Person Filing Report _____

Date of Report _____

Signature of Supervising Teacher _____

Signature of School Nurse _____

Signature of School Principal _____

FIGURE 17.1   Sample accident report form.

From *Developmental Physical Education for All Children* (4 ed.) by David L. Gallahue and Frances Cleland Donnelly, 2003, Champaign, IL: Human Kinetics.

by a detailed description of the emergency care given and the personnel involved. It is important to include a brief description of the nature of the injury, including, if applicable, the name of the physician or school nurse providing treatment. How and when the student's parents were contacted should also be included. When the form is completed, it should be signed and dated (Pastore, 1994). The original should be retained in the principal's office, and the teacher should keep a copy for his files. At no time should the teacher discuss the injury with others unless directed to do so by a school official. No attempt should be made to diagnose the injury or to provide treatment beyond emergency first aid until qualified medical personnel can take over. The injured student should not be left alone while the teacher summons help. The procedure for obtaining help, as a matter of written policy, should be to send a trusted student to the central office of the school.

Supply/Equipment Reports

Some schools utilize a district-approved form for inventorying the condition and reporting the status of supplies and equipment. If such a form is not available, the sample form presented in figure 17.2 may be adopted or modified to suit your needs. The **supply/equipment report** should contain a complete inventory of all the supplies, equipment, and facilities under the teacher's jurisdiction. At the beginning and end of each semester, there should be a complete accounting of all equipment and supplies. The number and condition of all the balls, bats, bases, ropes, hoops, beanbags, and other supplies should be noted on the form. Defective materials, such as splintered bats, frayed climbing ropes, or broken playground equipment, should be specifically noted and immediately repaired or removed from use. Unsafe conditions should be brought immediately to the attention of the proper building official, in writing. You should retain a copy of this correspondence in your files, along with your completed, signed, and dated supply/equipment report.

Facility Reports

The physical education teacher frequently has several facilities under her jurisdiction. Along with the gymnasium or multipurpose room, the physical education teacher is frequently responsible for supervising and reporting on the condition of the playground and athletic fields. The use of a **facility report** for regular, systematic inspection of each of these facilities is recommended. Filling out the report takes only a few minutes and may identify potential safety hazards such as improperly placed or stored equipment, dirty or unsafe floors, broken glass, potholes, and other unsafe conditions. Many of these potential hazards can be immediately rectified; rectifying others may take time. In any case, activity should not continue when conditions are unsafe, and the appropriate school official should be notified, in writing, of unsafe conditions.

Written Policies

Written policies that are clearly stated and strictly adhered to will do much to limit the extent of one's exposure to liability. Among the most important written policies are the emergency care policy and the extracurricular activity policy. Written excuses and insurance coverage are also important ways of reducing liability.

Emergency Care

Along with the accident report form, it is of utmost importance to have a written policy describing what is to be done in the event of an emergency. The **emergency**

Supply/Equipment Condition Report

Supplies/Equipment	Quality	Condition		Recommendations	
		Satisfactory	Unsatisfactory	Repair	Destroy

The above supplies and equipment were inventoried by _____ on _____ .
The items checked "Unsatisfactory Condition" have been removed from use. The items marked "Repair"
should be repaired by the earliest possible date or destroyed. I hereby acknowledge receipt of this
Supply/Equipment Report:

_____   _____
Signature of Report Preparer   Date   Principal's Signature   Date

FIGURE 17.2   Sample supply/equipment report.

care policy should reflect carefully thought-out risk management procedures detailing exactly what will be done in the event of an accident or injury. A copy of this procedure should be made available to all teachers, approved by appropriate school officials, and placed on file with the building principal or superintendent (Almquist, 2001).

Extracurricular Activities

Participation in extracurricular activities frequently exposes teachers to increased liability. To reduce this exposure, it is important to have a written **extracurricular activity policy** governing the conduct and supervision of these events. **Parent permission slips** that clearly spell out the nature of the activity are a must, whether the activity is a school-sponsored field trip or an athletic event at another school. Although the parent permission slip does not remove or reduce the limits of liability, it does provide a clear indication that the child's parents are aware of and approve of participation (Judd & Goldfine, 2000). Even with the permission slip on file, you

TEACHING TIP 17.1

The following questions need to be addressed in developing an *emergency care policy:*

- *Who should administer emergency first aid?* Ideally, all teachers should be certified in first aid and CPR, but this is rarely the case.
- *How will help be summoned?* The on-site teacher should not leave the injured child.
- *Who will determine if the injured student can be moved?* When in doubt, this decision should be left to a physician or emergency medical technician.
- *Who will determine if the child needs additional medical attention?* If emergency treatment is required, help should be summoned immediately.
- *Who will contact the child's parents, and what information will be given over the phone?* An

updated file with the home and business phone numbers of all parents and their family physicians should be maintained in the central office.

- *Who will fill out the accident report, and where and when is it to be filed?* The supervising teacher should be responsible for filling out the accident report, which should be filed by the end of the school day with the principal and other appropriate officials.
- *Who will take responsibility for follow-up on the injury, and what procedures will be used?* The principal, school nurse, or other school officials should be responsible for follow-up.

as the physical education teacher have the same responsibility for proper supervision as at any other time.

Written Excuses

Children frequently ask to be excused from participating in a physical education class for health reasons or because of religious beliefs. The law is clear in indicating that it is the teacher's duty to honor **written excuses** requesting nonparticipation or modified participation if they have been written by parents or medical officials. Failure to honor these written requests and insisting that the child take part are an open invitation to a lawsuit.

TEACHING TIP 17.2

Important points to consider in formulating an *extracurricular activity policy:*

- *Who is in charge of supervision?* This person should be a teacher operating with the permission of the appropriate school official.
- *Who will be assisting in the supervisory duties?* Adults, preferably parents of the children involved, should assist with supervision and should have specific written responsibilities.
- *What is the ratio of children to adult supervisors?* Although no clear legal precedent has been established, it is assumed that the teacher will operate in a reasonable and prudent manner in determining the number of supervisors needed.
- *Who will arrange for transportation, and how*

will it be supplied? This is a critical point that must be determined in conjunction with the school attorney and insurance officials. It should not be assumed that children can be transported in private automobiles from the school to school-sponsored events without the school's incurring additional liability. The law varies from state to state on this issue and should be clarified locally.

- *How will the nature of the activity and the quality of supervision be assessed?* To prevent difficulties in the future, it is important to have some means of determining if the supervisory policies enacted are adequate and are being followed.

Even if you suspect that the reasons for the written excuse are not valid and that, based on your judgment, it would be in the best interests of the child to participate, you must honor the written request that the child be excused. It is perfectly appropriate to question the validity of the request, but the child should be excused from participation while you are doing so.

Children are sometimes forbidden to take part in certain activities because of religious beliefs. Often parents request that their child be excused from all dancing, coeducational activities, or mass showering. These requests must be honored and carried out in a way that does not bring ridicule or attention to the child.

Requests from parents for their child to be excused from participation for minor medical reasons should be carefully scrutinized. As a general rule, requests for nonparticipation for over one week should be accompanied by a physician's excuse. If a child needs to be excused from physical education for only a day or two, a written excuse from a parent should be sufficient.

Insurance Coverage

CONCEPT 17.9

Professional liability insurance coverage is available through a variety of sources for a reasonable cost.

Despite all the precautions advocated and all the professionally responsible efforts made by concerned, caring teachers, accidents and injuries still occasionally occur. Any time an injury occurs, the possibility of some form of legal action exists. Therefore, it is wise to be certain that you have adequate insurance coverage in the unlikely event that you should be found legally liable due to negligence, contributing to an attractive nuisance, or malpractice.

Teachers may obtain insurance in a variety of ways. First, in some states, adequate liability insurance coverage is automatically provided for all teachers. Second, there are local school districts that carry liability insurance coverage on all their teachers. Third, professional teachers' organizations, including the American Alliance for Health, Physical Education, Recreation and Dance (AAHPERD) and the National Education Association (NEA), offer low-cost liability insurance policies to their members. A fourth source of liability insurance coverage is commercial insurance companies. Many companies offer liability coverage as a rider to home insurance and health insurance policies for little additional cost. Be certain to make yourself aware of the liability coverage available to you and the terms of the coverage. Because of astronomical settlement sums, many teachers are finding it prudent to take out additional liability coverage through their professional education association or through commercial insurance carriers even if they are already covered by their state or school district.

Even though the number of lawsuits has been on the rise for several years, the likelihood of a teacher's being sued and of the plaintiff's recovering damages is still small. Nevertheless, the peace of mind that you'll have for a moderate cost makes liability insurance worth the investment.

Summary

In order for a teacher to be proven negligent in a court of law, established duty must be determined, breach of duty must be proven, proximate cause must be established, and damage must have been caused. Negligence may take three forms: malfeasance (failure to comply with and implement a law, e.g., violating a student's rights), misfeasance (improper performance of a lawful act, e.g., use of improper first aid techniques), and nonfeasance (failure to perform a required act, e.g., failure to administer needed emergency first aid). An attractive nuisance is a place or object such as a swimming pool or a weight-training device that is left unattended or unsupervised. Teachers can avoid contributing to an attractive nuisance by properly supervising and locking facilities and properly storing equipment and supplies.

Malpractice is negligent, improper, or unethical behavior that results in mental, social, emotional, or physical injury or damage to the student. Educators may reduce the risk of liability by following the law, providing proper instruction and supervision, and maintaining a safe and healthful environment—that is, by adhering to basic principles of all quality education. However, they may further reduce liability by keeping good records, having written and enforced policies for emergency care and extracurricular activities, heeding legitimate excuses, and having liability insurance coverage.

Certain types of lawsuits have commonly been brought against physical education teachers. Failure to comply with the requirements of Title IX has resulted in numerous lawsuits. Other types of actions against teachers typically involve ignoring other mandated legislation, providing improper instruction, providing inadequate supervision, and failing to provide a safe environment. Becoming aware of and following the guidelines outlined in many professional publications will help you avoid legal action.

Terms to Remember

Excellent Readings

Hart, J., & Ritson, R. (2001). *Liability and safety in physical education and sport.* Reston, VA: NASPE.

Holford, E. (1992). Prayer on the playing field. *JOPERD, 63,* 29-32.

Mitchell, M. (1998). Reading between the lines: Interpreting notes from home. *Strategies, 12* (2), 21-23.

Piletic, C.K. (1998). Transition: Are we doing it? *JOPERD, 69* (9), 46-50.

Sawyer, T.H. (1999). Assumption of risk. *JOPERD, 70* (3), 18-19, 21.

Sawyer, T.H. (1999). Proximate cause and foreseeability. *JOPERD, 70* (8), 11-12.

Sawyer, T.H. (1999). Supervision. *JOPERD, 70* (5), 11-12.

Sawyer, T.H. (1999). Title IX. *JOPERD, 70* (4), 9-10.

Sawyer, T.H. (2000). Negligence and willful and wanton misconduct. *JOPERD, 71* (9), 10-11.

Sawyer, T.H. (2000). Negligent supervision. *JOPERD, 71* (8), 8.

The Skill Themes

As field professionals as well as authors, Part IV, "The Skill Themes," is near and dear to our hearts. Much of our professional lives has been involved in working with others who firmly believe that fundamental movement skills are important and convincing those who do not that mature fundamental movement skills do indeed make a difference. We have worked with athletes and their coaches from the youth sport level all the way to the Olympic and professional levels. We have also worked extensively with those who have significant movement deficits. Based on our professional experiences and the testimony of others, we know that skill themes focusing on fundamental movement skill development are critically important to what lies beyond. Each of these chapters, Fundamental Stability, Locomotor and Non-Locomotor, and Manipulative Skill Themes **(chapters 18, 19, 20),** focuses on fundamental movement skills critical to the later learning of complex, or specialized, movement skills. In short, these chapters are important because they serve as the basis for what goes beyond. If you grasped the concepts emphasized in the previous chapters, and if you appreciate what we are trying to accomplish by advocating a developmental approach to teaching children's physical education, then these chapters will be as important to you as they are to us.

18

Fundamental Stability Skill Themes

Key Concept

▶ Stability is the most basic of the three categories of movement because all locomotor and manipulative movements require an element of stability.

Chapter Objectives

This chapter will provide you with the tools to do the following:

▶ Define the word *stability* and discuss how and why it is considered a category of movement.

▶ Examine the stabilizing aspects of a variety of locomotor and manipulative skills at both the fundamental and specialized movement skill phases.

▶ List and describe the subcategories of stability.

▶ Demonstrate knowledge of and ability to plan and implement a developmental movement skill theme around one or more stability abilities.

▶ Identify the initial, elementary, and mature stages for a variety of fundamental stability abilities.

▶ Become familiar with the essential skill concepts and movement concepts that children should know about their developing stability abilities.

▶ Describe common developmentally based difficulties that children encounter in mastering fundamental stability abilities, and identify appropriate teaching strategies for overcoming these difficulties.

▶ Examine how to incorporate a variety of exploratory and guided discovery activities into a stability skill theme.

Stability represents the most basic of the three categories of movement. In fact, there is an element of stability in *all* locomotor and manipulative movements. Children who are exposed to a variety of movement situations usually have little difficulty in developing fundamental stability abilities. On the other hand, children who do not have a varied background of movement experiences frequently lag behind in the development of basic stability abilities.

The idea of stability as a category of movement goes beyond the notion of non-locomotor movements and static and dynamic balance. **Stability** is the ability to sense a shift in the relationship of the body parts that alter one's balance, as well as the ability to adjust rapidly and accurately for these changes with appropriate compensating movements. Stabilizing movement skills place emphasis on either gaining or maintaining balance in either static or dynamic movement situations. Therefore, the concept of stability encompasses axial movements, springing movements, upright supports, and inverted supports, all of which involve static or dynamic balance.

Axial movements, sometimes referred to as non-locomotor movements, are stability skills in which the **axis of the body** revolves around a fixed point. Movements such as twisting, turning, or spinning are generally considered to be axial movements that emphasize maintaining one's balance. **Springing movements** involve forceful projection of the body into space in either an upright or an inverted position. Movements such as a jump and turn in the air, jumping to catch a kick-on-goal in soccer, or a round-off in gymnastics are considered springing movements. Emphasis in these tasks is on the sudden loss and regaining of contact with one's base of support.

Upright supports are static or dynamic balance skills in which emphasis is on maintaining one's equilibrium when the body is placed in unusual positions. Individual supports or balances on different body parts such as in a "V-sit" or a front scale are upright postures. Partner stability movements using counterbalance or counter-tension (see chapter 23) can also involve upright supports.

Inverted supports involve supporting the body momentarily or for a sustained period in an inverted position. The tripod, headstand, and handstand are all sustained inverted supports. Momentary inverted supports include forward and backward rolls, cartwheels, and the round-off.

The concept of stability is broad. For the purposes of this discussion, the movement category of stability includes any movement in which a premium is placed on gaining or maintaining one's equilibrium. Figure 18.1 provides a partial listing of stability skills.

For this chapter, walking on a gymnastics bench or beam and the one-foot balance have been selected as representative samples of the many dynamic and static balance skills, along with body rolling and dodging. We provide a verbal and a visual description for each, along with teaching tips and concepts children should know. The chapter also presents a sampling of developmentally appropriate skill development activities and a variety of skill application activities for body rolling and dodging.

STABILITY SKILL SEQUENCING

Because stability is basic to all that we do, fundamental stability abilities begin developing early in life. But the extent to which these abilities are developed and refined depends largely on environmental factors.

When you are working on stability skill development, it is important to follow a logical progression of activities from simple to complex, building skill upon skill. Axial movements are a good place to start. Experimenting with how the body can bend, stretch, twist, and turn places children in new and unusual positions. Upright supports are good activities to include next. These provide practice in supporting

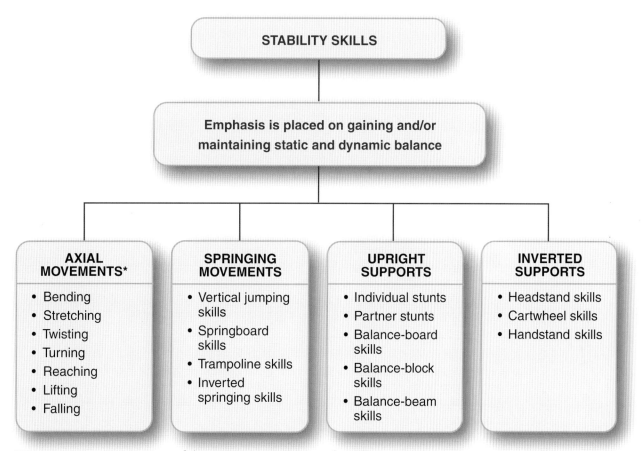

FIGURE 18.1 Components of the movement category of stability. *Axial movements are sometimes incorporated under the term *non-locomotor movements*. Non-locomotor movements, however, are a subset of the movement category of stability.

the body in progressively more difficult ways on the floor, on the mat, or on various pieces of large and small apparatus. Springing activities, in which the body is projected into the air in an upright posture, should be the third level of stability skill sequencing. These activities permit the body to be projected into the air for a short time, and they require progressively more sophisticated coordination as well as dynamic balance abilities. Inverted supports and inverted springing activities should be the last skills to be incorporated into the skill progression. Text Box 18.1 outlines the steps in developing a stability skill theme.

Stability skills require considerable coordination and kinesthetic sensitivity to where the body is in space. All stability skill development activities should follow a logical sequence of progression from beginning- to intermediate- to advanced-level activities. Not following a logical sequence will lead only to frustration and failure on the part of students and to the development of splinter skills that have little use.

CONCEPT
18.4

Proper progression and skill sequencing are especially important in the development and refinement of stability skills.

DYNAMIC AND STATIC BALANCE

Balance is commonly defined as the ability to maintain one's equilibrium in relation to the force of gravity, whether in a static posture or during performance of a dynamic activity. For a person to be in balance, the **line of gravity** that passes through

---

TEXT BOX 18.1

Developing a Stability Skill Theme

When planning a developmental movement skill theme around fundamental stability skills you will find it helpful to follow this sequence.

1. Preplan.
   a. Determine what fundamental stability skills will be grouped together for each skill theme. The following grouping my be considered:
      1) Axial movements and springing movements
      2) Rolling and transfer of weight
      3) Small apparatus skills
      4) Large apparatus skills
   b. Determine when to include each stability skill theme in your yearly curriculum.
   c. Decide approximately how many total lessons you will spend on fundamental stability skill development in relation to the total curriculum.
2. Observe and assess.
   a. Observe the static and dynamic balance skills of the group to be taught.
   b. Assess whether students are at the initial, elementary, or mature stage in their static and dynamic balance abilities. Study the verbal descriptions and visual descriptions for stability skills on the pages that follow for help.
3. Plan and implement.
   a. Plan appropriate movement activities geared to the needs, interests, and ability level of the group. Study the teaching tips and concepts children should know in the pages that follow for assistance.
   b. Implement a planned program of activities that stress progressive skill development.
4. Evaluate and revise.
   a. Informally evaluate progress in the stability skills being stressed in terms of improved mechanics. The questions found in figure 18.12 at the end of the chapter will be helpful.
   b. Revise subsequent lessons as needed, based on student progress.

CONCEPT 18.5

Individuals progress through a series of developmental stages in acquiring their stability skills, but they must have abundant opportunities for practice, encouragement, and instruction in an ecologically appropriate setting if they are to progress to the mature stage and beyond.

the individual's **center of gravity** must also lie within the base of support. If the line of gravity falls outside the base of support, the person cannot remain in balance and will fall unless compensating movements are made.

A **static balance** activity may be defined as any stationary posture, upright or inverted, in which the center of gravity remains stationary and the line of gravity falls within the base of support. Standing in place, balancing on a board, and standing on one foot are all examples of static balance from an upright posture. Examples of static balance activities using inverted postures include the tripod, tip-up, headstand, and handstand. Maintenance of the body in a stationary position for a specified period of time is the essential factor in any static balance activity.

Dynamic balance involves control of the body as it moves through space. In a dynamic balance activity, the center of gravity is constantly shifting. Locomotor and manipulative movements involve an element of dynamic balance. Virtually all movement involves an element of static balance. Therefore, balance is the basis from which

At Mary C. Howse School, fifth graders create static balances on different body parts.

all controlled movement emanates. As a result, the balance experiences engaged in by children play an important role in the development of total-body control.

This section focuses on those activities that clearly place a premium on the gaining and maintaining of one's equilibrium. The beam walk and the one-foot balance have been selected as representative fundamental dynamic and static balance movement patterns, respectively.

This first grade student is hopping in and out of a hula hoop. Does hopping demonstrate static or dynamic balance?

Low Beam Walk

Walking on a narrow object is a favorite activity of children. It tests their dynamic balance and challenges their ability to remain in an upright position. Children enjoy walking on a low beam, benches, tires, and anything else that either tests or disrupts their equilibrium (see figures 18.2 and 18.3).

I. Beam walk
  A. Initial stage
    1. Balances with support
    2. Walks forward while holding on to a spotter for support
    3. Uses follow-step with dominant foot leading
    4. Eyes focus on feet
    5. Body rigid
    6. No compensating movements
  B. Elementary stage
    1. Can walk a 2-inch low beam but not a 1-inch low beam
    2. Uses a follow-step with dominant foot leading
    3. Eyes focus on apparatus
    4. May press one arm to trunk while trying to balance with the other
    5. Loses balance easily
    6. Limited compensating movements
    7. Can move forward, backward, and sideways but requires considerable concentration and effort
  C. Mature stage
    1. Can walk a 1-inch low beam
    2. Uses alternate stepping action
    3. Eyes focus beyond beam
    4. Both arms used at will to aid balance
    5. Can move forward, backward, and sideways with assurance and ease
    6. Movements are fluid, relaxed, and in control
    7. May lose balance occasionally
II. Developmental difficulties
  A. Overdependence on spotter
  B. Visually monitors stepping leg
  C. Tying one arm in
  D. Rigid, hesitant movement
  E. Failure to actually negotiate the problem of balance
  F. Inability to perform without holding on to a spotter
  G. Poor rhythmical coordination of both sides of body
  H. Overcompensating for loss of balance

Figure 18.2 Developmental sequence for the low beam walk.

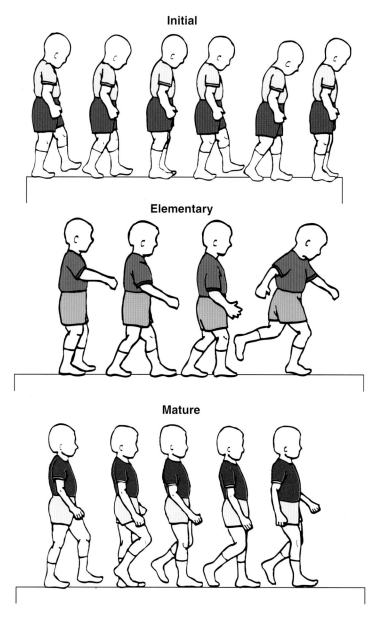

Initial

Elementary

Mature

FIGURE 18.3 Stages of the low beam walk.

TEACHING TIP 18.1

When you are working on *dynamic balance:*

- Have students practice balance activities on the floor and on various types of apparatus (benches, tires, crates) before using a balance beam or balance board.

- Spot activities carefully, but only as needed.

- Offer your hand for assistance, encouraging the child to grasp it less securely as balance is gained.

- Use a long pole to aid in balancing with use of both sides of the body.

- Encourage proper focusing of attention by having the child identify numbers that are held up.

At Hillsdale Elementary School, students are challenged to maintain their balance as they maneuver their bodies across the tires!

TEACHING TIP 18.2

When you are working on *static balance:*

- Work for good body control in different directions and at different levels.
- Have children try to pick up objects while balancing in order to alter the balance problem and to change level.
- Provide plenty of variety and opportunity for experimentation, remembering that the primary objective is to enhance balance and not

just to walk a balance beam or balance on a board.

- Provide numerous balance experiences, using various forms of equipment.
- Have children do low-level activities before introducing high-level activities.
- Practice on a low bench and low balance beam prior to using a regulation beam.

I. One-foot balance
   A. Initial stage
      1. Raises nonsupporting leg several inches so that thigh is nearly parallel with contact surface
      2. Is either in or out of balance (no in-between)
      3. Overcompensates ("windmill" arms)
      4. Inconsistent leg preference
      5. Balances with outside support
      6. Only momentary balance without support
      7. Eyes directed at feet
   B. Elementary stage
      1. May lift nonsupporting leg to a tied-in position on support leg
      2. Cannot balance with eyes closed
      3. Uses arms for balance but may tie one arm to side of body
      4. Performs better on dominant leg
   C. Mature stage
      1. Can balance with eyes closed
      2. Uses arms and trunk as needed to maintain balance
      3. Lifts nonsupporting leg
      4. Focuses on external object while balancing
      5. Changes to nondominant leg without loss of balance
II. Developmental difficulties
   A. Tying one arm to side
   B. No compensating movements
   C. Inappropriate compensation of arms
   D. Inability to use either leg
   E. Inability to vary body position with control
   F. Inability to balance while holding objects
   G. Visual monitoring of support leg
   H. Overdependence on outside support

FIGURE 18.4   Developmental sequence for the one-foot balance.

One-Foot Balance

Balancing on one foot is an activity that challenges children's static balance (see figures 18.4 and 18.5). Static balance abilities are basic to myriad sport activities and are enjoyed by children in a practice setting. Balancing should be practiced using a variety of different "environmental conditions." For example, balancing on one foot on different types of equipment challenges students. Changing the task conditions also motivates students to practice. Sample environmental or task conditions include using benches, crates, hula hoops, foam blocks, and so on.

FIGURE 18.5   Stages of one-foot balance development.

BODY ROLLING

Body rolling is a fundamental movement that requires the person's body to move through space around its own axis while momentarily inverted. Rolling may be forward, sideways, or backward. Children love to roll. The thrill of being upside down, the uncertainty of where they are in space, and the dizziness all combine to make rolling an enjoyable activity for most children. Body rolling is a fundamental movement pattern that is integral to the sports of gymnastics and diving. It is found in various forms in the martial arts, wrestling, and acrobatic skiing. The body aware-

DYNAMIC AND STATIC BALANCE CONCEPTS CHILDREN SHOULD KNOW

Skill concepts:

- Holding your arms out to the side will help you balance.
- Focusing on an object will help you balance.
- When walking on the beam, you should try to use an alternate stepping pattern.
- Be sure to have a spotter at your side.
- Do not rely on your spotter too much.
- The lower your center of gravity, the greater your stability.
- The wider your base of support, the greater your stability.
- Your line of gravity must stay within your base of support in order to balance.
- Balancing on one body part is usually more difficult because of a narrower base of support.

Movement concepts:

- You can balance your body at many different levels.
- You can balance on many different objects.
- You can balance while holding many different objects.
- You can move in different directions while balancing.
- You can balance while moving with others.
- You can widen your base when you balance for greater stability.
- You can lower your body when you balance for greater stability.

CONCEPT 18.6

Children must be able to apply many stability movement concepts and skill concepts in their daily lives if they are to be effective movers.

ness and space awareness demanded of the individual in any activity that involves rotating the body around its own axis are tremendous. Therefore, it is important that children have many and varied opportunities to develop their body rolling abilities.

Forward Roll

A forward roll can also be performed on a variety of different pieces of equipment or in different "environmental contexts." Children at a beginning level of movement skill learning should practice forward rolls on a gymnastics mat. Those students at an intermediate or advanced level of movement skill learning can perform a forward roll down an incline mat or on a padded bench. Advanced skill level movers can perform a forward roll on a beam or on a bench (see figures 18.6 and 18.7).

The forward roll, for many children, is their first inverted skill activity. It is important to remember that being "upside down" is a new and sometimes "scary" experience. It is critically important that you recognize the individual differences among your students when presenting this new, fun, and exciting skill. Be sure to take care in spotting and working through a developmental progression that takes all of the varying levels of competence and confidence into consideration.

I. Body rolling
  A. Initial stage
    1. Head contacts surface
    2. Body curled in loose "C" position
    3. Inability to coordinate use of arms
    4. Cannot get over backward or sideways
    5. Uncurls to "L" position after rolling forward
  B. Elementary stage
    1. After rolling forward, actions appear segmented
    2. Head leads action instead of inhibiting it
    3. Top of head still touches surface
    4. Body curled in tight "C" position at onset of roll
    5. Uncurls at completion of roll to "L" position
    6. Hands and arms aid rolling action somewhat but supply little push-off
    7. Can perform only one roll at a time
  C. Mature stage
    1. Head leads action
    2. Back of head touches surface very lightly
    3. Body remains in tight "C" throughout
    4. Arms aid in force production
    5. Momentum returns child to starting position
    6. Can perform consecutive rolls in control
II. Developmental difficulties
  A. Head forcefully touching surface
  B. Failure to curl body tightly
  C. Inability to push off with arms
  D. Pushing off with one arm
  E. Failure to remain in tucked position
  F. Inability to perform consecutive rolls
  G. Feeling dizzy
  H. Failure to roll in a straight line
  I. Lack of sufficient momentum to complete one revolution

FIGURE 18.6   Developmental sequence for body rolling.

Initial

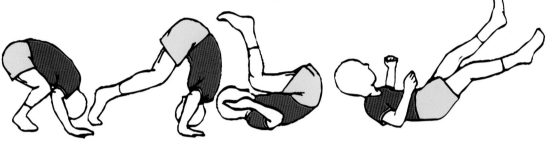

Elementary

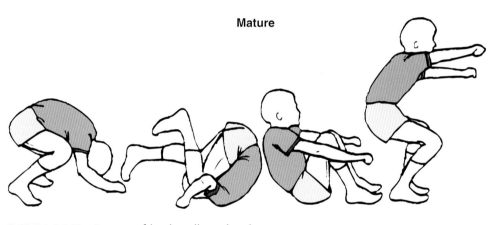

Mature

FIGURE 18.7   Stages of body rolling development.

These Hillsdale Elementary School students are at the intermediate level of movement skill learning as they perform a forward roll down an incline mat. These students need to tuck their chins to their chests more so that the top of their heads do not touch the mat and learn to recover with their knees tucked tightly to their chests.

When teaching *body rolling:*

- A grassy area or carpet is adequate if mats are not available.

- Provide careful spotting whenever needed.

- It is not necessary to spot every child individually. If individual spotting is desired, show the children how it is done.

- When spotting is used, insist that it be careful.

- Work crossways on the mats to permit maximum practice.

- Use a block of wood and a tennis ball to demonstrate the difference between a round object (our curled body) and a nonrounded object (our uncurled body) during rolling.

- Set up four or five mat stations (forward roll mat, backward roll mat, combination mat, advanced mat, and trouble mat), stationing yourself wherever children need specific instruction.

- Begin with an exploratory approach, but be sure the movement challenges that you present are within the ability level of your children.

- Use a guided discovery approach to facilitate an understanding of why the body moves as it does and how it moves when rolling.

- Children are often at diverse levels of ability within a class. Be sure to provide experiences that meet the individual needs of each child. This will require diversity and creativity in teaching.

BODY ROLLING CONCEPTS CHILDREN SHOULD KNOW

Skill concepts:

- Stay tucked in a small ball throughout your roll.

- Use your hands to support or push off so as little of your head touches the floor as possible.

- Keep your chin against your chest.

- Push off evenly with both hands.

- If you stay tucked during your roll, you can come all the way back to your starting position.

- Focus your eyes on an object in front of or behind you to help you roll in a straight line.

- Rolling is basic to the sports of gymnastics and diving and plays an important part in wrestling and the martial arts.

Movement concepts:

- You can roll in many directions.

- You can roll from different levels.

- You can roll using a variety of body positions.

- You can roll with objects and with people.

- You can roll at different speeds and with different amounts of force.

- Your roll can use different shapes—wide, narrow, bent.

- You can combine rolling with a variety of other activities.

Dodging

Dodging is a fundamental movement skill common to the game, sport, and play activities of children and adults. Dodging is similar to sliding, but dodging is often accompanied by running and involves quick, deceptive changes in direction. In the running dodge the knees bend, the center of gravity moves lower, and the body weight is shifted rapidly in a sideways direction. Dodging may occur from a stationary position and may involve a number of axial movements, including bending, twisting, stretching, or falling (see figures 18.8 and 18.9).

At Mary C. Howse Elementary School the student guarding the player with the ball demonstrates dynamic balance, while the player with the ball must dodge her opponent.

TEACHING TIP 18.4

When teaching *dodging*:

- Stress bending at the knees in anticipation of dodging.
- Begin with activities that require changing direction on a cue or verbal command.
- Explore various aspects of dodging in conjunction with effort, space, and relationships.
- Avoid dodgeball activities as a central focus of the lesson.
- Use a limited number of dodgeball-type activities, but only after the child has reached the mature level. Always use a foam ball or a partially deflated ball.
- Stress the necessity for quickness and deception.
- Work on dodging in all directions. Avoid activities in which only one direction is stressed.
- You may effectively combine dodging as a skill theme with running and leaping or with throwing and catching.

I. Dodging
   A. Initial stage
      1. Segmented movements
      2. Body appears stiff
      3. Minimal knee bend
      4. Weight is on one foot
      5. Feet generally cross
      6. No deception
   B. Elementary stage
      1. Movements coordinated but with little deception
      2. Performs better to one side than to the other
      3. Too much vertical lift
      4. Feet occasionally cross
      5. Little spring in movement
      6. Sometimes outsmarts self and becomes confused
   C. Mature stage
      1. Knees bent, slight trunk lean forward (ready position)
      2. Fluid directional changes
      3. Performs equally well in all directions
      4. Head and shoulder fake
      5. Good lateral movement
II. Developmental difficulties
   A. Inability to shift body weight in a fluid manner in direction of dodge
   B. Slow change of direction
   C. Crossing of feet
   D. Hesitation
   E. Too much vertical lift
   F. Total-body lead
   G. Inability to perform several dodging actions in rapid succession
   H. Monitoring of body
   I. Rigid posture

FIGURE 18.8   Developmental sequence for dodging.

Dodging is an important element in chasing and fleeing games. It is an important element in several sports, such as basketball, soccer, and lacrosse. Because of the natural combination of running with dodging, you may wish to group these two movement patterns into a common skill theme.

Initial

Elementary

Mature

FIGURE 18.9   Stages of the dodging pattern.

DODGING CONCEPTS CHILDREN SHOULD KNOW

Skill concepts:

- Stop your movement suddenly and shift your body weight rapidly to one side.
- Keep your center of gravity low for better balance.
- Keep your center of gravity over your base of support for balance, but put your body weight outside your base momentarily to dodge with quickness and deception.
- Turn your head, shoulders, eyes, or trunk to face the new direction of your intended movement.

(continued on following page)

(continued from preceding page)

Movement concepts:

- You can alter the effort that you use in your dodging to fit the demands of the situation.
- Your dodge can be altered in the amount of force applied, speed of performance, and flow.
- You can alter the space in which you dodge from place to place.
- You can dodge in different directions and at different levels.

CONCEPT 18.7

A variety of exploratory and guided discovery activities can be effectively used in developing the stability abilities of individuals at the initial and elementary stages.

SKILL DEVELOPMENT ACTIVITIES

Before you select specific **stability skill development** activities for a lesson, you will need to determine the typical stage of motor development displayed by the class. This will also provide important cues to your students' level of movement skill learning. With this information, you will be able to determine whether the lesson should focus on exploratory and guided discovery activities, skill application activities, or skill refinement activities.

Exploratory Activities

With **stability exploratory activities,** students at the initial or elementary stage of developing their stability abilities have an opportunity to learn how their bodies can balance alone and in relation to other objects or people. Exploration of the movement elements of effort, space, and relationships helps children develop a more complete idea of their stability potentials. Tables 18.1 and 18.2 provide a sampling of exploratory ideas for body rolling and for dodging. The same types of exploratory experiences may be used with a wide range of static and dynamic balance skills.

Guided Discovery Activities

The **stability guided discovery activities** in figures 18.10 and 18.11 comprise various problem-solving activities that will enhance rolling and dodging abilities. With guided discovery activities, children at the intermediate level of learning a new stability skill get the opportunity to practice the skill, learn more about it, and focus on it in a variety of movement situations. An infinite variety of guided discovery activity ideas can easily be devised for all types of static and dynamic balance skills.

SKILL APPLICATION ACTIVITIES

Once children have developed basic abilities to balance their bodies in static and dynamic situations, it is appropriate to begin focusing on **stability skill applica-**

TABLE 18.1 — EXPLORATORY ACTIVITY IDEAS FOR BODY ROLLING

Effort awareness	Space awareness	Relationship awareness
Force	**Level**	**Objects**
Can you roll . . . – as quietly as you can? – as loudly as you can? – so I cannot hear you? – (rock) back and forth very hard? – (rock) very softly?	*Can you roll . . .* – from as low as you can go? – from as high as you can go? – in a medium position?	*Can you roll . . .* – on the mat? – between the colored panels? – through the hoop? – down the mat? – over the rolled mat? – on the bench? – while holding onto a ball?
Time	**Direction**	**People**
– very quickly? – very slowly? – in slow motion? – at your regular speed? – (rock) quickly? – (rock) slowly?	– forward? – sideways? – backward? – in a straight line?	– with a partner? – at the same time as your partner? – together? – and move apart? – like twins?
Flow	**Range**	**Combinations**
– in a tight ball? – in four separate steps? – in one smooth motion? – in a jerky motion? – (rock) to my beat?	– from a wide base? – from a narrow base? – in your own space? – with your head touching the ground? – without your head touching the mat?	After you have provided ample opportunities for students to explore the various elements of rolling, you may want to combine them. For example, "Can you roll forward with a wide base from a high level?"

tion activities. Static and dynamic balance abilities can be developed through practice in a variety of educational gymnastic challenges using different types and sizes of equipment. Stability skills may be applied to a number of game- and dance-related activities. Chapter 22 highlights several skill themes related to dance activities, and chapter 23 highlights several skill themes related to gymnastics activities.

SAMPLE STABILITY GAMES

Although most games of low organization are thought of as locomotor or manipulative games, several activities can help to develop and reinforce fundamental stability abilities. Many of the stability games that follow use locomotor or manipulative tasks,

TABLE 18.2—EXPLORATORY ACTIVITY IDEAS FOR DODGING

Effort awareness	Space awareness	Relationship awareness
Force	**Level**	**Objects**
Can you dodge . . . – with great force? – with no force? – with some force?	*Can you dodge . . .* – from a high level? – from a low level? – from a high to a low level? – from a low to a high level? – keeping yourself at a medium level?	*Can you dodge . . .* – a fleece ball? – a playground ball? – a tossed ball? – a rolled ball?
Time	**Direction**	**People**
– as quickly as you can? – as slowly as you can? – alternating fast and slow dodges? – at a medium speed? – with a burst of energy?	– in different directions? – sideways? – to your left? – to your right? – backward? – forward?	– a person chasing you from behind? – a person in front of you? – in the same direction as your partner? – in the opposite direction as your partner?
Flow	**Range**	**Combinations**
– smoothly? – roughly?	– and concentrate on making different body shapes? – while staying in your own space? – and assess all the space you need? – while on one foot? – without using your arms?	After you have provided ample opportunities for students to explore the various elements of dodging, you may want to combine them. For example, "Can you dodge a rolled ball as quickly as you can from a low level to a high level?

CONCEPT 18.8

Skill application activities involving low-level games can be used effectively with individuals who have mastered the prerequisite skills.

but their primary feature is that they stress one or more aspects of stability (see table 18.3). Several tag games are included. Tag is a great activity for reinforcing dodging and feinting skills. Most tag games can be adapted to the particular skill and interest level of the group. These are the primary objectives of the **stability game activities** that follow:

- To enhance fundamental stability abilities
- To improve dynamic and static balance abilities
- To promote body, space, and directional awareness
- To foster cooperative behaviors

1. First explore several of the movement variations and combinations of rolling.

2. Then begin to place limitations on the response possibilities to the following movement challenges:

General
    a. Try rocking back and forth from many different positions. How many ways can you find? Did you notice anything special when you were rocking on your front, or your back, or your side? Did you keep your body straight or did you curve your body? Why?

Trunk
    b. Does your head do anything special when you rock? Why do you think you tuck your chin in when you rock on your back or from side to side? Try it with your head up. Does it work as well? Why not?

    c. When we do a forward roll, do we keep our body curved or straight? Can anyone show me how curved you make your body when getting ready for a forward roll?

Head
    d. What do you do with your head? Do you keep it up or curve it way down to your chest? Show me how your body and your head look when you do your forward roll. Practice rolling.

Arms
    e. What do we do with our hands and arms when we roll forward? Try it, and then tell me. So our hands help us? How? See if you can use your hands more as you roll. Try it.

Feet
    f. Can our feet help us when we roll? What can they do? Why does a good push-off help? Show me.

Combination
    g. Let's put it all together. Make a tight ball with your body and head, push off with your feet, and use your hands to catch your weight as you come over.

Finish
    h. If we want to come right back to our feet, what should we do? Try it. Can you get to your feet, without using your hands to push you off?

3. After the mature rolling pattern comes under the child's control, provide numerous opportunities for varying the pattern and combining it with other activities.

    a. Consecutive forward rolls.

    b. Wide-base forward rolls.

    c. One-handed rolls.

    d. Non-handed rolls.

    e. Rolls along a bench.

    f. Partner rolls (Eskimo rolls).

You will also find it helpful to introduce the sideways and backward rolls, using many of the same activities used for the forward roll. Variations and combinations of these body-rolling patterns also can be elaborated on once the mature stage has been obtained.

    a. Backward roll to a squat.

    b. Backward roll to a stand.

    c. Backward straddle roll.

    d. Backward roll to a momentary handstand.

    e. Combination forward and backward rolls.

FIGURE 18.10   Guided discovery activity ideas for body rolling.

1. First have the students explore several variations of dodging. Then begin to place limitations on the response possibilities to the following movement challenges:

General

a. Can you run forward and change direction quickly? Try it while running backward and sideways. What do you do when you change directions quickly? Do you do the same thing when moving in different directions? Why?

Leg action

b. Try to tag your partner who is facing you. How does your partner try to avoid your touch? What does she or he do with the feet and legs? Why are the knees bent and the feet apart? Now you try it, but try dodging your partner's touch from a position with your legs straight and starting with your feet together. Which way do you think works better? Try both ways. You're right, but why is it better to dodge from a standing position with your feet apart and your knees bent?

c. Now try dodging your partner while being chased. How do you avoid being tagged? When you dodge to the right, what do you do with your legs? Why does your right leg step out to one side as you pivot? Show me how you can do it to the opposite side.

d. Do you find it easier to dodge from a run in one direction than the other? Why? Let's practice dodging to our weak side.

Faking

e. From a position facing your partner, try to avoid his or her tags while using deceptive (feinting) movements of your head, eyes, or trunk. Does it work? What do you do with these body parts when you want to fake out your partner? Look at your starting position. Are your feet apart and your knees slightly bent? Don't forget to use that as your ready position, and then use other body parts to give the impression that you are going one way when you actually are going to the other.

2. When the mature dodging action has been reasonably well mastered, combine dodging with other activities. Often children can dodge satisfactorily in an isolated experience. However, when placed in a situation that requires them to dodge an oncoming object or in a complicated game in which dodging is only one of many elements of the game, children often become confused and unable to dodge with proficiency. Activities such as the ones that follow will help develop more integrated use of dodging.

a. Dodge one or more persons while running across the playfield.

b. Dodge oncoming objects. Be sure to use foam balls.

c. Use dodging maneuvers to advance a ball downfield or down court. You can run, dribble, or kick a ball while dodging.

FIGURE 18.11   Guided discovery activity ideas for dodging.

Scarf Tag or Rip-Flag Tag

Movement Skills

Dynamic balance, dodging, and feinting. Prerequisite skill is the ability to control one's body while moving through general space among other players (moving to music around polyspots and stopping on cue, bending knees, lowering center of gravity, etc.).

TABLE 18.3—SELECTED STABILITY GAMES SEQUENCED IN TERMS OF COMPLEXITY

Game title	Dodging/ Feinting	Dynamic balance	Static balance	Axial movements
Scarf Tag	X	X	X	X
Beanbag Boogie		X	X	X
Crazy Shape Tag	X	X	X	X
Mirror Touch Tag	X		X	
Grab the Goodies!		X		X
Travel to the Center of the Earth	X	X		X
Fly Trap				X
Lightning Quick!		X		X

Movement Concepts

Space: direction changes. Effort: changes in speed. Relationships: moving with other players.

Formation

Scatter formation; small groups of 8 to 10 students per play area.

Equipment

Several scarves or rip flags (new rip flags actually make a "popping" sound when stolen). Have more of these than the number of students in the class.

Procedures

All players are "it." The goal is to take another player's rip flag or scarf off of his belt (or waist). Dynamic balance is developed as children twist, turn, and dodge each other in order to prevent having their scarf or flag taken. If a player's scarf or flag is taken, that player can go over to a designated area (hula hoop off to side of play area) and get another scarf or rip flag. All players remain in the game at all times.

Beanbag Boogie

Movement Skills

Dynamic balance, leading with different body parts.

Movement Concepts

Space: level changes, direction changes. Effort: slow, controlled. Relationships: moving with other players and equipment.

Formation

Scattered.

Equipment

Obstacles and beanbags.

Procedures

Children place a beanbag on any body part and attempt to move through an obstacle course. The children could also construct the obstacle course, using foam shapes to move through, cones with ropes across them to go under, mats or shapes to go over, and so forth.

Crazy Shape Tag

Movement Skills

Balancing on different body parts, running/fast walking.

Movement Concepts

Space: general and personal space, levels, direction, pathways. Effort: slow, medium, fast. Relationships: moving with other players.

Formation

Scattered within a bounded space.

Equipment

Cones.

Procedures

Within each group of players, one or more are designated to be "it." Cards with numbers written on them have been placed on cones. When a player is tagged, that player balances on the number of body parts designated on the cone closest to where the player was tagged. To set a tagged player free, another player who has not been tagged matches the tagged player's shape. Then both players are free to begin play again. A possible variation is for the teacher to designate specific balances a player must perform when tagged. The teacher must change the player or players who are "it."

Mirror Touch Tag

Movement Skills

Dodging, feinting, and balancing.

Movement Concepts

Space: general and personal, levels, directions, pathways. Effort: fast, medium, slow. Relationships: moving with other players.

Formation

Scatter formation.

Equipment

None.

Procedures

One player is "it" and tries to touch another player. Players are "safe" when they are performing a counterbalance (hands to hands, shoulder to shoulder, back to back, etc.). The teacher could designate the counterbalance to be performed, or players could decide on their own. After holding the counterbalance for 5 seconds, players are free to resume play. The player or players designated to be "it" must be periodically changed by the teacher.

Grab the Goodies!

Movement Skills

Dynamic balance, walking/running.

Movement Concepts

Space: personal. Effort: quick, sharp, controlled. Relationships: moving with players and equipment.

Formation

Groups of four to six players; two players, "Xs," are positioned about 20 yards apart. Other two to four players, "Os," are between the players who are Xs:

X   O   O   X

Equipment

Beanbags or "the goodies."

Procedures

Players designated as Xs each have a beanbag placed on the floor between their legs. These players assume a wide base of support. Players designated as Os attempt to take the beanbag or the "goodies" out from between the legs of the Xs. A player who is successful at grabbing a beanbag then becomes a "defensive" player or an X. The X whose beanbag was taken becomes an O. The beanbag is placed back on the floor between the new defensive player's legs. As Os attempt to grab a beanbag, they should not touch any part of an X's body.

Travel to the Center of the Earth

Movement Skills

Dodging/dynamic balance, walking/running.

Movement Concepts

Space: personal, direction. Effort: quick changes. Relationships: moving within circles and with other players.

Formation

Three concentric circles.

Equipment

Polyspots.

Procedures

Three or more concentric circles are created on the floor with polyspots. Two or more defensive players are positioned within each circle. Offensive players (three to four), the "geologists," attempt to move through the circles and make it to the center circle, or the center of the earth! Defensive players, "aliens," attempt to tag the offensive players.

Fly Trap

Movement Skills

Axial movements.

Movement Concepts

Space: general/personal, extensions of body. Effort: quick with sudden slow to stop. Relationships: moving with other players.

Formation

Scatter, with half the players seated cross-legged.

Equipment

None.

Procedures

The players who are seated are the "traps." The remaining players are the "flies." The flies run throughout the traps, being sure to stay in the designated playing area. On the teacher's signal to "freeze," the flies immediately stop. The traps, from their seated position, stretch out and try to touch the flies. If a fly is touched, she changes places with that trap. The game continues.

Lightning Quick!

Movement Skills

Shift of weight, trapping a ball with body.

Movement Concepts

Space: personal, level changes, body extensions. Effort: quick changes. Relationships: moving with an object.

Formation

Two players per goal area.

Equipment

"Goals," foam ball or indoor soccer ball, gator-skin balls.

Procedures

Two players, one offensive and one defensive; or three players, one offensive and two defensive. Offensive player attempts to roll a ball into the designated goal area (width of goal should be developmentally appropriate). The defensive player or players attempt to react to the oncoming ball by shifting their weight quickly and trapping the oncoming ball with their body.

ASSESSING FUNDAMENTAL STABILITY SKILLS

Ongoing assessment of children's stability skills will help teachers in planning lessons as well as in evaluating the effectiveness of their instruction. Figure 18.12 is an example of authentic assessment technique (discussed in chapter 12). It provides a

	Yes	No	Comments

One-foot balance

1. Can the child balance for 30 seconds on one foot?
2. Does the child make adjustments with the arms as needed to maintain balance?
3. Can the child balance for 10 seconds with both eyes closed?
4. Does the child keep the nonsupport leg free?
5. Does the child focus forward rather than downward?
6. Can the child balance on either foot?
7. Is there observable improvement?

Beam walk

1. Can the child walk unaided across a 10-foot-long beam that is 4 inches wide?
2. Does the child use an alternating step?
3. Can the child travel backward and sideways as well as forward?
4. Does the child focus forward rather than downward?
5. Can the child use both arms to compensate for changes in balance?
6. Can the child easily change levels and directions?
7. Can the child walk independently of a spotter?
8. Is there observable improvement?

Body rolling (forward, backward, and/or sideways)

1. Does the child curve the body adequately?
2. Does the child tuck the head?
3. Does the child push off evenly with both feet?
4. Does the child take the body weight on the hands and arms?
5. Do the head and body stay tucked in throughout the roll?
6. Is the child able to keep the front and top of the head from touching the mat?
7. Can the child come to his or her feet unaided immediately after the roll?
8. Is the child able to travel in a straight line?
9. Can the child perform consecutive rolls?
10. Is there observable improvement?

Dodging

1. Can the child dodge a partner from a facing position?
2. Can the child effectively dodge a partner from a fleeing position?
3. Does the child dodge well in all directions?
4. Is the child able to combine dodging with other game skills?
5. Does the child use deceptive movements when dodging?
6. Is the action quick, fluid, and in control?
7. Is there observable improvement?

FIGURE 18.12 Self-questions chart for fundamental stability skill development.

series of questions that you can use to do an initial assessment of children's current stage of stability skill development. Chapter 12, "Assessing Progress," provides a wealth of information on assessing children's progress in physical education.

Summary

Stability is the most basic of the three categories of movement. All locomotor and manipulative movements involve an element of stability. Therefore, it is essential for teachers to put considerable time and effort into planning and implementing stability skill themes. It is critically important that the sequencing of skills progress from axial movements to upright supports, then from upright springing skills to inverted supports, and finally to inverted springing skills.

Children need to learn a variety of movement concepts and skill concepts associated with dynamic and static balance in general and with specific stability skills. You will need to ensure that fundamental stability abilities are developed and refined in conjunction with fundamental locomotor and manipula-

tive skills. You should also make sure that these concepts and abilities are integrated in a way that encourages motor control and movement coordination.

Exploratory and guided discovery activities are especially beneficial for children at the initial and elementary stages in the development of their fundamental stability skills. These types of activities permit children to experiment with the movement potential of their bodies and to problem-solve for themselves essential concepts of both dynamic and static balance. Children who have mastered the essential aspects of stability benefit from various skill application activities that permit them to use their stability abilities in a myriad of related low-level games. Remember, however, not to focus on skill application too early in the learning process. It is essential that children master stability skills and related locomotor and manipulative skills in terms of body mechanics before moving on to other important aspects.

Terms to Remember

Excellent Readings

Belka, D. (1993). Educational gymnastics: Recommendations for elementary physical education. *TEPE, 4,* 1–6.

Hammett, C. Totsky. (1992). *Movement activities for early childhood.* Champaign, IL: Human Kinetics.

Pica, R. (1993). *Upper elementary children moving and learning.* Champaign, IL: Human Kinetics.

Pica, R. (1994). *Early elementary children moving and learning.* Champaign, IL: Human Kinetics.

Rikard, G.L. (1992). Developmentally appropriate gymnastics for children. *JOPERD, 63, 44–46.*

Torbert, M., & Schneider, L.B. (1994). *Follow me too: A handbook of movement activities for three-to-five year olds.* Reading, MA: Addison-Wesley.

Wall, J., & Murray, N. (1990). *Children and movement.* Dubuque, IA: Brown.

19

Fundamental Locomotor and Non-Locomotor Skill Themes

Key Concept

▶ Mature fundamental locomotor and non-locomotor skills may be developed through a skill theme approach that uses a variety of appropriate movement experiences.

Chapter Objectives

This chapter will provide you with the tools to do the following:

▶ List and describe the steps in planning and conducting a locomotor movement skill theme.

▶ Describe essential aspects of several fundamental locomotor movement patterns at the initial, elementary, and mature stages.

▶ Provide the skill concepts for several fundamental locomotor movements.

▶ Describe fundamental non-locomotor skill themes.

▶ Become familiar with several skill application activities appropriate for children who are acquiring fundamental locomotor and non-locomotor skills.

Total-body movements in which the body is propelled in an upright posture from one point to another in a roughly horizontal or vertical direction are called **locomotor skills**. Movements such as walking, running, leaping, jumping, hopping, skipping, galloping, and sliding are generally considered to be fundamental locomotor skills. **Non-locomotor skills** include bending, stretching, twisting, and curling actions. These actions do not travel through space but are performed within one's personal space at a high, medium, or low level. Both locomotor and non-locomotor skills are necessary for purposeful and controlled movement through our environment and are basic to the numerous skills necessary for games, dance, and gymnastics activities.

Locomotor and non-locomotor skills do not develop automatically. Although there may be a **phylogenetic** (hereditary) basis for the appearance of the initial and even the elementary stage of several fundamental locomotor movements, attainment of the mature stage depends on **ontogenetic** (environmental) factors. Factors within the environment, such as opportunities for practice, encouragement, and

instruction, play a major role in the acquisition of mature patterns of locomotor movement. If people fail to develop these mature skills, they will have great difficulty in achieving acceptable levels of performance during the specialized movement skill phase of locomotor skill development. This chapter examines the importance of skill sequencing and the process of developing fundamental locomotor skill themes. We examine several locomotor skills and provide verbal and visual descriptions for each, as well as the concepts that children should know (Gallahue & Ozmun, 2002). We also provide teaching tips applicable to locomotor skill development and a sampling of appropriate skill development activities. This chapter concludes with a sampling of locomotor and non-locomotor game ideas.

LOCOMOTOR SKILL SEQUENCING

Although children are generally considered to have the developmental potential to perform most fundamental locomotor skills at the mature stage by age six or seven, in fact this is often not the case. Because of many factors, elementary school children often exhibit immature fundamental movement patterns. As a general rule, children at the preschool and primary grade level benefit most from a progressive program of fundamental locomotor skill development. But numerous children in the upper grades can also be identified as exhibiting immature stages of development in several locomotor skills.

It is important to know where your students are in terms of their locomotor skill development if you are to plan effectively for all. Remember, **skill sequencing** is a process of building skill upon skill. This means that you will need to carefully analyze the complexity of the skills and the activities in which they are to be incorporated.

RUNNING AND LEAPING

The running and leaping patterns begin developing early in childhood. Around the first birthday, the infant achieves an upright gait and begins to walk. Skill in walking develops rapidly until about age six, by which time a child's walking pattern resembles an adult's in many ways. It is important, though, to monitor the child's walking posture and provide movement experiences that help her focus on the proper walking pattern. The child is attempting to **run** by the age of 18 months, but there is no flight phase (phase in which the body is airborne). The initial attempts at running resemble a fast walk. A flight phase, marking the onset of true running, generally appears between the second and third birthday. With proper amounts of practice, encouragement, and instruction, the running pattern should continue to improve and should reach the mature stage by age seven.

Leaping is a fundamental movement that may be viewed as an extension of the running pattern. The development of mature leaping is dependent somewhat on efficient running. The **leap** is similar to the run except that a longer flight phase is involved and the leap is usually performed as a single rather than a repeated skill. In

TEXT BOX 19.1

Developing a Locomotor Skill Theme

To make the most efficient use of your time, the following sequence is recommended:

1. Preplan.
   a. Determine what locomotor skills will be grouped together for each skill theme. The following works well:
      1) Running and leaping
      2) Jumping and hopping
      3) Galloping, sliding, and skipping
   b. Determine when to include each locomotor skill theme in the yearly curriculum. You will need to consider whether to space out lessons on each skill over the entire school year (distributed practice) or to group lessons together into concentrated units of instruction (massed practice).
   c. Decide on the approximate total number of lessons that you will spend on locomotor skill development in relation to the entire curriculum.

2. Observe and assess.
   a. Observe fundamental locomotor abilities of the children to be taught.
   b. Assess whether children are at an initial, elementary, mature, or sport skill stage in each of the skills to be included as a skill theme. Study the verbal and visual descriptions for each locomotor skill on the following pages for help with this.

3. Plan and implement.
   a. Plan appropriate movement activities geared to the needs, interests, and ability levels of the group. For guidance, study the teaching tips and concepts children should know on the pages that follow.
   b. Implement a planned program of activities, stressing progression in skill development.

4. Evaluate and revise.
   a. Formally or informally evaluate progress in the locomotor skills being stressed in terms of improved mechanics (process) and performance (product). The questions in figure 19.25 at the end of this chapter will be helpful.
   b. Revise subsequent lessons as needed, based on student progress.

other words, when you leap, you do so either from a stationary position or following a run. It is possible to perform consecutive leaps, but a momentary hesitation from one leap to the next is easily observable in all but the most skilled. Leaping is used in the play and recreational activities of children (hopscotch, crossing a brook). Leaping is also a part of creative dance and developmental gymnastics activities; and it is used in combination with several manipulative skills, as in leaping into kicking on goal in soccer and leaping over a hurdle in track and field. Because the movement patterns of leaping and running are basic to our everyday activities, it is

This young boy demonstrates an elementary stage run.

This young lady demonstrates a mature stage leap as she soars through the air.

essential that they be developed to the mature level. Once the mature pattern has been attained, these skills may be applied to various educational games, dance, and gymnastics content. Practice in running and leaping will enhance one's performance abilities. Speed and endurance will also continue to improve with practice and will enable the individual to use these abilities in a variety of sport skills.

Running

Running is what children do. When given the chance, it's their preferred mode of moving from one place to another. In physical activity settings, your responsibility is

TEACHING TIP 19.1

When teaching *running*:

- Determine the characteristic stage in running ability.
- Plan activities designed to move the child to the next stage.
- Include plenty of activities involving movement exploration at the beginning level of skill learning.
- Work on good listening skills during running.

- Use the commands "freeze" and "melt" to develop listening skills.
- Stress not bumping into others.
- Stress stopping without sliding on the knees.
- For tagging games, teach proper tagging techniques.
- Incorporate activities that gradually increase aerobic capacity.
- Provide a wide variety of running activities.

to provide frequent opportunities, supportive encouragement, and fun reasons for running. Keep in mind: *If we make it fun, they will run.* As teachers, our responsibility is to provide developmentally appropriate activities that are enjoyable and encourage the fitness benefit of running but that also help children learn how to run with greater efficiency and control (see figures 19.1 and 19.2).

I. Running
   A. Initial stage
      1. Short, limited leg swing
      2. Stiff, uneven stride
      3. No observable flight phase
      4. Incomplete extension of support leg
      5. Stiff, short swing with varying degrees of elbow flexion
      6. Arms tend to swing outward horizontally
      7. Swinging leg rotates outward from hips
      8. Swinging foot toes outward
      9. Wide base of support
   B. Elementary stage
      1. Increase in length of stride, arm swing, and speed
      2. Limited but observable flight phase
      3. More complete extension of support leg at takeoff
      4. Arm swing increases
      5. Horizontal arm swing reduced on back swing
      6. Swinging foot crosses midline at height of recovery to rear
   C. Mature stage
      1. Stride length at maximum; stride speed fast
      2. Definite flight phase
      3. Complete extension of support leg
      4. Recovery thigh parallel to ground
      5. Arms swing vertically in opposition to legs
      6. Arms bent at approximate right angles
      7. Minimal rotary action at recovery leg and foot
II. Developmental difficulties
   A. Inhibited or exaggerated arm swing
   B. Arms crossing the midline of the body
   C. Improper foot placement
   D. Exaggerated forward trunk lean
   E. Arms flopping at the sides or held out for balance
   F. Twisting of the trunk
   G. Poor rhythmical action
   H. Landing flat-footed
   I. Flipping the foot or lower leg in or out

FIGURE 19.1   Development sequence for running.

Initial

Elementary

Mature

FIGURE 19.2   Stages of the running pattern.

RUNNING CONCEPTS CHILDREN SHOULD KNOW

Skill concepts:

- Keep your head up when you run.
- Lean into your run slightly.
- Lift your knees.
- Bend your elbows and swing the arms freely.
- Contact the ground with your heels first.
- Push off from the balls of your feet.
- Run lightly.
- Running is good for your heart and lungs.
- Your stride length is determined by the force of your push-off.

(continued on following page)

(continued from preceding page)

Movement concepts:

- You can run at many different speeds and levels.
- You can land heavily or lightly.
- Your run can be smooth or jerky.
- You can run in many different directions and paths.
- Your leg speed is influenced by your arm speed.
- The length of your running stride is determined by the force of your push-off.

I. Leaping
  A. Initial stage
    1. Child appears confused in attempts
    2. Inability to push off and gain distance and elevation
    3. Each attempt looks like another running step
    4. Inconsistent use of takeoff leg
    5. Arms ineffective
  B. Elementary stage
    1. Appears to be thinking through the action
    2. Attempt looks like an elongated run
    3. Little elevation above support surface
    4. Little forward trunk lean
    5. Stiff appearance in trunk
    6. Incomplete extension of legs during flight
    7. Arms used for balance, not as an aid in force production
  C. Mature stage
    1. Relaxed rhythmical action
    2. Forceful extension of takeoff leg
    3. Good summation of horizontal and vertical forces
    4. Definite forward trunk lean
    5. Definite arm opposition
    6. Full extension of legs during flight
II. Developmental difficulties
  A. Failure to use arms in opposition to legs
  B. Inability to perform one-foot takeoff and land on opposite foot
  C. Restricted movements of arms or legs
  D. Lack of spring and elevation in push-off
  E. Landing flat-footed
  F. Exaggerated or inhibited body lean
  G. Failure to stretch and reach with legs

FIGURE 19.3 Developmental sequence for leaping.

Leaping

Leaping is a skill much like running but involving a longer flight phase in taking off on one foot and landing on the other (see figures 19.3 and 19.4). Leaping is an exhilarating experience for children, and the use of imagery enhances the experi-

Initial

Elementary

Mature

FIGURE 19.4 Stages of the leaping pattern.

When teaching *leaping:*

- Provide definite objects or barriers to leap over.
- Combine leaping with two or three running steps.
- Have children leap over very low objects and then higher objects up to midthigh level.
- Encourage leading with either foot.

- Young children enjoy imagery when leaping "over deep canyons," "across raging rivers," or simply "over the brook."
- Use Velcro® straps or other devices that give way if the child comes in contact with the object he is leaping over.

LEAPING CONCEPTS CHILDREN SHOULD KNOW

Skill concepts:

- Push upward and forward with your rear foot.
- Stretch and reach with your forward foot.
- Keep your head up.
- Lean forward at the trunk as you leap.
- Alternate your arm action with your leg action.
- Push off of your back foot to extend trail leg.

Movement concepts:

- Push upward and forward with your rear foot.
- Stretch and reach with your forward foot.
- Keep your head up.
- Lean forward at the trunk as you leap.
- Alternate your arm action with your leg action.
- Push off of your back leg to extend trail leg.

---

ence. Leaping over "raging rivers" and "deep crevasses" adds to the excitement of being airborne for an extended period of time.

JUMPING AND HOPPING

Jumping and hopping are fundamental movement skills that are used in a variety of sport, recreational, and daily living experiences. Jumping and hopping may take many forms, all of which involve a takeoff, a flight phase, and a landing. A **jump** differs from a hop in that a jump involves taking off on one or both feet and landing on both feet, whereas a **hop** involves taking off on one foot and landing on the same foot. Jumping may occur in a roughly horizontal plane, in a vertical plane, or from a height. Hopping may occur in place, or it may occur over a roughly horizontal plane.

The fundamental movement patterns of jumping and hopping are basic to numerous games, dance, and gymnastics activities. It is essential for people to attain the mature stage of each of these patterns at an early date. Once a child has achieved the mature stage, the teacher and the child may begin to focus on improved performance scores and combine hopping and jumping with a variety of other locomotor and manipulative skills.

Horizontal Jumping

The horizontal jump is often used for the purpose of jumping for distance and is executed from one to two feet or two to two feet (see figures 19.5 and 19.6). As a fundamental locomotor skill, it can be practiced on the gymnasium floor, over low obstacles, or outside. A running approach is typically used when jumping from one to two feet. This combination skill is used in educational gymnastics when taking off of a springboard and later in the running long jump, an event in the sport of track and field.

This fifth grade student at Hillsdale Elementary School demonstrates a horizontal jump. At what stage of development is this jump?

I. Horizontal jumping
  A. Initial stage
    1. Limited swing; arms do not initiate jumping action
    2. During flight, arms move sideward-downward or rearward-upward to maintain balance
    3. Trunk moves in vertical direction; little emphasis on length of jump
    4. Preparatory crouch inconsistent in terms of leg flexion
    5. Difficulty in using both feet
    6. Limited extension of the ankles, knees, and hips at takeoff
    7. Body weight falls backward at landing
  B. Elementary stage
    1. Arms initiate jumping action
    2. Arms remain toward front of body during preparatory crouch
    3. Arms move out to side to maintain balance during flight
    4. Preparatory crouch deeper and more consistent
    5. Knee and hip extension more complete at takeoff
    6. Hips flexed during flight; thighs held in flexed position
  C. Mature stage
    1. Arms move high and to the rear during preparatory crouch
    2. During takeoff, arms swing forward with force and reach high
    3. Arms held high throughout jumping action
    4. Trunk propelled at approximately 45-degree angle
    5. Major emphasis on horizontal distance
    6. Preparatory crouch deep, consistent
    7. Complete extension of ankles, knees, and hips at takeoff
    8. Thighs held parallel to ground during flight; lower leg lands vertically
    9. Body weight forward at landing
II. Developmental difficulties
  A. Improper use of arms (that is, failure to use arms opposite the propelling leg in a down-up-down swing as leg flexes, extends, and flexes again)
  B. Twisting or jerking of body
  C. Inability to perform either a one-foot or a two-foot takeoff
  D. Poor preliminary crouch
  E. Restricted movement of arms or legs
  F. Poor angle of takeoff
  G. Failure to extend fully on takeoff
  H. Failure to extend legs forward on landing
  I. Falling backward on landing

FIGURE 19.5   Developmental sequence for horizontal jumping.

Initial

Elementary

Mature

FIGURE 19.6   Stages of the horizontal jumping pattern.

TEACHING TIP 19.3

When teaching *horizontal jumping:*

- Start with exploratory activities and progress to more directed techniques as skill develops.
- Children should not jump in socks or in gym shoes with poor traction.
- Use carpet squares or newspapers as a challenge for children to jump over.
- Emphasize the coordinated use of the arms and legs.

- Children like to measure the length of their jump. This is a good time to reinforce measuring with a yardstick or meter stick.
- See if children can jump a distance equal to their height.
- Have children try jumping from various types of surfaces. Discuss differences.

JUMPING AND HOPPING CONCEPTS CHILDREN SHOULD KNOW

Skill concepts:

- Crouch halfway down.
- Swing your arms back and then forward forcefully.
- Explode forward from a coiled position.
- Push off so that your toes leave the ground last.
- Stretch and reach forward.
- Bring your knees to your chest as you prepare to land.
- Your heels contact first upon landing.
- "Give" with your landing and fall forward.

Movement concepts:

- You can land heavily or lightly, but it is best to land lightly.
- If you swing your arms quickly, you will travel farther than if you swing them slowly.
- Your jump can be smooth or jerky, free or bound.
- You can jump in different directions and at different levels.
- You can combine your jump with other movements.
- You can jump in place, for height, for distance, or from a height.
- A jump requires taking off on one or two feet, but the landing must be on both feet.
- Jumping while holding an object will alter your pattern.

CONCEPT 19.4

Children need to learn both movement concepts and skill concepts—that is, how the body *can* move and how the body *should* move.

Vertical Jumping

Vertical jumping involves taking off on one or both feet in an upward direction and landing on one or both feet. The vertical jump is sometimes used as a measure of explosive strength (power). Although power is involved in vertical jumping, so too is skill and coordination of movement (see figures 19.7 and 19.8).

TEACHING TIP 19.4

When teaching *vertical jumping*:

- Some children may be "earthbound" and require special assistance.
- Stress coordinated action of legs and arms.
- Remind children to stretch and reach with the arms and head as they jump.
- Use plenty of exploratory activities at the initial stage, progressing to more directed techniques as needed.

- Have children try jumping on different surfaces. Inner tubes, mattresses, and trampolines provide exciting experiences.
- Have children chalk their fingers to mark their vertical jumps.
- Have children jump and place a piece of tape to mark their jumps.
- Have children jump up and grab an object, keeping eye contact with the object.

I. Vertical jumping
   A. Initial stage
      1. Inconsistent preparatory crouch
      2. Difficulty in taking off with both feet
      3. Poor body extension on takeoff
      4. Little or no head lift
      5. Arms not coordinated with the trunk and leg action
      6. Little height achieved
   B. Elementary stage
      1. Knee flexion exceeds 90-degree angle on preparatory crouch
      2. Exaggerated forward lean during crouch
      3. Two-foot takeoff
      4. Entire body does not fully extend during flight phase
      5. Arms attempt to aid in flight (but often unequally) and balance
      6. Noticeable horizontal displacement on landing
   C. Mature stage
      1. Preparatory crouch with knee flexion from 60 to 90 degrees
      2. Forceful extension at hips, knees, and ankles
      3. Simultaneous coordinated upward arm lift
      4. Upward head tilt with eyes focused on target
      5. Full body extension
      6. Elevation of reaching arm by shoulder girdle tilt combined with downward thrust of non-reaching arm at peak of flight
      7. Controlled landing very close to point of takeoff
II. Developmental difficulties
   A. Failure to get airborne
   B. Failure to take off with both feet simultaneously
   C. Failure to crouch at about a 90-degree angle
   D. Poor coordination of leg and arm actions
   E. Swinging of arms backward or to the side for balance
   F. Failure to lead with eyes and head
   G. One-foot landing
   H. Inhibited or exaggerated flexion of hips and knees on landing
   I. Marked horizontal displacement on landing

FIGURE 19.7 Developmental sequence for vertical jumping.

Initial

Elementary

Mature

FIGURE 19.8 Stages of the vertical jumping pattern.

VERTICAL JUMPING CONCEPTS CHILDREN SHOULD KNOW

Skill concepts:

- Crouch about halfway down for your takeoff and landing.
- "Explode" upward.
- Forcefully swing and reach upward with your arms.
- Stretch, reach, and look upward.
- Extend at the shoulder of your reaching arm.

(continued on following page)

(continued from preceding page)

CONCEPT 19.5

Children typically encounter a variety of developmental difficulties as they progress from one stage to another in the quest for mature fundamental movement skills.

Movement concepts:

- Vertical jumping requires a two-footed takeoff in an upward direction and a landing on both feet.
- You must time your jump so that all body parts work together.
- You can jump high or low and with or without use of your arms.
- You jump higher if you use your arms.
- Your movements must be quick and forceful for the highest jumps.
- You can jump while holding objects, but your height will be less.
- You can jump only as high as the force of gravity will let you.

Jumping From a Height

Jumping from a height is another of those airborne experiences that children enjoy. When jumping from a height the individual takes off from both feet and lands on both feet, absorbing the force of the jump in a manner commensurate with the height of the jump (see figures 19.9 and 19.10). Be sure to spot carefully and to have a soft landing area when working on this skill.

This young lady demonstrates a wide shape as she jumps from a medium height. After this type of jump, it is important for students to bring their arms and legs back together, land on two feet simultaneously, and bend their knees to absorb force.

I. Jumping from a height
  A. Initial stage
    1. One foot leads on takeoff
    2. No flight phase
    3. Lead foot contacts lower surface prior to trailing foot leaving upper surface
    4. Exaggerated use of arms for balance
  B. Elementary stage
    1. Two-foot takeoff with one-foot lead
    2. Flight phase, but lacks control
    3. Arms used ineffectively for balance
    4. One-foot landing followed by immediate landing of trailing foot
    5. Inhibited or exaggerated flexion at knees and hip upon landing
  C. Mature stage
    1. Two-foot takeoff
    2. Controlled flight phase
    3. Both arms used efficiently out to sides to control balance as needed
    4. Feet contact lower surface simultaneously, with toes touching first
    5. Feet land shoulder-width apart
    6. Flexion at knees and hip congruent with height of jump
II. Developmental difficulties
  A. Inability to take off with both feet
  B. Twisting body to one side on takeoff
  C. Exaggerated or inhibited body lean
  D. Failure to coordinate use of both arms in the air
  E. Tying one arm to side while using the other
  F. Failure to land simultaneously on both feet
  G. Landing flat-footed
  H. Failure to flex knees sufficiently to absorb impact of landing
  I. Landing out of control

FIGURE 19.9   Developmental sequence for jumping from a height.

TEACHING TIP 19.5

When teaching *jumping from a height:*

- Start with a low height and gradually work up.
- Observe carefully for children who may be landing stiff-legged. Provide an alternative activity if they are unable to bend appropriately at the knees.
- Place a mat on the floor.
- Spot all jumping carefully.
- Encourage exploration and then gradually focus on the skill element.
- Begin with single-task skills; then combine two or three tasks (e.g., jump, clap your hands, land, and roll forward).
- Stress proper landing techniques.
- Emphasize control while in the air.
- Provide different heights for different ability levels.
- Keep equipment well spaced for safety reasons.

Initial

Elementary

Mature

FIGURE 19.10   Stages of the jump from a height.

JUMPING-FROM-A-HEIGHT CONCEPTS CHILDREN SHOULD KNOW

Skill concepts:

- Push off with both feet.
- Your toes are the last part of your body to leave the ground.
- Lean forward slightly.
- Move your arms forward or sideward in unison for balance.
- Keep your legs shoulder-width apart to prepare for landing.
- Give at the ankles, knees, and hip joint upon landing.

(continued on following page)

(continued from preceding page)

Movement concepts:

- Jumping from a height requires taking off and landing on both feet.
- You can land either heavily or lightly.
- Your jump can be from many different heights.
- The extent of your crouch upon landing is based on the height of your jump.
- You can jump in many different directions, going forward, backward, or to the side.
- Your jump should be smooth, but it can be jerky and awkward.
- Your jump can be far or near, high or low.
- You can jump and land while holding objects, but you must make adjustments for the weight and size of the object.

CONCEPT 19.6

Movement exploration and guided discovery experiences are especially beneficial to children at the initial and elementary stages of the fundamental movement phase.

Hopping

Although hopping is a rhythmical, unilateral activity, it involves both sides of the body to a greater or lesser extent. Hopping involves rhythmical loss and regaining of support in an upward, forward, sideward, or backward direction on the same foot. The "non-hopping" side of the body assists by adding balance and thrust. Hopping, if performed over a distance, can be an exhausting activity in terms of muscle fatigue with younger children. Make certain that you limit the distance to be hopped to the individual abilities of your learners (see figures 19.11 and 19.12).

This young lady demonstrates the preparation, force phase, and follow-through components of a hopping pattern.

I. Hopping
  A. Initial stage
    1. Non-supporting leg flexed 90 degrees or less
    2. Non-supporting thigh roughly parallel to contact surface
    3. Body upright
    4. Arms flexed at elbows and held slightly to side
    5. Little height or distance generated in single hop
    6. Balance lost easily
    7. Limited to one or two hops
  B. Elementary stage
    1. Non-supporting leg flexed
    2. Non-supporting thigh at 45-degree angle to contact surface
    3. Slight forward lean, with trunk flexed at hip
    4. Non-supporting thigh flexed and extended at hip to produce greater force
    5. Force absorbed on landing by flexing at hip and by supporting knee
    6. Arms move up and down vigorously and bilaterally
    7. Balance poorly controlled
    8. Generally limited in number of consecutive hops that can be performed
  C. Mature stage
    1. Non-supporting leg flexed at 90 degrees or less
    2. Non-supporting thigh lifts with vertical thrust of supporting foot
    3. Greater body lean
    4. Rhythmical action of non-supporting leg (pendulum swing aiding in force production)
    5. Arms move together in rhythmical lifting as the supporting foot leaves the contact surface
    6. Arms not needed for balance but used for greater force production
II. Developmental difficulties
  A. Hopping flat-footed
  B. Exaggerated movement of arms
  C. Exaggerated movement of non-supporting leg
  D. Exaggerated forward lean
  E. Inability to maintain balance for five or more consecutive hops
  F. Lack of rhythmical fluidity of movement
  G. Inability to hop effectively on both left and right foot
  H. Inability to alternate hopping feet in a smooth, continuous manner
  I. Tying one arm to side of body

FIGURE 19.11 Developmental sequence for hopping.

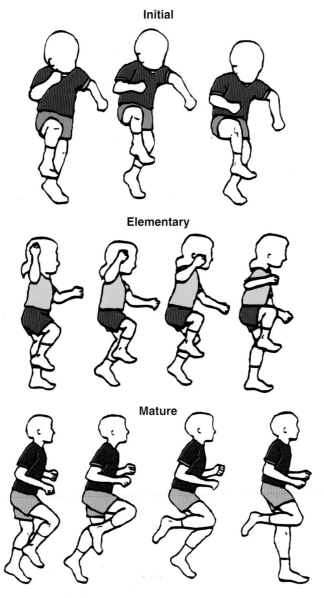

Initial

Elementary

Mature

FIGURE 19.12   Stages in the hopping pattern.

HOPPING CONCEPTS CHILDREN SHOULD KNOW

Skill concepts:

- Take off and land on the same foot.
- Lift your arms slightly as you spring up from your hop.
- Push off from your toes and land on the ball of your foot.
- Land softly.

Movement concepts:

- You can land heavily or lightly when you hop.
- You can hop in place or move in different directions.
- You can hop at different speeds.
- You can hop at different heights and levels.
- You can hop over objects and in different pathways.
- You can hop smoothly and freely, or the movement can be bound and jerky.
- You can hop with either foot.
- You can alternate hopping feet.
- Hopping requires a takeoff and a landing on one foot.

SKIPPING, SLIDING, AND GALLOPING

Skipping, sliding, and galloping are fundamental movement abilities that begin developing during the preschool years and that children should master by the first grade. The **gallop** occurs in a forward direction with one foot leading and the other trailing behind. **Sliding** is the same action but is performed in a sideways direction. Children are generally able to gallop and slide before being able to skip. Part of the

Two young girls demonstrate the gallop.

explanation may be that galloping and sliding are unilateral activities and require less differentiation and integration of neural mechanisms than the neurologically more complex, cross-lateral action of skipping. The term *differentiation* refers to the individual's ability to distinguish among the muscle groups required to perform a movement task. *Integration* refers to the harmonious working together of the motor and sensory systems. Integration is sometimes referred to simply as eye-foot, eye-hand, or eye-body coordination depending on the primary muscle groups used.

The action incorporated in **skipping** requires rhythmically alternating steps followed by a hop on the lead foot. Before you introduce skipping, it is advisable to give children opportunities to explore the many movement variations of galloping and sliding. You should incorporate guided discovery activities with galloping and sliding so that these patterns are at the mature stage before you introduce a teaching progression for skipping. In other words, if the child is not yet at the mature stage of galloping or sliding (with either foot leading), it is unwise to develop lessons that focus on skipping.

These Hillsdale Elementary School students enjoy skipping during an instant activity.

Sliding is similar in many ways to galloping but is conducted in a sideward direction. Once again, it is generally more appropriate to introduce sliding after the child has experienced some success with galloping. The sliding pattern is used extensively in a variety of game, dance, and gymnastics activities that require rapid lateral movement. Lateral movements need to be smooth, and the child should be able to make rapid changes in direction. Be sure to point out specific instances of the use of sliding in sports and to have students master sliding in relation to its specific use.

Skipping

Skipping is a complex bilateral rhythmical activity involving coordinated alternate use of both sides of the body. Because of the neurological organization required, it is a real challenge for children who are not developmentally ready and an easy task for those who are. Knowing more about the typical stages of skipping will enable you to design movement experiences that are individually appropriate (see figures 19.13 and 19.14).

These students demonstrate a sideward sliding pattern as they participate in a locomotor lesson at Hillsdale Elementary School.

I. Skipping
  A. Initial stage
    1. One-footed skip
    2. Deliberate step-hop action
    3. Double hop or step sometimes occurs
    4. Exaggerated stepping action
    5. Arms of little use
    6. Action appears segmented
  B. Elementary stage
    1. Step and hop coordinated effectively
    2. Rhythmical use of arms to aid momentum
    3. Exaggerated vertical lift on hop
    4. Flat-footed landing
  C. Mature stage
    1. Rhythmical weight transfer throughout
    2. Rhythmical use of arms (reduced during time of weight transfer)
    3. Low vertical lift on hop
    4. Toe-first landing
II. Developmental difficulties
  A. Segmented stepping and hopping action
  B. Poor rhythmical alteration
  C. Inability to use both sides of body
  D. Landing flat-footed
  E. Exaggerated, inhibited, or unilateral arm movements
  F. Inability to move in a straight line
  G. Inability to skip backward and to side

FIGURE 19.13   Developmental sequence for skipping.

Initial

Elementary

Mature

FIGURE 19.14   Stages of the skipping pattern.

When teaching *skipping:*

- Children should be able to gallop with either leg leading before they learn skipping.
- Children should be able to hop well on either leg before attempting to skip.
- Introduce skipping when child is ready.
- You may need to provide slow-motion demonstrations.

- Once the basic pattern is mastered, encourage exploration of variations of skipping.
- Use rhythmical activities that require skipping.
- Work for a rhythmical, flowing motion.

SKIPPING CONCEPTS CHILDREN SHOULD KNOW

Skill concepts:
- Step forward and then hop up on the same foot.
- Do the same with the other foot.
- Lift your knees sharply upward.
- Swing your arms upward in time with your legs.

Movement concepts:
- You can skip in different directions and along different pathways.
- You can skip at different speeds.
- You can skip in a smooth and free manner, or the movement can be jerky and bound.
- You can skip at different levels and land heavily or lightly.
- You can skip with a partner and while carrying objects.
- Skipping is a combination of two movements—stepping and hopping.
- Skipping requires you to use both sides of your body in a rhythmic fashion.

Sliding and Galloping

Sliding and galloping are similar. Sliding occurs in a sideward direction, galloping is generally forward. Although galloping has limited direct utility in most sports settings, sliding is basic to making quick lateral movements in many sports. In fact, the elements of sliding are used as the basic "ready" or "athletic" anticipatory movement patterns used in sports such as tennis, racketball, basketball, and soccer. Galloping, on the other hand, is frequently introduced as a precursor to skipping, which is an important fundamental movement used, in part, in later, more complex activities such as the layup shot in basketball and the triple jump in track and field (see figures 19.15 and 19.16).

SLIDING AND GALLOPING CONCEPTS CHILDREN SHOULD KNOW

Skill concepts:
- Step to the side and draw the other foot up quickly to the first foot.
- Repeat the action, landing with the same foot.
- Use your arms only as needed for balance.
- Move on the balls of your feet.
- Keep your knees bent slightly.
- Lean slightly forward at the waist.

Movement concepts:
- You can slide to the left or right.
- When you slide forward or backward, the movement is called a gallop.
- Your movements can be fast or slow, smooth or jerky, free or bound.
- You can slide at different levels and for different distances.
- You can slide with a partner.
- You can dodge while sliding.
- When sliding sideways, remain on your feet and don't fall to your knees.

I. Galloping and sliding
  A. Initial stage
    1. Arrhythmical at fast pace
    2. Trailing leg often fails to remain behind and often contacts surface in front of lead leg
    3. Forty-five degree flexion of trailing leg during flight phase
    4. Contact in a heel-toe combination
    5. Arms of little use in balance or force production
  B. Elementary stage
    1. Moderate tempo
    2. Appears choppy and stiff
    3. Trailing leg may lead during flight but lands adjacent to or behind lead leg
    4. Exaggerated vertical lift
    5. Feet contact in a heel-toe, or toe-toe, combination
    6. Heel-toe contact combination
    7. Arms not needed for balance; may be used for other purposes
  C. Mature stage
    1. Moderate tempo
    2. Smooth, rhythmical action
    3. Trailing leg lands adjacent to or behind lead leg
    4. Both legs flexed at 45-degree angles during flight
    5. Low flight pattern
    6. Heel-toe contact combination
    7. Arms not needed for balance; may be used for other purposes
II. Developmental difficulties
  A. Choppy movements
  B. Keeping legs too straight
  C. Exaggerated forward trunk lean
  D. Overstepping with trailing leg
  E. Too much elevation on hop
  F. Inability to perform both forward and backward
  G. Inability to lead with non-dominant foot
  H. Inability to perform to both left and right
  I. Undue concentration on task

FIGURE 19.15 Developmental sequence for galloping and sliding.

TEACHING TIP 19.8

When teaching *sliding/galloping:*

- Work on sliding in both directions.
- Stress not crossing the feet.
- Begin with exploratory experiences and then progress to skill drills and other activities involving sliding.
- Stress keeping the knees slightly bent and the trunk forward, as well as staying on the balls of the feet ("ready position").
- Rhythmic accompaniment aids sliding.
- Work for ease of movement in both directions.

Initial

Elementary

Mature

FIGURE 19.16   *Stages of the sliding pattern.*

SKILL DEVELOPMENT ACTIVITIES

Mastery of fundamental locomotor skills requires environmental conditions that permit practice and provide instruction. Instruction may take many forms. However, when viewing children from a developmental perspective, you must first determine their phase and stage of motor development, which will provide cues to their level of movement skill learning (beginning, intermediate, or advanced). When children are at the initial and elementary stages of **locomotor skill development,** activities should be designed to encourage exploration of the range of movement possibilities. Children at either the initial stage or the elementary stage should have an opportunity to learn *how* and *where* their body can move when performing locomotor movements. Equipment can actually be set up, or placed, so as to elicit or prompt specific locomotor movement skills.

Exploratory Activities

The primary purpose of incorporating **locomotor exploratory activities** into the movement lesson is to provide children at either the initial or the elementary stage an opportunity to learn how and where their body can move when performing locomotor movements. Exploratory activities are intended to help children get in touch with their bodies and to lead them to experiment with the many variations in effort, space, and relationships that they can experience. Combinations of locomotor skills can be successfully included in the lesson once children are progressing toward the mature stage in the movement skill. Tables 19.1 through 19.8 provide easy-to-use charts to help get you started in presenting movement challenges that permit children to explore their locomotor potential.

TABLE 19.1 – EXPLORATORY ACTIVITY IDEAS FOR RUNNING

Effort awareness	Space awareness	Relationship awareness
Force	**Level**	**Objects**
Can you run . . . – like a pixie? – like an elephant? – on your tiptoes? – flat-footed? – as if you were floating? – as if you weighed a million pounds? – as softly as you can? – as hard as you can?	*Can you run . . .* – very tall? – very small? – at a high level? – at a low level? – at a medium level? – fast or slow at a high level? – smoothly at a high level?	*Can you run . . .* – on the line? – across the line? – under the bars? – behind the chair? – over the hoop? – through the hoop? – carrying a ball? – carrying a suitcase? – with boots on?
Time	**Direction**	**People**
– as quickly as you can? – as slowly as you can? – starting slowly and showing form? – alternating fast and slow?	– forward? – backward? – to the left or right? – diagonally? – and change direction once? – and change direction three times? – in a straight line? – in a curvy line? – in a zigzag line? – in a pattern (show shapes)?	– all by yourself? – in front of a partner? – behind a partner? – beside a partner? – holding a partner's hand? – with the class? – without touching anyone? – with two others? – in formation?
Flow	**Range**	**Combinations**
– as smoothly as you can? – with jerky movements? – like a machine? – like a robot? – like a deer? – like a football player? – without using your arms?	– in your own space? – throughout the room? – as far as you can? – and not bump anyone? – with your feet wide? – with big steps? – with tiny steps?	An infinite variety of exploratory experiences can be devised simply by combining various effort, space, and relationship challenges.

TABLE 19.2—EXPLORATORY ACTIVITY IDEAS FOR LEAPING

Effort awareness	Space awareness	Relationship awareness
Force	**Level**	**Objects**
Can you leap . . . – and land lightly? – and land without a sound? – and land forcefully? – alternating hard and soft landings? – and swing your arms forcefully? – and keep your arms at your side? – holding your arms in different positions?	*Can you leap . . .* – as high as you can? – as low as you can? – at many different levels? – alternating low and high leaps?	*Can you leap . . .* – over a rope? – over a hurdle? – over a partner? – across two outstretched ropes? – over two outstretched ropes? – from one carpet square to the next? – from one footprint to a corresponding footprint?
Time	**Direction**	**People**
– and stay in the air as long as you can? – and land as quickly as you can? – and swing only one arm? – in time to the accented beat of the drum? – in time to the accented beat of the music?	– forward? – backward? – diagonally? – with your left foot leading? – with your right foot leading? – alternating left and right foot lead?	– the same distance as your partner? – over your partner? – the length of your partner's body? – in unison with your partner?
Flow	**Range**	**Combinations**
– from a three-step approach? – from a two-step approach? – from a one-step approach? – from a stationary position?	– as far as you can? – and keep one leg bent? – and bend both legs in the air? – and keep both legs straight? – and twist your trunk in the air? – and find different things to do with your arms while in the air? – on different surfaces?	After several variations of leaping have been explored singly, try combining various aspects of effort, space, and relationships. For example, "Can you leap lightly as high as you can over a rope held by two partners?"

TABLE 19.3—EXPLORATORY ACTIVITY IDEAS FOR HORIZONTAL JUMPING

Effort awareness	Space awareness	Relationship awareness
Force	**Level**	**Objects**
Can you jump . . . – as quietly as possible? – as loudly as possible? – alternating loud and soft jumps? – like a pixie? – like a giant?	*Can you jump . . .* – from as small a position as you can? – from as big a position as you can? – and stay under my hand?	*Can you jump . . .* – over the box? – across the rope? – through the hoop? – like a frog or a rabbit? – while holding this ball?
Time	**Direction**	**People**
– very fast? – very slow? – alternating fast and slow jumps? – as if you were stuck in molasses? – as if you were on ice?	– forward or backward? – sideways? – in a straight line? – several times in a zigzag or circular pattern? – making various geometric shapes or letters of the alphabet?	– with a partner? – as far as your partner? – over your partner? – at the same time as your partner jumps?
Flow	**Range**	**Combinations**
– with your arms and legs held stiffly? – keeping your arms out? – with your legs out? – in a relaxed manner? – like a wooden soldier?	– as far as you can? – as near as you can? – landing with your feet wide apart? – landing with your feet close together?	Numerous combinations of effort, space, and relationships are possible. For example: – for distance and then for height? – as short and as low as possible? – as fast and as far as possible? – as quietly and as far as you can? – and toss a ball? – and catch a ball? – to my rhythm? – to the music?

TABLE 19.4—EXPLORATORY ACTIVITY IDEAS FOR VERTICAL JUMPING

Effort awareness	Space awareness	Relationship awareness
Force	**Level**	**Objects**
Can you jump up . . . – and land lightly? – and land heavily? – like an elephant? – like a robot?	*Can you jump up . . .* – as high as you can? – as low as you can? – alternating high and low jumps? – and touch the same spot five times? – from a crouched position? – from an extended position?	*Can you jump up . . .* – and strike the hanging ball? – with a weighted object? – with a ball? – on a trampoline? – on a bounding board? – over a jump rope?
Time	**Direction**	**People**
– as quickly as you can? – as slowly as you can? – like a rocket? – like a growing flower?	– and land in the same spot? – and land in a different spot? – and land slightly forward, backward, or to the side? – and turn?	– with a partner? – and alternate jumping up with a partner? – while holding hands? – and touch your partner's spot?
Flow	**Range**	**Combinations**
– without using your arms? – and use only one arm? – and keep your head down? – and remain stiff? – as relaxed as you can?	– and land in your own space? – and land outside your space? – and land with your feet wide apart? – and land with your feet close together?	Numerous combinations of effort, space, and relationships are possible. For example: – and toss a ball? – and shoot a basket? – and catch a basket? – and hop over a jump rope? – and turn? – and turn and catch? – as lightly, as high, and as fast as you can?

TABLE 19.5—EXPLORATORY ACTIVITY IDEAS FOR JUMPING FROM A HEIGHT

Effort awareness	Space awareness	Relationship awareness
Force	**Level**	**Objects**
Can you jump . . . – and land as lightly as you can? – and land as forcefully as you can?	*Can you jump . . .* – from a crouched position? – from a tucked position?	*Can you jump . . .* – over the wand? – through the hoop? – and catch the ball in the air? – and throw the ball in the air? – and catch a ball you toss while in the air?
Time	**Direction**	**People**
– and land as quickly as possible? – and stay in the air as long as possible? – in slow motion?	– forward? – backward? – sideways? – and make a quarter turn? – and make a half turn? – and make a full turn?	– at the same time as a partner? – and land at the same time as your partner? – and do what your partner does? – and do the opposite of your partner?
Flow	**Range**	**Combinations**
– with different arm actions? – without using your arms? – while holding one arm to your side?	– and land with your feet together? – and land with your feet apart? – and land in this spot? – and make yourself as big as you can?	Numerous combinations of effort, space, and relationship activities involving exploration of jumping from a height are possible and should be used after the child has gained control of single movements.

TABLE 19.6—EXPLORATORY ACTIVITY IDEAS FOR HOPPING

Effort awareness	Space awareness	Relationship awareness
Force	**Level**	**Objects**
Can you hop . . . – as quietly as you can? – as noisily as you can? – alternating hard and soft landings? – hard four times on your left, then softly four times on your right?	*Can you hop . . .* – in a small ball? – in a crouched position? – with little crouched hops? – as high as you can? – at a medium height? – staying lower than my hand? – staying at the same level as my hand?	*Can you hop . . .* – over the rope? – in a hoop? – over the cones? – around the cones? – while bouncing a ball? – while catching a tossed ball? – while tossing and catching a self-tossed ball?
Time	**Direction**	**People**
– as quickly as possible? – as slowly as possible? – starting slowly and getting slower? – in time to the music?	– in place? – forward? – backward? – sideways? – and turn in the air? – and make a quarter (half, three-quarter, full) turn?	– in rhythm with a partner? – forward holding hands? – facing each other and hopping to the wall in unison? – imitating your partner's arm actions?
Flow	**Range**	**Combinations**
– without using your arms? – using only the arm opposite your hopping foot? – alternating feet every eight (four, two) beats?	– in your own space? – from spot to spot? – and land on a different carpet square each time? – and land on the same spot? – and land in as small a spot as possible? – and land in as large a spot as possible?	Numerous combinations of effort, space, and relationships can be explored for hopping after children have gained control in single-problem tasks. For example, "Can you hop as quietly as you can over the rope?"

TABLE 19.7—EXPLORATORY ACTIVITY IDEAS FOR SKIPPING

Effort awareness	Space awareness	Relationship awareness
Force	**Level**	**Objects**
Can you skip . . . – as quietly as you can? – as a giant would? – as loudly as you can? – landing heavily on one foot and lightly on the other? – alternating loud/quiet and hard/soft skips?	*Can you skip . . .* – while making yourself very small? – and gradually get smaller? – as tall as you can? – with a high knee lift? – barely raising your feet off the ground?	*Can you skip . . .* – without touching any of the lines on the floor? – without touching any cracks in the cement? – and try to step on each line or crack? – while carrying a heavy object?
Time	**Direction**	**People**
– as fast as you can across the room? – as slowly as you can? – as if you were on a sandy beach? – downhill? – uphill? – to the beat of the drum?	– forward or backward? – sideways (left or right)? – in a straight line? – in a curved or zigzag pattern? – in a circle?	– with a partner? – going backward while your partner moves forward? – in unison with a partner? – while holding both of your partner's hands?
Flow	**Range**	**Combinations**
– without using your arms? – swinging your arms outward, inward, or diagonally? – like a toy soldier? – in a relaxed manner?	– and see how many complete skips it takes to cross the room? – and measure how much space you cover in one complete skip? – with your legs wide apart?	Numerous ingenious combinations of effort, space, and relationships can be explored. For example, "Can you skip as quietly as you can while making yourself very big and without touching any of the lines on the floor?"

TABLE 19.8—EXPLORATORY ACTIVITY IDEAS FOR SLIDING AND GALLOPING

Effort awareness	Space awareness	Relationship awareness
Force	**Level**	**Objects**
Can you slide/gallop . . . – landing flat-footed? – landing on your toes? – very quietly? – while pretending you are dragging an elephant? – while pretending you are trying to escape a charger elephant?	*Can you slide/gallop . . .* – sideways and get smaller? – sideways and get bigger? – somewhere in between big and small? – and change levels as I raise or lower my hand?	*Can you slide/gallop . . .* – from one line to the other? – from one line to the other and return? – from one line to the other as many times as you can in 30 seconds? – in either direction while bouncing and catching a ball? – in either direction while dribbling a ball? – in either direction to catch a ball?
Time	**Direction**	**People**
– in either direction? – as quickly as you can? – as slowly as you can? – to the beat of the drum? – in time to the music?	– sideways? – forward or backward (gallop)? – to the left or right? – to the left four steps and then to the right four steps? – to the left two steps and then to the right two steps? – alternating left and right? – in the direction I point?	– facing a partner and travel in the same direction? – facing a partner and travel in the opposite direction? – facing a partner and travel four steps in the opposite direction and then four steps in the same direction?
Flow	**Range**	**Combinations**
– keeping both legs stiff? – keeping one leg stiff? – keeping your trunk erect? – bending forward at your waist?	– to your right (or left) as far as you can until I say "Stop"? – taking big steps? – taking small steps?	After exploring the many variations of sliding or galloping in isolation, you will want to combine various aspects of effort, space, and relationships. For example, "Can you slide in either direction four steps and touch the line while bouncing and catching a ball?"

Guided Discovery Activities

The primary purpose for including **locomotor guided discovery activities** (see chapter 10,"Teaching Styles") in the lesson is to provide children at the elementary stage of developing their fundamental locomotor abilities an opportunity to practice the skill. Practice, using a problem-solving technique, permits children to learn more about the skill and how their bodies should move. Emphasis at this level is on discovering the proper mechanics and the usefulness of various locomotor movements. Figures 19.17 through 19.24 present a sampling of guided discovery experiences that you will find helpful in getting started.

---

	1. Have the children first explore the numerous variations of running.
	2. Then begin to put limitations on the possible responses to the following movement challenges:
General	a. Run around the gym in a clockwise direction, then in a counterclockwise direction.
Arm action	b. Run as quickly as you can one time around the gym. What do your arms do? Do they move quickly or slowly?
	c. When you run slowly, do your arms move quickly or slowly? Why?
	d. How do you swing your arms when you run? Do they cross your chest, or do they stop before crossing?
	e. Run with your arms crossing your chest. Now try it without crossing. Which is better? Why?
Leg action	f. What part of your foot lands first when you are running as fast as you can? What about when you are jogging at a slower pace?
	g. Run uphill. Run downhill. How does your stride change? Why does it change?
Trunk action	h. Lean forward when you run. Now try to stay very straight. Now try something in between. Which feels the best for you? Why?
Total	i. Show me how you would run a 5-mile race. How would you run a mile race, a quarter mile, 50 yards?
	j. Why is your run slightly different for each distance?
	k. Can you run to the rhythm made by the drum?
	l. What happens to your run when the beat speeds up or slows down?
	3. Now combine running with other activities to achieve a more automatic pattern.
	a. Can you tag someone lightly while running?
	b. Can you dodge someone who is trying to tag you?
	c. Run barefooted. Now try it with your street shoes. How does it feel? Which is more comfortable? Safer way?
	d. Run on different surfaces. How does it affect your running pattern? Why?

FIGURE 19.17   Guided discovery activity ideas for running.

1. First explore the movement variations of leaping.

2. Then begin to put limitations on the response possibilities to the following movement challenges:

Leg action

    a. Try to leap as far as you can. What do you do when you want to go far? Can you show me? If you don't want to leap far, what do you do? Show me. Try pushing off forcefully with your trailing foot and stretching out with your lead foot. Does it make a difference?

    b. Try leaping and pushing off from different parts of your trailing foot. Try pushing off flat-footed and off the ball of your trailing foot. Which works better? See if there is any difference in the distance leaped trying both ways.

Trunk action

    c. Try leaping and bending your trunk at different angles. Now try keeping your trunk erect. Which way feels more comfortable? Do you bend your trunk differently for different purposes? Watch your partner and see if he or she bends at the waist differently when trying to leap different heights and various distances.

    d. What do we know about bending at the waist? When is it best to bend far forward? When is it best to have very little bend at the waist? Experiment with a partner and then let me know your answer.

Arm action

    e. Try leaping with your arms in a much different position. How does it feel? Which way helps you leap the farthest or the highest? Experiment and find out.

General

    f. See if you can leap and coordinate the use of your arms, legs, and trunk. What are some important things we should remember when leaping?

    g. Try leaping from a standing position. Now try it from a running approach. Which way helps you go farther? Why?

    h. Try leaping off one foot. Now try the other. Is there a difference? Why? Practice both ways.

3. After a mature leaping pattern has been reasonably well mastered, combine it with other exploratory and guided discovery activities to reinforce the pattern and make it more automatic.

    a. Listen to the beat of the drum and leap on every hard note.

    b. Beginning at one end of the gym, perform three leaps in combination with running.

    c. Try to leap over the outstretched ropes placed on the floor.

    d. Let's try to run across the gym alternating leaping off our left and right feet.

    e. Can you leap and catch a tossed ball while in the air?

    f. Try leaping across the outstretched ropes and touching the balloon overhead (ringing a suspended bell is a real challenge).

    g. Using carpet squares (on a nonstick surface only) or hoops, practice leaping from spaceship to spaceship, being sure that no other astronaut is in a spaceship that you leap to.

FIGURE 19.18 Guided discovery activity ideas for leaping.

	1. First explore several of the numerous variations of horizontal jumping.
	2. Now begin to place limitations on the responses to the following movement challenges:
General	a. Try to jump over the unfolded newspaper, outstretched ropes, or tape lines on the floor. Can you get over the short part without touching? How about the long part?
Arm action	b. What happens when you jump and don't use your hands? Why don't you go as far? What should we do with our arms when we jump? Show me.
	c. Show me how you would use your arms. Several are doing this (demonstrate) with their arms. Why? Oh, I see. It helps you keep your balance.
Landing	d. Can you show me several different ways to land? Try it now just doing different things with your feet. Now try landing with your feet way apart, close together, and in between. Which worked best for you? Why? What happens to your knees when you jump? Why? Should there be any difference if I jumped from a very high height or from a very low height?
Total	e. When you put the entire jump together, what do you do with your head and eyes? Try three different things with your head (look up, down, straight ahead). Which works best? Now try jumping with your eyes closed. Scary, isn't it? Why? What should we remember about the use of our head and eyes when we jump from a height?
	3. When the mature pattern has been reasonably well mastered, combine jumping from a height with other activities to reinforce the pattern and make it more automatic. For example:
	a. Jump and assume different postures in the air.
	b. Jump and perform turns in the air.
	c. Jump, land, and roll.
	d. Jump, turn, land, and roll.

FIGURE 19.19   Guided discovery activity ideas for horizontal jumping.

1. First explore several of the numerous variations of vertical jumping.

2. Now begin to place limitations on the response possibilities to the following movement challenges:

Arm action

a. What happens when you jump without using your arms? Does one arm help? When you use both arms, which way is best? Try three ways, and then tell me which works best for you. Many of you thought that swinging your arms up as your legs uncoiled was best. Why is that so?

b. Try bending your knees at three different levels when you jump. Which is best? Why? Measure the height of your jumps from three different leg positions. Why is there a difference with each jump?

Trunk action

c. Does your trunk stay bent forward when you jump or does it extend? Try both ways. Which is better? Why?

Head action

d. Jump as high as you can with your head and eyes in three different positions. Which is best for you? Many thought looking up was best. You're right. Think of yourself as a puppet with a string attached to your nose. Every time you jump up, you stretch your entire body out and reach up to the sky with your nose.

Landing

e. Try landing in different ways. Which do you think is best? Why do you bend your knees when you land? How much should you bend them? Why? Did you land in the same spot you took off from? See if you can. Some people are landing in front of their takeoff spot. Do you get more height or less height when that happens? Why?

3. When the mature pattern has been reasonably well mastered using these and other guided discovery challenges, combine vertical jumping with other activities to reinforce the pattern and make it more automatic. For example:

a. Try jumping on different surfaces.

boundary board

tires

trampoline (spot carefully)

b. Try jumping with other objects.

hoops (for small children only)

jump ropes

high jumping

stretch ropes

c. Play jumping games.

FIGURE 19.20   Guided discovery activity ideas for vertical jumping.

	1. First explore several of the variations of jumping from a height.
	2. Now begin to place limitations on the response possibilities to the following movement challenges:
Takeoff	a. How do you take off when you jump? Do you take off with one foot leading or do both feet leave at the same time? Try it both ways. Which way gives you more control or balance? Why? Try turning in the air after you take off, or try a two-footed takeoff.
Flight	b. What do you do while you are in the air? Try different things with your arms. What happens to your body when it is in the air? Can anyone show me what it looks like? Do you jump straight up? Do you just skim over the floor? Do you do something different?
	c. What happens when you swing your arms forward very hard as you jump? Very softly? What happens when your arms swing all the way to your head? Try it different ways and see which is best. Is it better to swing hard or soft, all the way up or only partway up when we jump as far as we can? Why? Show me.
Leg action	d. When you jump, do you leave the ground with both feet at the same time? Try both. Why is it better to use both feet for a standing long jump? Try jumping as far as you can using both feet. Now put a beanbag on one foot and, while trying to keep it there, jump as far as you can. Which works better, one foot or both feet? Why?
Landing	e. How do you land? Should you land and sit back or fall forward? What happens to your knees when you land? Are they stiff or do you bend them? Why?
Total	f. Let's put it all together. Jump as far as you can. How does it feel? Can you get your legs and arms to work together? What happens when they do? Should you jump quickly (explosively), or is it better to jump more slowly? Try both. Which works better? Why?
	3. When the mature pattern has been reasonably mastered, combine it with other activities to reinforce the pattern and make it more automatic.
	a. Play jumping games.
	b. Conduct cooperative jumping contests where partners try to jump the same distance.
	c. Jump from different surfaces. What happens to your distance when you jump from a very soft surface? Why?

FIGURE 19.21   Guided discovery activity ideas for jumping from a height.

	1. First explore several of the variations of hopping.
	2. Now begin to place limitations and questions on the following response possibilities:
General	a. Hop in place on one foot. Can you do the same on the other foot? Can you hop to the wall on one foot and come back on the other?
Leg action	b. Try hopping and putting your free leg in different positions. Which is easiest when you are hopping in place? For distance? Why? Try the same experiment with the other leg. Why do some people hop better on one leg than on the other? Do you have a better leg?
Arm action	c. Try hopping as far as you can, using your arms in three different ways to help. Try it without using your arms at all. Which works best for you? Several students seem to lift and swing the arms forward when they hop for distance. Try it. How does that feel?
	d. Let's try that same arm action while hopping in place. What happened? Why? What do you want to do with your arms when hopping in place? Show me.
	3. Once the mature hopping pattern has been reasonably well mastered for both the left and the right leg, move on to activities that use hopping in combination with other skills. Incorporation of hopping with other skills will reinforce the pattern and make it more automatic. For example:
	a. Step-hops.
	b. Various dance steps (schottische, step-hop, polka).
	c. Jump rope activities.
	d. Track and field event activities.

FIGURE 19.22 Guided discovery activity ideas for hopping.

	1. First explore several of the movement variations of skipping.
	2. Then help the children discover how their body works when they skip. For example:
Leg action	a. Try skipping around the room. Experiment with big steps, little steps, and in-between steps. When would you want to use each?
	b. Be a detective and see if you find out what two movements with your legs the skip is made up of. Who knows the answer? Good! Show me. Let's all take it apart.
Arm action	c. What do you do with your arms when you skip? Try four or five different things. How does it feel when your arms swing as you skip?
	d. Watch your partner. Do his or her arms swing with the same arm and leg?
	3. Once the mature skipping pattern has been reasonably well mastered using these and other guided discovery challenges, combine skipping with other activities to reinforce the pattern and make it more automatic. For example:
	a. Play skip tag.
	b. Skip to a drum beat.
	c. Skip to selected musical accompaniment.
	d. Modify chasing and fleeing games to incorporate skipping rather than running.
	e. Teach the children folk dances that incorporate skipping.

FIGURE 19.23 Guided discovery activity ideas for skipping.

Galloping	1. First explore several of the numerous variations of galloping.
	2. Then begin to place limitations on the response possibilities to the following movement challenges:
General	a. Put one foot forward and gallop around the room. Try it with the other foot leading. Which is easier? Why?
Leg action	b. Try galloping with your legs stiff. Then try with them very bent. Now try different amounts of knee bend. What works best for you? Why do you think some knee bend is good?
Foot action	c. What happens to your back foot when you gallop forward? Does it come up to meet your front foot, or does it overtake it and move in front? Which do you think is better? Try both. Why is it better not to overtake your front foot with the rear foot?
Arm action	d. Gallop across the room. What did you do with your arms? Now gallop back as fast as you can. Did your arms do anything that time?
	e. How can your arms help you when you gallop? Let's time our partner going across the room, first using his or her arms and then without using them. Which was faster? Which was more comfortable? Why?

3. After the mature pattern has been reasonably well mastered, combine it with other activities to reinforce the pattern and make it more automatic.
   a. Experiment with the wide variety of combinations of effort, space, and relationships that are possible.
   b. Conduct a story play or mimetic activities that use imagery with galloping horses.
   c. Practice galloping to the uneven beat of a drum or tambourine.
   d. Gallop to some form of musical accompaniment. Can you gallop to an even beat or an uneven beat?

Sliding	1. First explore the numerous movement variations of sliding.
	2. Then begin to place limitations on the response possibilities to the following movement challenges:
Leg and trunk action	a. When you slide sideways, try doing it with your legs stiff. How does it feel? How do you think you could slide better? What happens when your knees are slightly bent and your trunk is bent forward. How do you think you could slide better? What happens when your knees are slightly bent? Which is better – legs straight and back straight, or knees bent slightly and trunk bent slightly? Try both ways.
Foot action	b. Do you cross your feet when you slide? Have a partner watch you and check. Now watch my finger and slide in the direction I point, changing direction as fast as you can when I point in the opposite direction.
	c. It's best not to cross your feet. Right? Why? When moving to your left, which foot should move first? What about to the right?

3. After the mature pattern has been reasonably well mastered, combine it with other exploratory and guided discovery activities to reinforce the pattern and make it more automatic.
   a. Watch my hand and slide in the direction I point.
   b. Close your eyes and listen to my call of "left" or "right." Then move in that direction.
   c. Count for your partner and see how many times he or she can slide left and right between these two lines (indicate two parallel lines 10 feet apart) in 30 seconds.
   d. Slide left or right to catch the ball thrown to you in that direction. Why don't you cross your feet? What happens when you do?

FIGURE 19.24 Guided discovery activity ideas for galloping and sliding.

Skill application experiences involving developmentally appropriate games are suitable for students at the mature stage of the fundamental movement phase.

SKILL APPLICATION ACTIVITIES

After children have mastered fundamental locomotor skills and can perform them at the mature stage with reasonable consistency, it becomes appropriate to focus on skill application activities. **Locomotor skill application** activities permit practice and refinement of locomotor skills under dynamic conditions. These skills should be practiced within a variety of games (see chapter 21), dance (see chapter 22), and gymnastics activities (see chapter 23). Emphasis on technique is now important, as well as on combining single skills with others. Locomotor skill application activities should be introduced into the program *only after* the basic elements of these fundamental skills have been mastered.

SAMPLE LOCOMOTOR GAMES

Many of the low-level locomotor games presented here have been used for generations and may be found in numerous textbooks. We have selected them for inclusion here for several reasons:

- They provide for maximum activity.
- They promote inclusion rather than exclusion.
- They are easily modified and varied.
- They aid in the development of a variety of locomotor skills.
- They are fun for children to play.

Although some of the activities that follow have traditionally been played as elimination games, we encourage you to modify them to ensure that children are not eliminated and that activity is maximal for everyone. In presenting each game we first identify the particular movement skills that it incorporates and then outline the formation, equipment, and procedures for playing the game.

Children enjoy an almost endless variety of locomotor games. The vast majority of locomotor games, however, are designed around running as the primary mode of movement. The alert teacher will feel free to substitute other locomotor movements as they suit the nature of the lesson and the skills being stressed. Each of the games described here may be modified in a variety of ways (see table 19.9). These are the primary objectives of **locomotor game activities:**

- To enhance fundamental locomotor movement abilities
- To enhance agility and general body coordination
- To enhance rhythmic performance of locomotor movements
- To enhance the ability to participate cooperatively
- To develop listening skills and enhance the ability to follow directions and obey rules

TABLE 19.9 — SELECTED LOCOMOTOR GAMES SEQUENCED IN TERMS OF COMPLEXITY

	Walking/Running	Jumping/Hopping	Skipping/Sliding/ Galloping	Leaping
Movement Maps	X	X	X	X
Crows and Cranes	X			
Magic Carpet	X	X	X	X
Partner Power	X	X	X	
Outer Space	X			
Where's My Partner?	X	X	X	
Quick As Lightning	X	X	X	
Crossing the Brook		X		X
Jump the Shot		X		

Movement Maps— "When Are We Going to Get There?"

Movement Skills

Any locomotor skill.

Movement Concepts

Space: pathways, levels, directions. Effort: smooth. Relationships: mapping pathways.

Equipment

Maps constructed by children in the classroom or in physical education; 11- by 14-inch paper or poster board can be used. Crayons or magic markers are needed. Each child draws a "movement map." This map uses three to four different pathways. Each pathway should be a different color. The map also has a start and a finish destination.

Sample Movement Map

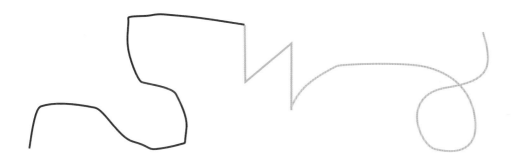

Procedures

Referring to their own movement map, students choose locomotor skills to perform along the route of their map. Each color should represent a different locomotor skill. For example, red = skipping; green = jumping; yellow = sliding. Music or a drumbeat could accompany the children's movements. Children can trade maps and learn to "read" their classmates' maps.

Variation

Various obstacles are placed along the pathway—foam shapes, cones with jump ropes hung across them, and foam shapes/styrofoam cylinders. Students then perform different locomotor skills over, through, or off of these obstacles.

Crows and Cranes

Movement Skills

Running, dodging, pivoting, starting, and stopping.

Movement Concepts

Space: direction changes. Effort: quick, light. Relationships: moving with partners.

Formation

Two lines of children facing each other, about 10 feet apart.

Equipment

None.

Procedures

Students each have a partner. One partner is a "crow"; the other is a "crane." These names could be changed to meet the objectives of the lesson or to suit the interests of the students (e.g., "apples" and "oranges"; "CDs" and "ROMs"). The crows and cranes line up on the designated center lines across the width of the playing space. The teacher designates either the crows or the cranes as "chasers" for a specific round. When the teacher calls out "crows" (i.e., the designated chasers), all crows chase after their partners (cranes). The crow attempts to tag the crane before the crane runs across a designated end line. For another round, the players' roles can be reversed. The instructor calls out various "names" beginning with the syllable "cra" before calling "crows" or "cranes" (e.g., "cra . . . ckers," "cra . . . yfish," "cra . . . yons").

Variation

Children in one partner line are designated as the "odd numbers." Those in the other partner line are "even numbers." Using one or two dice, the teacher rolls the dice between the two lines. Whether the number comes up odd or even determines which partner line gets to do the chasing. For example, if a three is rolled, the children in the odd-number partner line chase their "even partners." Math problems can be calculated if two dice are used.

End line
(about 20 feet from center line)

_____

XXXXXXXXXXXXXXXXXXXXXXXXXXXXXXXX (odd-numbered line)

_____

(10 feet between center lines)

_____

OOOOOOOOOOOOOOOOOOOOOOOOOOOOOOOO (even-numbered line)

_____

End line

Magic Carpet

Movement Skills

Any locomotor skill.

Movement Concepts

Space: directions. Effort: quick, sharp. Relationships: moving with other players and with equipment.

Formation

Scatter formation with lines, circles, and spots drawn on the floor, or equipment to this effect (e.g., plastic floor shapes, polyspots).

Equipment

Hula hoops or ropes tied into circles, polyspots, plastic floor shapes, carpet squares.

Procedures

The entire play area is considered the "carpet." Spots, circles, and other markings on the play area represent the "magic spots." In pairs, one student is the leader and the other a follower. When the leader stops, all students run to a magic spot. As the activity continues, the teacher gradually takes away one or more of the magic spots. Students must then share magic spots. Students can be asked to share the magic spots in different ways such as knee to knee or back to back, or with one student at a high level and the other at a low level, or with one student making a wide shape and the other a narrow shape, and so forth.

Partner Power

Movement Skills

Running, skipping, hopping, jumping, and sliding.

Movement Concepts

Space: general/personal. Effort: quick, light. Relationships: moving body parts with partners.

Formation

Partners standing back-to-back, with one extra child.

Equipment

None.

Procedures

The number of children should be uneven. On signal, each child stands back-to-back with another child. One child will be without a partner. This child can clap his hands and call out the next position to be taken, such as face-to-face or side to side, and all children then change partners, with the extra player seeking a partner. Other commands can be given, such as "Everybody run [hop, skip, jump, slide]" or "Spiral like a top." When the teacher signals (e.g., with a drumbeat, a whistle), children immediately find a partner and perform the stated body orientation.

Outer Space

Movement Skills

Running, starting, and stopping.

Movement Concepts

Space: directions, pathways. Effort: forceful bursts of energy, speeding up and slowing down. Relationships: moving with other students, equipment, and music.

Formation

Each student begins this game by standing on a green polyspot scattered on the floor. The green polyspots are numbered 1 through 10 and are placed third in their distance from the "sun" (yellow hula hoops). The sun is positioned at one end of the playing area. The equipment representing each planet, including Earth, is positioned relative to its distance from the sun.

Equipment

Objects to represent the earth and other planets (cones, specific colors of polyspots, etc.), outer-space music.

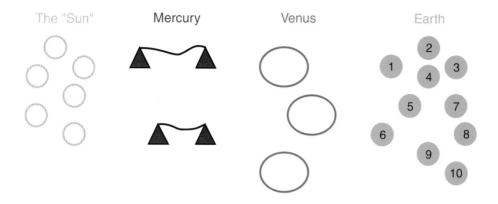

Procedures

Five to 10 players, or rocket ships, begin on Earth. Players can begin standing, but each time they return to Earth they must assume a new non-locomotor position as announced by the teacher (e.g., twisted shape on three body parts). The game begins on the teacher's signal, and designated rocket ships (e.g., numbers 3, 6, and 8) blast off and travel to Mercury and back to Earth. As children return to Earth, the teacher announces the type of non-locomotor skill to perform on the green polyspots. The teacher should call out different numbers for each round of play so that all children are included. More students (or rocket ships) can blast off at one time depending on the children's space awareness skills.

Order of Planets From Sun

(1) Mercury: cones with ropes to travel over. (2) Venus: styrofoam shapes to travel through. (3) Earth: green polyspots. (4) Mars: cones to skip around. (5) Jupiter: red polyspots to hop on. (6) Saturn: sturdy foam shapes to jump off of. (7) Uranus: red hula hoops to balance part of the body inside and outside of. (8) Neptune: balance boards to balance on top of. (9) Pluto: jump ropes placed on the floor to walk over as if they're tight ropes. (Reference: The Eugene Oregon Space Project.)

Where's My Partner?

Movement Skills

Skipping, galloping, walking, running, and hopping.

Movement Concepts

Space: pathways, directional changes. Effort: changes in speed. Relationships: moving with other players.

Formation

Scatter.

Procedures

Children are scattered throughout general space (bounded by markers). As music is played, the children perform a chosen locomotor skill throughout the general space and attempt to move to open spaces. When the music stops, the children find a partner (the nearest person; the teacher becomes a partner if the number of students is uneven). Once all the players are with a partner, the teacher states a way to "greet" their partner (e.g., with an "ankle shake"—partners simultaneously, side by side, shake each other's ankles by balancing on one foot and grasping the other's ankle with their hand), hip bumping, high five, do-si-do, and so forth. Each greeting is performed with a new partner, and each time the music stops the players must find their first (e.g., ankle-shake partner), then their second (bumping partner), then their third partner (high-five partner), and so on.

Quick As Lightning

Movement Skills

Any locomotor skill.

Movement Concepts

Space: general. Effort: quick changes of speed. Relationships: moving with lines on the floor and with other players.

Formation

Scatter.

Equipment

Music, lines on floor.

Procedures

Students, moving (forward direction) to music, must change direction (to backward or sideways or diagonal) every time they come to a line on the floor. Size of playing area can be decreased to a smaller space as children become better at using general and personal space.

Crossing the Brook

Movement Skills

Jumping and leaping (with a running approach).

Movement Concepts

Space: wide, narrow. Effort: strong. Relationships: leaping across the "brook."

Formation

Three to four students line up along the length of the "brook."

Equipment

Chalk, tape, or rope.

Procedures

Several lines or ropes are positioned to represent brooks. The children try to jump (one to two feet or leap) over. If they fall in, they must return home and pretend to change shoes and socks. The width of the brook should vary from narrow to wide so that all children will find a degree of success. You may try placing an object in the brook to be jumped on, such as a stepping-stone (mat or large plastic floor shape).

Jump the Shot

Movement Skills

Jumping.

Movement Concepts

Space: circular pathway. Effort: quick, light. Relationships: jumping over the moving rope.

Formation

Small groups of students or partner groups.

Equipment

Beanbag on the end of 10-foot line or jump rope.

Procedures

A student swings the rope about 3 to 6 inches off the ground at a moderate pace. To accomplish this, the student moves around in a circle as she simultaneously swings the rope for her partner. The children jump over the rope as it comes to them. Be sure to warn the children of the dangers of tripping, and do not allow the rope to be turned too fast. The children can perform tricks over the rope (tap ankles together in the air) or jump sideways or backward.

NON-LOCOMOTOR SKILL THEMES

Non-locomotor skill themes include bending, stretching, twisting, and curling, as well as swinging actions. These movements do not travel through space but are "stationary." The non-locomotor skills are essential skills to develop and apply to all three content areas of elementary physical education (i.e., games, dance, and gymnastics). For example, a child may stretch when performing a jump off of a low foam shape (gymnastics). Stretching actions are also used in retrieving an object far away from the body, as in catching a ball (games). Or a child may perform a stretched shape when involved in a dance lesson using elastic bands as props.

Non-locomotor skills may also be used in combination. Passing an object to an offensive teammate requires bending, twisting, and stretching in order to evade one's opponent. Dribbling a soccer ball around an opponent may also demand bending and twisting actions. Vaulting or jumping over a foam shape could require stretching on the takeoff, bending (knees to chest), and stretching for the landing. In the creative dance, "The Museum Game" (lesson plan on CD-ROM), you might ask children to make different shapes, thereby prompting the use of non-locomotor skills.

In game play situations, players may use mature non-locomotor skills to evade an opponent. For example, dodging an opponent consists of quick bending and twisting actions. These movements are performed by quick upper body "feints": the offensive player pretends to move in a certain direction by leaning the torso or quickly moving the head or shoulders in that direction, which is opposite the actual direction intended. These "feintings" involve isolated actions of specific body parts, but since they do not travel they are categorized as non-locomotor skills.

The initial stage mover must develop the non-locomotor skills within predictable, stationary, and individualized movement contexts. The following activities are suggested for children who are just beginning to "get the idea" or who are at the *initial stage* of motor skill development.

SAMPLE NON-LOCOMOTOR GAMES

Games that enhance non-locomotor skills are designed to include bending, stretching, twisting, curling, or swinging actions. You will notice that the following games also include locomotor skills. However, the emphasis during the game should be placed on performance of the non-locomotor skills.

Rock'n Stop

Movement Skills

Non-locomotor: quick stops and starts; dodging (lower body's center of gravity; bend at waist, lean torso).

Movement Concepts

Space: quick directional changes. Effort: slow, medium, fast. Relationships: moving around others.

Equipment

CD player and CD with "Rock'n Stop Music," song #2, on *Music for Creative Dance-3*, Ravenna Ventures Inc., Seattle, WA; composer: Eric Chapelle.

Procedures

Class is in a scattered formation throughout general space. As music plays, the teacher asks the students to perform various locomotor skills throughout general space. When the music stops, students respond by stopping in their own self-space. You should emphasize the correct mechanics of safely stopping (i.e., wide base of support, using arms for balance, bending knees). During a second round of play, you can also ask students to execute different types of balances (on differing numbers of body parts or differing types of shapes such as wide, narrow, twisted, straight, bent) at a high, medium, or low level.

Junkyard Dodging

Movement Skills

Non-locomotor: using body or torso to fake (bend; curl) going in one direction while traveling in another; using head to fake direction. Locomotor: walking, running.

Movement Concepts

Space: pathways. Effort: fast, medium, slow speeds. Relationships: moving around obstacles.

Equipment

Obstacles to maneuver: foam shapes, carpet squares, bowling pins, cones, ropes, or hoops.

Procedures

Children begin by standing beside or behind an object placed on the floor within a bounded area. Teacher demonstrates how to "fake" or lean in one direction and then travels in the other direction around an obstacle. A drumbeat can be used to prompt students to "fake" using head, shoulders, or torso. The task can be extended by having one student "shadow" a partner (i.e., follower, leader).

What's My Name? or Our Spelling List

Movement Skills

Non-locomotor: bending, stretching, twisting, curling, swinging.

Movement Concepts

Space: levels. Effort: bound movement. Relationships: moving to music, to elastic band, and to a partner.

Equipment

Music, tape player, stretchy bands.

Procedures

The teacher holds up large poster-size letters of the alphabet. Students make the letter with their bodies. Children may use any body part and create the letter at any level. The teacher can divide children into groups and have each group make a "secret" letter. Other groups try to guess what letter is being formed. The teacher has children discover what non-locomotor movements their letters are formed with. Older groups of children can spell out words. Children can also spell out their own names. A variation of this activity uses elastic bands. Children form the letters, using different body parts, as they stretch an elastic band. Finally, letters can be formed by partners, with or without elastic bands. Music can accompany any aspect of these activities. Children try to move to the beat of the music; for example, each letter of a child's name is formed to the tempo of the music.

Stuck to the Dot Tag

Movement Skills

Non-locomotor: bending, twisting. Locomotor: walking, running, galloping.

Movement Concepts

Space: pathways, directions, levels. Effort: slow, medium, fast speed. Relationships: moving with others.

Equipment

Polyspots, cones for boundary markers, scarves or flag belts.

Procedures

Seventy-five percent of the children, scattered throughout general space, must keep one foot on a polyspot at all times—stay "stuck to the dot." The remainder of the children travel around stationary players. The traveling players wear "rip-flag belts." The object of the game is for the stationary players to take the flags off the travelers' flag belts. Once they have taken a flag, they stick it onto their own Velcro flag belt. The teacher announces when the game is over. Scarves tucked into shorts can replace flag belts. Player's roles must be rotated on each round. For children at the initial stage of motor skill development, the use of flag belts can be omitted, and tagging the backs or arms of traveling players can be substituted.

Cats

Movement Skills

Non-locomotor: bending, twisting, curling. Locomotor: walking, running.

Movement Concepts

Space: general. Effort: fast, medium, slow speeds. Relationships: moving around others.

Equipment

Felt "cattails" of varying colors and designs (e.g., spotted, striped, brown, black, white). Cones to be used as boundary markers.

Procedures

Children tuck one or two "cattails" in their shorts. Extra cattails are kept at the side of the playing space in a hula hoop, or "cat dish." The object of the game is to steal cattails from other cats. In order to evade other cats, the students must use twisting, bending, and curling non-locomotor skills.

Frisbee Quick Catch

Movement Skills

Non-locomotor: stretching and bending. Manipulative: catching and throwing.

Movement Concepts

Space: quick direction changes. Effort: quick, light. Relationships: moving with a Frisbee and with cone/saucer.

Equipment

Cones or plastic "saucers," Frisbees, and foam balls.

Equipment Setup

Cone or saucer with a foam ball on top.

Procedures

One student stands behind and to the side of each cone. Player A throws the Frisbee to player B. Player B attempts to catch the Frisbee and simultaneously knock the ball off the cone. The distance between players can be determined by each pair of students (i.e., inclusion style teaching as discussed in chapter 10). Each time a player retrieves the Frisbee and simultaneously knocks the foam ball off the cone (or appropriate "tee"), the player scores a point. Children must stretch to retrieve the Frisbee and bend to knock off the foam ball.

Identical Twins

Movement Skills

Non-locomotor: bending, stretching, twisting, curling, swinging.

Movement Concepts

Space: levels. Effort: smooth, slow. Relationships: moving with a partner.

Equipment

Wands, small hula hoops, or Dynabands are used along with slow music.

Procedures

In pairs, children mirror their partner's non-locomotor movements. Partner A begins by creating, for example, a medium-level stretched shape. Partner B mirrors that non-locomotor movement. The song "Breath" by composer Eric Chapelle (*Music for Creative Dance*, Revenna Ventures Inc., Seattle, WA) is appropriate for slow, controlled non-locomotor performance. Native American flute music and slow classical music are also appropriate as accompaniment.

CONCEPT 19.8

Children should explore the range of movement possibilities within a skill theme. The movement concepts provide the tools for enabling children to develop a greater repertoire of movement skills.

ASSESSING PROGRESS

Assessing students' performance of both non-locomotor and locomotor skills serves multiple purposes. Assessment gives teachers critical knowledge about their students' abilities and provides helpful information about the effectiveness of a lesson. This in turn assists teachers in planning new and meaningful learning activities. Assessment can also enhance learning as students participate in a lesson. Formative authentic assessment conducted by the teacher, by peers, or by oneself is most effective in enhancing students' learning during a physical education lesson. Authentic assessments must be related to the learning objectives of the lesson in addition to being age and developmentally appropriate. Summative assessment, conducted at the beginning and end of a skill theme unit of instruction, is also useful in that it provides entry-level information about students' stage of skill development, helpful diagnostic information, and information relative to student improvement and learning as a result of the unit activities. Both formative and summative assessments are explained in greater detail in chapter 12, "Assessing Progress."

CONCEPT 19.9

Comparison of exit-level assessments with entry-level assessments is essential to diagnostic developmental teaching.

For children at the fundamental phase of developing their movement abilities, observational assessment works quite well. The sample assessment charts in chapter 12 are a practical means of charting individual and group progress. A second way to assess progress in locomotor skill development is to answer a self-question survey similar to the one shown in figure 19.25. If you are unable to answer "yes" to each question, you will need to modify subsequent lessons to more closely fit the specific needs of the individual or group.

Authentic assessments should be designed to address whether specific lesson or unit objectives have been met. Schiemer (2000) provides several assessment examples. For example in the skill application locomotor game, Crossing the Brook, students could be asked to differentiate between a leap and a jump. Students could view two pictures (drawings or clip art) of the landing phase of each and circle the appropriate choice. Asking students which locomotor skill they enjoy performing the most could also assess students' affective domain.

| | Yes | No | Comments |

Running

1. Are the children able to run from point to point with good postural control?
2. Are they able to make smooth transitions in direction, level, and speed?
3. Can they run about the gym or play yard without bumping into each other?
4. Can they use the running patterns in conjunction with other basic skills?
5. Do they run without undue attention focused on the process?
6. Are their movements relaxed, fluid, and rhythmical?
7. Is there observable improvement?

Leaping

1. Can they leap leading with either foot?
2. Can they make adjustments in height and distance with ease?
3. Is appropriate body lean used for the distance leaped?
4. Are the arms used properly in conjunction with the legs?
5. Is there observable improvement?

Jumping/Hopping

1. Can the children jump or hop with good control of their bodies?
2. Can the children take off simultaneously with both feet and land on both feet at the same time in all three jumping patterns?
3. Can the children take off on one or both feet and land on one foot when hopping?
4. Can they hop equally well on either foot?
5. Are the hopping and jumping actions smooth, fluid, and rhythmical?
6. Is there improved summation of force used to produce a hop or jump?
7. Is there any easy transition from one pattern to another?
8. Is there observable improvement?

Galloping

1. Can they gallop while leading with either the left or right foot?
2. Does the toe of the trailing foot remain behind the heel of the leading foot?
3. Is the action smooth and rhythmical?
4. Is there observable improvement?

Sliding

1. Can the children slide equally well in both directions?
2. Do they slide without crossing the feet?
3. Is the action smooth and rhythmical?
4. Is there observable improvement?

Skipping

1. Is the skipping action smooth and rhythmical?
2. Is there rhythmical alteration of both sides of the body?
3. Is there sufficient knee lift?
4. Is the arm action appropriate for the purpose of the skip?

FIGURE 19.25   Self-question chart for fundamental locomotor skill development.

Summary

Mature fundamental locomotor and non-locomotor skills are basic to the effective functioning of the individual and permit movement through the environment using efficient and effective means of travel. Locomotor movement skill themes focus on helping children progress from the initial to the elementary and finally to the mature stage in basic skills such as running, leaping, jumping, hopping, galloping, sliding, and skipping. Entry-level assessment of children's present stages of locomotor and non-locomotor skill development is essential prior to planning lessons that are both developmentally and age group appropriate.

Teaching strategies that help children learn the skill concepts and the movement concepts involved in locomotor and non-locomotor movements give children the tools for knowing how the body should move and how the body can move. Exploratory and guided discovery experience is particularly appropriate for children who are functioning at less than the mature stage. Games involving particular locomotor and non-locomotor skills are effective to use with children at the mature stage of these skills. Remember, overemphasis on the product of the game (i.e., winning) is frequently counterproductive when children have not yet mastered consistent use of the mature mechanics of a fundamental skill. Be certain to focus first on the process and work toward mastery of the body mechanics, using a variety of individually appropriate techniques, before emphasizing the product of the movement.

Terms to Remember

Excellent Readings

Hopple, C.J. (1995). *Teaching for outcomes in elementary physical education: A guide for curriculum and assessment.* Champaign, IL: Human Kinetics.

Schiemer, S. (2000). *Assessment strategies in elementary physical education.* Champaign, IL: Human Kinetics.

20

Fundamental Manipulative Skill Themes

Key Concept

▶ Fundamental manipulative skills may be developed and refined through a skill theme approach using movement experiences that are both individually appropriate and age group appropriate.

Chapter Objectives

This chapter will provide you with the tools to do the following:

▶ Describe the steps in developing a fundamental manipulative movement skill theme.

▶ Illustrate the importance of fundamental manipulative skill sequencing.

▶ Identify the initial, elementary, and mature stages of a variety of fundamental manipulative skills.

▶ Describe developmental difficulties that children encounter in their fundamental manipulative skill development and appropriate strategies for overcoming these deficits.

▶ Discuss the movement concepts and skill concepts that children should know concerning a variety of fundamental manipulative skills.

▶ Be able to incorporate exploratory and guided discovery activities into the fundamental manipulative skill theme lesson.

▶ Discuss the role of developmentally appropriate games in skill application of fundamental manipulative skills.

▶ Demonstrate knowledge of how to informally assess progress in a fundamental manipulative skill theme.

Manipulative skills, as referred to here, are gross body movements in which force is imparted to or received from objects. Manipulative movements such as throwing, catching, kicking, trapping, striking, volleying, bouncing, and ball rolling are generally considered to be fundamental manipulative skills. These skills are essential to purposeful and controlled interaction with objects in our environment. In their refined form, they are also necessary for successful playing of many of the sports of our culture.

Manipulative skills do not develop automatically. Opportunities for practice, encouragement, and instruction are essential in order for most children to develop mature patterns of manipulative movement. Achievement of the mature stage in many fundamental manipulative skills generally occurs somewhat later than for most locomotor skills because of the many complex visual-motor adjustments that are required for intercepting a moving object, as with catching, trapping, striking, and volleying. Therefore, as the instructor you should be alert both to children's perceptual abilities and to their movement abilities when focusing on manipulative skill development. Modification of the object to be intercepted through the use of balloons, beach balls, or foam balls frequently works well during the initial and

CONCEPT 20.1

Object manipulation permits the individual to come into meaningful contact with objects in the environment.

elementary stages of the skill. This chapter focuses on the importance of skill sequencing and on ways to develop a manipulative skill theme. We provide verbal and visual descriptions of several gross motor manipulative skills, identify common developmental difficulties, and present teaching tips and concepts that children should know (Gallahue & Ozmun, 2002). We then present a sampling of appropriate skill development activities that focus on exploratory, guided discovery, and developmentally appropriate game activities. Suggestions for assessing progress conclude the chapter.

TEXT BOX 20.1

Developing a Manipulative Skill Theme

When planning a fundamental manipulative skill theme, you will find it helpful to follow this sequence:

1. Preplan.
   a. Determine which manipulative skills will be grouped together for each skill theme. The following grouping generally works well:
      1) Throwing and catching
      2) Kicking and trapping
      3) Striking and volleying
      4) Dribbling and ball rolling
   b. Determine when in the yearly curriculum to include each manipulative skill theme. You will need to decide whether to space out lessons on each skill theme over the entire school year or to group lessons into longer units of instruction. Distributed practice tends to work better than massed practice during the beginning level of movement skill learning.
   c. Decide approximately how many lessons you will spend on fundamental manipulative skill development in relation to the total curriculum.

2. Observe and assess.
   a. Observe the fundamental manipulative skills of the children to be taught.
   b. Assess whether the students are at the initial, elementary, or mature stage of skill development with respect to each manipulative skill theme. Study the verbal and visual descriptions of each manipulative skill for guidance.

3. Plan and implement.
   a. Plan appropriate movement activities geared to the needs, interests, and ability level of the group. For help, study the teaching tips and concepts children should know in the pages that follow.
   b. Implement a planned program of activities, stressing progression in skill development.

4. Evaluate and revise.
   a. Informally evaluate progress in the manipulative skills being stressed in terms of improved mechanics and performance. The questions in figure 20.25 at the end of the chapter will be helpful.
   b. Based on student progress, revise subsequent lessons as needed.

MANIPULATIVE SKILL SEQUENCING

Fundamental manipulative skills begin developing early in children. Young children's interaction with objects and their gross attempts at throwing, catching, and kicking are generally the first forms of gross motor manipulation. Simply by virtue of maturation, most children progress to the elementary stage in their manipulative abilities. Progress to the mature stage largely depends on environmental stimulation. Because of the sophisticated perceptual requirements of most fundamental manipulative skills, children often lag behind in the development of their ability to strike a pitched ball or to volley a ball repeatedly. Therefore, attainment of the mature stage in manipulative skills depends on the combination of maturational readiness, environmental openness, and teacher sensitivity.

Although most children have the developmental potential to perform at the mature stage in their fundamental manipulative skills by about seven years of age, many lag behind. In fact, it is not unusual to see numerous older children, and even college students, who are unable to throw, catch, volley, bounce, or strike a ball at the mature stage. In order to plan effectively for all your students, it is important to know where they are in terms of their manipulative skills.

> **CONCEPT 20.2**
>
> Preparing for a developmental movement skill theme requires preplanning, observing and assessing, specific planning and implementing, and evaluating and revising.

THROWING AND CATCHING

Throwing and catching are two fundamental movements that fit together especially well in the presentation of a skill theme. **Throwing** involves imparting force to an object through use of the hands. The throw may take many forms: in an overhand, underhand, or sidearm pattern and with either one or both hands, depending on the purpose of the throw. Here we deal with the overhand throwing pattern because it is probably the pattern most frequently used by both children and adults. Throwing abilities begin developing early in life, and it is common to see individuals who have not received any formal instruction, and have had only limited opportunity for practice, functioning at the elementary level in the overhand throw. Most children progress

> **CONCEPT 20.3**
>
> Although most children have the developmental potential to be at the mature stage of manipulative skills by age five or six, many lag behind because of inadequate instruction, opportunities for practice, and encouragement.

This young girl demonstrates the preparation, execution, and following components of an elementary stage overhand throwing pattern, using a beanbag.

to the elementary stage more as a function of maturation than experience. In most cases, however, they will continue to perform at this stage even as adolescents and adults unless they receive sufficient practice and instruction. Throwing for distance promotes the mature pattern. Throwing for accuracy should be stressed only after the mature pattern is well learned.

Catching involves receiving force from an object and retaining the object in the hands. Practice in catching can be facilitated by the use of objects of varying sizes, shapes, colors, and firmness. Children at the initial stage, for example, typically experience greater success with catching a soft, brightly colored beanbag, yarn ball, or beach ball than with a hard ball of comparable size. They are able to grip a beanbag more securely than the ball, and there is little fear of injury if a child is hit in the face or on a finger by a beanbag, yarn ball, or beach ball. Wise teachers provide opportunities for children to practice catching with a variety of objects. They also take care to set up experiences that will not result in an avoidance reaction of the head or a closing of the eyes out of fear as the object approaches. During the early stages of learning, you should not require the child to adapt to the equipment; rather, you should modify the equipment to the developmental needs of the child.

a

b

(a) This second grade student demonstrates a mature two-hand catching pattern. *(b)* This young boy prepares to catch a beanbag by reaching out for the oncoming object. Keep your eye on the beanbag!

Overhand Throwing

Overhand throwing is what we visualize young boys and girls doing with their moms, dads, and friends. Overhand throwing is the process of imparting force to an object, usually a ball, to another person or object using an overhand pattern. The pattern of movement varies according to the requirements of the movement task. For example, if the task requires throwing the ball to a partner who is 6 feet away, an initial pattern will suffice. If the partner is 15 to 20 feet away, an elementary pattern may do. But if the task requires throwing for a distance of 30 feet or more, the thrower will most likely use a mature pattern if it is within his present level of movement sophistication to do so (see figures 20.1 and 20.2).

I. Throwing
   A. Initial stage
      1. Action is mainly from elbow
      2. Elbow of throwing arm remains in front of body; action resembles a push
      3. Fingers spread at release
      4. Follow-through is forward and downward
      5. Trunk remains perpendicular to target
      6. Little rotary action during throw
      7. Body weight shifts slightly rearward to maintain balance
      8. Feet remain stationary
      9. There is often purposeless shifting of feet during preparation for throw
   B. Elementary stage
      1. In preparation, arm is swung upward, sideward, and backward to a position of elbow flexion
      2. Ball is held behind head
      3. Arm is swung forward, high over shoulder
      4. Trunk flexes forward with forward motion of arm
      5. Shoulders rotate toward throwing side
      6. Trunk flexes forward with forward motion of arm
      7. Definite forward shift of body weight
      8. Steps forward with leg on same side as throwing arm
   C. Mature stage
      1. Arm is swung backward in preparation
      2. Opposite elbow is raised for balance as a preparatory action in the throwing arm
      3. Throwing elbow moves forward horizontally as it extends
      4. Forearm rotates and thumb points downward
      5. Trunk markedly rotates to throwing side during preparatory action
      6. Throwing shoulder drops slightly
      7. Definite rotation through hips, legs, spine, and shoulders during throw
      8. Weight during preparatory movement is on rear foot
      9. As weight is shifted, there is a step with opposite foot
II. Developmental difficulties
   A. Forward movement of foot on same side as throwing arm
   B. Inhibited back swing
   C. Failure to rotate hips as throwing arm is brought forward
   D. Failure to step out on leg opposite the throwing arm
   E. Poor rhythmical coordination of arm movement with body movement
   F. Inability to release ball at desired trajectory
   G. Loss of balance while throwing
   H. Upward rotation of arm

FIGURE 20.1 Developmental sequence for overhand throwing.

Initial

Elementary

Mature

FIGURE 20.2   Stages of the overhand throwing pattern.

TEACHING TIP 20.1

When teaching *overhand throwing:*

- Provide numerous opportunities for practice. One or two sessions will not be enough to develop a consistent mature pattern.

- Focus first on throwing for distance, not accuracy.

- Work for speed of movement and good hip rotation.

- Use carpet squares or hoops as cues for stepping out on the opposite foot.

- Be sure to have an ample supply of balls or beanbags that can be easily thrown.

- Beanbags, newspaper balls, yarn balls, and stocking balls work well and add variety.

- Use beanbags for wall drills to emphasize the throwing action and not catching or retrieving.

- Speed, accuracy, and distance are the performance elements of throwing. Work first for distance, then speed, and finally accuracy.

- Follow a logical teaching progression, using the preceding recommendations as a guide.

- There should be 100% participation.

THROWING CONCEPTS CHILDREN SHOULD KNOW

Skill concepts:

- Stand so that the leg on the other side of the throwing arm is leading.
- Turn your shoulder toward the target.
- Raise your free arm and point toward the target.
- Raise your throwing arm and hold the ball close to and behind your ear.
- Lead with your elbow on the forward swing.
- Bring your rear foot forward and follow through.

Movement concepts:

- The effort that you give to your throw will influence how fast the ball travels and the smoothness of your throwing motion.
- When you throw a ball, it can travel through space in a variety of directions and at various levels.
- A ball may be thrown using throwing patterns ranging from overhand and underhand to a variety of sidearm patterns.
- You can throw many different types of objects. The size, shape, and weight of the object will affect the distance it travels, as well as the pattern you use.
- The coordinated use of your arms, trunk, and legs will affect the speed and distance of your throw.

CONCEPT 20.4

Children can be accurately assessed as being at the initial, elementary, or mature stage in a variety of fundamental manipulative movement skills.

Catching

Catching is a visual task as well as a motor task. Because it requires sophisticated coordinated use of both processes, catching develops somewhat later than other fundamental movement skills in children. Catching involves making the fine visual-motor adjustments required to locate, anticipate, initiate, and intercept a moving object. As easy as it seems to us, it is a formidable movement task for many children (see figures 20.3 and 20.4).

TEACHING TIP 20.2

When teaching *catching:*

- Use soft objects for initial catching experiences. Yarn balls and beanbags work best.
- Provide verbal cues such as "Ready? Catch" to avoid surprises.
- Begin with large balls and progress to smaller sizes.

- Use brightly colored balls.
- Be aware of the background against which the ball is to be caught. Avoid figure-ground blending.
- Vary the speed, level, and trajectory of the ball as skill increases.

I. Catching
   A. Initial stage
      1. There is often an avoidance reaction of turning the face away or protecting the face with arms (avoidance reaction is learned and therefore may not be present)
      2. Arms are extended and held in front of the body
      3. Body movement is limited until contact
      4. Catch resembles a scooping action
      5. Use of body to trap ball
      6. Palms are held upward
      7. Fingers are extended and held tense
      8. Hands are not utilized in catching action
   B. Elementary stage
      1. Avoidance reaction is limited to eyes closing at contact with ball
      2. Elbows are held at sides with an approximately 90-degree bend
      3. Since initial attempt at contact with child's hand is often unsuccessful, arms trap the ball
      4. Hands are held in opposition to each other; thumbs are held upward
      5. At contact, the hands attempt to squeeze ball in a poorly timed and uneven motion
   C. Mature stage
      1. No avoidance reaction
      2. Eyes follow ball into hands
      3. Arms are held relaxed at sides, and forearms are held in front of body
      4. Arms give on contact to absorb force of the ball
      5. Arms adjust to flight of ball
      6. Thumbs are held in opposition to each other
      7. Hands grasp ball in a well-timed, simultaneous motion
      8. Fingers grasp more effectively
II. Developmental difficulties
   A. Failure to maintain control of object
   B. Failure to "give" with the catch
   C. Keeping fingers rigid and straight in the direction of object
   D. Failure to adjust hand position to the height and trajectory of object
   E. Inability to vary the catching pattern for objects of different weight and force
   F. Taking eyes off object
   G. Closing the eyes
   H. Inability to focus on or track the ball
   I. Improper stance, causing loss of balance when catching a fast-moving object
   J. Closing hands either too early or too late
   K. Failure to keep body in line with the ball

FIGURE 20.3 Developmental sequence for catching.

Initial

Elementary

Mature

FIGURE 20.4   Stages of the catching pattern.

CATCHING CONCEPTS CHILDREN SHOULD KNOW

Skill concepts:

- Get directly in the path of the ball.
- Place one foot ahead of the other.
- Adjust your hand position for the height of the ball—thumbs in for balls above the waist, thumbs out for balls below the waist.
- Curve your fingers and keep your eyes on the ball. Pull the ball in toward your body.

(continued on following page)

(continued from preceding page)

CONCEPT 20.5

Children need to learn the skill concepts and movement concepts associated with fundamental movement skill acquisition.

Movement concepts:

- You can catch an object in many different ways.
- You can catch with different body parts.
- You can catch from a variety of positions.
- The objects you catch may vary in size, shape, color, or texture.
- The objects you catch can come toward you at different levels and with varying degrees of speed.
- You can play a variety of games that involve catching.

KICKING AND TRAPPING

Kicking and trapping are two fundamental movement patterns that fit nicely together into a common skill theme. Basically, **kicking** involves imparting force to an object with use of the foot and leg. Kicking may take the form of kicking a pebble, a can, or a ball; it is a part of some low-level games and of the sports of soccer and football. As individuals develop a mature pattern of kicking, emphasis should be on kicking for distance. Distance kicking (or kicking as forcefully as possible) promotes the mature pattern. More complete action of the kicking leg on the windup and follow-through, as well as the coordinated action of the trunk and arms, is necessary for a long kick versus shorter kicks. Kicking for accuracy should not be of concern until after the mature pattern has been mastered.

The kicking pattern is demonstrated by this Hillsdale Elementary student, who is at the elementary stage of skill development.

Trapping, or *collecting* as it is sometimes called, is a fundamental movement pattern that requires use of various parts of the body to stop the forward momentum of an oncoming object. With children, trapping a rolled ball should precede trapping a tossed object. The focus of the lessons on trapping should be on gaining control of the ball and being able to make appropriate adjustments relative to the speed of the ball and the level of contact.

This fifth grade boy at Hillsdale Elementary School demonstrates a mature stage kicking pattern in soccer, using the inside of his foot.

There are many ways to receive or collect a soccer ball. This young boy demonstrates trapping with his shins and feet.

Kicking

Kicking, like catching, is a sophisticated visual-motor task. In this instance it is coordination of the eyes with the feet that is required. Once again, anticipation, initiation, and interception are all important events in successful performance. This movement task is used primarily in the sports of American soccer and football (see figures 20.5 and 20.6).

I. Kicking
   A. Initial stage
      1. Movements are restricted during kicking action
      2. Trunk remains erect
      3. Arms are used to maintain balance
      4. Movement of kicking leg is limited in backswing
      5. Forward swing is short: there is little follow-through
      6. Child kicks "at" ball rather than kicking it squarely and following through
      7. A pushing rather than striking action is predominant
   B. Elementary stage
      1. Preparatory backswing is centered at the knee
      2. Kicking leg tends to remain bent throughout the kick
      3. Follow-through is limited to forward movement of the knee
      4. One or more deliberate steps are taken toward the ball
   C. Mature stage
      1. Arms swing in opposition to each other during kicking action
      2. Trunk bends at waist during follow-through
      3. Movement of kicking leg is initiated at the hip
      4. Support leg bends slightly on contact
      5. Length of leg swing increases
      6. Follow-through is high; support foot rises to toes or leaves surface entirely
      7. Approach to the ball is from either a run or leap
II. Developmental difficulties
   A. Restricted or absent backswing
   B. Failure to step forward with non-kicking leg
   C. Tendency to lose balance
   D. Inability to kick with either foot
   E. Inability to alter speed of kicked ball
   F. Jabbing at ball without follow-through
   G. Poor opposition of arms and legs
   H. Failure to use a summation of forces by the body to contribute to force of the kick
   I. Failure to contact ball squarely or missing it completely (eyes not focused on ball)
   J. Failure to get adequate distance (lack of follow-through and force production)

FIGURE 20.5   Developmental sequence for kicking.

Initial

Elementary

Mature

FIGURE 20.6 Stages of the kicking pattern.

TEACHING TIP 20.3

When teaching *kicking:*

- Focus on kicking for distance rather than accuracy. Accuracy kicking will not promote use of the mature pattern.
- If possible, have a ball for every other child.
- Begin with a variety of exploratory experiences, but progress to guided discovery experiences without too much delay.
- Encourage kicking with the nonpreferred foot after the mature stage has been reached with the preferred foot.
- Work jointly with kicking and trapping, using a peer teaching approach.
- Be sure to work for control of the height of the

ball. This will make it necessary to teach the instep and inside-of-foot kick as well as the popular toe kick.
- After the mature kicking pattern has been achieved, introduce accuracy kicking activities.
- Incorporate kicking into low-level games and lead-up games after the mature stage has been reached.
- Work for total-body control in kicking.
- Have children practice kicking a stationary ball prior to a moving ball.
- Be sure to use balls about the same size as a standard soccer ball.

KICKING CONCEPTS CHILDREN SHOULD KNOW

Skill concepts:

- Stand behind the ball and slightly to one side.
- Step forward on the non-kicking foot.
- Keep your eyes on the ball.
- Swing your kicking leg back and then forcefully forward from the hip.
- The snap down from the knee gives the ball its speed.
- Contact the ball with the top portion of your foot (low ball), with your toe (high ball), or with the inside portion of your foot (ground ball).
- Follow through in the direction that the ball is to go.
- Use your arms for balance and force production.
- The kicking pattern is basic to the sport of soccer and is used in kicking games such as kick ball.

Movement concepts:

- You can kick a ball at different levels (high, medium, low) by contacting it with different parts of your feet.
- You can kick either for distance or for accuracy, but the two processes will look different.
- The manner in which you coordinate the use of your entire body will influence the direction, distance, level, and path that the ball takes.
- You can kick the ball at objects and to people. Great precision is needed for kicking at or to something.
- It is important for you to keep your eyes on the ball when it is about to be kicked.
- Your kicks can be long or short, fast or slow, hard or soft, and they may travel in a variety of directions and at different levels.

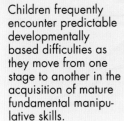

CONCEPT 20.6

Children frequently encounter predictable developmentally based difficulties as they move from one stage to another in the acquisition of mature fundamental manipulative skills.

Trapping or Collecting

Trapping, or collecting, is also a sophisticated fundamental skill involving use of the feet and eyes in a coordinated manner. Collecting is a movement task in which the individual gains control of a moving object without use of the hands. It is a basic skill essential to successful performance in the game of American soccer (see figures 20.7 and 20.8).

I. Trapping/Collecting
   A. Initial stage
      1. Trunk remains rigid
      2. No "give" with ball as it makes contact
      3. Inability to absorb force of the ball
      4. Difficulty getting in line with object
   B. Elementary stage
      1. Poor visual tracking
      2. "Gives" with the ball, but movements are poorly timed and sequenced
      3. Can trap a rolled ball with relative ease but cannot trap a tossed ball
      4. Appears uncertain of what body part to use
      5. Movements lack fluidity
   C. Mature stage
      1. Tracks ball throughout
      2. "Gives" with body upon contact
      3. Can trap both rolled and tossed balls
      4. Can trap balls approaching at a moderate velocity
      5. Moves with ease to intercept ball
II. Developmental difficulties
   A. Failure to position body directly in path of ball
   B. Failure to keep eyes fixed on ball
   C. Failure to "give" as ball contacts body part
   D. Failure to angle an aerial ball
   E. Causing body to meet ball instead of letting ball meet body
   F. Inability to maintain body balance when trapping in unusual or awkward positions

FIGURE 20.7   Developing sequence for trapping/collecting.

TEACHING TIP 20.4

When teaching *trapping/collecting*:

- Begin with collecting activities that involve the feet and legs (foot trap and single- and double-knee trap).
- Teach how to collect a rolled ball before using an elevated ball.
- Stress eye contact with the ball throughout.
- Introduce trapping a tossed ball only after the concepts involved in collecting a ground ball are mastered.
- Use a foam ball, beach ball, or partially inflated ball in the beginning.
- Foam balls work nicely to introduce collecting an elevated object.
- Work for control with the stomach and chest traps by teaching how to deflect the ball downward.
- Emphasize the importance of getting in the path of the ball, "giving" with it, and absorbing its force over as much surface area as possible.
- Do not introduce kicking and trapping drills until both partners are at the mature stage.

Initial

Elementary

Mature

FIGURE 20.8 Stages of the trapping/collecting pattern.

TRAPPING/COLLECTING CONCEPTS CHILDREN SHOULD KNOW

Skill concepts:

- Get directly in the path of the ball.
- Keep your eyes on the ball.
- "Give" with the ball as it touches the body.
- Deflect an elevated ball downward.
- Let the ball meet your body.
- The trapping pattern is basic to the sport of soccer and any other activity in which the trunk, legs, or feet are used to stop an object.

(continued on following page)

(continued from preceding page)

Movement concepts:

- You can use any part of your body to trap a ball except your hands and arms.
- You can trap a ball at different levels.
- You can trap objects other than balls.
- You and your partner can practice trapping and kicking together.
- Your control of the ball will influence the success of your trapping.

This group of Hillsdale Elementary students practice bouncing a basketball as they move through general space around others.

BALL BOUNCING AND ROLLING

Ball bouncing is a fundamental movement that involves receiving force from an object and immediately imparting force from that object in a downward (hand bounce or dribble) or a ground-level, horizontal (foot dribble) direction without the use of an implement. The developmental sequence for hand bouncing appears to consist of the following:

1. Bouncing and catching
2. Bouncing and ineffective slapping at the ball
3. Basic bouncing with the ball in control of the child
4. Basic bouncing while stationary with the child in control of the ball
5. Controlled bouncing while moving

Bouncing is applied primarily to the sport activities of basketball, soccer, and speedball and in rhythmic gymnastics. Bouncing is unique in that it is of only limited direct value to most recreational and daily living skills. It does, however, provide the individual with important experiences in interrupting an object and requires the sophisticated interaction of sensory and motor processes at a precise moment in time. Therefore, when we view bouncing as a fundamental movement, we may also view it as an ideal task for helping people learn how to coordinate the use of the eyes with the hands.

The movement pattern of **ball rolling** involves imparting force to an object in such a way that it travels in a forward direction on the ground. There has been limited scientific study of ball rolling using controlled experimentation, so we know little about the emergence of ball-rolling abilities. But ball rolling is a fundamental movement pattern that is often applied to the sport and recreational activities of bowling, curling, bocce, and shuffleboard. The basic ball-rolling pattern may be observed in underhand tossing, softball pitching, and lifesaving rope-tossing techniques.

Ball Bouncing

For many people, ball bouncing is a formidable task. After all, it involves giving force in a downward direction to an object and receiving force in an upward direction from that same object, usually a rubber ball, that often seems to have a mind of its own. The visual acuity requirements, as well as the figure-ground and depth perception requirements of this task, are complex. Think of it: after pushing a rubber ball forcefully downward, you have only a split second to instantaneously react to your initial action by making contact with the upward-moving object and sending it downward again in a manner that will repeat itself over and over. This is an amazingly sophisticated perceptual-motor task that, with practice, soon becomes "automatic" (see figures 20.9 and 20.10).

TEACHING TIP 20.5

When teaching *ball bouncing:*

- Use a playground ball or other ball that does not require as much force in bouncing as a basketball.
- Use balls of different colors or striped balls to avoid blending of figure and ground.
- Work first for controlled bouncing and catching.
- Provide plenty of opportunities for practice in an atmosphere of exploration and experimentation.

- As skill develops, challenge the children with a variety of guided discovery activities that focus on being more aware of the process.
- Do not introduce low-level games, relays, or lead-up games until the mature stage of bouncing has been reasonably well achieved.
- Have students master bouncing with the dominant hand prior to practicing with the nondominant hand.

I. Ball bouncing
  A. Initial stage
    1. Ball held with both hands
    2. Hands placed on sides of ball, with palms facing each other
    3. Downward thrusting action with both arms
    4. Ball contacts surface close to body, may contact foot
    5. Great variation in height of bounce
    6. Repeated bounce and catch pattern
  B. Elementary stage
    1. Ball held with both hands, one on top and the other near the bottom
    2. Slight forward lean, with ball brought to chest level to begin the action
    3. Downward thrust with top hand and arm
    4. Force of downward thrust inconsistent
    5. Hand slaps at ball for subsequent bounces
    6. Wrist flexes and extends and palm of hand contacts ball on each bounce
    7. Visually monitors ball
    8. Limited control of ball while dribbling
  C. Mature stage
    1. Feet placed in narrow strike position, with foot opposite dribbling hand forward
    2. Slight forward trunk lean
    3. Ball held waist high
    4. Ball pushed toward ground, with follow-through of arm, wrist, and fingers
    5. Controlled force of downward thrust
    6. Repeated contact and pushing action initiated from fingertips
    7. Visual monitoring unnecessary
    8. Controlled directional dribbling
II. Developmental difficulties
  A. Slapping at ball instead of pushing it downward
  B. Inconsistent force applied to downward thrust
  C. Failure to focus on and track ball efficiently
  D. Inability to dribble with both hands
  E. Inability to dribble without visually monitoring ball
  F. Insufficient follow-through
  G. Inability to move about under control while dribbling

FIGURE 20.9   Developmental sequence for ball bouncing.

Initial

Elementary

Mature

FIGURE 20.10   Stages of the ball-bouncing pattern.

BALL-BOUNCING CONCEPTS CHILDREN SHOULD KNOW

Skill concepts:

- Push the ball down.
- Your wrist controls the bounce.
- Use your fingertips.
- Follow through.
- Push the ball slightly forward.
- Keep the ball below your waist.

(continued on following page)

(continued from preceding page)

Movement concepts:

- You can bounce the ball at different levels.
- You can bounce the ball with different amounts of force.
- You can control the amount of time between bounces by using different amounts of force and bouncing at different levels.
- The rhythmic flow of the bounced ball is important for controlled bouncing.
- You can bounce many kinds and sizes of balls.
- The density of the ball will influence its bouncing capabilities.

Ball Rolling

You can roll a ball from a sitting or a standing position. From a sitting position, ball rolling simply involves imparting force to an object that is currently in position on a supporting surface. From a standing position, however, the requirements of the task become somewhat different. Now the task involves specific elements of stability, namely twisting, bending, and stretching, employed in coordinated unison with the locomotor skill of stepping forward (walking) to impart controlled force to an object, typically in a forward direction. Ball rolling is, of course, used in complex static sport skills such as bowling and curling and as a means of verifying visual images with motor responses. In other words, it is a means of making the perceptual and motor match so essential to all visual-motor events (see figures 20.11 and 20.12).

TEACHING TIP 20.6

When teaching *ball rolling:*

- Have children practice with large balls prior to smaller ones.
- Do not stress accuracy during the initial experiences.
- Work for proper body mechanics by having the children roll the ball at a wall from increasing distances.
- After the basic pattern has been mastered, begin working for increased accuracy.
- Begin with large targets to promote success, and progress to smaller ones as skill warrants.
- Gradually increase both distance and accuracy requirements.
- Children should not roll heavy objects such as a bowling ball until they have developed skill.
- Practice ball rolling from a stationary one-step position prior to adding an approach.

I. Ball rolling
   A. Initial stage
      1. Straddle stance
      2. Ball is held with hands on the sides, with palms facing each other
      3. Acute bend at waist, with backward pendulum motion of arms
      4. Eyes monitor ball
      5. Forward arm swing and trunk lift with release of ball
   B. Elementary stage
      1. Stride stance
      2. Ball held with one hand on bottom and the other on top
      3. Backward arm swing without weight transfer to the rear
      4. Limited knee bend
      5. Forward swing with limited follow-through
      6. Ball released between knee and waist level
      7. Eyes alternately monitor target and ball
   C. Mature stage
      1. Stride stance
      2. Ball held in hand corresponding to trailing leg
      3. Slight hip rotation and trunk lean forward
      4. Pronounced knee bend
      5. Forward swing with weight transference from rear to forward foot
      6. Release at knee level or below
      7. Eyes are on target throughout
II. Developmental difficulties
   A. Failure to transfer body weight to rear foot during initial part of action
   B. Failure to place controlling hand directly under ball
   C. Releasing the ball above waist level
   D. Failure to release ball from a virtual pendular motion, causing it to veer to one side
   E. Lack of follow-through, resulting in a weak roll
   F. Swinging the arms too far backward or out from the body
   G. Failure to keep eye on target
   H. Failure to step forward with foot opposite hand that holds ball
   I. Inability to bring ball to side of the body

FIGURE 20.11   Developmental sequence for ball rolling.

Initial

Elementary

Mature

FIGURE 20.12   Stages of the ball-rolling pattern.

BALL-ROLLING CONCEPTS CHILDREN SHOULD KNOW

Skill concepts:

- Stand with opposite foot leading.
- Swing your arm straight back as you rock back on your rear foot.
- Let go of the ball when it is 6 to 12 inches in front of your leading foot.
- Follow through with your swing in the direction of the target.
- Keep your eyes on the ball.
- The rolling pattern is basic to the sports of bowling, curling, and bocce. It is also used in games such as Tunnel Ball (p. 556) and Guard the Castle (p. 559).

(continued on following page)

(continued from preceding page)

Movement concepts:

- You can roll a ball at different speeds.
- The force you apply to the ball will control its speed.
- The coordinated use of your muscles as you roll the ball will influence the force of the ball and its speed.
- You can place your body in many different positions when rolling an object.
- You can roll a ball in many different directions and cause it to travel in different pathways.
- You can roll balls of different sizes.
- You can devise many challenging game activities that use ball rolling.

OBJECT STRIKING AND VOLLEYING

Object striking is a fundamental movement pattern that may be performed in several different planes, with or without the use of an implement. Striking may involve contact with a stationary or moving object. However, even though the plane, implement, and nature of the object to be struck may differ in a number of ways, striking in all these cases is governed by the same mechanical principles of movement. First, the amount of momentum generated depends on the length of the backswing, the number of muscles involved, and the proper sequential use of the muscles. Second, the object to be struck must be contacted at the precise moment that maximum speed of the swing has been reached. Third, the striking implement must follow through toward the intended target. Fourth, the striking implement should make contact at a right angle to the object. Fifth, the implement should be held out and away from the body to achieve maximum momentum.

The forms that striking takes are many, and its application to sports varies. The horizontal striking pattern is found in baseball. The vertical striking pattern is found in tennis, golf, volleyball, badminton, handball, and racketball. Only the horizontal striking pattern with an implement is described here. You should, however, be quick to recognize that the description, teaching tips, and concepts children should know apply equally well to striking an object in other planes or without an implement.

Volleying is a specialized striking-pattern skill that involves receiving force from an object and immediately imparting force to that object in a roughly vertical direction, as with volleyball or with heading and juggling in soccer. Volleying is characterized by the fact that it can be repeated more than once in the same sequence with the same ball. The developmental sequence for effective volleying is much like that for striking, beginning with ineffective, uncontrolled efforts followed by gradual control and increased proficiency. Volleying involves the complex interaction of visual and motor processes. It is helpful to initiate striking and volleying activities with the use of balloons, beach balls, or other light objects that allow children a longer visual tracking period. The size and color of the ball may influence volleying and striking activities. Be sensitive to these possible influencing factors, and be ready to make adjustments in ball type, size, or color to maximize the child's success potential.

Horizontal Striking

Horizontal striking is probably the most complex of all of the fundamental movements. It involves anticipating, reacting to, and imparting force to an object approaching the body in a horizontal plane. When done at the fundamental movement phase, striking of a stationary ball in a horizontal plane is difficult enough because of the visual-perceptual requirements of the task. Striking a moving object is a doubly difficult task (see figures 20.13 and 20.14).

I. Striking
   A. Initial stage
      1. Motion is from back to front
      2. Feet are stationary
      3. Trunk faces direction of tossed ball
      4. Elbow(s) fully flexed
      5. No trunk rotation
      6. Force comes from extension of flexed joints in a downward plane
   B. Elementary stage
      1. Trunk turned to side in anticipation of tossed ball
      2. Weight shifts to forward foot prior to ball contact
      3. Combined trunk and hip rotation
      4. Elbow(s) flexed at less acute angle
      5. Force comes from extension of flexed joints; trunk rotation and forward movement are in an oblique plane
   C. Mature stage
      1. Trunk turns to side in anticipation of tossed ball
      2. Weight shifts to back foot
      3. Hips rotate
      4. Transfer of weight is in a contralateral pattern
      5. Weight shift to forward foot occurs while object is still moving backward
      6. Striking occurs in a long, full arc in a horizontal pattern
      7. Weight shifts to forward foot at contact
II. Developmental difficulties
   A. Failure to focus on and track the ball
   B. Improper grip
   C. Failure to turn side of the body in direction of intended flight
   D. Inability to sequence movements in rapid succession in a coordinated manner
   E. Poor backswing
   F. "Chopping" swing

FIGURE 20.13 Developmental sequence for object striking.

Initial

Elementary

Mature

FIGURE 20.14   Stages of the horizontal striking pattern.

TEACHING TIP 20.7

When teaching object *striking:*

- Follow a sequence of teaching that progresses from striking with the hand and other body parts to using short-handled implements and then long-handled implements.
- Use balloons and beach balls at the initial stages.
- Practice hitting stationary objects prior to moving objects.
- Work with striking large objects and then progress gradually to striking smaller objects.
- Experiment with striking in horizontal and vertical planes.

HORIZONTAL STRIKING CONCEPTS
CHILDREN SHOULD KNOW

Skill concepts:

- Be sure that your hands are touching when you grip a baseball bat and that your right hand is on top of your left (right-hand-dominant pattern).
- Keep your eyes on the ball at all times.
- Always contact the ball at the point of complete arm extension.
- Shift your weight back and forward as you swing.
- Swing in a level fashion.
- Follow through across the chest.

Movement concepts:

- You can strike a ball with different amounts of force.
- You can make the ball go fast or slow.
- The sequential and rhythmic use of your muscles will affect the force of your swing and the speed of the ball.
- The ball can be struck at many different levels.
- The ball may be contacted in a horizontal or vertical plane.
- You can hit a ball in many different directions.
- Objects other than balls can be struck.
- You don't always need to use an implement to strike something. You can effectively use your hand(s), your head, or your foot.
- Striking a moving object is a complex task, requiring precise coordination of your eyes and muscles.
- The success of your striking will be influenced by the size, shape, and color of the ball, as well as the size and shape of the implement and the speed of the object.

Horizontal striking at the elementary stage of movement skill development is demonstrated by this young girl.

Volleying

Volleying, for many children, is a scary task. After all, it involves intercepting a downward-moving object with the hands and imparting force to that object in a manner that moves it onward in the desired direction. If done improperly, volleying results in jammed fingers and a real fear of the ball. But learned in a developmentally appropriate manner using what we know about children's perceptual and motor development, volleying is something even the youngest of school-age children can do (see figures 20.15 and 20.16).

I. Volleying
  A. Initial stage
    1. Inability to accurately judge path of ball or balloon
    2. Inability to get under the ball
    3. Inability to contact ball with both hands simultaneously
    4. Slaps at ball from behind
  B. Elementary stage
    1. Failure to visually track ball
    2. Gets under the ball
    3. Slaps at ball
    4. Action mainly from hands and arms
    5. Little lift or follow-through with legs
    6. Unable to control direction or intended flight of ball
    7. Wrists flex and ball often travels backward
  C. Mature stage
    1. Gets under the ball
    2. Good contact with fingertips
    3. Wrists remain stiff and arms follow through
    4. Good summation of forces and utilization of arms and legs
    5. Able to control direction and intended flight of ball
II. Developmental difficulties
  A. Failure to keep eyes on ball
  B. Inability to accurately judge flight of ball and to properly time movements of body
  C. Failure to keep fingers and wrists stiff
  D. Failure to extend all of the joints upon contacting ball (lack of follow-through)
  E. Inability to contact ball with both hands simultaneously
  F. Slapping at ball
  G. Poor positioning of body under ball

FIGURE 20.15   Developmental sequence for volleying.

Initial

Elementary

Mature

FIGURE 20.16   Stages of the volleying pattern.

VOLLEYING CONCEPTS CHILDREN SHOULD KNOW

Skill concepts:

- Get into position directly beneath the ball.
- Watch the flight of the ball between the opening formed by your two hands.
- Extend the arms and legs as the ball touches your fingertips.
- Keep the fingers and wrists stiff throughout.
- Follow through in the direction that the ball is to go.
- Keep your eyes on the ball.
- Volleying is a striking pattern that is used in many games and in the sport of volleyball.

Movement concepts:

- You can vary your body position when you control the ball.
- You can alter the level of your body.
- You can make changes in the force that you apply to the ball.
- The coordinated contact of the ball will be influenced by how well all of your body works together.
- You can give direction to the ball.
- You can control the distance that the ball travels.
- You can volley many different objects.
- You can play volleying games with other people.

CONCEPT 20.7

A wide variety of exploratory, guided discovery, and skill application activities can be successfully used to enhance fundamental manipulative abilities.

SKILL DEVELOPMENT ACTIVITIES

Before selecting **manipulative skill development** activities to include in the lesson, you should determine the typical stage of motor development displayed by the class. Knowing the stage of motor development will provide cues to their level of movement skill learning. With this important information, it becomes possible to determine whether the lesson should focus on exploratory, guided discovery, skill application, or skill refinement activities.

Exploratory Activities

Manipulative exploratory activities provide children at the initial or elementary stage an opportunity to learn how their body can move, where it can move, and how it moves in relation to other objects (see chapter 10 "Teaching Styles": "Divergent Production Style" section). Children should explore the movement elements of effort, space, and relationships to develop a more complete idea of their manipulative movement potential. Tables 20.1 through 20.8 provide a sampling of exploratory activities that can be used as movement challenges for children at the beginning level of manipulative skill learning. You should present these challenges separately at first. However, you can combine them into many types of challenges after children have mastered the basic elements of the skill.

Guided Discovery Activities

The sampling of manipulative guided discovery activities presented in figures 20.17 through 20.24 should provide children with a variety of activities designed to lead them to mature manipulative patterns of movement. This guided approach permits children to learn more movement characteristics about the skill and how their body should move. Guided discovery activities give children an opportunity to practice the skill and to focus on its use in many types of movement situations. Have children practice using different sizes, colors, and textures to promote skill development. Also, it is helpful to use nonthreatening objects such as fleece balls, beach balls, or foam balls. Practice with catching different-sized objects is also important.

SKILL APPLICATION ACTIVITIES

Once the mature stage has been attained in a manipulative skill, it is appropriate to focus on skill application activities. The use of manipulative skill application activities with a variety of games, dances, and educational gymnastics permits practice and refinement of manipulative skills under dynamic conditions in a constantly changing environment. Overlearning of manipulative skills and practice in a variety of situations are important to ensure that the mature patterns of movement can be performed consistently. Several manipulative skill application game ideas that are appropriate for elementary school children start on page 552.

CONCEPT 20.8

Low-level manipulative games and relays are effective tools for applying newly learned fundamental manipulative skills.

Sample Manipulative Games

Several game activities may be used to reinforce fundamental manipulative abilities. You must keep in mind the desired outcomes of the game and feel free to modify the activity whenever necessary to ensure maximum participation and practice of the skills being stressed. Table 20.9 lists the manipulative games included in this chapter and the movement skills stressed. The following are the basic objectives of manipulative game activities:

- To enhance fundamental manipulative abilities in throwing, catching, kicking, trapping, volleying, striking, bouncing, and rolling
- To enhance eye-hand and eye-foot coordination
- To encourage working together in a group effort
- To enhance listening abilities
- To encourage following directions and obeying rules

Once again, remember to modify these games to maximize participation and player safety. Modify the activity in creative ways so that all students receive maximum benefit from the skill reinforcement potential of the game.

TABLE 20.1—EXPLORATORY ACTIVITY IDEAS FOR THROWING

Effort awareness	Space awareness	Relationship awareness
Force	**Level**	**Objects**
Can you throw . . . – as soft as you can? – as hard as you can? – so that the ball makes a loud noise when it hits the wall? – alternating hard and soft throws? – stepping forward with a loud noise?	*Can you throw . . .* – up high? – down low? – as low as you can? – at the wall as high as you can? – at high-, low-, and medium-height targets? – alternating high and low throws?	*Can you throw . . .* – a Wiffle ball? – a fluff ball? – a softball? – a baseball? – a football? – a newspaper ball? – a playground ball? – at a target? – into the bucket? – over the rope? – from inside a hoop or inner tube?
Time	**Direction**	**People**
– as slowly as you can? – as fast as you can? – moving your throwing arm as fast as you can? – and twist your body (hips) as fast as possible?	– forward? – backward? – to the side? – at an angle?	– to a partner? – as far as your partner? – as hard or soft as your partner? – the same way as your partner?
Flow	**Range**	**Combinations**
– using as little movement as possible? – using as much of your body as possible? – like a robot? – like a plastic person? – without using your legs? – without using your trunk? – using only one other part of your body besides your throwing arm? – as smoothly as you can?	– as far as you can? – as near as you can? – with your right hand? – with your left hand? – with both hands? – with both feet? – overhand? – underhand? – sidearm? – with your arm going through short and long ranges of motion?	Initial experiences should focus on exploring the various aspects of effort, space, and relationships in isolation before you structure experiences involving combinations. For example, "Can you and your partner find three different ways to throw at the target from a far distance?"

TABLE 20.2—EXPLORATORY ACTIVITY IDEAS FOR CATCHING

Effort awareness	Space awareness	Relationship awareness
Force	**Level**	**Objects**
Can you catch . . . – with your arms in different positions? – without making a sound with your hands? – as loudly as you can? – keeping your arms straight? – keeping your arms bent?	*Can you catch . . .* – a ball tossed at a low level? – a ball tossed at waist level? – a ball tossed at a high level? – at many different levels? – from a sitting position? – from a lying-down position? – in many different positions?	*Can you catch . . .* – a playground ball? – a small ball? – a large ball? – a beanbag? – five different objects? – five different types of balls?
Time	**Direction**	**People**
– and go with the ball? – without going with the ball? – the ball as quickly as you can? – after waiting for the ball as long as you can?	– a ball tossed from in front of you? – a ball tossed from an angle? – a ball tossed from the side? – a ball coming down from above? – a tossed ball coming at you from different directions?	– a ball while holding both hands with a partner? – while holding one hand with a partner?
Flow	**Range**	**Combinations**
– a ball as smoothly as you can? – with varying degrees of smoothness?	– using different body parts? – from different positions? – with one eye closed? – with both eyes closed?	Exploratory experiences should begin with these and other activities, first in isolation. Later, combinations of effort, space, and relationships should be added. For example, "Can you catch a self-tossed ball at waist level while jumping in the air?"

TABLE 20.3—EXPLORATORY ACTIVITY IDEAS FOR KICKING

Effort awareness	Space awareness	Relationship awareness
Force	**Level**	**Objects**
Can you kick the ball . . . – as hard as you can? – as soft as you can? – with a forceful leg swing but a light hit? – with a lazy leg swing for a forceful hit?	*Can you kick the ball . . .* – high? – low? – as high as you can? – so it stays on the ground? – so it doesn't go higher than your waist?	*Can you kick the ball . . .* – and hit the wall? – and hit a big target? – and hit a small target? – over the goal? – into the goal? – under the stretched rope? – through the chair legs? – around the cones using several controlled kicks?
Time	**Direction**	**People**
– so it goes quickly? – so it goes very slowly? – from here so it hits the wall in 5 seconds? – from here and turn around before it hits the wall? – and touch the floor before it hits the wall?	– forward? – backward? – sideways? – diagonally? – alternating left and right feet (dribbling)?	– to a partner? – to a partner while walking (passing)? – at different levels to a partner? – with different amounts of force to a partner? – at different speeds to a partner?
Flow	**Range**	**Combinations**
– with a big leg swing? – with no knee bend? – without using your arms? – while swinging both arms back? – while swinging both arms forward? – with no follow-through? – with no backswing?	– as far as you can? – as near as you can? – with your feet wide apart? – with your body in different positions? – with your other foot?	Numerous exploratory activities that combine elements of effort, space, and relationships can be explored after they are first tried in isolation. For example, "Can you find ways to kick the ball with different amounts of force and at different levels with your partner?

TABLE 20.4—EXPLORATORY ACTIVITY IDEAS FOR TRAPPING

Effort awareness	Space awareness	Relationship awareness
Force	**Level**	**Objects**
Can you trap . . . – a ball that is rolled slowly toward you? – a ball that is tossed lightly at you? – a ball that is rolled rapidly toward you? – a ball that is tossed forcefully at you (use a fleece ball)?	*Can you trap . . .* – a ball that is rolling toward you? – a ball that is rolling off to one side? – a ball at waist level? – a ball at stomach level? – a ball at chest level?	*Can you trap . . .* – a beanbag? – a beach ball? – a fleece ball? – a playground ball? – different-size balls? – a soccer ball?
Time	**Direction**	**People**
– in slow motion? – a fast-moving ball? – a slow-moving ball?	– a ball moving toward you? – a ball moving away from you? – a ball moving in front of you? – a ball moving to one side?	– a ball and kick it back to your partner? – a ball and have your partner count the number of different ways you can do it?
Flow	**Range**	**Combinations**
– a ball and "give" with the ball? – a ball without "giving" with the ball?	– a ball with your foot? – a ball with your shin? – a ball with your stomach? – a ball with your chest? – a ball with either foot? – a ball with a large body part? – a ball with a small body part?	Combinations of effort, space, and relationships can be devised and explored after a variety of isolated activities are explored. For example, "Experiment with how much you must 'give' with your body when trapping five different types of balls."

TABLE 20.5—EXPLORATORY ACTIVITY IDEAS FOR BALL BOUNCING

Effort awareness	Space awareness	Relationship awareness
Force	**Level**	**Objects**
Can you bounce (or dribble) the ball . . . – as hard as you can? – as soft as you can? – changing from hard to soft?	*Can you bounce (or dribble) the ball . . .* – at knee level? – at waist level? – at leg level? – higher than your head? – lower than your knees? – and change levels with each bounce?	*Can you bounce (or dribble) the ball . . .* – around the chairs? – under the outstretched rope? – over the outstretched rope? – while walking close to the wall? – if it is a basketball? – if it is a playground ball? – and notice any difference with different types of balls?
Time	**Direction**	**People**
– as quickly as you can? – as slowly as you can? – alternating fast and slow? – and allow as much time as you can between bounces? – as many times as you can until I say "Stop"?	– in front of you? – to one side? – behind you? – in different pathways? – in a straight line? – in a circle? – in a curved line? – in a zigzag line?	– to your partner? – alternating with a partner? – in time with your partner's bounce? – in time with your partner, with the two of you moving away and back together with the same number of bounces?
Flow	**Range**	**Combinations**
– and catch it? – repeatedly after catching it repeatedly? – without catching it (dribbling)?	– in your space? – hitting the same spot each time? – while moving around the room? – as far away from you as you can? – as close to you as you can? – with other body parts? – with your other hand?	As the child gradually gains control of the ball rather than the ball controlling child, add various combinations of effort, space, or relationships. For example, "Can you dribble the ball at waist level but to one side of your body as you go around the field?"

TABLE 20.6—EXPLORATORY ACTIVITY IDEAS FOR BALL ROLLING

Effort awareness	Space awareness	Relationship awareness
Force	**Level**	**Objects**
Can you roll the ball . . . – softly? – as hard as you can?	*Can you roll the ball . . .* – while lying on the floor? – from your knees? – from a sitting position?	*Can you roll the ball . . .* – no matter what size it is? – on the balance beam? – on a line? – between the boxes? – into the can? – through the tube? – under a wicket? – at the pins?
Time	**Direction**	**People**
– as slowly as possible? – as quickly as you can?	– in a straight line? – so that it curves?	– to a partner? – alternating back and forth? – mirroring your partner? – shadowing your partner?
Flow	**Range**	**Combinations**
– using your arms only? – using only one side of your body? – smoothly? – like a robot? – like a champion bowler?	– around yourself? – with your other hand? – as far as you can? – as accurately as you can? – without moving off the line? – with an approach?	Numerous combinations of effort, space, and relationships related to rolling are possible as well as combinations with other fundamental movements. For example, "Can you roll the ball with differing amounts of force?" "Can you roll the ball at a low level with a partner?"

TABLE 20.7—EXPLORATORY ACTIVITY IDEAS FOR STRIKING

Effort awareness	Space awareness	Relationship awareness
Force	**Level**	**Objects**
Can you strike the ball (balloon, beach ball) . . . – as hard as you can? – as softly as you can? – so it makes a loud noise? – like a strong monster? – squarely?	*Can you strike the ball (balloon, beach ball) . . .* – so it travels at different levels? – with your body at different levels? – from a high level to a low level? – from a low level to a high level?	*Can you strike the ball (balloon, beach ball) . . .* – off different height cones? – off a batting tee? – over the rope? – under the rope? – through the chairs? – around the chair? – into the bucket? – using different-sized objects? – with different implements?
Time	**Direction**	**People**
– slowly? – quickly? – firmly?	– in a straight line? – with a level swing? – up? – down? – forward? – backward? – in different pathways?	– to a partner? – as your partner does? – tossed by your partner?
Flow	**Range**	**Combinations**
– limply? – with jerky movements? – with smooth movements?	– using different body parts? – and keep it in your space? – with your other hand? – from the other side? – with a wide base? – with a narrow base?	After exploring the many variations of striking in isolation, it will be helpful to combine various aspects of effort, space, and relationships. For example, "Can you hit the balloon as hard as you can so that it travels at a low level to a partner?"

TABLE 20.8—EXPLORATORY ACTIVITY IDEAS FOR VOLLEYING

Effort awareness	Space awareness	Relationship awareness
Force	**Level**	**Objects**
Can you volley the ball . . . – very hard? – very softly? – high? – low?	*Can you volley the ball . . .* – when you are at different levels? – from a seated position? – from a kneeling position? – without it going above your head? – with it going as high as possible?	*Can you volley the ball . . .* – if it is a beach ball? – if it is a balloon? – if it is a large ball? – it it is a small ball? – if it is a volleyball? – over the rope? – over the net? – with different body parts? – with your head (heading)? – with your knees (juggling)?
Time	**Direction**	**People**
– as many times as you can until I say "Stop"? – as few times as you can in 30 seconds?	– forward? – backward? – to the side? – in a circle?	– to a partner? – tossed by a partner? – back and forth to a partner?
Flow	**Range**	**Combinations**
– alternating hard and soft volleys? – but relax your fingers? – but tense your fingers? – and "give" with the ball? – without "giving" with the ball?	– and have it drop in your personal space? – and have it drop outside your space? – from a position directly under it? – from a position off to one side?	Simple exploratory activities with light objects (balloons and beach balls) are essential prior to using volleyballs. Combine activities only after reasonable control has developed. For example, "Can you find ways to volley the ball to your partner so that your partner can volley it back at different levels?"

	1. First explore the movement variations of throwing.
	2. Now begin to place limitations on the response possibilities to the following movement challenges. (You may want to use a beanbag rather than a ball for these activities to promote a minimum of confusion when retrieving the thrown objects.) For example:
General	a. Stand about a body length from the wall and throw your beanbag at it. Now try the same thing from here (15 to 20 feet). Try it again from here (30 to 50 feet). Do you have to do anything different to hit the wall each time? Why?
Leg action	b. Experiment with different ways of using your legs as you throw. Try throwing with your feet together (initial stage). Now try it by stepping out on the foot on the same side as your throwing arm (elementary). Try it this time by stepping out on the opposite foot (mature). Did you notice any difference in how far the ball went? Which way does a baseball player use? Why?
Trunk action	c. Try throwing without twisting your trunk. Now try it with twisting. Experiment with different combinations of twisting your trunk and using your legs. Now show me the best combination. Can you stand facing this wall but throw the ball at the wall to your left? Try it first without bringing your hips around. Now try it bringing your hips around to the left (for right-hand throw). Now try it with stepping out on your left foot and turning to your left.
Arm action	d. Experiment with different ways of using your arms when you throw. Can you find three different arm patterns you can use when throwing? Let's work on the overhand throw. Throw the ball overhand without rotating your hips. Try it while rotating your hips. Which way caused the ball to go the farthest? Throw the ball so that it hits high on the wall. Throw it now so that it hits the wall as hard as possible. Now throw the ball as far as you can. Now throw far but over the outstretched rope (6 to 8 feet high).
Total	e. Let's see if we can put it all together. Try throwing while stepping forward on the opposite foot and turning your trunk while your arm moves forward. Practice throwing with a partner. Now pretend that it is a hot potato that you must throw back as fast as you can. What happens when you try to get rid of the ball quickly? Some of you went back to the elementary stage instead of throwing at the mature stage. Why? Will it help to practice?

3. After the mature throwing pattern has been reasonably well mastered in practice sessions, begin to combine it with other activities. Apply it to numerous situations to make it more automatic.

    a. Introduce basic throwing and catching games that will provide plenty of opportunities for practice.

    b. Throw different objects.

    c. Throw at distances that encourage mature use of the pattern.

    d. Throw at a stationary target.

    e. Throw at a moving target.

    f. Combine distance and accuracy throwing.

FIGURE 20.17 Guided discovery activity ideas for throwing.

	1. First explore the movement variations of catching.
	2. Then begin to place limitations on the response possibilities to the following movement challenges. You may find it helpful to experiment with brightly colored balls.
General	a. Experiment with catching a lightly tossed ball. How many ways can you catch the ball? Try experimenting with different arm positions. Now try catching the ball without it touching your body. Can you catch the ball with your hands only?
Arm action	b. What should your arms do when they catch a ball? Do they stay straight? Do they stay bent as if you were making a basket, or are they first straight and then bend as you catch the ball? Why do they "give" (bend) when you catch the ball? Try catching a softly thrown ball and a ball thrown hard. Is there any difference in how much your arms give as you catch? Why?
Hand action	c. Experiment with different ways of holding your hands when you catch. Is there a difference in how you place them for a high ball and for a low ball? Can you catch a low ball with your little fingers together side by side? Now try it with your hands facing each other. Are there times when you want to use one ball-catching method and times when you use another? Let's try the same experiment while catching a ball that is above the waist.
Eyes	d. We all know it's best to catch a ball with your eyes open and looking at the ball, but sometimes we close our eyes or turn our head away. Why do you think some people do that? What are some things we can do to help people look at the ball and not turn away? Let's play catch with a partner and see if we can find some ways to help our partner if he or she has this problem. Should we use a large ball or small ball? Why? Should we tell them we are going to toss the ball or not? Why? Let's try each and see what works better. Find what works better for your partner and practice until he or she feels comfortable. Then begin to try out different-sized balls, speeds, and heights.

3. After the mature catching pattern has been mastered in a structured environment, you will want to provide further practice experiences that permit use of catching in various situations. The attempt now should be to help make the mature pattern more automatic and adaptable to a variety of backgrounds, ball sizes, color, objects, speeds, and positions in relationship to the body.

a. Introduce basic catching and throwing games.

b. Stress variations in ball size and hardness.

c. Try fielding grounders, fly balls, and balls not directly in line with the body.

FIGURE 20.18 Guided discovery activity ideas for catching.

1. First explore the movement variations of kicking.

2. Then begin to place limitations on the response possibilities to the following movement challenges:

Leg action

    a. Try kicking the ball without bending your leg. Now bend first at your kicking knee. Then kick the ball. Which way caused the ball to go farther? Which felt better? Try kicking the ball as far as you can, using different amounts of knee bend but no follow-through (that is, stopping your leg as soon as you contact the ball). Now try the same thing, but follow all the way through. Which amount of knee bend works best? Does a follow-through on your kick help the ball go farther?

    b. Try different ways of approaching the ball before you kick it, using a full bend at the knee of your kicking leg and extending at the hip. Does the ball go farther after a kick from standing still, or does it help to take a step or two? Why? Let's practice kicking as far as we can, using a step to the ball.

Trunk action

    c. Do you think it will help if you move your trunk backward when you kick the ball? Try it. Now keep your body straight and then try leaning far forward. Do you notice any difference? Let's try to kick the ball as far as we can and practice leaning back a little as we make contact with the ball.

Arm action

    d. What do you do with your arms when you kick the ball? Watch your partner. What does she or he do? Experiment with different arm positions as you kick. Which way works best? Let's practice kicking as hard as we can and swing our arms so that the arm opposite our kicking leg is swung forward while the other moves backward.

Total

    e. Try kicking the ball as far as you can and as hard as you can. Now try kicking at the target (a suspended hula hoop works fine). Did you notice any changes in how you kick when you kick for accuracy rather than for distance?

    f. Try kicking a rolling ball. Try kicking while on the run. Experiment with kicking the ball, but first tell your partner if it will be a high, medium, low, or ground kick. Can you control the level of your kick? What must you do to control the level? Show me. Try using different parts of your foot when you kick. Use your toe, your instep, the inside of your foot. What differences do you notice in level, in speed, in accuracy, in distance?

3. After a mature kicking pattern has been reasonably well mastered, it is important to combine it with other activities to reinforce the pattern and make it more automatic.

    a. Make quick kicks.

    b. Kick at a stationary target.

    c. Kick at a moving target.

    d. Kick at a target from a run.

    e. Kick for control in high-, low-, and ground-level kicks.

    f. Kick back and forth to a partner while moving in the same direction (passing).

    g. Maneuver and kick at a target against a defense.

    h. Play kicking relays.

    i. Play kicking games.

FIGURE 20.19   Guided discovery activity ideas for kicking.

1. First explore several of the movement variations of trapping. Remember that a primary purpose of these exploratory activities is to lead the child to a better understanding of the movement concepts of effort, space, and relationships as applied to trapping an object.

2. Then begin to place limitations on the response possibilities to the movement challenges that you present. Remember that your reason for doing this is so that you may lead the individual to the mature pattern of movement through his or her own discovery of the solution to the movement problems that you structure. Trapping, for example, may be performed in a variety of ways, such as the foot trap, knee trap, stomach trap, and chest trap. Although each uses a different part of the body to intercept and stop the oncoming object, all incorporate the same principles of movement, namely (1) absorbing the force of the ball over the greatest surface area possible and (2) absorbing the force of the ball over the greatest distance required for successful trapping. The following are examples of several movement challenges that you can use to help bring out these movement principles.

General

   a. Try to stop a rolling ball with your feet. What happens to the ball when you let it hit your feet without "giving" when it hits? Why does this happen? How can you cause the ball to stop right after it hits your feet? What do you have to do?

   b. Let's try the same thing with the ball being tossed at your legs (stomach, chest, etc.). What must you do each time to get the ball to drop and stop right after it hits you? Try different ideas and then show me the one that works best for you. Did you notice how you had to "give" with the ball to get it to stop?

   c. Do you have to "give" with the ball as much if the ball is traveling slowly as when it is traveling quickly? Why? Show me how you "give" with the ball when it is coming quickly and then when it is coming slowly.

   d. Is it better to try trapping the ball with a small body part or a large body part? Try both ways. Which works better? Why?

   e. If a ball is traveling fast, would you want to "give" with the ball over a longer distance or a shorter distance? How about over a large part of your body or over a small part? Experiment with the different ways of trapping and let me know which is best.

3. After trapping has been reasonably well mastered in controlled guided discovery lessons, you will find it helpful to structure experiences that demand greater control and rapid decision making. For example:

   a. Trap a ball kicked by a partner and then kick it back.

   b. Trap a ball coming from different directions and levels and at different speeds.

   c. Play games involving kicking and trapping.

FIGURE 20.20   Guided discovery activity ideas for trapping/collecting.

	1. First explore several of the movement variations of ball bouncing.
	2. Then begin to place limitations on the response possibilities to the following movement challenges:
General	a. Try dribbling your ball in your own space with your feet together, legs straight. How does it feel? Now try it several different ways. Which way feels best? Why?
Trunk action	b. When you dribble the ball in place, what do you do with your feet? Your trunk? Is it easier to control the ball one place standing straight or bent slightly forward at the waist? Try both. Which was better? Why?
Leg action	c. Experiment with different foot positions when you dribble in place. Are there any differences? Why?
	d. Try moving about the room while dribbling the ball. Is it easier or harder than when you are standing in your space? Why is it harder?
	e. Listen to my commands and move only in the direction I call out. Can you do it? Why is it hard for some people and easier for others? All those who are "experts" try the same thing but use your opposite hand to dribble the ball. Did you "experts" notice any difference in how well you did? Why?
Arm and hand action	f. Experiment with using your hand and arm in different ways as you dribble the ball. What do we do with our fingers, our wrists, and our arms when we dribble the ball? Show me. Why do we push the ball down rather than slap at it? Can you keep your wrist stiff and dribble the ball off your fingertips? Try it.
	g. Try to stay in your own space, dribbling the ball off your fingertips with a stiff wrist and good follow-through. Now try it by slapping at the ball. Which way gives you the most control? Show me. Why?
Eyes	h. Look at the ball as you dribble. Now try the same thing looking up here at me. Try it now with your eyes closed. Which was easier? Which was harder? When you are playing basketball, is it better to look at the ball as you dribble, or is it better to be looking where you are going? Let's try to dribble without looking at the ball.
General	i. Let's practice dribbling with the opposite hand. Now let's alternate dribbling first with one hand then the other. Is it harder with one hand than with the other? Why?
	j. See if you can dribble around an object, changing hands each time you change direction.
	3. After the mature dribbling pattern has been fairly well mastered, it should be combined with other activities to reinforce the pattern and make it more automatic.
	a. Dribble around obstacles.
	b. Dribble the ball while touching different body parts and changing hands, levels, or directions.
	c. Keep the ball away from an opponent while dribbling.

FIGURE 20.21   Guided discovery activity ideas for ball bouncing.

| | 1. First explore several of the numerous variations of rolling. |
| | 2. Then begin to place limitations on the response possibilities to the movement challenges you present. Focus on how the body should move and why when rolling an object. For example: |

General

    a. Let's experiment with different ways of rolling the ball. How many ways can you find? Show me. Why?

    b. What should we do if we want the ball to go as fast as possible? Show me. Why?

    c. What can you do to make the ball go as straight as possible?

    d. If you want the ball to go both fast and straight, how would you roll it? Why?

Arm action

    e. Try rolling the ball from between your legs. Now try placing it by your side and rolling. Which way allows the ball to go faster? Which is the more accurate? Why?

    f. What happens when you use a small ball and then a large ball? Which ball will go faster? Which ball travels more accurately? Try both and then tell me.

Leg action

    g. Why do you think bowlers bowl like this (demonstrate)? Try doing different things with your legs as you roll the ball. Try standing with your feet together and your knees locked. Does it work well? What happened to the ball? Why did it bounce before it began to roll?

    h. See what you can do to prevent the ball from bouncing as it is rolled. Can you do anything with your trunk? Can you do anything with your legs that will help? Show me. Why does it help to bend forward and step out on the leg opposite the ball? Let's all try it and see how straight we can roll our ball.

3. After a mature ball-rolling pattern has been reasonably well mastered, begin to focus on accuracy and increasing the distance to the target. A variety of low-level games and lead-up activities to bowling can be incorporated at this point. You will also want, however, to combine rolling with a variety of other movements to reinforce the proper pattern and make it more automatic. For example:

    a. Roll different-sized balls.

    b. Roll the balls on different surfaces.

    c. Try to control the direction of a rolled ball.

FIGURE 20.22   Guided discovery activity ideas for ball rolling.

| | 1. First explore several of the numerous variations of striking. Emphasize the idea of striking in terms of effort, space, and the ball's relationship to objects and people. |
| | 2. Then begin to place limitations on the response possibilities to the following movement challenges: |

1. First explore several of the numerous variations of striking. Emphasize the idea of striking in terms of effort, space, and the ball's relationship to objects and people.

2. Then begin to place limitations on the response possibilities to the following movement challenges:

Arm action

a. Try hitting the ball off the tee using your hand, a paddle, a bat. Which way caused the ball to go the farthest? Why?

b. Now try using a bat, but keep your arms bent. Then try it with your arms straight when the bat hits the ball. Did you notice a difference? Which works better and why?

c. See if you can find different ways to swing your bat. Experiment with different ways of holding the bat. Can anyone tell me the best way to hold the bat and the best way to swing it if I want what I'm hitting to go as far as possible?

d. Now we want to have our right hand on top (right-handed batter) and our left on the bottom, and we want our swing to be level. Let's try it.

Leg action

e. Let's try standing in different ways when we strike the ball. Try to find five ways to stand as you hit the ball off the tee. Which helps the ball go the farthest? Show me.

f. Now let's see what you can do with your feet when we hit the ball. Try standing with your feet together, wide apart, and less apart. Which feels best?

g. Will it help to step out as we swing at the ball? Try it. Why do you think that it helps?

General

h. Try hitting the balloon with your hand, a Ping-Pong paddle, a Wiffle ball bat. Which was easiest? Hardest? Why?

i. Now try to hit the beach ball the same way—first with your hand, then a Ping-Pong paddle, then a bat. Which was easiest? Hardest? Why?

3. After a mature striking pattern has been reasonably well mastered, you will want to begin practicing hitting a tossed ball. To maximize skill development, you may want to:

a. Use a large ball, then gradually work down to a small ball.

b. Use an oversized bat prior to using a regulation bat.

c. Use a bat that is slightly shorter or have the child "choke up" on the bat.

d. Toss the ball slowly and then gradually increase its speed.

e. Experiment with different pitching distances.

f. Experiment with different ball colors and background.

g. Incorporate the striking pattern into a variety of low-level and lead-up games.

FIGURE 20.23 Guided discovery activity ideas for horizontal striking.

1. First explore several of the movement variations of volleying, taking care to use an object appropriate to the ability of the individual.

2. Then begin to place limitations on the response possibilities to the question you ask. Focus on eliciting the mature volleying pattern, first using a balloon, then a beach ball, and finally a volleyball. To aid children with tracking and accurately interrupting the ball, you may permit an intermediate bounce of the ball before it is actually volleyed in the following activities:

General
   a. Can you hit the balloon, beach ball, or other type of ball into the air so that it comes right back to you? Try hitting it several times in a row, staying in your own space. What must you do to be sure that the ball comes back to you? What about your hands? Do you have more control with one or both hands?

Hand and arm action
   b. Try volleying your balloon with both hands as many times as you can. What must you do to keep it up over your head? Show me. What do you do with your hands and fingers and wrists when you volley the balloon?

   c. Try volleying a beach ball or volleyball. Is it easier or harder than the balloon? Why?

   d. Use your volleyball to volley with, but let it bounce once before you try hitting it again. Is that easier than before? Why?

   e. Let's try volleying different-sized balls. Is there any difference? Can you use two hands as easily with a small ball?

   f. Experiment with different foot positions as you volley. Now try it with your knees locked, with them apart, with them bent slightly. Which works best?

3. You will need to spend considerable time with discovery activities to help the children focus on control of the object. Intercepting a ball and volleying or striking it are extremely complicated tasks requiring sophisticated interaction of visual and motor processes and exact timing. Be patient in your approach and be sure to use objects and activities that permit the beginner ample opportunity to track the ball visually before intercepting it. Once the volleying pattern has been mastered to a reasonable degree and the individual is exhibiting mature control of the ball, it will be wise to focus on a combination of activities that reinforce the correct pattern and make it more automatic.

   a. Volley the ball to different heights.
   b. Volley from different body levels.
   c. Volley continuously without an intermediate bounce.
   d. Volley against a wall.
   e. Volley with a partner.
   f. Volley with a group.
   g. Volley the ball in a direction different from that in which it came.

FIGURE 20.24   Guided discovery activity ideas for volleying.

TABLE 20.9—SELECTED MANIPULATIVE GAMES

	Striking/ Rolling	Throwing/ Catching	Kicking/ Trapping	Bouncing/ Volleying
Swinging Hoops!	X			
Silly Zilly Zones	X	X		
Three in a Row!		X		
Falling Stars	X			
Popcorn Popper	X			
Boundary Ball		X		X
Quick Feet!	X	X		X
Tunnel Ball		X		X
Magic Triangle	X	X	X	
Cross the Line		X		
Hoop Tricks			X	
Kick the Can		X		
Zigzag "Zoccer"		X		
Guard the Castle	X	X		
Zone B!	X	X	X	

Swinging Hoops!

Movement Skills

Underhand or overhand throwing.

Movement Concepts

Space: levels, direction. Effort: varying amounts of force. Relationships: moving with a moving hoop.

Formation

One to two children per hoop.

Equipment

Rope, hula hoops, balls of varying sizes, beanbags, polyspots or floor markers. Hoop is hung from a basketball hoop or from a long rope suspended horizontally across the gymnasium (I-hooks can be used on the walls of the gymnasium and wire strung across; ropes can then be vertically hung down from the wire with hoops attached).

Procedures

Maximum of three children per throwing station. Children choose their distance from a hula hoop. Partners can make the hoop swing from side to side. Students attempt to throw an object through the hoop. The level of the hoop can be varied.

Silly Zilly Zones

Movement Skills

Overhand throwing or kicking (for distance).

Movement Concepts

Space: levels. Effort: strong. Relationships: moving within a defined area.

Formation

Children (three to four per group) are assigned to an outside general space.

Equipment

Rag balls, foam footballs, or any type of ball small enough for a child to grip that also has density and weight.

Procedures

Zones (silly zilly zones) are formed by cones. These zones may be squares, circles, triangles, and so forth. The object of the game is to throw from a stationary position into the zones. The zones are large enough for initial and elementary stage throwers to successfully throw into (about 10-15 yards in diameter). A variation is for the thrower to receive a pass from another player and then throw to a zone. Kicks, from a stationary position, with a running approach, or after receipt of a pass (as in soccer), can also be executed toward the zones. Kicks could be lofted or low kicks.

Three in a Row!

Movement Skills

Overhand throwing, catching on the move.

Movement Concepts

Space: general, pathways. Effort: strong. Relationships: moving with other players on the move.

Formation

Students in groups of four; three students will be moving out to receive an overhand pass.

Equipment

Cones and balls.

Procedures

Small groups of students are assigned to a general space. One student is the designated "thrower," and the remaining three students are "receivers." The object is for the thrower to successfully pass three balls, one at a time, to each receiver as that player moves out away from the thrower. Throwers can determine how far they would like the receiver to move before attempting to catch the thrown ball. A cone can mark the approximate spot where the receiver should move.

Falling Stars

Movement Skills

Overhand throwing, catching on the move.

Movement Concepts

Space: levels, directions. Effort: light, medium, or strong. Relationships: determining where the ball will bounce in relationship to the wall.

Formation

Three to four children per group; single-file line.

Equipment

Wall, different types of balls that will rebound off of a wall.

Procedures

One child in the group begins by throwing the ball of her choice to a wall. The group can predetermine distance. On the rebound, another child moves into position to catch the rebounding ball. Play continues with each child throwing to the wall for another child to catch. Groups can keep score in a variety of ways, including (1) the number of catches made during the game, (2) the number of consecutive catches before a miss, or (3) achievement of a set number of catches as decided by the group. The teacher should provide feedback about throwing mechanics and can ask "What if" questions about angle of projection—for example, "If the ball is thrown very high off of the wall, where might the ball rebound?"

Popcorn Popper

Movement Skills

Overhand throwing and catching.

Movement Concepts

Space: levels. Effort: strong. Relationships: moving among the mats.

Formation

Four players are inside and six to eight players are outside of gymnastic mats that are positioned to stand on their sides (four mats—can create a triangle or square).

Equipment

Four-inch yarn balls (15 or more), mats, cones.

Procedures

Three to four players stand inside the area created by the mats, and six to eight players are outside of the mat barrier. Cones are placed in a circle about 15 feet away from the mat barrier. The outside players must throw the balls back into the "popcorn popper" from behind the cones; they may retrieve fleece/yarn balls from in front of the cones. Inside players throw balls out of the popcorn popper, one at a time, while outside players throw the balls back into the popper. The teacher can set a specific amount of time for each round of play. Inside and outside players switch roles after each round of play. In a variation, inside players throw "high pop-ups," and outside players earn a point for every ball caught in the air. If a ball is not caught in the air, it must be thrown back into the popper. Therefore, the object of this variation is to see how many points the outside group can earn per round.

Boundary Ball

Movement Skills

Rolling, trapping.

Movement Concepts

Space: directions. Effort: strong. Relationships: moving with other players and oncoming objects.

Formation

Two teams, seven to eight players, each standing on an end line.

Equipment

Beach balls, "slow-mo" balls, medium-size cage ball, playground balls.

Procedures

Two equal teams of seven to eight players are positioned 15 yards or so apart. The players are spread, width-wise, across two end lines. Each player has a playground ball. The goal is to roll the playground balls toward one of the beach balls (or "slow-mo" balls, etc.) that have been placed in the middle of the playing area at the beginning of each round and to eventually cause one of more of these balls to go over the opposite team's end line. No "middle-space ball" (i.e., beach ball, "slow-mo," or cage ball) can be touched with the hands. The only way players can stop a ball from rolling over an end line is with another playground ball (by rolling it at an oncoming ball or holding the playground ball and using it to stop the oncoming ball). Teams earn points by making a ball roll over the opposing team's end line. Players on the end lines can switch positions during play. Players must also communicate and share playground balls. Sideline players may be used to retrieve "out-of-bounds" balls and roll them back to their team. A variation of Boundary Ball is to use indoor soccer balls or deflated playground balls and for players to use inside-of-the-foot passes and trapping with the feet versus rolling and stopping with a playground ball.

Quick Feet!

Movement Skills

Underhand or overhand throwing, bouncing, kicking.

Movement Concepts

Space: levels, directions. Effort: quick changes of speed. Relationships: moving with another player and about the target.

Formation

Two children, one offense and the other defense. One player faces target (hula hoop taped to wall or a large target at a medium or high level) and the other faces away from the target. Both players should be positioned 5 feet or more away from the wall.

Equipment

Beanbag, fleece or rag ball, large target, jump rope or floor tape.

Procedures

The offensive player with the beanbag or yarn ball must stand so that the jump rope or line taped on the floor is between that player's body and the wall. Defense faces the offensive player and also is positioned so that the jump rope is between his body and the wall. The object of the game is for the offensive player to use quick side-to-side sliding steps to evade the defensive player. The offensive player should use shoulder and head feints to try to trick the defense regarding which direction he's going to slide in. The offensive player's goal is to throw the beanbag or yarn ball and hit the wall target. The defensive player's role is to prevent the offensive player from accomplishing this by guarding him with the arms and denying space.

Tunnel Ball

Movement Skills

Rolling and trapping.

Movement Concepts

Space: levels, directions. Effort: quick, smooth. Relationships: moving with the space or goals made by player's legs.

Formation

Single circle of 8 to 10 players facing in, two to three children in center.

Equipment

Foam balls.

Procedures

Eight to 10 players form a circle with 2 to 3 players in the center of the circle. The players forming the circle spread their feet apart, and a player in the center tries to roll the ball through the legs of the players forming the circle or between the players. If successful, the player in the center takes the place of the player in the circle. The player in the circle must try to "collect" or trap the ball with her feet. The teacher has students change roles after an appropriate amount of playing time has elapsed.

Magic Triangle

Movement Skills

Passing a ball with the feet or hands; receiving a ball with feet or hands.

Movement Concepts

Space: general, zigzag pathways, directions. Effort: quick, sharp. Relationships: moving with others and to a triangular shape.

Formation

Several groups of three students each, forming triangles.

Equipment

One 8-inch playground ball or foam ball per group.

Procedures

One player begins with the ball. The goal is to pass the ball using the feet or a bounce pass to another player (thus players trap with their feet or catch with their hands). As the three team members move the ball among one another, they must also change their position on the field or court. The goal is to always maintain a "magic triangle" (width, depth, and support). Prior to using a ball, students could be asked to simply run and change playing positions. The teacher then randomly freezes students and checks to see if they are still in a triangular formation. During this version of "magic triangle," students stay within their own general space or area. An extension of this activity is to have students cover space or move down a field or gymnasium as they pass back and forth. Adding one defensive player would again increase the level of complexity of the game.

Cross the Line

Movement Skills

Kicking and trapping.

Movement Concepts

Space: pathways. Effort: quick, strong. Relationships: moving with players on the line.

Formation

Three to four players per group, each facing a kicker.

Equipment

One 8-inch playground ball per group.

Procedures

The goal line is a 25-foot line drawn a distance of 20 to 40 feet from a kicking circle or area. Eight to 10 other players who are designated to trap the oncoming ball scatter in the playing field between the kicking circle and the goal line. The kicker places the ball on the ground inside the kicking circle. The player calls out, "Cross the line," and kicks the ball toward the 25-foot goal line. Any fielder who can trap or catch the ball before it goes over the line is the new kicker. If the ball crosses the line, the original kicker kicks again. If no one stops the ball after she has kicked three times, another student rotates to become the kicker.

Hoop Tricks

Movement Skills

Volleying.

Movement Concepts

Space: level changes. Effort: light touches. Relationships: moving with hoops, partners, and other players within general space.

Formation

Scattered pairs; hula hoops are placed on floor randomly throughout the playing area.

Equipment

Balloons (one for each pair) and hula hoops.

Procedures

Play begins with one player volleying the balloon toward a hula hoop. The player's partner has picked the hula hoop up off of the floor and is holding it in the air as a target for the player to volley the balloon through. As soon as the balloon goes through the hula hoop, the player holding the hoop quickly puts it back on the floor while simultaneously attempting to keep the balloon up in the air. Players alternate volleying. Both players then walk to another hula hoop while continuing to volley the balloon back and forth to each other. The goal of the game is to see how many hoops they can volley the balloon through in the time allotted. Players can take turns holding the hula hoops up in the air.

Kick the Can (or Pinball Soccer)

Movement Skills

Kicking and trapping.

Movement Concepts

Space: straight/angular pathways, low level. Effort: strong, medium force. Relationships: moving among targets.

Formation

Two parallel lines 30 feet apart with four to six players per group.

Equipment

Foam balls, soccer ball, and five large cans, cones, bowling pins, or cartons.

Procedures

Divide players into two teams (small groups of six to eight), each team standing on its own kicking line. Kicking lines are 30 to 60 feet from center line, depending on the skill of players. Give soccer balls to players of one team, or you can divide balls equally between the two teams at the start of the round. Players begin by kicking their ball, from their own kicking line, at a can (cone, carton, or bowling pin) that has been placed in the center of the playing area. Opponents trap the ball with their feet as it rolls to them, and then they kick from their line. The game continues until all the cans are down. A team makes one point for each can it knocks down. When all the cans are down, the team with the higher score is the winner (or total both team's points together to reach an all-time class high!). A player may block the ball with his body but may not touch it with the hands unless it goes out of bounds, in which case it is carried to the kicking line and the game is started again.

Zigzag "Zoccer"

Movement Skills

Passing with feet and trapping.

Movement Concepts

Space: zigzag pathway. Effort: controlled, medium force. Relationships: moving with other players and with the cones.

Formation

Zigzag groups of players.

Equipment

One soccer-type ball per group; cones.

Procedures

Each group of players (three to four) is spread out along a zigzag line (the line can span the width or the length of the playing area or field), marked by cones. Players are positioned at every other cone; cones are about 10 yards apart depending on skill level of students. On the signal "Go!" the first player in the zigzag line dribbles the soccer ball to the next cone in the zigzag line. When arriving at that cone the player passes the ball to the next player in the line. That player collects the ball, dribbles it to the next cone, and then passes the ball to the next player. The last player receiving the ball dribbles it up the field or playing area to the beginning of the zigzag line. Play continues.

Guard the Castle

Movement Skills

Throwing, kicking, and trapping.

Movement Concepts

Space: low level, medium-size general space. Effort: bound, strong. Relationships: moving with the other player and with the target.

Formation

Two players.

Equipment

Foam or playground balls, bowling pins, cones.

Procedures

One player throws the ball at the cone or bowling pin, trying to knock it down. The other player tries to prevent the cone from being knocked down by stopping the ball in any manner. Players switch roles after a designated time or after the thrower scores (knocks cone or pin down).

Zone B!

Movement Skills

Passing, catching, and bouncing.

Movement Concepts

Space: general. Effort: quick changes in speed. Relationships: moving in the zone created as a goal and with other players.

Formation

Three offensive and three defensive players.

Equipment

Pinnies, playground ball, four cones to mark a large zone next to wall area.

Procedures

Two teams, using the skills of bouncing, passing, and catching, attempt to move the ball down the playing area (one-third the width of a basketball court). The ball may be intercepted at any time, which will switch defense to offense. The object of the game is to score in the zone by relaying the ball to a player located in the zone, who then touches the wall with the ball (a wide goal area created by cones next to wall space about 10 yards in width; cones about 2 feet away from wall). The ball cannot be thrown toward the scoring area or zone but must be passed to a player in the zone. A rule can be made that all three players on a team must receive a pass before trying to score in the zone.

Manipulative Relays

Manipulative relays are designed to reinforce fundamental manipulative skills and sport skills that have been acquired during the skill development portion of the lesson. No more than two or three students should be on a relay team. This maximizes time-on-task. In addition, relays can be cooperative activities if team members total the points earned to achieve a collective goal. It is appropriate to use relays only after the basic elements of the skill have been mastered. Remember, control should be achieved prior to speed and accuracy. These are the primary objectives of **manipulative relay activities**:

- To practice and reinforce fundamental manipulative abilities
- To practice and reinforce manipulative sport skills
- To test one's abilities in selected manipulative skills against others in a controlled, gamelike situation
- To improve selected fitness components
- To be able to handle a ball with speed, control, and accuracy

Obstacle Relays

In this type of relay, players attempt to maneuver an object, using the skills designated, around, through, over, or alongside obstacles positioned in general space. It is important that there be enough space between obstacles to ensure control of the body and of the object being manipulated.

Goal-Scoring Relays

In this type of relay, each player manipulates an object through general space with the end product being an attempt to score on goal. For example, players could be challenged to see how many goals they can score in 60 seconds given five soccer balls. The five soccer balls would be positioned, for example, 15 yards away from a goal. The player, taking one soccer ball at a time, dribbles the ball to a designated spot or area and attempts to kick the ball into a goal. You can make this relay more difficult by adding a goaltender and/or a defender.

Team Relays

In this type of relay, all players are sequentially involved. One player begins the relay and then sends the object being used to the next player. The object is subsequently passed on to the next player using designated locomotor and manipulative skills. The two or three players involved can then be challenged to repeat the pattern a specified number of times without losing control or can be challenged to see how many times they can complete a pattern within a designated period of time.

ASSESSING PROGRESS

CONCEPT
20.9
Progress may be assessed in fundamental manipulative skill acquisition through a process assessment approach.

It is important to assess children informally at the beginning of a manipulative skill theme and again at the end. Once you know the children's entry level of ability, it is a relatively easy matter to determine the types of activities to include in the lesson. Figure 20.25 is a sample checklist or rubric for assessing manipulative skill

	Yes	No	Comments
Throwing			
1. Does the child throw consistently with a preferred hand?			
2. Is the child able to control the trajectory of the ball?			
3. Is there noticeable humerus lag of the forearm?			
4. Does the child use arm and leg opposition?			
5. Is there definite hip rotation?			
6. Is there efficient summation of forces in use of the arms, trunk, and legs?			
7. Is there noticeable improvement in throwing ability?			
Catching			
1. Does the child maintain eye contact with the ball throughout?			
2. Is the child able to adjust easily to a ball thrown at different levels?			
3. Is the child able to adjust easily to a ball thrown at different speeds?			
4. Are proper adjustments made in the arm and hand action of large and small balls?			
5. Is the catching action smooth, coordinated, and in good control?			
6. Is there observable improvement in catching abilities?			
Kicking			
1. Does the child make consistent contact with a stationary ball?			
2. Can the child make good contact with the ball from an approach?			
3. Can the child control the direction, level, and distance of his or her kick?			
4. Is there an acute bend at the knee and backward extension at the hip when the child is kicking for distance?			
5. Are the entire trunk and the arms brought into play for a forceful kick?			
6. Can the child consistently kick a moving ball?			
7. Is there noticeable improvement in the kicking pattern?			
Trapping			
1. Can the child trap a rolled ball?			
2. Can the child trap a tossed ball?			
3. Does the child make easy adjustments for trapping balls traveling at different speeds?			
4. Does the child make adjustments for the surface area used to trap the ball based on the speed of the ball?			
5. Are the movements of the child fluid and in control?			
6. Is there observable improvement in trapping abilities?			

(continued)

FIGURE 20.25   Self-question chart for fundamental manipulative skill development.

development. Such charts are a practical means for recording individual and group progress. You should be able to answer "yes" to each of the questions. If you cannot, you will need to modify subsequent lessons to more closely fit the specific needs of the individual, group, or class. Chapter 12, "Assessing Progress," provides more information on assessing children's skill development.

	Yes	No	Comments

Ball bouncing
1. Is the child in control of the ball?
2. Is the child able to dribble in her or his own space?
3. Can the child dribble while moving about the room?
4. Can the child dribble the ball without stopping to catch it?
5. Does the child properly use the fingers, wrist, and arms while dribbling?
6. Is the trunk bent forward slightly while dribbling?
7. Is the action smooth and rhythmical?
8. Can the child vary the height and direction of the ball at will?
9. Can the child dribble with either hand?
10. Is there observable improvement in the child's ability to dribble with control?

Ball rolling
1. Does the child use a rolling pattern to one side of the body?
2. Can the child make adjustments for different-sized balls?
3. Does the child adjust to the distance and accuracy required?
4. Does the child exhibit a good backswing?
5. Is there sufficient follow-through?
6. Can the child control the path of the ball?
7. Is there observable improvement?

Striking
1. Can the child strike a balloon with good control (does the child control the balloon or does the balloon control the child)?
2. Can the child strike a ball off a batting tee?
3. Does the child use a level horizontal swing?
4. Does the child grip the implement properly?
5. Is the stance appropriate for the task?
6. Does the child show evidence of proper summation of forces?
7. Is there observable improvement?

Volleying
1. Can the child volley a balloon repeatedly with good control?
2. Can the child volley a beach ball with good control?
3. Can the child volley and remain in his or her own space?
4. Can the child control the direction of the volley?
5. Can the child volley a ball that has been permitted to bounce one time?
6. Does the child exhibit controlled use of the fingers, hands, and arms?
7. Does the child maintain eye contact throughout?
8. Is there observable improvement?

FIGURE 20.25 *(continued)*

Summary

Developing a fundamental manipulative skill theme includes planning, organizing, implementing, and assessing fundamental manipulative movements. Developmentally appropriate skill sequencing is important in that attainment of the mature stage in manipulative skills depends not only on maturational readiness but also on environmental openness and teacher sensitivity.

As an example of the developmental sequence for manipulative skills, the initial, elementary, and mature stages for throwing differ greatly in such aspects as arm action and position, trunk movement, shifting of body weight, rotation during the throw, and foot placement. Again in throwing as an example, developmental difficulties include forward movement of the "wrong" foot, inhibited backswing, poor coordination of arm and body movement, and loss of balance during throwing. Children need to know throwing concepts such as which leg should lead, how to turn the shoulder, where to hold the ball, and how to follow through.

Developmentally appropriate games help children practice and refine fundamental manipulative skills under dynamic conditions in a constantly changing environment. Manipulative game activities enhance fundamental manipulative abilities, enhance eye-hand and eye-foot coordination, encourage working together, enhance listening abilities, and encourage following directions. Teachers should use charts such as those provided in the chapter to assess individual and group progress in manipulative skill development.

Terms to Remember

Excellent Readings

Bowyer, G. (1996). Effective methods for developing throwing. *TEPE, 7* (1), 24-25.

Buscher, C. (1994). *Teaching fundamental movement skills.* American Master Teaching Series. Champaign, IL: Human Kinetics.

Butler, G. (1996). "Volley-loon"—Ball skills with balloons. *TEPE, 7* (1), 26-27.

Hammett, C.T. (1992). *Movement activities for early childhood.* Champaign, IL: Human Kinetics.

Kraft, R.E., & Smith, J.A. (1993). Throwing and catching: How to do it right. *Strategies, 6,* 24-29.

Manross, M. (2000). Learning to throw in physical education class—What I learned from fourth and fifth graders. *TEPE, 11* (1), 12-13.

Manross, M. (2000). Learning to throw in physical education class: Part 2 The results. *TEPE, 11* (2), 34-35.

Morton-Jones, P. (1990). Skill analysis series: Part I, analysis of the place kick. *Strategies, 3,* 10-12.

Morton-Jones, P. (1990). Skill analysis series: Part II, analysis of the over arm throw. *Strategies, 3,* 22-23.

Morton-Jones, P. (1991). Skill analysis series: Part VI, catching. *Strategies, 4,* 23-24.

Worrell, V. (1994). Tennis skills for young students. *Strategies, 7,* 9-11.

The Content Areas

Part V, "The Content Areas," is unique as presented in this text. Rather than providing an endless variety of games, dances, and gymnastics activities, these chapters look at the content areas of physical education from a developmental perspective. Each chapter provides you with a developmental progression for teaching games, dance, and gymnastics activities. This is coupled with other critical information on such topics as assessing the educational value of games, applying movement concepts to creative dance, and selecting appropriate teaching methods for developmental gymnastics. We are reminded of the proverb: "Give a man a fish and he will have food for a day. Teach him how to fish and he will have food for a lifetime." So it is with developmental games, dance, and gymnastics. If you understand and can apply the critical concepts inherent in each content area, you will have little difficulty in devising an endless variety of developmentally appropriate movement activities that are both educational and fun. Games, dances, and gymnastics activities are the "tools" of our profession. They are important in that they are a means to an end, many ends, rather than an end in themselves. So take pride in your "tool kit." Take time to learn a variety of developmentally appropriate activities that can be applied to children's learning in educationally sound ways.

21

Developmental Games

Key Concept

▶ In the developmentally based physical education program, games are incorporated for the purpose of offering children opportunities to apply mature fundamental movement skills, along with movement concepts, within dynamic learning environments.

Chapter Objectives

This chapter will provide you with the tools to do the following:

▶ View games from a developmental perspective.

▶ Understand the purpose of games in a developmental physical education curriculum.

▶ Understand and apply the different ways games can be categorized and defined.

▶ Know the developmental levels of game play.

▶ Become familiar with salient features of teaching games.

"Let's play the game!" Children's natural desire to move—their desire to test their own limits as well as their hunger for excitement, challenge, and novelty—often compels them to ask, "When can we play a game?" Games are an integral component of an elementary physical education curriculum. If developmentally appropriate practices are reflected within this curricular area, game experiences can make a positive contribution toward children's desire to lead active lives. *Appropriate Practices for Elementary School Physical Education*, a NASPE-COPEC position paper (National Association for Sport and Physical Education, Council on Physical Education for Children, 2000a), presents *appropriate* and *inappropriate* guidelines for the implementation of games in the curriculum. For example, we should select and sequence games based on the skill themes and movement concepts fostered within the game. We should also consider the concept of "moving to open spaces" (space concept) or "maintaining width, depth, and support" among players (relationship concept) when sequencing educational games. Additionally, teachers and children should select, design, sequence, and modify games in ways that maximize learning and enjoyment. It is inappropriate to teach games with no obvious purpose or goal other than to keep children "busy, happy, and good."

National Content Standards for Physical Education #5, #6, and #7 can be reinforced through the careful selection and design of games that promote the behaviors advocated by these standards:

- Content Standard #5: Demonstrates responsible personal and social behavior in physical activity settings
- Content Standard #6: Demonstrates understanding and respect for differences among people in physical activity settings
- Content Standard #7: Understands that physical activity provides opportunities for enjoyment, challenge, self-expression, and social participation

CONCEPT 21.1

Developmentally appropriate games that are properly integrated into the curriculum can make a positive contribution to the instructional physical education program.

Teaching children games as well as sequencing games into a meaningful series of lessons or unit of instruction is a complex challenge. It is challenging because several factors affect the educational value of teaching games. In this chapter we take up this challenge by examining what makes an activity a "game." We also discuss the purpose of games in the developmental physical education program, various games classification schemes, and questions to ask in assessing the value of a specific game. Finally, we provide you with a developmental progression for successfully teaching games and discuss the dynamics of teaching games, as well as best practices for games teaching.

WHAT IS A GAME?

Games have been defined as "activities in which one or more children engage in cooperative, collaborative, or competitive play, with or without an object, within the structure of certain rules and boundaries" (Allison & Barrett, 2000, p. 84). Games give children an opportunity to utilize single motor skills or combinations of motor skills (i.e., stability, locomotor, and manipulative) and movement concepts (i.e., awareness of space—changes of direction; awareness of effort—changes in speed; and awareness of relationships—to objects, goals, boundaries, other players) in order to accomplish a goal.

College students often answer the question "What is a game?" by saying that a game involves team competition. Competition is a natural aspect of game play; however, *developmentally appropriate competition* often differs from the "adult" view of competition. In the physical education classes you teach, children may be at differing stages of emotional and social development. Some children may thrive on competition while others shy away from team competition. The competitive aspects of a game may need to be modified to suit children's stages of social-emotional development. Teachers need to understand how to vary the degree of competition in a game and should be sensitive to their students' developmental needs. For example, a game may involve only one player so that competition is doing "one's personal best." The following "solo games" are examples:

- **Throwing underhand to a moving hula hoop suspended from a backboard.** The object is to see how many beanbags or yarn balls the child can successfully throw through the hula hoop.

- **Bouncing a playground ball around cones.** The object of the game is to see how many cones the child can bounce the ball around in 30 seconds.

- **Striking to zones.** From a pitched ball or a ball placed on a tee, the object is to hit the ball to different areas or zones.

These primary grade students play a manipulative game as they practice underhand and overhand throwing patterns toward a stationary target.

THE PURPOSE OF GAMES

The inclusion of games in the physical education lesson generally begins during the preschool and primary grade years. Astute teachers use games as an educational tool. Every game that is played should be chosen for specific reasons that depend on the nature of the lesson. These may range from practicing specific movement skills and enhancing various components of physical fitness to promoting social learning or academic concept development. If the teacher has clearly defined objectives for the use of one or more particular games in a lesson, then we may be sure that games will serve an educational purpose.

In a developmental physical education program, games are incorporated for the purpose of offering children opportunities to apply mature fundamental movement skills along with movement concepts within dynamic learning environments. In this type of program, the teacher considers the developmental status of children when selecting, designing, and sequencing games. Teachers should have ample information about the following characteristics of the students:

CONCEPT 21.2

Games should be fun, but fun is not a primary reason for including them in the developmental physical education program.

- Stage of motor skill and movement concept development
- Physical fitness development
- Stage of cognitive understanding
- Present level of social skills

Children will gain limited benefits from playing a game for which they have not acquired the prerequisite motor, cognitive, social, or fitness skills. Therefore it's essential that teachers assess their students' motor skill development (see chapter 12, "Assessing Progress"). Teachers can also gain useful information from other relevant sources (e.g., classroom teacher; informal observations of children during lunch, recess) about children's cognitive and social development. Understanding children's overall developmental profile will lead to enjoyable game experiences and make positive contributions to their movement repertoire. Allison and Barrett (2000) reinforce this idea in stating that "game experiences, to be an integral and valuable part of the physical education curriculum, must clearly be meaningful and hold educational value for each child" (p. 81).

TEXT BOX 21.2

Are Your Children Ready for the Game? "The Scarf Tag Scenario"

I was teaching four- and five-year-old children attending a preschool. Several stations were designed, one of which was "scarf tag." In considering this game I estimated that the six children had acquired the necessary prerequisite motor skills and movement concepts.

But as I watched them play, I quickly realized they had not! Although they chased each other, their movement was limited to a circular pattern. This did not promote the quick changes in direction, stops and starts, and changes in speed that I had anticipated would occur in this game. Why didn't it work? Well, the children simply had not yet developed these skills and concepts. So, the moral of the story: Know what the demands of the game are! Chasing and fleeing games require combinational skills (running/walking, pivoting, dodging) and concepts (speed and directional changes). The following are the requirements of scarf tag:

1. Knowledge of different directions and ability to physically change direction
2. Ability to change the speed of one's body
3. Understanding that changing directions is strategically beneficial
4. Willingness to chase someone other than your friend!

Games also challenge children to think critically. Critical thinking in our context has been defined as "reflective thinking used to make reasonable and defensible decisions about movement" (McBride & Cleland, 1998, p. 42). McBride (1992) conceptualized critical thinking in physical education using a four-phase schema (see chapter 25, figure 25.1, p. 662). Phase I involves *cognitive organization,* such as focusing on a problem and asking questions. Phase II is *cognitive action*—for example, utilizing previous information and making deductions. Phase III involves generating *cognitive outcomes* such as alternative responses and criteria to judge responses. Phase IV represents the *psychomotor outcomes*—that is, the actual performance of the movement or motor skills. Children utilize these critical thinking processes when learning a new game or playing an already known game. For example, children must "focus on a problem" or on the rules of the game. During game play, children are prompted to analyze a situation and subsequently develop a plan of action based on their analysis (Nichols, 1994). Game play also challenges children to generate movement responses and to evaluate these responses based on selected criteria (e.g., the rules of the game) (see table 21.1).

CONCEPT 21.3

Games, when properly used, can be an effective means for enhancing children's critical thinking skills.

TABLE 21.1—MODIFIED CRITICAL THINKING SCHEME APPLIED TO GAME PLAY

Critical thinking process	Application to game play
1. Focusing on a problem	1. Focusing on rules of a game
2. Asking questions	2. Students asking teacher to clarify rules, how to use equipment, what their "job" is
3. Making inferences	3. If we try this, then "this" might happen (as children group to make "hunches")
4. Generating alternative responses	4. Using different skills to accomplish goals; trying out new playing
5. Selecting criteria to judge solutions	5. Using rules or making up new rules to facilitate play or to evaluate success

Based on McBride's "Schema of Critical Thinking in Physical Education" (1992).

Playing games also fosters children's social and emotional development. For example, games offer opportunities for children to share ideas, cooperate to achieve goals, and encourage one another. Emotional development can be nurtured if game play stimulates children to take new risks, assess their strengths and weaknesses, and recognize that individuals have different abilities. Encouraging appropriate game play can offer a way for children to express themselves. Through games children can express joy, anticipation, and desire to achieve, among other feelings. As Nichols (1994) states, "Games allow the children to move into areas of uncertainty and insecurity without the real threat of failure because the outcome is not an important life-and-death matter" (p. 450).

CLASSIFYING GAMES

A game has five critical components. These are boundaries, rules, the use of motor skills and movement concepts, strategies, and player roles. There are four basic approaches to classifying games: the game categories approach, the games for understanding approach, the core content approach, and the developmental games approach. In the following paragraphs we discuss the first three of these. The fourth, the developmental approach, is discussed in detail in the next section. Figure 21.1 depicts the four approaches for classifying games.

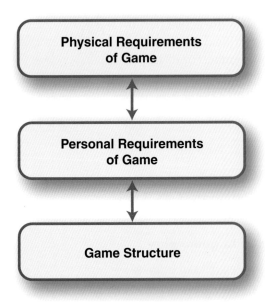

Game categories classification approach
(Nichols, 1994)

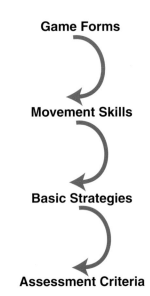

Core content of games classification approach
(Allison & Barrett, 2000)

Developmental games classification
approach (Gallahue & Cleland, 2003)

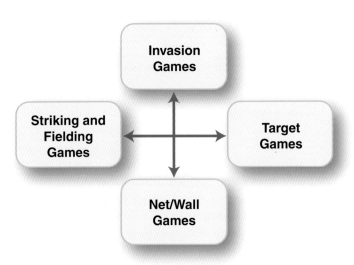

Games for understanding classification approach
(Werner & Almond, 1990)

FIGURE 21.1   Games classification schemes.

CONCEPT 21.4

A variety of methods may be used for classifying game activities.

The **game categories** approach is a popular way to classify games. Based on Nichols' (1994) method of classifying games, the various components of games may be organized into three major categories: the physical requirements of the game (i.e., equipment, space, organizational pattern/boundaries), the game structure (i.e., game classification, number of participants, modifications, and strategy), and the personal requirements of the game (i.e., motor skills, movement concepts, fitness requirements, and social skills).

In the **games for understanding** approach, games are categorized according to the strategies used. This model classifies games as target games (bowling, archery), net/wall games (tennis, badminton, volleyball), invasion games (basketball, soccer), and striking/fielding games (baseball, softball). When the games for understanding approach is used to teach games, children learn not only the skills of a game but also the tactical aspects of game playing. When playing a particular game, children need to learn not only *what* to do (bounce or pass) and *how* to do it but also *why* and *when* to do it (Werner, 2001).

Allison & Barrett (2000) use the **core content of games** as a classification system. They categorize games around four broad interrelated content areas including:

1. **Game forms**
   a. **Conventional games:** already existing in a culture such as basketball or soccer
   b. **Original games:** those created by the teacher, children, or both
2. **Movement skills:** locomotor, stability, manipulative
3. **Movement concepts:** body, space, effort, and relationship (also called movement awarenesses); and *game tactics:* strategies used when playing games such as moving to open space to "get open"
4. **Game criteria:** criteria used to judge the educational value of games such as does the game maximize participation, does it promote positive social interactions?

All three of these approaches to classifying games have merit. Each can be used to understand the nature of games and to incorporate them effectively into the instructional physical education program. However, with use of a developmental approach to the teaching of children's physical education, we believe that it is important to view games from a developmental perspective. In the next section we describe the developmental approach to classifying and teaching games.

A DEVELOPMENTAL PROGRESSION FOR TEACHING GAMES

CONCEPT 21.5

In the developmental physical education program, games are viewed as belonging to different developmental levels.

In the developmental approach to teaching children's physical education, games are viewed mainly as a tool for applying, reinforcing, and implementing a variety of fundamental movement skills and sport skills. Games are *not* viewed as a primary means for learning new movement skills. Although movement skill acquisition is a primary objective of the movement lesson, games from a developmental perspective serve mainly as a means for applying and utilizing present skill levels.

But other important objectives can still be achieved through proper game selection and good teaching. From a developmental perspective, games are frequently classified as simple low-level games (Level I games), complex games (Level II games), lead-up games (Level III games), and official sports (Level IV games). We'll take a look at each of these next.

Level I Games

Level I games are low-level game activities that are easy to play, have few and simple rules, require little or no equipment, and may be varied in many ways. Games at this developmental stage may be viewed as familiarization games. That is, they are games that help the learner become acquainted with the basic skills involved in an activity. They may also be viewed as discovery games because in playing them the learner is

Developmental Level I Games

- Use limited or no equipment
- Have easily perceived boundaries
- Employ limited rules
- Focus on single skills or movement concepts
- Are playable by one person alone or by a small group (three)
- Emphasize low level of competition
- Are often categorized by the fundamental movement skill involved
- Utilize one or two game strategies

Developmental Level II Games

- Use combinations of motor skills and/or movement concepts
- Use approximately two rules of the official sport
- Employ slightly more complex strategies
- May involve skill challenge games (i.e., "how far," "how fast")

Developmental Level III Games

- Also known as small-sided games (six-sided in soccer, three-on-three in basketball)
- Majority of the official sport rules used
- Several motor skills and movement concepts involved
- Multiple game strategies involved
- Often a greater role for physical fitness in the success of game play

Developmental Level IV Games

- Official team sports, dual sports, and individual sports
- Sports governed by a set of rules by an official governing body
- Not appropriate for the instructional physical education program

establishing an awareness of the spatial requirements of the game while at the same time experimenting with how the game is played. Both familiarization and discovery games are particularly appropriate for learners who are at the beginning/novice level of learning the skills being used in the game.

Level I games, which can be viewed as either familiarization or discovery games, may be easily modified to suit the objectives of the lesson, the size of the room, and the number of participants. Because they are easy to learn and can be enjoyed by both children and adults, they are often used as an educational tool primarily during the preschool and primary grades. When viewed from a skill reinforcement and application perspective, Level I games are classified as fundamental locomotor, stability, and manipulative games. That is, Level I games are classified according to the primary category of movement skill that they promote.

Let's slice the pizza! These primary grade children are participating in a Level I spatial awareness game. Each student has a number. The instructor calls out two or more numbers and these students perform a sliding action, with arms extended, as they slide across the circle to slice the pizza.

Beanbag Thank-You

Movement Skills

Walking, dynamic balance.

Movement Concepts

Space: general and personal space, curved pathways. Effort: medium/slow speed. Relationships: to other players.

Equipment

Beanbags, boundary markers, music.

These first grade students participate in Beanbag Thank-You. What fun!

Directions for Play

Children are each given one beanbag. They are asked to balance it on a body part. All players find their own personal space. The object of the game is to walk through general space without dropping one's beanbag. If a player drops his beanbag onto the floor, he must freeze. He stays "frozen" until another player offers to pick up the beanbag and give it back to him. When the player gets his beanbag back he says, "Thanks!" Players who are retrieving a dropped beanbag must pick it up while simultaneously balancing their beanbag on their own body.

Many tag games can also be categorized as Level I games if one movement skill and/or movement concept is the focus of the game. Rules of play should also be minimal.

Bounce Through the Maze

Movement Skill

One or two-handed bouncing.

Movement Concepts

Space: pathways, general/personal space, changes in direction. Effort: changes in speed. Relationships: to other players and to objects.

Equipment

Polyspots, cones, or other obstacles.

Directions for Play

Each child is given a playground ball (8 inches), and children begin play in their own personal space. The object of this game is to see how many obstacles children can bounce their ball around without losing control of the ball. Children count for themselves, thus keeping track of their own "personal best." The teacher can facilitate game play by asking children to change speeds. Changing speeds could be prompted by a drumbeat or with music.

Level II Games

Level II games are active games that involve the use of two or more motor skills and movement concepts. They have two or more rules, or procedures used in playing the official sport, and may be relatively simple or quite complex. In their simplest form they are skill challenge games in which players have an opportunity to test their developing skills. Formal games represent the more complex aspects of Level II games. Skill challenge games are those in which the rules are few and simple and the focus is on "how far," "how fast," or "how many?" Horse is a basketball shooting skill challenge game. Circle soccer is a soccer kicking and trapping skill challenge game. Bounce Through the Maze could become a Level II game if stationary defenders were added to play. The defender would be required to keep one foot on a polyspot at all times. Defenders would not be permitted to steal a ball but simply to "deny space" to the player attempting to bounce the ball through the maze.

These intermediate grade students are engaged in a Level II game involving striking and catching. The object of the game is for the batter to hit and then run around the three bases placed in the outfield as many times as possible before the outfielders retrieve the hit and throw the ball around the bases three consecutive times. Batter up!

Level III Games

Level III games are made up from the more complex aspects of Level II games. In these activities the rules and strategies of the game have more significance, as well as meaningful use of the skills required. Half-court basketball and six-a-side soccer are Level III games. Level III games may be viewed as a means to an end or as an end in themselves. As a means to an end, they are preparatory to playing the official sport and are used as a way of further developing one's ability to master the skills,

These intermediate grade students are involved in a Level III basketball game. This game involves three offensive players and two defensive players. Modified rules are being employed. For example, all offensive players must touch the ball prior to taking a shot at the basket. In addition, traveling is not a violation.

rules, and strategies of the official sport. As an end in themselves, they represent a less complex version of the official sport that is more suited to one's skill level (intermediate/practice level) and to the available facilities and equipment.

It's a beautiful fall day and these Hillsdale intermediate grade students participate in a Level III striking game with long-handled implements, namely field hockey. The object of this game is to pass to a teammate through one of several goals created by placing cones about 4 feet apart (multiple goals are set up in a medium-sized general space). Dribbling, running, and passing are the skills involved, and moving to open space and getting into position to receive a pass are the movement concepts being emphasized in this Level III game.

Level III games play an important role among upper elementary and middle school students, and they are frequently more fun to play than the official sport itself. These games allow students to practice and perfect sport skills in a modified environment. Most youngsters are not thrilled with the repetitive practice of skill drills. They are, however, interested when these same skills are used in gamelike situations. There-fore, after the skill has been reasonably mastered, it's advisable to modify skill drills to take on game form: give it a name and make it a game. As students gain profi-ciency, you can make the Level III games more complex by incorporating a greater number of skill elements and more involved strategies and by requiring a closer approximation of the regulations of the official sport.

Level IV Games

Level IV games represent the many and varied official sport games played through-out the world. They are most frequently classified as team sports, dual sports, and individual sports. Sometimes, however, they are classified according to the (1) facili-ties used (court sports, aquatic sports), (2) type of team interaction (contact sports,

CONCEPT 21.6

Level IV games, official sports, are inappropriate for inclusion in the instructional physical education program.

noncontact sports, combative sports), and (3) equipment used (racket sports, ball sports). An *official sport game* is one governed by a set of rules and regulations that are recognized and interpreted by an official governing body as the standard for play.

Official sports have *no* place in the instructional elementary school physical education program. Official sport games are particularly appropriate for individuals at the advanced/fine-tuning level of movement skill learning. Few elementary school students are at this level; instead elementary grade students need considerable instruction and practice in movement skill learning. Children may, however, engage in these sports during the intramural program, the interscholastic sport program, or the agency-sponsored youth sport program. The physical education period is a learning laboratory for learning, practicing, and putting new skills to use in a variety of movement situations.

TEACHING TIP 21.1

Enabling ideas for *modifying ball-type games:*

Modify equipment
- Suitably sized and weighted balls for each child
- Soft and/or textured balls which can be gripped
- Balls with lower bounce speed
- Reachable goals or targets

Modify the rules
- Time ball may be held before passing
- Ball can/cannot be taken from opponent's hands
- Players may run holding the ball or may dribble the ball or may not travel with the ball
- Players play in zones or may travel anywhere
- Only certain people may shoot, or anyone may shoot
- Vary type of goals/targets

Modify the number and grouping of participants
- Keep team size small but workable
- Sometimes form mixed ability groups
- Sometimes form teams with players of similar ability
- Try to match teams of equal potential

Teacher joins in to help
- Work alongside players
- Distribute the ball to engage players that may not be as involved as you would want them to be
- The teacher does not compete

ASSESSING THE EDUCATIONAL VALUE OF GAMES

Allison and Barrett (2000, pp. 144-145) highlight helpful assessment criteria for determining the educational value of a game. As a teacher you should ask the following questions, based on Allison and Barrett's discussion:

CONCEPT 21.7

Assessment of the educational value of games prior to, during, and after their inclusion into the curriculum is of critical importance.

• **Does the game allow for active participation by all?** All game participants should have equitable playing time and roles within the game. More specifically, children should have reasonable opportunity to be involved in the game, to run, to dodge, to handle a ball, to score, and so on. As a result, children should feel that they have made a valuable contribution to the game.

- **Are the children successfully challenged—does the game work?** During game play, you should observe the children and ascertain whether or not they are able to use the strategies and movement skills necessary to play the game successfully. For example, can they move to open spaces, perform skills in combination (e.g., throwing/catching), make quick changes of direction?

- **Does the game promote positive social behaviors?** Several aspects of children's emotional and social behavior can be evidenced during game play. In a positive atmosphere of play, children should encourage and support one another's efforts. Their tone of voice, although often animated, should be positive and nurturing toward others. Responses to game outcomes should also be positive. Arguing over a rule may indicate that the game is too complex or confusing for the children's stage of motor or skill development.

- **Does the game flow?** This is sometimes a subjective aspect to assess; but if the game appears to be continuous, with few stops and starts, it is described as one that "flows." For example, if a ball goes out-of-bounds, can children quickly retrieve, adapt, and begin play again without difficulty?

- **Is the game safe?** One aspect of safety is physical safety. Is there adequate space to play the game safely? Is the direction of travel safe? The pattern of travel should not promote "racing" or bumping into others. Is the equipment the appropriate size, weight, and texture? If several objects are used in the game, will objects interfere with players' motor performance or movement through space? Once targets are "hit," are they in a safe position relative to players' movement patterns?

  Emotional safety is another aspect of safety. Are any children singled out during play? Are children developmentally ready for the level of competition involved in the game? Does the game promote treating others with dignity and respect?

- **Is learning occurring?** In order for you to determine whether the children are learning, you must carefully construct the objectives for the game prior to the lesson. Through formal or informal assessment, you must determine whether or not the children are achieving the lesson objectives. Teacher observation is the most common method of assessing children's motor performance during game play. Rubrics can also be constructed to assess particular aspects of game play, including skill performance and use of game strategies/tactics (see figure 21.2).

Students' names	Can move to open spaces to receive object				Passes object to teammate when teammate is open				Supports a teammate by moving behind them, beside them, or in front of them			
No. of observations →	1	2	3	4	1	2	3	4	1	2	3	4
Zach Cattell	☐	☐	☐	☐	☐	☐	☐	☐	☐	☐	☐	☐
Jennifer Eaton	☐	☐	☐	☐	☐	☐	☐	☐	☐	☐	☐	☐
Ryan B. King	☐	☐	☐	☐	☐	☐	☐	☐	☐	☐	☐	☐
etc. ↕												

FIGURE 21.2 Rubric for assessment of game play. This assessment is for a manipulative Developmental Level II or III game and assesses only offensive play. The teacher could observe one group of three offensive players using an interval of "every 2 minutes" throughout the game. A square is checked (✓) if the student displays the skill being observed during the 2-minute interval.

THE DYNAMICS OF TEACHING GAMES

CONCEPT 21.8

Before including a game in the lesson, the teacher must make decisions about the teaching style to be used and determine what tactical decisions students must make during game play.

When teaching a game, you may do so from a variety of perspectives that can be reduced to two critical decisions. First, you must select the teaching style or styles you will use to present the game; and second, you will need to determine what tactical decisions students should learn to master the game.

Teaching Style Decisions

Games can be presented to children using a variety of teaching methods and/or models of instruction. Based on the objectives of the lesson, one or more teaching styles are selected (see discussion in chapter 10 on the spectrum of teaching styles). If you want children to discover or explore a skill, movement concept, tactic, or game strategy, the production cluster of teaching styles (i.e., guided discovery, convergent discovery, divergent production styles) is appropriate. If the objectives of the lesson are to have children replicate, peer teach, monitor their own progress, or make informed choices about game play, then the reproduction cluster of teaching styles (i.e., practice, reciprocal, self-check, inclusion styles) is best to use. The following is an example of a Level III game using the guided discovery teaching style.

Figure Out the Defense

Movement Skills

Dribbling, passing, feinting, dodging, guarding.

Movement Concepts

Space: pathways, levels, and directions. Effort: changes in speed. Relationships: to other players and to a goal.

Equipment

Playground ball or basketball, cones, pinnies.

Directions for Play

This game is a modified three-on-three basketball game in which the number and complexity of rules can be determined by the skill level of the children playing. The purpose of the game is to foster the discovery of zone or person-to-person defense. Which of these the children learn about depends on the type of goal used in the game (see figure 21.3). In one version of the game, the goal is a tall cone inside a circle (radius of 8 feet) of smaller cones (or polyspots). Two of these goals are set up, one at each end of the playing area (width of gymnasium floor). The object in this version of the game is to dribble the ball and, from the outside of the small circle, execute a bounce pass in order to touch the tall cone inside of the circle. Defensive and offensive players may not enter the circle; therefore, the tall cone or goal may not be defended. In the second version of the game, the goal is a wide area of wall space (about 15 feet). Cones are placed on the floor to specify the width. The height (8-10 feet) can be marked by tape. Polyspots can mark the distance players must stay from the wall (about 3 feet). The object in this version of the game is to pass the ball to the wall, thus touching the ball to the wall. Neither offense nor defense may be inside the 3-foot area from the polyspots to the wall. Defending the goal (tall cone inside circle) in the first version of the game requires person-to-person defense, whereas the second version of the game (wall goal) requires zone defense.

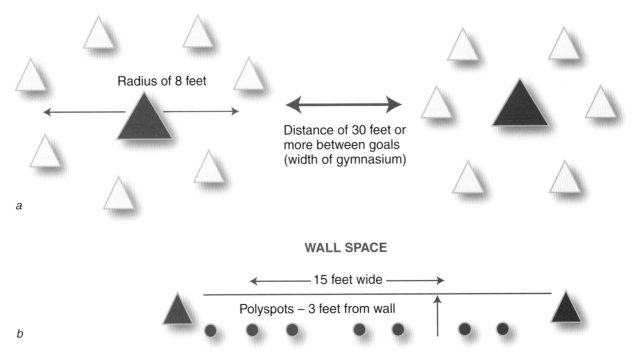

Radius of 8 feet

Distance of 30 feet or more between goals (width of gymnasium)

a

WALL SPACE

15 feet wide

Polyspots – 3 feet from wall

b

FIGURE 21.3 Figure Out the Defense. *(a)* Goal #1: person-to-person defense. *(b)* Goal #2: zone defense (one at each end of playing area).

Figure Out the Defense is a Level III game involving passing and dribbling. Offensively, students are practicing passing and bouncing on the move, as well as moving to open spaces. Defensively, students are learning how to deny space, or guard, when on defense.

Have children play each version of the game and then ask, "How did you defend the goal? Did you defend a person or an area?" In addition to having the children play the game, you may also choose to have children observe each other playing before you ask these questions.

TEACHING TIP 21.2

When *selecting and presenting a game:*

- Choose games that are appropriate to time, space, class size, available equipment, and specific objectives of the lesson.
- Choose teaching style(s) based on objectives of the lesson.
- Make explanations brief, clear, and simple.
- Correct outstanding faults, but avoid fine details in the beginning in order to get the game going.
- If applicable, demonstrate the "parts of the game" or combine demonstrations with explanation.
- Ask "What if" questions.
- Ask questions during a pause in game play to encourage children to reflect on their play.
- Have children modify a teacher-designed game or create their own game.
- Avoid stopping the game too frequently.
- Do not overplay the game. Stop at the height of interest and when players are successful.

Tactical Decisions

Traditional large-side, zero-sum games in which winners and losers are obvious, and active participation is minimal for many students, lead to failure, frustration, and minimal learning in physical education (Griffin, Mitchell, & Oslin, 1997). An alternative to the traditional model of teaching games, emphasizing skill acquisition through drills that are often "boring" and unrelated to the "real game," is the **tactical approach.** With use of this model, motor skills are taught within the tactical context of a game. "Tactical awareness is the ability to identify tactical problems that arise during a game and to select the appropriate responses to solve them" (Griffin et al., 1997, p. 8). In the tactical model, also called the "games for understanding" model, the emphasis is on *why* to execute a specific motor skill and *when* to use it—in other words, on the tactics or strategies needed for successful play. Game play involves "decision-making, supporting, marking and guarding, covering teammates, adjusting position as game play unfolds, and ensuring adequate court or field coverage by a base position" (Griffin et al., 1997, p. 12). When games are classified according to their inherent strategies (i.e., net/wall, invasion, striking/fielding, and target), teachers can emphasize tactics that apply to many game forms within a specific category. For example, ball possession and attacking the goal in soccer can also be applied to ultimate Frisbee and floor hockey. Students are encouraged to transfer their understanding from one game to another. The tactical model is rich with possibilities and helps children to apply movement skills and movement concepts within meaningful game activities.

Howarth (2001) presents one example of use of the tactical model to teach children about space awareness. Space awareness, through the use of personal and general space, is a critical feature of all games in the tactical model category (i.e., invasion, net/wall, striking/fielding, and target games). Where to move when one is in possession of the game object (e.g., a ball) and, even more challenging, when one is not in possession of the ball (Howarth, 2001, p. 8), is often very difficult for young, "egocentric" players. Howarth (2001) presents several concepts that will help children develop an understanding of space required to play invasion games. These are the key spatial concepts in playing an invasion game:

• **You need to respond to the space between yourself and others.** How far away is the other person? In which direction should the ball be thrown or kicked? How high or low should I throw the ball? The suggested games for reinforcing this concept are Monkey in the Middle or Keep Away.

• **The number of players shapes the game formation.** Progressing from two to three offensive players creates a triangular formation for game play. This formation creates more options for passing the ball. Players can now pass left or right, up or back. Adding even more players creates a circular formation. Children must learn how to change their position and maintain the circular shape—for example, creating space in an attack or denying space in a zone defense.

• **Creating patterns changes the dynamics of the game.** Patterns affect speed and accuracy. If a child has a ball and a goal, she will travel in a straight pathway toward the goal. However, if a defender is added, the child must use a zigzag or curved pathway to evade the opponent. Howarth (2001) explains that "the teacher can help the child understand that the zigzag caused by the position of the defender is really an attempt to go in a straight line, the quickest way to the goal" (p. 10). Patterns are created by the player, team, and game object.

• **The space between players and object affects the game.** Dribbling a soccer ball against a defender requires a player to use quick taps, changes of direction, and different parts of his feet to keep the soccer ball away from the defender. When the player is dribbling in an open space, his movements may be larger and stronger, as

These Hillsdale students are playing a Level III, multiple-goal soccer game. The emphasis in this game is on getting open to receive a pass. Four to six goals (two cones, approximately 4 feet apart make a goal) are spread out within a grid measuring 20 yards by 20 yards. The size of this playing area is based on the level of skill proficiency of these students.

he wants to keep the ball "out in front" of him as he quickly runs and dribbles down the field. When shooting on goal, children should understand that shooting from an angle is more difficult for the goalkeeper to defend against than shooting "straight on" because of the amount of space the goalkeeper must defend.

- **Utilizing space on the field or court modifies the game.** Children need to understand the different areas that are created on the playing field or court. These are the goal being defended, clearing space (defending area) in front of this goal, the transition area (midfield), shooting space (or attack zone), and the goal to attack.

BEST PRACTICES FOR TEACHING CHILDREN GAMES

CONCEPT 21.9

Wise teachers use a variety of proven "best practices" when including games in the lesson.

When using a developmental child-centered approach to teaching games, you should keep a number of "best practices" in mind.

- **Use part-whole teaching.** When presenting a game, you can use a "part-whole" teaching method. The part-whole method involves breaking the game into logical parts, teaching each one separately, and then gradually adding these parts, or aspects of game play, together.

- **Vary the game.** There are several ways of modifying or varying a game. The most common method of modifying a game is by varying the number of players to increase or decrease complexity. Aspects of game play can be practiced individually, with a partner, with a small group, or when one or more defenders are added (if having offense and defense is applicable). Formation of teams can also be varied. Team composition can include players of mixed ability or of similar ability levels. Additional game variables include the size of the playing area, the type of equipment used, the size of the goal or target, the pace of the game (the duration of each round of play), and the number of rules.

TEACHING TIP 21.3

Games may *be modified* in a variety of ways:

- Change or add to the movement skills used to play the game.
- Alter the rules to more closely suit the objectives of the lesson.
- Modify the equipment being used.
- Change the duration of the game.
- Intensify the game by stepping up the pace of the activity.

- Alter the game to encourage problem-solving.
- Modify the game to stimulate creativity in making up new games.
- Redesign the game to promote maximum active participation of all students.
- Modify the game to represent a special holiday or event.
- Redistribute teams during the game.

- **Explain and demonstrate.** Be sure to use demonstrations if you want children to replicate how to play the game. You may also combine demonstrations with explanations. Providing a demonstration of the game formation visually on a chalkboard (for older students) and in the playing area is also helpful. An excellent guided discovery learning experience is to provide students with a visual representation of the game formation or a game play and ask them to replicate it on their own. It is important, however, not to "overteach" or provide lengthy explanations that students cannot remember or reproduce.

- **Use instant replays.** Having children "freeze" during play, along with doing **instant replays,** also helps children understand individual aspects of game play. For example, if a child executes a successful lead pass, the teacher may choose to run an instant replay to reinforce the importance of passing to teammates who are moving toward the goal and who are open or unguarded by a defender. It is important not to let the instant replays detract from the flow of the game. Also, you should not use replays exclusively to point out players' errors.

- **Ask questions.** Questions are also an excellent teaching tool to use when there is a pause in game play or, of course, if children are confused or are playing unsafely. Having children think about what they did and why they did it is an excellent way to promote critical thinking. Presenting "What ifs?" is a valuable teaching strategy. A teacher can ask players, for example, "If you move to open spaces when you do not have possession of the ball, what might occur?"

- **Let children create and modify games.** Children are also eager to create their own games by modifying one or more aspects of game play. In the game of Boundary Ball (see chapter 20), for example, players might brainstorm with their team how to make the game "easier." Building a problem into the game facilitates creativity. For example, in Boundary Ball, at least one or two players should be covering the sidelines. These players retrieve stray or out-of-bounds balls and roll them back to their respective teams. If sideline players are not initially introduced, an inherent game "problem" exists. Children can simply modify one or more aspects of the game to create yet a new game. Once children have had experience modifying games, they can create their own games based on specified criteria provided by the teacher. The teacher must have clear lesson objectives, and the determination of game criteria should be based on these objectives.

- **Provide feedback.** It is important to provide feedback to your students regarding game strategies or specific movement skills. Be sure to limit feedback and to provide it as close in time to the activity as possible. It is much better to target one or two aspects of game play than to give feedback on many aspects. When we give too much feedback, students often forget it.

This teacher is providing feedback to a student regarding the direction and technique of his soccer pass.

Summary

Games are an integral part of the elementary physical education program, and it is critical to use developmentally appropriate practices when teaching children games. Games should be chosen based on the objectives of the lesson—that is, what motor skills and movement concepts does the teacher want children to develop? Games therefore provide opportunities to use one or more fundamental motor skills and movement concepts in dynamic settings. Playing games can also reinforce social skills, such as cooperation among team players, and cognitive skills, such as how to modify or create a game. There are several classification schemes for describing games. A developmental stage approach considers children's psychomotor, cognitive, and social status and, when employed, enables children to successfully engage in game play. The tactical model is a valuable model for teaching games. Finally, a variety of teaching methods and teaching styles lend themselves to the teaching of games.

Terms to Remember

Excellent Readings

Belka, D. (2000). Developing competent game players. *TEPE, 11* (3), 6-7.

Mitchell, S. (2000). A framework and sample games for go-through-go to games. *TEPE, 11* (3), 8-11.

Werner, P. (1992). *Teaching children games—becoming a master teacher.* Champaign, IL: Human Kinetics.

Werner, P., & Almond, L. (1990). Models of games education. *JOPERD, 61* (4), 23-27.

Williams, L., & Ayers, S. (2000). Teaching go to the goal games. *TEPE, 11* (3), 12-14.

22

Developmental Dance

Key Concept

▶ Dance is an expressive movement form through which children are encouraged to communicate their thoughts, feelings, and ideas. A well-balanced elementary physical education program offers children varied opportunities to express themselves through dance.

ance, unlike games and educational gymnastics, offers children an opportunity to utilize their movement repertoire (i.e., movement skills and concepts) to express themselves in a unique fashion. Games and gymnastics are functional movement forms in which movement skills and concepts are used to accomplish specific objectives, such as kicking a soccer ball into a goal or performing a forward roll on a bench. Dance, on the other hand, is an **expressive movement** form. A well-balanced elementary physical education program offers children varied opportunities to express themselves through dance. Both in structured dance (i.e., existing dances including folk, square, and social forms of dance) and in creative dance, children use their body as an instrument of communication and for self-expression, much the same way a painter uses line, color, shape, and texture to express ideas on canvas.

Dance accomplishes multiple outcomes in the developmental physical education program. "Dance can be a powerful tool toward peace because people learn to solve problems, express feelings, cooperate, accept and value individual differences, gain an awareness of their own and other's cultures and engage in an activity that increases, rather than decreases, self esteem" (Gilbert, 1992, p. 4).

Incorporation of rhythmic fundamentals into the creative dance lesson provides an important movement foundation for children. This

This chapter will provide you with the tools to do the following:

▶ Distinguish between functional and expressive movement.

▶ Understand rhythmic fundamentals.

▶ Identify the concepts of creative dance.

▶ Describe the components of a creative dance lesson.

▶ Understand the "progressive approach" to teaching creative dance.

▶ Justify the role of dance in the elementary physical education program.

▶ Understand the components of a creative dance lesson.

▶ Become familiar with several lessons highlighting rhythmic fundamentals and creative dance.

▶ Understand the role of assessment in dance.

▶ Discuss the importance of children being participants, observers, and performers of dance.

TEXT BOX 22.1

Teaching children dance supports National Content Standards for Physical Education #1 and #6:

- Content Standard #1: A physically educated person demonstrates competency in many movement forms and proficiency in a few movement forms.
- Content Standard #6: A physically educated person demonstrates understanding of and respect for differences among people in physical activity settings.

---

chapter defines rhythmic fundamentals and presents activities for developing rhythm, but first we examine the learning outcomes of dance. Later in the chapter we discuss the ingredients of creative dance, the creative dance lesson, a developmental progression for teaching creative movement, and finally a variety of stimuli and lesson ideas for creative dance.

TEXT BOX 22.2

Dance is a way of moving, different from other types of movement taught in the physical education curriculum. It is the only form of moving that meets the child's innate need to express thoughts, feelings, and ideas through movement. All other type of movements in the curriculum are functional—students learn them to perform a specific skill.

THE LEARNING OUTCOMES OF DANCE

Dance is an amazing learning tool. The following learning outcomes applicable to all dance forms are based on those originally generated by Anne Green Gilbert (1992). In the psychomotor domain, dancers enhance the health-related fitness components of muscular strength and endurance, cardiovascular endurance, and flexibility; apply the concepts and principles of dance through lessons designed to develop dance skills; learn body awareness, control, balance, and coordination; release stress through positive physical activity; increase their personal movement vocabulary as they work with other dancers and learn from other cultures; and learn to respect the role dance has in lifelong well-being.

Within the cognitive domain of learning, dancers increase their knowledge and vocabulary through an understanding of the elements and principles of dance; learn to solve movement problems, using convergent and divergent thinking skills; gain an understanding of the dance histories and cultures of the world's peoples; sharpen their skills of observation and learn how to make informed judgments regarding dance performances and choreography; increase their learning in other curricular areas as dance lessons are based on other academic subjects in the curriculum; and expand their creative skills through choreography and improvisation.

Within the affective domain, dancers express their feelings through movement, becoming more attuned to the inner self; experience contrasting movements that help them define their feelings; and express their feelings verbally about their own and other people's dances, helping them to put feelings and thoughts into words. They also increase their self-esteem through self-expression and the mastery of movement concepts while being engaged in a positive and noncompetitive dance form; learn self-discipline as they develop skills and create dances; and learn to take risks by mastering movement challenges, as well as learning trust through activities that involve weight-sharing, partnering, and group cooperation.

With regard to social skills, dancers learn to cooperate with others through partner and small-group work; bond with one another through positive physical contact and the sharing of ideas and space; and learn poise before a group through informal showings of formal performances. Additionally, they increase leadership skills through partner and group work; learn appropriate ways of touching others through gentle physical contact and weight-sharing; and discover the value of individual differences through creative exploration, problem-solving, and the study of other dance forms and cultures.

TEXT BOX 22.3

"For years I have been hiding inside myself. Today I found out what it was like to really be ME inside myself . . . " (quote from an elementary school student in *Sure I Can Dance*, a video produced by Ririe-Woodbury Company, Salt Lake City, UT).

RHYTHMIC FUNDAMENTALS

Rhythmic fundamentals involve developing an understanding of and feel for the elements of rhythm, namely underlying beat, tempo, accent, intensity, and rhythmic pattern. Each of these may be achieved effectively through movement. When teaching children about the elements of rhythm, you may use a drum, a tambourine, two sticks, a record player, or a piano to supply the musical phrasing. In fact, the children may provide the musical accompaniment themselves through sounds, body percussion, or homemade rhythm instruments.

Using movement as a way to develop the elements of rhythm reinforces fundamental movement skill development and fosters an understanding of and feel for rhythm. This is an important point because all coordinated, purposeful movement requires an element of rhythm, and practice in rhythmic fundamentals and singing rhythms reinforces the development of coordinated movement. Through practice with certain fundamental movements, children begin to understand the structural elements of rhythm and are able to express this understanding through coordinated, purposeful movement.

CONCEPT 22.1
Rhythmic fundamentals are an important means for children to learn about and respond to the elements of rhythm.

Understanding the Elements of Rhythm

When teaching the **rhythmic elements**, namely accent, tempo, intensity, rhythmic pattern, and underlying beat, you might use a drum, lummi sticks, or any percussive instrument while the children perform. The children may even provide the rhythmic accompaniment themselves, or you can play a record. Jumping rope to music or bouncing balls to the beat of the music often aids in developing an understanding of the elements of rhythm.

Underlying beat is the steady, continuous sound in any rhythmical sequence. Teachers can promote listening and responding to the underlying beat by having children respond to the beat of a drum or tambourine with appropriate locomotor or axial movements. Children can also provide their own beat and move to it; march to recordings by John Philip Sousa, the Marine Band, and other march recordings; jump rope to the beat of music; bounce balls to the beat of music; or keep time with the beat of music with a homemade rhythm instrument.

Rhythmic pattern is a group of beats related to the underlying beat. The underlying beat may be even or uneven. Children may develop and express an understanding of rhythmic pattern by walking, running, hopping, or jumping to an even beat; skipping, sliding, or galloping to an uneven beat; clapping rhymes; playing "echo"; playing "names in rhythm"; using wooden sticks; or tinikling.

Tempo refers to the speed of the movement, music, or rhythmic accompaniment. Children may increase their understanding of tempo by responding to speed changes in the beat of a drum with various locomotor and stability movements, performing animal walks at various speeds, bouncing a ball at various speeds, or jumping rope to different tempos.

Accent is the emphasis that is given to any one beat. The accented note is usually the first beat of every measure. Children may develop a keener awareness of accent by listening to music and clapping on the accented beat; moving about the room with the appropriate rhythmic pattern and changing direction or level on each accented beat; clapping on every beat except the accented one; or varying the response to the accented beat with a specific locomotor, stability, or manipulative movement.

Intensity is the quality of the music in terms of its loudness or softness. Children can develop an understanding of intensity by altering their movements for various intensities, changing their level for different intensities, changing the amount of

CONCEPT 22.2

The elements of rhythm are found in all forms of coordinated movement.

These two teachers lead a class in urban folk dance. This type of dance emphasizes rhythmic stepping patterns, tempo changes, and accent.

force they use to move for different intensities, bouncing a ball with appropriate amounts of force, or dribbling a ball as softly as possible and then as loudly as possible.

Discovering Rhythm

The following compilation of fundamental rhythmic activities is designed to help children discover rhythm. Most of the activities may be used from grades one through grade six, depending on the rhythmic sophistication of the group. Practice in activities that permit children to discover rhythm will help them develop an understanding of the elements of rhythm, express the elements of rhythm through movement, "feel" the beat of a musical composition, and translate the beat of a musical composition into action.

In Beat

Formation
Any number of children seated in a semicircle, facing the teacher.

Equipment
A well-known song such as "Itsy Bitsy Spider," performed by Little Richard (primary level), or any pop song that has a distinct beat (upper level). A chalkboard or large piece of writing paper and either chalk or a magic marker.

Procedures
Lead in with a discussion of rhythms around us and things that have a steady beat (heartbeat, a clock, and so on). Then have the children sing or listen to the song, and follow up by asking the children to keep the steady beat of the song by slapping their thighs. Help children discover the length of the song by putting a chalk mark on the board for each time the beat occurs in the song. Have the children use a different "body instrument" every time the song is sung (clap, slap stomach, tap feet). Have them discover new body sounds (snap fingers, pat jaw). Combine these body percussion instruments into a particular sequence such as feet-thighs-clap-snap (repeat).

Suggestions
Use a currently popular song and let the children make up their own patterns of body percussion as well as varying the old patterns. Younger children may start with only clapping and thigh slapping until they can add the others without difficulty.

Body Talk

Formation
The group seated in a semicircle, facing the teacher.

Equipment
A list of several easy poems or nursery rhymes, written either on a chalkboard or on a large piece of paper. Shel Silverstein poetry offers many possibilities.

Procedures

Have children listen to the poem, song, or nursery rhyme to feel the rhythm of the composition. Decide on appropriate body instruments for the children to use and what pattern or sequence they should follow. Say the poem or rhyme, letting the children put their body instruments to work.

Suggestions

The children can make up their own short compositions and create new patterns or sequences of body percussion. Simple melodies can be used to enhance the composition. Some appropriate rhymes or sayings are "April showers bring May flowers"; "Birds of a feather flock together"; "An apple a day keeps the doctor away"; "Rain, rain, go away, Little Johnny wants to play"; "A stitch in time saves nine"; "Early to bed, early to rise, makes one healthy, wealthy, and wise"; "If at first you don't succeed, try, try again."

Copycat

Formation

Group seated in a circle, square, or arc formation.

Equipment

A good recording suitable for the age of the children involved. Older children might enjoy a currently popular record with a lot of percussion sound.

Procedures

With a partner, children perform an assortment of axial movements called for by the music. Their partner mirrors or "copycats," doing exactly what the leader does.

Suggestions

Older children can be encouraged to give the movement separate form or pattern, such as a basic round form (A, B, A, C, A, D, A; A for bending, B for stretching, A for bending, C for twisting, and so on).

The Accent

Formation

Class seated in a semicircle.

Equipment

A chalkboard or large piece of paper on which to write several series of numbers.

Procedures

Put the following number pattern on the board:

1234567812345678123456781234 5678

Children clap only on the red numbers. They can clap as a round in two parts, three parts, or up to six parts. They might use rhythm instruments (tambourine, cymbals, shakers, and so on) instead of clapping.

Suggestions

Let the children make up their own patterns. They can use a different body part for each section. You can change the meter from fours to sixes.

Echo

Formation

Groups seated in a semicircle.

Equipment

A set of rhythm instruments for each group of six to eight.

Procedures

The teacher beats out a certain rhythmic pattern that could use silent beats or rests. Children try to duplicate the pattern by clapping their hands or using other body instruments. The teacher sings a pattern. The children respond, either with their voices or with a body instrument. Rhythm instruments may be substituted.

Suggestions

In smaller groups, have children take turns being the "teacher" and making up the rhythmical patterns.

Names in Rhythm

Formation

Groups seated in a semicircle.

Equipment

None required.

Procedures

This activity helps the children discover the rhythm of their own names by saying them and clapping them aloud.

Suggestions

A song can be used to enhance the name patterns. The class sings "What Is Your Name?" to a tune made up by the teacher, and the children sing back their answer by singing the same tune. Several of the names can be put together and organized into a chant or a song.

Conversations

Formation

Small groups in a circle.

Equipment

None required.

CONCEPT 22.3

Children internalize the elements of rhythm through activities that permit them to discover and apply rhythm.

Procedures

One person begins with a rhythmic pattern and tells it to the next person by using body language. The next person repeats what the first person did and adds his or her own rhythmic phrase. This can continue until each child has had a turn.

Suggestions

This is a good activity for memory, but it probably should be saved for the upper grades.

Applying Rhythm

The following rhythmic activities are designed to help children apply their knowledge of rhythmic fundamentals to a variety of fun and challenging activities. Each of these activities is appropriate throughout the elementary grades, depending more on the rhythmic sophistication of the children than on their movement abilities. Practice in applying rhythms will help children develop an understanding of the elements of rhythm; the ability to express rhythm through controlled, measured movement; listening skills; and fine motor control.

Sound Compositions

Formation

Groups of six to eight in a scatter formation.

Equipment

Rhythm instruments such as wood block, cymbal with mallet, drum, ratchet, and xylophone.

Procedures

Have the children decide on the movements to use and the rhythm instruments to play for each movement, such as neutral position = drum; lifting arms = xylophone (ascending); lowering arms = xylophone (descending); twisting = cymbal with mallet; nodding head = wood block. Choose children to play the various instruments, and give them time to decide what order they will play in. Have the children play their instruments one at a time, and allow the class to respond in the agreed-on fashion. Then have the children try the activity without looking at the instrument players.

Suggestions

When the activity has been mastered, have the children write their composition so that it can be saved and used later. Have the children read the symbols and perform the movements without the instruments. Create sound montages and have the children perform them. Have them make the sounds indicated in figure 22.1.

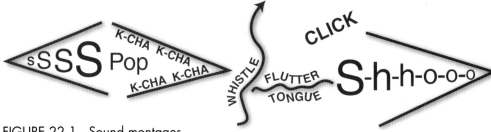

FIGURE 22.1   Sound montages.

Tampering With the Elements

Formation

Class in a scatter formation.

Equipment

A large sheet of paper or chalkboard containing the words of the army wake-up song "Reveille" and an accompaniment instrument (e.g., drum, piano).

Song

I can't get 'em up, I can't get 'em up, I can't get 'em up in the morning (repeat). The corporal's worse than privates; The sergeant's worse than corporals; Lieutenant's worse than sergeants; and the captain's worst of all!

Procedures

The children chant the words in rhythm. Then they sing the words with accompaniment. Once they have learned the words, have them begin experimenting with the expressive qualities. Remember, though, to keep the beat steady. Have the children go from quiet to loud and back to quiet again, then go from loud to quiet to loud again. They can begin slowly and accelerate to the end; they can begin fast and get slower. For color and mood, have them sing in the major key (the normal way) and then in the minor key (variation).

Suggestions

So the children can visualize intensity (i.e., softness, loudness), have them move their bodies to their expressions. Have them extend their arms very far apart and bring their arms together when the music becomes softer. Have them place their hands together and then extend their hands to show a crescendo (increasing loudness). Or they can bend down in a crouching position and as the song gets louder, extend upward to a standing position then reverse the procedure when the music gets softer.

Conducting the Beats

Formation

Six to eight per group, seated in a semicircle.

Equipment

A conductor's baton if available or a pencil will be fine as a substitute. A CD player and disc with a selection of strong, steady beat patterns, such as "Stars and Stripes Forever" (2/4) and "Dixie" (4/4). Chalkboard with chalk or a large piece of paper and a magic marker.

Procedures

Have the children discover the meter (how the song is counted), whether it is in groups of twos, threes, fours, or sixes. Don't use unusual groups such as fives, sevens, or elevens at first. Diagram on a chalkboard or piece of paper the conductor's beat patterns (figure 22.2). Let the children take their preferred hand and trace the patterns in the air. Then they should use the nonpreferred hand to do the same. After both hands have traced the patterns, children can do the same exercise with a conductor's baton. Play a recording and let them conduct with the music.

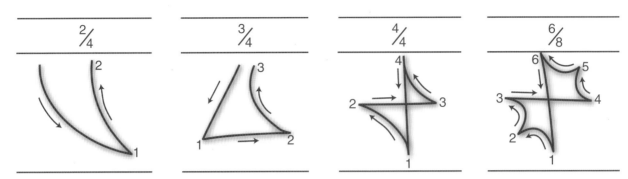

FIGURE 22.2   Conductor's beat pattern.

Suggestions

Let the children conduct each other in singing, and let them see the importance of keeping the beat constant. Use a variety of meters as well as a variety of songs.

Percussion Instrument Stories

Formation

Groups of 8 to 10 in a circle formation.

Equipment

The following story can be written either on a chalkboard or on a large piece of paper so that the children can easily read it. Or have the story duplicated on individual sheets so that each child may have a copy. Rhythm instruments are needed.

Story

One day I went for a walk. As I walked along on the sidewalk, I could hear my footsteps going . . . walk, walk, walk. Some other people came by there and their footsteps went . . . walk, walk, walk, walk. I passed a new house. The men were fixing the roof. I could hear their hammers going . . . tap, tap, tap, tap. I heard a train coming, so I ran to the corner to watch it. My feet went . . . run, run, run. Oh, it was a big, long train. The wheels were going 'round and 'round, 'round and 'round while they went . . . clickety-clack, clickety-clack. Then I heard some bells . . . tinkle, tinkle, tinkle. Where were they coming from? I turned around, and there, coming down the street, was an ice cream man. He was ringing the bells . . . tinkle, tinkle, tinkle. He didn't have a truck. He was riding in a wagon being pulled by a horse. The horse's hooves went . . . clip-clop, clip-clop. The bell and the horse and the train all together sure made a lot of noise . . . clip-clop, tinkle, tinkle, and clickety-clack. It was getting very late. My watch said . . . tick, tick, tick. It was very late for my dinner. I ran all the way home. My feet went . . . run, run, run. I came to my house and knocked on the door . . . knock, knock, knock. My mother opened the door and slammed it shut . . . slam. I washed my hands and sat down to eat. Everyone was talking . . . yak, yak, yak, yak. It sounded like a broken television . . . noise!

Procedures

Let the children choose instruments (rhythm and body) to imitate the sounds mentioned in the story (such as a triangle for the tinkling sound of the ice cream man's wagon). Let them have fun exploring with the different sounds. They might even want to bring some sound instruments from home. Have someone read or tell the story. As a particular sound is mentioned, let that sound be heard the number of times indicated. At the end, all the instruments can make the noise.

Suggestions

Have the children make up their own story. Older children particularly enjoy this. Let some of the children act out the motions implied within the story that are being sounded (e.g., sizzling egg = shaking one's shoulders).

Orchestration

Formation

Entire class seated in a circle formation. Later the class breaks into smaller groups.

Equipment

Rhythm instruments, a recording of a song.

Procedures

Sing the selected simple song for the children, or have everybody listen to a song on a recording. Let them sing or chant along and learn the words and the tune. Have the class practice all rhythms to be played before you pass out the instruments. They should play body instruments first, and then switch to others: drum, maracas (rattlers), balls, sand blocks. Pass out instruments to only a few children who seem to have the idea. Let these children have "understudies" who will concentrate only on that part and will eventually get to have a turn when they catch on. Have the drum begin as an introduction. When the child has established the proper beat, gradually add the other instruments. After the instrument players are settled into their parts, add the singers. End the composition in reverse order: singers, the last instrument to the first, and finally the drum. Let the drumbeat fade out gradually.

Suggestions

Have singers work out a body percussion ensemble to join in with the rhythm instrument ensemble. Vary the rhythm patterns as well as the instruments. Make up a dance to go along with the chant or song.

APPLYING MOVEMENT CONCEPTS TO CREATIVE DANCE

To begin learning creative dance, children need to acquire a dance vocabulary. They need letters to form words; words to form sentences; and sentences to form paragraphs, or complete dance pieces. The "vocabulary" or "A, B, C's" of both structured and creative dance are based on skill themes and movement concepts just as the content of games and gymnastics is. The skill themes of dance are embedded within *body awareness* and the movement concepts of *space, effort,* and *relationship awareness* (figure 22.3). Gilbert (1992, p. 5) uses a slightly different framework, "concepts of dance," for describing dance vocabulary. These concepts, discussed next, include *space, time, force, body, movement,* and *form.*

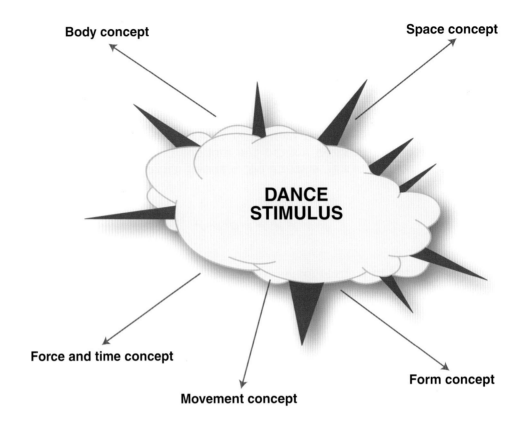

Body concept

Space concept

DANCE STIMULUS

Force and time concept

Movement concept

Form concept

FIGURE 22.3 The first step in building a dance lesson: Determine the stimulus. Note: The idea or stimulus for the creative dance lesson can be "translated" into logical movement tasks using the concepts of dance. For example, if the lesson stimulus is "Robots," percussive movement would be appropriate. Percussion is a quality or dynamic of movement and within the concept of force. Isolation of body parts and movements of head, shoulders, arms, legs, and so on are within the body concept. Mirroring a partner's actions is also from the body concept—specifically, relationships (i.e., between dancers).

The Concept of Space

Space refers to *where* the body can move. Learning to perform locomotor or non-locomotor skills within personal and general space, along different pathways, at various levels, and in different directions is essential for building children's movement repertoire. Subsequent lessons can emphasize the size or range of a movement, as well as a single focus in space or on a specific body part (e.g., on one's own hand as it moves within space) or a multiple focus throughout space (e.g., visually looking around the entire dance space).

- **Place.** Self-space/general space
- **Size.** Big/small, far reach/near reach
- **Level.** High/medium/low
- **Direction.** Forward/backward, right/left, up/down
- **Pathway.** Curved/straight/zigzag
- **Focus.** Single focus/multi-focus

These students at Mary C. Howse soar through general space, running and leaping, as they participate in a lesson about flying.

The Concepts of Time and Force

Time and force relate to *how* the body moves and are commonly referred to as the dynamics of movement. When one is developing a movement or movement phrase, time and force are sometimes prompted by the dance idea or theme (e.g., moving like lightning) but are often part of refining or enhancing the quality of a movement or movement phrase.

Time:

- **Speed.** Fast/medium/slow
- **Rhythm.** Pulse/pattern/breath

Force:

- **Energy.** Sharp (sudden)/smooth (sustained)
- **Weight.** Strong/light
- **Flow.** Free/bound

The Concept of Body

This concept includes the many body parts that can move as well as how they relate to one another. Individual parts of the body can move, or several parts can move together. Relationships among body parts or to other dancers are also part of this concept. Dancers, for example, can move together or apart; however, parts of one's own body can also move together or apart from each other (folding and unfolding).

- **Parts.** Head, neck, arms, wrists, elbows, hands, fingers, pelvis, spine, trunk, legs, knees, feet, toes, ankles, heels, shoulders, and so on

- **Shapes.** Curved/straight, angular/twisted, symmetrical/asymmetrical
- **Relationships.** Body parts to body parts, individuals to groups, body parts to objects, individuals and groups to objects: near/far, meeting/parting, alone/connected, mirroring/shadowing, unison/contrast, over/under, above/below, around/through, beside/between, on/off, gathering/scattering, in/out, and so forth
- **Balance.** On balance and off balance

The Concept of Movement

The activities of the body compose the concept of movement. The body can travel from one place to another, or locomote; and the body can perform movements that stay in self-space and do not travel. Locomotor and non-locomotor movements are often thought of as the "core" of a dance or the *what* of the dance.

- **Locomotor movements.** Basic—walk, run, jump, hop, leap, gallop, slide, skip, crawl, roll; combined—step-hop, waltz, schottische, two-step, grapevine, jog, prance, slither, creep
- **Non-locomotor movements.** Bodily movements from the stability category that occur in a fixed place on the ground—bending, twisting, stretching, swinging, pushing, pulling, falling, curling, melting, swaying, turning, spinning, dodging, poking, lifting, carving, lunging, slashing, dabbing, punching, flicking, floating, pressing, wringing, shaking, rising, sinking, bursting, wiggling, and so forth

The Concept of Form

The design or pattern of a dance makes up a particular dance form or style of choreography. Young children who are in the concrete stage of thinking may not be able to grasp this concept, so teachers may need to model the dance form. Older or more experienced dancers who can think in more abstract terms may be able to apply a dance form to a series of movements or movement phrases.

- **Recurring theme.** The dance has a theme in variation, canon, round (ABA: A = one phrase, B = different phrase)
- **Abstract.** The dance doesn't relate to a specific idea
- **Narrative.** The dance is based on a story, making it interpretive or representational
- **Suite.** The dance has a moderate beginning, slow center, and a fast end
- **Broken form.** The parts of the dance are unrelated ideas, often making the dance humorous

These concepts of dance provide children with the necessary foundation and enable them to develop a comprehensive movement repertoire. If children have not established this foundation (physical and mental experience with the concepts of *space, time, force, movement, body,* and *form*), their ability to create movement will be restricted. The situation would be analogous to asking children to play a modified game of small-sided soccer when they have not been taught the prerequisite skills of inside-of-the-foot pass, soccer dribble, or moving to an open space. Creative dance therefore is *not* simply turning on music and asking children to move "how they feel," *nor* is it interpreting or pretending to be something such as a "tree in the wind." "Interpretive dance limits students' ability to fully explore and understand all the ways the body can move" (Gilbert, 1992, p. 45), as illustrated by the following movement tasks:

- **Interpretive movement task:** "Boys and girls, please explode like a rocket ship!"
- **Creative movement task:** "Boys and girls, jump into the air using different body shapes and changes in the size of your jump! Now try jumping in different directions!"

The imagery of a rocket ship may excite your students and may be a relevant academic concept to integrate into your physical education dance lesson, but if students do not have the prerequisite movement vocabulary, their movement responses to imagery will be limited. Imagery, therefore, should not precede instruction about the concepts of dance. When using imagery to stimulate movement ideas, be sure to use a variety of images coupled with the elements of dance. For example, ask the students to "burst like a little bubble," "burst like a big balloon," "burst like a firecracker," or "burst like a ripe tomato." In this learning experience, the emphasis is on "ways to burst" versus asking the students to imitate an object.

**CONCEPT
22.4**

To successfully create movement, children must acquire a dance vocabulary.

a

b

(a) Students on an imaginary springboard jump up into the air during this creative dance lesson on flying at Mary C. Howse Elementary School. *(b)* These two young girls make shapes, like airplanes after a landing.

DEVELOPING THE CREATIVE DANCE LESSON

Similar to a games or gymnastics lesson plan, a developmental dance lesson must build from simple to more complex. The components making up a dance lesson

**CONCEPT
22.5**

The creative dance lesson follows a step-by-step progression that enables both the teacher and the learners to engage in a meaningful and worthwhile educational experience.

differ slightly from those for a games or gymnastics lesson. In the following paragraphs we briefly describe each portion of the dance lesson.

Step I: Set Induction

As in a games or gymnastics lesson, the teacher should begin with a **set induction**. The purpose of a set induction is to introduce the dance concept (e.g., canon form; making shapes) and capture the students' interest. This introductory portion of the lesson may also include warm-up activities, dance exercises, or both. As a result of the set induction, students should understand what the lesson is about.

The set induction helps children focus and center their thoughts and energy toward the upcoming lesson. The set induction can serve to motivate children to move, as well as communicate the purpose and objectives of the day's lesson, and can do so in a variety of ways. For example, if the lesson is about finding different ways to "burst," balloons can be suspended from the ceiling or scattered about on the floor. In their art class the children could construct rocket ships, firecrackers, and tomatoes to be used to create the "bursting environment." An inviting and unique environment can excite and stimulate the children's interest. Other possibilities are to evoke each of the images to be used during the lesson by playing sound effects as children enter or to show a videotape of a rocket ship taking off into space.

The set induction is also a time to physically prepare the children for the day's lesson. **Technique exercises** are appropriate to teach at this time. Technique exercises emphasize body alignment, stretching of large-muscle groups, isolation of body parts, and strengthening of major muscle groups.

Finally, the set induction may be a time for review of a previous lesson activity such as mirroring or translating one or more of the action words into movement (e.g., glide, float, press, slash, dab).

Step II: Exploring a Dance Concept

Next the students explore the specific dance concept being emphasized in the lesson. This may be done individually, in pairs, or in small groups. During this part of

The teacher in this creative dance lesson on shape is providing constructive criticism about different ways to make shapes while inside of a body sock.

the lesson the teacher employs divergent or guided discovery teaching styles to foster students' creative exploration (see chapter 10, "Teaching Styles").

In this portion of the lesson, children are guided in exploring the lesson concept or concepts. For example, if the concepts being taught are *shape (body concept)*, *level (space concept)*, and *use of different body parts (relationship concept)*, the teacher could provide the following movement tasks:

- **Exploratory task—shape.** "Boys and girls, in your own personal space, please make three different shapes." The teacher then leads a brief discussion about the exploratory activity. "What types of shapes did you create? Can anyone describe their shape?" Another example of exploring might be based on *rising* and *sinking (relationship concept)* and leading these actions using different body parts.

- **Exploratory task—relationship.** "Begin on the floor in any shape you choose. Slowly rise from your low level to a high level and then back down." After a brief movement exploration (2-3 minutes), the teacher leads a discussion about rising and sinking actions.

Students in this lesson create "duet shapes" with one dancer inside of a body sock and the other dancer sculpting their shape around the body sock. This is an exciting and novel lesson for students. Partners not in the body socks can dance from one shape to another using locomotor patterns or traveling movements based on action words such as "spiral," "flow," or "dart."

Step III: Developing and Practicing New Movement Skills

The third part of the creative dance lesson involves students in practicing and developing movement skills (both locomotor skills and non-locomotor stability movements) through the dance concepts. For example, if the lesson is about the concept of *free movement* (i.e., movement that is indirect and does not have a distinct ending) and *bound movement* (i.e., movement that is direct and has a distinct ending), the students can practice spinning or turning on different body parts as a free movement and jumping as a bound movement.

In this part of the lesson, students practice specific non-locomotor or locomotor skills. They can practice these using a center-floor movement phrase or using across-the-floor movement phrases. For example, students may practice run-run-leap across the floor, gradually making each leap bigger (concept of space). A center-floor phrase would involve a movement combination. This combination is one the teacher would choreograph and would teach using the command style or the practice style (see chapter 10, "Teaching Styles"). Movement combinations are based primarily on non-locomotor skills: swinging, carving, spoking, shape-flow, bend, stretch, twist, and curl.

Step IV: Creating Movement Phrases

During this lesson segment the students create **movement phrases,** which are "dance sentences," through improvisation. Structured movement tasks presented by the teacher facilitate the improvisational process. For example, you might say, "Boys and girls, let's use free or unbound non-locomotor movements to the slow music and bound locomotor movements to the fast music." Students improvise using non-locomotor and locomotor movement skills in response to the instructional task.

When movement phrases are created, the concept explored briefly at the beginning of the lesson is developed further. Using the first lesson idea about shapes, for example, the following instructional tasks could be presented:

- **Introductory task.** "Begin with creating a shape at a high, medium, or low level."
- **Extending task.** "What other types of shapes can you make with your body?"
- **Refining task.** "Do all shapes have to be made on your feet, or can you make shapes while supporting yourself on different parts of your body?"
- **Application task.** "Now, let's see if you can connect three shapes in a row by moving smoothly from one shape to another! Perform each of your shapes at a different level." (Music can accompany students at this point, or instruments can be played by other students.)

Feedback, or refining tasks, should be about the lesson concepts. Are the students using different levels, different body parts, and different types of shapes? It is important for the teacher to use a guided discovery or divergent production teaching style in order to foster students' exploration.

The following instructional tasks could be used to develop the second lesson idea, rising and sinking:

- **Introductory task.** "Begin by rising to a drumbeat of eight counts."
- **Extending task.** "Now sink to the floor during the next eight counts of the drum."
- **Refining task.** "Be sure to move slowly, using all eight drumbeats."
- **Extending task.** "This time when you rise, lead the action with only one body part. Choose a different body part when sinking back to the floor."
- **Extending task.** "The next time you rise, rise quickly to the drumbeat and sink slowly to the drumbeat." (Play the rhythm first so that students are familiar with the speed of the quick eight counts of rising and the slow eight counts of sinking.)

The number of extending and refining tasks used in this portion of the lesson will depend on your time constraints and the ability of your students to conceptualize the objectives of the lesson.

Step V: Lesson Closure

The creative dance lesson culminates with a lesson closure. During **lesson closure** the teacher may conduct a cool-down using specific dance exercises, or the lesson closure can be a time for viewing some of the improvisational ideas and choreography of students. This portion of the lesson can also be a time to review with the students, evaluate the day's lesson, and preview the next lesson.

In addition to review, lesson closure can include observation and assessment. For example, so that students can observe one another's movement ideas, half of the class may perform for the other half. On the basis of criteria provided by the teacher

---

Authentic assessment of the individual movement(s) created, dance phrase, or entire dance piece can be done in several ways. Students could watch themselves on videotape and critique themselves according to the constructs of the lesson. A checklist could be provided for students to conduct a "self-check" or self-assessment. Students may also write in journals about their dance learning experience. Classmates could view each other's responses and assess their classmates based on criteria provided by the teacher. A sample peer checklist is described below.

Assessment Example: Dance Concepts: Shapes and Levels

Performer's Name: _____ **Date:** _____

Observer's Name: _____

Grade: _____ **Class:** _____ **(Classroom Teacher's Name)**

1. Place a checkmark ✓ next to the shapes included in your dance.

    _____ Straight ———   _____ Bent ⌐   _____ Round ◯

    _____ Wide �ču   _____ Twisted ∞   _____ Narrow |

2. Place a checkmark ✓ next to the levels used in your dance.

    _____ High   _____ Medium   _____ Low

3. Place a checkmark ✓ by the body parts used as "bases of support" for the shapes made.

    _____ Knees   _____ Hands   _____ Bottom   _____ Stomach

    _____ Feet   _____ Head   _____ Side   _____ Elbow

    _____ Shoulder

FIGURE 22.4 Sample peer assessment of a creative dance lesson.

about the lesson constructs, students observe fellow classmates for specific movement responses. Appreciation for individual differences and of the creative process may be the focus of discussion in response to student observation. Lesson closure can also include self-assessment and teacher assessment. A sample peer assessment on shapes and levels is presented in figure 22.4. Assessment is also discussed in greater detail in chapter 12, "Assessing Progress."

When planning for and conducting the creative dance lesson, take time to think of the following four key words:

- **Plan.** First, pre-assess where your students are, then plan accordingly.
- **Participate.** Strive for maximum student participation focused on the objectives of the lesson.
- **Create.** Set up a learning environment that is open to and supportive of children's expressive efforts.
- **Evaluate.** Take time with your students to review what has been taught and the extent to which it has been learned.

All four of these ingredients are essential to the successful creative dance lesson.

CONCEPT 22.6

Effective teaching of creative dance requires awareness of and respect for where students *are* in the creative dance process rather than where they *should* be.

A DEVELOPMENTAL PROGRESSION FOR TEACHING CREATIVE DANCE

Children in your classes will have varying levels of experience with dance. Nicholes (1991) provides a developmental or "progressive approach" to teaching children creative movement that accommodates the heterogeneous makeup of physical education classes. Nicholes uses four levels to describe both the characteristics of children and the teaching methodology best suited for teaching children at a specific level. Table 22.1 highlights the essential characteristics of these four developmental levels.

Level I Dance

Level I dance is a teacher-dependent experience with the emphasis on awareness, exploration, and discovery. Lessons foster creativity through single movement challenges in which the teacher provides the stimulus for movement (verbally, through music, visuals, stories, etc.). The teacher must provide appropriately timed cues that are simple and specific. For example, action words might be the stimulus for movement. On the basis of lesson objectives, the teacher selects specific words to elicit movement. If the aim is to have the children explore the use of contrasting efforts, the teacher might provide the following action words: plop/float, shrivel/grow or expand, tight/loose.

Level II Dance

Level II dance is a teacher-student-interdependent experience. The teacher gives the students a movement problem (a combination of movement tasks) to solve and offers guidance and feedback as needed. These movement problems should stimulate divergent thinking and provide children time to create several physical responses. Level II movement tasks are combined dance elements and are more comprehensive than Level I tasks. You might say, for example, "When you hear the music, begin

TABLE 22.1—ESSENTIAL CHARACTERISTICS OF THE DEVELOPMENTAL PROGRESSION FOR TEACHING CREATIVE DANCE

Developmental level	Teacher/Student orientation	Focus	Teacher's role
Level I	Teacher dependent	Teacher challenges students to be aware of and explore single movement challenges	Provides simple and specific cues
Level II	Teacher-student dependent	Teacher challenges student to explore and "solve" more complex movement problems by stimulating divergent thinking.	Provides movement challenges Gives guidance and feedback
Level III	Teacher initiated Student directed	Teacher provides the initial movement stimulus. Students develop the idea.	Supports Clarifies Suggests
Level IV	Student initiated Student directed	Students generate and test out their own ideas.	Creates an emotionally safe and noncompetitive environment

working with your partner and create an action word transition into a connecting shape." Basic terms such as "action word," "transition," and "connecting shape" have been independently explored in Level I activities. The teacher follows the initial movement challenge by stating, "Keep the shapes and transitions going, and freeze when the music stops."

Level III Dance

Level III dance is teacher initiated and student directed. The teacher provides the stimulus and leaves the development up to the students. Level III emphasizes form and the development of selected ideas to a greater extent and challenges students to repeat and perform what they have practiced. Students must have a good grasp of the dance elements and their components (e.g., space: direction, level, range, pathways, general space, personal space) in order to be successful in exploring and developing their ideas. A sample Level III movement challenge might be, "Working with your partner, create a short dance that has three dependent and connecting shapes, and an action word transition between each shape." In Level III experiences, the students should create dances that have a beginning, middle, and end. The teacher's role in Level III learning experiences is to support, clarify, and offer aesthetic suggestions to students.

Level IV Dance

Level IV dance, the highest on the developmental progression, is student initiated and student directed. At this level students generate and develop their own ideas.

The teacher needs to establish a nonthreatening, noncompetitive environment that fosters creative work. The teacher provides guidance and feedback as needed. Level IV demands a mature willingness and ability to commit to working on a dance for an extended period of time. Intermediate-grade students who have experienced creative dance throughout their elementary physical education program can progress to Level IV.

This progressive approach to teaching children creative dance considers children's developmental status, taking into account their experience and knowledge of the "ingredients" or concepts of dance. Children are more likely to be motivated and successful as they discover the joy of creating their own dances.

STIMULI AND LESSON IDEAS FOR CREATIVE DANCE MAKING

Life is a dance! Yes, there are many different stimuli for facilitating creative dances. Poetry, academic ideas or concepts, props, and themes represent sample stimuli for developing a dance lesson. Remember, a dance stimulus needs to be "translated" through use of the dance concepts as described earlier in figure 22.3. For example, if the lesson theme is "referee signals," the teacher should present a series of tasks that use the dance concepts as a means of developing the theme into actual movement problems or tasks to perform. To begin with, students might observe the teacher modeling a movement phrase composed of various referee signals to a musical selection. The students might then be asked to generate different types of signals. Subsequently they might be asked to take a specific movement and make it bigger, perform it while traveling, or perform it from a high to a low level. The CD-ROM accompanying this textbook provides full-length lesson plans based on a variety of types of stimuli.

Summary

It is important for teachers to incorporate creative dance into the elementary physical education program. The concepts of dance include space, time, force, body, movement, and form. It is essential that children understand these concepts, which are the ingredients of creative dance, and thus develop a dance vocabulary. The components of a dance lesson include set induction, exploring a dance concept, developing and practicing new movement skills, and creating dance movements. The physical education program can provide children with the opportunity to be participants, observers, and performers of creative dance. Nicholes' developmentally based progressive approach to teaching creative movement or dance is a teaching method that accommodates the heterogeneous makeup of physical education classes.

Terms to Remember

Excellent Readings

AAHPERD. (1994). *National dance standards.* Reston, VA: Author.

Fleming, G.A. (Ed.). (1990). *Children's dance.* Reston, VA: AAHPERD.

Joyce, M. (1980). *First steps in teaching creative dance to children.* Mountain View, CA: Mayfield.

Rovegno, I., & Bandhauer, D. (2000). Teaching elements of choreography. *TEPE, 11* (5), 10.

Stinson, S. (1988). *Dance for young children: Finding the magic in movement.* Reston, VA: AAHPERD.

TEPE feature edition on dance. (September, 2000). *TEPE, 11* (5).

Williams, L. (2001). Creative writing is a moving experience. *TEPE, 12* (1), 25-26.

23

Developmental Gymnastics

Key Concept

▶ Developmental gymnastics accommodates children's unique individual differences by using a variety of teaching styles that develop and enhance fundamental movement skills within varied learning environments.

Developmental gymnastics uses both direct and indirect teaching approaches. Through developmental gymnastics, children are encouraged to explore a variety of ways to use fundamental movement skills and movement concepts for the purpose of learning efficient management of their bodies. Developmental gymnastics focuses on skills within the ability and understanding of the individual student and is consistent with the principles of the developmentally based physical education curriculum. In addition to enhancing movement skills and body coordination, teaching children developmental gymnastics enhances their ability to do the following:

- Use higher-order thinking skills (i.e., convergent and divergent thinking)
- Develop the health-related fitness components of cardiovascular respiratory endurance, muscular strength, muscular endurance, and flexibility
- Develop social skills through partner and small-group collaboration
- Learn to manage the body against gravity

This chapter will provide you with the tools to do the following:

▶ Understand the role of gymnastics in the developmental physical education program.

▶ Become familiar with the content of developmental gymnastics.

▶ Learn how to use aspects of the movement framework to vary movement tasks.

▶ Understand the methodology best suited for teaching developmental gymnastics.

▶ Learn how to design different learning environments in developmental gymnastics.

▶ Become familiar with the performance-related criteria for several gymnastics skills.

▶ Become familiar with developmentally appropriate equipment for teaching children gymnastics.

▶ Become familiar with spotting techniques.

▶ Become familiar with sequencing gymnastics content.

- Apply movement skills and movement concepts to movement tasks
- Develop performance-related abilities including agility, power, and coordination

In this chapter we explain the difference between Olympic-style gymnastics and developmental gymnastics. We then briefly examine teaching methods appropriate for developmental gymnastics instruction. Next we take a look at a four-level developmental progression for gymnastics content; and finally, we discuss assessment of progress, provide safety tips, and offer our thoughts on developmentally appropriate gymnastics equipment.

TEXT BOX 23.1

National Physical Education Content Standards #1 and #2 can be reinforced by carefully selecting educational gymnastics activities that are developmentally appropriate and promote the behaviors advocated by these standards:

- Content Standard #1: Demonstrates competency in many movement forms and proficiency in a few movement forms.
- Content Standard #2: Applies movement concepts and principles to the learning and development of motor skills.

DEVELOPMENTAL GYMNASTICS

Developmental gymnastics, frequently called educational gymnastics, is better suited for the instructional physical education program than Olympic-style gymnastics. The equipment, which includes both small equipment (e.g., hula hoops, wands, ropes, balls) and large equipment (e.g., foam shapes, benches, trestles, ladders), is designed to fit the physical dimensions of preschool and elementary school children. Furthermore, developmental gymnastics is self-testing, meaning that competition is with oneself rather than against an opponent.

Olympic-style gymnastics traditionally utilizes direct or reproduction teaching styles (e.g., command or practice styles; see chapter 10, "Teaching Styles") and a set progression for skill acquisition. Emphasis is on the perfection of gymnastics skills based on established performance criteria. In addition, Olympic-style gymnastics uses specific types of equipment, including the vaulting horse (set at specified heights for various competitive levels), parallel and uneven bars, horizontal bar, rings, pommel horse, balance beam, and a floor exercise mat. Most of the equipment of Olympic-style gymnastics is expensive, requires advanced levels of knowledge for safe use and proper instruction, and is difficult to modify to fit the physiques of most elementary grade children. For these reasons, Olympic-style gymnastics is most appropriately taught in private clubs and gymnastics centers.

CONCEPT 23.1

Although Olympic-style gymnastics is generally inappropriate in the elementary physical education program, developmental gymnastics can be of great value.

APPROPRIATE TEACHING METHODS

CONCEPT
23.2

Depending on the needs of the learner and the objectives of the lesson, both direct (i.e., reproduction) and indirect (i.e., production) styles of teaching can be effectively used in the developmental gymnastics lesson.

The teaching styles associated with developmental gymnastics allow children to progress at their own rate; they also accommodate varied levels of interest and experience, as well as various body types and levels of physical fitness. The use of both direct (i.e., reproduction) and indirect (i.e., production) teaching styles provides children with choices about which movement skills to practice or create. After children have responded to a movement challenge presented by the teacher, refinement of the skill becomes important.

The practice, reciprocal, and inclusion styles of teaching facilitate skill practice. In the reciprocal style, the teacher designs a task card that highlights the critical cues or performance-related criteria specific to the skill being practiced. The teacher or the child may determine the conditions or learning environment in which the child practices the skill (e.g., on a mat, on a bench). This direct or reproduction style helps children develop and refine specific gymnastics skills.

The inclusion style of teaching gives children an opportunity to select the skills that they want to practice. Their selections will vary in difficulty; but children soon learn to make decisions, with teacher guidance, about the level of skill difficulty they should attempt. For example, if the skill theme is jumping and landing, children might choose from the following array of skills:

- Jumping and landing over a rope on the floor
- Jumping and landing over a rope suspended between two cones
- Jumping and landing with turns in the air
- Jumping and landing off of a foam shape (18-24 inches)

The point is that if children are responding to a divergent movement task, several movement solutions are acceptable. All children are challenged at their own level of ability and are more likely to experience success.

As a teacher you must select the teaching style or styles appropriate for accomplishing the lesson objectives. In all cases, you should give children meaningful feedback about the efficiency of their movement solutions and should assist (i.e., spot) children when necessary. It is appropriate to provide demonstrations (e.g., video, computer, or teacher or student demonstrations) when you are using either the

---

TEXT BOX 23.2

Eleven Critical Educational Gymnastics Skills

1. Five basic jumps
2. Sideways roll
3. Hand balance/body curled
4. Shoulder balance
5. Head/hand balance
6. Jump/land/roll basic sequence
7. Forward roll/shoulder roll
8. Backward roll/shoulder roll
9. Hand balance/body extended
10. Cartwheel
11. Jump for height

Allison, P.C., & Barrett, K. (2000). *Constructing children's physical education experiences.* Boston: Allyn and Bacon, pp. 154-155.

production or reproduction teaching styles, or after students have produced several movement solutions to a task and need clarification on how to execute a specific skill. You can also use a variety of teaching styles within the same gymnastics lesson. The key is to provide developmentally appropriate and successful learning experiences for all children.

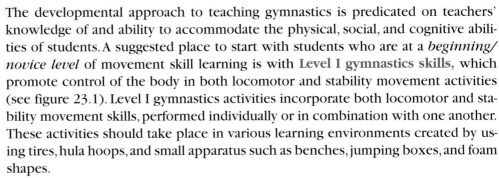

A TEACHING PROGRESSION
FOR DEVELOPMENTAL GYMNASTICS

**CONCEPT
23.3**

Gymnastics activities that are developmentally based focus on body control (Level I), balancing and rolling (Level II), weight transfer (Level III), and body flight (Level IV).

The developmental approach to teaching gymnastics is predicated on teachers' knowledge of and ability to accommodate the physical, social, and cognitive abilities of students. A suggested place to start with students who are at a *beginning/novice level* of movement skill learning is with **Level I gymnastics skills,** which promote control of the body in both locomotor and stability movement activities (see figure 23.1). Level I gymnastics activities incorporate both locomotor and stability movement skills, performed individually or in combination with one another. These activities should take place in various learning environments created by using tires, hula hoops, and small apparatus such as benches, jumping boxes, and foam shapes.

After children have begun to master a progression of Level I gymnastics activities, they can move on to Level II. **Level II gymnastics skills** focus on balancing and

These students perform partner balances stimulated by photos on a task card. Are they having fun yet?

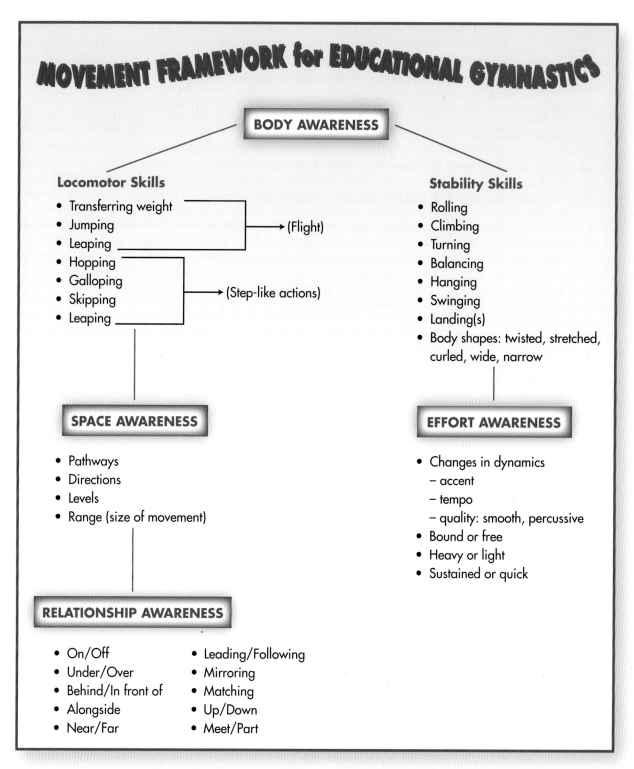

FIGURE 23.1 Core content of developmental gymnastics. Note that the skills and concepts shown are not exclusive of one another. For example, you can roll using different body shapes, quickly or slowly, big or small, and/or meeting or parting.

rolling. Children who are at this level are at a slightly higher point in the beginning/novice level of movement skill learning in that they have a developing sense of body awareness and motor control.

Level III gymnastics skills deal mainly with transfer of weight. Children doing activities at this level should be at the intermediate/practice level of movement skill learning. As such they are ready to experience the exciting sensations that accompany learning to perform wheeling actions, inverted supports, and a variety of springing movements.

Level IV gymnastics skills involve the body in flight. These activities are reserved for children at the advanced/fine-tuning level of movement skill learning. Activities at this level, such as in-flight rolls and advanced springing movements, focus on loss of contact with the supporting surface.

Level I Skills: Body Control

When children are at Level I of movement skill development in educational gymnastics, it is important for them to acquire body control through a series of lessons aimed at developing locomotor and stability skills. At Level I, children's performances are sometimes exaggerated (too big or too small), uncoordinated, and lacking in rhythmical timing, and often parts of the skill are missing. Therefore it is important that lessons emphasize space awareness (e.g., personal space and general space; using different pathways) and effort awareness (e.g., starting and stopping with control). The following are examples of a variety of lesson activities for facilitating skill development in Level I.

- Moving individually:
  - Skipping along a curvy pathway
  - Balancing on different body parts
- Moving with others:
  - Leading/following
  - Mirroring
  - Meeting/parting
- Emphasizing effort:
  - Changing speeds
  - Sudden stops and starts
  - Moving to an external beat
  - Light versus strong energy
- Emphasizing space:
  - Along different pathways
  - In different directions
- Moving in combination:
  - Gallop and turn (on any body part)
  - Skip, hop, walk along a curved pathway
  - Run, jump from one to two feet, stretch, make a twisted shape on one foot
  - Run and leap
- Moving on small and large apparatus:
  - In and out of hula hoops
  - Over ropes placed on the floor or elevated

- On low foam shapes or benches
- Off low obstacles: foam shapes, jumping boxes, benches

With the activities listed, movers can use a safety roll when they lose control after a jump or do not control their body upon a sudden stop. The safety roll uses a round or curled body shape; the knees are bent and tucked into the chest, the chin is tucked to the chest, and the back is used to roll across the surface.

After children have practiced locomotor skills such as skipping, leaping, galloping, running, and sliding, as well as axial movements such as turning and twisting, they should begin a series of lessons on jumping and landing. Body shapes combined with jumping create several movement options. A *star jump* is a jump off of two feet with the arms and legs spread out or wide while the person is in the air, and a two-foot landing (see photo). A *seat kicker* is a jump in which the knees bend so that the heels can be touched to the buttocks while the person is in flight; this jump also uses two feet for takeoff and landing. In another jump variation, the jumper has a curved or stretched body shape while in flight and does a quarter, half, or full turn in the air before landing on two feet. During a jump, children can also touch their toes or heels in a variety of ways. Jumps can be performed on, over, off, and back and forth across equipment or over a partner or other movers (see photos). Jumps can cover space horizontally or project the body vertically into the air.

Children can also perform manipulative activities (e.g., using ribbons, wands, hoops) while jumping. They can jump in unison with a partner or mirror or match a partner; they can jump as partners or in small groups, both together and apart.

A star jump is demonstrated by this Mary C. Howse fifth grade student. Wow!

Tuck your knees! This jump involves a tight body shape or a tucked position as she jumps off of a foam trapezoid shape.

This young boy performs a jump over his partner and achieves great "hang time!"

Fundamental movement skills are commonly broken down into three phases or parts: the preparation, the execution or force phase, and the recovery phase or follow-through. For jumping, the critical performance cues involve preparing the body by contracting it and bending to gather energy with the arms low at the sides of the body. During the force phase the arms swing vigorously from low to high, in to out (depending on type of jump), as the legs straighten or bend; during the recovery phase the landing should be on two feet simultaneously, while the knees are bent to absorb force and the arms are lowered for balance.

Level II Skills: Balancing and Rolling

At Level II, children are expanding their movement repertoire and beginning to learn about weight-bearing skills, namely balancing and rolling. The skill themes of balance and rolling can be varied using the movement framework (refer to figure 23.1). The following are some possible options for both nontraditional and traditional balancing and for rolling.

Nontraditional Balancing

Nontraditional balancing occurs within the movement framework of effort, space, relationships, and body awareness and is used as a means of enhancing children's static and dynamic balance abilities. The following are ways in which these balances can be performed:

- Individually:
  - In self-space on a mat
  - Upright or inverted
- Emphasizing different body shapes:
  - Wide or narrow
  - Twisted, bent, straight, or round
  - Symmetrical/asymmetrical
- Emphasizing relationships:
  - Between body parts (near/far; under/over)
  - With a partner or a group: matching or mirroring
- In combination with locomotor skills:
  - Gallop in a zigzag pathway, stop and perform a balance on three body parts (on a mat)
  - Jump and perform a turn in air, stretch, balance on one body part
  - Leap over a rope, turn, balance on two body parts while inverted
- With equipment:
  - Part of body in a hula hoop, part of body out of a hula hoop
  - Part of body on a bench, part of body off bench
  - On a partner; partner in an "all-fours" position

A static balance is a stability skill in which the center of gravity remains in a stable position. The weight-bearing skills in Level II of the developmental progression emphasize static balance. Like all skill themes, weight-bearing skills can be prompted by a variety of learning environments, created by purposeful arrangement of equipment, including benches, beams, ropes, tires, ladders, and bridges. For example, when you assign an open-ended task by saying something like "Touching three body parts, create as many different balances as possible," you will elicit a variety of responses from children. Such techniques challenge students at their

CONCEPT
23.5

Level II developmental gymnastics activities are most appropriate for those who have mastered Level I skills and are somewhat further along in the beginning/novice level of movement skill learning.

This young girl performs a static balance on one foot while on top of a balance board. Quite elegant! Many different static balances could be made on the board by balancing on different body parts.

individual level of skill. Some children may respond with a headstand, while others may create a balance using their head, a hand, and one foot.

Counterbalancing and Counter-Tension

Many aspects of the movement framework depicted in figure 23.1 can be applied to balancing. When designing movement tasks, the teacher poses challenges that lead children from balances on larger body parts to balances on smaller body parts. When equipment is being used, children can execute balances with part of their body on

Stretch! Counter-tension is demonstrated by these students participating in a developmental gymnastics lesson at Hillsdale Elementary School.

the equipment (e.g., a bench) and part of their body off the equipment (on another child or on the floor). When the task involves balancing with a partner, children can perform two types of balances—counterbalances and counter-tensions.

Counterbalancing with a partner occurs when weight and force are distributed inward, or toward one's partner. A popular way in which children attempt to counterbalance is from a standing position, with hands pressed against their partner's hands. Other body parts can be used as well, including back, sides of the body, feet, shoulders, or bottom.

Counter-tension is the opposite of counterbalance, with the weight and force being distributed away from one's partner. Holding hands and leaning away from one's partner is the most common form of counter-tension with a partner. The feet of the partners should be as close together as possible, with legs kept straight. The use of different body parts, levels, and directions (see photo) can vary counter-tension.

Traditional Balancing

Traditional balancing includes skills such as the knee scale, front scale (some children call this an "airplane balance"), tripod, and headstand. The critical performance-related cues for a headstand, corresponding to the preparation, execution, and recovery phases, are as follows:

- **Preparation phase.** The head (forehead area) touches the mat; hands are placed behind head (fingers spread and facing straight ahead [not sideways]) and about shoulder-width apart; elbows are bent at a right angle.

- **Force or execution phase.** One leg lifts up into the air (leg can be straight or bent), and then the other leg follows. Legs should be squeezed together once both are extended in the vertical plane.

A partner balance is fun when performed with control, as these two Mary C. Howse students demonstrate. The teacher spots to aid the students' balance.

- **Recovery phase.** Legs come down to the floor one at a time while straight or bent.

- **Safety tips and spotting.** Before attempting a headstand, students should be able to execute a tripod or a headstand while in a round or tucked position for 3 seconds or more. They can perform a headstand against a large foam shape, which supports them while they are inverted and ensures that they will not tilt over. A spotter should grasp the first leg of the performer as it is lifted into the vertical plane and then the other leg. Sometimes a performer's back should be supported to keep her from tilting over. If a child feels as if she's going to fall over, she should learn to immediately tuck her knees into her chest to recover.

All of these traditional balances can be elicited through carefully designed movement problems. Many pieces of gymnastics equipment will aid children in performing these skills. For example, a handstand can be performed up against a foam block, which will support the torso and legs.

Rolling

Rolling is a dynamic aspect of weight bearing in developmental gymnastics. The following elements of the movement framework (see figure 23.1) can be used to create varied learning tasks based on the skill theme of rolling:

- Performed individually or in combination:
  - On a mat
  - In different directions (space)
- Using different body shapes and different relationships between body parts:
  - Forward roll with wide legs
  - Roll with legs narrow and straight
  - Roll with legs bent, body curled
- Using different relationships:
  - Alongside equipment
  - In unison with a partner
  - Through a foam obstacle
  - Using small manipulative equipment
- Performed in combination with other movement skills:
  - Arabesque scale into a roll
  - Jump vertically, land, stretch, and roll
  - Jump off of equipment and roll

Rolls can also be performed on a bench, off of a bench or foam shape, or through a foam shape. Manipulating a ball, ribbon, or hoop during rolling is another variation. Ribbons, hoops, and balls can be projected into the air during the rolling action and caught during recovery. Several other movement combinations or sentences are possible when rolling is combined with other aspects of the movement framework. The critical performance-related cues for a sideward, forward, and backward roll are the following:

Sideward Roll

- **Preparation phase.** The body is stretched out while the child is on a mat or bench; muscles are contracted and as tight as possible, and arms reach above head.

- **Force phase.** The performer generates momentum by using hips and energy from the center of the body (hips/stomach), as well as the arms, to move sideways from stomach to back to stomach.

- **Recovery phase.** The performer returns to the initial preparation position.

Forward Roll

- **Ready position.** The hands are flat on mat; the hips are lifted up; the head is tucked under (chin to chest); and weight of body is slightly forward.

- **Force phase.** The feet push off floor evenly; hips must be pushed over head with use of the hands to generate force; back of head, then shoulders, then back should touch mat; knees stay bent and tucked into chest.

- **Recovery phase.** Knees stay tucked into chest; arms stretch out and reach forward, lifting the chest and body up into the vertical plane.

Forward rolls are difficult for tall, lanky children because of the length of their legs and are challenging for students who are overweight. For these reasons it is important to offer choices by posing open-ended tasks when rolling is a lesson objective. This enables children to choose another type of roll.

Beginning a forward roll requires a simultaneous takeoff from two feet, proper hand placement, and tucking the head (chin to chest). This boy and girl begin a forward roll down an incline mat, an inviting piece of gymnastics equipment.

Backward Roll

- **Preparation phase.** The body is round, with knees tucked into chest (like a ball); the head is down, with chin tucked into chest; hands are positioned by ears with fingers spread out (thumbs in).

- **Force phase.** The performer pushes evenly with the feet to generate momentum, rocks backward onto the lower back, keeps chin tucked into chest; knees stay tucked into chest; the hands, placed flat on the mats (like pizza!), push forcefully to generate momentum.

- **Recovery phase.** The landing is on both feet simultaneously; hands and arms recover and are positioned by the ears, and knees remained tucked into chest.

This student at Mary C. Howse Elementary School is practicing her backward roll. An incline mat assists students in performing a backward roll by increasing the momentum, thus taking the weight off of their neck and shoulders.

CONCEPT 23.6

Level III developmental gymnastics activities involve transfer of weight and are appropriate for those at the intermediate/practice level of movement skill learning.

Level III Skills: Transfer of Weight

Children at Level III are progressing into the intermediate/practice level of movement skill learning. Motor skill performance is now more rhythmically coordinated and controlled, and children generally have more muscular strength and endurance than previously. Discussing **weight transfer,** Mauldon and Layson (1979) state, "In transference of weight the stress is on what happens between weight being removed from one part and arriving on another; in other words, how the body moves between two points of support. Whereas weight bearing is concerned with relative stillness, transference of weight involves locomotion" (pp. 76-77). There are many possible ways of transferring weight from the hands to the feet, including the following:

- Varying space:
  - With different body shapes—straight, bent, curled, wide, narrow
  - At different levels
  - Covering general space (cartwheel)
  - Staying in personal space (handstand)
- Varying effort:
  - Slow or fast
  - Landing as lightly as possible
- Varying relationships:
  - Individually
  - With a partner—in unison, mirroring, matching, following/leading
  - On/off equipment; in/out of equipment; alongside equipment

When we ask children to transfer weight from their hands to their feet, it is important to delimit their movement responses so that they do not use the middle part of their body (i.e., the stomach or back) on the floor or on equipment to bear weight. Most movement responses position the body in an inverted or "upside-down" position. It is important, therefore, that we teach children how to bear weight on their hands, while inverted, so that the elbows are locked, fingers are spread, and their weight is evenly distributed. Teaching children how to do a "mountain" can help with this. In a mountain, the majority of the body's weight is on the hands. The stomach faces the floor, the buttocks are high, and the body is bent at the waist with the head low.

When the learning environment includes a gymnastics mat or floor exercise mat, possible ways of transferring weight from hands to feet include the following:

- **Crab walk.** The performer walks on the hands and feet with the stomach facing up.
- **Bear walk.** The performer walks on the hands and feet with the stomach facing down.
- **Corkscrew.** Starting with a crab walk (stomach facing up), the performer rotates the body while in the horizontal plane to assume the bear walk (stomach facing down).
- **Wheel.** The performer transfers weight from two hands to two feet with the legs below the hips.
- **Cartwheel.** The performer transfers weight from hand to hand and foot to foot with the legs above the hips. A cartwheel leading with the right hand follows the pattern of right hand, left hand, left foot, right foot with the legs elevated over the head. A cartwheel leading with the left hand follows the pattern of left hand, right hand, right foot, left foot with the legs elevated over the head.
- **Dive cartwheel.** While doing a cartwheel, usually following a forceful gallop, slide, or run, the performer momentarily loses contact with the supporting surface.
- **Round-off.** The performer transfers weight from two hands to two feet with a half turn while inverted. A round-off also includes a momentary flight phase with the push-off coming from the hands, which creates force. The snap-down executed also generates force in the flight phase by bending at the waist with both legs squeezed and snapping them down toward the floor.
- **Handstand.** The performer transfers weight from two feet to two hands.
- **Front walkover.** The performer transfers weight from both hands to one foot and then the other foot while curving and bending over in a forward direction.
- **Back walkover.** The performer transfers weight from both hands to one foot and then the other foot while curving and bending the body over in a backward direction.
- **Handspring.** The performer springs from hands to feet in a forward and backward direction.
- **Valdez.** Beginning from a seated position on the floor with one leg straight and the other leg bent, the body is thrust up and backward with force generated as the performer lifts and swings the legs, lifts up with the hips, and reaches with the arms. Legs are thrust backward, one at a time, and landing is on one foot at a time.

Many of these ways of transferring weight on the floor are also possible on or over equipment. For example, a cartwheel can be done on a bench or a low beam. The performer can use a round-off when dismounting or coming off a bench or low beam. Performers can transfer weight by walking on hands and feet on tires, benches, or a beam. Experienced competitive gymnasts can execute a handspring and Valdez on a balance beam.

A learning environment that includes obstacles can elicit additional movement. Obstacles may include ropes placed on the floor, a hula hoop placed on the floor (hands go into hoop, landing is outside of hoop), a rope horizontally suspended between two cones, long foam shapes, or foam vaulting boxes (trapezoid shapes). Obstacles can be different sizes, widths, and heights.

Belka (2000, p.17) provides a helpful teaching progression for transferring weight using wheeling actions.

1. The learner performs a squat, places hands to the sides, and shifts weight and hips over the hands.

2. Step 1 is repeated, but the landing is as controlled and quiet as possible.

3. Step 1 is repeated, but the learner moves the hips as directly over the base of support as possible.

4. Step 3 is repeated, but the learner maintains as straight a pathway of the hips over the head as possible during the entire weight transfer.

5. Step 4 is repeated, but the learner moves the knees away from the chest and as directly over the base of support as possible.

6. Step 5 is repeated but from a semi-stand position instead of a crouch:

   a. The learner tries to keep legs as straight as possible.

   b. The learner permits the legs to separate and move as freely and naturally as possible.

7. The learner gradually moves toward taking several steps into the wheeling action while focusing on turning to maintain the side position.

8. Step 7 is repeated, but the learner moves toward straight legs and as close to a hand-hand-foot-foot weight transfer as possible.

9. Step 8 is repeated, but the learner tries to keep the action in as straight a line as possible.

Transfer of weight from hands to feet is tricky when you travel over a low jump rope. This student is in the recovery phase or ending part of a cartwheel.

10. Step 9 is repeated, but the learner quickly brings the legs together at the inverted point, turns hips, and lands facing the direction of the takeoff (round-off).

There are preliminary skills that children should be able to perform when developing the ability to do a handstand:

- **Hands-on-floor handstand.** The performer begins with hands placed on the mat and proceeds to kick or swing only one leg into the air. This type of handstand involves a "rock-up" with one leg straight and one leg maintaining contact with the floor.

- **Switch-a-roo handstand.** In this version of the handstand, the hands again begin on the floor; but both legs, one at a time, are lifted or kicked into the air. Some refer to this as a "scissor kick handstand." The rhythm is up-up-down-down. The legs *do not* stay up in the air.

These are the critical performance-related cues for a handstand:

- **Preparation phase.** The performer begins from a standing position.
- **Force phase.** Motion is initiated as the performer rocks weight forward and downward toward the mat and onto the hands (this can be practiced as a separate part); arms swing up and reach out and then down toward the supporting surface. At the same time, one leg swings up or kicks into the air as the body is being inverted and weight is placed on the hands. The other leg quickly follows. The head should be positioned straight down and between elbows. The legs and buttocks should be squeezed together to maintain balance.
- **Recovery phase.** The performer brings one leg down at a time; arms push off or "block" off the mat and reach out and upward to lift the body back into a standing position.

Level IV Skills: The Body in Flight

Children in Level IV, the advanced/fine-tuning level of movement skill learning, are capable of performing gymnastics skills that involve the **body in flight.** Flight entails momentary or suspended loss of contact with the supporting surface, such as the floor or apparatus. Several of the skills of the previous levels can be performed in such a way that there is a suspended or momentary loss of contact with the supporting surface. Level IV skills can be further categorized as Stage B flight skills and Stage A flight skills. **Stage B flight skills,** which are less demanding, do not require much force upon takeoff, muscular strength, or overall coordination of body parts (jumping off of a bench is an example). **Stage A flight skills** are more demanding. They require children to be experienced and kinesthetically able to invert their bodies as well as to know where their body is in space. Stage A skills also require the mover to generate more force upon contact as well as a higher degree of body coordination and timing of movement. For example, a roll can be performed so that there is a momentary loss of contact with the floor or other supporting surface. Using a preparatory run and two-foot takeoff, the mover can project the body into the air in a stretched-out (layout) position before landing on the hands and absorbing force through the arms and the body as it rolls forward.

The critical cues for performing a roll in flight are the following:

CONCEPT 23.7

Because Level IV developmental gymnastics activities involve the body in flight, they are most appropriate for those at the advanced/fine-tuning level of movement skill learning.

- **Preparation phase.** The performer runs into a two-foot takeoff; the arms swing forcefully from low to high and are lifted up and stretched forward simultaneously with takeoff.
- **Force phase.** In flight the body is stretched out into a layout position: the entire body is straight and narrow, and the head is level with and positioned between the arms.
- **Recovery phase.** On impact, weight is absorbed by the arms (which gradually bend at the elbow). The performer controls the roll onto the upper and lower back while bending the body in half or piking at the waist, then tucking knees into chest and recovering onto both feet.
- **Safety tips and spotting.** Lead-up tasks should precede a roll with flight. First, the running takeoff should be omitted and the child should practice a two-foot takeoff from a standing position into a forward roll, learning to absorb force with the arms. Obstacles can then be used for the child to roll over, creating greater periods of flight.

Movers should be spotted while in flight—just as they are beginning to contact the floor—so that their impact with the floor is controlled. Spotting is on the back of the neck and lower back area so that the spotter controls the child's weight.

- Stage B skills:
  - Jumping
  - Leaping
  - Galloping
  - Sliding sideways
  - Scissor kick
  - Skipping
- Stage A skills:
  - Cartwheels
  - Walkovers
  - Handsprings
  - Round-off
  - In-flight rolls

TEXT BOX 23.3

"I used to go to the park near my house and try to fly by jumping off the 'bandstand' while holding my umbrella. Northern Indiana was very flat and I had visions of staying in the air forever." (Fran Cleland Donnelly, 2003)

Vaulting

In vaulting, the mover transfers weight from feet to hands to feet. During the vault, the body assumes different positions while in flight over an obstacle. Vaulters go through three movement phases when transferring weight over an obstacle and supporting their body weight on the hands and arms: the approach phase, the flight phase, and the after-flight phase. For example, as the performer transfers weight to his hands and contacts the obstacle or supporting surface (18-inch foam shape), he can swing the legs parallel and straight out to the sides of the obstacle (flank vault), lift them straight up into the vertical plane (the head is low) (handspring vault), or swing them wide or far apart while vaulting forward (straddle vault). In other words, the legs can make different shapes in the air. A springboard assists the mover in generating momentum for transferring weight from the hands to the feet. Many of these skills can also include turns in the air after takeoff, prior to contact with the surface for support, and during the after-flight. This type of weight transfer is difficult, requiring the mover to gain a great deal of height over the obstacle and to generate enough momentum at the moment of takeoff to sustain flight. The takeoff from one to two feet off of a gymnastics springboard is a difficult task for many movers at Level I or II.

A sideward vault is demonstrated by this student as she transfers weight from feet to hands to feet over a foam trapezoid vault.

Movement Combinations

Children can be prompted to combine movements from one category (e.g., balancing) or from a variety of categories (e.g., rolling, balancing, transferring weight), with and without equipment, individually, with a partner, or in a small group. It is important to design movement tasks appropriate for the developmental level of the children you teach. You may need to make modifications for children with physically limiting conditions such as spina bifida or cerebral palsy (see chapter 7, "Children With Disabilities"). The following are examples of instructions for open-ended movement tasks that combine skills:

• "Combine a step-like action in a sideward direction with a step-like action that uses hands and feet only. Repeat combination using a piece of equipment" (Belka, 2000, p. 18).

• "Combine a rolling action with a wide shape with a wheeling step-like action" (Belka, 2000, p. 18).

- Combine a series of rolls with different body shapes, using acceleration and deceleration.
- Combine a balance on a piece of equipment and transfer of weight off of the equipment.
- Combine a transfer of weight over three different pieces of equipment, a balance, and a roll.

Hanging, Swinging, and Climbing Skills

Hanging, swinging, and climbing skills are also important skills for children to develop that can be safely included in developmental gymnastics instruction. These skills can be effectively integrated into the educational gymnastics lesson for children at all four developmental levels. The problem for most physical educators is having a budget that allows the types of equipment needed to facilitate these skills.

This student demonstrates an inverted position as she hangs between two ropes.

Gerstung Manufacturers makes a product line, Developmental Equipment, that is designed to enhance children's climbing, balance, hanging, and swinging skills. This equipment includes "trestles" or A-frame metal structures that connect to other pieces of gymnastics equipment, including cargo nets, ropes, a curved bridge, a triangular climbing frame, wooden planks, metal poles, and benches. Excellent instructional materials are available, and the equipment folds up so that it can be stored in most equipment room facilities. Another company, Laurentian Gymnastics Industries Ltd., manufactures a climbing frame that mounts on the gymnasium wall. The climbing frame opens out from the wall and is excellent for climbing, hanging, and swinging skill development.

ASSESSING PROGRESS

As in developmental games and dance, children's psychomotor, cognitive, and affective learning can be assessed in developmental gymnastics. Alternative forms of assessment in gymnastics include peer observations (e.g., reciprocal task card—please refer to pp. 234-237 for a discussion on the reciprocal teaching style), videotape analysis, student journals, and checklists. All three domains of learning should be assessed. Tools designed to assess *motor competencies* should target individual skills, combinations of skills, and use of the skills in relationship to equipment. Assessment strategies aimed at evaluating children's *cognitive understanding* of gymnastics content should pinpoint their general understanding of movement concepts and skill themes; knowledge about factors that influence the appropriate execution and refinement of individual skills; and knowledge of safe setup, use, and design of learning environments and equipment. The affective domain should also be evaluated. Assessment of this domain should include strategies to assess children's feelings about themselves regarding gymnastics competency (self-concept), ability to work cooperatively with others, and appreciation of gymnastics content. Examples of psychomotor, cognitive, and affective assessment tools for developmental gymnastics are provided in text boxes 23.4, 23.5, and 23.6, respectively. The psychomotor assessment tool is a generic rubric that teachers can use to assess any gymnastics skill. Additionally, Lathrop and Murray (2000) contribute several ideas for designing developmental gymnastics assessment tools and provide specific examples.

CONCEPT 23.8

A variety of means are available for assessing children's progress in developmental gymnastics.

TEXT BOX 23.4

Psychomotor Assessment of Gymnastics Skills

Excellent:

- Coordination of body parts is excellent.
- Timing is smooth, and skill is rhythmically controlled.
- Range (amplitude) of skill is appropriate (covers space if applicable or stays in place if applicable).
- Skill is muscularly controlled.
- Form and body mechanics are correct.
- Speed of skill can be controlled.

Good:

- Form is good, but skill amplitude is not as developed.
- Skill can be performed in appropriate but not varied speeds.
- Coordination of body parts good and sequenced correctly.

Needs improvement:

- Parts of skill may still be missing.
- Coordination and sequencing of body parts needs work.
- Muscular control is weak.
- No amplitude.

TEXT BOX 23.5

Cognitive Assessment Sample for Gymnastics

1. When rolling backwards, you should:
   a. keep feet, knees, legs straight
   b. round your back, tuck chin to chest
   c. swing arms upward for good height

2. When performing a cartwheel, both hands contact the floor at the same time.
   True _____   False _____

3. Video clip: The teacher shows a short video clip of a gymnastics sequence and then asks children to fill out the following checklist:
   a. The balances in the sequence were:
      Counterbalances _____   Counter-tension _____
   b. Did the mover use:
      _____ a lot of amplitude in performing skills
      _____ a medium amount of amplitude
      _____ no amplitude in performing skills

Based on example by Lathrop & Murray, 2000, p. 31.

TEXT BOX 23.6

**Affective Assessment Sample for Gymnastics:
Personal Feelings Checklist**

Circle the word or words that describe how you feel about your rolling ability:

Great	Excited	OK
In control	Unsure	Confident
Strong	Tired	Confused

SAFETY TIPS

To ensure a successful and enjoyable gymnastics experience, the learning environment must first be safe. The teacher must have a strong knowledge base and be able to design movement tasks that are appropriate for the children being taught. Teachers should adhere to the following safety measures when teaching developmental gymnastics.

All teachers have established teaching protocols. Stopping and starting cues are important for children. In gymnastics instruction, stopping cues should not demand immediate cessation of all activity as in other areas of the curriculum. Rather, since many movements cannot be suddenly curtailed, "Rest" may be a better command to use in this situation.

You should expect an appropriate low level of noise when children are working at different stations or learning environments. Too much noise can lead children to lose concentration and can jeopardize their body control. Some teachers use the "three-cone" strategy. As class begins, three cones are standing in a place on the floor where the children can see them. If the students become too loud, one cone is laid down on the floor. The second and third cones are laid down if students persist in being too loud. When all three cones are laid down on the floor, all class activity is stopped. Whatever your protocol, you need to expect a reasonable level of noise but should also monitor the noise level carefully.

As in other content areas, students should receive guidance on how many of them can safely use one piece of equipment in a single learning environment. Distances among children as they move about are also important.

Another safety priority is to prepare children physically and emotionally to engage in gymnastics. Children often need help in focusing on the day's lesson. Designing interesting and invigorating warm-up activities can get them focused. Because many gymnastics lessons include ballistic movements, children should be involved in moderate to vigorous warm-up activities that elevate their heart rate and include flexibility activities. Emphasis on the lower body through a game of Secret Exercises (p. 646) can also be the focal point of a warm-up. Twisting, stretching, and curling exercises can be used to prepare the upper body.

How the physical learning environment is structured is also very important. Equipment must be properly positioned. Additionally, since children sometimes misinterpret how to use a piece of equipment, you should teach and stress the proper use of all equipment. The height and width of equipment are also important and should be modified to ensure that all children can maneuver their bodies safely on, off, or over equipment.

Landing mats, 12 inches thick, should be used under equipment at heights of 5 feet or greater (e.g., trestles, cargo nets). All mats should be cleaned regularly with a mild disinfectant, should not have tears in them, and should not overlap when placed on the floor.

It is important to observe children carefully, not only for proper space and equipment usage but also for their energy levels. When the lesson emphasizes weight bearing, transferring weight, or flight (e.g., jumping and landing), children may tire more rapidly. Muscular endurance and cardiovascular endurance are factors in children's ability to effectively manage their body weight.

EQUIPMENT IDEAS

CONCEPT 23.9

In order to maximize safety, teachers should instruct children in proper use of equipment and learning environments and should expect children to adhere to the instructions.

An ideal inventory for a complete developmental gymnastics program is listed in table 23.1. However, small manipulative equipment (hoops, wands, ribbons, balls, jump ropes, cones), mats (flat and incline), and foam shapes (for balancing and jumping) are sufficient for developmental gymnastics within the elementary physical education program. With this equipment you can design several learning environments. Of course, additional pieces will offer students a richer and broader array of movement experiences.

TABLE 23.1 – REQUIRED EQUIPMENT FOR DEVELOPMENTAL GYMNASTICS SKILL THEMES FOCUSING ON ROLLING, JUMPING/LANDING, BALANCE, TRANSFER OF WEIGHT, AND HANGING/SWINGING

Equipment items	Equipment size	Quantity for class size of 20-25
Foam vaulting trapezoid	3-4 sections	1
Styrofoam shapes (circles, triangles, ovals, wedge, etc.)		8
Mats	4' × 6' or 5' × 10', 2" thick, 100ILD foam	3-4 students per mat; 7-8 mats
Balance beams/benches	12'L, 12"W	1 or more
Balance boards	9"W × 29 1/2"L	12-13
Jumping boxes (foam shapes of varying heights)	12"-24"	4-6
Trestles	5"6' × 7"	2 or each
Sliding boards to connect to trestles	12"L, 10-12"W	2
Connecting ladder		1
Hanging ropes		1-2
Landing mats	4" thick	Minimum of 1
Incline mats	36"W × 72"L	1
Jump ropes	7', 8', 9', and 16' length (plastic segments for beginners; speed rope for experienced jumpers)	13
Stretch jump ropes ("magic ropes")		8-12
Wands		12-13

Summary

Teaching children developmental gymnastics is a rewarding experience. Children are stimulated by the exciting learning opportunities created through well-designed lessons and varied learning environments, and by the chance to solve movement problems in their own unique way. Through gymnastics, children increase movement efficiency and body control. Health-related fitness components of cardio-vascular endurance, muscular strength, endurance, and flexibility are also enhanced.

In the developmental approach to teaching gymnastics, movement skills are organized into four content levels. *Level I*, emphasizing body control, is best suited for those at the beginning/novice level of movement skill learning; *Level II*, focusing on balancing and rolling skills, is suited for children at a slightly higher point in the beginning/novice level of movement skill learning. *Level III*, in which weight-bearing skills are emphasized, is best suited for children at the intermediate/practice level of movement skill learning; and *Level IV,* focusing on weight transference, is most appropriate for those at the advanced/fine-tuning level of movement skill learning. Performance-related cues for movement skills in each developmental area are highlighted.

The content within this developmental progression is based on the skill themes of (1) jumping and landing; (2) balance; (3) rolling; (4) transfer of weight;

and (5) hanging, swinging, and climbing. Teachers need to sequence gymnastics content carefully and assess children's learning just as in other areas of instruction. Safety issues, which are an important part of gymnastics instruction, include such aspects of the learning environment as noise level, proper use of equipment, and appropriate warm-up activities.

Terms to Remember

Excellent Readings

Allison, P.C., & Barrett, K.R. (2000). *Constructing children's physical education experiences: Understanding the content for teaching.* Boston: Allyn and Bacon.

Hardin, B. (2000). Facilitating inclusion in educational gymnastics. *TEPE, 11* (4), 33–35.

Nilges, L.M. (2000). Teaching educational gymnastics. *TEPE, 11* (4), 6–9.

Nilges, L.M., & Lathrop, A.H. (2000). Eleven safety tips for educational gymnastics. *TEPE, 11* (4), 10.

TEPE Feature Edition on Gymnastics. (July, 2000). *11* (4).

The Program Strands

The aim of part VI, "The Program Strands," is to provide you with a wealth of information and sample activities for developing the active child, the thinking child, and the feeling child. The activities presented are a mere sampling of the many that are available from a variety of excellent written and Web resources. Take time to learn more about what we present here and what is available elsewhere on your journey to becoming an effective teacher.

Chapter 24, "Developing the Active Child," provides developmentally appropriate and fun activities for enhancing children's aerobic endurance, muscular strength and endurance, and joint flexibility. Important tips for motivating children to participate in fitness activities conclude this chapter. **Chapter 25,** "Developing the Thinking Child," deals with the cognitive domain and with structuring the learning environment to promote critical thinking skills in the gymnasium. **Chapter 26,** "Developing the Feeling Child," addresses the role of physical education teachers in the affective domain in helping children take personal and social responsibility for their actions.

24

Developing the Active Child

Key Concept

▶ The notion of enhancing children's physical activity and fitness is a primary strand woven throughout the developmental physical education program.

Chapter Objectives

This chapter will provide you with the tools to do the following:

▶ List and discuss techniques for motivating children to engage in positive fitness behaviors.

▶ List and describe essential fitness principles of frequency, intensity, and time that children should know, and provide examples of how each may be taught.

▶ Provide examples of developmentally appropriate aerobic endurance activities for children.

▶ Provide examples of developmentally appropriate muscular strength and endurance activities for children.

▶ Provide examples of developmentally appropriate joint flexibility activities for children.

▶ Discuss what is meant by "weaving" fitness throughout the developmental physical education program.

▶ Examine strategies for teaching fitness to children.

▶ List and discuss the 4 C's for motivating children for fitness.

Fitness activities are included in the physical education program for the specific purpose of contributing to the health-related aspects of physical development. Cardiovascular respiratory endurance (i.e., aerobic endurance), muscular endurance, muscular strength, and joint flexibility are the primary components of health-related physical fitness. Virtually all of the activities presented in part IV, "The Skill Themes," and part V, "The Content Areas," contribute in some measure to the development or maintenance of one or more aspects of physical fitness. The majority of these activities, however, focus on movement skill acquisition as their primary objective, with fitness benefits as a worthy but unspecified by-product.

As discussed in chapter 4, "Physical Activity and Fitness Enhancement," low levels of physical fitness have been repeatedly demonstrated among many children across North America. Therefore, it is vitally important that the instructional program intentionally include movement activities designed to promote physical fitness and increased physical activity for their own sake.

A portion of the physical education lesson should be devoted to instruction in fitness as well as skill development. Ideally, an in-school, home, or community-based daily fitness program should be available to every child. Unfortunately, this is not always the reality. Therefore, the physical education program has the following responsibilities:

CONCEPT 24.1

Because of its transient nature, health-related fitness needs to be woven throughout the developmental physical education program.

- To increase children's knowledge base about fitness and develop positive attitudes toward its importance
- To motivate children to take part in regular moderate to vigorous physical activity
- To teach children how to exercise and what to do to improve their personal levels of fitness
- To provide opportunities for children to enhance their physical fitness

Physical education is *not* physical fitness or physical activity but involves elements of both. Fitness activities should be integrated throughout the entire physical education curriculum. We recommend that rather than focusing on fitness as a theme for a single unit of instruction, teachers include some form of fitness instruction as a part of each lesson throughout the school year. Fitness is not an isolated part of the physical education program; it should be fostered continually through an active program of movement skill acquisition and fitness enhancement for its own sake.

In this chapter we examine the health-related components of fitness development and provide a sampling of developmentally appropriate activities for promoting increased levels of physical activity and fitness development. We conclude with teaching strategies for motivating children to engage in a more active way of life. A personal fitness profile suitable for use with children is presented in figure 24.1. Also, you may find it helpful to refer back to chapter 4, "Physical Activity and Fitness Enhancement," for additional information about children's fitness.

CONCEPT 24.2

Children frequently need to be motivated to engage in positive fitness behaviors. Giving an activity a name and making it a game helps ensure that they will be eager to take part in vigorous fitness activities.

AEROBIC ENDURANCE

Aerobic endurance is the ability of the heart, lungs, and vascular system to supply oxygen to the working muscles during exercise. Most experts consider aerobic endurance the most important component of total fitness. Any activity resulting in a sustained elevated heart rate is considered aerobic. The keys to developing increased aerobic capacity are frequency, intensity, duration, and variety.

For children to receive the most benefit from physical activity, it must be of sufficient **activity intensity** to elevate the heart to about 150 beats per minute or more. The average daily routine of most North American children provides few occasions for the heart rate to reach such levels.

Activity duration is important. The length of time the heart rate is elevated is the second key to aerobic endurance in children. Experts agree that it is not enough to

Name: _____ Grade: _____

Body Build Profile

	Trial 1	Trial 2	Trial 3	Trial 4
Date				
Age				
Height				
Weight				
Frame size				

Aerobic Fitness Profile

	Trial 1	Trial 2	Trial 3	Trial 4
Distance run				
Resting heart rate				
Exercise heart rate				
1-minute recovery rate				
5-minute recovery rate				

General Fitness Profile

	Trial 1	Trial 2	Trial 3	Trial 4
Arm endurance: push-ups				
Abdominal endurance: sit-ups				
Leg power: standing long jump				
Arm power: softball throw				
Flexibility: sit and reach				
Speed: 50-yard dash				
Agility: shuttle run				
Coordination: cable jump				
Balance: one-foot stand				

Summary

I am: _____ overweight _____ about right _____ underweight

I have: _____ too much fat _____ about right _____ too little fat

My aerobic condition is: _____ excellent _____ good _____ fair _____ poor

My general fitness is: _____ excellent _____ good _____ fair _____ poor

My goals are

1. _____

2. _____

3. _____

FIGURE 24.1 Personalized fitness profile.

From *Developmental Physical Activity for All Children* (4 ed.) by David L. Gallahue and Frances Cleland Donnelly, 2003, Champaign, IL: Human Kinetics.

simply achieve an elevated heart rate—the higher heart rate must be sustained for 10 minutes or longer to produce a positive training effect. Again, the normal daily routine of many children does not provide for situations in which high heart rates are sustained for a long enough duration to produce an aerobic benefit.

Activity frequency is the third key to increased aerobic capacity. In addition to elevating one's heart rate for a sustained period of time, aerobic exercise must occur no less than three times per week for a positive training effect. In fact, most experts recommend five times per week as the ideal. A daily physical activity program in the schools is the only place where we can guarantee that every child will have the frequency of exercise needed.

The fourth, and probably most important, key to increasing aerobic endurance is **activity variety**. Children respond favorably if there is variety in the aerobic activities program. For children, the activity must be fun. If it isn't, most will soon tire of the activity and quit.

The following are the primary objectives of the aerobic endurance activities to be discussed next:

- To improve children's aerobic endurance
- To help children internalize the four keys to improved aerobic endurance (intensity, duration, frequency, and variety)
- To help children identify vigorous physical activities that contribute to increased aerobic endurance
- To encourage children to select one or more aerobic endurance activities to take part in on a regular basis

The following is a sampling of aerobic activities designed to enhance children's aerobic endurance.

Toss and Tag

Pairs of students are spread throughout general space. Within pairs, children roll or toss a yarn ball back and forth to each other (pairs choose the distance between partners). When the music stops, whoever has the yarn ball in his possession chases his partner (players may also use a fast walk). Once he tags his partner, the "tagger" gives the yarn ball to the other player and "takes off" as the roles reverse. The teacher stops play randomly.

Shadow

One player attempts to get away from another player by running, dodging, and feinting. The partner attempts to be a "shadow" by staying directly behind. This activity can be played by an entire class (i.e., 25 or fewer students) if space allows.

Shipwreck

The play area is marked off as the bow, stern, port, and starboard of a ship. The leader calls out a part of the ship, and the children (six to eight) run to that area.

Rabbit and Turtle

The leader tells a story about the rabbit and the turtle. Every time the word "rabbit" is mentioned, children run in place as fast as they can. Every time "turtle" is mentioned, they run slowly in place. This activity can be played by an entire class.

Toss and Tag! In this activity, students toss a yarn ball back and forth with a partner. Music can be played. When the music stops, the student with the yarn ball chases the student without the yarn ball through general space. If they tag their partner, the roles reverse. The chaser becomes the chased and the chased becomes the chaser. This is an aerobic activity that motivates students to move!

Freeze and Melt

Players run around the perimeter of the gymnasium or the play area. Each time the leader says "Freeze!" they stop in their tracks and hold a motionless position until they hear the leader say "Melt." Cones can be used to mark the perimeter of the gymnasium, and music can be used to guide the speed of the children's run. This activity can be played by an entire class or a smaller group of students.

Four Corners

A cone is placed in each of the four corners of the gymnasium. Four posters, each listing three or four locomotor skills, are placed on the cones (one on each cone). Children (25) are divided into four groups, and each group begins at a specified cone. Groups travel to the next cone using the first locomotor skill listed on their poster. When they reach the second cone, they change to the first locomotor skill listed on that poster. Once members of a group reach their "home" cone they continue traveling, but now they perform the second locomotor skill listed on the poster, then the third and fourth. Music accompanies this activity.

Sunny Side Up

Children jog around an oval (created by cones or polyspots) in one direction. Every 15 to 30 seconds when a signal is given, the children all drop, touch their stomach to the ground, flip over (like an egg), touch their back to the ground, then get up and begin jogging in the opposite direction. Different locomotor skills can be used. To facilitate muscular strength and endurance, children can do an exercise (e.g., push-up, sit-up) each time they drop to the floor (Hinson, 1995). This activity can be played by an entire class.

Picture Fun Run (Outdoor Activity)

Children choose a laminated photograph of a piece of equipment (swings, slide) or a place (drinking fountain) that is located in the playground area. They walk briskly or jog to the object or location shown on the chosen picture. After returning, they choose another photograph. In a variation, the pictures are inside a paper bag and the children play "grab bag" to get their photograph. If they do not want to go to the location chosen, they can "grab" another photo. The places and equipment pictured must be in the teacher's range of vision at all times (Hinson, 1995). This activity can be played by an entire class.

Hoop-a-Long

Hula hoops are placed throughout the movement area. Music is played. The teacher calls out different movements to perform inside of the hula hoop as children jog, walk, or skip to get to the hoops. The movements may include putting one foot or one hand inside the hoop and quickly taking it back out, putting two feet inside, two hands inside, whole body inside, and so on. Children attempt to move to as many hula hoops as possible. This activity can be played by an entire class.

Slice the Pizza

Each child "takes a pizza" (cut-out clip art of a pizza) out of the pizza box. This "pizza" has a number written on the back. The children put their pizza back into the box and remember their number. They then form a circle designated by polyspots (big circle). To begin the activity, children walk clockwise around the circle to the music. The teacher calls out two to three "pizza numbers," and the children with those numbers slide sideways across the circle. Then they find a new place in the circular formation. Play continues and new numbers are called. The circle of students can perform a designated locomotor skill while the "pizza people" slide sideways across the circle, or they can remain stationary. This activity can be played by an entire class.

In variations, children go counterclockwise or do a new locomotor skill, or several "pizza people" slide across the circle at the same time.

Secret Exercises

Children move to music. When the music stops, a child is asked to go to the center of the circle and pick up a "secret exercise card" (placed facedown on the floor in the middle of the circle). Stationary aerobic dance steps are written on the exercise cards. A picture can accompany the written description. All children then perform the exercise with the teacher's guidance. Play continues. Muscular endurance and strength are incorporated into the exercise if the secret exercise cards specify this health-related component (Hinson, 1995). This activity can be played by an entire class.

Shapes

Students are asked to make a big shape using any combination of body parts as they balance and make these shapes on the gymnasium floor. If students are "color coded" or given stickers, specific colors or stickers can then be designated by the teacher to move over, under, or through the obstacles or shapes made by a specified group of students (e.g., all students with a red sticker). Music can be played. This activity can be played by an entire class.

Variations include having two students hold hands or a ring-toss and move through obstacles together cooperatively, and having two students make a shape/obstacle together.

Surprise! Disks of cardboard with exercises written on them as well as math problems are randomly placed in the gymnasium. Students perform locomotor patterns to music as they travel from one disk to the next. When the music stops, students turn over the disk closest to them and perform that exercise. Repetitions are determined by the answer to the mathematics problem.

MUSCULAR STRENGTH AND ENDURANCE

Muscular strength is the maximum force that a muscle can exert in one effort. The benefits of increased muscular strength include reduced risk of injury and improved posture. Resistance training can be beneficial for young children and can improve their muscular strength. Teachers should emphasize dynamic concentric contractions as opposed to eccentric overload exercises using full range of motion (Cahill, 1988).

This intermediate grade student demonstrates muscular strength as she supports her entire body weight while pushing up into a straddle position on the balance board. Awesome!

These students demonstrate muscular endurance and flexibility as they sustain balances while their partners move through their shapes!

Muscular endurance is the ability of a muscle to sustain a contraction or perform numerous contractions over an extended period against a submaximal load. Calisthenics and locomotor skills help to develop muscular endurance. "Being able to participate in activity for longer periods without muscle fatigue is the primary objective of developing muscular endurance in children" (Hinson, 1995, p. 7).

For children, the use of a circuit or station approach to muscular strength and endurance exercises is recommended. Movement from station to station and achievement of specific individual goals for each exercise frequently heighten interest in conditioning activities.

The primary objectives of the conditioning exercises discussed next are the following:

- To enhance children's muscular endurance and muscular strength
- To help children become knowledgeable about the differences between strength and endurance and the ways in which each is developed
- To teach children about the major muscle groups of the body and how to exercise each
- To enable children to determine their own level of strength and endurance and to make individual improvement
- To help children develop an appreciation for and desire to be involved in vigorous physical activity

Arm and Shoulder Activities

Arm and shoulder activities are too frequently absent from the lives of children. As a result many North American children are weak in these areas, and teachers need to give arm and shoulder activities special attention. The activities that follow should be presented in a manner that is developmentally appropriate and that emphasizes the fun in doing the activity. These activities are most successful when conducted with a class size of 25 or fewer students.

Seal Crawl

From a push-up position with the arms extended and toes pointed, children drag their body forward, using only their arms.

Coffee Grinder

From a side-support lying position with the body's weight supported on one arm (hand flat on floor), children walk around their support arm several times. Have them repeat with the opposite arm.

Spread-Eagle Walk

From a push-up position with the arms extended and wide apart and the legs wide apart, children walk forward, then back.

Modified Pull-Ups

From a back-leaning position with their feet on the floor and their hands gripping a low horizontal bar, children perform pull-ups bringing the nose to the bar.

Bent-Knee Push-Ups

From a push-up position with the knees bent and the arms extended, the children do push-ups, bringing their nose to the floor in front of their hands.

Push-Ups

From a push-up position, children do repeated push-ups, keeping the back flat and touching the chest to the floor.

Abdominal Activities

The abdominal muscles form the strength core of the body. Strong abdominal muscles are critically important for proper posture as well as maximizing children's potential in games, sports, and other vigorous activities. Don't be fooled by all of the gadgets and gizmos on the market today that promise to be just the device you need for stronger abs and a flatter stomach with little or no effort. The activities that follow work just as well as, or better, than these unproven shortcuts to greater abdominal strength and endurance.

Shoulder Curl

From a bent-knee sit-up position with the arms folded across the chest, children raise their head and shoulders off the surface and hold for three counts. They return and repeat several times.

Half Curl

This is the same as the shoulder curl except that the upper back is raised entirely off the surface. Be certain that the lower back remains in solid contact with the surface. Have children repeat several times.

Half-V-Sits

From a sitting position on the floor with the legs straight and together and the hands supporting the hips, children raise one leg, hold for three counts, and return. Have them repeat with the opposite leg. They should repeat the activity several times.

Hillsdale Elementary School fifth graders participate in an instant activity designed to enhance a variety of fitness components.

Bent-Knee Sit-Ups

From a bent-knee back-lying position with the feet flat on the surface and the arms crossed in front of the chest or behind the head (more difficult), the students perform repeated sit-ups.

Alternate-Knee-Touch Sit-Ups

From a back-lying, bent-knee sit-up position with the hands behind the head, children sit up and twist to one side, touching the elbow to the opposite knee.

V-Sits

This is the same as the half-V except that both legs are raised at the same time. Have the students repeat.

Lower Back Activities

Low back pain is a frequent complaint of children and adults alike. Involving children in activities that make unusual demands on the muscles of the lower back can result in severe and lasting injuries. Too often, people give little attention to the muscles of the lower back, and as a result these muscles are not strong enough to withstand the demands of daily living activities, let alone game and sport activities. As a teacher you should take special care to have your program include activities like the following that progressively improve lower back strength and endurance.

Alternate Leg Lifts

From a back-lying position with their legs straight and their hands at their side, have the children raise one leg at a time to a vertical position and return. Students repeat several times.

Back Arch

From a front-lying position with their arms extended overhead, students raise their head and legs off the ground, hold, and return. They then repeat.

Rocking Horse

This exercise is the same as the back arch, except that the body is rocked back and forth from the arched position.

Leg Activities

Leg strength and endurance are fundamental to all that we do as we move through our world. The too-often sedentary lifestyles of children place few demands on leg strength. Sitting in front of the television for hour upon hour or playing an endless variety of computer games does little for the muscles of the legs. The activities that follow, applied in a manner that is both fun and developmentally appropriate, will do much to improve leg strength and endurance. These activities are most successful when conducted with a class size of 25 or fewer students.

Rabbit Hop

Have students assume a squat position and then reach forward with their hands. Students then kick the heels up and forward to reach their hands. Have them repeat the action several times.

Blast Off

From a stand with the arms extended overhead and touching, count down "5, 4, 3, 2, 1" as the children gradually assume a half-squat position. On the signal "Blast off," they spring high into the air. They repeat several times.

Sprinter

From a squat position with one leg extended back and their hands placed on the surface outside the knees, students alternate bringing one leg forward and then the other. They should repeat rhythmically several times.

Heel Lifts

From a stand, have the children rise up on the toes as high as possible and return. They should repeat several times.

Heel Drops

From a standing position on the edge of a stair, on a block of wood, or on a book, children drop the heels as low as possible, hold, and then slowly push up onto the toes. They repeat several times.

Pogo Jumps

From a stand with the hands laced behind the head, have the children alternate jumping with a half squat, placing one foot forward and then the other.

Games for Strength and Endurance

Putting the various muscular strength and endurance exercises into a game-type situation will make becoming fit much more fun for children.

Clubs, Diamonds, Spades, and Hearts

Muscular strength and endurance exercises are listed on four large poster boards. Each poster board is designated as a spade, heart, diamond, or club (draw the shapes at the

CONCEPT
24.4

Although a variety of exercise activities are available for enhancing aerobic endurance, muscular strength, and muscular endurance, children frequently find it more fun to pursue fitness through developmentally appropriate game activities.

tops of the posters). One poster board is placed on each sideline and end line of the movement space. A deck of cards is scattered in the middle of the space. Children choose a card, and on the basis of what suit it is they travel to that poster board. They remember the number of their playing card and perform the exercise (e.g., "bear hugs" or lunges) corresponding to their number as listed on the poster board. Jacks equal 11, queens equal 12, and kings equal 13. Each poster board therefore lists 13 exercises.

Fitness Bags

Each fitness bag (baggie) contains laminated puzzle pieces. Pairs or small groups of children put the puzzle together and then perform the exercise specified in writing or pictured on the puzzle. Teachers can integrate mathematics into this game by also writing math problems on the puzzle pieces. The children solve the math problem and perform the exercise the number of times corresponding to the answer to the math problem (Hinson, 1995).

Beat the Bell

Before starting the game, choose an exercise, such as modified push-ups, to be used for the first "round." When you begin playing music, the children perform a locomotor skill around the movement area. When the music stops, all children quickly move to a polyspot (placed randomly throughout the movement space) and begin doing the exercise. A child's name is called; this child goes to the center of the space, stands up two bowling pins (placed on their sides next to a bell in the middle of the movement space), and rings the bell. The object is to see how many exercise repetitions children can complete before the bell is rung. The children informally keep track of their own repetitions. When the bell rings, a new exercise is chosen for the second round. When the music begins again, children once again move throughout the space (Hinson, 1995).

All-Fours Hockey

Children assume a push-up position and face, or mirror, their partner from a distance of approximately 3 to 5 feet. Using one beanbag, children attempt to slide the beanbag on the floor through their partner's arms as their partner maintains the push-up position. If necessary, depending on children's fitness level, children may place one or both knees on the floor. A child scores by sliding her beanbag through her partner's arms. Players stop a goal with their hands. Children keep their own scores. Play continues after each goal is scored (Hinson, 1995).

JOINT FLEXIBILITY

CONCEPT
24.5

Static stretching is a key to maintaining and improving joint flexibility.

Joint flexibility refers to the range of motion of a joint. Although children are generally thought to be flexible, research clearly indicates that flexibility is related to the type and amount of physical activity an individual engages in. Joint flexibility diminishes without sufficient stretching activities. The activities that follow are designed to maintain and improve flexibility in the back and trunk, the upper arms and shoulders, and the lower limbs. These activities should be performed in a static stretching manner; that is, passive stretch should be placed on the muscles rather than the ballistic action of dynamic stretching. Each activity will contribute to improved flexibility if properly and regularly performed. Stretching exercises should be held for approximately 20 to 30 seconds.

These are the primary objectives of the joint flexibility activities that follow:

- To improve flexibility in the back and trunk, upper arms and shoulders, and upper and lower leg
- To become knowledgeable about the importance of flexibility
- To learn how to maintain and improve flexibility at a joint
- To take part in a variety of static stretching activities

Back and Trunk Stretching Activities

As we build strength and endurance in the upper body, it is equally important to incorporate activities that promote flexibility in these areas. There is a reciprocal dialogue between strength and endurance. Don't let your students engage in one at the expense of the other.

Side Stretch

Standing with the feet spread, children bend at the waist slowly to one side and hold. They then repeat to the opposite side. Holding a hoop, rope, or wand overhead aids in performance. The stretches are repeated.

Windshield Wiper

Have the children start in a standing position with the feet spread and arms out from the sides. They twist first in one direction slowly as far as possible without moving the feet, then twist in the opposite direction.

Simon Says

Modify the traditional game of Simon Says to emphasize bending and stretching in a wide variety of ways.

Students prepare for soccer activities as they stretch and manipulate a soccer ball around their legs while in a standing straddle position.

Knee Lifts

From a stand, students bring one knee up and pull to the chest with both arms, then stretch and hold. They repeat with the other leg.

Ankle Pull

From a stand with the feet together, the children bend forward at the waist as far as possible while keeping the legs straight, but slightly bent at the knee joint, and grasp their ankles or reach for the ankles. Have them hold for 15 seconds and return slowly to an upright position. They should repeat several times.

Bicycle

From a back-lying position, children extend the hips upward and pretend to pedal a bicycle with the legs.

The Rainbow Arch

From a kneeling position on a mat, children stretch their arms vertically overhead and reach backward and overhead toward the ankles (as in a back bend), or around the legs, in order to grasp around the ankles. In this way the back is arched while the torso (chest, stomach, and hips) is lifted up and forward into space.

Willow Bend

Have the children start from a kneeling position on one knee with the other leg extended to the side. They then bend to the extended side at the waist and hold, and repeat to the other side.

Arm and Shoulder Stretching Activities

Stretching activities for the arm and shoulder muscles should be incorporated into the program along with strength- and endurance-building activities. As you present these activities, be sure to emphasize practicing them properly. This means that the children should focus on doing the activity in a slow and sustained manner rather than in an all-out frenzy.

Super Circles

From a standing position with the arms out from the sides, students make small circular motions first in one direction, then in the other. For variety and challenge, they can try moving one arm in one direction and the other in the opposite direction.

Star Burst

From a standing position with the hands clasped in front of their body, students keep their arms and body straight and raise their arms above their head. They then slowly push their arms back past their head to stretch the muscles spanning the shoulder joint and also the chest muscles.

Giraffe

Students start from a stand with their hands clasped behind the back, then bend forward at the waist while raising the arms to a vertical position, and hold.

Chicken Hawk

From a stand or seated with the hands clasped behind the neck, children press the elbows back and hold, and repeat.

Greet Yourself

Have the children, from a stand, try to clasp their hands behind their back by putting one arm over the shoulder and bending the opposite arm behind the back. They stretch and hold.

Towel Stretch

From a stand with their arms grasping a towel or rope overhead about shoulder-width apart, the students pull outward on the towel and stretch the arms back. They should hold and repeat.

Towel Magic Trick

Students start from a stand with the arms greater than shoulder-width apart. They grasp a towel or rope overhead and try to bring the towel down behind them without bending the elbows. The wider the grip, the easier the exercise. Students repeat the exercise.

Leg Stretching Activities

Taking time to "stretch out" before engaging in explosive activities with the legs, such as running and jumping, is a time-honored tradition backed up by a limited amount of science but considerable conventional wisdom. The conventional wisdom is that leg stretching activities "warm up" the muscles and reduce the chances of injury. With children, there is little hard evidence that this is so, but stretching out before performance is a good habit that may have later benefits. Remember that stretching exercises should be held for approximately 20 to 30 seconds.

Toe-Toucher

From a stand with the feet crossed, students bend forward slowly at the waist and try to touch the toes. They should bend as low as possible with only a slight bend at the knees.

Straddle Stretch

Have the children start from a sitting position with the legs spread and the toes facing skyward. They then bend forward at the waist, grasp one leg, and try to pull their chin to one knee. They repeat to the other leg.

Center Stretch

The center stretch is the same position as the straddle stretch except that the pull is toward the center while the child grasps both ankles at the same time. The child bends, stretches, and holds.

Fencer's Lunge

From a fencer's on-guard position, the child lunges forward, stretches, and holds for approximately 20 to 30 seconds, then repeats in the opposite direction.

Heel Drop

Have the children stand on the edge of a step or object 4 to 6 inches high. They then drop the heels over the edge and hold.

Heel Stretch

From a feet-together standing position about 3 feet from a wall, students lean forward to a bent-arm position against the wall, stretching the lower calf and ankles.

Ankle Circles

From a sitting position, children grasp one ankle and slowly rotate it, first in one direction and then in the other.

Games for Promoting Joint Flexibility

Embedding these flexibility exercises within a game, dance, or gymnastics activity will be of real interest to children.

Flexibility Tag

Make flexibility tag cards (e.g., butterfly stretch—soles of feet together while in a seated position on buttocks; knees to chest—in a supine position while lying down on the floor; fencer's lunge). Children should already be familiar with each exercise and know how to perform it correctly before engaging in the game of tag. In Flexibility Tag, children are spread out throughout general space, and approximately one-half of them have tag cards. When the music begins, the children with the tag cards attempt to tag someone without a card. When a child is tagged, he takes the tag card from the tagger and performs the stretching exercise written on it for 15 seconds. The exercisers then become taggers and try to tag someone who does not have a card (Hinson, 1995, p. 133).

Grid Flexibility

On a large or small poster board, a grid is drawn. In each cell an exercise is pictured or specified in writing. Children (groups of three to four) draw two numbers out of a number basket and plot these numbers on the grid. When they come to the correct cell, they perform the exercise indicated in that cell. See figure 24.2.

CONCEPT 24.6

A wide variety of simple joint flexibility exercises and game activities can be incorporated into the program in a manner that is both beneficial and fun for children.

FIGURE 24.2 Grid flexibility.

	1	2	3	4	5
2		Straddle stretch	Butterfly	Draw bridge	Windshield wiper
3		Heel drop	Side stretch	Greet yourself	Towel stretch
4		Fencer's stretch	Toe toucher	Chicken wings	Giraffe
5		Center stretch	Star burst	Willow bend	Bicycle

MOTIVATING CHILDREN TO PARTICIPATE IN FITNESS ACTIVITIES

It is essential to motivate children to engage in physical fitness activities and help them to conceptually understand the meaning of each health-related fitness component. The components of health-related fitness are abstract, so using concrete examples enhances conceptual understanding. For example, you might explain range of motion at a joint (flexibility) by using a model of one of the joints in the body; or children might construct a replica using pipe cleaners. A little or a lot of joint flexibility could be demonstrated using the pipe cleaners. Picking up a bag of groceries or the family cat is an example of muscular strength, whereas walking up a flight of stairs while carrying a bag of groceries represents muscular endurance. Aerobic endurance is easier for children to understand because performing aerobic exercise leads to one or more physical responses (heavier breathing, faster heartbeat). Bulletin board displays are an excellent teaching tool to use to foster a conceptual understanding of health-related physical fitness.

An excellent teaching style to accommodate children's varying levels of physical fitness is the inclusion style (see chapter 10, "Teaching Styles"). The principle is to challenge all children at the level that they decide is appropriate to their ability. Hinson (1995, p. 22) points out that teachers must address two questions when using the inclusion style. First, are the children able to select levels of participation that match their individual differences? Second, does the activity involve all children all the time?

As happens with many academic experiences, if the challenge is too easy, children may become bored. If the challenge is too difficult, they become frustrated. Thus, teachers must select and design fitness activities carefully; they must also give children the opportunity to make decisions about how much of a particular fitness activity to perform and how long to perform it.

It is easier to motivate children to engage in moderate to vigorous physical activity if the activities are intrinsically appealing. Children must want to participate. As discussed in chapter 4, intrinsically motivating activities have four characteristics in common: *challenge, curiosity, choice,* and *creativity* are the 4 C's of motivating children for fitness (Raffini, 1993). First, activities must have a developmentally appropriate *challenge* for each child. Then, if children are *curious* and are stimulated by the activity, they are more likely to be intrinsically motivated to participate. Third, children must have some degree of *choice* over their own fitness development. Inclusion style teaching and offering alternative fitness activities give children a measure of control. Finally, the activities must be *creative* or novel. Most children enjoy something that is new and exciting.

CONCEPT 24.7
The inclusion style is an excellent teaching style for motivating children toward increased participation in physical activity.

CONCEPT 24.8
The 4 C's of motivating children for participation in fitness activities are *challenge, choice, curiosity,* and *creativity.*

Summary

The generally poor fitness level of today's children should concern us all. Recent research clearly indicates that children are less fit and more fat than their counterparts of just 20 years ago. This statistic seems even more alarming when we recognize that American children of a generation ago were already considered by most experts to be unfit and overfat. Clearly it would be in the best interest of all to correct this deplorable situation. Quality physical education, with a portion of each instructional period spent in the quest for physical fitness, is the only reasonable answer. By helping children become fit movers, informed movers, and eager movers, teachers do much to provide the means for healthful living and an active way of life.

The health-related components of physical fitness are transient and highly susceptible to change. Children need to learn and to apply the essential fitness principles of exercise frequency, intensity, duration, and variety. Adherence to these principles in the quest for cardiovascular endurance, muscular strength and endurance, and joint flexibility will provide children with the knowledge and skills required for a lifetime of physical activity and positive fitness behaviors. The fitness strand in the developmental physical education program is necessary and critically important if we are serious about the need and potential for fitness literacy among the children and youth of North America.

Terms to Remember

Excellent Readings

Allsbrook, L. (1992). Fitness should fit children. *JOPERD, 63*, 47-49.

Blakemore, C., Hawkes, N.R., & Hilton, H.G. (1992). Making fitness work for students. *Strategies, 5*, 26-29.

Conkell, C., & Askins, J. (2000). Integrating fitness into a skill themes program. *TEPE, 11* (1), 22-25.

Darby, L.A., & Pohlman, R.L. (1993). Heart rates help personalize fitness. *Strategies, 7*, 9-15.

Gabbard, C. (1990). Health-related fitness in elementary physical education. *Strategies, 3*, 14-18.

Hester, D., & Dunaway, D. (1990). Beyond calisthenics: Fitness and fun in elementary physical education. *Strategies, 3*, 25-28.

Kuntzelman, C., Kuntzelman, B., McGlynn, M., & McGlynn, G. (1996). *Aerobics with fun.* Reston, VA: AAHPERD.

Levitt, S. (1993). Motivate your students: Participate. *Strategies, 6*, 10-11.

Mitchell, M. (1999). Teaching fitness intensity concepts to young children. *TEPE, 10* (3), 17-19.

Ratliffe, T. (2000). Children's fitness—Teaching fitness concepts. *TEPE, 11* (6), 22-24.

Tenoschok, M. (1993). Jog around the world. *Strategies, 6*, 18-20.

TEPE Feature Edition on Children's Fitness. (March, 2000). *11* (2).

25

Developing the Thinking Child

Key Concept

▶ Creating rich, exciting, and meaningful learning experiences that foster *thinking*, as well as moving, empowers children to become critical thinkers.

This chapter will provide you with the tools to do the following:

▶ Justify the role of critical thinking (i.e., problem solving or higher-order thinking) processes in a developmental physical education program.

▶ Define critical thinking as it applies to physical education.

▶ Become familiar with the benefits of student-centered learning that promotes critical thinking.

▶ Describe the role of the teacher in fostering critical thinking in physical education.

▶ Structure the learning environment to promote critical thinking.

▶ Become familiar with activities designed to foster children's critical thinking in the gymnasium.

Children are naturally curious. They enjoy solving riddles and puzzles or finding the answer to a unique and challenging question. Physical education activities, whether they constitute dance, games, or gymnastics content, are rich with opportunities to engage children in "thinking." Creating rich, exciting, and meaningful learning experiences that foster moving *and* thinking empowers children and helps them to be excited about physical education.

In this chapter, we examine the cognitive domain of learning as it applies to teaching physical education. To this end we define "thinking" terminology, discuss the predispositions necessary for critical thinking, examine how to structure learning environments to foster thinking, and provide several activity ideas for promoting critical thinking in children's physical education.

CONCEPT
25.1

Critical thinking
involves the use of
higher-order thought
processes.

DEFINING THINKING

It seems so simple—don't children automatically think as they move? Yes, degrees of thinking do accompany voluntary movement. However, thinking as we define it later in this chapter requires greater focus and intention on the part of the mover. Suppose, for example, that Dan is practicing an overhand throw toward a partner "on the move." We assume that Dan may be thinking, "How high should I throw the ball so that it reaches my partner? Did I follow through correctly on that last throw? How can I generate more force behind my throw to keep from throwing short?" But there's a question for us. How do we know that Dan is thinking as he is practicing throwing to his partner? The answer: We don't. For this reason, teachers must use specific strategies to monitor children's thinking and to nurture its development within the cognitive domain.

CRITICAL THINKING

We can define **higher-order thinking** processes as those processes that engage the learner in one or more of the following:

- Comparing and contrasting ideas
- Making deductions
- Generating alternative responses

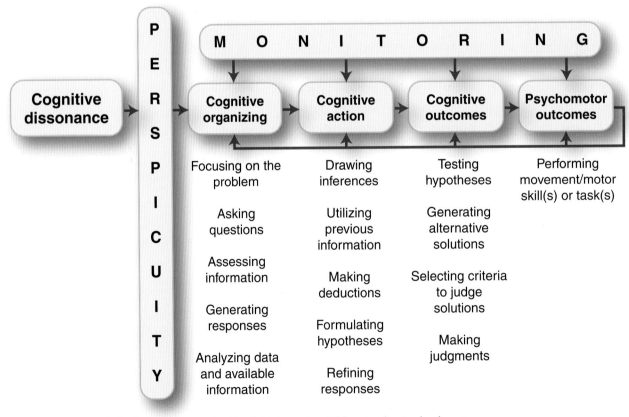

FIGURE 25.1   McBride's schema of critical thinking in children's physical education.
Adapted, by permission, of R. McBride, 1992, "Critical thinking—an overview with implications for physical education," *JTPE* 11: 112–125.

- Analyzing a situation
- Synthesizing information and/or applying information

Lower-order thinking involves much more simplified cognitive processes such as simple recall and recognition. Higher-order thinking is also called *critical thinking*. McBride (1992) was the first to consider how we could foster critical thinking in physical education. He defined **critical thinking** in physical education as "reflective thinking that is used to make reasonable and defensible decisions about movement" (p. 115). Critical thinking has also been defined as the process of estimating, evaluating, noting similarities and differences, or offering opinions with reasons (Lipman, 1988).

McBride (1992) developed a four-phase schema to represent the process of critical thinking in physical education (see figure 25.1). Each of the four phases—cognitive organization, cognitive actions, cognitive outcomes, and psychomotor outcomes—includes several critical thinking components. This schema serves as a *template* for helping teachers address critical thinking within physical education activities.

CRITICAL THINKING DISPOSITIONS

Engaging children in activities designed to foster problem-solving and critical thinking requires that they be receptive and eager to do these things. In other words, children's **critical thinking dispositions** or habitual ways of behaving must be conducive to engaging in critical thinking activities. The dispositions favorable to critical thinking include (1) trying to be well informed, (2) being open-minded, (3) being sensitive to others' ideas, (4) being patient, and (5) being willing to share ideas. These dispositions must be nurtured and are a product of children's social-emotional, cognitive, and psychomotor development. As a paraphrase of the saying goes, "You can lead a horse to water, but you can't make it *think*." Teachers, therefore, must be sensitive to children's overall development and, after assessing their students' dispositions, determine how much, for how long, and when to integrate thinking within physical education activities.

TEXT BOX 25.1

"Learners must first be predisposed to the process in order to be successful critical thinkers in physical education. Many students used to traditional styles of teaching that rely on facts, recall, and demonstration/replication may resist adopting a more active role in the learning process."

McBride, R., & Cleland, F. (1998). Critical thinking in physical education. Putting the theory where it belongs: In the gymnasium. *JOPERD, 69* (7), 42–46.

CONCEPT 25.2

Teachers can structure the learning environment in the gymnasium in such a way that it promotes critical thinking skills among all learners.

STRUCTURING THE LEARNING ENVIRONMENT

When you are preparing to promote critical thinking in physical education, it is important to give considerable thought to the following:

- Identifying your goal and objectives

- Determining the most appropriate teaching styles
- Properly sequencing each critical thinking experience
- Asking questions
- Organizing the learning environment

Each of these is briefly discussed in the paragraphs that follow.

Identifying Goals and Objectives

**CONCEPT
25.3**

Indirect teaching
styles that focus on
self-discovery of move-
ment solutions are
most appropriate for
fostering critical
thinking in physical
education.

Highlighting specific components of the critical thinking process helps physical educators choose activities and teaching methods that develop a specific aspect of critical thinking. For example, if one aspect of the lesson is to help students learn to focus on a problem, the teacher might use task cards specifying a written movement task or problem in order to facilitate this part of the cognitive organization phase of critical thinking. Posted instructions could also prompt students to focus on a problem. If the objective is for students to utilize previously learned concepts and motor skills, an open-ended problem that stimulates them to draw upon this knowledge would be appropriate.

Selecting Appropriate Teaching Styles

Teachers are the catalysts or facilitators of critical thinking in physical education. "To become an effective catalyst, teachers must shift their role from controller of information to facilitator of information. In physical education, this means we must rely less on the traditional demonstration/replication (direct) mode of instruction and use other modes of indirect instruction associated with fostering critical thinking" (McBride & Cleland, 1998, p. 42).

This teacher is distributing self-check task cards (see chapter 10) for students to use for the purpose of analyzing their own progress relative to developing soccer skills. These task cards can serve as a form of assessment as well as promote critical thinking with the physical education lesson.

What you want to note about this recipe is the use of the production cluster of teaching styles (for a complete discussion of these indirect teaching styles, please refer to chapter 10, "Teaching Styles"). The production cluster involves children in many higher-order thinking processes and fosters critical thinking.

TEXT BOX 25.2

A "Piece of Cake Recipe" for Fostering Critical Thinking in Physical Education

Utensils:

- 20-25 willing students (or students who have discussed and participated in activities that have helped them to develop the dispositions that support the CT process)
- Cupboards full of equipment
- Large gymnasium-sized pan
- Teacher "to stir things up"

Cake:

- 4 cups of indirect teaching styles
- 3 cups of knowledge about McBride's schema of CT-PE
- 2 cups of knowledge about the dispositions that support CT
- 6 eggs filled with strategies promoting CT-PE (compare/contrast egg; similarities/differences egg)
- 1 cup of conveying student expectations
- 1 cup of providing prompting questions
- 3 tbsp. of "wait time"
- 2 tsp. of praise
- Several dashes of patience

Directions:

Combine first three "dry" ingredients in a giant bowl. Use teacher to stir things up. Add the cup of student expectations, cup of prompting questions, and tablespoons of wait time. Add one egg at a time until all six have been thoroughly stirred into dry ingredients by teacher. Add the teaspoons of praise and pour into a gymnasium-sized pan. Bake within an "accepting atmosphere" for 10 to 15 minutes. Take out of oven and gently shake pan. Put back into oven for another 30 minutes.

Frosting:

- 1 cup of students defending ideas
- 1 stick of teacher response
- 2 tsp. of closure and summary

Combine all ingredients and stir for several minutes until smooth. Take out and frost while hot!

McBride, R., & Cleland, F. (1998). Critical thinking in physical education. Putting the theory where it belongs: In the gymnasium. *JOPERD, 69* (7), 42–46.

Sequencing Learning Experiences

Adhering to a sequential progression (e.g., moving from simple to more complex), as we do when teaching movement skills, also applies to infusing critical thinking into physical education lesson content. As you begin to foster critical thinking within your physical education lessons, you will find the following guidelines helpful:

- Children at the beginning/novice level of movement skill learning may need to establish domain-specific knowledge, or a foundation of motor skills and movement concepts, that they can draw on when presented with a critical thinking challenge.
- The amount and complexity of critical thinking tasks and the time allotted can gradually increase. Begin with simple tasks and devote brief time periods to movement tasks demanding critical thinking.
- Sequence critical thinking tasks within a series of ongoing lessons.
- When using critical thinking strategies for the first time, students need encouragement, and teachers must be observant of the students' responses. For example, if you present an open-ended question or movement task and students cannot think of any response, you may need to provide two or three alternatives that they can choose from. Success is the key. We do not want students to become overly frustrated with the process.

Asking Questions

In addition to employing guided discovery, convergent discovery, and divergent production teaching styles, teachers ask higher-order questions to encourage critical thinking. Questions with simple yes or no answers do not foster critical thinking. Instead, teachers need to design questions that provoke thought and that stimulate the components of critical thinking. These are some examples:

What could you ask these two young girls about their striking pattern? Perhaps you could ask, "When you strike, how do you create more force?"

- "What happens when you release the throw too soon?"
- "How can you create support in your soccer formation?"
- "If I kick the ball so that the shoelaces part of my foot contacts the underneath part of the ball, what will happen?"
- "Does a follow-through in kicking a lofted ball need to be high? Why or why not?"
- "What are the similarities and differences among the different ways of striking that we practiced today?"

- "Can you create three different ways of jumping and landing using this learning environment? What will assist you in jumping higher?"

- "Watch your partner perform a cartwheel. What suggestions do you have to help your partner improve her performance?"

- "Our creative dance theme today is about the ocean. What things in the ocean move? How do they move? What locomotor or stability movements could you do to represent one aspect of the ocean?" (Response could be ocean waves—they advance and turbulently retreat.)

- "Please observe this group perform their shape dance. What would you suggest they do to create more variety or surprise in their dance?"

Of course, questions should reflect your lesson objectives and the target concepts you want your students to learn. Questions may be incorporated into several parts of the lesson and should not be limited to the lesson closure or the review of the day's lesson. It is important also that you give children time to answer questions or to collaborate with a partner or in small groups on answers, and that you recognize children's ideas, whether right or wrong.

You should also encourage children in your classes to ask questions. They may need help in generating questions that are relevant and meaningful to the lesson objectives.

Asking questions and prompting students to generate questions take time. If we are to address critical thinking in physical education, as teachers we need to inform administrators that sufficient time must be allotted for our physical education classes (remember that daily quality physical education is our ultimate goal). In addition, we must organize our classes so that they provide critical thinking opportunities as well as accomplishing our main objective, namely to engage children in physical activity.

CONCEPT 25.4

Specific questions designed to foster critical thinking in physical education should reflect lesson objectives and address concepts that are important for students to learn.

Organizational Strategies

Using partner and small-group activities also accommodates higher-order thinking among children. In "think-pair-share," students respond to a problem or task by collaborating with a partner. They discuss possible movement responses or answers to a question, and cooperate to "think together" and subsequently share their answer with peers and/or the teacher.

In small-group activities, having students play the following roles can encourage thinking and problem-solving:

CONCEPT 25.5

Children can be organized into groups and take on specific roles that will promote critical thinking.

- *Monitor*—the person who makes sure the group is focused and is staying on task

- *Challenger*—the person who encourages everyone in the group to contribute an idea or movement response

- *Task definer*—the person who reads a task from a task card or explains and repeats the task to the group

- *Strategist*—the person who summarizes the group's ideas and strategies (Cleland & Pearse, 1995)

You can rename these roles to make them more inviting and understandable to younger children (e.g., "detective" for the strategist).

TEXT BOX 25.3

✏✏✏✏✏✏✏✏

Critical Thinking Small-Group Roles

- **Monitor:** the child who makes sure the group is focused on staying on task
- **Challenger:** the child who encourages everyone in the group to contribute an idea or movement response
- **Task definer:** the child who reads a task from a task card or explains and repeats the task to his group
- **Strategist:** the child who summarizes the group's ideas and strategies

Cleland, F.E., & Pearse, C. (1995). Critical thinking in elementary physical education: Reflections on a yearlong study. *JOPERD, 66*, 31–38.

PUTTING THEORY WHERE IT BELONGS— IN THE GYMNASIUM

Critical thinking can be infused in many different ways within games, dance, or gymnastics activities. The activities outlined in this section feature critical thinking in all three physical education content areas. We begin with activities appropriate for primary grade children (kindergarten through grade two) and conclude with activity ideas typically appropriate for intermediate grade children (grades three to five).

Critical Thinking in Physical Education Content: Kindergarten Through Grade Two

Questions promoting analysis of any fundamental movement skill or group of skills give students opportunities to analyze, make inferences, discuss similarities and differences, or make comparisons. For example, as students perform the underhand toss or throw, parts of the throw can be the focus for student analysis. Students can compare two different stances: feet together and opposite foot forward. The teacher might ask which stance helps create momentum or energy, and why. The teacher might also focus on the release of the ball by asking students to think about what occurs when they want to throw the ball at a low level versus a high level. After a period of practice, students might share ideas and then discuss similarities and differences they noticed in performing the underhand throw.

In a dance lesson based on the eight effort actions (see Developmental Dance Lesson 5 on the CD-ROM), students can analyze the types of "efforts" that various machines or electrical appliances perform. First they would explore the eight effort actions (i.e., movements based on the combination of weight [as an aspect of force], space, and time movement factors). For example, children may perform "floating" (light weight, indirect space, slow time) or "punching" (strong weight, direct space, quick time), "pressing" (strong, direct, slow), and so forth. To establish domain-specific knowledge or knowledge about the effort actions, the teacher may need to initially demonstrate the effort actions. The teacher might then present pictures of various machines (washer, pasta maker, toaster, etc.). Children could then discuss the types of movement factors involved: "What actions do these machines perform?"

After discussing what actions machines do, children could explore these actions with their bodies—using the whole body or individual body parts. The essential critical thinking strategy in this scenario is the use of previous knowledge, along with the application of knowledge.

A third scenario highlights the content area of educational gymnastics. The teacher may ask pairs of students to create symmetrical and asymmetrical shapes and balances using different body parts to support their weight (students are already familiar with the terminology being used in the lesson). The teacher then takes Polaroid snapshots of the children's favorite shapes and balances and puts all the snapshots in a box. Pairs of students play the game of Fish and select two photographs, perform the selected balances, then determine whether they are symmetrical (even) or asymmetrical (uneven). A class discussion should follow. In this critical thinking learning experience, children are comparing, contrasting, and applying previous knowledge to a problem.

In this developmental gymnastics lesson the teacher has designed task cards that depict specific partner balances. Students must determine how to get safely into and out of the balances, thus creating a movement sentence.

Critical Thinking in Physical Education Content: Grades Three to Five

Children in the intermediate grades may be ready to modify games or create their own games. When asking children to create games, you typically need to provide very clear guidelines. A clear set of guidelines for children who will be creating a game might look like this:

- The game will include bouncing, passing, and/or rolling.
- Scoring *cannot* be accomplished by sending the object into a target or zone.
- All players must be active and involved.

- Boundaries must be designated.

As students design their games, the teacher acts as a facilitator and questions group members to stimulate their thinking:

- "If you do this, then what might happen next?"
- "How large is your playing area? Why?"
- "When playing your game, are you bouncing correctly?"
- "How could you determine this?"
- "Do you have an offense and defense in your game? Why?"

Students in this basketball lesson are challenged to interpret a "give and go" play by analyzing a diagram. After identifying the problem, students must determine their playing positions and the actions that should take place and subsequently attempt to run the play. The teacher serves as the facilitator in this learning experience. Students must have domain-specific knowledge before attempting this type of critical thinking activity, including how to pass and dribble, how to guard, and how to move to open space.

These and many other questions stimulate children to think about what they are creating and why.

A developmental gymnastics critical thinking scenario for intermediate grade children could involve making collages. This activity could be done in collaboration with the classroom teacher, the art teacher, or both. It would be valuable for students to know what a collage is and to learn about the aesthetic principles that contribute to a well-designed collage. Within the physical education lesson, students (five to six per group) could be asked to create a collage of different types of balances. Teachers could specify criteria before the students make the collage, or students could generate their own criteria for assessing their collage. A teacher might instruct students to make sure the collage included elements such as these:

- Depth
- Inverted and upright balances

- Symmetrical and asymmetrical balances
- Different levels
- Different shapes

Again, the teacher could take Polaroid snapshots of collages, and groups might evaluate their own and another group's collage.

In developmental dance, students might analyze their own locomotor skills on videotape (e.g., run-run-leap) and assess them using specified criteria. Students could observe dances on video and determine what choreographic principles were used (e.g., entrances/exits; stillness; repetition; canon form), or students could compare and contrast different forms of dance (e.g., "What is similar among the dance forms?" "What is different?" "Why do you think these differences exist?").

Physical education content presents plentiful opportunities to challenge students to employ critical thinking strategies. It is imperative that teachers strive to foster critical thinking and do so in an intentional and developmentally appropriate manner. For younger or less experienced students, or children who have special needs, teachers should not design lessons that are too complex. Success is the key, and teachers need to be sensitive to all children's cognitive and social development.

Summary

Critical thinking in the context of physical education is reflective thinking used to make reasonable, defensible, and logical decisions about a movement problem or task. Physical education activities are rich with opportunities to promote critical thinking. Certain predispositions need to be developed among students before teachers can engage them in critical thinking activities. Structuring the learning environment to promote critical thinking involves identifying goals, selecting the most appropriate teaching style, sequencing the critical thinking experiences, asking questions, and organizing the learning environment. Thinking activities such as analysis of skills, comparison and contrast, and use of previously learned concepts can be incorporated into lessons using developmental games, dance, and gymnastics activities.

Terms to Remember

Excellent Readings

Cleland, F.E., & Pearse, C. (1995). Critical thinking in elementary physical education: Reflections on a yearlong study. *JOPERD, 66,* 31-38.

Lipman, M. (1988). Critical thinking—What can it be? *Educational Leadership, 46* (1), 38-43.

McBride, R. (1992). Critical thinking—an overview with implications for physical education. *JTPE, 11,* 112-125.

McBride, R., & Cleland, F.E. (1998). Critical thinking in physical education. Putting the theory where it belongs: In the gymnasium. *JOPERD, 69,* 42-46.

TEPE Feature Edition. (May, 2001). *12* (3).

26

Developing the Feeling Child

Key Concepts

▶ Children are thinking, feeling, and moving beings. The developmental physical education program recognizes the importance of nurturing children's understanding of themselves and others with a goal of helping them develop positive social behaviors.

This chapter will provide you with the tools to do the following:

▶ Understand the importance and meaning of teaching personal and social responsibility.

▶ Examine strategies for fostering social responsibility in developmental physical education.

▶ Become familiar with activities that promote personal and social responsibility.

For many years the physical education profession has acknowledged that we teach the "whole child," implying that children's self-concept (i.e., a nonjudgmental view about one's personal attributes) is enhanced through participation in physical activity. However, engaging in sport, physical activity, or a physical education lesson does not automatically ensure that children's self-concept or their social skills will be addressed. Research demonstrates that physical educators must *consciously* and *deliberately* use teaching strategies, as well as specific lesson content, in order to facilitate greater personal and social responsibility among children (Hellison, 1995). Teaching the "whole child" may require teachers to rethink their teaching philosophy as well as their overall understanding of children. Noddings (1992) summed this up in stating, "The physical self is only part of the self. We must be concerned also with the emotional, spiritual, and intellectual self, and clearly these are not discrete. We separate and label them for convenience in discussion but it may be a mistake to separate them sharply in curriculum" (p. 48).

In this chapter, we begin by answering the question: Why address the affective domain? Then we propose a four-level developmental model for helping children achieve greater personal and social control. Next we take a look at teaching strategies designed to foster children's affective development, and a final

section of the chapter deals with ways to structure activities for personal and social responsibility.

ADDRESSING THE AFFECTIVE DOMAIN

Children's view about themselves and others is shaped by many factors. One's family structure, culture, ethnicity, geographic location, socioeconomic status, and religion are among the most powerful factors. As a consequence, in our diverse communities children may display myriad attitudes and behaviors that affect their learning. In physical education, little can be accomplished if children's attitudes and behaviors negatively influence their ability to monitor and control their own behavior. It is imperative, therefore, that as a physical educator you consider children's affective development as you seek to create more positive and effective learning environments. Addressing the affective domain, or the "feeling child," is a worthy goal in physical education and is an important strand woven throughout the developmental physical education program.

PERSONAL AND SOCIAL RESPONSIBILITY: A DEVELOPMENTAL PROGRESSION

The affective domain of development encompasses children's personal understanding of and views about themselves (e.g., their concept of self), as well as their attitudes and feelings toward others (i.e., their social views and their understanding of others). One approach to enhancing children's affective development has been addressed through a model developed by Hellison (1995) termed the *personal and social responsibility model.*

Hellison dedicated much of his professional career to exploring how teachers can encourage students to take personal and social responsibility through carefully designed lessons in physical education. Using physical education as the "vehicle," Hellison's two primary goals are to (1) help students take more **personal responsibility** for their own well-being and (2) help students accept greater **social responsibility** by being more sensitive and responsive to the well-being of others. Hellison's framework for addressing the affective domain, or "the feeling child," has been embraced by many physical educators across the nation.

In Hellison's model, taking personal and social responsibility is defined by two values related to **personal well-being,** *effort and self-direction,* and two values related to **social well-being,** *respecting others' rights and feelings* and *caring about others.* Hellison has expanded upon these values and created awareness levels, or developmental levels, to help children focus on and understand their own behavior. In this chapter we will examine how physical educators can teach children about these levels of personal and social responsibility. With this knowledge, children can think about and assess their own levels of responsibility. We should continually strive to help children progressively achieve higher levels of personal and social responsibility.

- Level 0/Irresponsibility
- Level I/Respect

- Level II/Participation
- Level III/Self-Direction
- Level IV/Caring

Each developmental level helps clarify what responsibility means and what children are to take responsibility for. Each is briefly discussed in the following paragraphs.

Level I/Respect

In a physical education class where children are at **Level I/Respect**, they exhibit self-control, can take turns, work cooperatively with others, and learn to resolve conflicts peacefully. **Self-control** refers to regulating one's own behavior so that the rights and feelings of others are respected. Self-control also means that respectful behavior is "self-initiated" and "self-governed," in other words, that teachers do not have to ask the student to control his behavior. As an example, you are demonstrating self-control when you respond civilly to a person who is verbally abusing you or criticizing you, instead of retaliating with similar verbal abuse or physical abuse.

Conflict resolution is a complex process, and some schools subscribe to specific procedures for all students to follow in dealing with conflict (see chapter 9, "Facilitating Learning"). Generally speaking, conflict resolution refers to negotiating differences with others. Children should be guided in dealing with conflict and should be given conflict resolution strategies and perhaps steps to follow.

Inclusion in this context refers to allowing all in a group or a class to participate and make meaningful contributions in an activity. Taking turns, assisting others, working cooperatively with a partner or group, and playing a specific role in a game activity are all examples of group inclusion.

Level II/Participation

In **Level II/Participation**, students are encouraged to put forth effort by trying new things and new activities. At Level II, students begin to realize that they must exert

CONCEPT 26.3

The development of children's sense of responsibility can be viewed as occurring in a progression or along a developmental continuum, encompassing Level I/Respect; Level II/Participation; Level III/Self-Direction; and Level IV/Caring.

These students are participating in an instant activity and cooperating well with their partners.

personal effort in order to improve themselves, both in physical activity settings and in all aspects of their lives. Children at Level II are also exploring what success means to them and how to handle both victory and defeat. Teachers, therefore, should be helping students develop internal standards for success, standards that the children themselves set versus standards imposed by parents, teachers, or coaches. It's important to note that at Level II, students are still dependent on the teacher in order to stay on task and that they require assistance in shaping their participation in wholesome ways.

Level III/Self-Direction

Students at **Level III/Self-Direction** are capable of staying on task without being prompted by a teacher. At this level they are for the most part self-directed and capable of being independent learners. Students at this level are able to resist the sometimes negative influence of peer pressure. They resist the need to be "one of the gang," to "look cool," or to "do their own thing" when the associated behaviors are clearly improper. The new challenges in Level III/Self-Direction require students to learn appropriate assertive behaviors and social behaviors for accomplishing their plans and expressing their ideas. Students in Level III know how and want to take responsibility for themselves but don't always have the skills needed to act independently of social or group pressure. At this level, teachers need to stay involved and help students learn to cope with outside pressures (i.e., of friends or classmates) so that they can become more self-directed and self-reliant.

This student demonstrates self direction by helping to put equipment away, no matter how big it is!

Level IV/Caring

At **Level IV/Caring**, students show compassion for others and do so without expecting something in return. Students at Level IV possess interpersonal listening skills, are nonjudgmental, and consistently demonstrate a wholesome absence of arrogance. They are truly empathetic toward others and strive to make positive contributions to the group or class. Teachers can take advantage of "teachable moments" in order to help students get to this level—to help the individuals and the class understand and identify with the feelings and needs of others.

Many teachers use the personal and social responsibility model and have adapted the levels to more closely match the cognitive understanding and social development of the children they teach. Masser's (1990) application of the four levels is appropriate for elementary school children.

TEXT BOX 26.1

Level 0—Irresponsibility

Home: Blaming brothers or sisters for problems

Playground: Calling other students names

Classroom: Talking to friends when teacher is giving instructions

Physical education: Pushing and shoving others when selecting equipment

Level 1—Self-control

Home: Keeping self from hitting brother even though really mad at him

Playground: Standing and watching others play; not getting mad and calling someone names if they take your playground ball away

Classroom: Waiting until appropriate time to talk with friends

Physical education: Practicing, but not all of the time

Level 2—Involvement

Home: Helping to clean up supper dishes

Playground: Playing with others; playing a new game

Classroom: Listening and doing class work

Physical education: Trying new things without complaining and saying, "I can't"

Level 3—Self-responsibility

Home: Cleaning room without being asked; practicing piano without being asked

Playground: Returning equipment during recess

Classroom: Doing a science project not part of any assignment

Physical education: Undertaking to learn a new skill through resources outside the physical education class

Level 4—Caring

Home: Helping take care of a pet or younger child

Playground: Asking others (not just friends) to join them in play

Classroom: Helping another student with a math problem

Physical education: Willingly working with anyone in the class

---

INTERPRETING THE LEVELS

One way of interpreting the four levels of personal and social responsibility is to see them as a cumulative progression. Students are taught that each level builds on and encompasses all lower levels. The advantage of this interpretation is that it is simple; students can quickly set personal goals regarding responsibility and can easily evaluate their progress. The disadvantage is that students may display more than one level of behavior within the same lesson so that the levels become less personally meaningful. Some teachers have countered this disadvantage by implementing specific rules. For example, if students demonstrate behaviors at more than one level within the same lesson, they must evaluate themselves at the lowest level. Others have suggested averaging the different levels that a student displays. For example, Level II behaviors plus Level III behaviors = Level 2-1/2. With this system, students know that they are making progress but that they still have a way to go in order to get to the next level.

ASSESSING PERSONAL AND SOCIAL BEHAVIORS

CONCEPT 26.4

Assessing where children are in the developmental progression relating to personal and social responsibility is difficult because progress is often inconsistent.

Your students can assess their level of personal and social responsibility in many different ways. Reflection time gives children an opportunity to evaluate their behavior and attitudes. You can provide time for reflection either at the conclusion of a lesson or during the lesson—you would do it during the lesson if you wanted children to concentrate on how a specific activity or event contributed to their sense of personal and social responsibility. Students can share their self-reflections publicly with others, can reflect privately, or can record their reflections in a journal. The following strategies have been effectively used with children:

• During lesson closure, students sit in a circle and tell the group which level they are at; if time permits they can explain why they chose a specific level.

• As the children exit the gymnasium they touch (perhaps jump up to touch) their level (numbers are painted on or taped to the wall adjacent to the door).

• Children place a colored card into a wall pocket as they exit the gymnasium or during lesson closure; the pockets are labeled with the numbers of the levels or are color-coded (red = Level 0; blue = Level I; green = Level II; yellow = Level III; white = Level IV).

• The children record their level on an index card or small piece of paper and place this in their physical education folio.

• Children check off (✓) or circle a character (see figure 26.1).

TEACHING STRATEGIES

Several strategies are available to help teachers put the levels of personal and social responsibility into action. At Level I, for example, teachers can use inclusion games to help students understand the importance of giving everyone a chance to partici-

FIGURE 26.1 Sample index card/handout for physical education folio.

pate and make contributions. In addition, games can have specific rules—for example, "Everyone must touch the ball before a goal can be scored." Teachers might have children play a game in which the design and rules of the game have an inherent "problem." The children could be challenged to solve the problem by modifying the game (e.g., choice of equipment, rules, players' roles). In this "game problem" scenario, all children would be asked to contribute their ideas, so participation would be enhanced.

Another strategy commonly used in physical education is **time-out.** Hellison's (1995) suggestions regarding the use of time-out involve "progressive separation from the group" (p. 28). This progression includes the following choices:

CONCEPT 26.5

Teachers need to carefully consider the teaching strategies and teaching styles for their lessons when attempting to help children take greater personal and social responsibility for their actions.

1. The student can either sit out or get immediately under control.
2. The student sits out with the choice of returning when ready to put Level I into practice.
3. The student sits out until the teacher and student can negotiate a plan.
4. The teacher and student renegotiate a different plan.
5. The student is referred for appropriate counseling.
6. The student is offered the right of exit from the class or program (but note that it is often not possible in physical education to allow children to leave a class; this choice necessitates collaboration with the classroom teacher, principal, and perhaps parents).

For students at Level I, involving them in the process, when possible, can facilitate individual decision making. If time-out is necessary, the student is asked to determine the time to rejoin class activity.

The **talking bench** can be used at Level I to resolve conflicts. Children literally go to a bench and discuss the problem. Then they report back to the teacher on how they resolved the problem.

In Level II, the inclusion style of teaching (see chapter 10, "Teaching Styles") can be used to provide students with choices. Choices permit students to be involved in self-paced activities and to work at their own rate and level of challenge. This is an excellent way to encourage participation. Other techniques for encouraging students to participate include sending home "happygrams," giving a shoelace token for accomplishing a specific task, and giving "the golden shoe award." (The golden shoe is an old tennis shoe that has been spray painted gold and mounted on a piece of wood.)

Another strategy highlighted by Hellison (1995) is **Grandpa's** or **Grandma's law.** According to this law, if children behave appropriately for half of the class time, they get to help choose an activity for the second half of class time, or the teacher chooses activities that students have identified as favorites.

The 0-10 **intensity scale** is yet another strategy. The scale can be posted on the gymnasium wall to be used by students to assess their effort and willingness to participate at Level II. The scale represents the amount of effort a student is willing to put forth in an activity. Young children who do not yet think in abstract terms may have difficulty with this strategy. Although there are various ways of implementing the intensity strategy, the primary aim is to make success a reachable goal. For example, the teacher might tell students that a particular activity requires an intensity level of 5. Students who have privately assessed themselves as lower than a 5 can choose an alternate activity. They will be less likely to fail or to frustrate peers who do want to participate in an activity requiring more effort.

At Level III, children have opportunities to develop a personal plan and carry out that plan (e.g., trying or designing a new activity; playing with a new friend). The teacher can apply the **accordion principle** for giving or taking away time. If children carry out their plan (e.g., staying on task without needing to be prompted while attempting a new skill), they are rewarded with independent time. If they cannot work productively on their own or carry out their plan, then the teacher takes away independent time and reverts to a more teacher-directed lesson plan.

In Level IV physical education lessons, students can use reciprocal style (see chapter 10, "Teaching Styles"). Within this style, students teach or coach each other somewhat independently of the teacher. Task cards and teaching cues must be used to facilitate this style. The **Giraffe Club** is a Level IV strategy created for those "who stick their necks out for the common good" (Lickona, 1991, p. 309). Sticking one's neck out, or being sensitive and responsive to the needs of peers, must be operationally defined for children so that they understand what behaviors constitute this action. Group goals also promote Level IV behaviors. Formation of group goals might entail having each student in a group offer a suggestion for creating a dance or a game.

We encourage you to customize these sample strategies and invent new ones for promoting personal and social responsibility among your students. After all, you know your students better than anyone else does. Remember, though, that all strategies for helping children gain increased personal and social control have certain elements in common. You must design these strategies so that they empower children toward a better understanding of themselves and others and also promote success within the physical education lesson.

CONCEPT 26.6

A variety of strategies are available to teachers in developing the "feeling child"; but in the final analysis, all teachers are responsible for developing strategies that are effective with their particular children in the context of their specific program.

STRUCTURING ACTIVITIES

When structuring activities to foster personal and social responsibility, teachers should first consider the range of developmental factors (i.e., physical, social, and cognitive factors) that may affect children's readiness.

As a teacher you will need to consider general age-related characteristics and developmental factors when figuring out how to foster personal and social responsibility among students. For example, primary grade children are frequently limited by their cognitive development to thinking in the "here and now." They can reason well about things that are physically present but have difficulty with abstractions or hypothetical propositions. Because they think in clear-cut terms, they need "hands-on" or **concrete representations** of abstract concepts. For example, kindergarten and first grade children may not be able to conceptually grasp a statement like "You need to think about how you treat your friends." Why? This statement invites children to think about an abstract concept, "how to treat friends." It might be more appropriate to ask a child, "What did you just do during the Beanbag Thank-You game that was nice to your friends? Yes, you picked up beanbags that fell to the floor and gave them back to the person who dropped the beanbag." The teacher in this case is referring to the situation in concrete terms—in the here and now.

Young children also tend to be egocentric, typically thinking in terms of what they need or how they feel. They have difficulty thinking how others may feel or demonstrating empathy. For these reasons, teachers must provide children with developmentally appropriate examples of acceptable behavior. To get across the idea of empathy, you might say, "What do you need to remember in order to take good care of your dog? Yes, you need to feed and walk your dog every day. So, at school what might you do to 'take care' of your classmates? Yes, maybe your classmate needs a friend to play with during recess, or perhaps you might share your dessert with a friend at lunchtime."

Intermediate grade students are beginning to enter into the **formal operations** stage of cognitive development. That is, students in fourth and fifth grade begin to think in more abstract terms and develop the "ability to reason about hypothetical problems—about what might be—as well as real problems, and to think about possibilities as well as actualities" (Newcombe, 1996, p. 134). Children may now be able to understand and perhaps accept another person's point of view. For these reasons, we can ask students to take part in class discussions that reflect on activities

CONCEPT 26.7

Understanding and adapting to where children are in their cognitive comprehension is important in structuring meaningful activities for personal and social responsibility.

Providing students with opportunities to share their ideas and to express concerns can lead to positive personal and social behavior in physical education.

conducted during that day's physical education class, previous classes, and future classes. These discussions may help children understand more about themselves and others.

As a teacher you must also analyze and determine what level of personal and social responsibility specific physical education activities facilitate or require. The

---

TEXT BOX 26.2

Cooperative Game, Dance, and Gymnastics Activities

Cooperative game: "Recycling"

Movement Skills: Locomotor skills—walking, skipping, galloping

Movement Concepts: Pathways, levels, speed, directions, relationship to others

Equipment: Recyclable materials, recycling bins, music

Social Responsibility: Working with others to figure out a problem

Personal Responsibility: Willingness to help determine the answer

Procedures: Several small recyclable "things" are spread out all over the gymnasium floor. Four recycling bins are positioned at each of the four sides of the movement space. Children are divided into four recycling teams. Play begins by having team players walk quickly throughout the space to gather recyclable materials. Each team is provided their own "Recycling Clue Sheet" and must gather items that are described and specified on this clue sheet or task card. The first team to successfully gather the correct recyclables receives a "commendation" from the city mayor!

Sample Clue Sheet:

1. This item is round, connected, and used to keep many things together. (plastic rings for soda, water bottles)
2. This item could be used when sending a package through the mail to a friend. (paper bag)
3. This item is used to help you have a nice hairstyle! (shampoo bottle)
4. This item is a condiment. (old catsup bottle)
5. These can be used over and over again for storing things in your refrigerator. (baggies)

Cooperative dance/gymnastics: "The Seven Wonders of the World"

Movement Skills: Locomotor skills, balance/stability skills

Movement Concepts: Levels, shapes, sizes

Equipment: Music

Social Responsibility: Working together to form a shape or balanced sculpture

Personal Responsibility: Providing suggestions and making new shapes or balances

Procedures: Dance. Students are asked to find out about the Seven Wonders of the World. Then each group is assigned or chooses one of these "Wonders." The goal of each group is to move into and out of a shape that represents their Wonder. Each student must be actively involved and contribute at least one idea to "creating" their Wonder shape. Music can accompany this dance.

Variation for Gymnastics: Have students use rolling or transfer of weight for their Wonder shape sculpture. The shape sculpture could also be restricted to counterbalances, inverted balances, or any appropriate balance for the skill level of the students in class.

---

following are questions that you can consider when selecting or designing physical education lesson content to promote personal and social responsibility:

- Does the activity offer students an opportunity to accept the decisions and/or actions of others? (Level I/Respect)
- Does the activity provide an opportunity for each person to contribute? (Level II/Participation)
- Does the activity offer students an opportunity to participate with differing amounts of effort? (Not all students are at the same place at the same time!) For example, children could play one of three different versions of a Level III soccer game (see chapter 21, "Developmental Games"). Children would select the game that matches the level of effort they wish to put into the game. (Level II/Participation and Level III/Self-Direction)
- Does the content offer children opportunities to try out ideas or activities they have never been exposed to before? (Level III/Self-Direction)
- Does the activity provide opportunities for group or partner activity and promote cooperation among students? (Level III/Self-Direction and Level IV/Caring)
- Does the activity elicit "caring for others," perhaps as a partner or small-group activity that involves peer teaching or peer assessment? (Level IV/Caring)

You can address many of these questions by applying the spectrum of teaching styles (see chapter 10, "Teaching Styles"). As you saw in chapter 10, these styles give children progressively more responsibility in the decision-making process. Cooperative learning also provides many opportunities to foster personal and social responsibility. Steven Grineski's (1996) work in this area is exemplary. The text box provides examples of cooperative games, dance, and gymnastics activities that teachers can use to facilitate children's personal and social responsibility. It is important to remember that after the activity, students should have the opportunity to assess how they did or did not demonstrate specific level behaviors.

Summary

Physical educators should address all three domains of learning (i.e., cognitive, affective, and psychomotor). The purpose of addressing the affective domain within the developmental physical education program is to help develop positive attitudes and behaviors on the part of the children, which in turn promote a more positive and effective learning environment. The affective domain of development encompasses children's self-concept (i.e., *personal understanding* and *views about themselves*) as well as their attitudes and feelings toward others (i.e., *social views* and *understanding of others*).

Teachers need to be familiar not only with developmental factors that affect children's ability to demonstrate personal and social responsibility but also with strategies for fostering a sense of responsibility. Using inclusion games and rules, using the inclusion style of teaching, offering choices to encourage participation, allowing children to "earn" independent time, and using the reciprocal teaching style are examples of such strategies. Among activities that promote responsibility are those that provide opportunities to accept the decisions or actions of others, opportunities for each person to contribute, opportunities for students to participate with differing amounts of effort, and opportunities for cooperation between partners or within a group.

Terms to Remember

Excellent Readings

Cochran, D. (2001). The three T's of conflict resolution. *TEPE, 12* (1), 20-21.

Gruber, J.J. (1985). Physical activity and self-esteem development in children: A meta-analysis. *Academy Papers, 19,* 30-48.

Hartinger, K. (1997.) Teaching responsibility. *TEPE 3* (5), 15-17.

Horrocks, R. (1978). Resolving conflict in the gymnasium. *JOPERD, 49,* 61.

Lickona, T. (1991). *Educating for character: How our schools can teach respect and responsibility.* New York: Bantam.

McHugh, E. (1995). Going "beyond the physical": Social skills and physical education. *JOPERD 66* (4), 18-21.

Newcombe, N. (1996). *Child development—change over time.* New York: Harper Collins.

Glossary

academic concept learning: Using movement activities as a learning tool for *reinforcing* knowledge concepts in language arts, mathematics, science, and social studies.

accent: The emphasis given to any one beat, usually the first beat of each measure.

accident report: A means of minimizing legal liability that involves filling out and filing a detailed report on the nature of a specific injury, specific procedures followed, and the events leading up to the injury.

accordion principle: A social behavior shaping technique in which time is given to or taken away from students based on their level of successful self-direction.

active learning time: The amount of time actively engaged in learning activities directly related to the objectives of the lesson.

active listening: Using various means to convey your attention to the verbal messages of another through the use of eye contact, directly facing the speaker, and verbal feedback.

activity concept learning: Learning about *where* the body should move in terms of patterns, formations, rules, and strategies for recreational and sport activities.

activity duration: A key component of fitness enhancement referring to the length of time the heart rate is elevated.

activity frequency: A key component of fitness enhancement referring to the number of times per week that moderate to vigorous physical activity is engaged in order to achieve a training effect.

activity intensity: A key component of fitness enhancement that refers to an elevated heart rate of about 150 beats per minute required in order to achieve an aerobic training effect.

activity variety: Sometimes called "activity type"; a key component of fitness enhancement referring to taking part in several different types of fitness enhancing activities.

act of nature: A legal defense referring to something completely unexpected and totally unforeseen occurring that was totally out of the control of the defendant.

adapted physical education: A program of physical activities that have been modified to meet the needs of individuals diagnosed with a specific disability or limiting condition.

advanced/fine-tuning level: The third and final level of learning a new movement skill in which the learner refines performance and individualizes the task.

advocacy: The process of informing others of the benefits of our profession and the art of making the views of our profession count when it comes to offering quality physical education programs offered daily.

aerobic dance: Exercise to music led by an instructor who cues the participants on the proper exercise for each phrase of music.

aerobic endurance: The ability of the heart, lungs, and vascular system to supply oxygen to the working muscles during exercise.

aerobic exercise: Participation in physical activities in which the heart rate is elevated above a threshold of training (about 140-180 bpm in children) and maintained at that level for an extended period of time (about 15 minutes or more), as in long distance running and swimming.

affective growth: In a movement sense, the ability to act, interact, and react effectively and appropriately with others and self in movement situations.

age-group appropriateness: The inclusion of learning experiences into the physical education experience based on chronological age or grade level.

age of reason: A chronological age, usually age 12, in which an individual without mitigating factors is considered to be capable of complying to imposed rules and regulations.

aggressive behavior: Teacher or student behaviors that among other things are nagging, accusative, argumentative, and bullying.

agility: The ability to change direction of the entire body quickly and with accuracy while moving from one point to another, as in negotiating an obstacle course for time.

aim: The overarching intent or purpose of what we do. In the case of physical education: learning-to-move and learning-through-movement.

anaerobic exercise: High intensity exercise of short duration that does not depend on the body's ability to supply oxygen, as in sprinting in track and swimming.

analysis paralysis: A term sometimes given to what happens to an individual when a previously well-learned and automatically performed movement skill is brought back to a conscious cognitive level.

antecedents: A behavioral approach to discipline that links the behavior to be changed to actions occurring directly before the behavior to the consequences that will occur after the behavior.

anticipatory set: See *lesson introduction.*

application stage: The second stage within the intermediate/practice level of learning a new movement skill in which the individual utilizes the skill in some form of recreational or sport setting.

arthritis: A painful musculoskeletal limitation characterized by inflammation of the joints.

assertive behavior: Teacher or student behaviors that among other things are respectful, persistent, honest, and straightforward.

assumption of risk: A legal defense indicating that in certain situations one assumes responsibility for his or her own safety that is heavily dependent upon the nature of the activity and if it is engaged in as a requirement or on a voluntary basis.

asthma: A pulmonary limitation affecting the bronchial tubes that interferes with normal breathing and may range from mild to severe.

ataxia: A form of cerebral palsy characterized by very poor balance and coordination resulting in slow, deliberate, and wobbly movements.

athetosis: A form of cerebral palsy characterized by involuntary, jerky, uncoordinated, random, and almost constant movement.

atrophy: Decreases in muscle size brought about by lack of regular use.

attitudes: Opinions about something or someone that is evidenced in one's behavior through compliance, identification, and internalization.

attractive nuisance: A place or a thing that if left unsupervised is deemed to be a contributing factor to the injury or death.

authentic assessment: Sometimes called "alternative assessment"; contextually relevant means of evaluating student progress in the cognitive, affective, and motor domains.

authority style: The manner in which a teacher exerts specific behaviors to affect positive discipline on the part of students.

autism: An emotional disorder that manifests itself prior to age three, persists throughout life, and is characterized by significant delays in both language and social development.

axial movements: Sometimes called "non-locomotor movements"; they are stability skills in which the axis of the body revolves around a fixed point and includes movements such as bending, stretching, twisting, turning, reaching, lifting, and falling.

axis of the body: An imaginary point, center of gravity, around which the body would be perfectly balanced.

balance: The ability to maintain one's equilibrium, in static postures or dynamic activities, in relation to the force of gravity and to make minute alterations in the body when it is placed in various positions.

ball bouncing: Receiving force from an object and immediately imparting force from that object in a downward motion (hand bounce or dribble) or at ground level in a horizontal direction (foot dribble), without the use of an implement.

ball rolling: Imparting force to a ball in a forward direction, at ground level, in a horizontal direction using one or both hands.

beginning/novice level: The first level of learning a new movement skill in which the learner gains a general awareness of the requirements of the task, explores various movement possibilities, and discovers more efficient ways of performing.

behavioral approach to discipline: Teacher-centered discipline that relies on external control techniques, specified consequences for misbehavior, positive reinforcement for good behavior, and direct teacher control.

behavioral learning theory: A learning theory that contends that learning occurs from the outside in through the correct reproduction of events.

behavioral objectives: A form of specific objectives that are observable, measurable, and establish the criterion for performance.

being a good sport: The process of behaving in a moral fashion within a sport context.

belonging: An aspect of self-esteem that involves a feeling of being accepted and valued as a member of a defined group such as a class or team.

benchmark objectives: A form of specific objectives that represent a sampling of specific marker objectives to be achieved by a certain time.

body awareness: A three-component learning process that involves knowledge of the body parts, knowledge of what they can do, and knowledge of how to make them move in the process of gaining greater understanding of the nature of the body and its movement in space.

body composition: Lean body mass in proportion to fat body mass.

body in flight: Momentary or suspended loss of contact with the supporting surface.

body of the lesson: The third part of the lesson plan that contains the central focus of the lesson and emphasizes both skill development and skill application.

body rolling: A fundamental stability skill in which the body moves through space around its own axis while momentarily inverted, as in a forward or backward roll.

breach of duty: The second of four requirements for an individual to be declared negligent in a court of law that demonstrates the accused has breeched the expected standard of behavior.

bulletin board: Displays in the gymnasium and school hallways that provide a message, create interest, impart knowledge, and record information specific to the physical education program.

cardiovascular endurance: The ability to perform numerous repetitions of an activity requiring considerable use of the circulatory and respiratory systems.

cardiovascular limitations: A limiting condition that includes reduced or restricted physical activity due to congenital heart disease, rheumatic heart disease, coronary heart disease, and hypertensive heart disease.

catching: Receiving force from an object and retaining it in the hands.

categories of movement: One of a variety of ways of classifying movement. In this case by its intended function: locomotion, manipulation, and stability.

center of gravity: In geometric shapes the exact center of the object. In asymmetrical shapes such as the human body, it is a constantly changing point when the body is in motion and always moves in the direction of the movement or the additional weight.

cephalocaudal development: The general tendency toward gradual downward progression in increased motor control, especially during infancy, from the head to the feet.

cerebral palsy: A nonprogressive, permanent neuromuscular limitation caused by damage to the motor area of the cortex resulting in paralysis, weakness, tremor, or uncoordinated movement depending on type and severity.

character: In a social sense, how one lives in response to what is held to be important, meaningful, and worthwhile.

checking for retention: A process by which the instructor asks questions about or requires a demonstration of the just completed lesson or previous lesson to determine what the student remembers.

checking for understanding: A process in which the instructor asks recall-type questions of the learner or asks for a brief demonstration of the material previously taught to determine if the material was comprehended.

child-centered methods: Sometimes called "indirect teaching methods," in which emphasis is placed on the learning process by the teacher with emphasis on the concept of learning-to-learn.

childhood obesity: Being at or above the 95th percentile of weight for height. A condition that has reached near epidemic proportions in many developed countries, especially the United States.

class protocols: Predetermined ways of handling situations that frequently arise in classroom settings.

classroom management: The process of organizing students for learning, using class protocols and rules for good behavior.

club programs: Similar to intramurals except greater emphasis is placed on further instruction rather than competition.

cognitive concept learning: The process by which information is organized, put into memory, and made available for recall and application in a variety of settings.

cognitive learning: In a movement sense, progressive change in the ability to think, reason, and act to new movement settings.

cognitive learning theory: A learning theory that contends learning is an internal process occurring from the inside-out through incorrect mastery attempts.

cognitive maps: Mental images of how movement skills are to be performed that are retained in memory and can be recalled, as necessary, in a split second.

cognitive set: See *lesson introduction.*

combination stage: The first stage within the intermediate/practice level of learning a new movement skill in which the learner puts two or more movement skills together and practices for greater efficiency and control.

command style: A reproduction teaching style in which the teacher makes all of the decisions concerning what is to be performed, how it is to be done, and when it is to be performed; and the learner practices the "correct" performance.

competence: An aspect of self-concept that deals with the actual ability to accomplish the achievement demands of a particular task.

compliance: In a social setting, doing something with the hope of getting a positive response from someone else.

concept learning: In a movement setting, permanent change in one's motor behavior brought about by experiences designed to foster understanding of the movement concepts, skill concepts, fitness concepts, and activity concepts of the developmental physical education program.

conceptual framework: The essential concepts upon which a particular curricular approach is based. Certain concepts, theories, and research findings form the conceptual framework of the developmental physical education curriculum.

concrete operations phase: Jean Piaget's third phase of cognitive development, occurring during the elementary school years, characterized by curiosity, exploration, experimentation, and self-discovery of new cognitive structures usually through games, play, and general physical activity.

concrete representations: The typical cognitive level of elementary school students, indicating the need for use of clear-cut terms and "hands-on" learning.

concurrent feedback: Process cues provided to the learner during performance of a movement task.

conditions for implementation: The reality of the terms under which a curriculum is to be put into action.

conflict resolution: A specific problem-solving technique involving communication dialogue between two disagreeing students that involves gathering information, clarification, identification, brainstorming, agreement, and closure.

constructivist approach to discipline: A cognitive approach to learning that permits the learner to construct and actively derive personal meaning in terms of how to act or behave.

Content Standards: A subsection of the National Standards for Physical Education (NASPE, 1995) that focuses on what students should be able to do in terms of both movement skills and movement knowledge.

contingency contracts: Signed individual or group behavior codes designed cooperatively by students and teachers outlining expected behaviors and the corresponding consequences of their violation.

continuous movements: Movements that are repeated for a specified period of time, as in swimming, running, and cycling.

contributory negligence: The plaintiff being held partially or wholly at fault for the injury received or loss incurred, and heavily influenced by one's age, and physical and mental capabilities.

conventional games: Games that exist in a culture, often passed down from generation to generation, and that are available for anyone to use.

convergent discovery style: A production teaching style in which students solve task-related problems assigned by the teacher but without guiding clues. The teacher provides feedback to the learner but does not provide the solution for "correct" performance.

cooperative games: Developmental Level II games that minimize competition and place emphasis on group interaction, positive socialization, and working together.

cooperative learning: A process of positive socialization that involves working with others to achieve a common goal.

coordination: The ability to integrate separate motor systems with varying sensory modalities into efficient movement, as in kicking or dribbling a ball.

core content of games: A way of classifying games around interrelated ideas or content areas including: game forms, movement skills, basic strategies/tactics, and criteria for assessing the educational value of a game.

counterbalancing: The process of keeping two individuals in balance by moving their weight and force inward, or toward one another.

counter-tension: The process of keeping two individuals in balance by moving their weight and force away from one another.

country and western dances: A form of folk dance that reflects the culture of the early settlers and includes activities such as line dances and square dances.

creative dance: A form of rhythmic movement that permits the expression and interpretation of ideas, emotions, and feelings.

critical thinking: Skillful and responsible thinking that facilitates good judgment. Also called *higher-order thinking*.

critical thinking dispositions: Habitual ways of behaving that are conducive to critical thinking such as being well informed, open-minded, sensitive to other's ideas, patient, and willing to share ideas.

cultural norms: Acceptable standards of behavior expected of all members of a society no matter what their status or perceived role.

cultural socialization: The process of modifying one's behaviors to conform to the expectations of an individual or group.

curricular balance: The relative emphasis of the program in terms of time spent in specific content emphases.

curricular goals: An outgrowth of the mission statement consisting of broad areas of continuing importance and curricular emphasis.

cystic fibrosis: A progressive noncurable pulmonary limitation in which the lungs fill with mucus over time, causing difficulty in breathing and eventual death.

daily fitness programs: A specific time set aside daily, in addition to the physical education program, in which the entire school (students, faculty, and staff) engages in a variety of planned fitness activities.

daily lesson plan: A more specific subset of the unit plan, based on developmental appropriateness and age appropriateness of your students, that contains the specific objectives and detailed learning activities of the lesson.

damage: The fourth of four requirements for an individual to be declared negligent in a court of law that refers to a proven injury or loss as a result of the combined effects of the preceding three conditions.

development: The continuous process of change, both positive and negative, throughout the life cycle from conception to death.

developmental curricular model: The curricular model of children's physical education based on the concept that development of one's fundamental and specialized movement skills occurs in distinct but often overlapping phases and stages of motor development, in each of the three categories of movement, stability, locomotion, and manipulation.

developmental gymnastics: Also referred to as

"educational gymnastics" and not to be confused with "Olympic gymnastics," is self-testing in nature and permits the learner to test fitness, skill, body awareness, and movement coordination in an individualized manner.

developmental physical education: Physical education programs that place emphasis on movement skills acquisition and increased physical competence based on the developmental level of the learner (individual appropriateness) and characteristics of the group (age-group appropriateness).

developmental sequence: The orderly, predictable sequence of increased motor control and movement competence in the normally developing individual.

developmental skill theme: A movement skill or group of related movement skills upon which a lesson or unit of study is based in order to achieve the goals of the program.

developmental variability: Typical age variations in the rate of movement skill acquisition seen among normally developing children.

differentiation: Gradual progression, over time, in the ability to distinguish between various muscle groups moving from gross globular motor control to increased refinement and precision of movement.

directing the learner: The second level of teacher intervention in the learning process in which the teacher, because of the complexity of the movement task or the inability of the learners to comply, uses one or more reproduction teaching styles.

directional awareness: A two-component learning process that involves direction in space that is made up of laterality and directionality.

directionality: The name given to the actual meaning of directional terms such as left, right, up, down, in, out, among, behind, between, and so forth.

direction of movement: Moving from one point to another in various directions such as forward or backward, right or left, up or down, and into or out of.

discipline: The process of enabling students to use their time effectively to meet the learning objectives of the lesson without interfering with the attempts of others to achieve the goals of the lesson.

discovery games: Another term used for low-level familiarization type games that help the learner become aware of the spatial requirements of the activity while at the same time experimenting with how the game is played.

discovery stage: The second stage within the beginning/novice level of learning a new movement skill in which the learner begins to find more efficient ways of performing the task.

discrete movement: Any movement that has a definite beginning and ending, as in throwing a ball.

distance messages: Nonverbal communication conveyed to others by one's physical distance from the learner.

distractibility: A behavioral condition typified by inattention, failing to finish tasks, difficulty in concentrating, and difficulty in staying on task with play activities.

divergent production style: A production teaching style in which the teacher decides on the content of the lesson and structures movement problems while the learner explores and self-discovers a variety of movement solutions.

dodging: A fundamental stability skill in which quick, deceptive changes in direction are made in either a forward, sideward, or backward direction, often accompanied with axial movements such as bending, stretching, and twisting.

dynamic balance: A component of any locomotor or manipulative movement skill in which the body moves through space, causing the center of gravity to constantly shift; the ability to maintain one's equilibrium while the body is in motion, as in walking on a balance beam.

dynamic endurance: The ability of a muscle or group of muscles to shorten and lengthen repeatedly through progressive resistance training using light to moderate resistance with a moderate number of repetitions.

eager movers: Children who are active movers and playful movers willing to participate in a variety of physical activities.

early puberty: Beginning the preadolescent growth spurt and the development of secondary sex characteristics two or more years earlier than one's age-mates.

echolalia: The involuntary repetition of the words of others.

effective teachers: Individuals who through planned instruction are able to bring about positive change in the learner in school or community settings, within the classroom or gymnasium, and in recreational or sport settings.

effort awareness: How the body moves in terms of the amount of force applied as well as the timing and flow of movement.

elementary stage: The second stage within the fundamental movement phase, primarily dependent on maturation, during which major elements of the movement task begin to become more coordinated and controlled, but some elements are missing or performed in an awkward manner.

elements of rhythm: The five rhythmic fundamentals of underlying beat, tempo, accent, intensity, and rhythmic pattern.

emergency care policy: A carefully thought-out written set of risk management procedures to be followed in the event of an accident or injury occurring in the gymnasium, playground, or other facilities.

emotional disorder: The inability to learn that cannot be explained by sensory problems, health factors, or intellectual deficits and leaves the person unable to make and maintain satisfactory interpersonal relationships with peer and adults; characterized by inappropriate behaviors, unhappiness, depression, or physical symptoms in response to school or personal problems.

encouraging others: Giving positive support to others and celebrating their "victories."

entry-level assessment: The second step in planning a movement skill theme that involves informal observation and assessment of students' current level of movement skill functioning. Sometimes called "formative assessment."

environmental retardation: A secondary cause of mental retardation caused by factors such as infections and toxins to the expectant mother, the infant, or the young child.

environmental setting: The ecology of the immediate surroundings in which an individual is attempting to learn.

epilepsy: A condition caused by electrochemical imbalances in the brain that is typified by seizures ranging from mild to severe.

error correction: Changing a well-learned but habitually incorrect movement performance.

established duty: The first of four requirements for an individual to be declared negligent in a court of law that establishes that the accused has a duty to follow certain standards of practice that protect others from unreasonable risks.

exit-level assessment: Evaluation conducted at the conclusion of a movement skill theme to determine if learning has occurred. Sometimes called "summative assessment."

exploration stage: The first stage within the beginning/novice level of learning a new movement skill in which the learner develops an initial awareness of the requirements of the task by experimenting with a variety of movement possibilities.

expressive movement: The essence of what dance is.

extended curriculum: Program responsibilities of the teacher that go beyond the basic instructional program. In physical education this may include club programs, recess and noon-hour programs, as well as before-school and after-school extended care programs.

external feedback: Sometimes called "augmented feedback," takes the form of verbal cues from the instructor or cues from some form of mechanical device.

externally paced: Movement activities that involve making rapid responses to a constantly changing and unpredictable environment, as in performing a layup shot during a game of basketball.

extracurricular activity policy: A written policy governing the conduct and supervision of students attending an event outside the normal school day, either on school grounds or at another location.

facial expressions: Nonverbal messages involving changes in facial features.

facility report: A means of minimizing legal liability that involves periodic inspection of all facilities under one's control.

fair play: Taking part in an activity in a manner consistent with the rules and commonly accepted behavioral expectations of the game.

familiarization games: The type of low-level games that are used to help the learner become acquainted with one or two fundamental movement skills involved in playing the game.

feedback: Information received as the result of some form of response either during performance of a movement task, known as knowledge of performance (KP), or after performance of the task, known as knowledge of results (KR).

field day: Informal all-school participation in a variety of fun activities, usually near the end of the school year.

fine motor manipulation: Movement skills that involve imparting force, using one or more small muscle groups, to objects and/or receiving force from objects, as in playing the violin, playing darts, or writing a letter.

fit movers: Individuals who take responsibility for gaining, maintaining, and enhancing both their health-related and performance-related fitness.

fitness awards: Extrinsic motivators used to recognize individuals who have achieved a predetermined standard of fitness excellence.

fitness breaks: A set period of time outside of the regular physical education program, usually 15-20 minutes, set aside for all students, faculty, and staff to participate in fitness enhancing activities.

fitness concept learning: Learning about *what* to do to gain and maintain one's personal level of fitness.

fitness education: The process by which children become fit movers while at the same time becoming informed movers and eager movers.

fitness education materials: Educational and motivational fitness information ranging from comic books and videotapes to Web sites and CD-ROM applications.

fitness homework: A technique for motivating children to increase levels of physical activity by assigning them fitness tasks to do at home or at school with a parent or friend.

fitness training: The process by which children become fit movers with little or no regard to helping them become informed movers and eager movers.

FITT principle: An acronym that stands for Frequency, Intensity, Timing (duration), and Type of exercise, closely associated with the principles of overload, specificity, and progression.

flow of movement: The continuity of a movement.

folk dances: Structured dance activities typical of different cultures around the world.

formal games: A complex lead-up game involving significant use of rules and strategies.

formal operations: A stage of cognitive development described by Jean Piaget as the ability of the child to think and reason in more abstract terms, beginning around age 10.

fundamental movement phase: The period of time, typically ranging from 2-6 years of age, during which children learn a wide variety of basic locomotor, manipulative, and stability movement skills.

fundamental movement skill: An organized series of basic movements that involve the combination of movement patterns of two or more body parts.

gallop: A combination of two fundamental locomotor skills involving a brief flight phase and repeated action involving stepping forward on the lead foot and a leaping-like action of the trailing foot as it is brought up to but not in advance of the lead foot.

game categories: A way of classifying games by which the various components of a game are grouped by its physical requirements, structure, and personal requirements.

game forms: Either conventional or original games.

games: Activities in which one or more children engage in cooperative, collaborative, or competitive play, with or without an object, within the structure of certain rules and boundaries (Allison & Barrett, 2000).

games for understanding: A way of classifying games based on the strategies used, including target games, net/wall games, invasion games, and striking games.

general objectives: An outgrowth of curricular goals that represents broadly based desired outcomes for the learner to achieve.

general space: The total space that is available in a room, gymnasium, or playground.

genetic retardation: A tertiary cause of mental retardation brought about by chromosomal abnormalities, of which Down syndrome is the most common.

gestures: Movement of the body, head, arms, hands, or face that expresses a nonverbal idea, opinion, or emotion.

Giraffe Club: A social behavior shaping technique recognizing those that "stick their neck out" for others by helping their peers during class learning sessions.

goal: A standard toward which one continually expends effort in an attempt to achieve.

goal setting: Establishing a standard to achieve. Goal setting must be individual, set in relation to past performance, and have an end in view.

grand mal seizures: A severe form of epilepsy resulting in convulsions and unconsciousness and characterized by aura, tonic, and clonic phases.

Grandpa's/Grandma's law: A social behavior shaping technique in which the class, if properly behaved for the first half of the class, is permitted to choose the activity for the second half from among "class favorites" identified by the students.

gross motor manipulation: Movement skills that involve imparting force, using one or more large muscle groups, to objects and receiving force from objects, as in throwing, catching, kicking, and volleying activities.

group affiliation: The overwhelming need to belong or to be part of an identified group that begins in childhood and peaks during later adolescence.

group initiatives: A type of cooperative game that emphasizes small or large groups working together to accomplish a given task.

group problem-solving: A type of cooperative game similar to group initiative activities except with the addition of group problem-solving for movement challenges posed by the instructor.

growth retardation: Delayed or impaired growth resulting from severe, chronic malnutrition. The extent of impairment depends upon the severity, duration, and time of onset of undernourishment.

guided discovery style: A production teaching style in which the teacher guides the learner through assigned tasks using a sequence of movement questions that permit individualized problem-solving on the part of each learner.

gym shows: A formal demonstration involving all or most of the students in the school that highlights the learning activities of the year and serves as an opportunity to showcase the physical education program.

health-related fitness: That aspect of physical fitness composed of the following: muscular strength, muscular endurance, cardiovascular endurance, joint flexibility, and body composition.

Healthy People 2000: A major U.S. federal government report first released in 1990 proposing an agenda for targeting the prevention of disease in which physical activity and physical fitness play a prominent role. More recently, *Healthy People 2010* has further extended this important health agenda into the 21st century.

hearing impairment: A sensory impairment in which the child has difficulty processing verbal information with or without amplification in such a way that it interferes with educational performance.

higher-order thinking: The process of involving the learner in comparing and contrasting ideas, making deductions, generating alternative responses, analyzing situations, or synthesizing information. Also called *critical thinking.*

hop: A fundamental locomotor skill in which the body takes off and lands on the same foot in a horizontal or vertical direction.

hyperactivity: A behavioral condition characterized by extreme difficulty in sitting still long enough to complete a task.

hypertrophy: Increases in muscle size brought about by regular use.

identification: In a social setting, adopting another's attitude or values.

improper instruction: A claim of negligence due to inadequate or improper use of teaching techniques.

impulsivity: A behavioral condition characterized by acting before thinking, difficulty in getting organized, and needing considerable supervision.

inadequate supervision: A claim of negligence due to failure to properly supervise an individual or class.

inclusion: The process of integrating children with disabilities into the regular classroom and physical education program.

inclusion style: A reproduction teaching style in which the teacher determines the content of the lesson and the learners determine the level of performance based on individual ability.

individual appropriateness: The inclusion of learning experiences into the physical education program geared to learner's phases and stages of motor development and the levels and stages of movement skill learning.

individualized assessment: A personalized progress report that the teacher can send home periodically so that parents can keep abreast of their children's progress in the developmental physical education program.

Individualized Education Program (IEP): A provision of P.L. 105-17 (Individuals with Disabilities Act) mandating that all children diagnosed with disabilities be offered educational experiences in the "least restrictive environment" as determined by this personalized evaluation of their present level of functioning.

individualized stage: The second and final stage within the advanced/fine-tuning level of learning a new movement skill in which the learner personalizes the movement performance around specific strengths and limitations.

informed movers: Individuals who know about and are able to apply fitness concepts to their own lives.

initial stage: The first stage within the fundamental movement phase during which the individual makes the first observable and purposeful attempts at performing a particular movement task. Although the movements are uncoordinated and often lack major components of the skill, there is a definite attempt to achieve the goal of the movement task.

in-school violence: Acts of aggression from one or more children directed at fellow students, teachers, and/or staff.

instant replays: A technique for using a relay-type activity as an on-the-spot means of bringing attention to and reinforcing particular aspects of a movement skill in a game situation.

integration: Coordinated interaction of sensory and motor mechanisms as found in eye-hand, eye-foot, and eye-body coordination activities.

intensity: The loudness or softness of the movement or music.

intensity scale: A social behavior shaping technique consisting of a 0-10 scale posted on a gymnasium wall that helps students personally access their level of effort and willingness to participate in the class activities of the day.

intermediate/practice level: The second level of learning a new movement skill in which the learner begins to combine and apply movement skills into more complex movement forms.

internal feedback: Sometimes called "intrinsic feedback," is obtained by the learner as a result of performing the task itself.

internalization: In a social setting, taking on a particular behavior as part of one's own value system.

internally paced: Movement activities that require a fixed performance under a given set of environmental cues, as in making a free-throw shot in basketball.

interscholastic program: Competitive sport programs, usually conducted after school hours, between groups of students from different schools.

intramurals: Competitive sport programs conducted before, during, or after school between groups of students from the same school.

inverted supports: Either static or dynamic balance skills in which emphasis is placed on maintaining one's equilibrium when placed in inverted positions, as in performing a headstand (static), or body rolling movement, such as a forward or backward roll (dynamic).

inviting the learner: The first level of teacher intervention in the learning process in which the teacher uses production teaching styles to satisfy the learning objectives of the lesson.

isokinetic strength: The ability of a muscle or group of muscles to accommodate to variable resistance throughout the full range of the process of alternately shortening and lengthening.

isometric strength: The ability of a muscle or group of muscles to maintain a contracted state over a period of several seconds.

isotonic strength: The ability of a muscle or group of muscles to perform a maximal or near-maximal effort once or for a limited number of repetitions, in which the muscles alternately shorten and lengthen.

Jacksonian seizures: A form of epilepsy with intermittent contraction and relaxation of the muscles in one part of the body and spreading to others, similar to grand mal seizures but lacking the aura and tonic phases.

joint flexibility: The ability of the various joints of the body to move through their full range of potential motion.

jump: A fundamental locomotor skill involving an explosive takeoff and landing on both feet in either a forward, downward, or upward direction.

juvenile rheumatoid arthritis: The most common form of arthritis found in children, it varies greatly in severity. It attacks the entire skeletal system and results in inflammation, stiffness, and acute pain in the joints.

kicking: Imparting force to an object with the use of the foot and leg.

knowledge of performance (KP): Information provided to the learner during the movement task leads to error correction and the desired response.

knowledge of results (KR): Information provided to the learner as a result of performance.

kyphosis: A postural deviation characterized by an exaggerated curve in the thoracic region of the spine that may result in rounded shoulders, winged scapula, and forward head tilt.

large apparatus: Equipment traditionally used in developmental gymnastics such as parallel bars, balance beam, turning bar, indoor climbers, and cargo nets.

laterality: An internal "feel" for direction that enables one to know left from right and top from bottom without giving conscious attention to the task.

lead-up games: Developmental Level III games that make use of two or more sport skills, rules, or procedures used in playing the official version of the game.

leap: A fundamental locomotor skill similar to a run but with a sustained loss of contact with the supporting surface and with greater elevation and distance covered.

learning: A process that results in a relatively permanent change in behavior brought about as a result of practice or experience.

learning disability: One who is restricted in the ability to read, write, think, speak, spell, or do mathematical operations due to the inability to fully utilize basic psychological processes involved in using spoken or written language. Individuals with learning disabilities do not have their difficulty traced to visual, auditory, or motor disabilities, or to mental retardation.

learning readiness: The convergence of the requirements of the task to be learned with the biology of the individual and the conditions of the learning environment.

learning-through-movement: The aim of physi-cal education that focuses on the cognitive and affective aspects of children's development.

learning-to-move: The aim of children's physical education that centers on promoting movement skill acquisition, increased motor control and movement competence, and enhanced levels of physical fitness and physical activity.

legal liability: Also called "tort liability," a term meaning that someone is at fault, that this fault caused injury or loss to another person, and that someone is legally responsible.

lesson closure: The last step in a creative dance lesson in which the teacher may conduct a cool-down session, view some students' dance ideas, review the lesson, evaluate the lesson, and/or preview the next lesson.

lesson introduction: A more specific subset of the lesson plan, sometimes called *set induction, anticipatory set,* or *cognitive set,* that sets the tone for the lesson to come and provokes student interest and enthusiasm for the lesson.

lesson review: The second part of the lesson plan following the lesson introduction that provides a brief focus on the highlights of the previous lesson.

lesson summary: The last part of the daily lesson that includes review of the highlights of the current lesson and organized class dismissal.

level: A term used in movement settings to denote where the body moves, as in a high, medium, or low level.

Level I dance: Teacher-dependent rhythmic activities in which the learner is provided some form of rhythmic accompaniment, along with simple movement challenges, with the intent of promoting a greater sense of self-awareness and motor creativity through use of movement exploration and guided discovery techniques.

Level I games: Low-level games that are easy to play, have few and simple rules, require little or no equipment, and may be varied in many ways.

Level I gymnastics skills: Activities for learners at the beginning/novice level of movement skill learning that promote control of the body in both locomotor and stability movement skills, individually and in combination with one another.

Level I/Respect: The first level of developing personal and social well-being that reflects self-control, peaceful conflict resolution, and inclusion by working cooperatively with others.

Level II dance: Teacher-student interdependent rhythmic activities in which the teacher provides a movement problem and offers guidance and feedback to the learner as needed.

Level II games: Active games involving the use of two or more movement skills and movement concepts, and are more complex than Level I games taking the form of skill challenge games.

Level II gymnastics skills: Activities for learners at a slightly higher level than those at Level I that emphasize body balancing and body rolling.

Level II/Participation: The second level in developing personal and social well-being that involves all learners making an effort to try new activities in a cooperative and respectful manner.

Level III dance: Teacher-initiated but student-directed rhythmic activities in which the teacher provides the stimulus and leaves development of the idea up to the learner.

Level III games: Active games that are more complex than Level II games in that they involve more rules and complex strategies as well as greater skill development in order to be successful.

Level III gymnastics skills: Activities for learners at the intermediate/practice level of movement skill learning that emphasize wheeling actions, inverted supports, and a variety of springing movements.

Level III/Self-Direction: The third level in developing personal and social well-being in which students are independent learners who stay on-task without being prompted by the teacher.

Level IV/Caring: The fourth level in developing personal and social well-being in which students show genuine compassion for others without expecting something in return.

Level IV dance: Student-initiated and student-directed rhythmic experiences in which learners generate and develop their own ideas. Guidance and feedback are provided only as needed or requested.

Level IV games: Active games that take the form of official individual, dual, and team sport games played throughout the world.

Level IV gymnastics skills: Activities for learners at the advanced/fine-tuning level of movement skill learning that focus on the body in flight, including in-flight rolls and advanced springing movements.

level of movement: See *level.*

lifelong utilization stage: The third stage within the specialized movement skill phase in which individuals select a small set of physical activities to pursue for fun, fitness, and perhaps competition during their adult years.

line of gravity: An imaginary line that extends vertically through the center of gravity, through the base of support when the body is in balance and outside of the base of support when the body is out of balance.

locomotor exploratory activities: Movement activities designed for individuals at the initial and elementary stages in their fundamental locomotor skills that use the movement framework of effort, space, and relationship awareness.

locomotor game activities: Low-level game activities designed for the application and enhancement of fundamental locomotor skills.

locomotor guided discovery activities: Movement activities designed for individuals at the elementary stage of developing their fundamental locomotor abilities that use a guided problem-solving approach.

locomotor movement skills: Movement skills that involve transporting the body in a horizontal or vertical direction from one place to another, as in walking, running, jumping, and skipping activities.

locomotor skill application: Movement activities designed for individuals at the mature stage of developing their fundamental locomotor abilities that focus on utilizing these skills in developmental game, dance, and gymnastics activities.

locomotor skill development: Movement activities designed to enhance fundamental locomotor skills that utilize movement exploration and guided discovery activity experiences.

locomotor skills: Total-body movements in which the body is propelled in an upright posture from one point to another in a roughly horizontal or vertical direction.

lordosis: A postural deviation characterized by an exaggerated curve of the lower back resulting in a forward tilt of the pelvis and weak abdominal muscles.

lower-order thinking: The process of involving the learner in simple recall and recognition.

low-impact aerobics: A form of aerobic dance developmentally appropriate for children that reduces the stress and strain placed on bones and joints.

low-level games: Developmental Level I games that are easy to play, have few and simple rules, require little or no equipment, and may be varied in a variety of ways.

loyalty: In a movement context, being a supportive member of the team or group for the intent of achieving the goals of the activity.

malfeasance: Committing an illegal act.

malpractice: Negligent behavior, improper behavior, or unethical behavior on the part of an individual, resulting in injury or damage to an individual.

mandated legislation: Federal and state laws concerning certain procedures and requirements in the design and implementation of educational programs.

manipulating the learner: The third level of teacher intervention in the learning process in which the teacher physically manipulates the learner or the learning environment using reproduction teaching styles to effect learning.

manipulative exploratory activities: Movement activities designed for individuals at the initial and elementary stages in their fundamental manipulative skills that use the movement framework of effort, space, and relationship awareness.

manipulative game activities: Low-level games designed to enhance fundamental manipulative skills.

manipulative guided discovery activities: Movement activities designed for individuals at the elementary stage of developing their fundamental manipulative abilities that use a guided problem-solving approach.

manipulative relay activities: Cooperative and competitive group activities designed to enhance and reinforce fundamental manipulative skills and specific object manipulation skills in various sports.

manipulative skill application: Movement activities designed for individuals at the mature stage of developing their fundamental manipulative abilities that focus on utilizing these skills in developmental game, dance, and gymnastics activities.

manipulative skill development: Movement activities designed to enhance fundamental manipulative skills that utilize movement exploration and guided discovery activity experiences.

mature stage: The third stage within the fundamental movement phase, primarily dependent on practice and experience, characterized by motor control, movement coordination, and complete integration of all of the components of a particular fundamental movement skill.

mental retardation: A condition typified by faulty development of intelligence to the point that it interferes with one's ability to learn and is classified as being either mild retardation or severe retardation.

mild retardation: A category of mental retardation denoting individuals who need only limited or intermittent external support to function appropriately in society and are generally included in the regular physical education program.

misfeasance: Improper performance of a lawful act by failing to perform within the established standard of practice.

mission statement: An outgrowth of the values statement that clearly and concisely delineates what the curriculum or program attempts to do.

moral behavior: Acting on one's moral reasoning and operating in a consistent manner.

moral dilemma: A teachable moment for bringing about moral growth (out of a situation that is either real or manufactured) through moral reasoning that results in moral behavior.

moral dissonance: Personal questioning brought about by attention given to a moral dilemma.

moral growth: One's potential for the need for higher levels of moral reasoning and moral behavior.

moral reasoning: Making intelligent decisions about what is right and what is wrong.

motor development: Progressive change in movement behavior throughout the life cycle, brought about by interaction among the requirements of the movement task, the biology of the individual, and the conditions of the learning environment.

movement challenges: A means of developing and refining movement skills that uses word challenges that begin with terms such as "Who can," "Let's try," "Can you," and so forth.

movement concept learning: Learning about how the body *can* move.

movement framework: The four movement concepts originally described by Rudolph Laban as body, space, effort, and relationship awareness.

movement pattern: An organized series of related movements that involve the performance of an isolated movement that by itself is too restricted to be classified as a fundamental or specialized movement skill.

movement phrases: Combining elements of stability, locomotor, and/or manipulative skills into a coordinated and rhythmical sequence, as in hitting a pitched ball and running to first base. In dance, they are movement sequences put together through improvisation and performed to some type of rhythmic accompaniment. Sometimes called "dance sentences."

movement skill: The acquisition of motor control, precision, and accuracy in the performance of both fundamental and specialized movement skills.

movement time: The amount of time elapsed from the initial movement to completion of the task, as in the time it takes to swim or run a 100 meters.

moving to rules: An aspect of relationship awareness that refers to limiting one's movement to conform with the rules of games, patterns of structured dances, and patterns of gymnastic activities.

moving with equipment: An aspect of relationship awareness referring to moving with traditional objects such as hoops, balls, benches, and foam cubes.

moving with others: An aspect of relationship awareness referring to moving with one or more partners.

moving with props: An aspect of relationship awareness referring to moving with nontraditional equipment such as body stockings, elastic bands, and streamers.

muscular endurance: The ability to exert force against an object external to the body for several repetitions without fatigue.

muscular strength: The ability of the body to exert maximum force against an object external to the body.

musculoskeletal limitation: A disease or condition of the bones or muscles that limits the child's ability to move effectively and efficiently, as in Osgood-Schlatter condition and arthritis.

myelin: A fatty substance that surrounds the neurons in which increased myelination from infancy through early childhood results in the more efficient transmission of nerve impulses.

National Standards: Performance indicators, commonly established by national professional associations or accrediting agencies. National Standards for Physical Education have been adopted by the National Association for Sport and Physical Education (NASPE, 1995) and serve as the basis for quality physical education programs in the United States.

naturalistic observation: Unobtrusive observation of child or adult behavior in real-world settings such as the classroom or gymnasium, rather than in artificial laboratory settings.

negligence: Failure on the part of an individual to act in a manner judged to be reasonable, careful, and prudent for someone of essentially equal training or status.

neuromuscular limitations: Limiting conditions characterized by damage to the brain or spinal cord, as in cerebral palsy and epilepsy.

nonfeasance: Failure to perform a required act deemed appropriate under the circumstances, such as failure to administer emergency first-aid.

non-locomotor skills: Sometimes called "axial movements," these are stability skills in which the axis of the body revolves around a fixed point, and include movements such as bending, stretching, twisting, turning, reaching, lifting, and falling.

nontraditional balancing: Balancing activities that use the movement framework of effort, space, and relationship awareness as a basis for enhancing the learner's static and dynamic balance skills.

nonverbal communication: Sometimes called "body language," is the projection of messages through subtle and often unconscious changes in body postures, gestures, and facial expressions.

noon-hour programs: An extension of the in-school lunch program in which children are permitted an opportunity to engage in free-choice activity selection.

norms: Standards of performance statistically derived from large population samples.

objective: The observable, measurable, and quantifiable means used to achieve a goal.

objective localization: That aspect of spatial awareness referring to the ability of older children and adults to locate objects independent of their own body.

object striking: Making contact with a stationary or moving object, either with or without an implement, in a horizontal or vertical plane in activities such as batting in baseball and serving in tennis.

official sport game: Developmental Level IV games governed by a set of rules and regulations recognized and interpreted by an official governing body as the accepted standard for performance and play.

ontogenetic: Fundamental or specialized movement skills thought by most experts to require an environmental component to achieve the mature stage, as in swimming and bicycle riding.

original games: Entirely new game activities created by the teacher, the students, or both to help achieve the specific learning objectives of the lesson.

Osgood-Schlatter condition: A musculoskeletal limitation characterized by pain and swelling around the knee joint and typically found in prepubescent boys and girls.

otitis media: Inflammation of the inner ear frequently occurring in young children due to the flat angle of the Eustachian tubes.

overcorrection: A discipline technique in which a student exhibiting an inappropriate behavior is required to repeatedly practice the positive desired behavior.

parent permission slips: A non-legally binding but important written okay from a parent or legal guardian agreeing to the participation of their child in an activity outside the normal activities of the school day.

pathways: A term used in movement settings to denote moving through space, as in straight, curved, and zigzag pathways.

pathways of movement: Where the body can move in terms of straight, curved, zigzag, and diagonal directions.

perceived competence: An aspect of self-esteem that involves a personal self-evaluation of competence in comparison with others.

perception: The ability to know or to interpret, brought about by the process of combining incoming sensory information (visual, auditory, tactile, kinesthetic, olfactory, and taste) with past information that has been stored in the brain that leads to a modified response pattern.

perceptual-motor: A hyphenated term that signifies the close link between all voluntary movement and the perceptual information that is received prior to, during, and after a motor performance.

perceptual-motor activities: Gross and fine motor activities designed to enhance the perceptual-motor components of body awareness, spatial awareness, directional awareness, and temporal awareness.

perceptual-motor learning: The interaction of perceptual and motor processes through movement experiences resulting in improved spatial and temporal integration.

perceptual-motor process: The continuous closed-loop process of voluntary motor behavior that involves the five-step process of sensory input, sensory integration, motor interpretation, movement activation, and sensory feedback.

Performance Benchmarks: Descriptors for assessing behaviors that objectively demonstrate progress toward a Performance Standard of the National Standards for Physical Education (NASPE, 1995).

performance-related fitness: That aspect of physical fitness, sometimes called "skill-related" or "motor fitness," composed of the following: body balance, movement coordination, movement speed, agility, and power.

performance stage: The first stage within the advanced/fine-tuning level of learning a new movement skill in which the learner further refines the elements of the task, working for greater precision and utilizing the skill in various sport settings.

Performance Standards: Objective assessment criteria for assessing pupil progress for achieving the National Standards for Physical Education (NASPE, 1995).

personal responsibility: A process by which the learners take ultimate responsibility for their own welfare.

personal space: The immediate area in all directions around one's body at its furthest possible span.

personal well-being: Taking responsibility for one's own effort and self-direction in matters of particular importance to one's effective integration into a democratic society.

petit mal seizures: A form of epilepsy resulting in nonconvulsive seizures characterized by a momentary loss of consciousness.

phylogenetic: Fundamental or specialized movement skills thought by some experts to require only a genetic or hereditary basis for achieving the mature stage, as in running and jumping.

physical disability: Any physical condition that interferes with a child's educational performance, including disabilities caused by disease, congenital factors, and other unspecified causes.

physical education helpers: Older more mature student volunteers or paid paraprofessionals who assist with many of the routine chores of the physical education program.

physical fitness: In a generic sense, the ability to perform daily tasks without fatigue and to have sufficient energy reserves to participate in additional physical activities and to meet emergency needs. In a specific sense, a set of attributes that one possesses related to the ability to perform physical activity, coupled with one's genetic makeup, and the maintenance of nutritional adequacy.

physical growth: Structural increases in size. In childhood, steady increases in height, weight, muscle mass, and oftentimes fat mass.

physically educated: As defined by NASPE, a physically educated person: "HAS learned skills necessary to perform a variety of physical activities; IS physically fit; DOES participate regularly in physical activity; KNOWS the implications of and the benefits from involvement in physical activities; VALUES physical activity and its contributions to a healthy lifestyle."

P.L. 94-142: The Education for All Handicapped Children Act of 1975 requires that all children with disabilities be provided a free and appropriate public education. Students with limiting conditions must be mainstreamed as much as possible, and an Individualized Education Program must be prepared and implemented.

P.L. 99-457: The updated "cousin" of P.L. 94-142. The Education of the Handicapped Amendments Act of 1986 extended the mandates of P.L. 94-142 to children aged 3-5 years.

play day: A special day of activities, often near the end of the school year, involving children randomly assigned to teams from the same school or different schools competing informally together.

positive discipline: Exhibiting self-control and the assumption of responsibility for one's actions.

positive socialization: Behaviors in a physical activity setting resulting in fair play, honesty, cooperation, teamwork, self-control, and other moral behaviors.

postural deviations: A limiting condition typified by either functional or structural deviations to the body, as in scoliosis, lordosis, and kyphosis.

postures: Nonverbal messages that are conveyed through one's stance and placement of the arms and hands.

power: The ability to perform one maximum effort in the shortest period of time possible, as in striking or throwing a ball for distance.

practice style: A reproduction teaching style similar to the command style in that the teacher controls the content, but the learner is now provided with opportunities for individualized pacing within given boundaries.

preoperational phase: Jean Piaget's second phase of cognitive development, occurring during early childhood, characterized by egocentric thinking in the formation of cognitive structures, and facilitated through movement.

principle of individuality: Each person improves in terms of fitness at her or his own personal rate.

principle of overload: A muscle must do more work than it is accustomed to doing by either increasing the load or decreasing the time in which the same amount of work is done in order to enhance its strength and/or endurance.

principle of progression: Improvement in strength and/or endurance increases over time in response to the individual's threshold of training and target zone.

principle of specificity: A muscle that is overloaded in terms of increased work or decreased time for the same load will increase in strength and/or endurance specific to the muscles worked.

process assessment: An observational approach to motor assessment that places emphasis on the qualitative aspects of movement, including mechanics, form, and style.

product assessment: A quantitative approach to motor assessment concerned with the end results of ones' movement in terms of how far, how fast, how high, or how many.

production cluster: A series of teaching styles that require higher-order thinking processes on the part of the learner that facilitate the discovery of concepts as well as the development of alternative concepts, including the guided discovery, convergent discovery, and divergent production teaching styles.

proficiency barrier: A term first coined by Vern Seefeldt (Michigan State University), signifying the difficulty in performing a specialized movement skill if the prerequisite fundamental movement skill has yet to be mastered.

program preplanning: The first step in planning a movement skill theme that involves determining available resources such as facilities and equipment, and the conditions of the learning environment such as the number of students, frequency of class meetings, and so forth.

program scope: In curriculum construction, the breadth or range of the program in terms of content during one school year.

program sequence: In curriculum construction, the timing and depth of the program in terms of progression from year to year.

proprioceptors: Nerve endings located in the muscles, joints, tendons, and the skeletal muscles that provide clues to one's body position and balance in space.

proximate cause: The third of four requirements for an individual to be declared negligent in a court of law that demonstrates a reasonable relationship between the injury received or loss incurred and a breach of expected duty.

proximodistal development: The general tendency toward gradual outward progression in increased motor control, especially during infancy, from the center of the body (trunk and shoulder girdle) to its most distant parts (arms, wrists, hands, fingers).

psychomotor seizures:A form of nonconvulsive epilepsy characterized by short-term changes in normal behavior, such as temper tantrums, incoherent speech, and aggressive behaviors, in which there is no memory of the atypical behavior.

public demonstration: A formal demonstration involving a select group of students to display their skills in specific activities such as jumping rope, tumbling, juggling, or unicycling.

public relations: The process of telling others what you are doing, why you are doing it, and how it benefits your students.

range of movement: The actual size of the movement and the extent to which the body can reach from a fixed point on the supporting surface.

reaction time: The amount of time elapsed from the stimulus ("go") to the first movement of the body, as in one's quickness off the blocks in swimming or running.

readiness: The convergence of conditions within both the biology of the individual and the conditions of the environment that make for greater ease and efficiency in the learning of a new movement task.

recess: A defined period of time, outside when possible, usually 10-20 minutes in length in the midmorning and/or midafternoon, in which elementary school children are permitted a break from the normal learning activities of the day to engage in unstructured free play.

reciprocal style: A reproduction teaching style, sometimes called "peer teaching," in which students work in pairs or groups of three on a specified teacher-designed task. The teacher provides feedback to the "mini teacher" during the teaching-learning episode.

relationship awareness: A term used in movement settings to denote moving with something, usually with other people or objects.

relative endurance: Endurance adjusted for the child's body weight.

remedial physical education: A corrective program of physical activities designed to improve body mechanics.

remediation: The process of using various intervention strategies to overcome or mitigate a particular learning difficulty.

reproduction cluster: A series of teaching styles that require lower-order thinking processes on the part of the learner that involve memory, recall, identification, and sorting, and include the command, practice, reciprocal, self-check, and inclusion teaching styles.

restricted space: A specifically prescribed or limited space in which one is permitted to move.

revisiting: Coming back to a skill theme at different times throughout the school year in order to take advantage of both physical, cognitive, and/or social maturation.

rhythm: The regulated flow of energy organized in both duration and intensity, resulting in balance and harmony, and possessing sufficient repetition of regular groupings of sights, sounds, and/or movements.

rhythmical stereotypes: In infants, regular rhythmic head, torso, leg, and arm actions thought to be precursors of voluntary controlled forms of movement with these body parts. In childhood and beyond, viewed as pathological behavior indicative of developmental disabilities.

rhythmic elements: The group of interrelated components that make up rhythm—accent, tempo, intensity, rhythmic pattern, and underlying beat.

rhythmic fundamentals: Developing an awareness of and the ability to respond to the five elements of rhythm (underlying beat, tempo, accent, intensity, rhythmic pattern).

rhythmic pattern: A group of beats related to the underlying beat.

rigidity: A form of cerebral palsy characterized by extreme stiffness and absence of a stretch reflex resulting in restricted movement and hyper-extension.

role: In a social setting, an individual behavior that one uses to carry out a particular status.

rolling: See *body rolling*.

rules for good behavior: Guidelines for expected student behaviors, usually written and mutually agreed upon by teacher and students.

run: A fundamental locomotor skill that is essentially an exaggerated form of walking, but with a brief flight phase during each step, in which the body is out of contact with the supporting surface.

scoliosis: A postural deviation characterized by lateral curvature of the spine.

scope and sequence chart: In curriculum construction, a large chart outlining the breadth (scope) and depth (sequence) of the program throughout the school year and from year to year.

secular trends: Changes, both positive and negative, in measures of height, weight, and sexual maturity associated with differences in lifestyle factors and nutritional habits from one generation to another.

security: In a social sense, the knowledge that one is loved, valued, and accepted by one or more significant others.

segmental assessment: An individualized observational assessment technique used to determine the specific location of developmental difficulties in performing a particular fundamental or specialized movement skill.

self-acceptance: An aspect of self-concept that in-

volves recognizing and accepting one's weaknesses and limitations as well as strengths and abilities.

self-assessment: A realistic evaluation of oneself.

self-check style: A reproduction teaching style in which the learners use a standardized task sheet while the teacher observes their performance and provides feedback.

self-concept: A value-free description of self that is a personal judgment of worth or value. Often used interchangeably with *self-esteem*.

self-confidence: An aspect of self-concept that involves an inner belief in one's ability to accomplish a given task.

self-control: Self-initiated and regulated behavior that respects the rights and feelings of others. In a movement context, maintaining the standards of acceptable behavior when placed in a competitive situation.

self-encouragement: A teachable process by which teachers help children learn that it is okay to feel good about their accomplishments, by letting them see teachers humbly encourage themselves.

self-esteem: A description of self that is rooted in what one thinks others think of him- or herself. Often used interchangeably with *self-concept*.

self-referenced assessment: A method by which a learner's exit level of achievement is compared with his or her entry level.

self-regulatory growth: The unexplained ability of the body to compensate and over time make up for temporary interruptions in the normal pace of growth.

self-space: Also known as "personal space," is the area immediately surrounding one's body, generally up to 3 feet.

sensitive period: A broad time frame, or window of opportunity, when learning a new skill is easier and quicker, as in learning to speak a foreign language or to swim during early childhood.

sensorimotor phase: Jean Piaget's first phase of cognitive learning, occurring during infancy and toddlerhood, during which the child's motor activities and perceptual abilities are brought together into a tenuous whole to form cognitive structures.

sensory impairment: A condition in which the sensory receptors are unable to transmit or interpret stimuli in a manner conducive to educational performance, as in visual impairments and auditory impairments.

serial movements: Any movement involving the repetitive performance of a single discrete movement in rapid succession, as in dribbling a basketball.

set induction: See *lesson introduction.*

set-to-learn: The learner's preparation for and expectation of a learning session to occur, often facilitated by checking for children's understanding.

severe retardation: A category of mental retardation denoting individuals in need of extensive long-term or even constant support to survive and are generally not part of the regular physical education program.

shape: A term used in movement settings to denote the body assuming specific positions, as in a narrow, wide, curvy, bent, or straight shape.

Shape of the Nation Report: First released in 1997, this regular report highlights the status of physical education offered in public schools throughout the United States. The 2001 report indicated that Illinois is still the only state to offer daily physical education.

shared negligence: A legal defense that compares the level of negligence between the plaintiff and the accused and awards damages on a proportional basis.

singing rhythms: Rhythmic expression, including rhymes, poems, finger plays, and singing dances in which words are combined with music and movement to help children better understand music phrasing.

skill application: The part of the daily lesson that comes after the skill development portion of the lesson that enables students to use their newly acquired movement skill in a developmentally appropriate game, dance, or gymnastics activity.

skill challenge games: A form of lead-up game in which there are few and simple rules and the focus is on maximum performance for time, distance, or number, as in playing the basketball skill challenge game of Horse.

skill charts: Homemade or commercially purchased wall displays of the various elements of a particular skill or activity.

skill concept learning: Learning about how the body *should* move.

skill development: The single most important part of the daily developmental physical education lesson contained within the body of the lesson that emphasizes new skill learning.

skillful movers: Individuals who move with efficiency, control, and coordination in the performance of fundamental or specialized movement skills.

skill sequencing: The process of building skill upon skill.

skipping: A combination of two fundamental locomotor skills in which there is a rhythmically alternating stepping and hopping action.

sliding: A fundamental locomotor skill similar to galloping but in a sideward direction.

small apparatus: Small handheld equipment used in developmental gymnastics such as hoops, wands, beanbags, and balls.

social dance: Partner dances that reflect the mores of the particular culture at the time of its popularity.

social inclusion: The process by which students allow all in the group or class to participate and make meaningful contributions to an activity.

social responsibility: A process by which learners take on a greater role in being sensitive and responsive to the well-being of others.

social well-being: Respecting the rights and feelings of others, and possessing a genuine sense of caring for the welfare of others.

space awareness: Not to be confused with *spatial awareness,* involves knowledge of where the body moves in terns of level, direction, and range.

spasticity: A form of cerebral palsy characterized by limited voluntary control of movement as a result of hypertonia of the muscles.

spatial awareness: Not to be confused with *space awareness,* is a two-component learning process that is developmentally based and involves the process of subjective localization and objective localization in terms of where the body can move, how much space it occupies, and the ability to use the body effectively in external space.

SPEAK II: A Sport and Physical Education Advocacy Kit packed full of useful information, position papers, medical reports, and government documents in support of increasing physical activity through quality physical education programs offered daily.

specialized movement phase: The time period typically beginning around age seven in which individuals begin to combine and apply a variety of fundamental movement skills into more complex patterns of movement for use in a variety of sport, dance, and other activities.

specialized movement skill: A fundamental movement skill or combination of fundamental movement skills that have been applied to the performance of activities related to sport, dance, or performance of some other complex activity.

specific objectives: The portion of the curriculum that extends from the general objectives of the program, indicating precisely what is to be taught and learned. Specific objectives may be stated as behavioral objectives, terminal objectives, or benchmark objectives.

specific planning: The third step in planning a movement skill theme that involves specific curricular planning in terms of developing a scope and sequence chart, yearly plans, unit plans, and daily lesson plans.

spectrum of teaching styles: A term used to denote a variety of teaching styles first identified by Muska Mosston (Mosston & Ashworth, 2001).

speed: The ability to move from one point to another in the shortest time possible, as in the 50-meter dash.

sports day: Similar to a play day except that children compete against each other as intact classes or schools in a tournament-like atmosphere.

springing movements: Stability skills involving forceful projection of the body into space in either an upright or inverted position, as in performing a round-off or basketball dunk shot.

squad leaders: A rotating responsibility given to an individual to serve as the person responsible for maximizing the active learning time of the group.

squads: A small grouping of learners, usually six to eight, organized by the teacher to promote cooperative learning.

stability: The most basic of the three categories of movement, locomotion and manipulation being the other two, is the ability to sense a shift in the relationship of the body parts that alter one's balance and the ability to adjust rapidly and accurately for these changes with appropriate compensating movements.

stability exploratory activities: Movement skill activities emphasizing stability enhancement that are specifically designed for learners at the initial or elementary stage of the fundamental movement skill phase of development.

stability game activities: Low-level game activities designed to reinforce specific fundamental movement skills.

stability guided discovery activities: Movement skill activities emphasizing stability that are specifically designed for learners at the intermediate/practice level of learning a new stability skill.

stability movement skills: Movement skills that place a premium on gaining and/or maintaining one's equilibrium in relationship to the force of gravity, as in bending, stretching, twisting, turning, or performing a forward roll or a headstand.

stability skill application: Movement skill activities designed for learners who have developed their fundamental stability skills.

stability skill development: Movement activities specifically intended to enhance fundamental stability skills using movement exploration, guided discovery, skill application, or skill refinement activities.

Stage A flight skills: Body in flight skills that involve inverting the body in midair and require a high degree of strength and coordination, as well as explosive power.

Stage B flight skills: Body in flight skills, such as jumping from a height, that are somewhat limited in the amount of force applied and strength and coordination required.

Stages of Change Model: Five hypothesized stages that one goes through in changing a health behavior (precontemplation, contemplation, preparation, action, and maintenance stages).

static balance: Any stationary posture, upright or inverted, in which the center of gravity remains stationary and the line of gravity falls within the base of support.

static endurance: The ability of a muscle or group of muscles to stay flexed for an extended period of time, usually measured in seconds, and is improved through progressive resistance training using light to moderate resistance.

status: In a social sense, one's perceived position in a particular group such as the family, classroom, and team.

subjective localization: That aspect of spatial awareness referring to the tendency of young children to locate objects in space relative to themselves.

supply/equipment report: A means of minimizing legal liability that involves a periodic inventory and status report of all the supplies and equipment under one's control.

Surgeon General's report: The landmark U.S. federal government report that for the first time recognized physical activity as a significant factor in improving one's overall health.

tactical approach: Sometimes called "games for understanding approach," emphasizes improving movement skills through games instruction by stressing the *why* and *when* of using a particular movement skill in a game situation.

talking bench: A technique to resolve issues of students respecting one another in which two students go to a designated place (a bench) to discuss a problem and then report back to the teacher how they resolve the problem.

target zone: The point at which maximum benefits are obtained for an individual's personal level of fitness.

task card: A written verbal or visual description of what skill or movement activity is to be performed.

taxonomy: A classification scheme.

teacher-centered methods: Sometimes called "direct teaching methods," in which emphasis is on the product, and the teacher makes all or most of the decisions concerning what, how, and when the learner is to perform.

teaching episode: A part of the daily lesson that focuses on a particular aspect of skill development and incorporates a predetermined teaching style to help effect learning.

teaching styles: The result of a series of decisions made by the teacher prior to, during, and after a teaching episode that impacts the relationship between the teacher and the learning process.

teamwork: Working together with others in a cooperative manner.

technique exercises: Exercises, appropriately taught during the set induction, that emphasize body alignment, stretching of large-muscle groups, isolation of body parts, and strengthening of major muscle groups.

tempo: The speed of the movement, music, or accompaniment.

temporal awareness: A three-component movement learning process that involves developing an internal time structure composed of movement synchrony and sequencing in a rhythmical manner, the product of which is referred to as *coordination.*

terminal feedback: Information provided to the learner after performance of the movement task that emphasizes the product of one's actions.

terminal objectives: A form of specific objectives that represent, in list form, the major cognitive, affective, and motor objectives to be achieved in the program.

threshold of training: The minimum amount of physical activity required to produce fitness gains.

throwing: Imparting force to an object in an overhand, underhand, or sidearm pattern using either one or both hands, depending on the goal of the task.

time-out: A discipline technique that involves sending a disruptive student to an easy-to-monitor, safe, and neutral place for a period of time before being permitted to reenter the learning activity.

timing of movement: The speed at which a movement occurs.

Title IX: A federal law that makes it illegal to discriminate among students in matters of education based on gender.

total-body assessment: An observational assessment technique used with groups of learners in which the teacher, in an informal setting, observes the body mechanics of a particular fundamental or specialized movement skill in order to get a general picture of the group's present level of functioning and to identify particular learners who may be experiencing difficulties.

traditional balancing: Balance skills, frequently used in Olympic gymnastics that involve static balances, such as a front scale, tripod, tip-up, headstand, and handstand, and dynamic balances, such as a variety of balance beam walking skills.

transition stage: The first stage within the specialized movement phase during which children attempt to apply their movement skills to a wide variety of game, sport, and dance activities.

trapping: Sometimes called "collecting," involves using various parts of the body to stop the forward momentum of an oncoming object, usually a ball.

traumatic brain injury: The primary cause of mental retardation, characterized by damage to the central nervous system before, during, or after birth.

tremor: A form of cerebral palsy characterized by tremor and rhythmic but involuntary movement.

trust activities: A type of cooperative game that requires the participants to work cooperatively to overcome a challenge that involves a real or imagined element of risk.

underlying beat: The steady, continuous sound of any rhythmical sequence.

uniqueness: An aspect of self-concept that involves recognizing, respecting, and celebrating one's personal characteristics.

unit plan: A more specific subset of the yearly plan that represents the National Standards for Physical Education and the theme of instruction for that unit.

upright supports: Either static or dynamic balance skills in which emphasis is placed on maintaining one's equilibrium when the body is placed in unusual upright positions, as in performing a front scale (static) or snow skiing (dynamic).

values: The first step in curriculum and program building, which involves developing a list of critically important indicators of the success of the curriculum or program. The value statement provides the framework for the mission statement.

verbal clarity: An important element of effective verbal communication in which the speaker is concise, doesn't ververbalize, and uses good grammar and pronunciation to foster understanding.

verbal communication: The projection of messages through the voice; a crucially important tool for teachers for explanations and presentations of movement challenges. It is essential that the teacher get and maintain students' attention and provide clarity in the instruction.

videotaped performances: An excellent means for providing learners with a visual model of the movement skills to be learned and to record individual progress throughout a unit of work.

virtue: An aspect of self-concept that involves one seeing him- or herself operating consistently within an established moral code.

visual impairment: A sensory impairment in which a child's educational performance is adversely affected even when corrective lenses are worn.

volleying: A specialized striking pattern that involves receiving force from an object with both hands and immediately imparting force to that object in a roughly vertical direction, as in volleyball or heading in soccer.

weight of movement: The strength or force with which a movement occurs.

weight transfer: Shifting the body weight from one base of support to another.

worthiness: An aspect of self-esteem that involves seeing yourself as deserving and valued for who you are rather than for what you are both in your own estimation and in the estimation of others.

written excuses: Notes from home or from a physician requesting that the child be excused from a scheduled activity, usually due to health or religious reasons.

yearly plan: A more specific subset of the scope and sequence chart that represents the scope of activities to be included in the curriculum for any grade for the entire school year, geared both to age and developmental appropriateness.

References

Allison, P.C., & Barrett, K. (2000). *Constructing children's physical education experiences.* Boston: Allyn and Bacon.

Allsbrook, L. (1992). Fitness should fit children. *JOPERD, 63,* 47-49.

Almquist, S. (2001). The emergency room. *Strategies, 14* (5), 30-32.

American Alliance for Health, Physical Education, Recreation and Dance. (2001). *Guidelines for facilities, equipment and instructional materials in elementary physical education.* Reston, VA: AAHPERD.

American Alliance for Health, Physical Education, Recreation and Dance. (2002a). *Physical Best activity guide: Elementary level.* Champaign, IL: Human Kinetics (American Fitness Alliance).

American Alliance for Health, Physical Education, Recreation and Dance. (2002b). *Physical education for lifelong fitness: The Physical Best teacher's guide.* Champaign, IL: Human Kinetics (American Fitness Alliance).

American Association on Mental Retardation. (1992). *Mental retardation: Definition, classification, and systems of support* (9th ed.). Washington, DC: Author.

American Fitness Alliance (2002a). *Activitygram.* Champaign, IL: Human Kinetics.

American Fitness Alliance. (2002b). *Fitnessgram.* Champaign, IL: Human Kinetics.

American Obesity Association. (2000). *AOA fact sheets.* Washington, DC: Author.

Arlin, P.K. (1999). The wise teacher: A developmental model of teaching. *Theory into Practice, 38* (1), 12-17.

Association for Childhood Learning Disabilities. (1987). The Childhood for Learning Disabilities position statements: Measurement and training

of perceptual and perceptual-motor functions. *Journal of Learning Disabilities, 20,* 349-350.

Ayers, W. (1993). *To teach: The journey of a teacher.* New York: Teachers College Press.

Beighle, A., Pangrazi, R.P., & Vincent, S.D. (2001). Pedometers, physical activity, and accountability. *JOPERD, 72* (9), 16-19, 36.

Belka, D. (2000). Teaching step-like actions. *TEPE, 11* (4), 15-18.

Benham-Deal, T., Byra, M., Jenkins, J., & Gates, W.K. (2002). The physical education standards movement in Wyoming: An effort in partnership. *JOPERD, 73* (3), 25-28.

Blair, S.N. (1992). Are American children and youth fit? The need for better data. *Research Quarterly for Exercise and Sport, 63* (1), 120-123.

Burton, A.W., & Rodgerson, R.W. (2001). New perspectives on the assessment of movement skills and motor abilities. *Adapted Physical Activity Quarterly, 18,* 347-365.

Cahill, B. (Ed.). (1988). *Proceedings of the conference on strength training and the prepubescent.* Chicago: American Orthopaedic Society for Sports Medicine.

Carpenter, L.J. (2000). *Legal concepts in sport: A primer.* Reston, VA: AAHPERD.

Centers for Disease Control and Prevention. (1997). Guidelines for school and community programs to promote lifelong physical activity among young people. *MMWR, 46,* No. RR-6.

Centers for Disease Control and Prevention. (2000). *Clinical growth charts.* National Center for Health Statistics. Washington, DC: Author. (**http://www.cdc/growthcharts**)

Centers for Disease Control and Prevention. (2001). Increasing physical activity: A report on recommendations of the task force on community preventative services. *MMWR, 50,* No. RR-18.

Charles, C.M. (1992). *Building classroom discipline.* White Plains, NY: Longman.

Cleland, F., & Gallahue, D.L. (1993). Young children's divergent movement ability. *Perceptual & Motor Skills, 77,* 535-544.

Cleland, F.E., & Pearse, C. (1995). Critical thinking in elementary physical education: Reflections on a yearlong study. *JOPERD, 66,* 31-38.

CompTech Systems Design. *Fit America and physical skills manager* [Computer software]. P.O. Box 516, Hastings, MN 55033.

Corbin, C.B., & Pangrazi, R.P. (1998). *Physical activity for children: A statement of guidelines.* Reston, VA: NASPE.

Deci, E.L., & Ryan, R.M. (2000). The "what" and "why" of goal pursuits: Human needs and the self-determination of behavior. *Psychological Inquiry, 11* (4), 227-268.

Dollard, N., & Christensen, L. (1996). Constructive classroom management. *Focus on Exceptional Children, 29* (2), 1-12.

Dougherty, N.J. (Ed.). (2002). *Principles of safety in physical education and sport.* Reston, VA: NASPE.

Dougherty, N.J., Auxter, D., Goldberger, J.D., & Heinzmann, G.S. (2002). *Sport, physical activity, and the law.* Reston, VA: AAALF/ Sagamore.

Dunn, J.M. (Ed.). (1991). PL 99-457 Challenges and opportunities for physical education. *JOPERD, 62,* 33-48. (Series of articles)

Epanchin, B.C., Townsend, B., & Stoddard, K. (1994). *Constructive classroom management: Strategies for creating positive learning environments.* Pacific Grove, CA: Brooks/Cole.

Fay, T., & Doolittle, S. (2002). Agents for change: From standards to assessment to accountability in physical education. *JOPERD, 73* (3), 29-33.

French, R., Silliman, L., & Henderson, H. (1990). Too much time out! *Strategies, 3,* 5-7.

Gabbard, C. (2000, October). Investing in life. *American School Board Journal,* 56-58.

Gabbei, R., & Hamrick, D. (2001). Using physical activity homework to meet the National Standards. *JOPERD, 72* (4), 21-26.

Gallahue, D.L., & Ozmun, J.C. (2002). *Understanding motor development: Infants, children, adolescents, adults.* Boston: McGraw-Hill.

Garcia, A.W., Broda, M.A.N., Frenn, M., Coviak, C., Pender, N.J., & Ronis, D.L. (1995). Gender and developmental differneces in exercise beliefs among youth and prediction of their exercise behavior. *Journal of School Health, 65,* 213-219.

Garrahy, D. (2001). To integrate or not to integrate? That is the question. *Strategies, 14* (4), 23-25.

Gerstung Manufacturers, Baltimore, MD. (**www.Gerstung.com**)

Gilbert, A.G. (1992). *Creative dance for all ages.* Reston, VA: AAHPERD.

Griffin, L.L., Mitchell, S.A., & Oslin, J.L. (1997). *Teaching sports concepts and skills: A tactical games approach.* Champaign, IL: Human Kinetics.

Grineski, S. (1995). Students can learn to cooperate. *JOPERD, 9,* 27-29.

Grineski, S. (1996). *Cooperative learning in physical education.* Champaign, IL: Human Kinetics.

Helion, J. (1996). If we build it, they will come: Creating an emotionally safe physical education environment. *JOPERD, 67,* 40-44.

Hellison, D. (1995). *Teaching responsibility through physical activity.* Champaign, IL: Human Kinetics.

Henderson, H.L., French, R., Fritsch, R., & Lerner, B. (2000). Time-out and over correction: A comparison of their application in physical education. *JOPERD, 71* (3), 31-35.

Hinson, C. (1995). *Fitness for children.* Champaign, IL: Human Kinetics.

Howarth, K. (2001). Space, the final frontier. *TEPE, 12* (1), 8-11.

Johnson, D.W., & Johnson, R.T. (1995). Why violence prevention programs don't work—and what does. *Educational Leadership, 52* (5), 63-70.

Judd, M.R., & Goldfine, B. (2000). Playing it safe with student travel. *Strategies, 13* (3), 5-7.

Kerby, S. (1997). Making the case for teaching social skills. *TEPE, 8* (5), 8-9.

Kohn, A. (1996). *Beyond discipline: From compliance to community.* Alexandria, VA: Association for Supervision and Curriculum Development.

Kozub, F. (1998). Recent amendments to the Individuals with Disabilities Act: Implications for physical education. *JOPERD, 69* (8), 47–50.

Kwak, C. (1993). *The initial effects of various task presentation conditions on students' performance of the lacrosse throw.* Unpublished doctoral dissertation, University of South Carolina, Columbia.

Lathrop, A.H., & Murray, N.R. (2000). Assessment in educational gymnastics. *TEPE, 11* (4), 28–31, 40.

Laurentian Gymnastics Industries Ltd., 15 Melanie Drive, Brampton, Ontario, Canada L6T 4K8. (800-354-0071)

Lavay, B.W., French, R., & Henderson, H.L. (1997). *Positive behavior management strategies for physical educators.* Champaign, IL: Human Kinetics.

Lickona, T. (1991). *Educating for character: How our schools can teach respect and responsibility.* New York: Bantam.

Lipman, M. (1988). Critical thinking—What can it be? *Educational Leadership, 46* (1), 38–43.

Logsdon, B.J., Alleman, L.M., Straits, S.A., Belka, D., & Clark, D. (1997). *Physical education unit plans for grades 3-4. Learning experiences in games, gymnastics, and dance.* Champaign, IL: Human Kinetics.

Lund, J. (1997). Authentic assessment: Its development & applications. *JOPERD, 68* (7), 25–28, 40.

Magill, R.A. (2001). *Motor learning: Concepts and applications.* Dubuque, IA: Brown.

Martens, R., & Seefeldt, V. (1979). *Guidelines for children's sports.* Reston, VA: AAHPERD Publications.

Masser, L. (1990). Teaching for affective learning in elementary physical education. *JOPERD, 64,* 17–20.

Mauldon, E., & Layson, J. (1979). *Teaching gymnastics* (2nd ed.). London: Macdonald and Evans.

McBride, R. (1992). Critical thinking—an overview with implications for physical education. *JTPE, 11,* 112–125.

McBride, R., & Cleland, F. (1998). Critical thinking in physical education. Putting the theory where it belongs: In the gymnasium. *JOPERD, 69* (7), 42–46.

McClenaghan, B.A., & Gallahue, D.L. (1978). *Fundamental movement: A developmental and remedial approach.* Philadelphia: Saunders.

Melograno, V. (1996). *Designing the physical education curriculum* (3rd ed.). Champaign, IL: Human Kinetics.

Melograno, V.J. (1998). *Professional and student portfolios for physical education.* Champaign, IL: Human Kinetics.

Mosston, M., & Ashworth, S. (2001). *Teaching physical education* (5th ed.). New York: Macmillan.

NASPE News. (winter 2002). *Surgeon general leads call for physical education.* Reston, VA: National Association for Sport and Physical Education.

National Association for Sport and Physical Activity. (1992). *The physically educated person.* Reston. VA: Author.

National Association for Sport and Physical Education. (1995). *Moving into the future: National standards for physical education.* Reston, VA: Author.

National Association for Sport and Physical Education. (1998). *Physical activity for children: A statement of guidelines.* Reston, VA: Author.

National Association for Sport and Physical Education. (1999). *Sport and physical education advocacy kit II.* Reston, VA: Author.

National Association for Sport and Physical Education. (2000a). *Appropriate practices for elementary school physical education.* Reston, VA: Author.

National Association for Sport and Physical Education. (2000b). *Appropriate practices in movement programs for young children ages 3-5.* Reston, VA: Author.

National Association for Sport and Physical Education. (2000c). *Opportunity to learn—Standards for elementary physical education.* Reston, VA: Author.

National Association for Sport and Physical Education. (2001a). *Benefits and importance of physical education in the K-12 curricula.* Reston, VA: Author.

National Association for Sport and Physical Education. (2001b). *Guidelines for facilities, equipment and instructional materials in elementary physical education.* Reston, VA: Author.

National Association for Sport and Physical Education. (2001c). *Shape of the nation report.* Reston, VA: Author.

National Association for Sport and Physical Education. (2002). *Physical activity guidelines for infants and toddlers.* Reston, VA: Author.

National Consortium for Physical Education and Recreation for Individuals with Disabilities. (1995). *Adapted physical education national standards.* Champaign, IL: Human Kinetics.

Newcombe, N. (1996). *Child development—change over time.* New York: HarperCollins.

Nicholes, V. (1991). Creative dance for the primary child: A progressive approach. In *Early childhood creative arts: Proceedings of the International Early Childhood Creative Arts Conference* (pp. 144-159). Reston, VA: AAHPERD.

Nichols, B. (1994). *Moving and learning. The elementary school physical education experience.* St. Louis: Mosby.

Nilges, L.M. (1997). Educational gymnastics: Stages of content development. *JOPERD, 68* (3), 50-55.

Nilges, L.M. (2000). Teaching educational gymnastics. *TEPE, 11* (4), 6-9.

Noddings, N. (1991). Stories in dialogue: Caring and interpersonal reasoning. In C. Ratliffe, T. Ratliffe, & B. Bie, Creating a learning environment: Class management strategies for elementary PE teachers. *JOPERD, 62,* 24-27.

Noddings, N. (1992). *The challenge to care in schools: An alternative approach to education.* New York: Teachers College Press.

Pastore, D.L. (1994). A checklist for accident report forms. *Strategies, 7,* 15-17.

Patrick, K., Spear, B., Holt, K., and Sofka, D. (2001). *Bright futures in practice: Physical activity.* U.S. Department of Health and Human Services, Washington, DC: National Center for Education in Maternal and Child Health.

Payne, V.G., & Isaacs, L.D. (2001). *Human motor development: A lifespan approach.* Mountain View, CA: Mayfield.

Peterson, R., & Felton-Collins, V. (1986). *The Piaget handbook for teachers and parents.* New York: Teachers College Press.

President's Council on Physical Fitness and Sports. (2000). *Fitness Tracker* [President's Challenge Physical Fitness Test software]. Micro Services, 14 Harmony Lane, Danville, NJ 07834. (943-627-1781)

President's Council on Physical Fitness and Sports. (2002-03). *The President's Challenge: Physical fitness program packet.* 400 E. 7th Street, Bloomington, IN 47405 (800-258-8146). (**www.indiana.edu/~preschal**)

Purcell Cone, T., Werner, P., Cone, S., & Mays Woods, A. (1998). *Interdisciplinary teaching through physical education.* Champaign, IL: Human Kinetics.

Raffini, J.P. (1993). *Winners without losers: Structures and strategies for increasing student motivation to learn.* Boston: Allyn and Bacon.

Rauchenbach, J. (1994). Checking for student understanding—Four techniques. *JOPERD, 65* (4), 60-63.

Rink, J. (1993). *Teaching physical education for learning.* St. Louis: Mosby.

Rink, J. (1996). Effective instruction in physical education. In S.J. Silverman & C.D. Ennis (Eds.), *Student learning in physical education: Applying research to enhance instruction* (pp. 171-198). Champaign, IL: Human Kinetics.

Rink, J., Mitchell, M., Hohn, R., Templeton, J., Barton, G., Hewitt, P., Taylor, M., & Dawkins, M. (2002). High stakes assessment in South Carolina. *JOPERD, 73* (3), 21-24, 33.

Rizzo, T.L., & Lavey, B. (2000). Inclusion: Why the confusion? *JOPERD, 71* (4), 32-36.

Rosenshine, B., & Stevens, R. (1986). Teaching functions. In Wittrock, M.C. (Ed.), *Handbook of research on teaching* (3rd ed.) (pp. 376-391). New York: Macmillan.

Sallis, J.F., Strikemiller, P.K., Harsha, D.W., Feldman, H.A., Ehlinger, S., Stone, E.J., Williston, J., & Woods, S. (1996). Validation of interviewer- and self-administered physical activity checklists for fifth-grade students. *Medicine and Science in Sports and Exercise, 28* (7), 840-851.

Scantling, E., Lackey, D., Strand, B., & Johnson, M. (1998). Maintaining physical education's place in our schools. *Strategies, 11* (4), 13-16.

Schiemer, S. (1996). Pursue excellence. Promoting quality physical education programs and physical activity for all. *TEPE, 7* (4), 24.

Schiemer, S. (2000). *Assessment strategies for elementary physical education.* Champaign, IL: Human Kinetics.

Seefeldt, V., & Haubenstricker, J. (1976). Developmental sequence of fundamental motor skills. Unpublished research, Michigan State University.

Senne, T.A., & Housner, L. (2002). NASPE standards in action—part I. *JOPERD, 73* (3), 19-20, 33.

Siedentop, D., & Tannehill, D. (2000). *Developing teaching skills in physical education.* Mountain View, CA: Mayfield.

Solomon, G.B. (1997). Fair play in the gymnasium: Improving social skills among elementary school students. *JOPERD, 68* (5), 22-25.

Thompson, D., Hudson, S.D., & Bowers, L. (2002). Play areas and the ADA: Providing access and opportunities for all children. *JOPERD, 73* (2), 37-41.

Turner, B., & Turner, S. (1998). The jog-a-thon. A fundraiser for physical education. *TEPE, 9* (3), 5.

Ulrich, D.A. (2000). *Test of gross motor development.* PRO-ED, 5341 Industrial Oaks Blvd., Austin, TX 78735. (512-892-3142)

U.S. Department of Education. (1998). Federal Register, 34 C.F.R. Ch. III, July 1, 1998.

U.S. Department of Health and Human Services. (1996). *Physical activity and health: A report of the Surgeon General.* Washington, DC: U.S. Government Printing Office.

U.S. Department of Health and Human Services. (2000). *Healthy people 2010: National health promotion and disease prevention objectives.* Washington, DC: U.S. Government Printing Office.

Vigil, D. (1997). Hear no evil, see no evil. *TEPE, 8* (5), 4-5.

Wasielewski, R.A., & Scruggs, M.Y. (1997). Student groups conducted by teachers. The teachers as counselors (TAC) program. *Journal for Specialists in Group Work, 22* (1), 43-51.

Watson, D.L., & Hildebrand, K. (2000). Advocacy: Changing our professional behaviors. *JOPERD, 71* (3), 46-49.

Welk, G.J., & Wood, K. (2000). Physical activity assessments in physical education. A practical review of instruments and their use in the curriculum. *JOPERD, 71* (1), 30-40.

Werner, P. (2001). More tactical approaches to playing games. *TEPE, 12* (1), 6-7.

Werner, P., & Almond, L. (1990). Models of games education. *JOPERD, 61* (4), 23-27.

Weston, A.T., Petosa, R., & Pate, R.R. (1997). Validation of an instrument for measurement of physical activity in youth. *Medicine and Science in Sports and Exercise, 29* (1), 138-143.

Zahn-Waxler, C., & Radke-Yarrow, M. (1992). Development of concern for others. *Developmental Psychology, 28* (1), 126-136.

Index